**PAGE
30**

ON THE
ROAD

YOUR COMPLETE DESTINATION GUIDE
In-depth reviews, detailed listings
and insider tips

**The Cordilleras
& Yungas**
p91

**Lake
Titicaca**
p71

Amazon Basin
p271

**La Paz
& Around**
p32

**Santa Cruz &
Gran Chiquitania**
p238

**Central
Highlands**
p166

**Southern
Altiplano**
p128

**South Central
Bolivia &
the Chaco**
p220

D1334035

**PAGE
327**

SURVIV
GUIDE

ATION TO
MOOTH TRIP

Health

000000683708

welcome to
Bolivia

DUDLEY LIBRARIES

000000683708

Askews & Holts	
	£18.99
DU	

Adventure

Every second of every day is an adventure in Bolivia. Just finding your way from summit to city can be a challenge in itself. Then there are the peaks, the rivers, the treks, the jungles, the gut-bursting mountain-bike descents, and the vast, impenetrable and remote expanses that tug you ever further into the wild. It's a place that calls for a boldness and braveness of spirit, the kind of drive that took early explorers to the next rise on the horizon and the next turn on the river. For climbers, the steep mountain peaks offer a lifetime's worth of adventure. Plunging from the Andes down to the edge of the Amazon, multiday journeys follow ancient Inca paving, making this one of the world's top trekking destinations, while trips along rivers deep in the heart of the Amazon take you past the riotous barks of monkeys and a thriving mass of biodiversity that will leave you awestruck.

Culture

The cultural, historical and spiritual depths and richness of Latin America's most indigenous nation are astounding. Officially declared a Plurinational State, Bolivia is a place to visit, learn from and experience a diverse mix of peoples. There are at-risk cultures and languages that could disappear within our lifetime, and traditions and beliefs that reach back to the days of the Inca kings and Tiwanaku cosmologist priests.

Rough around the edges, superlative in its natural beauty, rugged, vexing, complex and slightly nerve-racking, Bolivia is one of South America's most diverse and perplexing nations.

(left) Laguna Colorada (p155), Los Lípez
(below) Aymará people on Isla del Sol (p83), Lake Titicaca

There are pastoralists and independent miners in the highlands whose marked pride in Quechua, Aymará and Uru roots is displayed in their ongoing patchwork of cultural traditions. In the forested depths and low-lying plains, you'll find a laid-back attitude in remote Guaraní communities which are slowly changing and adapting with the arrival of Quechua-speaking and mestizo settlers. In the cities, culture can change quickly – or purposefully slowly – as you move through a remarkably stratified society that includes both rich and poor, educated and underprivileged. At every corner a new snapshot, a new understanding will disrupt every stereotype, paradigm and truism you ever had.

Nature

Bolivia is a wild place and nature lovers, aesthetes and poets alike will find landscapes, views, and nature-born experiences not seen in many other places on the planet. The sheer amount of geographic, topographic, climatic and biological diversity will astound you. Then there are the playful bands of monkeys, the elegant and reclusive herds of vicuña and more than 1000 unique bird species to entertain, inspire and elevate you to a new proximity to the natural world.

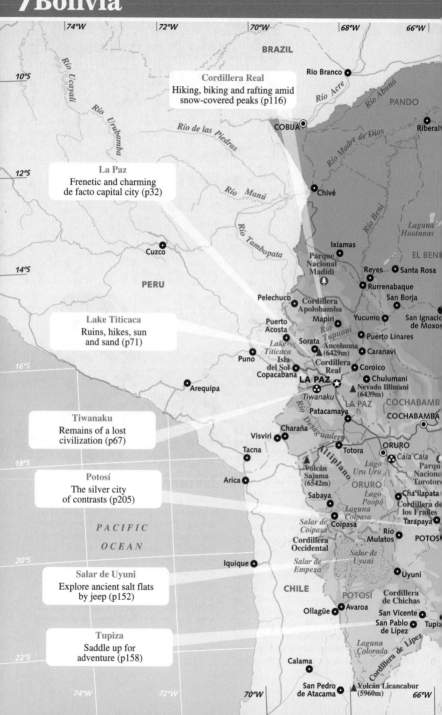

Bolivia

Cordillera Real
Hiking, biking and rafting amid snow-covered peaks (p116)

La Paz
Frenetic and charming de facto capital city (p32)

Lake Titicaca
Ruins, hikes, sun and sand (p71)

Tiwanaku
Remains of a lost civilization (p67)

Potosí
The silver city of contrasts (p205)

Salar de Uyuni
Explore ancient salt flats by jeep (p152)

Tupiza
Saddle up for adventure (p158)

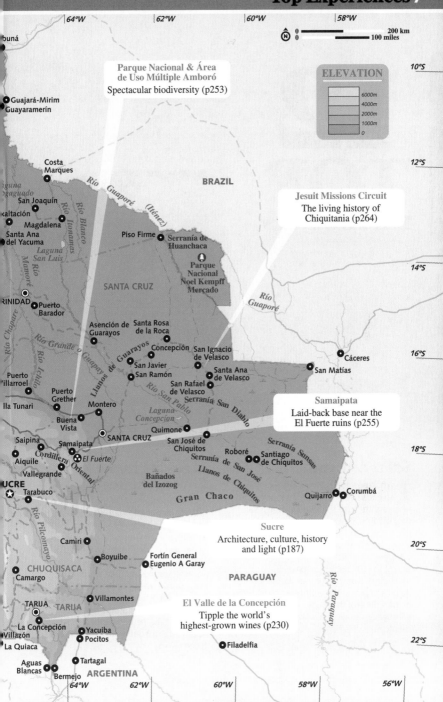

64°W   62°W   60°W   58°W

0   200 km
0   100 miles

10°S

Parque Nacional & Área de Uso Múltiple Amboró
Spectacular biodiversity (p253)

ELEVATION

6000m
4000m
2000m
1000m
0

buná

Guajará-Mirim
Guayaramerín

Costa
Marques   12°S

Laguna
Rogaguado   BRAZIL

San Joaquín   Río Guaporé (Iténez)

xaltación
Magdalena   **Jesuit Missions Circuit**
Santa Ana   The living history of
del Yacuma   Piso Firme Serranía de   Chiquitania (p264)
                                Huanchaca
Laguna
San Luis   Parque
Río Mamoré   Nacional   14°S
                                Noel Kempff
RINIDAD Puerto   Mercado
         Barador   SANTA CRUZ   Río
                                          Guaporé

Río Chapare   Río Grande o Guapay

Asención de Santa Rosa
Guarayos   de la Roca

Concepción San Ignacio   Cáceres   16°S
                         de Velasco
San Javier   San Matías
Puerto   San Ramón   Santa Ana
illaroel   de Velasco
            San Rafael
Ila Tunari Puerto   de Velasco
            Grether   Montero Serranía San Diablo
            Buena
Saipina   Vista   SANTA CRUZ **Samaipata**
                     Quimone   Laid-back base near the
Samaipata   San José de El Fuerte ruins (p255)
Aiquile El Fuerte   Chiquitos   Roboré Serranía Sunsas
         Cordillera Oriental   Santiago   18°S
Vallegrande   Serranía de San José de Chiquitos
                     Llanos de Chiquitos
UCRE Tarabuco   Bañados
                  del Izozog
Río Pilcomayo   Gran Chaco   Quijarro Corumbá

Sucre
Camiri   Architecture, culture, history
                    and light (p187)   20°S
Boyuibe   Fortín General
CHUQUISACA Eugenio A Garay
Camargo   **PARAGUAY**

Villamontes   **El Valle de la Concepción**
TARIJA   TARIJA   Tipple the world's
La Concepción Yacuiba highest-grown wines (p230)
illazón Pocitos
La Quiaca   Filadelfia   22°S

Aguas   Tartagal
Blancas **ARGENTINA**
Bermejo 64°W   62°W   60°W   58°W   56°W

12
TOP
EXPERIENCES

Salar de Uyuni

1 Who knew feeling this cold could feel so good? While a three- to four-day jeep tour through the world's largest salt flat (p152) will leave your bones chattering, it could quite possibly be the defining experience of your Bolivian adventure. The vastness, austerity and crystalline perfection of the salt flat will inspire you. An early morning exploration of rock gardens, geyser fields and piping hot springs along with the camaraderie of three days on the road with your fellow 'Salterians' will create a lasting memory.

Trekking in the Cordillera Real

2 Walk in the path of the Inca along the many trekking routes that weave their way from the Andes into the Amazon Basin, through the remarkable skyward-bound wilderness of the Cordillera Real (p116). These four- to 14-day treks are no small undertaking, but it will be worth every step, every drop of sweat and every blister. Along the way, you'll have the chance to dine with indigenous families, cool off beside cascading waterfalls and connect with Pachamama (Mother Earth) deep within her potent green realm.

M G THERIN WEISE/GETTY IMAGES ©

CUAN HANSEN/GETTY IMAGES ©

Tiwanaku

3 Bolivia's hallmark archaeological site (p67) sets your imagination on fire. Despite lacking the power and prestige of other ruins in Latin America – those who have visited Machu Picchu or Tikal will be hard-pressed not to strike comparisons – this pre-Inca site has a lot to offer. A massive celebration is held on the winter solstice, with smaller ones taking place for the other solstice and equinoxes. The on-site museum provides a thought-provoking glimpse into life in this religious and astronomical center. An easy day trip from La Paz, Tiwanaku is a good place to start your Andean odyssey.

Parque Nacional & Área de Uso Múltiple Amboró

4 Sandwiched between the old and new roads to Cochabamba is one of Bolivia's most biodiverse, and fortunately most accessible, protected areas – the breathtaking Parque Nacional Amboró (p253). Here the lush, leafy Amazon kisses the thorny, dusty Chaco, and the sweaty lowlands greet the refreshing highlands. Stunning scenery, wonderful wildlife and the assistance of professional tour agencies make this a wilderness just begging to be explored. Red howler monkeys

ANDRAS JANCSIK/GETTY IMAGES ©

DANITA DELIMONT/GETTY IMAGES ©

JOHN ELK/GETTY IMAGES ©

Isla del Sol, Lake Titicaca

5 Plopped onto sprawling Lake Titicaca like the cherry on top of an ice-cream sundae, Isla del Sol (p83) is considered to be the birthplace of Andean civilization. You can easily spend four days here, tracking down forgotten Inca roads to small archaeological sites, removed coves and intact indigenous communities. At the end of the day, take in the sunset with a *cerveza* (beer) from your ridge-top lodge. The lake itself has a magnetism, power and energy unique in this world – no wonder many claim the ancient civilization of Atlantis was found here.

Jesuit Missions Circuit

6 Though traveling around the missions circuit (p264) is a challenge in itself, the fantastically ornate reconstructions of Jesuit churches that are the centerpieces of the villages along the route make it well worth the effort. Lovingly restored by professional artisans and historians to offer a glimpse of their former glory, the churches of the missions circuit are testimony to the efforts of the missionaries who, against all odds, managed to establish communities in remote Chiquitania before being expelled from the Spanish colonies in 1767. Art at San Javier

Sucre

7 Glistening in the Andean sun, the white city of Sucre (p187) is the birthplace of the nation and a must-see for any visitor to Bolivia. It's an eclectic mix of the old and the new, where you can while away your days perusing historic buildings and museums, and spend your nights enjoying the city's famous nightlife. Visitors to Sucre invariably fall in love with the place. Convento de San Felipe Neri (p191)

BRENT WINEBRENNER/GETTY IMAGES ©

La Paz Markets

8 The whirling engine that feeds and fuels a nation, the markets of La Paz (p35) are so crazy, so disjointed, so colorful and mad and remarkable that you'll end up spending at least a few afternoons wandering from stall to stall. There are sections for food, sections for sorcery, sections where you can buy back your stolen camera, sections for pipes and Styrofoam – in every shape and form imaginable – and sections packed with fruits, flowers and smelly fish that will push you to olfactory overload.

Samaipata

9 Cosmopolitan Samaipata (p255) manages to retain the air of a relaxing mountain village, despite becoming an increasingly unmissable stop on the Bolivian tourist trail. But it's not just the great-value accommodations and top-class restaurants that bring in the visitors. Samaipata's proximity to the mystical El Fuerte ruins and a series of worthy day trips to nearby areas of outstanding natural beauty mean that many visitors find themselves staying for a lot longer than they planned.
El Fuerte

Potosí

10 Said to be the highest city in the world, lofty Potosí (p205) once sat upon a land laden with silver that funded the Spanish empire for centuries. Though the mines now lay all but barren and the city has long been in economic decline, the remnants of the wealthy past can still be seen through the cracked brickwork of the ornate colonial-era buildings and wonderfully preserved churches. Potosí's most famous museum, the Casa de la Moneda, was once Bolivia's national mint and offers a fascinating insight into the rise and fall of a city that once described itself as 'the envy of kings.'

Wine-Tasting near Tarija

11 Take a deep breath of the thin mountain air and prepare to get dizzy sampling wine from the world's highest vineyards (p231). Though rarely sold outside Bolivia, Tarija wines, produced in a Mediterranean-like climate at altitudes of up to 2400m, are sold throughout Bolivia and have received international plaudits for their fresh, aromatic taste. Whether you prefer *tinto* (red), *rosado* (rosé) or *blanco* (white), you are likely to be pleasantly surprised by the quality on offer and may find yourself taking a bottle or two home for your friends. El Valle de la Concepción (p230)

Tupiza

12 Cut from the pages of a Wild West novel, the canyon country around Tupiza (p158) is an awesome place for heading off into the sunset (in a saddle, atop a mountain bike, on foot or in a 4WD). From town you can ramble out into the polychromatic desert wonderlands and canyons, visiting hard-cut mining villages and the town where Butch Cassidy and the Sundance Kid met their end. The pleasant weather and lyrical feel of the town make it a welcome retreat after a bit of hardship in the highlands.

PETER LANGER/CORBIS ©

IDEALINK PHOTOGRAPHY/ALAMY ©

need to know

Currency
» Boliviano (B$)

Languages
» Spanish, Quechua and Aymará

When to Go

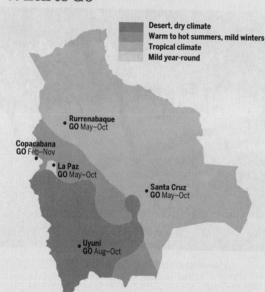

Desert, dry climate
Warm to hot summers, mild winters
Tropical climate
Mild year-round

Rurrenabaque
GO May–Oct

Copacabana
GO Feb–Nov

La Paz
GO May–Oct

Santa Cruz
GO May–Oct

Uyuni
GO Aug–Oct

High Season
(May–Oct)

» Expect mostly sunny days, but it's cooler in the Altiplano.

» Reliable weather makes for easier transit, and better climbing, trekking and mountain biking.

» Prices are generally higher. August is the most popular month.

Shoulder Season

» August to October is a great time to visit the Salar de Uyuni.

» This is a good period for budget hunters.

Low Season
(Nov–Apr)

» The rainy season; it can be miserable in the lowlands.

» Overland transportation is hard or impossible in some areas.

» Climbing is dangerous, trekking and biking tedious. February to April have lots of religious festivals.

Your Daily Budget

Budget less than
B$175

» Dorm/budget beds: B$30-50

» Set lunch and supplies bought from the market

» Museum entrances, limited guided trips

» Second-class transit

Midrange
B$175-630

» Hotel: B$160-400

» Continental breakfast in hotel, set lunch and dinner out

» Extra cash for beers, guided trips and tours

» First-class transit

Top End over
B$630

» Hotel: over B$400

» Breakfast buffet, lunch and dinner at high-end eatery

» Plenty of extra cash for guided trips

» First-class transit and occasional air transfers

Money

» Cash is king, dollars are better than euros, but watch for counterfeits. ATMs and credit cards are accepted in big cities. Small towns have cash advances.

Visas

» Generally free for visits up to 90 days. US citizens need to pay.

Cell Phones

» Local SIM cards work on most modern phones. Roaming rates are high. Data rates are even higher.

Transportation

» Harrowing bus rides, some trains in the Altiplano, boats on the rivers of the Amazon. Beware bogus taxis.

Websites

» **Bolivian Express** (www.bolivianexpress. org) English magazine focusing on cultural coverage.

» **Bolivia Online** (www. bolivia-online.net) Solid portal in English, Spanish and German.

» **Bolivia Web** (www. boliviaweb.com) Good portal with a variety of cultural and artistic links.

» **Bolivia Weekly** (www. boliviaweekly.com) Weekly news in English.

» **Lonely Planet** (www. lonelyplanet.com/ Bolivia) Destination info, hotel bookings, traveler forum etc.

Exchange Rates

Australia	A$1	B$7.24
Canada	C$1	B$6.99
Europe	€1	B$8.92
Japan	¥10	B$0.84
New Zealand	NZ$1	B$5.76
UK	£1	B$11.07
US	US$1	B$6.91

For current exchange rates, see www.xe.com.

Important Numbers

Country code	☏591
International access code	☏00
Ambulance	☏118
Fire	☏119
Operator	☏104

Arriving in Bolivia

» **El Alto International Airport, La Paz**
It's very high (4050m). Taxi is B$50 (US$7) to the airport from the city center. Minibuses are B$6 (US$1) during the day.

» **Viru-Viru International Airport, Santa Cruz**
Buses are the way to go. Taxi is B$70 (US$10) to the airport from the city center. Minibuses are B$3 (US$0.50) during the day.

Don't Leave Home Without

Bolivia is a tough travel destination. Specific travel warnings are included within the chapters. Make sure you are prepared before your trip by checking the visa situation and travel advisories, and packing the following:

» Proof of vaccination for yellow fever; first aid kit and bug spray

» Copy of your passport and of your travel insurance policy

» Plug adapter for your camera battery charger

» Binoculars for wildlife watching, plus an all-purpose knife or tool and a headlamp

» A little extra cash to pay for emergencies or once-in-a-lifetime trips

» Sunscreen and a hat for high altitudes; warm clothes and a rain jacket year-round

» Ear plugs for disco nights you want to sleep through and a pack lock or other luggage security for peace of mind

» Sense of humor – your patience and courage will be tested in queues and on buses

if you like...

Adventure Sports

You're in luck. This Andean nation has kick-ass mountain biking, lost summits that have only seen a handful of ascents, 'easy' 6000m climbs for beginners, and plenty of opportunities for white-water rafting, plus adrenaline-charged activities such as paragliding, ziplining, rappelling and rock climbing.

Climbing Step into this mountaineer's dreamland with steep, glaciated peaks that see little traffic (p23)

Mountain biking With elevation drops of 4000m, Bolivia offers some of the best mountain-bike descents in the world – we suggest you take a bus back up (p24)

Paragliding While it can be hard to find a qualified guide, paragliding in the Cordillera Real and Central Highlands is as good as it gets (p26)

Boating Whether you take a flat-water Amazon cruise or power your way through white-water rock gardens, there's plenty to get you on the water (p25)

Festivals

Bolivia shines during the myriad Catholic and folk festivals. It seems there's something happening nearly every month. The unique costumes, traditions, dances, music and lore take you to another time.

Carnaval It's celebrated throughout the country, but Oruro's festivities, costumes and giant water fight are not to be missed (p136)

Fiesta de la Cruz Tarija comes to life with the Festival of the Cross, while in the countryside *tinku* (ritual fighting) prevails (p17)

Fiesta de la Virgen de Candelaria Pilgrims descend on Copacabana for three days of drunken revelry and to honor the town's patron saint (p77)

Phujllay For a look at Bolivia's Inca roots, check out this two-day celebration that includes a Quechua mass and feast (p16)

Willkakuti On the winter solstice Bolivians celebrate Aymará New Year with offerings at Tiwanaku (p17)

Fiesta del Santo Patrono de Moxos The Amazon's biggest bash includes fireworks, masses, dancing, feasts and wild costumes (p288)

Cultural Exploration

Extraordinary cultural experiences are to be had across Bolivia. The culturally curious will love learning about the nation's unique indigenous imprint, history and modern-day trends by exploring archaeological sites, well-preserved colonial cities, markets and mystical cathedrals and missions.

Sucre Bolivia's white city remains an intellectual stronghold, home to some of the nation's best museums and architecture (p187)

Potosí This colonial city fueled Bolivia's economy for hundreds of years – the city center is not to be missed (p205)

Tiwanaku Bolivia's best-known pre-Inca site has large ceremonial platforms, monoliths and a mysterious arch that may have been an ancient calendar (p67)

Markets Culture lives on every day in La Paz' markets, where Quechua, Aymará, Spanish, English and German are heard on nearly every corner (p35)

Jesuit Missions Circuit There's a mystical air to the missions of the Chiquitania region outside Santa Cruz (p264)

Tarija Indulge your senses in Bolivia's wine country (p231)

ESCUDERO PATRICK/GETTY IMAGES ©

» Offerings for Pachamama (Mother Earth), Sucre (p187)

Wildlife Watching

Nature is everywhere, making Bolivia a hands-down favorite for nature lovers, bird-watchers and anyone curious about wildlife. Large national parks and nature preserves protect (to a degree) the country's endemic and at-risk species. There's a remarkable variety at your doorstep. And with amazingly varied geography (high plains, deserts, mountains, forests, grasslands, jungle) you can see a world's worth of critters in a short time.

Parque Nacional Madidi The Amazon comes to you in Bolivia's best-known national park (p285)

Parque Nacional Tunari Easily accessed wilderness area just outside Cochabamba (p179)

Parque Nacional Amboró This remote national park is home to rare species, such as the spectacled bear, and is a bird-watcher's paradise (p253)

Parque Nacional Sajama The bleak landscape of Sajama is home to rhea, vicuña and even some Andean wildcats (p142)

Parque Nacional Carrasco Explore the cloud forest and encounter a variety of mammals and birds in this isolated national park (p278)

Trekking

For long-distance hauls and shorter day trips along ancient Inca paving, down cloud-encased valleys and through vast swaths of untamed wilderness, you can't beat Bolivia's treks. Many start in the Andes, finishing just above the Amazon Basin, while others take you through lost forests, past remote rural communities and into the heart of the Bolivian countryside.

El Choro Traversing Parque Nacional Cotopata, the Choro trek is the most popular trip around (p100)

Takesi Memorable cultural experiences await in the remote rural villages along this fun and easily accessible option (p102)

Yunga Cruz The most demanding of the Inca treks, this five- to six-day trip takes you over the shoulder of Illimani down into the warm climes of the Yungas (p103)

Cordillera de los Frailes Immerse yourself in Jalq'a culture on this fun village-to-village trek outside Sucre (p200)

Mapiri Further off the beaten track, this six-day romp is for the hard core only (p114)

Crafts

Take a little piece of Bolivia home from this treasure-trove of fine artisan goods. There are intricate textiles, coca products, witches' talismans, high-quality silver products, baskets, scarves, shawls and more. Better yet, most of the shopping is done in resplendent open-air markets, making for a unique cultural and sensory experience.

Musical instruments This is a lyrical place, and La Paz' Sagárnaga market has great deals on instruments such as *pifano* (indigenous flute), *charango* (ukulele-like instrument) and those famous pan pipes (p58)

Woven wear Cruise through the markets in nearly any Altiplano town for fine woven scarves, sweaters and shawls made from alpaca, llama and vicuña wool (p321)

Silver One of the country's prime exports takes art form in the crafts shops of Potosí (p217)

Ceramics The towns around Cochabamba, such as Huayculli, specialize in ceramics, often with an Andean twist (p182)

Jalq'a weaving Head out from Sucre to visit remote Jalq'a villages and explore some of the finest woven wall hangings around (p201)

month by month

Top Events

1 **Fiesta de la Virgen de Candelaria** February

2 **Carnaval** February

3 **Phujllay** March

4 **Gran Poder** May

5 **Fiesta del Santo Patrono de Moxos** July

January

Although part of summer, this is the rainiest month of the year, making getting around tough. Climbing is basically out of the question, but you could rough it on hikes and other outdoor activities.

★ New Year's Eve
Watch out for street vendors selling underwear leading up to January 1. Red underwear will help your love life, yellow is for money and pink is for health. With the chiming of the gongs at midnight, 12 grapes are choked down for good luck and fake money is counted to signal the wealth that will come in the new year.

★ Día de los Reyes Magos
'Kings' Day' (Epiphany) is celebrated on January 6 as the day the three wise kings visited the baby Jesus after his birth. The largest celebrations are in Reyes (in the Beni region), Sucre, Tarija, and rural villages in the departments of Oruro, Cochabamba and Potosí.

★ Alasitas
Taking place in La Paz and Copacabana on January 24 and for two weeks after, this giant fair celebrates Ekeko, the Aymará god of abundance, with stalls and street vendors selling miniatures of items people are longing for (tiny houses, cars, banknotes etc).

February

This wet and warm month sees important celebrations for Pachamama (Mother Earth), especially in traditional communities, with ceremonies and rituals taking place in her honor.

★ Fiesta de la Virgen de Candelaria
This week-long festival is held during the first week of February in Aiquile (Cochabamba), Samaipata (Santa Cruz), Angostura (Tarija) and Cha'llapampa (Oruro). The biggest celebration kicks off on February 2 in Copacabana.

★ Carnaval
Celebrations are held nationwide the week before Lent. Oruro is known for having the most colorful Carnaval fiesta; Santa Cruz, Sucre and Tarija follow suit. Carnaval dates change each year, depending on when Lent falls, so check your calendar.

March

The rain starts to taper off, making it slightly easier to get around. You could consider heading out for a trek or mountain bike. River rafting is getting good.

★ Semana Santa
One of the most impressive of the nationwide Holy Week activities is the Good Friday fiesta in Copacabana, when hundreds of pilgrims arrive on foot from La Paz. It's a fun time across the country.

★ Phujllay
On the second Sunday in March, indigenous people gather in Tarabuco to celebrate the 1816 victory of local armies over Spanish

troops with ritual dancing, song, music and *chicha* (fermented corn) drinking.

May

Winter is here! It's starting to cool off. The weather is nice in the lowlands, but transit can still be a mess. The rains are nearly gone, and trekking, climbing and mountain-biking season begins.

Fiesta de la Cruz

The Festival of the Cross (May 3) brings revelry to Tarija for two weeks. The fiesta is also big in Vallegrande (Santa Cruz), Cochabamba and Copacabana. *Tinku* (ritual fighting) takes place in rural communities around Potosí.

Gran Poder

Held in late May/ early June, this La Paz festival involves candle processions, elaborate costumes and dancing.

June

It's getting a little too cold for comfort in the Altiplano, but the rains are basically gone. Transportation in the lowlands should be getting easier and temperatures are cooling off.

Willkakuti

On June 21, the Aymará celebrate the winter solstice – the return of the new sun – and their New Year. The biggest ceremony takes place overnight at Tiwanaku.

San Juan

This Christian holiday is held nationwide (June 24), with bonfires, fireworks and traditional burning of wood. The largest celebrations take place around Santa Cruz, with firewalkers in the village of Porongo.

July

High season is in full swing. It's dry and cold in the Altiplano, cooler and drier in the lowlands, and just nice in the areas in between.

Fiesta del Santo Patrono de Moxos

Running from July 22 to the end of the month, this kickass festival is the biggest in Beni. Expect outrageous costumes, plenty of drinking and some hard partying.

August

This is the height of the tourist season. It's starting to warm up a little in the Altiplano, making it a good time for a trip to Salar de Uyuni. Important religious and indigenous festivals also take place.

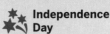 Independence Day

This lively public holiday (August 6) sees lots of gunfire in the air and parades galore. It's celebrated everywhere, but is especially boisterous in Copacabana.

September

Some of the tourists head home, making this cool, dry time perfect to pick up deals. Conditions for adventure sports continue to be excellent, though expect a slight increase in rains.

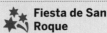 Fiesta de San Roque

One of Tarija's biggest fiestas, San Roque celebrates the end of the plague and leprosy in the area. It kicks off on August 16, but most of the celebrations begin on the first Sunday of September, lasting eight days.

October

At the end of winter (and the high season), rainfall spikes in the lowlands, while it's still relatively tolerable in the Altiplano. Deals can be had, but it's getting tougher to climb, trek and generally be outdoors. It will stay rainy until April.

itineraries

Whether you've got six days or 60, these itineraries provide a starting point for the trip of a lifetime. Want more inspiration? Head online to lonelyplanet.com/thorntree to chat with other travelers.

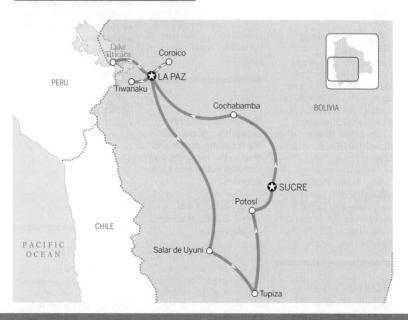

Two Weeks
Best of Bolivia

> This bare-bones itinerary will take you to the best of Bolivia at a head-rattling pace. Start out with a day of acclimatization in **La Paz** visiting the markets. History buffs can take a side trip to **Tiwanaku**. From La Paz, head to **Lake Titicaca**. Allow up to three days on the lake to take in the sites of Copacabana and Isla del Sol and continue your acclimatization. From there, circle down the Altiplano (via La Paz) to the **Salar de Uyuni** for a bone-chatteringly cold three-day jeep tour. You can extend your trip to take you to the former territory of Butch Cassidy in the pleasant cowboy town of **Tupiza**. Swing up to **Potosí**, a starkly beautiful Unesco World Heritage city, situated at 4070m, where you can visit the mint and mines. After a day or two, head to the white city of **Sucre** to hang out with students in grand plazas. Return to La Paz via **Cochabamba**, taking in the good views along the way. On your last day in La Paz, consider a day of museum-hopping or a mountain-bike ride down the World's Most Dangerous Road to **Coroico**.

Four to Five Weeks
The Whole Country

A month allows more time to acclimatize to the high altitude, take in one of Bolivia's signature treks, climb a peak, do a mountain-bike trip or simply dive into Bolivian culture. From **La Paz** you can choose from a variety of day trips, including a visit to **Tiwanaku** or hiking in nearby **Chacaltaya** or **Valle de la Luna**. The adventurous can take on the Takesi or Choro treks, or ride a bike (or bus) down the World's Most Dangerous Road to **Coroico** in the Yungas. Next, head north to **Rurrenabaque** and the famous **Parque Nacional Madidi** – depending on your time and budget you can get here by land, air or boat. Take the time to explore this wild, little-trodden utopia. From 'Rurre,' you can puddle-jump or take a boat to some of the more remote parks, such as the **Reserva Biosférica del Beni**, or simply head over to **Santa Cruz**. From here you'll kick off a multi-day road trip through the **Jesuit Missions Circuit**, curling back via Santa Cruz to the unique ruins near the cooler-than-thou village of **Samaipata** and the spectacular **Parque Nacional & Área de Uso Múltiple Amboró**. Head back toward **Cochabamba** for good market buys. From there you'll start gaining some altitude as you pass through the culturally charged towns of **Sucre** and **Potosí**. After you've had your fill of these colonial masterpieces, cruise down to wine country near **Tarija** for a few days of warm weather, wine and chilled-to-perfection Zen. You can then loop across to **Tupiza** for a day or two of mountain biking, while you arrange your four-day **Salar de Uyuni** trip, going the back way to avoid the crowds. On the way back toward La Paz, adventurous spirits may wish to stop near **Curahuara de Carangas**, before heading on to the high-plains wonderland of **Parque Nacional Sajama**, where hot springs and wildlife watching await. But you're not done yet: if you still have time, continue through La Paz to **Copacabana** for a day or two of beachfront fun on **Lake Titicaca**. Cruise over on the ferry, stopping at Isla de la Luna for an afternoon on your way to Isla del Sol. It's easy to spend five days here, trekking to lost valleys, ruins and small indigenous villages.

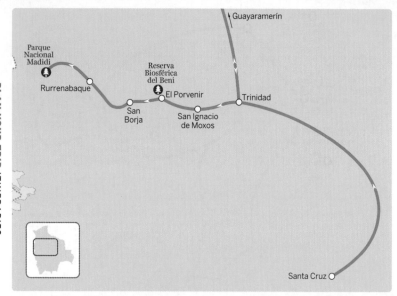

Amazon

More than half of Bolivia's territory lies in the Amazon, and yet this is one of the least visited parts of the country. Sounds amazing! Waterway adventures here are good (and wet) in the rainy season, but if you plan on any type of road travel you should stick with the dry months. Start in **Santa Cruz**, a sophisticated and cosmopolitan city with a dreamy (sometimes steamy) climate and tropical atmosphere. From here fly or catch the overnight bus to **Trinidad**, a sleepy town with a pretty plaza. With enough time, the trip down the Río Mamoré from Trinidad to **Guayaramerín** is highly recommended. If you don't have the time, stay in town for a bit, whirling around on a motorcycle for a local fish meal, a visit to a museum or two and a much-needed siesta or three – it gets hot. A three-hour bus ride will take you to the Jesuit mission village of **San Ignacio de Moxos** – plan your trip around the town's colorful, not-to-be-missed festival in July. From here, wildlife watchers should make a detour from **El Porvenir** into **Reserva Biosférica del Beni**, where the trained eye can spot up to 500 species of birds. There are around 100 different mammals in the reserve, also home to Chimane people. It's a long slog from here via **San Borja** to **Rurrenabaque**, hammock country, from where you can set out for a couple of days on a jungle or pampas tour. One option is to get your jungle fill at the San Miguel del Bala eco-resort, just upriver from Rurrenabaque. Whatever you do, don't miss a trip to **Parque Nacional Madidi**. Bolivia's best-known national park offers a week's or a lifetime's worth of adventures in more than 1.8 million hectares. The park's remarkable biodiversity is best enjoyed at a slow pace, and you should leave enough time to stay at the highly regarded, community-run Chalalán Ecolodge. An option into the Amazon region from La Paz is via a hiking, boating and biking route from the Yungas town of Sorata or on a rough ride through the remote Cordillera Apolobamba.

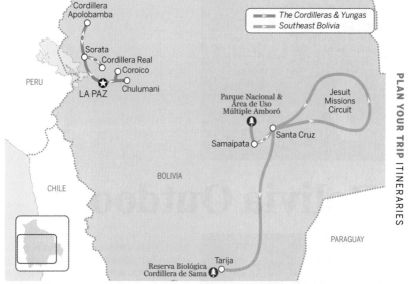

Cordillera
Apolobamba

Sorata
Cordillera Real
Coroico
PERU
LA PAZ   Chulumani

The Cordilleras & Yungas
Southeast Bolivia

Parque Nacional &
Área de Uso
Múltiple Amboró

Jesuit
Missions
Circuit

Santa Cruz
Samaipata

BOLIVIA

CHILE

PARAGUAY

Tarija
Reserva Biológica
Cordillera de Sama

Two Weeks
The Cordilleras & Yungas

Three Weeks
Southeast Bolivia

Trapped between the heights of the Andes and the Amazon, this fascinating area is a wonderland for trekkers, climbers, hikers and bikers. Getting here is half the fun. Trekkers can start from outside **La Paz**, traveling by foot via the Takesi or Choro treks into the heart of the Yungas. You can also get into the southern Yungas on a butt-busting daylong mountain-bike ride down the World's Most Dangerous Road. Be sure to spend a few days at the end of your descent in the pleasant Yungas villages of **Coroico** or **Chulumani**, which offer plenty of day hikes, swimming and a chilled-out traveler vibe. From there, it's back to the capital (or via a tough circuitous jungle route) for climbing and trekking in the **Cordillera Real**, stopping in the cool-air, soft-spirited Andean town of **Sorata**. Adventurers could take on any number of treks from Sorata, good mountain-bike adventures or head up to the glaciated peaks of the Cordillera. Then, if you have the time, you could extend this trip to the seldom-explored **Cordillera Apolobamba** for visits to lost tribes or wildcat miners and loads of deep wilderness trekking. Otherwise, think about linking from Sorata by land or boat north into the Amazon Basin.

This trip will get you away from the main tourist track and into Bolivia's warm southern comforts. Along the way, there are a few trekking options, interesting cultural centers and energetic cityscapes. Start with a few days of partying in **Santa Cruz**, Bolivia's second-largest city. It's great fun just wandering around the streets as you dive into *camba* (lowlands) culture. Then make your way out of the city for a weeklong dusty adventure through the **Jesuit Missions Circuit**, a series of beautiful mission villages where baroque music and faith meld with the chilled-out culture of the Guaraní, which is punctuated by contented smiles, simple connection with the land and unique cultural experiences. Cruise back through Santa Cruz on your way to the pre-Inca ruins at **Samaipata** and tip-top wildlife watching at the **Parque Nacional & Área de Uso Múltiple Amboró**. From the park (backtracking via Samaipata and Santa Cruz) make your way down to the relaxed wine-country town of **Tarija**. After a few days in town, you can customize the tail end of your adventure with hikes along the Inca Trail in the **Reserva Biológica Cordillera de Sama** or in any of the numerous national parks and reserves of the Chaco region.

Bolivia Outdoors

Best Treks

El Choro Two- or three-day classic trek
Takesi Bolivia's Inca Trail passes small villages on a two-day journey.
Yunga Cruz A five- or six-day thigh buster with fewer crowds and more adventure.
Cordillera de los Frailes Bring a guide on this off-the-beaten-track hike.

Best Biking Trips

World's Most Dangerous Road It's a classic mountain-biking adventure.
Zongo Valley Experts only at this downhill mecca.
Sorata Less traveled, with more single track.
La Paz Get steep near Chacaltaya and the Zona Sur.

Best Climbs

Huayna Potosí Good for beginners, but it's no cake walk.
Illimani Experts will love this amazingly beautiful climb.
Cordillera Apolobamba Far from civilization, this is where adventure begins.

Bolivia is like a theme park for grown-up adventurers. It offers multiday treks, relatively easy day hikes, mountain biking that'll leave your teeth chattering, climbs to lost Andean peaks, rivers to raft, rugged 4WD trips to the corners of the old Inca empire, and just about anything else you could ask for.

Dry season (May through October) makes for safer climbs, drier bike trails and easier hikes. Plan to get wet the rest of the year.

Hiking & Trekking

Hiking and trekking are arguably the most rewarding Andean activities. Add a porter, llama train and experienced guide, and you have all the makings for a grand adventure. Some of the most popular hikes and treks in Bolivia begin near La Paz, traverse the Cordillera Real along ancient Inca routes and end in the Yungas. These include the well-known and well-used **El Choro**, **Takesi** and **Yunga Cruz** treks.

Sorata is a trekker's dream come true, offering a variety of options from don't-leave-home-without-a-machete-type hikes such as the **Mapiri Trail** to more pleasant walks on Inca trails surrounding the Illampu massif. The **Área Natural de Manejo Integrado Nacional (Anmin) Apolobamba**, which includes the four- to five-day **Lagunillas to Agua Blanca** trek, is becoming more popular but is best visited with a guide. Be aware that the treks near Sorata and in the Cordillera Apolobamba have largely fallen into disuse, and there has been an increase in reports of robberies.

Bolivia's national parks are also paradise for hikers, with hiking opportunities in **Parque Nacional & Área de Uso Múltiple Amboró** and **Parque Nacional Sajama**. A few hikes outside **Charazani** are also worth checking out.

For a shorter jaunt, hire a guide and cruise the cultural and historic sites and hot springs around **Cordillera de los Frailes** outside Sucre or **El Nido de los Condores** near Samaipata.

Many treks can be done by experienced outdoors travelers without a guide (you should know how to use a map, compass and GPS, build a fire – even in the rain – and open a bottle of wine with a pocket knife). Nevertheless, hiring a guide provides an added level of security. No matter what, check out the security situation before heading out. Solo female travelers need to be extra careful.

Trekking in Bolivia by Yossi Brain is a good resource.

Mountaineering & Climbing

Climbing in Bolivia is an exercise in extremes – like the country itself. In the dry southern winter (May to October) temperatures may fluctuate as much as 40.5°C in a single day. Once you're acclimatized to the Altiplano's relatively thin air (you'll need at least a week), there is still 2500m of even thinner air above.

A plus for climbers is the access to mountains; although public transportation may not always be available, roads pass within easy striking distance of many fine peaks.

The most accessible and spectacular climbing in the country is along the 160km-long **Cordillera Real** northeast of La Paz. Six of its peaks rise above 6000m and there are many more gems in the 5000m range. Because of the altitude, glaciers and ice or steep snow, few of the peaks are 'walk-ups,' but some are within the capability of an average climber, and many can be done by beginners with a competent guide. **Huayna Potosí** is one of the most popular climbs for nonprofessionals, but be aware that although it's on the La Paz agency circuit, it's no walk (or climb) in the park! La Paz operators also take climbs up the magnificent **Volcán Sajama**, Bolivia's highest peak.

Around **Cordillera Quimsa Cruz** there is a variety of lesser-known climbing opportunities. **Volcán Illimani** is for serious climbing expeditions and popular among advanced climbing groups.

RESPONSIBLE TREKKING

To help preserve the ecology and beauty of Bolivia, consider the following tips when trekking.

» **Carry out all your trash** Yes, many tracks in Bolivia are already littered, but this doesn't mean that you should contribute to it.

» **Never bury your rubbish** Digging disturbs soil and ground cover, encourages erosion, affects local wildlife and the rubbish may take years to rot.

» **Keep water sources clean** Contamination of water sources by human feces can lead to the transmission of all sorts of nasties. Where there is a toilet, use it. Where there is none, best practice is to carry waste out. If you decide to bury it, dig a deep hole away from water sources.

» **Be clean, but not too clean** Don't use detergents or toothpaste in or near watercourses.

» **Stick to existing trails** Avoid cutting corners – it contributes to erosion.

» **Don't depend on open fires for cooking** Cook on a lightweight kerosene, alcohol or Shellite (white gas) stove and avoid those powered by disposable butane gas canisters. Continuous cutting of wood by local communities and trekkers can cause deforestation, plus wildfire risks.

» **Do not feed the wildlife** Don't touch them either. It can lead to animals becoming dependent on handouts, to unbalanced populations and to disease.

» **Always seek permission to camp** Ask in the village if you can camp.

Staying Safe

Dangers include getting lost, avalanches, crevasses, snow blindness, dehydration, altitude sickness, and occasional muggings on the way up. To avoid these things be careful when hiring a guide, buy mountaineering insurance, drink lots of water, protect your skin, dress properly and wear sunglasses. Altitude sickness is a very real thing – watch for signs of fatigue, dizziness and nausea. Proper acclimatization and hydration will help. If you think you are getting sick, head down.

Socorro Andino Bolivia (p117) provides rescue assistance for around US$100 per day, per guide.

Hiring a Guide

Many travel agencies in La Paz and larger cities organize climbing and trekking trips in the Cordillera Real and other areas. Not all, however, are everything they claim to be. Some guides have gotten lost, several have died, and others have practiced less-than-professional tactics, such as stringing 10 or more climbers on the same rope. Always do your research and go with professionally accredited guides such as those registered with the **Asociación de Guias de Montaña** (☑2-214-7951; www.agmtb.org; Sagárnaga 189, Edificio Doryan, La Paz), an internationally certified association of registered mountain guides. They're more expensive, but it's worth the cost.

When choosing an agency, ask to see the equipment you will be using and meet the guide. If harnesses are worn, double-boots are broken down or the ropes are frayed, demand they be replaced. Talk with the guide and make sure you feel comfortable with them. When you hit the mountain, the guide should teach you how to travel on a rope (two people and a guide per rope, no more) and self-arrest with your ice ax.

Agencies can provide almost everything you will need – from just organizing transportation to a full service with guide, cook, mules, porters, an itinerary and so forth – but you should bring warm clothes (avoid cotton and stick to wool or synthetics), a headlamp and extra batteries, plenty of water and snacks. The guides will generally prepare three meals a day.

Professional trekking guides generally charge US$40 to US$60 per day (plus food).

Maps

Historically, maps of Bolivia's climbing areas have been poor in quality and difficult to obtain. Even now, elevations of peaks are murky, with reported altitudes varying as much as 600m – it seems the rumor that Ancohuma is taller than Argentina's Aconcagua won't die.

Maps are available from Los Amigos del Libro, which has branches in **La Paz** (Map p38; ☑22-220-4321; www.librosbolivia.com; Mercado 1315), Cochabamba (p177) and **Santa Cruz** (Map p242; ☑3-336-0709; Ingavi 114), and other bookstores. In La Paz try the trekking agents and tourist shops along Sagárnaga.

The *Travel Map of Bolivia,* one of the best country maps, and *New Map of the Cordillera Real,* which shows mountains, roads and precolonial routes, are published by O'Brien Cartographics. They are out of print, but still available at various tourist hangouts, including the postcard kiosks within La Paz' central post office (p61).

Government 1:50,000 topographical and specialty sheets are available from the **Instituto Geográfico Militar (IGM)**, which has offices in most major cities, including a branch in La Paz (p60).

Walter Guzmán Córdova has produced 1:50,000 colorful contour maps of El Choro-Takesi–Yunga Cruz, Mururata–Illimani, Huayna Potosí–Condoriri and Sajama, but those other than the El Choro-Takesi–Yunga Cruz map are in short supply. The Deutscher Alpenverein (German Alpine Club) produces the excellent and accurate 1:50,000 maps *Alpenvereinskarte Cordillera Real Nord (Illampu),* which includes the Sorata area, and *Alpenvereinskarte Cordillera Real Süd (Illimani),* which centers on Illimani.

Guidebooks

The best mountaineering guide is *Bolivia: A Climbing Guide* by Yossi Brain; the late author worked as a climbing guide in La Paz and served as secretary of the Club Andino Boliviano. *The Andes of Bolivia* by Alain Mesili was recently translated into English.

Mountain Biking

Bolivia is blessed with some of the most dramatic mountain-biking terrain in the world, and offers seven months a year of near-perfect weather and relatively easy access to mountain ranges, magnificent lakes, precolonial ruins and trails, and myriad eco-zones connected by an extensive network of footpaths and jeep roads.

The Bolivian Andes are full of long and thrilling descents, as well as challenging touring possibilities – but most people opt for downhill rides because of the altitude. One of the world's longest downhill rides will take you from **Parque Nacional Sajama** down to the Chilean coast at Arica. In the dry season you can even tackle the mostly level roads of the vast Amazon lowlands.

Some rides from La Paz can be done by riders of any experience level. There are more combinations than on a bike lock as trails lead through Inca roads, tropical tracks, jeep roads and scree chutes. The best known (but not necessarily the best for serious riders) is the thrilling 3600m trip down the **World's Most Dangerous Road** from La Cumbre to Coroico. Another popular route near La Paz is the lush **Zongo Valley** ride, which can be started from **Chacaltaya** (5395m).

The town of Sorata is emerging as the mountain-bike mecca of Bolivia, with scores of downhill single-track trails and jeep road rides near town, including a combination bike-and-boat trip from Sorata to Rurrenabaque. For the hardcore rider, scree chutes to biker-built single track and jump zones abound. Every year, typically in October, Sorata is host to the longest downhill race on a hand-built course, the **Jach'a Avalancha (Grand Avalanche) Mountain Bike Race**. Other epic descents begin in Sorata and head into the hinterland of the Cordillera Muñecas, or start in Copacabana and La Paz and head to Sorata.

More and more travelers are taking up the cycling challenge and heading on two wheels from the north of the country to the south, or vice versa. Those with their own bikes need to consider several factors. During part of the rainy season, particularly December to February, some roads become mired in muck and heavy rain can greatly reduce visibility, creating dangerous conditions. Also worth noting is Bolivia's lack of spare parts. Comprehensive repair kits are essential. In the southern Altiplano and Uyuni regions, water is very scarce; you must be able to carry at least two days' worth of water in some places.

4WD Tours

Heading out in 4WD vehicles is becoming an increasingly popular activity. It allows you access to places that are tricky to get to and, although sometimes on the pricier side, may be the only feasible way of visiting a region. As well as the standard **Southwest Circuit** tours (setting off from Uyuni, Tupiza or La Paz), you can cruise out to the *quebradas* (ravines or washes, usually dry) beyond Tupiza, visit the **Tarabuco market** on a tour from Sucre or the **Inca ruins** near Cochabamba.

Tours in 4WDs are a great way to enter some of the country's national parks. Current trips include those around **Parque Nacional Torotoro** (from Cochabamba) and **Parque Nacional Sajama** (from La Paz), or into the **Cordillera de los Frailes** (from Sucre).

Those keen to arrange trips themselves should consider hiring a driver. This can be an efficient and good-value way of seeing specific areas, especially in a group.

White-Water Rafting & Kayaking

One of Bolivia's greatest secrets is the number of white-water rivers that drain the eastern slopes of the Andes between the Cordillera Apolobamba and the Chapare. Here, avid rafters and kayakers can enjoy thrilling descents. While access will normally require long drives and/or treks – and considerable expense if done independently – there are a few fine rivers that are relatively accessible.

Some La Paz tour agencies can organize day trips on the **Río Coroico**. Other options include the **Río Unduavi** and numerous wild Chapare rivers.

A more gentle but fun rush in the Chuquisaca region is a float downriver in rubber inner-tubes. This trip is often coupled with mountain biking. One of the greatest thrills along the same biathlon idea is to cruise 4000m downhill on mountain bike to Mapiri and then raft your way for several days, camping en route, to Rurrenabaque. Amazon canoe tours along the **Río Beni** are unforgettable, as are the trips along the **Río Mamoré** from Trinidad.

GO WITH THE FLOW

Numerous tour operators are combining rafting, biking, hiking and 4WD trips. These trips can be costly, but it's great fun to mix things up a bit.

» **Sorata to Rurrenabaque** A double-action trip comprising a five-day ride-and-river jaunt. This full-on adventure includes a two-day biking trip, which culminates in an exciting 4000m descent on single track via Consata and Mapiri, followed by three days of floating down the Río Beni on a riveting expedition in a motorized dugout canoe, with side hikes to waterfalls and to Parque Nacional Madidi for wildlife watching. It's offered by Andean Epics (p110).

» **Coroico** You can custom-build trips with guides from Coroico that will take you to waterfalls by dawn, in an all-terrain vehicle (ATV) by noon and to visit canyons by sunset.

» **Tupiza** Travel by horse, ATV and mountain bike on innovative triathlons.

» **Copacabana** Paddle a swan boat across the bay, cycle to Yampupata, row to Isla del Sol, run across the island, then take the boat back. It's never been done in one day (according to legend).

Horseback Riding

For some, a horse saddle sure beats a bus seat, and it's a great way to absorb the sights, sounds and smells of a country. Horseback-riding trips are a new, increasingly popular way to reach otherwise inaccessible wilderness areas. The best place to try it is in Tupiza, former territory of Butch Cassidy and the Sundance Kid. You get to see the multicolored desert landscape, *quebradas* and cacti-dotted countryside. Other pleasant options for horseback riding are through cloud forest in Coroico, around La Paz – see **Calacoto Tours** (Map p38; ☎2-211-2524; www.calacoto tours.com; cnr Murillo & Sagárnaga, La Paz) – and in the *cerrado* (savanna) of the **Reserva Biosférica del Beni**.

Wildlife Watching

Flora and fauna fanatics are spoilt for choice in this extraordinary country where world-class wildlife watching abounds. The diversity of intact habitats throughout the country accounts for the huge number of surviving species.

Parque Nacional Madidi, for example, home to more than 1000 bird species as well as wildlife endemic to the majority of Bolivia's ecosystems, from tropical rainforest and savanna to cloud forest and alpine tundra, is arguably one of the most biodiverse places on the planet. Agencies, often run by scientists or environmentalists, run nature trips out of Santa Cruz, Cochabamba and Samaipata and, to a lesser extent, from La Paz.

Bird-watching hot spots include the highlands around La Paz and Cochabamba, Parque Nacional & Área de Uso Múltiple Amboró and the Reserva Biosférica del Beni. Contact Asociación Armonía (p261), the Bolivian partner of BirdLife International, for further information. Other organizations with bird knowledge include Fundación Amigos de la Naturaleza (p250) and Michael Blendinger Tours (p257).

Other Activities

» **Paragliding** is a recently introduced activity, so it should be done with care – not all local guides are experts of years' standing. Most paragliding is done around Sucre.

» More relaxing hot spots are the many *termas* (**hot springs**) that bubble away in various parts of the country. You don't have to go to the ends of the earth to immerse yourself in this less energetic activity – there are springs in **Tarapaya** just outside Potosí, **Talula**, **San Javier** and **Sajama**.

» **Ziplining** and **canopy tours** are just starting up, with ziplines near Coroico and 'The Biggest Canopy in Bolivia' near Rurrenabaque. Then there's **fishing**, **canyoneering**, driving **ATVs** (noise and pollution pots that they are), and **rappelling** off buildings in La Paz.

regions at a glance

La Paz & Around

History ✓✓
Shopping ✓✓✓
Nightlife ✓✓

Walking the Town
La Paz' history and culture come to life on every corner. Head up the preposterously steep hills to the myriad museums celebrating Bolivia's archaeology, natural history, culture, crafts, music, revolutions and more. The town is really an open-air museum itself, with churches dating back hundreds of years, and living, breathing, seething markets that reflect the nation's cultural currents.

Crafts Shopping
The markets of La Paz are some of the most compelling in the world. In the tangle of open-air stalls, covered malls, crafts kiosks and witches' markets you can find just about everything under the sun, including crafts and textiles from across Bolivia, llama fetuses, aphrodisiacs, woodcarvings, free-trade wares, metal pipes and tin pans. It's all part of the great whirl of commerce that drives the nation's economy and culture.

Bring the Party
La Paz loves to party. And at 3660m, just about everybody's a lightweight. Diverse religious and civic festivals are held throughout the year and bring plenty of daytime parades and pageantry. Come sunset, a parade of different sorts takes hold in the lounges, discos and bars of Sopocachi. It's about as high-octane as you can get without breaking the law.

p32

Lake Titicaca

History ✓✓
Hiking ✓
Scenery ✓✓✓

Birthplace of the Sun
The Tiwanaku and Inca believed the sun and their civilization were born from this remarkable body of water, and it remains a great spot to explore pre-Columbian history.

Island Traverse
In a day or two you can hike from tip to tail of the mystical Isla del Sol. On the way you'll encounter numerous ruins dating from before the Spanish conquest. There are also intact indigenous villages, plenty of fun, family-run restaurants and a chilled-out vibe that's a traveler's dream.

Water and Ice
There are no bad views over Lake Titicaca. Crossing between islands, you'll be entranced by mirrored reflections of the nearby Cordillera Real, while the sunsets and sunrises will burn their imprint into your soul.

p71

The Cordilleras & Yungas

Trekking ✓✓✓
Climbing ✓✓✓
Biking ✓✓✓

Inca Trails
Ancient Inca trails lead from the high Andes to the edge of the Amazon, taking you through diverse eco-systems, past squawking riots of tropical birds, indigenous villages, waterfalls and impressively sheer cliffs.

Step into Vertical
Strap on your crampons and ice ax for an ascent of the glaciated peaks of the Cordilleras Real, Apolobamba and Quimsa Cruz. There are peaks that have been summited only a handful of times and trade routes good for novice climbers.

Downhill Biking
With elevation drops of more than 3000m, this is one of the best downhill mountain-biking spots in the world. Push the envelope on arm-busting descents of the World's Most Dangerous Road, past waterfalls near Sorata or down seldom-visited single tracks.

p91

Southern Altiplano

Wildlife ✓✓
Adventure ✓✓
Scenery ✓✓✓

High-Plains Fauna
Bolivia's Altiplano is a wilderness of bleak and vast proportions. Up here, under the sheltering sun, wild herds of vicuña are on the rise. Lucky visitors will also spot South America's aloof version of the ostrich, the rhea, plus any number of Andean camelids.

Salar de Uyuni
Adventure abounds on a three- or four-day jeep tour of the Salar de Uyuni. There are mountain-bike trips and ATV tours from nearby Tupiza, as well as climbs up massive volcanic peaks and descents into centuries-old mines.

Extraordinary Views
As you make your way across this remarkable and remote wilderness, you'll marvel at the world's largest salt flat, whimsical rock formations, cacti-filled valleys straight out of the Old West, volcanic peaks, technicolor lakes and a sky that seems to stretch forever.

p128

Central Highlands

Climate ✓✓✓
History ✓✓
Mines ✓

Cool Breeze
Cochabambinos (residents of Cochabamba) claim that their year-round spring-like climate makes it the ideal place to live. Whether you are coming from the sultry lowlands or the freezing highlands, you might just agree.

Colonial Charms
There is no place in Bolivia that can match the historic majesty of Sucre, a wonderfully understated town in the foothills of the Andes that gave birth to the nation's independence. The museums, cathedrals and open plazas make this one of Bolivia's grandest colonial cities.

Silvery Past
A visit to the silver mines of Potosí offers an evocative journey into the region's past, and an insight into the realities of treasure hunting in any century.

p166

South Central Bolivia & the Chaco

Scenery ✓
Wine ✓✓✓
Food ✓✓

Windswept Highlands

The arid, thorny hills of the baking-hot Chaco give way to a windswept highlands landscape peppered with pink-flamingo lakes. There's a delightful vibe to the sights around Tarija's wine country, and plenty of wild national parks and reserves in between.

Oenophilia

Bolivian wine doesn't often get the credit it deserves, but a few days spent sampling the goods in El Valle de la Concepción wineries near Tarija will quickly turn you into a convert, as will the friendly folks that call this land of wine and honey home.

Food

Chapaco (Tarija local) cuisine is unique and inventive and, while some of the dishes sound more appealing than others, you won't find a similar menu elsewhere in the country.

p220

Santa Cruz & Gran Chiquitania

Food ✓✓
History ✓
Missions ✓✓

Food

The city of Santa Cruz is low on sights but big on eats, and its cosmopolitan population offers up a variety of culinary options that will whet the appetite of even the fussiest eaters.

Revolution

Che pilgrims will make a beeline for La Higuera, where the revolutionary's Bolivian project finally came to an end when he was captured and executed, and Vallegrande, where his body was then displayed.

Jesuit Missions

Wonderfully ornate churches which have been reconstructed in their original style are the centerpieces of the remote towns that make up the Jesuit Missions Circuit, one of the country's most surprising and entrancing highlights.

p238

Amazon Basin

Adventure ✓✓
Culture ✓✓
Wildlife ✓✓✓

Outdoor Adventure

The very word 'Amazon' is synonymous with adventure. Progress is slow and the insects can be a distraction, but this is a land where nature rules and you are just a guest.

Festivals Unfettered

The exuberant festivals in Trinidad and San Ignacio de Moxos are famous nationwide for their color and chaos and will leave you no doubt that you are in the heart of the Amazon.

Wild Explorer

Hands down the most biodiverse region on the planet, the Amazon has almost mythical status among ecotourists, who are tempted by the possibility of a fleeting glimpse of a jaguar and wooed by the morning chorus of howler monkeys.

p271

Every listing is recommended by our authors, and their favourite places are listed first

Look out for these icons:

 Our author's top recommendation

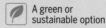 A green or sustainable option

FREE No payment required

See the Index for a full list of destinations covered in this book.

On the Road

La Paz & Around

Best Places to Eat

» Pronto (p52)

» Mercado Uruguay (p54)

» Mongo's (p55)

Best Places to Stay

» Hotel Rosario (p48)

» Casa Fusion (p48)

» Wild Rover (p50)

» A La Maison Appart-Hotel (p49)

Why Go?

La Paz is a city of Gothic proportions, world-class views and a multi-ethnic cultural imprint unique to the Americas. It's sinister and serendipitous – often at the same time. While there's plenty of petty crime, traffic and pollution, La Paz is somehow so unique and so odd that it could very well become the highlight of your trip.

Most of the city lies within a preposterously steep valley at around 3660m. Medieval-looking buildings ascend the slopes with Seussian haphazardness finally spilling over the edge into the rough commerce hub of El Alto, while to the south the three-peaked Illimani (6402m/21,003ft) watches over it all in stately serenity.

A few days wandering the frenetic markets, high-quality museums, crafts stalls, cloistered nightclubs and winding alleyways will not disappoint. This is also the staging center for many hikes, bike trips and excursions into the fascinating Andean wilderness areas that surround the city.

When to Go
La Paz

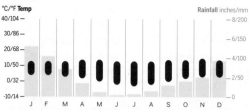

Nov–Apr Rain most afternoons turns the steep streets into torrents.

May–Oct Winter days are cool but sunny, making this La Paz' high season.

Jan–Jun Festival season includes Alasitas, Gran Poder, Carnaval and Aymará New Year.

Lay of the Land

The La Paz metropolitan area is divided into three very distinct zones. North of the city center is the separate municipality of **El Alto** (where you arrive if coming by plane). This fast-growing commercial and industrial city is the center for Aymará culture, has fascinating markets and few tourist attractions. Down from here in the valley is the city of **La Paz**, where most travelers spend their time. On the west side of the valley are the notable commercial districts Rosario, Belen, San Pedro and Sopocachi. To the east, the action centers on the Plaza Murillo, Santa Bárbara and Miraflores neighborhoods. If you get lost in La Paz, head downhill. You'll soon enough find yourself somewhere along the main thoroughfare, **El Prado**. Further down the valley to the south is the Zona Sur. This is where the city's wealthy live and, with safety a concern in the town proper, many businesses (and businesspeople) are moving here. There's a good collection of upscale restaurants and hotels.

IMMERSING YOURSELF

La Paz will give you what you put in. But the true heart of the city lies behind closed doors, and the only way to really break through is by learning the language and engaging with locals.

Several **language courses** will give you the vocabulary you need to learn about La Paz' unique history, culture and arts scenes. An especially recommended experience is setting up a homestay, which you can arrange through some hostels or language schools.

Volunteering is another way to learn about the city. Many travelers end up spending a few extra weeks in La Paz either working for their hostel or donating their time to one of the many nonprofits in the area.

La Paz' Best Views

» Mirador Laikakota (p41) is a *mirador* (lookout) set above the city's largest park. It's popular with young lovers and old dreamers alike.

» The Radisson Plaza Hotel's top-floor Aransaya Restaurant (p49) has spectacular city views. The food can be over-priced and formal, but the views more than make up for it.

» Get vertical with the new rappelling adventures hundreds of feet up a downtown skyscraper with Urban Rush (p45).

MAIN POINTS OF ENTRY

Most travelers will arrive either at El Alto International Airport or the main bus terminal. Buses from within Bolivia may also drop you in Villa Fátima or the Plaza 1 de Mayo area. For more information, see Getting There & Away (p61).

Fast Facts

» Telephone area code: 2
» Population: 1.4 million
» Elevation: 3660m (12,007ft)

Top Tips

» Bring a jacket as at this altitude it's cold at night year-round.

» Drinking lots of water helps with altitude sickness.

» There's quite a bit of petty theft in La Paz (and violent attacks are on the rise), so leave your valuables in the hotel. For more information, see p58.

Resources

» Lonely Planet (www.lonelyplanet.com/bolivia/la-paz)

» Boliviaweb (www.boliviaweb.com)

» Bolivia Online (www.bolivia-online.net)

» La Razón (www.la-razon.com/salimos-hoy.html) Events calendar in Spanish

» Eventos Bolivia (www.eventosbolivia.com.bo) Entertainment listings in Spanish

La Paz & Around Highlights

1 Wander up from **El Prado** through tight alleyways to the top of the valley

2 Buy aphrodisiacs as you have your fortune told in the **Mercado de Hechicería** (p36)

3 Get cultured at the **Calle Jaén Museums** (p39)

4 Go **shopping** (p58) till you drop in fair-trade boutiques along Illampu, El Prado and in the Zona Sur

5 Buy the ingredients for a picnic lunch from the street stalls of the bustling **Mercado Negro** (p35)

6 Eat to the beat of folklore music at a **peña** (folk music venue; p56)

7 Get dusty as you descend nearly 3600m (12,000ft) by mountain bike on the **World's Most Dangerous Road** (p46)

8 Dive into history's past at the **Tiwanaku ruins** (p67)

LA PAZ

History

La Ciudad de Nuestra Señora de La Paz (the City of Our Lady of Peace) was founded on October 20, 1548, by a Spaniard, Captain Alonzo de Mendoza, at present-day Laja situated on the Tiwanaku road. Soon after, La Paz was shifted to its present location, the valley of the Chuquiago Marka (now called the Río Choqueyapu), which had been occupied by a community of Aymará miners.

The Spaniards didn't waste any time in seizing the gold mines, and Captain Mendoza was installed as the new city's first mayor. Unions between Spanish men and indigenous women eventually gave rise to a primarily mestizo population.

If the founding of La Paz had been based on anything other than gold, its position in the depths of a rugged canyon probably would have dictated an unpromising future. However, the protection this setting provided from the fierce Altiplano climate and the city's convenient location on the main trade route between Lima and Potosí – much of the Potosí silver bound for Pacific ports passed through La Paz – offered the city some hope of prosperity once the gold ran out. And by the time the railway was built, the city was well enough established to continue commanding attention.

In spite of its name, the City of Our Lady of Peace has seen a good deal of violence. Since Bolivian independence in 1825, the republic has endured more than 190 changes of leadership. An abnormally high mortality rate once accompanied high office in Bolivia, and the job of president came with a short life expectancy. In fact, the presidential palace on the plaza is now known as the Palacio Quemado (Burned Palace), owing to its repeated gutting by fire. As recently as 1946 then-president Gualberto Villarroel was publicly hanged in Plaza Murillo.

Today La Paz is Bolivia's de facto capital (Sucre remains the constitutional capital).

☉ Sights

Most official sights, including museums, are closed during the Christmas holiday period (December 25 to January 6).

WEST OF EL PRADO

The areas west of the Prado include the fascinating markets around Rosario, Belen and San Pedro, the cemetery and the sophisticated Sopocachi neighborhood.

Markets   MARKET

La Paz' buzzing, frenetic markets are easily the highlight of any trip. It is here that the commerce and culture of this modern-day capital collide in a wonderful riot of honks, shrieks, smells, tastes and Kodachrome moments. There are open-air markets from Plaza Pérez Velasco uphill to the cemetery – past Mercado Lanza, and Plazas Eguino and Garita de Lima. The narrow cobblestone streets off Max Paredes are the center of the action. Locals call this section the **Mercado Negro** (Black Market; ☉6am-8pm). Every day is market day in La Paz, but Saturdays are especially fun.

Especially interesting are the sections near Graneros ('designer' clothes), Tumusla and Isaac Tamayo (everything and anything), and between Santa Cruz and Sagárnaga (tools and building materials). The best place for electronics is along Eloy Salmón. Be especially careful when wandering around this part of town: it's notorious for light fingers. It's best to take a taxi here at night.

North of Plaza San Francisco, on Calle Figueroa, the **Mercado Lanza** (Map p38; ☉6am-8pm) is one of La Paz' main food markets. It also houses the splendid **Flower Market**.

Iglesia de San Francisco   CHURCH

(Map p38; Plaza San Francisco) The hewed stone basilica of San Francisco, on the plaza of the same name, reflects an appealing blend of 16th-century Spanish and mestizo trends. The church was founded in 1548 by Fray Francisco de los Ángeles, and construction began the following year. The original structure collapsed under heavy snowfall around 1610, but it was reconstructed between 1744 and 1753. The second building was built entirely of stone quarried at nearby Viacha. The facade is decorated with stone carvings of natural themes such as *chirimoyas* (custard apples), pinecones and tropical birds.

The mass of rock pillars and stone faces in the upper portion of Plaza San Francisco is intended to represent and honor Bolivia's three great cultures – Tiwanaku, Inca and modern.

The cloisters and garden of **Museo San Francisco** (Map p38; ☎231-8472; Plaza San Francisco; entrance B$20; ☉9am-6pm Mon-Sat), adjacent to the basilica, beautifully revive the history and art of the city's landmark. There are heavenly religious paintings, historical artifacts, an interesting anteroom and a God-like, if quirky, view from the roof.

LA PAZ IN...

Two Days

Given the altitude and hills, La Paz is best explored at a leisurely pace. Allow a solid day to acclimatize before really hitting the town hard. You should be able to 'do' much of the city in just two days. Start your morning with breakfast on the **Prado** or a snack – try *salteñas* (meat and vegetable filled pastry shells) – around **Plaza Avaroa**, both perfect spots for watching one of the world's highest cities wake up. Stroll the historic cobblestone streets around **Iglesia de San Francisco** and Calle Jaén, home to the wonderful **Calle Jaén Museums**. Tie some cultural threads together at the **Museo de Textiles Andinos Bolivianos**, or wander through the interesting (if slightly over-the-top) artesanía alley **Calle Linares**, and **Mercado de Hechicería** (Witches' Market). From here, head up to the **Mercado Negro** (Black Market) for amazing sights, sounds, smells and tastes (but be sure to watch for pickpockets).

Come dusk, head back downhill along the Prado and, if you're traveling with a special someone, treat yourself to a sunset smooch at the **Mirador Laikakota** before donning your evening threads for a night of fine dining in one of the international eateries in Sopocachi. Alternatively, kick back in one of the many popular bars around town or enjoy a taste of traditional music at one of the **peñas**.

Four Days

Follow the two-day itinerary, then on your third day do a **guided walking tour** of La Paz or the wild rock gardens that surround the city in the **Valle de la Luna** or **Muela del Diablo**. It's always fun to bring a picnic of fresh foods from the markets. On the fourth day take a day trip out to **Tiwanaku** to explore the ruins. Or, depending on the season, you could visit **Chacaltaya** or do a day's **bike trip** on the outskirts of La Paz.

As one of the city's focal points, the plaza is often the staging ground for rallies and protests.

Museo Tambo Quirquincho MUSEUM
(Map p38; Plaza Alonso de Mendoza; admission B$3; ☺9:30am-12:30pm & 3-7pm Tue-Fri, 9am-1pm Sat & Sun) This intriguing museum is slated to re-open after renovations in October 2012. A former *tambo* (wayside market and inn), it houses temporary exhibitions. Past exhibitions include cultural photos of Mexico and Peruvian art.

Mercado de Hechicería MARKET
(Witches' Market; Map p38) The city's most unusual market lies along Calles Jiménez and Linares between Sagárnaga and Santa Cruz, amid lively tourist *artesanías* (stores selling locally handcrafted items). What is on sale isn't witchcraft as depicted in horror films and Halloween tales; the merchandise is herbal and folk remedies, plus a few more unorthodox ingredients intended to manipulate and supplicate the various malevolent and benevolent spirits of the Aymará world. An example of these types of ingredients is dried toucan beaks, intended to cure ills and protect supplicants from bad spirits.

If you're building a new house you can buy a llama fetus to bury beneath the cornerstone as a *cha'lla* (offering) to Pachamama (Mother Earth), encouraging her to inspire good luck therein. If someone is feeling ill or is being pestered by unwelcome or bothersome spooks, they can purchase a plateful of colorful herbs, seeds and assorted critter parts to remedy the problem. As you pass the market stalls, watch for wandering *yatiris* (witch doctors), who wear dark hats and carry coca pouches, and offer (mainly to locals) fortune-telling services.

Inquiries and photographs taken here may be met with unpleasantness – ask politely first.

Museo de la Coca MUSEUM
(Map p38; Linares 906, Rosario; admission B$10; ☺10am-7pm Mon-Fri) Chew on some facts inside the small, slightly tired Coca Museum, which explores the sacred leaf's role in traditional societies, its use by the soft-drink and pharmaceutical industries, and the growth of cocaine as a party drug. The displays (ask for a translation in your language) are educational, provocative and evenhanded.

Iglesia Indígena de San Pedro CHURCH
(Map p42; Plaza San Pedro, San Pedro) Founded in 1549 and finished at the end of the 18th century after the siege of La Paz by Tupac Katari, the 'Indigenous Church of San Pedro' has baroque and neoclassic touches.

**Museo de Arte
Contemporáneo Plaza** MUSEUM
(MAC, Contemporary Art Museum ; Map p42; 16 de Julio 1698, Prado; admission B$15; ◷9am-9pm) Better modern art may be found in various other collections around town, but this private museum wins the gold star for the most interesting building: a restored 19th-century mansion (one of only four left on the Prado) with a glass roof and stained-glass panels designed by Gustave Eiffel. The museum's eclectic collection housed over three floors is a mix of reasonable – although not mind-blowing – Bolivian and international work. You might catch an interesting temporary exhibition on the ground floor, sometimes free if you ask nicely.

La Paz Cemetery CEMETERY
As in most Latin American cemeteries, bodies are first buried in the traditional Western way or are placed in a crypt. Then, within 10 years, they are disinterred and cremated. After cremation, families purchase or rent glass-fronted spaces in the cemetery walls for the ashes, they affix plaques and mementos of the deceased, and place flowers behind the glass door. Each wall has hundreds of these doors, and some of the walls have been expanded upward to such an extent that they resemble three- or four-story apartment blocks. As a result the cemetery is an active place, full of people passing through to visit relatives and leave or water fresh flowers.

It's possibly most interesting on November 2, the Día de los Muertos (Day of the Dead), when half the city turns out to honor their ancestors.

Be aware that the area around the cemetery is a little unsavory.

Sopocachi NEIGHBORHOOD
Sopocachi has some of La Paz' best restaurants and nightspots. You can spend a few hours people watching on **Plaza Eduardo Avaroa**, before hoofing up to the wonderful views from **Monticulo Park**.

Be aware that express taxi robberies and muggings are common, especially at night near Plaza Avaroa and Plaza España. Take a radio taxi.

EAST OF EL PRADO
East of the Prado you'll find most of the city's museums, as well as the presidential palace.

Cathedral CHURCH
(Map p38; Plaza Murillo) Although it's a relatively recent addition to La Paz' collection of religious structures, the 1835 cathedral is an impressive structure – mostly because it is built on a steep hillside. The main entrance is 12m higher than its base on Calle

---

MARINA NÚÑEZ DEL PRADO

Bolivia's foremost sculptor, Marina Núñez del Prado, was born on October 17, 1910 in La Paz. From 1927 to 1929 she studied at the Escuela Nacional de Bellas Artes (National School of Fine Arts), and from 1930 to 1938 she worked there as a professor of sculpture and artistic anatomy.

Her early works were in cedar and walnut, and represented the mysteries of the Andes: indigenous faces, groups and dances. From 1943 to 1945 she lived in New York and turned her attentions to Bolivian social themes, including mining and poverty. She later went through a celebration of Bolivian motherhood with pieces depicting indigenous women, pregnant women and mothers protecting their children. Other works dealt largely with Andean themes, some of which took appealing abstract forms. She once wrote, 'I feel the enormous good fortune to have been born under the tutelage of the Andes, which express the richness and the cosmic miracle. My art expresses the spirit of my Andean homeland and the spirit of my Aymará people.'

During her long career she held more than 160 exhibitions, which garnered her numerous awards, and she received international acclaim from the likes of Pablo Neruda, Gabriela Mistral, Alexander Archipenko and Guillermo Niño de Guzmán. In her later years Marina lived in Lima, Peru, with her husband, Peruvian writer Jorge Falcón. She died there in September 1995 at the age of 84.

Central La Paz – The Prado

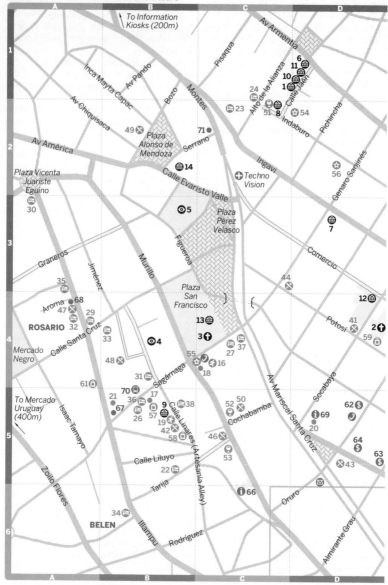

To Information Kiosks (200m)

LA PAZ & AROUND SIGHTS

Av Armentia
Pisagua
Inca Mayta Capac
Av Pando
Bozo
Montes
Alto de la Alianza
Calle Bueno
6
11
10
1
24
23
51 **8**
54
Indaburo
Pichincha
Av Chiquisaca
49
Plaza Alonso de Mendoza
Serrano
71
Ingavi
Techno Vision
Genaro Sanjinés
Av América
Calle Evaristo Valle
14
56
Plaza Vicenta Juariste Eguino
30
5
Plaza Pérez Velasco
7
Graneros
Figueroa
Murillo
Comercio
35
Jiménez
Plaza San Francisco
44
12
Aroma **68**
47
29
13
Potosí
41
2
ROSARIO
32
3
59
Mercado Negro
33
4
27 **37**
55
9 **16**
48
18
31
61
70 17
2
Socabaya
21 36
57 **9** **38**
52 50
62
To Mercado Uruguay (400m)
67
26
19
Cochabamba
69
20
42
58
46
64
43
63
Calle Liluyo
53
22
66
Oruro
Tarija
34
BELEN
Illampu
Rodríguez
Almirante Grau
Zoilo Flores
Isaac Tamayo
Calle Santa Cruz
Calle Linares (Artesanía Alley)
Sagárnaga
Av Mariscal Santa Cruz

Potosí. The cathedral's sheer immensity, with its high dome, hulking columns, thick stone walls and high ceilings, is overpowering, but the altar is relatively simple. Inside, the main attraction is the profusion of stained-glass work; the windows behind the altar depict a gathering of Bolivian politicos being blessed from above by a flock of heavenly admirers.

Beside the cathedral is the **Presidential Palace** (Map p38; Plaza Murillo), and in the center of **Plaza Murillo**, opposite, stands a

See Central La Paz – Sopocachi Map (p42)

Museo Nacional del Arte — MUSEUM

(National Art Museum; Map p38; www.mna.org.bo; cnr Comercio & Socabay, Casco Viejo; admission B$15; ⊘9:30am-12:30pm & 3-7pm Tue-Fri, 10am-5:30pm Sat, 10am-1:30pm Sun) Near Plaza Murillo, this museum is housed in the former Palacio de Los Condes de Arana. This stunning building was constructed in 1775 of pink Viacha granite and has been restored to its original grandeur, in mestizo (mixed) baroque and Andino baroque styles. In the center of a huge courtyard, surrounded by three stories of pillared corridors, is a lovely alabaster fountain. The various levels are dedicated to different eras, from pre-Hispanic works to contemporary art, with an emphasis on religious themes. Highlights include works by former *paceño* Marina Nuñez del Prado. There are regular temporary exhibitions on the ground floor.

FREE Museo de Etnografía y Folklore — MUSEUM

(Ethnography & Folklore Museum; Map p38; www. musef.org.bo; cnr Ingavi & Sanjinés, Casco Viejo; ⊘9am-12:30pm & 3-7pm Mon-Sat, 9am-12:30pm Sun) Anthropology buffs should check out this free museum. The building, itself a real treasure, was constructed between 1776 and 1790, and was once the home of the Marqués de Villaverde. The highlight is the Tres Milenios de Tejidos exhibition of stunning weavings from around the country – ask a guide for a look inside the drawers beneath the wall hangings. It also has a fine collection of Chipaya artifacts from western Oruro department, a group whose language, rites and customs have led some experts to suggest that they are descendants of the vanished Tiwanaku culture, and the Tarabucos, from near Sucre.

TOP CHOICE Calle Jaén Museums — MUSEUM

(Calle Jaén, Casco Viejo; combination admission B$4; ⊘9am-12:30pm & 2:30-7pm Tue-Fri, 9am-1pm Sat & Sun) These four small, interesting museums are clustered together along Calle Jaén, La Paz' finest colonial street, and can generally be bundled into one visit. Buy tickets at the Museo Costumbrista.

Also known as Museo del Oro (Gold Museum), the **Museo de Metales Preciosos** (Museum of Precious Metals; Map p38; Jaén 777) houses four impressively presented salons of pre-Columbian silver, gold and copper works and pieces from Tiwanaku.

Sometimes called the Museo de la Guerra del Pacífico, the diminutive **Museo del Litoral**

---

statue of President Gualberto Villarroel. In 1946 he was dragged from the palace by vigilantes and hanged from a lamppost in the square. Interestingly enough, Pedro Domingo Murillo, for whom the plaza was named, met a similar fate here in 1810.

Central La Paz – The Prado

(Map p38; Jaén 798) incorporates relics from the 1884 war in which Bolivia became landlocked after losing its Litoral department to Chile. The collection consists mainly of historical maps that defend Bolivia's emotionally charged claims to Antofagasta and Chile's Segunda Región.

Once the home of Pedro Domingo Murillo, a leader in the La Paz Revolution of July 16, 1809, the **Casa de Murillo** (Map p38; Jaén 790) displays collections of colonial art and furniture, textiles, medicines, musical instruments and household items of glass and silver that once belonged to Bolivian aristocracy. Other odds and ends include a collection of Alasitas miniatures.

The **Museo Costumbrista Juan de Vargas** (Map p38; cnr Jaén & Sucre) contains art and photos, as well as some superb ceramic figurine dioramas of old La Paz. One of these is a representation of *akulliko*, the hour of coca-chewing; another portrays the festivities surrounding the Día de San Juan Bautista (St John the Baptist's Day) on June 24; another depicts the hanging of Murillo in 1810. Also on display are colonial artifacts and colorful dolls wearing traditional costumes. A pleasant cafe is on the premises.

Museo de Instrumentos Musicales
MUSEUM

(Museum of Musical Instruments; Map p38; Calle Jaén 711, Casco Viejo; admission B$5; ☉9:30am-1pm & 2-6:30pm daily) The exhaustive, hands-on collection of unique instruments at this museum is a must for musicians. The brainchild of *charango* master Ernesto Cavour Aramayo, it displays all possible incarnations of the *charango* (a traditional Bolivian ukulele-type instrument) and other indigenous instruments used in Bolivian folk music and beyond. If you don't happen on an impromptu jam session, check out Peña Marka Tambo across the street. You can also arrange *charango* and wind instrument lessons here for around B$50 per hour.

Museo Nacional de Arqueología
MUSEUM

(National Archaeology Museum; Map p42; Tiahuanacu 93, Casco Viejo; admission B$10; ☉9am-12:30pm & 3-7pm Mon-Fri, 9am-noon Sat) Two blocks east of the Prado, this museum (closed for renovations at press time) holds a small but well-sorted collection of artifacts that illustrate the most interesting

aspects of Tiwanaku culture – those that weren't stolen or damaged during the colonial days, anyway. Some of the ancient stonework disappeared into Spanish construction projects, while valuable pieces found their way into European museums or were melted down for royal treasuries. Unfortunately there are no explanations in English, only Spanish.

Museo de la Revolución Nacional
MUSEUM

(Museum of the National Revolution; Plaza Villarroel, Casco Viejo; admission B$2; ☉9:30am-12:30pm & 3-7pm Tue-Fri, 10am-noon Sat & Sun) The first question to ask when approaching this museum is 'Which Revolution?' (Bolivia has had more than 100 of them). The answer is that of April 1952, the popular revolt of armed miners that resulted in the nationalization of Bolivian mining interests. It displays photos and paintings from the era. Located at the end of Av Busch.

FREE Parque Raúl Salmón de la Barra
PARK

(Map p42; off Bolívar, Miraflores; ☉daylight) La Paz' city park has interesting skyways and the **Mirador Laikakota** (Av del Ejército; admission US$0.15; ☉9am-5:30pm). Traveling circuses will often set up here, too.

Pipiripi
MUSEUM

(Map p42; Av del Ejército, Miraflores; admission B$3; ☉10am-6:30pm Sat, Sun & holidays; ⊞) La Paz' children's museum has interactive exhibits and plenty of stickiness and stinky sock smells over six rambling levels. The views are awesome, and exhibits include a word forest (English words count), a poet's corner, textile and market areas, and a giant scrabble game. To get here take the gondola from the Mirador Laikakota.

DON'T MISS

ARTE AL AIRE LIBRE

La Paz Mayor Juan del Granado created **Arte al Aire Libre** (on the Kantutani, btwn Calles 16 & 14, Obrajes, along the river, Zona Sur). This wonderful open-air art gallery features around 15 giant artworks that focus on La Paz and surrounds, from images of Illimani to notable painters of La Paz. Works change every three months.

Central La Paz – Sopocachi

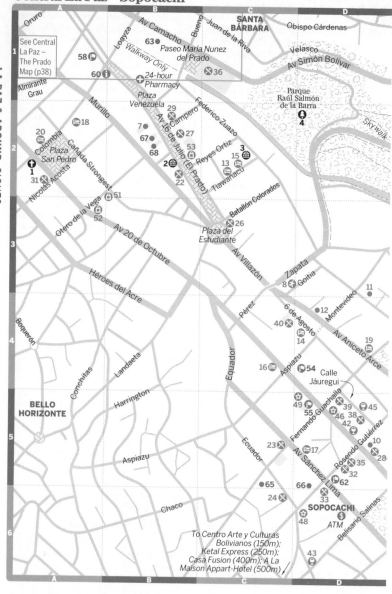

Museo de Textiles Andinos Bolivianos

MUSEUM

(Plaza Benito Juárez 488, Miraflores; admission B$15; 9:30am-noon & 3-6pm Mon-Sat, 10:30am-noon Sun) Fans of Bolivia's lovely traditional weaving consider this small textile museum a must-see. Examples of the country's finest traditional textiles (including pieces from the Cordillera Apolobamba, and the Jal'qa and Candelaria regions of the Central High-

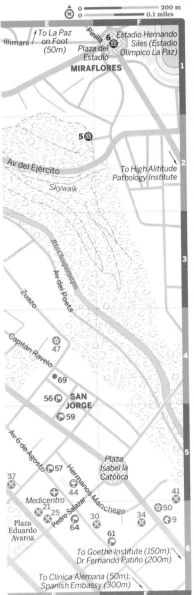

FREE | **Templete Semisubterráneo & Museo al Aire Libre** MUSEUM

(Map p42; Stadium, Miraflores) The open-pit Museo al Aire Libre opposite the stadium contains replicas of statues found in Tiwanaku's Templete Semisubterráneo. The show-piece Megalito Bennetto Pachamama (Bennett monolith) was moved to Tiwanaku's new site museum to avoid further smog-induced deterioration. This place is only worth seeing if you aren't able to visit the actual site. If you have some time while you're here, hoof your way up to the Killi Killi lookout for breathtaking views.

EL ALTO

A billboard in El Alto announces: 'El Alto is not part of Bolivia's problem. It's part of Bolivia's solution.' Not all would agree, but visiting here is an experience. Having once been a melting pot for *campesinos* (subsistence farmers) and people from all around the country, and with a population of 650,000, El Alto is now a city in its own right. It has a 5% to 6% growth rate per year and is considered the Aymará capital of the world.

If you arrive by air, below you are dozens of white church spires soaring up from the brown earth. These were built by a German priest, Padre Obermaier, renowned in the city for his past and current works (and longevity). From the canyon rim at the top of El Alto Autopista (toll road) or the top of the free route at Plaza Ballivián, the streets hum with almost perpetual activity. It's hard to distinguish one street from another – the miles of orange brick and adobe houses, shops, factories and markets create a hectic atmosphere at every corner.

Taxis to El Alto charge around B$50 from the center of La Paz. *Micros* marked 'Ceja' or 'El Alto' will get you here for B$3.

La Ceja NEIGHBORHOOD

In the lively La Ceja (Brow) district, which commands one of the highest real-estate prices in the region for its commercial value, you'll find a variety of electronic gadgets and mercantile goods. For an excellent market experience don't miss the massive Mercado 16 de Julio (⊙6am-3pm Thu & Sun), which stretches for many blocks along the main thoroughfare and across Plaza 16 de Julio. This shopaholic's paradise has absolutely everything, from food and electronics, to vehicles and animals, all at reasonable prices. Heads up: watch your wallet in both senses of the phrase.

lands) are grouped by region and described in Spanish. To get there, walk 20 minutes northeast from the Prado or catch *micros* (small buses or minibuses) *131* or *135*, or minibuses marked 'Av Busch.'

Central La Paz – Sopocachi

Cholitas Wrestling   WRESTLING
(www.cholitaswrestling.com; Polifuncional de la Ceja de El Alto (stadium); B$80; ⊙3:30pm Sun) Wrestling matches between indigenous women (derogatively called *cholitas*) has become popular in recent years. The staged bouts take part in El Alto on Sunday afternoons. You can go on your own, but for ease of mind, many choose to get there by booking online or through a Sagárnaga tour agency.

Tupac Katari Mirador   LOOKOUT

For a great view of La Paz head in a taxi to the Tupac Katari Mirador, situated right on the edge of the rim that plunges down the valley to La Paz. It was – and is – a sacred Inca site and ritual altar where Tupac Katari is believed to have been drawn and quartered by colonialists. The colonialists constructed and interred a statue of Christ on the same site, but that didn't stop locals from performing spiritual rituals here.

Around the *mirador* (lookout) and as far as the eye can see is a long line of small identical blue booths, distinguished only by a number. These house *curanderos* (healers) or *yatiris,* who provide sage advice. Note: the counsel of a *yatiri* is taken extremely seriously; please be sensitive to this – both photos and tourist appointments are considered inappropriate and are not appreciated.

🏃 Activities

You'll get plenty of exercise hoofing up and down the Prado but you don't have to head far out of town for a real adrenaline rush.

Urban Rush   RAPPELLING

(Map p42; ☎231-3849; www.urbanrushbolivia.com; 16 de Julio 1490 No 10, Edificio Avenida) Run by Gravity Assisted Mountain Biking, this company offers an urban rappel down the Hotel Presidente. Two rappels cost B$200.

Casa del Sol   YOGA

(Map p42; ☎244-0928; www.yogabolivia.com; Goitia 127, Prado; 2hr class B$35; ⏰6:30am-11pm) Casa del Sol offers Hatha yoga classes to get the kinks out.

Mountain Biking

There are tons of mountain-biking options just outside of La Paz. Intermediate riders can take on a thrilling downhill ride on the **World's Most Dangerous Road**, while advanced riders may wish to go for the less traveled **Chacaltaya to Zongo** route, the rides near **Sorata**, or include a bit of single track on the top of the Dangerous Road route for an extra B$100. Beginners not quite ready for the death road may wish to check out the **Balcón Andino** descent near the Zona Sur, a 2400m roller coaster on a wide dirt road.

Gravity Assisted Mountain Biking   MOUNTAIN BIKING

(Map p42; ☎231-3849; www.gravitybolivia.com; 16 de Julio 1490 No 10, Edificio Avenida, Prado) This knowledgeable, highly regarded and professional outfit has an excellent reputation among travelers and tip-top Kona downhill bikes. Its Dangerous Road Trip (B$750 per person) ends with hot showers, an all-you-can-eat buffet and a tour of the Senda Verde animal refuge.

B-Side   MOUNTAIN BIKING

(Map p38; ☎211-4225; Linares 943, Rosario) B-Side is recommended for the Coroico trip (B$310 to B$690 per person). It receives positive reports from travelers and hooks you up with a bike operator based on the type of bike you want, the size of the group and your experience level.

Andean Epics   MOUNTAIN BIKING

(☎712-76685; www.andeanepics.com) This operator is your best bet for rides near Sorata. It was moving at the time of writing, so check out the web for its new location.

Climbing

La Paz is the staging ground for most of the climbs in the Cordilleras. From here novice climbers can arrange trips to Huayna Potosi (two to three days, B$900 to B$1100), while more experienced climbers may look to climb Illimani (four to five days, US$485), Sajama (five days, US$650), Parinacota (four days, US$530) and beyond.

Andean Summits   CLIMBING

(Map p38; ☎242-2106; www.andeansummits.com; Muñoz Cornejo 1009, Sopocachi) Offers a variety of outdoor activities from mountaineering and trekking to 4WD tours in Bolivia and beyond. The owners are professional UIAGM/IFMGA mountain guides.

Asociación de Guias de Montaña   CLIMBING

(☎214-7951; www.agmtb.org) Certifies guides in Bolivia. It's worth checking out its information before deciding on a guide operation.

Climbing South America   CLIMBING

(Map p38; ☎297-1543; www.climbingsouthamerica .acom; Linares 940, 2nd fl, Rosario) Climbing South America is a reputable operator.

Hiking

Except for the altitude, La Paz and its environs are made for hiking. Many La Paz tour agencies offer daily 'hiking' tours to **Chacaltaya,** a rough 35km drive north of La Paz, and an easy way to bag a high peak without having to do any really hard-core hiking. Head to **Valle de la Luna, Valle de las Animas** or **Muela del Diablo** for do-it-yourself day hikes from La Paz. Other longer day trips

DEADLY TREADLIES & THE WORLD'S MOST DANGEROUS ROAD

Many agencies offering La Cumbre to Coroico mountain-bike plunge give travelers the T-shirts boasting about surviving the road. Keep in mind that the gravel road is narrow (just over 3.2m wide), with precipitous cliffs with up to 600m drops and few safety barriers.

In March 2007 a new replacement road opened. Prior to this, the road between La Paz and Coroico was identified as 'The World's Most Dangerous Road' (WMDR) by an Inter-American Development Bank (IDB) report. Given the number of fatal accidents that have occurred on it over the years, the moniker was well deserved. An average of 26 vehicles per year disappeared over the edge into the great abyss.

Crosses (aka 'Bolivian caution signs') lining the way testify to the frequency of vehicular tragedies from the past. The most renowned occurred in 1983 when a *camión* (flatbed truck) plunged over the precipice, killing the driver and 100 passengers in the worst accident in the sordid history of Bolivian transportation.

With the new road up and running, the old road – the WMDR – is now used almost exclusively by cyclists, support vehicles and the odd tourist bus.

Around 15 cyclists have died doing the 64km trip (with a 3600m vertical descent) and readers have reported close encounters and nasty accidents. Ironically, the road – now traffic-free – can be more dangerous to cyclists, especially for kamikaze freewheeling guides and overconfident cyclists who think they don't have to worry about oncoming vehicles. Other accidents are due to little or no instruction and preparation, and poor-quality mountain bikes; beware bogus rebranded bikes and recovered brake pads.

or guided tours take you to the **Hampaturi Valley** and **Parque Nacional Cotopata**.

La Paz on Foot ECOTOUR
(☎7154-3918, 224-8350; www.lapazonfoot.com; 400 Prolongación Posnanski, Miraflores) This is a tip-top operation run by the passionate English-speaking ecologist Stephen Taranto, and offers a range of activities, including walks in and around La Paz, Apolobamba, the Yungas, Chulumani, Madidi and Titicaca. The fascinating, fun and interactive La Paz urban trek (half-day tours B$160 to B$175, day tours B$295 to B$315, depending on group size) heads from the heights of El Alto to the depths of Zona Sur. Other tours include art and architecture, living history, stimulants (think coca, cocoa and coffee) and a mural explorer tour. Trips further afield include a three-day Pacha trek, a four-day Condor trek, a Yungas coca tour, and various nature trails. Multilingual guides are available.

🎵 Courses

For musical instruction (in Spanish) on traditional Andean instruments (such as the *zampoña, quena, charango*) inquire at the Museo de Instrumentos Musicales (p41).

Note that not everyone advertising language instruction is accredited or even capable of teaching Spanish, however well they speak it, so seek local and personal recommendations, and examine credentials before signing up. Plan on paying around B$60 per hour for individual instruction and B$30 to B$50 for group lessons. Many schools can offer homestays (on a weekly or monthly basis) that include three meals a day and cost around US$350 per month. Living with a Bolivian family is an amazing cultural experience and the best way to learn the language.

ie Instituto Exclusivo LANGUAGE COURSE
(Map p42; ☎242-1072; www.institutoexclusivo.com; 20 de Octubre 2315, Sopocachi) Specialized courses for travelers and professionals.

Pico Verde Languages LANGUAGE COURSE
(Map p38; ☎231-9828; www.pico-verde.com; Sagárnaga 363, 2nd fl, Rosario) Offers flexible schedules and homestays.

SpeakEasy Institute LANGUAGE COURSE
(Map p42; ☎244-1779; www.speakeasyinstitute.com; Arce 2047, Prado) Specialized courses for travelers and professionals.

🎫 Tours

Many of Bolivia's tour agencies are based in La Paz. Some are clearly better than others (note: many are not formally registered; check carefully if choosing between those on Sagárnaga), and many specialize in par-

Unfortunately, even though it is such an adventurous activity, there are no minimum safety standards in place for operators of this trip, and no controls over false advertising, or consequences for unsafe operating practices. In short, many agencies are less than ideal. As such the buyer has to be aware, even a bit paranoid; this is one activity where you don't want to be attracted by cheaper deals. Experienced and trained guides, high-quality bikes, well-developed risk-management systems, and adequate rescue equipment all cost money, and cheaper companies may stretch the truth about what they provide if it means making another sale. Cost cutting can mean dodgy brakes, poor-quality parts and, literally, a deadly treadly. This, plus inexperienced and untrained guides and little or no rescue and first-aid equipment, is a truly scary combination on the WMDR.

Nuts & Bolts

The trip begins around 7am in La Paz. Your agency will arrange a hotel pickup. From there, you bus it up to the *cumbre* (summit), about 45 minutes outside La Paz. Trips cost anywhere from B$310 to B$750, but you get what you pay for. Advanced riders can include a fun section of single track up top for an extra B$100. Most operations provide a solid buffet lunch in Coroico, and some even have arrangements with hotels for showers and swimming pool rights. There is a B$25 surcharge to use the old road. Bring sunscreen, a swimsuit and dust-rag (if they don't provide one), and ask about water allotments. The bus takes you back up in the early evening; expect to arrive in La Paz around 9pm.

ticular interests or areas. Most agencies run day tours (B$70 to B$500 per person) in and around La Paz, to Lake Titicaca, Tiwanaku, Zongo Valley, Chacaltaya, Valle de la Luna and other sites. See also p346 for more La Paz–based tour agencies.

Mundo Quechua   GUIDED TOUR
(☎279-6145; www.bolivia-travel.net; Circunvalación 43, Achumani, Zona Sur) French- and English-speaking owners who offer tailor-made tours around Bolivia, including Salar de Uyuni, Tiwanaku, Sajama – whatever you want. Prices vary according to group size and trip.

Viajes Planeta   BUS TOUR
(www.lapazcitytour.net) Viajes Planeta runs tours of the city and Zona Sur in a red, double-decker, city-tour bus (B$50 per person; around three hours). Stops on the Zona Sur trip include Valle de la Luna (admission B$15). The recorded narration is in seven languages. Tickets can be purchased in many travel agencies, or on the bus. Buses depart from Plaza Isabel Católica at 9am and 3pm for city tours, and 10:30am and 1:30pm from the Zona Sur.

Zig-Zag   HIKING
(Map p38; ☎245-7814; www.zigzagbolivia.com; Office 5, Illampu 867, Rosario) Offers a range of trekking tours (including Choro and Takesi), beginners' climbs and custom-made adventures around Bolivia.

Festivals & Events

La Paz is always looking for an excuse to celebrate. Check with the InfoTur (p61) for a complete list of what's on.

Alasitas   AYMARÁ
During Inca times the Alasitas (Aymará for 'Buy from me'; in Spanish it's *Cómprame*) fair coincided with the spring equinox (September 21), and was intended to demonstrate the abundance of the fields. The date underwent some shifts during the Spanish colonial period, which the *campesinos* weren't too happy about. In effect they decided to turn the celebration into a kitschy mockery of the original. 'Abundance' was redefined to apply not only to crops, but also to homes, tools, cash, clothing, cars, trucks, airplanes and even 12-story buildings. The little god of abundance, Ekeko ('dwarf' in Aymará), made his appearance and modern Alasitas traditions are now celebrated on January 24.

**La Festividad de Nuestro
Señor Jesús del Gran Poder**   RELIGIOUS
Held in late May or early June, El Gran Poder began in 1939 as a candle procession led by an image of Christ through the predominantly *campesino* neighborhoods of upper La Paz. The following year the local union of embroiderers formed a folkloric group to participate in the event. In subsequent

EKEKO

Ekeko is the household god and the keeper and distributor of material possessions. During Alasitas his devotees collect miniatures of those items they'd like to acquire during the following year and heap them onto small plaster images of the god. He's loaded down with household utensils, baskets of coca, wallets full of miniature currency, lottery tickets, liquor, chocolate and other luxury goods. The more optimistic devotees buy miniature souped-up *camiones* (trucks), 1st-class airline tickets to Miami and three-story suburban homes! Once purchased, all items must be blessed by a certified *yatiri* (witch doctor) before they can become real. If this apparent greed seems not to be in keeping with Aymará values – the community and balance in all things – it's worth noting that Ekeko is also charged with displaying that which a family is able to share with the community.

years other festival-inspired folkloric groups joined in, and the celebration grew larger and more lively. It has now developed into a unique La Paz festival, with dancers and folkloric groups from around the city participating. Embroiderers prepare elaborate costumes for the event and upwards of 25,000 performers practice for weeks in advance. El Gran Poder is a wild and exciting time, and offers a glimpse of Aymará culture at its festive finest. A number of dances are featured, such as the *suri sikuris* (in which the dancers are bedecked in ostrich feathers), the lively *kullasada, morenada, caporales* and the *inkas,* which duplicates Inca ceremonial dances.

Fiestas de Julio   CULTURAL
This month-long cultural series at the Teatro Municipal features much folk music throughout July.

Virgen del Carmen   CHRISTIAN
The patron saint of the department of La Paz gets her own public holiday (July 16), which includes many dances and parades.

Entrada Folklórica de Universitaria   FOLKLORE
Held on the last Saturday in July, and with an atmosphere alluding to Carnaval, hundreds of dance groups made up of students from around the country perform traditional dances through the streets of La Paz.

🛏 Sleeping

Most backpackers beeline for central La Paz to find a bed. The area around the Mercado de Hechicería (Witches' Market; between Illampu, Santa Cruz and Sagárnaga) is about as close as Bolivia gets to a travelers' ghetto. If you want to live closer to movie theaters, a wider array of restaurants and a bar or two,

consider staying closer to Sopocachi. For more upmarket luxury, look along the lower Prado and further south in the Zona Sur. The Lonely Planet effect is in full force in La Paz, and our top picks often require reservations.

All places reviewed here claim to have hot water at least part of the day; few have it all the time. Many are cheaper outside high season. Save big on business hotels by booking with an online aggregator.

WEST OF EL PRADO

TOP CHOICE **Hotel Rosario**   BOUTIQUE HOTEL $$
(Map p38; ☎245-1658; www.hotelrosario.com; Illampu 704, Rosario; s/d/tr/q/ste incl breakfast B$553/553/623/700/868; @🛜) The professional, English-speaking staff at La Paz' best three-star hotel pamper you with five-star treatment. The ultraclean rooms in the well-maintained colonial residence all have solar-powered hot showers, cable TV and heaters. There is free internet and a generous breakfast buffet at the Tambo Colonial. Groups love it, so reserve ahead.

Casa Fusion   BOUTIQUE HOTEL $$
(☎214-1372; www.casafusion.com.bo; Miguel de Cervantes 2725, Sopocachi; s/d incl breakfast B$280/370; @🛜) While it does lack a little personality, the Casa Fusion is probably your best midrange bet in town for comfort, value and convenience. The brand-spanking-new Sopocachi boutique has modern clean lines, more Scandinavian furnishings than you'll find in your local Ikea store, thick down comforters, blazing hot showers and friendly service. The top-story rooms have the best views.

La Casona   HISTORIC HOTEL $$$
(Map p38; ☎290-0505; www.lacasonahotelboutique.com; Mariscal Santa Cruz 938, Prado; incl breakfast

s B$490, d B$595-650, ste B$740-950; @🛜) A new entrant in the luxury boutique category, La Casona has 15 rooms in a beautifully restored colonial-era building surrounding a small courtyard. While the bathrooms could be a bit better designed (and we really wish there was a good common area other than the rooftop terrace), the rooms with high ceilings, exposed wood beams and thoughtful Andean textile accents are welcome retreats.

La Posada de la Abuela
HOTEL **$$**

(Map p38; 🖉233-2285; www.hostalabuelaposada. com; Linares 947, Rosario; s/d/tr incl breakfast B$210/280/350; @🛜) Readers praise this pleasant oasis in the heart of the artisan and tourist center. The rooms are sterile and clean (some have internally facing windows), and the plant-filled courtyard adds a colorful, if potentially noisy, touch. Reserve ahead – it's popular with groups.

Onkel Inn
HOSTEL **$$**

(Map p42; 🖉249-0456; www.onkelinn.com; Colombia 257, Sopocachi; dm/s/d/tr incl breakfast B$60/200/250/300; @🛜) This bright, HI-affiliated place is in a fabulous spot between San Pedro and El Prado. It's less of a scene than the hostels up by the terminal, making it good for tranquilo travelers. The dorm rooms are the nicest in La Paz with crispy-cream orange bedcovers and a bright modern feel. Some of the dorm bunks will leave you with vertigo.

A La Maison Appart-Hotel
B&B **$$**

(🖉241-3704; www.alamaison-lapaz.com; Pasaje Muñoz Cornejo 15, Sopocachi; s/d incl breakfast B$385/455; @🛜) While it's a bit difficult to find, this top-flight Sopocachi midrange choice has whimsical art throughout, funked-out and tasteful rooms complete with kitchenettes, cable TV and sitting areas, and a home-spun family friendliness that's especially attractive for long-stay visitors and families.

La Loge
HOTEL **$$**

(Map p42; 🖉242-3561; www.lacomedielapaz.com; Pasaje Medinacelli 2234, La Comédie Art-Cafe Restaurant, Sopocachi; apt B$400; @) *Oooh la la!* This one is tops. The attention to detail in these light, bright and airy self-catering, serviced apartments is French in flavor – and that means *bon goût* (good taste).

Radisson Plaza Hotel
BUSINESS HOTEL **$$$**

(Map p42; 🖉244-1111; www.radisson.com/lapazbo; Arce 2177, Prado; incl breakfast s/d US$160/180,

ste US$240-280; 🅿✶@🛜🏊) The Radisson has everything you'd expect in a five-star hotel, even if its pink walls are like totally 1983 and the lobby is quite smoky. Rooms include giant resort beds, great views and your typical hodge-podge of high-market amenities, making this the best business hotel option in the center. Ask for a south-facing room for the best views. The top-floor Aransaya Restaurant affords a superb view over the city and surrounding mountains.

Hostal Naira
HOTEL **$$**

(Map p38; 🖉235-5645; www.hostalnaira.com; Sagárnaga 161, Rosario; s/d/tr incl breakfast B$220/320/452; 🛜) You can't get a better location – right at the bottom of Sagárnaga near the Plaza San Francisco. The rooms are also quite comfortable with vaulted ceilings, slightly bowed mattresses and no dirt within sight. It can be a bit noisy at night.

Hotel Las Brisas
HOTEL **$$**

(Map p38; 🖉246-3691; www.hotelbrisas.net; Illampu 742, Rosario; s/d/tr incl breakfast B$150/250/340; @🛜) This is a solid budget bet with a 'Bolivia moderna' style – think stark, but neat rooms (some with internal windows), funky murals and crispy sheets coupled with a few shabby bits and external glassy walls. The rooms at the front have excellent views and the staff are friendly, but the whole place does smell a little like Thai food.

Arcabucero Hostal Inn
HISTORIC HOTEL **$$**

(Map p38; 🖉231-3473; Liluyo 307, Rosario; s B$95-155, d/tr B$180/200; 🛜) The nine quiet rooms at this restored colonial home are arranged around an ornate, plant-filled indoor courtyard. The saggy mattresses, however, should

❶ LUSTRABOTAS

Around La Paz and the rest of Bolivia *lustrabotas* (shoeshine men and boys) are a familiar sight and hound everyone with footwear, even those sporting sandals. Many *lustrabotas*, especially the older ones, wear ski masks and baseball caps – it's said that they often do so to avoid social stigma, as many are working hard to support families or pay their way through school. You can support their cause for between B$2 and B$3.

be relegated to the inn's otherwise quirky antique decorations, as should the pillows and electric showers.

Hotel Fuentes
HOTEL **$$**

(Map p38; ☑231-3966; www.hotelfuentesbolivia.com; Linares 888, Rosario; s/d/tr incl breakfast B$160/190/270; ☎) This cozy place is just-ever-so-slightly overpriced. Nevertheless, there's friendly service, and the basic rooms with bowed beds and parquet floors, cable TV and hot water are certainly do-able. Some rooms on the higher levels have superlative views. A book exchange is a nice bonus.

Hotel Berlina
HOTEL **$$**

(Map p38; ☑246-1928; www.hotelberlina.com; Illampu 761, Rosario; s/d/tr/q B$250/350/450/550; P@☎) While the lobby promises shiny things, the spacious rooms are stark and have a slightly unpleasant smell, though they do seem clean. It lacks a bit of personality, but seems a reliable bet. Ask for an east-facing room on an upper story for the best views. Road-front views can be noisy.

Hotel Madre Tierra
HOTEL **$$**

(Map p42; ☑241-9910; www.hotelmadretierra.com; Av 20 de Octubre, Sopocachi; s/d B$290/360; @☎) One of the newer additions in the stylish Sopocachi neighborhood, this modern, slightly overpriced offering has a very nice common area in which to meet other independent travelers. Unfortunately, the rooms are quite dark, and those facing the road can get noisy. Solid mattresses, cleanliness (after all, it is next to godliness), minibars and cable TV make up for the drawbacks.

Hotel Continental
HOTEL **$**

(Map p38; ☑245-1176; www.hotelcontinentalbolivia.com; Illampu 626, Rosario; s/d/tr $90/140/200, without bathroom B$60/120/170; ☎) This dark and slightly dreary downtown option is popular among thrift-sters. The detergent smell can be overpowering, but at least you know somebody was cleaning the place.

Hostal Maya Inn
HOTEL **$**

(Map p38; ☑231-1970; www.hostalmaya.com; Sagárnaga 339, Rosario; s/d incl breakfast B$90/160; @☎) This is a friendly, if basic, place. The most appealing rooms have windows (note: a few don't), although rooms at the front can be a little noisy. Nonsmokers may be bothered by the smokiness, and the electric showers can be rough for hot-water lovers.

Hotel Sagárnaga
HOTEL **$**

(Map p38; ☑235-0252; www.hotel-sagarnaga.com; Sagárnaga 326, Rosario; s/d/tr incl breakfast B$140/180/240; @☎) The knight in shining armor at the front desk (and no, we're not talking about the receptionist, although he *is* friendly) and the mirrors are the brightest things in this otherwise slightly tarnished and smoky, yet wholly adequate, '80s-style place. East-facing rooms are the best, and decent solar showers should keep you warm come bath-time.

Hotel Milton
HOTEL **$**

(Map p38; ☑235-3511; homilton@acelerate.com; Illampu 1126-1130, Rosario; s/d/tr incl breakfast $100/150/225; @☎) Tune in and drop out! This '70s pad truly is a paradise lost with red vinyl-studded walls, painted murals and funky wallpaper. Darker rooms at the back are a bit dingy, but the higher and lighter front rooms afford stupendous views over La Paz, making this a solid budget bet.

Residencial Sucre
HOTEL **$**

(Map p42; ☑249-2038; Colombia 340, Rosario; s/d B$90/140, r per person without bathroom B$60) This place hasn't been refurbished since the '50s, and it's pretty beat down, man. If it weren't so damned cheap, we'd boot it from the book.

Hotel España
HOTEL **$$**

(Map p42; ☑244-2643; 6 de Agosto 2074, Prado; s/d/tr B$190/270/360; @☎) This place is a bit like a great aunt – friendly with a colorful personality but ever-so-slightly worse for wear. It's a slightly overpriced colonial place, with a lovely, sunny courtyard and garden, and worn rooms. It's an easy stroll to many of the city's best restaurants and nightlife spots. Rates include cable TV.

Hotel Majestic
HOTEL **$**

(Map p38; ☑245-1628; hot.majestic@gmail.com; Calle Santa Cruz 359, Rosario; s/d/tr incl breakfast B$90/140/210; ☎) Calling yourself Majestic won't necessarily make it so. And while its pink bathrooms, smart parquet floors and cable TV provide some distraction from the dirty baths and stanky-like-a-field-mouse rooms, this is one of those last-ditch choices that's good for a night and not much more.

EAST OF EL PRADO

Wild Rover
HOSTEL **$**

(Map p38; ☑211-6903; www.wildroverhostel.com; Comercio 1476, Miraflores; dm B$45-65, s without bathroom $65; @🛜) Your best bet to meet fellow travelers, the Wild Rover has a high-octane take-no-prisoners vibe that 20-somethings will love and 30-somethings will loathe. The rooms at some other hostels are better, and the dorm rooms are too tightly packed, but you'll be spending most of your day at the boisterous Irish pub anyway.

Arthy's Guesthouse
GUESTHOUSE $

(Map p38; 🖉228-1439; arthyshouse@gmail.com; Ismael Montes 693, Bus Terminal; r per person without bathroom B$80; @) This clean and cozy place hidden behind a bright orange door deservedly receives rave reviews as a 'tranquil oasis,' despite its location on one of La Paz' busiest roads. The friendly, English-speaking owners will do all they can do to help you. Kitchen facilities are available. Note, though, that there is a midnight curfew.

Hostal República
HOSTEL $

(Map p38; 🖉220-2742; www.hostalrepublica.com; Comercio 1455, Miraflores; dm/s without bathroom B$50/140, d/apt B$229/553; @🛜) Three blocks from the historic heart of the city (up a seriously steep hill), this hostel occupies a lovely historic building that was home to one of Bolivia's first presidents. Its two large courtyards make for a quiet oasis, and it has an extremely chilled air. All the rooms are fairly basic (those downstairs can be dank and musty), but will make for a pleasant, if unremarkable, stay. The apartment sleeps five.

Café El Consulado
HISTORIC HOTEL $$$

(Map p42; 🖉211-7706; www.cafeelconsulado.com; Calle Bravo 299; s/d incl breakfast B$560/700, ste incl breakfast B$560-980; @🛜) You'll feel every bit the VIP in one of these five delightful rooms, housed in a converted consulate and stunning colonial building, above the cafe of the same name. This boutique place oozes European style (it's Danish run), with large, airy and spacious rooms in a quiet location. Those with private bathrooms have clawed baths.

Loki Hostel
HOSTEL $

(Map p38; 🖉211-9034; www.lokihostel.com; Loayza 420, Bus Terminal; dm B$44-60, d B$140-160; @🛜) This party hostel has a gilded bar, bean-bag hangout area and more than 180 beds. The rooftop terrace is dope and the rooms can get a bit dark, and all-in-all there's some sort of strange vibe going on.

Bacoo Hostel
HOSTEL $

(Map p38; 🖉228-0679; www.bacoohostel.com; Alto de la Alianza 693, Bus Terminal; dm B$40-60, d B$160; @🛜) This sprawling party-focused hostel has a bar and Jacuzzi (ooh-la-la), and plenty of travelers looking to hook up (both literally and figuratively). Welcomed touches include down comforters and thick mattresses. Dorm rooms range from four to 20 people, so book ahead or bring ear plugs. There's a rather unkempt feel to the place, but you're close to the bus station and Calle Jaén.

Hotel Europa
BUSINESS HOTEL $$$

(Map p42; 🖉231-5656; www.hoteleuropa.com.bo; Tiahuanacu 64, Prado; s/d/ste US$140/160/240; P✳@🛜🏊) One of the city's sleekest business hotels, the Europa's rooms aren't as nice as some of La Paz' other business hotels, but you do get an excellent spa and pool area (open to the public for a daily-use fee) and solid business-class rooms and service.

Hospedaje Milenio
HOTEL $

(Map p38; 🖉228-1263; hospedajemilenio@hotmail. com; Yanacocha 860, Casco Viejo; r per person B$35-40; 🛜) A simple, laid-back joint, run by friendly staff, with fun common areas, a book exchange and truly dirt-cheap rooms, the Milenio is a solid budget bet. The best rooms are upstairs and outward facing (note that most single rooms have internal windows). The mushy beds may leave you limping, though.

ZONA SUR

Camino Real
BUSINESS HOTEL $$$

(Map p52; 🖉279-2323; www.caminoreal.com.bo; Ballivián 369, cnr Calle 10, Calacoto; r incl breakfast B$1500; P✳@🛜🏊) The best business hotel in town, the towering Camino Real in the Zona Sur has a soaring atrium, and high-end rooms with flat-screens, updated modern furnishings and great views of the neighboring bluffs. It'd be nice if there were better common areas, but the onsite restaurant will do. Booking online through aggregators will save you big.

Tarapari La Paz
HOTEL $

(🖉7154-3918; www.lapazonfoot.com; r per person US$22) Fourteen kilometers from Zona Sur, in the very authentic village of Chicani, is this tranquil escape: an ecofriendly apartment in a secure location. It's made of adobe and its kitchen and bathroom is operated by solar water. It's the perfect place to base

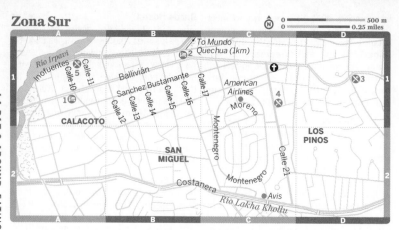

Zona Sur

Sleeping
1 Camino Real A1
2 Casa Grande.. B1

Eating
3 Chalet La Suisse D1
4 Coroico in Sur.. C1
5 Furusato... A1

yourself for day and overnight hikes into the Cordillera Real – the owner (of La Paz on Foot (p46) tours fame) says you can be at the base of a glacier within eight hours. Access is by an unsealed road, 45 minutes by minibus from central La Paz (B$4).

Casa Grande   BUSINESS HOTEL **$$$**
(Map p52; ☑279-5511; www.casa-grande.com.bo; cnr Ballivián and Calle 17, Calacoto; s/apt/f incl breakfast B$1255/1395/1675; P❄@☎) This business hotel is in need of a serious rehab – especially the lumpy oatmeal pillows – but with living rooms and kitchens in all the rooms, long-stay visitors may still want to give it a try.

✖ Eating

For local fare, your cheapest (and sometimes tastiest) bets are the *almuerzos* (set lunches) in the countless hole-in-the-wall restaurants; look for the chalkboard menus out front. As a general rule, the higher you climb from the Prado, the cheaper the meals will be. Markets and street stalls offer good prices and interesting experiences, but can

be challenging for your stomach. Sopocachi and the Zona Sur have most of the city's high-end eateries. *Chifas* (Chinese restaurants) are ubiquitous and cheap.

Vegetarians are increasingly well catered for these days, and there are some excellent vegetarian restaurants.

WEST OF EL PRADO
There are plenty of eateries around Sagárnaga. Upscale and international bites are found in Sopocachi.

TOP CHOICE Pronto   ITALIAN **$$$**
(Map p42; ☑244-1369; Jauregui 2248, Sopocachi; mains B$55-80; ☺6:30am-11pm Mon-Sat) We don't know where (or how) it gets its fresh ingredients, but this candlelit underground restaurant has figured it out, offering up dish after dish of thoughtfully prepared, well structured and delicately balanced antipasti, pasta and mains. The antipasta della casa is a remarkable mix of stewed tomatoes, walnuts and other wonderful treats. The alchemy of many of these dishes would leave many a 'developed world' chef red-cheeked and jealous. Call ahead for reservations on the weekends.

La Casona Restaurant   BOLIVIAN **$$**
(Map p38; Mariscal Santa Cruz 938, Prado; mains B$20-50, almuerzo B$45; ☺9am-9pm; ☎) The upscale executive set lunch here comes with an extensive salad bar, soup and your choice of mains like chicken in wine sauce or delicately crafted milanesas. The colonial atmosphere is quite comfortable, making this one of the best lunch spots in town. It goes à la carte at night.

Ángelo Colonial INTERNATIONAL $$
(Map p38; ✆236-0199; Linares 922, Rosario; mains B$20-50) This quirky, darkened colonial-style restaurant features a ramshackle collection of antiquities – pistols, swords and antique portraits – plus excellent soups, salads and luscious vegetable lasagna. You don't want to be in a hurry – service is slow.

Star of India INDIAN $$
(Map p38; Cochabamba 170, Rosario; mains B$32-45; ✎) Worthy of a London curry house (the owner is British), this place is hot. It receives rave reviews by foreign residents and travelers for its broad menu of tasty Indian foods. It also serves lassi breakfasts and snacks.

La Guinguette FRENCH $$
(Map p42; Fernando Guachalla 399, Sopocachi; mains B$45-70; ◷9am-11pm Mon-Sat) Hang out with the Sopocachi cool cats at this chic spot below the Alianza Francesa cultural center. The cozy bistro serves an excellent soup, sandwich and desert combo at lunch for B$45. There are steaks, fish and rather doughy pasta on the menu, too.

Martiani Pizza PIZZA $
(Map p38; Illampu 738, Rosario; pizzas B$20-35; ◷1-9:30pm Mon-Sat) If you believe the napkin reviewers (one day they'll put Lonely Planet writers out of a job for good), this is the best slice in La Paz. We wouldn't go that far, but this is a damn good pie, with crispy crust, fresh ingredients and plenty of savory thrust in the sauce. It's a small place, so expect to wait a bit.

Restaurant Paladar BRAZILIAN $$
(Map p42; Fernando Guachalla 359, Sopocachi; mains B$40-60, almuerzo Tue-Fri B$20; ◷lunch Tue-Sun) This cavernous place serves recommended Brazilian fare, including *feijoada* (a bean and meat casserole, typical of Portugal and Brazil). Heavy drapes, bow-tied waiters and smartly dressed locals would have you think it's a pricey joint. And you'd be fooled – all this for a mere B$20. À la carte dishes are served at weekend lunches.

Paceña La Salteña FAST FOOD $
(Map p42; 20 de Octubre 2379, Sopocachi; pastries B$5-10; ◷8:30am-2pm) Eating a *salteña* (a baked pastry stuffed with out-of-this-world meat and vegetable goodness) is a not-to-be-missed local experience. The peach walls, chintz curtains and gold trimmings give the fare a gilded edge at this award-winning

salteñería. Vegetarian *salteñas* are available on weekends only.

Armonía VEGETARIAN $
(Map p42; Ecuador 2284, Sopocachi; buffet B$29; ◷lunch Mon-Sat; ✎) A recommended all-you-can-eat vegetarian lunch is found above Libería Armonía in Sopocachi. Organic products are served when possible.

Kuchen Stube BAKERY $
(Map p42; Rosendo Gutiérrez 461, Sopocachi; cakes B$4-30) A favorite for sweet snacks with decadent German pastries, reasonable coffee, fresh juices and quiche lorraine.

Cafe Blueberries CAFE $$
(Map p42; Plaza Avaroa, Sopocachi; mains B$30-50; ☎) Tea lovers will enjoy this relaxed Japanese-owned place – it has a good selection of infusions and accompanying snacks, from salads to cakes. The pleasant front terrace overlooks Plaza Avaroa, and the back sunroom overlooks a pretty rose garden.

Pepe's Coffee Bar CAFE $
(Map p38; Jiménez 894, Rosario; snacks B$10-25) This cheery, inviting, artsy cafe is tucked away on a sunny bend in the Witches' Market. It's a cozy place for coffee or cocktails. Big breakfasts and veggie lunch options go down easily while browsing the library of guidebooks and English-language periodicals.

Sergiu's Pizza PIZZA $
(Map p42; 6 de Agosto 2040, Prado; slices from B$12; ◷from 5pm) Popular among students, this evening-only hole-in-the-wall near the Aspiazu steps serves up a reasonable New York–style pizza and fast food.

Restaurant Laza BOLIVIAN $
(Map p38; Bozo 244, Rosario; lunch B$8) Join the locals for cheap eats at this authentic joint.

EAST OF EL PRADO

Café Ciudad INTERNATIONAL $
(Map p42; Plaza del Estudiante, Prado; mains B$15-40; ◷24hr; ☎) This La Paz institution serves up warm coffee, surly service, yummy pizzas, hamburgers and other international favorites (plus one of the best *pique machos*, a Bolivian dish with sausages and french fries in sauce, in town) 24 hours a day, seven days a week.

Wagamama JAPANESE $$$
(Map p42; Pinilla 2257, Prado; meals B$45-90; ◷lunch & dinner Mon-Sat) This Japanese joint,

hidden up a quiet lane, has a classy atmosphere and impeccably presented food. Treat yourself to a *teishoku* (a feast featuring 'everything'; B$80).

El Arriero
ARGENTINIAN **$$$**

(Map p42; 6 de Agosto 2535, Prado; mains B$65-95, almuerzo $50; ⊘lunch & dinner) This Argentine grill restaurant has good steak but inattentive service. The chunky imported beef is kept warm on a tableside grill, while a series of even larger cuts feed three or four. There's a decent salad bar, but it's no vegetarian hangout! The fixed lunch is good value.

Confitería Club de La Paz
CAFE **$**

(Map p38; cnr Camacho & Mariscal Santa Cruz, Prado; mains B$10-30) For a quick coffee or empanada, join the well-dressed elderly patrons in their daily rituals. The cafe was formerly renowned as a literary cafe and haunt of politicians (and, formerly, of Nazi war criminals); today, it's better known for its strong espresso and cakes.

Confitería Manantial
VEGETARIAN **$**

(Map p38; Potosí 909, Hotel Gloria, Casco Viejo; buffet B$25; ⊘lunch Mon-Sat; ✍) This place has a good-value and popular veggie buffet. Arrive before 12:30pm or you risk missing the best dishes.

ZONA SUR
Calle Montenegro has a good collection of bars, restaurants and shops all within walking distance of each other.

EASY EATS

Popular with La Paz' yuppie set, these chain cafes serve java drinks, good fruit juices and tasty snacks, sandwiches and international favorites like quesadillas. While they are a bit saccharine, they're good spots if your stomach is easily upset.

» **Alexander Coffee & Pub** (www.alexandercoffee.com; mains B$16-40; ⊘6am-11pm) Branches in Prado (Map p42; 16 de Julio 1832), Socabaya (Map p38; Calle Potosí 1091) and Sopocachi (Map p42; 20 de Octubre 2463).

» **Cafe La Terraza** (mains B$10-40; ⊘late) Branches in Prado (Map p42; 16 de Julio 1615) and Sopocachi (Map p42; 20 de Octubre 2331, Montenegro Bloque).

Chalet La Suisse
SWISS **$$$**

(Map p52; ☎279-3160; www.chaletlasuisse.com; Muñoz Reyes 1710, Calacoto; mains B$60-120) This Swiss-run restaurant is as upscale as the name sounds – it's seriously expensive (by Bolivian standards), has a very old-style atmosphere and is extremely good. Imported cheeses, top local wines and trout dishes are merely part of the experience. Don't go here if you're after Bolivian atmosphere – it would be as at home in New York or London – but it's good fare.

Furusato
JAPANESE **$$$**

(Map p52; Inofuentes 437; mains B$50-109; ⊘12-3pm & 7-11pm Tue-Sun, dinner only Mon) This place is neater than an origami figure – and fittingly so. It's very formal, with exquisite Japanese fare and jaw-splitting views of the nearby cliff, although friendliness isn't always on the menu.

Coroico in Sur
BOLIVIAN **$**

(Map p52; Juli Patino 1526; almuerzo B$15; ⊘lunch & dinner Mon-Sat, lunch only Sun) A great place to join the locals for typical Bolivian lunch dishes of *plato paceño* (a dish of fried cheese, corn, beans and potato) and set lunches in a tranquil garden setting.

Self-Catering
If you don't mind the hectic settings and questionable hygiene, your cheapest and most interesting food options are found in the markets. The *comedor* (dining hall) at **Mercado Uruguay**, off Max Paredes, sells set meals (of varying standards and in basic surrounds) including tripe and *ispi* (similar to sardines) for less than B$8. Other areas to look for cheap and informal meals include the **street markets around Av Buenos Aires**, and the **Mercado Camacho** (Map p42; cnr Av Simon Bolivar & Bueno), known for its juice stands, fresh breads and puffy *llauchas* (cheese pastries). Chain supermarkets include the following:

Ketal Hipermercado
SUPERMARKET

(Map p42; Arce, nr Pinilla, Sopocachi) If you're off to a picnic, load up here on everything from olives to cheese, crackers and beer.

Ketal Express
SUPERMARKET

(Plaza España, Sopocachi) Ketal Express is a decent but basic supermarket.

Hiper Maxi
SUPERMARKET

(Map p42; Rosendo Gutiérrez, Sopocachi) A handy supermarket.

Irupana   SUPERMARKET
(Map p38; Murillo 1014, cnr Tarija, Rosario) Locally made organic produce is sold at this
health-food chain. There is another branch
in **Sopocachi** (Map p42; cnr Fernando Guachalla
& Av Sanchez Lima, Sopocachi).

Arco Iris   SUPERMARKET
(Map p42; Fernando Guachalla 554, Sopocachi;
⊙8am-8pm Mon-Sat) Arco Iris has an extensive
pastelería (cake shop) and deli featuring fine
specialty regional meat and dairy treats like
smoked llama salami, plus products such as
fresh palm hearts and dried Beni fruits.

Drinking

There are scores of inexpensive, local drinking dens where men go to drink *singani*
(distilled grape spirit, the local firewater),
play *cacho* (dice) and eventually pass out.
Unaccompanied women should steer clear
of these spots (even accompanied women
may have problems).

There are plenty of elegant bars, which
are frequented by foreigners and middle-
class Bolivians. Local, gilded youth mingle
with upmarket expats at clubs along 20
de Octubre in Sopocachi and in Zona Sur,
where US–style bars and discos spread along
Av Ballivián and Calle 21. These change as
often as fashions, so it's best to ask around
for the latest in-spot.

Bocaisapo   PUB
(Map p38; Calle Jaén, Casco Viejo; ⊙7pm-late Thu-
Sat) This bohemian favorite has live music,
a maddening elixir de coca drink, plenty
of affected La Paz artsters and a candlelit
ambience.

Green Bar   PUB
(Map p42; Salinas 596, Sopocachi) For a cloistered pub setting with intellectual types,
girls straight out of a Modigliani painting,
weirdos, rockers and other ne'er-do-wells,
check out this beloved hole in the wall.

Oliver's Travels   PUB
(Map p38; cnr Murillo & Cochabamba, 2nd fl, Rosario) The worst (or best?) cultural experience
in La Paz is to be had at this pub, thanks
to its crowd of mainly foreign revelers, good
beer selection, football, typical English food
(including curries) and popular music. It
has a good, if pricey, book exchange.

Mongo's   PUB
(Map p42; Manchego 2444, Sopocachi; mains B$30-
60; ⊙6pm-3am) The easiest spot to pull in La

ICE CREAM TIME

Despite its cool temps, La Paz is a good
spot for ice cream. These are some of
our faves:

Heladería Napoli (Map p38; Ballivián,
Casco Viejo; ice cream B$2-5; ⊙8:30am-
10:30pm) Italian-style on Plaza Murillo.

Helados Splendid (Map p42; cnr
Nicolás Acosta & Av 20 de Octubre, Plaza
San Pedro; ice cream B$2-5) Helados
Splendid has been scooping up splen-
did ice cream for nearly 50 years.

Dumbo (Map p42; 16 de Julio s/n, Prado;
ice cream B$2-5, mains B$35-50; 🏛) Kids
only need apply.

Paz – that's hook up to you Americanos –
Mongo's is a perennial favorite, with dancing
on the tables, excellent pub grub and a good
mix of locals and tourists.

Café Sol y Luna   PUB
(Map p38; cnr Murillo & Cochabamba, Rosario;
⊙9am-1am)   This is a low-key, Dutch-run
hangout offering cocktails, good coffee and
tasty international meals. It has three cozy
levels with a book exchange and an extensive guidebook reference library (many current Lonely Planet titles), talks, salsa nights,
live music and other activities.

Reineke Fuchs   BEER HALL
(Map p42; Jáuregui 2241, Sopocachi; ⊙from 6pm
Mon-Sat) This Sopocachi *brewhaus* features
imported German beers, *schnappsladen* and
hearty sausage-based fare. Also in Zona Sur.

Diesel Nacional   LOUNGE
(Map p42; 20 de Octubre 2271, Sopocachi; ⊙from
7:30pm Mon-Sat) The postmodern place to
escape reality for an overpriced drink with
the rich kids. It doesn't really get going until
late.

Entertainment

Pick up a copy of the free monthly book-
let *Kaos* (available in bars and cafes) for a
day-by-day rundown of what's on in La Paz.
Otherwise, watch hotel notice boards for bar
and live music posters, or check the newspapers. InfoTur (p61) can also help.

Centro Arte y Culturas Bolivianos LIVE MUSIC
(Ecuador 2582, Sopocachi) This arts complex
has rotating exhibits, live music (Thursday

BREAKING BAD IN BOLIVIA

Bolivia offers plenty of opportunities to 'Break Bad.' With its status as a major cocaine-producing nation and a reputation for lax law enforcement, Bolivia is a popular destination for drug and sex tourism. Travelers who come to Bolivia to engage in these and other marginal activities can find themselves in trouble, however, as these activities have serious consequences and legal ramifications.

Prostitution

Prostitution is legal for adults aged 18 and older, and is common throughout the country. While legal, there are few protections for sex workers or controls on the industry (raising the chances of contracting an STD). Child prostitution (the average sex worker starts at 16 years old) and human trafficking are also real issues in the country, especially in the Chapare and major urban centers. Young children are sold into prostitution, especially from the tropical lowlands, and brought to large urban centers or sold overseas either as slaves or prostitutes. Trafficking from Paraguay to Bolivia is on the rise for the 'mega brothels' being built near Santa Cruz. In Southern Bolivia, around 10 children every month are sold into prostitution or slavery, and across the globe some 1.2 million children are victims of human trafficking annually. It's a US$12 billion annual industry, and many advocacy organizations say consumers will control its end. Jail sentences for sex with a minor are 20 to 25 years in Bolivia, and those found guilty will also likely face criminal charges in their home country. (Sources: Unicef, 2008 US State Department Human Rights Report, UNHCR, EFE)

Cocaine & Other Drugs

Drug tourism is on the rise in Bolivia. The cocaine is pure, it's cheap (B$100 to B$150 a gram), it's easily attainable, and it remains illegal. The laws are a bit contradictory and ill-defined. Personal possession, while illegal, is not supposed to carry a jail sentence, but

---

through Saturday), a decent restaurant and terrace cafe. They call it the Luna Llena rock bar come 8pm.

Thelonious Jazz Bar JAZZ
(Map p42; 20 de Octubre 2172, Sopocachi; cover charge around B$25; ⊘7pm-3am Mon-Sat) Bebop fans love this charmingly low-key bar for its live and often impromptu performances and great atmosphere. A flier on the wall promotes upcoming sessions.

Traffic Dance DANCE
(Map p42; www.trafficsanjorge.com; Arce 2549, Prado) It has lost some pizzazz in recent times, but is still popular for cocktails, live music – from world beats to disco – and all the attitude and dancing you can muster.

Cultural Centers

Alianza Francesa CULTURAL CENTER
(Map p42; ☑242-5005; www.alianzafrancesa.org.bo; cnr Fernando Guachalla & 20 de Octubre, Sopocachi) This French cultural center has lectures, courses and rotating exhibits in French and Spanish. Thursday nights are movie nights.

Goethe Institute CULTURAL CENTER
(☑243-1916; www.goethe.de; Arce 2708, Prado) The German cultural center has a library, courses, exhibits and movie nights on Fridays.

Nueva Acropolis CULTURAL CENTER
(Map p42; ☑291-1172; www.acropolis.org.bo; Ecuador 2405, Sopocachi; ⊘7:30am-10:30pm) This locally run cultural center offers courses, talks and other intellectual exercises, mostly in Spanish.

Peñas

Typical of La Paz (and most of Bolivia) are folk-music venues known as *peñas*. Most present traditional Andean music, rendered on *zampoñas, quenas* and *charangos,* but also often include guitar shows and song recitals. Many *peñas* advertise nightly shows, but in reality most only have shows on Friday and Saturday nights, starting at 9pm or 10pm and lasting until 1am or 2am. Admission ranges from B$30 to B$80 and usually includes the first drink; meals cost extra.

Peña Marka Tambo TRADITIONAL MUSIC
(Map p38; ☑228-0041; Calle Jaén 710, Casco Viejo; cover charge B$35, mains B$35-50; ⊘from 8pm

trafficking carries a minimum eight-year sentence, according to the Andean Information Network. The only problem: there's no definition of personal possession. Your best bet is to not do it. If you get caught, your embassy will not help you. The only option for many travellers is to attempt to pay their way out of the situation, which is also risky since bribes are illegal, too. It's also worth noting that the same criminal organizations producing cocaine are also responsible for human trafficking; don't go down dark alleys after midnight looking to score. Moreover, cocaine can be deadly, especially at Bolivia's high altitudes.

Marijuana is also common here (and also illegal), while other high-end pharmaceuticals, like ecstasy, are hard to come by. Hallucinogenics, like the San Pedro cactus and ayahuasca, are becoming slightly more common and sit in a grey area of the law.

San Pedro Prison

It's likely you won't be in La Paz long before you'll hear about 'tours' to San Pedro prison – from other travelers, or sometimes operators and hostels. We strongly advise against participating in one of these unofficial – and, in fact, illegal – 'tours', which are organized by inmates, guards and dodgy operators. There are high risks associated with entering San Pedro prison. First, it's illegal, and the Bolivian authorities are cracking down on unofficial visits. Secondly, inside the prison, there's no protection or guarantee of your safety and, well, you're surrounded by criminals.

Bribes

Bribes are illegal in Bolivia, but common. With cops making just over US$115 a month, it's easy enough to see why it would be so ubiquitous. People stopped for minor traffic violations or more serious infractions sometimes ask if they can 'pay the fine now.' Watch out for false police – authentic police officers will always wear a uniform and will never force you to show them your passport, insist you get in a taxi with them, or search you in public.

Thu-Sat) A reasonably priced – and some claim quite traditional – *peña*. The food is OK, but the music is better.

Peña Huari   TRADITIONAL MUSIC
(Map p38; ☑231-6225; Sagárnaga 339, Rosario; cover charge B$105, buffet dinner B$100; ☉show 8pm nightly) The city's best-known *peña* is aimed at tourists and Bolivian businesspeople. The attached restaurant specializes in Bolivian cuisine, including llama steak, Lake Titicaca trout, *charquekan* (jerky) and salads. The show starts at 8pm.

Peña Parnaso   TRADITIONAL MUSIC
(Map p38; ☑231-6827; Sagárnaga 189, Rosario; cover charge B$80, mains B$35-40; ☉show 8:30pm) Also open for lunch (B$35) with no show.

Cinema

La Paz' cultural centers often show foreign-language films. Most movies are in English with Spanish subtitles and cost around B$30. There are several cinemas along the Prado.

Cinemateca Boliviana   CINEMA
(Map p42; cnr Zuazo & Rosendo Gutiérrez, Prado) Art films gone wild.

Theater

Teatro Municipal Alberto Saavedra Pérez   THEATER
(Map p38; cnr Sanjinés & Indaburo, Casco Viejo; tickets B$20-50) The Teatro Municipal Alberto Saavedra Pérez has an ambitious program of folklore shows, folk-music concerts and foreign theatrical presentations. It's a great old restored building with a round auditorium, elaborate balconies and a vast ceiling mural.

Spectator Sports

The popularity of *fútbol* (soccer) in Bolivia is comparable to that in other Latin American countries. Matches are played at Estadio Hernando Siles (Estadio Olímpico La Paz, Miraflores). Sundays (year-round) are the big game days, and Wednesdays and Saturdays also have games. Prices vary (B$20 to B$100) according to seats and whether it's a local or international game. You can imagine what sort of advantage the local teams have over mere lowlanders; players from elsewhere consider the high-altitude La Paz games a suicide attempt!

DANGERS, ANNOYANCES & COMMON SENSE

La Paz is not a safe city, especially at night. For years we've been saying that crime in Bolivia is no worse than in large US cities. Today, this is no longer true, and travelers should exercise caution while in La Paz. A little common sense goes a long way.

Simple Rules to Keep You Safe

Travel in groups, take cabs after 8pm (make sure it's a radio taxi with a bubble on top), don't walk down dark alleys, carry small amounts of cash, and leave the fancy jewelry and iPods at home or in the hotel safe. Also remember that you likely don't know anybody in Bolivia. It's sad to say, but you should be wary of strangers here.

What's Happening?

Fake police officers and bogus tourist officials exist. Note: authentic police officers will always be uniformed (undercover police are under strict orders not to hassle foreigners) and will never insist that you show them your passport, get in a taxi with them or allow them to search you in public. If confronted by an imposter, refuse to show them your valuables (wallet, passport, money etc), or insist on going to the nearest police station on foot. If physically threatened, it is always best to hand over valuables immediately.

In the last few years there have been many incidents of 'express kidnappings' by taxi drivers, where the driver and his accomplices (who board later or jump out from the trunk) kidnap you and beat you until you provide your ATM PIN details. The best way to prevent express kidnappings is to take a radio cab; these have a radio in the car and a promo bubble on the roof (do not take the informal cabs which merely have a 'taxi' sticker). At night, ask the restaurant or hotel to call a cab – the cab's details are recorded at a central base. Don't share cabs with strangers and beware of accepting lifts from drivers who approach you (especially around dodgy bus areas).

🔒 Shopping

La Paz is a shopper's paradise; not only are prices very reasonable, but the quality of what's offered can be astounding. The main tourist shopping area lies along the very steep and literally breathtaking Calle Sagárnaga between Santa Cruz and Tamayo, and spreads out along adjoining streets. Here, you'll also find Calle Linares, an alley chock-a-block with artisans' stores. Some stores specialize in *oriente* woodcarvings and ceramics, and Potosí silver. Others deal in rugs, wall-hangings, woven belts and pouches. Amid the lovely weavings and other items of exquisite craftsmanship, you'll find plenty of tourist kitsch, an art form unto itself: Inca-themed ashtrays, fake Tiwanaku figurines, costume jewelry and mass-produced woolens. Music recordings are available in small stores along Valle Evaristo and more established places on Linares. Or you can try your luck in the Mercado de Hechicería where there are figurines and Aymará good-luck charms, including frogs.

For less expensive llama or alpaca sweaters, bowler hats and other non-tourist clothing items, stroll Calles Graneros and Max Paredes. Reflecting its status as the more upmarket area, Zona Sur opts for designer clothing; several stores sell stunning llama and alpaca fashion items. The Montenegro area is especially good for shopping.

Many La Paz artisans specialize in traditional woodwind instruments such as *quenas, zampoñas, tarkas* and *pinquillos*. Several shops sell instruments along Sagárnaga, Linares and Illampu. Be aware, though, that there's a lot of low-quality or merely decorative tourist rubbish around.

For the few photographers who use slide and/or print films nowadays, these are available in some camera shops; be cautious about buying film at street markets where it is exposed to strong sun all day. Many photo shops cluster around Plaza Venezuela (El Prado); some of these do digital processing.

For all kinds of backpack protection – plastic sacks, chains, padlocks etc – check the street stalls along Calle Isaac Tamayo.

Artesanía Sorata   ARTS & CRAFTS
(Map p38; www.artesaniasorata.com; Sagárnaga 363) A community-focused project that spe-

Violent attacks, including strangling victims and assault with weapons like clubs, is on the rise.

Petty theft and pickpocketing is not uncommon in restaurants, bus terminals, markets and internet cafes. Keep a close eye on your stuff.

One popular scam involves someone spilling a substance on you or spitting a phlegm ball at you. While you or they are wiping it off, another lifts your wallet or slashes your pack; the perpetrator may be an 'innocent' granny or young girl. Similarly, make sure that you don't bend over to pick up a valuable item which has been 'dropped.' You risk being accused of theft, or of being pickpocketed.

Where It's Happening

It's everywhere. The Sopocachi and the areas around Sagárnaga have especially high rates of attacks on foreigners. You should avoid El Alto, the cemetery and higher-elevation neighborhoods altogether at night. Use special caution in the bus terminals.

Other Concerns

La Paz is a great city to explore on foot, but take the local advice 'camina lento, toma poco...y duerme solo' (walk slowly, drink little...and sleep by your lonesome) to avoid feeling the effects of soroche (altitude sickness). Soroche pills are said to be ineffective, and can even increase altitude sickness. Acetaminophen (also known as Tylenol or paracetamol) does work, and drinking lots of water helps, too.

In the last couple of years, it seems traffic has increased tenfold due in part to secondhand car imports – take care in crossing roads and avoid walking in busy streets at peak hours when fumes can be overwhelming.

Protests are not uncommon in La Paz, and they do sometimes turn violent. These center around Plazas San Francisco and Murillo.

cializes in export-quality handmade dolls, original alpaca products and other beautiful items.

Comart Tukuypaj   ARTS & CRAFTS
(Map p38; www.comart-tukuypaj.com; Linares 958, Rosario) Offers export-quality, fair-trade llama, alpaca and *artesanías* from around the country. Upstairs the Inca Pallay women's weaving cooperative has a gallery with justly famous Jal'qa and Candelaria weavings.

Kodak   ELECTRONICS
(Map p42; 211-7606; 16 de Julio s/n, Edificio Alameda) For camera fixes.

Tatoo   OUTDOOR EQUIPMENT
(Map p38; Illampu 828) Part of a South American chain, this outdoor outlet has climbing gear and name-brand outerwear.

**Spitting Llama Bookstore &
Outfitter**   OUTDOOR EQUIPMENT, BOOKS
(Map p38; www.thespittingllama.com; Linares 947) Inside Posada de la Abuela, this friendly one-stop shop stocks everything from maps to gear, including tents, backpacks and hiking boots.

El Ceibo   FOOD & DRINK
(Map p38; www.elceibo.org; Potosí 1147) Chocoholics mustn't miss El Ceibo, an ecologically friendly producer of fantastic local chocolates.

Bodega La Concepción   WINE
(Map p42; Cañada Strongest 1620, at Otero de la Vega, San Pedro) Award-winning, high-altitude vintages are available at wholesale prices from this outlet of the Tarija-based winery.

Campos de Solana/Casa Real   WINE
(Map p42; Otero de la Vega 373, at 20 de Octubre) A Tarija winery best known for its Malbec and Riesling.

ℹ Information

Emergency
Police (110)
Fire and ambulance (118)
Tourist police (Policía Turística; 800-140-071; Puerta 22, Plaza del Estadio, Miraflores) Next to Disco Love City. English-speaking. Report thefts to obtain a *denuncia* (affidavit) for insurance purposes – they won't recover any stolen goods. They also have a kiosk in front of the bus terminal.

Immigration

Migración (Map p42; ☑211-0960; www.migracion.gob.bo; Camacho 1468; ⊗8:30am-4pm Mon-Fri) Some call this place 'Migraine-ation' but this is where you must obtain your visa extensions.

Internet Access

La Paz has nearly as many cybercafes as shoe-shine boys. Charges range from B$1 to B$3 an hour, and connections are generally fastest in the morning or late evening. Many of the smarter cafes and most hotels now have wi-fi access.

Laundry

Lavanderías (laundries) are the cheapest and most efficient way of ensuring clean (and dry) clothes in La Paz. Higher-end hotels charge per piece (10 times the price), while budget digs may charge a fair per-kilo rate.

Calle Illampu, at the top of Sagárnaga, is lined with laundries. For quick, reliable same-day machine-wash-and-dry service (B$7 to B$12 per kilo), try the following options.

Lavandería Aroma (Map p38; Illampu 869, Rosario)

Lavandería Maya (Map p38; Sagárnaga 339, Hostal Maya, Rosario) Laundry service.

Laverap (Map p38; Aroma 730, Rosario)

Left Luggage

Most recommended sleeping places offer inexpensive or free left-luggage storage, especially if you make a return reservation. The main bus terminal has a cheap *depósito* (B$6 to B$8), but think twice about leaving anything valuable here.

Maps

Free city maps are available at the tourist offices. Inside the central post office, opposite the *poste restante* counter, there are gift shops that sell a range of maps.

La Paz is the best place to stock up on maps for the rest of your trip.

Instituto Geográfico Militar (IGM; Map p38; Juan Pablo 23, Edificio Murillo, San Pedro; ⊗8:30am-12:30pm & 2:30-6:30pm Mon-Fri) IGM offers original 1:50,000 topographic maps (B$40) or photocopies (B$35) if a sheet is unavailable.

Librería Olimpia (Map p38; ☑240-8101; Mariscal Santa Cruz, Galería Handal, Local 14) A stationery store that stocks a small but worthwhile collection of maps.

Servicio Nacional de Áreas Protegidas (SERNAP; ☑242-6272; www.sernap.gob.bo; Francisco Bedregal 2904, Sopocachi) Provides information and maps of Bolivia's 22 protected national areas.

Media

La Razón (www.la-razon.com), **El Diario** (www.eldiario.net) and **La Prensa** (www.laprensa.com.bo) are La Paz' major daily newspapers. National media chains **ATB** (www.bolivia.com) and **Grupo Fides** (www.radiofides.com) host the most up-to-date online news sites. English-language publications come and go. **Bolivia Weekly** (www.boliviaweekly.com) is a good source for up-to-date English headlines.

Medical Services

For serious medical emergency conditions, contact your embassy for doctor recommendations.

PHARMACIES

24-hour pharmacy (Farmacia 24 Horas; cnr Av 16 de Julio & Bueno; ⊗24hr) A good pharmacy on the Prado.

MEDICAL CENTERS

Centro Epidemiológico Departamental La Paz (Centro Pilote; ☑245-0166; Vásquez at Perú; ⊗8:30-11:30am Mon-Fri) Anyone heading for malarial areas can pick up antimalarials, and rabies and yellow fever vaccinations, for the cost of a sterile needle – bring one from a pharmacy.

Clínica Alemana (☑432-521; Vásquez at Perú, Sopocachi; ⊗24hr) Offers German efficiency.

Clínica Sur (☑278-4001; Hernando Siles, Zona Sur) Emergency service.

High Altitude Pathology Institute (☑7325-8026, 224-5394; www.altitudeclinic.com; Saavedra 2302, Miraflores) Bolivian member of the International Association for Medical Assistance to Travelers (Iamat). Offers computerized high-altitude medical checkups and can help with high-altitude problems. English spoken.

Medicentro (☑243-2521; 6 de Agosto 2821, Prado; ⊗24hr) Recommended for general care.

Techno Vision (☑240-9637; Comercio 844) Glasses and eye care.

DOCTORS

Dr Elbert Orellana Jordan (☑7065-9743, 242-2342; asistmedbolivia@hotmail.com) English speaker.

Dr Fernando Patiño (☑7724-3765; curare27@gmail.com; Edificio Curare, Calle 10, 8090, cnr Julio C Paiño, Calacoto) English speaker.

Dr Iturri Stroobandt Igor (☑7195-8595, 221-876; bolivianmedicine@latinmail.com) French and English speaker.

Money

ATMS

Cash withdrawals of bolivianos and US dollars are possible at numerous ATMs at major intersections around the city. For cash advances (bolivianos only, amount according to your limit in your home country) with no commission and little hassle, try the Lonely Planet–listed options.

Banco Mercantil (Map p38; cnr Mercado & Ayacucho)

Banco Nacional de Bolivia (Map p38; cnr Colón & Camacho)

MONEY TRANSFERS

Try **Western Union/DHL**, which has outlets scattered all around town, for urgent international money transfers.

MONEY CHANGERS

Casas de cambio (exchange offices) in the city center can be quicker and more convenient than banks. Most places open from 8:30am to noon and 2pm to 6pm weekdays, and on Saturday mornings.

Be wary of counterfeit US dollars and bolivianos, especially with *cambistas* (street money changers) who loiter around the intersections of Colón, Camacho and Santa Cruz. Traveler's checks can be virtually impossible to change, except at money changers and banks.

Cambios América (Map p38; Camacho 1223, Casco Viejo) Money-changing bureau.

Casa de Cambio Sudamer (Map p38; Colón 206 at Camacho, Casco Viejo; ☉8:30am-6:30pm Mon-Fri, 9:30am-12:30pm Sat) Also has MoneyGram service for money transfers.

Post

Many hotels now have post boxes.

Central post office (Ecobol; cnr Mariscal Santa Cruz & Oruro, Prado; ☉8am-8pm Mon-Fri, 8:30am-6pm Sat, 9am-noon Sun) *Lista de correos (poste restante)* mail is held for two months for free here – bring your passport. A downstairs customs desk facilitates international parcel posting.

Telephone

Convenient *puntos* (privately run phone offices) of various carriers – Entel, Cotel, Tigo, Viva etc – are scattered throughout the city, and some mobile services now have wandering salesmen who will allow you to make a call from their mobile phone. Street kiosks, which are on nearly every corner, also sell phone cards, and offer brief local calls for about B$1 per minute. You can buy cell phone sim cards (known as *chips*) for about B$10 from Entel or any carrier outlet. International calls can be made at low prices from the **International call center** (Galería Chuquiago, cnr Sagárnaga & Murillo; ☉8:30am-8pm).

Entel (Ayacucho 267, Casco Viejo; ☉8:30am-9pm Mon-Fri, to 8:30pm Sat, 9am-4pm Sun) The main Entel office is the best place to receive incoming calls and faxes.

Tourist Information

Information kiosks (Main bus terminal) Opening hours vary. The kiosks have maps and may help you find a hotel.

InfoTur (Map p42; ☎265-1778; www.visit bolivia.org; cnr Av Mariscal Santa Cruz & Colombia, Prado; ☉8:30am-7pm Mon-Fri, 9:30am-1pm Sat & Sun) Stop by to grab some maps and get detailed information. English is spoken by some staff.

❶ Getting There & Away

Air

El Alto International Airport (LPB) is 10km via toll road from the city center on the Altiplano. At 4050m, it's the world's highest international airport; larger planes need 5km of runway to lift off and must land at twice their sea-level velocity to compensate for the lower atmospheric density. Stopping distance is much greater too, and planes are equipped with special tires to withstand the extreme forces involved.

Airport services include oxygen tanks in the international arrivals area, newsstand, ATMs, internet, souvenir stores, a bookstore, a coffee shop, fast food, a bistro and a duty-free shop in the international terminal. The currency-exchange desk outside the international arrivals area gives poor rates on traveler's checks – if possible, wait until you're in town. The domestic departure tax is B$15, while the international departure tax is US$25 (payable in cash only in the airport lobby).

Times and schedules for flights change often. Check your airline's website or call.

AIRLINES

Aerocon (☎in Santa Cruz 3-351-1010; www.aerocon.bo) Flights to Cochabamba, Guayamerín, Riberalta, Rurrenabaque, Santa Ana, Santa Cruz, Sucre, Tarija, Trinidad and Yacuiba.

Amazonas (☎222-0848; www.amazonas.com) Daily flights to Cuzco, Rurrenabaque, Santa Cruz, Tarija, Trinidad and Uyuni.

American Airlines (☎235-1360; www.aa.com; Calle 18, Calacoto) International.

Boliviana de Aviación (BOA; ☎901-10-5010; www.boa.bo) Flights to Buenos Aires, Cobija, Cochabamba, Sucre, Santa Cruz, Sao Paolo and Tarija.

Lan Airlines (Map p42; ☎235-8377; www.lan.com; 16 de Julio 156, Suite 104, Edificio Ayacucho, Prado) International.

Taca (Map p42; ☎215-8202; www.taca.com; 16 de Julio 1616, Edificio Petrolero, Prado) International.

TAM Mercosur (Map p42; ☎244-3442; Gutiérrez 2323)

BUS COSTS & DISTANCES

From Main Terminal

DESTINATION	COST (B$)	DURATION (HR)
Arica	130	8
Buenos Aires	650	48–50
Copacabana	35	3–4
Cochabamba	43–90	7–8
Cusco	130	12–17
Iquique	150	11–13
Lima	500–600	27
Oruro	23–60	3.5
Potosi	52–110	8
Puno	100	8
Santa Cruz (new road)	85–170	17
Santa Cruz (old road)	95–180	20
Sucre	69–135	14
Tarija	115–215	24
Tupiza	90	20
Uyuni	72–155	10
Villazón	90–200	23

From Villa Fátima

DESTINATION	COST (B$)	DURATION (HR)
Caranavi	15–25	8
Chulumani	20	4
Coroico	20–30	3
Cumbre	20	1
Rurrenabaque	120	18–20
Yolosita	20	3

From Cemetery

DESTINATION	COST (B$)	DURATION (HR)
Copacabana	15	3
Desaguadero	15	2
Huarina (for Cordillera Apolobamba)	10	3
Sorata	17	5
Tiwanaku	6–15	1.5

Transporte Aéreos Militares (TAM; Map p38; ☑268-1111; www.tam.bo; Ismael Montes 738, Prado) Flights to Cobija, Cochabamba, Guayamerín, Puerto Suárez, Riberalta, Rurrenabaque, Santa Cruz, Sucre, Tarija, Trinidad, Yacuiba, Ixiamas and Uyuni.

Bus

La Paz has three bus terminals/bus areas. You can use the main bus terminal for most national and international destinations. If you are going to the Yungas or Amazon, you'll need go to Villa Fátima. For Sorata, Titicaca and Tiwanaku, head to the cemetery. Most national destinations are serviced hourly for major cities and daily for less visited spots. International departures generally leave once a week – check ahead as schedules change. You can get to all the bus areas by *micros*, but radio taxis are recommended for your safety.

Bolivia en Tus Manos (www.boliviaentus manos.com/terminal) Up-to-date information on buses from La Paz.

Cemetery (Baptista) Offers cheap buses to Tiwanaku, Titicaca and Sorata (via Desaguadero). This area is especially hairy at night, and you should watch your bags while boarding.

Main bus terminal (Terminal de Buses; Plaza Antofagasta) This services all national destinations South and East of Paz, as well as international destinations. It is a 15-minute uphill walk north of the city center. Fares are relatively uniform between companies. The station was designed by Gustave Eiffel.

Villa Fátima (Tejada Sorzano) Services Coroico and other Yungas and Amazon destinations, mostly via *micros*. It's about 1km uphill from Plaza Gualberto Villarroel. There's no central station, so ask around to find the buses servicing your particular destination. Offices on Yanacachi by an old gas station service Coroico, on Las Americas, also by a gas station, service the Amazon Basin, and on San Jorge, service Chulumani. There are more operations clustered along Virgen del Carmen, just west of Av Las Américas.

TOURIST SERVICES FROM MAIN TERMINAL

Tourist services to Copacabana, Puno (book with La Paz tour agencies), Tiwanaku, Uyuni and Valle de la Luna cut down on risk and up your comfort.

Diana Tours (Map p38; www.diana-tours.com; Main Terminal; B$60) Round-trip guided trips to Valle de la Luna, leaving at 8:30am.

Nuevo Continente (Main Terminal; B$60) Round-trip guided trips to Tiwanaku, leaving at 9am and returning at 4pm.

Todo Turismo (www.todoturismo.bo; Main Terminal; B$230) Overnight direct buses to Uyuni leaving at 9pm (10 hours).

Train

La Paz' old train station is defunct, but they are experimenting with a tourist service to Tiwanaku from El Alto. Trains for Chile and the Argentine border, via Uyuni and/or Tupiza, all leave from Oruro. For information and bookings, contact the **Empresa Ferroviaria Andina** (www.fca.com. bo). For information about rail services within Peru, contact **Peru Rail** (www.perurail.com).

ⓘ Getting Around

To/From the Airport

There are two access routes to El Alto International Airport: the *autopista* toll road (B$3), and the sinuous free route, which leads into Plaza Ballivián in El Alto.

Minibus 212 runs frequently between Plaza Isabel la Católica and the airport between around 7am and 8pm. Heading into town from the airport, this service will drop you anywhere along the Prado.

Radio taxis (around B$50 for up to four passengers) will pick you up at your door; confirm the price with the dispatcher when booking, or ask the driver to verify it when you climb in. For a fifth person, there is an additional B$10 charge. Transportes Aéreos Militares (TAM) flights leave from the **military airport** (☎212-1585, 237-9286) in El Alto. Catch a Río Seco *micro* from the upper Prado. Taxi fares should be about the same as for the main El Alto airport.

Car & Motorcycle

Driving the steep, winding, frenetic one-way streets of La Paz may be intimidating for the uninitiated, but for longer day trips into the immediate hinterlands, you could consider renting a car (but hiring a driver is probably easier and just as economical; for more information see the Transport chapter, p344).

Avis (☎211-1870; www.avis.com.bo; cnr Av Costanera & Calle 20, Zona Sur)

Budget (Map p42; ☎241-8768; www.budget. bo; Fernando Guachalla 639) Also a branch at the airport. Watch for unexpected extra expenses, like car washes.

Kolla Motors (Map p42; ☎241-9141; www.kolla motors.com; Rosendo Gutiérrez 502)

Public Transportation

MICRO & MINIBUS

La Paz' sputtering and smoke-spewing *micros*, the older three-quarter-sized buses, charge about B$2 per trip. Minibuses service most places as well, for a slightly higher cost. In addition to a route number or letter, *micros* plainly display their destination and route on a signboard posted in the front window. Minibuses usually have a young tout screaming the stops. Wave to catch the bus. They stop at signed *paradas* (official stops), or, if the cops aren't watching, whenever you wave them down.

TRUFI

Trufis are shared cars or minibuses that ply set routes. Destinations are identified on placards on the roof or windscreen. They charge approximately B$3 around town and B$4 to Zona Sur.

TAXI

Radio taxis (with roof bubbles advertising their telephone numbers) are recommended. They charge about B$10 around the center, B$12 to B$14 (more in peak hours) from Sagárnaga to Sopocachi or Sopocachi to the cemetery district, and B$15 to B$20 to Zona Sur. Charges are a little higher after 11pm. Normal taxi services (with just a taxi sign, no phone number and no bubble) work as collective cabs, charging each passenger around B$6; note, thought, that they are known for express kidnappings (see boxed text, p58).

If possible, ask your hotel or restaurant to ring for a taxi. Otherwise, taxis can be waved down anywhere, except near intersections or in areas cordoned off by the police. Always confirm the fare before you leave.

AROUND LA PAZ

Valle de la Luna

About 10km down the canyon of the Río Choqueyapu from the city center, Valle de la Luna is a slightly overhyped place, though it's a pleasant break from urban La Paz. It's the most accessible hiking spot near the city, with signed trails and regular patrols. It could be easily visited in a morning or combined with another outing such as a hike to **Muela del Diablo** to fill an entire day. It actually isn't a valley at all, but a bizarre, eroded hillside maze of canyons and pinnacles technically known as badlands. Several species of cactus grow here, including the hallucinogenic *choma* (San Pedro cactus).

Unfortunately, urban growth has caught up to the area, making it less of a viewpoint than it otherwise might have been. On your way here, take a pit-stop at the **Sendero del Aguila**, a 1.7km trail just up from the Rio Selva hotel.

Be aware that while they are upping patrols, robberies have been reported here. Travel in groups.

ⓘ Getting There & Away

Diana Tours (p63) offers round-trip guided trips to Valle de la Luna, leaving at 8:30am from the main bus terminal in La Paz. If on your own, from Av México in La Paz, which parallels the Prado, catch any form of transportation marked 'Mallasa' or 'Zoológico.' These will drop you off several meters from the entrance.

For a taxi from the center of La Paz, you'll pay around B$80 for up to three people, and the driver may wait for an hour or so while you look around.

Mallasa

The village of Mallasa is popular among *paceños* (people from La Paz) on weekends. Just east of Mallasa is La Paz' spacious, but sorely underfunded, **Vesty Pakos Zoo** (admission B$3.50; ◷10am-5pm). Animal lovers may be upset by the poor conditions, however.

Around La Paz

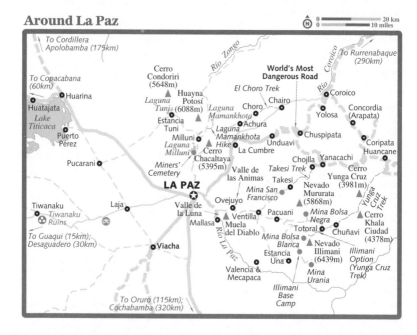

From the overlook immediately behind the zoo, you can take the clearly marked walking track that descends to and crosses the fetid Río Choqueyapu, before beginning a lung-bursting 600m climb to the Muela del Diablo.

To get to Mallasa from La Paz, take minibus 231 from Sagárnaga, or any form of transportation marked 'Mallasa' or 'Zoológico.' From the top of Valle de la Luna, catch a *micro* heading downvalley or continue a couple of kilometers on foot to Mallasa.

Valencia & Mecapaca

About 30km south of La Paz, and 15km from Mallasa, are two quaint, if increasingly urbanized, villages worth visiting for their authenticity and beautiful landscapes. Mecapaca boasts a beautifully restored church in its plaza (ask for Sra Ninfa Avendaño for keys; if you buy something from her store and add a donation to the church box, she'll likely oblige). The church is perched on the hillside of the small plaza with wonderful views of the fertile valley beyond. On the plaza, there are two small super-simple restaurants for lunch (mains B$15).

A great treat on the way back to La Paz is to stop for an Italian meal at **Trattoria Sant' Aquilina** (⊘weekends only), a Greek island–style restaurant, just before or after Jupapina, depending which direction you are coming from. The restaurant is renowned for its wood-fired pizza and gelato, and it's popular among the trendy *paceñan* crowds who converge on Sundays. If this doesn't take your fancy, join the *paceñans* at a number of other weekend eateries that have sprung up along the increasingly urbanized road south of La Paz.

Take minibus 253 to Mecapaca/Valencia from Plaza Belso in San Pedro (B$4) or from Mallasa. To return to La Paz take the same minibus 253 from Mecapaca; from anywhere else, catch anything that moves back up the valley. On weekends, *trufis,* minibuses and radio taxis leave constantly from Plaza Humboldt (Zona Sur) for points south.

Muela del Diablo

The prominent rock outcrop known as the Devil's Molar is actually an extinct volcanic plug that rises between the Río Choqueyapu and the suburban sprawl of Pedregal and Calacoto. A hike to its base makes a pleasant –

and easy to take on – half-day walking trip from La Paz; it offers incredible views of the city and valley of La Paz, and can be easily combined with a visit to Valle de la Luna.

From the cemetery in Pedregal, the trail climbs steeply (several times crossing the new road that provides access to the hamlet near the base of the *muela*). After a breathless hour or so, you'll reach a pleasant grassy swale where the 'tooth' comes into view, as well as some precarious pinnacles further east.

At this point the walking track joins the road and descends through the hamlet. About 300m further along, a side route branches off to the left and climbs toward the base of the *muela*. From the end of this route you can pick your way with extreme caution up to the cleft between the double summit, where there's a large cross. Without technical equipment and expertise, however, it's inadvisable to climb further.

After descending to the main track, you can decide whether to return the way you came, or follow the steep track that circles the *muela* in a counterclockwise direction and descends to the Río Choqueyapu before climbing the other side of the valley to the zoo in Mallasa. The latter option will turn this hike into a full-day trip, as it takes about six hours for the hike between Pedregal and Mallasa.

Be aware that several robberies have been reported here; inquire locally about safety before heading out and travel in pairs or groups, or with a local guide.

❶ Getting There & Away

From La Paz the best access to the start of the hike is on minibus 288, marked 'Pedregal,' from the lower Prado. The end of the line is the parking area a couple of hundred meters downhill from Pedregal's cemetery. Returning from Valle de la Luna, you can board these minibuses at Zona Sur's Plaza Humboldt or follow the difficult walking track from near the zoo in Mallasa, which involves a descent to the Río Choqueyapu and then a stiff 600m ascent to the eastern side of the *muela*. To return to La Paz from Pedregal, catch a 'Prado' minibus from the parking area.

Valle de las Ánimas

The name Valley of Spirits is used to describe the eerily eroded canyons and fantastic organ-pipe spires to the north and northeast of the barrios of Chasquipampa,

RÍO CHOKE

The Río Choqueyapu, which flows underground through La Paz and opens up in the Zona Sur, might as well be shortened to the Río Choke. It's the most contaminated river in all of Bolivia, containing high levels of industrial waste, urine, garbage and excrement. The industrial toxins include cyanide from tanneries and a cocktail of chemicals and dyes from textile and paper industries, which cause the river to flow bright orange in places, or red topped with a layer of white foam. The river also receives about a ton of heavy metals a day from upstream mines, according to the news outlets *El Diario* and *Gaia Noticias*. Despite recently passed environmental protection laws, most of the contamination comes from illegal industrial dumping.

Further downstream, the water is used by *campesinos* for washing, consumption and agriculture. Most people heat the water before drinking it, but few boil it, and even boiling wouldn't eliminate some of the chemical pollutants from industrial wastes. Several years ago there was an outbreak of cholera in La Paz, prompting people to blame the *campesinos* in a nearby valley, who grow vegetables in the fertile valley.

Ovejuyo and Apaña (which are rapidly being absorbed into the Zona Sur neighborhoods of La Paz). The scenery resembles that of Valle de la Luna, but on a grander scale. It's worth just getting out here.

There are two (long-day) walking routes through the valley: the Río Ovejuyo Route and the Quebrada Negra Route. The **Río Ovejuyo Route** requires a compass and 1:50,000 topography sheet *5944-II* and, for a very short section, topo sheet *5944-I*. This option can be challenging, especially because of the altitude. Make sure you carry plenty of water, a hat and snacks.

The **Quebrada Negra Route** heads up Quebrada Negra, over Cerro Pararani and down to Huni. Although only 7km, it's a demanding day hike that requires six to seven hours. It begins at the Quebrada Negra ravine, which crosses the road at the upper (eastern) end of Ovejuyo village.

The easy-to-follow 4km route up Quebrada Negra will take you through the most dramatic stretches of the eroded Valle de las Ánimas pinnacles. Near the head of the ravine, you need to traverse southeast around the northern shoulder of Cerro Pararani, until you find the obvious route that descends steeply to Huni village (not Huni chapel, which is also marked on topo sheets). In fine weather you'll have good views of Illimani along this section. For this route you'll need a compass and the 1:50,000 topo sheets *5944-I* and *6044-III*. To return to La Paz, follow the road for 2km up over Paso Huni and then for another 1.5km downhill to Apaña, where you'll catch up with regular *micros* and *trufis* returning to the city.

ℹ Getting There & Away

To get here, take minibus 42 (it must also say Uni) from Plaza Humboldt in Zona Sur. Ask the driver to drop you here.

Cañón de Palca

The magnificent Palca Canyon (marked on topo sheets as Quebrada Chua Kheri) brings a slice of Grand Canyon country to the dramatic badland peaks and eroded amphitheaters east of La Paz. A walk through this gorge makes an ideal day hike from La Paz. Note: go only in groups as assaults on single hikers at the time of research have been reported here. Check the safety status before setting out.

A good, safe alternative is to head out with La Paz on Foot (p46), which offers excellent guided day hikes through the canyon (US$45 per person including transportation and lunch).

🛏 Sleeping & Eating

Palca is a pleasant, basic town located relatively close to the exit of the canyon. It has a simple **hostal** (r per person B$20-40), which offers set meals and is popular with Bolivian tourists on weekends. Alternatively, you can camp around Palca or nearby Ventilla. Beware of the badly polluted surface water, and ask permission before you set your tent up in a field or pasture.

Huni is a small town above the entrance to Cañón de Palca. It has a store selling basic supplies, including bottled water and snack foods, and also provides Bolivian set-menu meals at lunchtime.

ℹ Getting There & Away

For the start of this hike, you need to reach Huni, which is served only by *micros* and *trufis* heading for Ventilla and Palca. These leave at least once daily from near the corner of Boquerón and Lara, two blocks north of Plaza Líbano in the San Pedro district of La Paz. There's no set schedule, but most leave in the morning – be there by 7am. You'll have the best luck on Saturday and Sunday, when families make excursions into the countryside. Alternatively, take *micro 42* or minibus 385, marked 'Ovejuyo/Apaña,' get off at the end of the line, and slog the 1.5km up the road to Paso Huni.

From Palca back to La Paz, you'll find occasional *camiones, micros* and minibuses, particularly on Sunday afternoon, but don't count on anything after 3pm or 4pm. Alternatively, you can hike to Ventilla, an hour uphill through a pleasant eucalyptus plantation, and try hitchhiking from there.

If you arrive in Palca geared up for more hiking, you can always set off from Ventilla along the Takesi trek.

Chacaltaya

The 5395m-high Cerro Chacaltaya peak atop a former glacier (it diminished over several decades and, tragically, had melted completely by 2009), is a popular day trip. Until the 'big melt,' it was the world's highest 'developed' ski area. It's a steep 90-minute ride from central La Paz, and the accessible summit is an easy 200m ascent from there.

You can get your thrills, spills (well, hopefully not) and great views on a 60km-plus mountain-bike trip from Chacaltaya to Zongo and beyond at descents of up to 4100m (vertical drop). La Paz bike outfitters run trips for around B$800 per person.

For visitors and hikers, Chacaltaya offers spectacular views of La Paz, Illimani, Mururata and 6088m Huayna Potosí. It's a high-altitude, relatively easy (but steep) 100m or so climb from the lodge to the summit of Chacaltaya. Remember to carry warm clothing and water, and take plenty of rests – say, a 30-second stop every 10 steps or so, and longer stops if needed – even if you don't feel tired. If you start to feel light-headed, sit down and rest until the feeling passes. If it doesn't, you may be suffering from mild altitude sickness; the only remedy is to descend.

From Chacaltaya it's possible to walk to Refugio Huayna Potosí, at the base of Huayna Potosí, in half a day. Before you set out, you must obtain maps from Instituto Geográfico Militar (p60) and instructions.

If it's open, snacks and hot drinks are available at Club Andino's lodge; if you want anything more substantial, bring it from town. Also bring warm (and windproof) clothing, sunglasses (100% UV proof) and sunscreen.

For overnight stays at Chacaltaya, you can crash in Club Andino's ski lodge, a '50s-style stone ski lodge. A warm sleeping bag, food and lots of water are essential for an overnight stay.

Those who fly into La Paz from the lowlands will want to wait a few days before visiting Chacaltaya or other high-altitude places.

ℹ Getting There & Away

There's no public transportation to Chacaltaya. Most La Paz tour agencies take groups to Chacaltaya for around B$50 to B$80 per person.

Tiwanaku

While it's no Machu Picchu or Tikal, a visit to the ruins of Tiwanaku (sometimes spelled Tiahuanaco or Tihuanaco) makes for a good day trip from La Paz. The site itself is less than outstanding, with a few carved monoliths, archways and arcades, and a decent museum, but history buffs will love diving into the myths and mysteries of this lost civilization. In the eponymous village, there are a number of hotels, restaurants, a fun little plaza with excellent sculptures inspired by Tiwanaku styles and a 16th-century church, built, no doubt, with stones from the Tiwanaku site.

Little is actually known about the people who constructed the ceremonial center on the southern shore of Lake Titicaca more than a thousand years ago. Archaeologists generally agree that the civilization that spawned Tiwanaku rose around 600 BC. Construction on the ceremonial site was under way by about AD 700, but around 1200 the group had melted into obscurity, becoming another 'lost' civilization. Evidence of its influence, particularly its religion, has been found throughout the vast area that later became the Inca empire.

The treasures of Tiwanaku have literally been scattered to the four corners of the earth. Its gold was looted by the Spanish, and early stone and pottery finds were sometimes destroyed by religious zealots who considered them pagan idols. Some of the work found its way to European museums; farmers destroyed pieces of it as they turned the surrounding area into pasture and cropland; the Church kept some of the statues or sold them as curios; and the larger stonework went into Spanish construction projects, and even into the bed of the La Paz–Guaqui rail line that passes just south of the site.

Fortunately, a portion of the treasure has been preserved, and some of it remains in Bolivia. A few of the larger anthropomorphic stone statues have been left on the site, and the onsite museum has a decent collection of pottery and other objects. Others are on display at the Museo Nacional de Arqueología (p41) in La Paz.

History

Although no one is certain whether it was the capital of a nation, Tiwanaku undoubtedly served as a great ceremonial center. At its height the city had a population of 20,000 inhabitants and encompassed approximately 2.6 sq km.

Some say the name roughly translates to 'the dry coast' or 'stone in the center,' and the 3870m (12,696 ft) city most likely sat on the edge of Lake Titicaca, serving as the ceremonial center for the regions south of the lake.

While only 30 percent of the original site has been excavated – and what remains is less than overwhelming – the Tiwanaku culture made great advances in architecture, math and astronomy well before the Inca ascendancy.

Archaeologists divide the development of the Tiwanaku into five distinct periods, numbered Tiwanaku I through V, each of which has its own outstanding attributes.

The Tiwanaku I period falls between the advent of the Tiwanaku civilization and the middle of the 5th century BC. Significant finds from this period include multicolored pottery and human or animal effigies in painted clay. Tiwanaku II, which ended around the beginning of the Christian era, is hallmarked by ceramic vessels with horizontal handles. Tiwanaku III dominated the next 300 years, and was characterized by tricolor pottery of geometric design, often decorated with images of stylized animals.

Tiwanaku IV, also known as the Classic Period, developed between AD 300 and 700. The large stone structures that dominate the site today were constructed during this period. The use of bronze and gold is considered evidence of contact with groups further east in the Cochabamba valley and further

west on the Peruvian coast. Tiwanaku IV pottery is largely anthropomorphic. Pieces uncovered by archaeologists include some in the shape of human heads and faces with bulging cheeks, indicating that the coca leaf was already in use at this time.

Tiwanaku V, also called the Expansive Period, is marked by a decline that lasted until Tiwanaku's population completely disappeared around 1200. Were they the victims of war, famine, climate change or alien abductions? Nobody knows, though most archaeologists point to climate change as the most likely cause of the civilization's rapid decline. During this period pottery grew less elaborate, construction projects slowed and stopped, and no large-scale monuments were added after the early phases of this period.

When the Spaniards arrived in South America, local indigenous legends recounted that Tiwanaku had been the capital of the bearded, white god-king called Viracocha, and that from his city Viracocha had reigned over the civilization.

Pieces from the three more recent Tiwanaku periods may be found scattered around Bolivia, but the majority are housed in archaeological museums in La Paz and Cochabamba. The ruins themselves have been so badly looted, however, that much of the information they could have revealed about their builders is now lost forever.

At the request of Unesco, they ceased excavations of the site in 2005, and are concentrating now on preserving what they've already dug up. About 100,000 visitors come to the site every year.

◉ Sights & Activities

Entrance to the site and museum (B$80; tickets 9am to 4pm, site open until 5pm) is paid opposite the visitor's center. If you go on your own, start your visit in the museum to get a basic understanding of the history, then head to the ruins.

The true star of the show at the onsite museum, **Museo Lítico Monumental**, is the massive 7.3m **Monolito Bennett Pachamama**, rescued in 2002 from its former smoggy home at the outdoor Templete Semisubterráneo (p43) in La Paz. You'll also find a basic collection of artifacts, pottery, exhibits on the practice of cranial deformation, and other items dug up on the site here. Labeling is in Spanish. Much of the collection is currently mothballed, as the roof of the recently built museum is already collapsing.

Scattered around the Tiwanaku site, you'll find heaps of jumbled basalt and sandstone slabs weighing as much as 25 tons each. Oddly enough, the nearest quarries that could have produced the basalt megaliths are on the Copacabana peninsula, 40km away the lake. Even the sandstone blocks had to be transported from a site more than 5km away. It's no wonder, then, that when the Spanish asked local Aymará how the buildings were constructed, they replied that it was done with the aid of the leader/deity Viracocha. They could conceive of no other plausible explanation.

At the entrance to the site two stone blocks can be used as **megaphones**. After entertaining yourself for a minute or two with this interesting pre-Columbian, pre-iPod technology, climb the hill up to Tiwanaku's most outstanding structure, the partially excavated **Akapana pyramid**, which was built on an existing geological formation. At its base this roughly square 16m hill covers a surface area of about 200 sq meters. In the center of its flat summit is an oval-shaped sunken area, which some sources attribute to early, haphazard, Spanish excavation. The presence of a stone drain in the center, however, has led some archaeologists to believe it was used for water storage. In the past few years, though, archaeologists have changed their minds. Recent findings include craniums, assumed to be war trophies, leading archaeologists to believe the pyramid was, in fact, a ceremonial temple.

North of the pyramid is **Kalasasaya**, a partially reconstructed 130m-by-120m ritual-platform compound with walls constructed of huge blocks of red sandstone and andesite. The blocks are precisely fitted to form a platform base 3m high. Monolithic uprights flank the massive entrance steps up to the restored portico of the enclosure, beyond which is an interior courtyard and the ruins of priests' quarters. Note the size of the top stair – a massive single block. The **Monolito Ponce** monolith, with his turban (no doubt covering up his deformed cranium), mask, ceremonial vase and walking stick, sits at the center of the first platform. Some say the stick and the vase are symbolic of the dualism of Andean culture (nature versus nurture).

Other stairways lead to secondary platforms, where there are other monoliths including the famous **El Fraile** (priest). At the far northwest corner of Kalasasaya is Tiwanaku's best-known structure, the **Puerta del Sol** (Gateway of the Sun). This megalithic gateway was carved from a single block of andesite, and archaeologists assume that it was associated in some way with the sun deity. The surface of this fine-grained, gray volcanic rock is ornamented with low-relief designs on one side and a row of four deep niches on the other. The gateway was most likely originally located in the center of Kalasasaya Platform and was used as a calendar, with the sun striking specific figures on the solstice and equinox. The structure is estimated to weigh at least 44 tons.

There's a smaller, similar gateway carved with zoomorphic designs near the western end of the site that is informally known as the **Puerta de la Luna** (Gateway of the Moon).

East of the main entrance to Kalasasaya, a stairway leads down into the **Templete Semisubterráneo**, an acoustic, red sandstone pit structure measuring 26m by 28m, with a rectangular sunken courtyard and walls adorned with 175 crudely carved stone faces. In the 1960s archaeologists tried to rebuild these and used cement between the stones.

West of Kalasasaya is a 55m-by-60m rectangular area known as **Putuni** or Palacio de los Sarcófagos (The Palace of the Sarcophagi). It is surrounded by double walls and you can see the foundations of several tombs. About 90% of the artifacts collected by amateur enthusiast Fritz Buck in the early 20th century from these tombs are found in La Paz' Museo de Metales Preciosos (p39).

The heap of rubble at the eastern end of the site is known as **Kantatayita**. Archaeologists are still trying to deduce some sort of meaningful plan from these well-carved slabs; one elaborately decorated lintel and some larger stone blocks bearing intriguing geometric designs are the only available clues. It has been postulated – and dubiously 'proven' – that they were derived from universal mathematical constants, such as pi, but some archaeologists simply see the plans for a large and well-designed building.

Across the railway line southwest of the Tiwanaku site, you'll see the excavation site of **Puma Punku** (Gateway of the Puma). In this temple area megaliths weighing more than 130 tons have been discovered. Like Kalasasaya and Akapana, there is evidence that Puma Punku was begun with one type of material and finished with another; part was constructed of enormous sandstone blocks and, during a later phase of construction, notched and jointed basalt blocks were added.

Note also, in the distance of the site's northern boundary, the *sukakollo,* a highly sophisticated system of terraced irrigation.

Tours

Guided tours (☏7524-3141; tiwanakuguias_turismo@hotmail.com; B$80 for 1-6 people) are available in English and Spanish, and are highly recommended.

✦ Festivals & Events

On June 21 (the southern hemisphere's winter solstice), when the rays of the rising sun shine through the temple entrance on the eastern side of the complex, the **Aymará New Year** (Machaq Mara) is celebrated at Tiwanaku. As many as 5000 people, including a large contingent of New Agers, arrive from all over the world. Locals don colorful ceremonial dress and visitors are invited to join the party, drink *singani* (alcoholic spirit), chew coca, sacrifice llamas and dance until dawn. Artisans hold a crafts fair to co-incide with this annual celebration.

Special buses leave La Paz around 4am to arrive in time for sunrise. Dress warmly because the pre-dawn hours are bitterly cold at this time of year.

Smaller, traditional, less tourist-oriented celebrations are held here for the other solstice and equinoxes.

🛏 Sleeping & Eating

You'll find several basic eateries near the ruins. Tiwanaku village, 1km west of the ruins, has several marginal restaurants and an incredibly colorful Sunday market.

Gran Hotel Tiahuanacu   HOTEL $$
(☏289-8548; www.tijuanacumystical.com; Bolívar 903; s/d incl breakfast B$120/240, s without bathroom incl breakfast B$60) Three blocks east of the Plaza, this is the nicest place to stay, with rooms that are clean, breezy and comfortable. There's a restaurant open daily. We only wish there were better views of the ruins.

Hotel Akapana   HOTEL $
(☏289-5104; www.hotelakapana; Ferrocarril; s/d incl breakfast B$80/150) Just 100m west of

the site, this friendly hotel has three levels, simple rooms with good views, hot water 24 hours a day, and a top-floor *mirador* with amazing views of the neighboring site.

Restaurante Cabaña del Puma   BOLIVIAN $$
(Ferrocarril; mains B$45-70; ☏) Next to the ruin entrance, this clean eatery offers basic country food, like trout and chicken. A vegetarian meal comes with veggies, potatoes and country cheese.

❶ Getting There & Away

Many La Paz agencies offer reasonably priced, guided, full- and half-day Tiwanaku tours (B$70 to B$140 per person), including transportation and a bilingual guide. These tours are well worth it for the convenience; most travelers visit Tiwanaku this way.

Nuevo Continente (Main Terminal; B$60) has round-trip guided trips to Tiwanaku, leaving at 9am and returning at 4pm from La Paz' main terminal.

For those who prefer to go it alone, buses from La Paz' cemetery leave every hour and cost from B$6 to B$15.

Minibuses, which are often crowded, pass the museum near the entrance to the complex. To return to La Paz, catch a minibus from the village's main plaza. Make sure it says Cemetario, otherwise, you'll get dropped off in El Alto's Ceja. Sometimes minibuses will pass the museum entrance if they're not full, looking for passengers. *Micros* to Guaqui and the Peruvian border also leave from the plaza in Tiwanaku village, or may be flagged down just west of the village – again, expect crowds.

Taxis to Tiwanaku from La Paz cost from B$210 to B$280 for the round trip.

Empresa Ferroviaria Andina (FCA; ☏2-241-6545; www.fca.com.bo) has started a pilot program to run occasional round-trip train trips from La Paz' El Alto to Tiwanaku (1.5-hour stop) and on to Guaqui on Lake Titicaca (two-hour stop). The train departs La Paz the second Sunday of each month at 8am and costs from B$10 to B$40. Check the website or call ahead.

Local guide **Franz Choque Quispe** (☏7-407-7252; fransua_tours@hotmail.com) is working on the permits to run a two-and-a-half-day walking, boating, busing tour from here to Lake Titicaca (just 12km away), that will include camping and stays with local families. Check it out.

Lake Titicaca

Best Places to Eat

» La Cúpula Restaurant (p79)

» La Orilla (p79)

» Isla Flotante Kalakota (p82)

Best Places to Stay

» Las Olas (p78)

» Hotel Rosario del Lago (p78)

» La Estancia Ecolodge (p87)

Why Go?

A visit to the world's largest high-altitude lake feels like a journey to the top of the world. Everything – and everyone – that sits beside this impressive body of water, from the traditional Aymará villages to the glacier-capped peaks of the Cordillera Real, seems to fall into the background as the singularity, power and sheer gravity of the lake draws all eyes. It is not hard to see how Inca legends came to credit Lake Titicaca with the birth of their civilization.

Set between Peru and Bolivia at 3808m, the 8400 sq km lake offers enough activities to keep you busy for at least a week. There are trips to the many islands that speckle the shoreline, hikes to lost coves and floating islands, parties in the tourist hub of Copacabana and chance encounters with locals that will provide new insight into the culture and traditions of one of Bolivia's top attractions.

When to Go
Copacabana

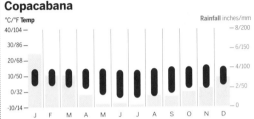

Feb–Nov Sunny by day, but there's often a cool wind off the lake and bitterly cold nights.

Feb–Apr Festivals include Semana Santa and the Fiesta de la Virgen de Candelaria.

May The Fiesta de la Cruz (Feast of the Cross) is popular around the lake.

History

When you first glimpse Lake Titicaca's crystalline, gemlike waters beneath the looming backdrop of the Cordillera Real in the clear Altiplano light, you'll understand why pre-Inca people connected it with mystical events. Those early inhabitants of the Altiplano believed that both the sun itself and their bearded white god-king, Viracocha, had risen out of its mysterious depths. The Incas, in turn, believed that it was the birthplace of their civilization.

Archaeological discoveries indicate that the areas around the lake have been inhabited since about 1500 BC by organized civilizations like the Tiwanaku, Aymará and

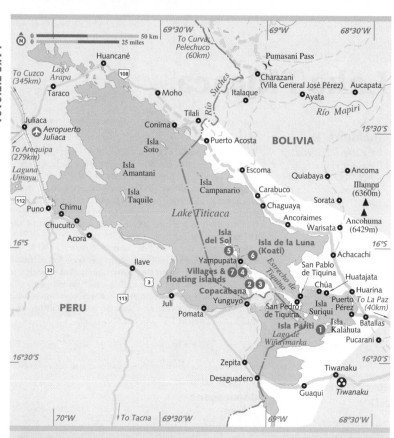

Lake Titicaca Highlights

❶ Visit the tiny island of Pariti, with its lovely **museum** (p90) featuring exquisite Tiwanaku finds from a recent excavation

❷ Discover vestiges of the Inca culture in and around **Copacabana** (p73)

❸ Check out a baptism (or even a vehicle blessing!) at Copacabana's **cathedral** (p75)

❹ Travel through **lakeside villages** (p82) between Copacabana and Yampupata, and take a spin in a reed boat

❺ Explore **Isla del Sol** (p83) on foot, hiking from tip to tail over a few days

❻ Head out to **Isla de la Luna** (p89) for spectacular lake views, ancient ruins and

landscapes straight out of the Mediterranean

❼ Eat fresh grilled trout on a **floating island** (p82) with a cold Paceña to keep you company

❽ Watch the **sunset** from the deck of your hotel, a humbling and truly awesome experience

Inca. The recent discoveries of a subaquatic temple and ancient wall have led some scientists to speculate that the lake area was inhabited as far back as 6000 BC, when it had much lower water levels. And while the nearby Tiwanaku ruins are the largest in the area, there are numerous pre-Columbian sites surrounding the lake.

From pre-Columbian times to present day, the Uru people have lived on man-made floating reed islands on the lake. The islands on the Peruvian side of the lake are still inhabited, while the Bolivian counterparts are made purely as tourist attractions. The Spanish arrived in the area in the mid-16th century, resurrecting cities like Puno and Copacabana on the shore.

From year to year, changes to the water level of Lake Titicaca are not uncommon; in the 1980s, a large flood displaced 200,000 people and it took several years for the Río Desaguadero, the lake's only outlet, to drain the floodwaters. Today, with melting glaciers and inconsistent rainfalls, the water is dropping to record-low levels.

Archaeological expeditions continue around – and beneath – the lake. At Isla Koa, north of Isla del Sol, 22 large stone boxes were found, containing a variety of artifacts: a silver llama, some shell figurines and several types of incense burners. And in 2004, the tiny island of Pariti hit world headlines when a team of Finnish and Bolivian archaeologists discovered elaborate and beautiful pottery there, which is now housed in a small museum on the island and in La Paz.

ⓘ Getting There & Away
The road journey between La Paz and Copacabana is impressive. Buses to La Paz have been hijacked, and it's recommended to travel by day. To get to Copacabana by bus, you'll need to cross the Estrecho de Tiquina (Tiquina Straits) on a ferry. The Islas de la Luna and del Sol are accessed by boat from Copacabana.

Copacabana
🎵 2 / POP 54,300 / ELEV 3808M
Nestled between two hills and perched on the southern shore of Lake Titicaca, Copacabana (also called Copa) is a small, bright and enchanting town. It was for centuries the site of religious pilgrimages and today local and international pilgrims still flock to its fiestas.

Although it can appear a little tourist-ready, the town is a pleasant place to wander

around. It has scenic walks along the lake and beyond, is the launching pad for visiting Isla del Sol and Isla de la Luna and makes a pleasant stopover between La Paz and Puno or Cuzco in Peru.

History
After the fall and disappearance of the Tiwanaku culture, the Kollas (Aymará) rose to power in the Titicaca region. Their most prominent deities included the sun and moon (who were considered husband and wife), Pachamama (Mother Earth) and the ambient mountain spirits known as *achachilas* and *apus*. Among the idols erected on the shores of the Manco Capac peninsula was Kota Kahuaña, also known as Copacahuana (meaning 'lake view' in Aymará), a deity with the head of a human and the body of a fish.

Once the Aymará had been subsumed into the Inca empire, Emperor Tupac-Yupanqui founded the settlement of Copacabana as a wayside rest for pilgrims visiting the *huaca* (shrine) known as Titi Khar'ka (Rock of the Puma), a former site of human sacrifice at the northern end of Isla del Sol.

Before the arrival of Spanish priests in the mid-16th century, the Incas had divided local inhabitants into two distinct groups. Those faithful to the empire were known as Haransaya and were assigned positions of power. Those who resisted, the Hurinsaya, were relegated to manual labor. It was a separation that went entirely against the grain of the community-oriented Aymará culture, and the floods and crop failures that befell them in the 1570s were attributed to this social aberration.

This resulted in the rejection of the Inca religion, and the partial adoption of Christianity and establishment of the Santuario de Copacabana, which developed into a syncretic mishmash of both traditional and Christian beliefs. The populace elected La Santísima Virgen de Candelaria as its patron saint and established a congregation in her honor. Noting the lack of an image for the altar, Francisco Tito Yupanqui, a direct descendant of the Inca emperor, fashioned a figurine of clay and placed it in the church. However, his rude effort was deemed unsuitable to represent the honored patron of the village and was removed.

The sculptor, who was humiliated but not defeated, journeyed to Potosí to study the arts. In 1582 he began carving a wooden image that took eight months to complete. In

LAKE TITICACA COPACABANA

Copacabana

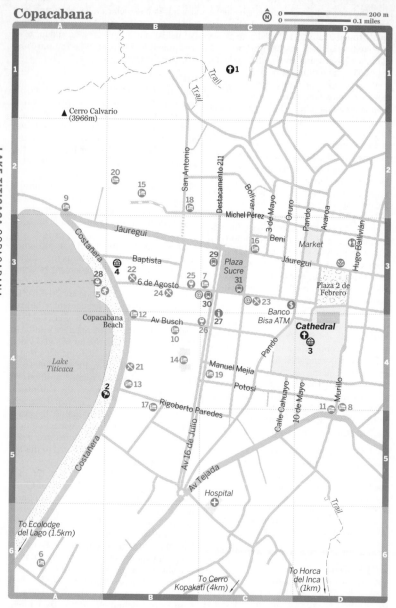

LAKE TITICACA COPACABANA

▲ Cerro Calvario
(3966m)

Lake
Titicaca

Copacabana
Beach

To Ecolodge
del Lago (1.5km)

To Cerro
Kopakati (4km)

To Horca
del Inca
(1km)

1583 *La Virgen Morena del Lago* (the Dark Virgin of the Lake) was installed on the adobe altar at Copacabana and shortly thereafter the miracles began. There were reportedly 'innumerable' early healings and Copacabana quickly became a pilgrimage site.

In 1605 the Augustinian priesthood advised the community to construct a cathedral commensurate with the power of the image. The altar was completed in 1614, but work on the building continued for 200 years. In 1805 the *mudéjar* (Moorish-style)

Copacabana

LAKE TITICACA COPACABANA

cathedral was finally consecrated, but construction wasn't completed until 1820. In 1925, Francisco Tito Yupanqui's image was canonized by the Vatican.

⊙ Sights & Activities

Copacabana's central attractions can be visited in one long but relaxed day, but there are some great trips further afield, including to the surrounding peninsulas. Much of the action in Copa centers around Plaza 2 de Febrero and Av 6 de Agosto, the main commercial drag, which runs east to west. The transportation hub is in Plaza Sucre. At its western end is the lake and a walkway (Costañera) that traces the shoreline.

Cathedral CHURCH
(6 de Agosto) The sparkling white *mudéjar* cathedral, with its domes and colorful *azulejos* (blue Portuguese-style ceramic tiles), dominates the town. Baptisms take place every Saturday at 4pm; check the notice board in front of the entrance for the mass schedule.

The cathedral's black Virgen de Candelaria statue, **Camarín de la Virgen de Candelaria**, carved by Incan Emperor Tupac-Yupanqui's grandson, Francisco Yupanqui, is encased above the altar upstairs in the *camarín* (shrine); note, visiting hours can be unreliable. The statue is never moved from the cathedral, as superstition suggests that its disturbance would precipitate a devastating flood of Lake Titicaca.

The cathedral is a repository for both European and local religious art and the **Museo de la Catedral** (per person B$10, minimum 4) contains some interesting articles – offerings from hopeful individuals. Unfortunately, the museum is open only to groups of four or more (unless you're happy to pay) and you'll most probably need to chase down a sister to arrange your visit.

Copacabana Beach BEACH
While Bolivia's only public beach can't hold a candle to the better-known beach of the same name in Rio de Janeiro, on weekends the festive atmosphere is a magnet for

families. You can take a pew at one of the many little eateries along (unfortunately) the drain-ridden shore front, play foosball against the local talent and rent all manner of watercraft, from paddleboat swans (B\$10 per hour) and canoes (B\$30 per hour) to small sailboats (B\$50 per hour). Also on offer are horseback rides (B\$40 per hour), bicycles (B\$10 per hour, B\$70 per day) and motorbikes (B\$50 per hour).

Cerro Calvario
LOOKOUT

The summit of Cerro Calvario can be reached in half an hour and is well worth the climb, especially in the late afternoon to watch the sun set over the lake. The **trail** to the summit begins near the **church** at the end of Calle Destacamento and climbs past the 14 Stations of the Cross.

Horca del Inca
RUIN

(admission B\$10) This odd gate is a fascinating pre-Inca astronomical observatory. Perched on the hillside, it is surrounded by pierced rocks that permit the sun's rays to pass through onto the lintel during the solstice of June 21, the Aymará New Year. Locals use the event to predict everything from the expected rainfall to the crop yields. During this time locals venture up before sunrise to celebrate. From near the end of Calle Murillo, a signposted trail leads uphill to the site.

Cerro Kopakati
RUIN

About 4km down the road from the Horca del Inca toward Kasani (near the turnoff to the floating islands) lies Cerro Kopakati, a carved stone featuring pre-Inca ruins and pictographs. The best known, though difficult to distinguish, is the **Escudo de la Cultura Chiripa**, a unique icon attributed to the pre-Inca Chiripa culture.

Tribunal del Inca (Intikala)
RUIN

(admission B\$5) North of the cemetery on the southeastern outskirts of town is the sadly neglected site of artificially sculpted boulders known as the Inca Tribunal. Its original purpose is unknown, but there are several carved stones with *asientos* (seats), basins and *hornecinos* (niches), which probably once contained idols.

Kusijata & Baño del Inca
MUSEUM, RUIN

(admission B\$10) A 3km walk northeast along the shoreline from the end of Calles Junín or Hugo Ballivián leads to the community of Kusijata, where there's a former colonial hacienda housing a small, dusty (read untouched) archaeological display. If you can see in the semi-dark – there's no electricity – seek out the long-deceased mummified corpse *(chullpa)* sitting in an upright fetal position, as he was buried. If no one is at the entrance, simply ask around. You can also enter the now-unkempt gardens where there's a pre-Columbian irrigation channel, originally used to access the subterranean water supply. Head past the first gushing pipe and follow the path to the carved-stone **Baño del Inca** (Inca Bath), the origins and meaning of which are a little unclear.

Museo del Poncho
MUSEUM

(www.museodelponcho.org; Baptista near Costañera; admission B\$15; ⏱10:30am-5pm Mon-Sat, 10:30am-3pm Sun) A visit to the Museo del Poncho will help you unravel the mysteries of the regional textiles (pun intended). The exhibits, spread over two floors, give a clear insight into the origins and meanings of the poncho and its associated crafts. Labels are in both English and Spanish. Hours are irregular.

FREE Museo Taypi
MUSEUM

(Hotel Rosario del Lago, Paredes near Costañera) Museo Taypi is a small, privately run cultural museum within the grounds of Hotel Rosario with a small but lovely collection of antiquities and cultural displays on the region. Here you'll also find Jalsuri, a fairtrade craft shop selling quality *artesanía*.

Tours

To visit Islas del Sol and de la Luna you can either take a ferry or go the luxury route with a La Paz–based tour operator for a guided excursion (adding a night or two in their hotels on Isla del Sol). Top guided trips include the following:

Balsa Tours
GUIDED TOUR

(☑244-0620; www.turismobalsa.com) Offers motor excursions from its resort at Puerto Pérez to Islas Pariti, Kalahuta and Suriqui.

Crillon Tours
GUIDED TOUR

(☑233-7533; www.titicaca.com; Camacho 1223, La Paz) An upmarket agency with a hydrofoil service offering various day and multiday packages kicking off from the lakefront village of Huatajata. Enquire at the Inca Utama Hotel and Spa in the village for info.

Transturin
GUIDED TOUR

(☑242-2222; www.transturin.com; Arce 2678, La Paz) This agency runs day and overnight cruises to

OUTDOOR ADVENTURES FROM COPA

The areas around Copacabana offer plenty of adventure. The trip to Yampupata is a worthwhile excursion by foot, bike or bus. And here are a few DIY activities that will take you beyond the standard tourist tracks.

Las Islas Flotantes (floating reed islands) Visit a community project at Sahuiña, approximately 6km from Copa, for a delightful spin on one of the most tranquil parts of the lake in a rowboat or a *totora*-reed boat (B$10 to B$15 per person per island). Hint: take the minibus towards Kasani (B$3) and ask to be dropped off at the entrance to the project (a 10-minute ride). The office is 15 minutes on foot from here and it's another 15 minutes to the boats.

Lost ruins Ask the Centro de Información Turística (p81) for a list of nearby Inca ruins and strike out on your own. Some, but not all, Inca sites are listed here. Admittedly, many are now neglected or rarely visited. Let us know what you find!

Hike south of town Hike around the stunning peninsula south of town to get a different perspective of the lake. To start your hike, head out 6km to the village of J'iska Q'ota, near the ex-*pista* (former airport strip). To get there, catch a minibus marked 'Kasani' (B$3) and after about 10 minutes you'll arrive at the strip. Follow the road towards the lake heading in a northeasterly – and then northerly – direction around the peninsula and back to Copa.

Bike from town Hire a bike at Copacabana Beach and head off into the hills or in the direction of Yampupata – a hilly, but beautiful, journey.

Isla del Sol in covered catamarans (and reed-boats) and has luxury accommodation on Isla del Sol.

Turisbus GUIDED TOUR
(☑245-1341; www.turisbus.com; Hotel Rosario del Lago, Paredes near Costañera) Book your tour with this well-run and professional agency through the Hotel Rosario in Copacabana or La Paz.

⭐ Festivals & Events

Copacabana hosts several major annual fiestas. The town also celebrates the **La Paz departmental anniversary** on July 15. Thursdays and Sundays are lively market days. Watch your belongings; with lots of partying – and people from out of town – there's plenty of petty theft during Copacabana's festivals.

Alasitas Festival SPIRITUAL
One local tradition is the blessing of miniature objects, such as cars or houses. Supplicants pray that the real thing will be obtained in the coming year. Held on January 24.

Fiesta de la Virgen de Candelaria RELIGIOUS
Honors the patron saint of Copacabana and all Bolivia. Copacabana holds an especially big bash and pilgrims and dancers come from Peru and around Bolivia. There's much

music, traditional Aymará dancing, drinking and feasting. On the third day celebrations culminate with the gathering of 100 bulls in a stone corral along the Yampupata road. The town's braver (and drunker) citizens jump into the arena and try to avoid being attacked. From February 2 to 5.

Semana Santa RELIGIOUS
As part of the Easter Week celebrations the town fills with pilgrims on Good Friday – some walk the 158km journey from La Paz – to do penance at the Stations of the Cross on Cerro Calvario. Beginning at the cathedral at dusk, pilgrims join a solemn candle-lit procession through town, led by a statue of Christ in a glass coffin and a replica of the Virgen de Candelaria. Once on the summit they light incense and purchase miniatures representing material possessions in the hope that they will be granted the real things by the Virgin during the year.

Fiesta de la Cruz RELIGIOUS
(Feast of the Cross) Celebrated over the first weekend in May (or on May 3 – check, as dates change) all around the lake, but the biggest festivities are in Copacabana.

Bolivian Independence Day NATIONAL HOLIDAY
Copacabana stages its biggest event during the first week in August. It's characterized

BENEDICIÓN DE MOVILIDADES

The word *cha'lla* is used for any ritual blessing, toast or offering to the powers that be, whether Inca, Aymará or Christian. On most mornings during the festival season from around 10am (and reliably on Saturday and Sunday), cars, trucks and buses hover in front of Copacabana's cathedral decked out in garlands of real or plastic flowers, colored ribbons and flags. They come for a *cha'lla* known as the Benedición de Movilidades (Blessing of Automobiles). Petitions for protection are made to the Virgin and a ritual offering of alcohol is poured over the vehicles – and sometimes into the driver – thereby consecrating them for the journey home. Between Good Friday and Easter Sunday, the *cha'lla* is especially popular among pilgrims and long-distance bus companies with new fleets. Drivers offer the priest donations for their blessings, but per vehicle it's still a cheap alternative to insurance!

by round-the-clock music, parades, brass bands, fireworks and amazing alcohol consumption. This coincides with a traditional pilgrimage that brings thousands of Peruvians into the town to visit the Virgin.

🛏 Sleeping

During fiestas accommodation fills up quickly and prices increase up to threefold. Ironically, given its lakeside position, Copacabana's water supply is unpredictable. Better hotels go to extreme efforts to fill water tanks in the morning (the supply is normally switched off at some time between 8am and noon).

A host of budget options abound, charging about B$30 per person (significantly more in high season and festivals), especially along Calle Jáuregui.

TOP CHOICE Las Olas   BOUTIQUE HOTEL $$

(📞7250-8668; www.hostallasolas.com; Michel Pérez 1-3; s B$210-224, d B$266-294; @📶) To say too much about this place is to spoil the surprise, so we'll merely give you a taste with a few simple descriptives: quirky, creative, stylish, ecofriendly, million-dollar vistas. Plus there are kitchens, private terraces with hammocks and a solar-powered Jacuzzi. You get the idea – a once-in-a-lifetime experience and well worth the splurge. Reserve one to two weeks ahead and get here by passing by its partner hotel, La Cúpula.

Hotel Rosario del Lago   HOTEL $$$

(📞862-2141, La Paz 2-245-1341; www.hotelrosario.com/lago; Paredes near Costañera; s/d/tr incl breakfast B$560/700/850; @📶) One of the smartest places in town, the hacienda-styled, three-star sister of Hotel Rosario in La Paz has charming modern rooms with solar-heated showers, double-glazed windows and lake views. Extras include mag-

netic locks, room safes and excellent service. The Altiplano light streams in and there's a pleasant sun terrace. An onsite museum, top-quality restaurant and a travel agency, Turisbus, add to the experience.

Hotel La Cúpula   HOTEL $$

(📞862-2029; www.hotelcupula.com; Michel Pérez 1-3; s/d/ste B$133/210/266; 📶) International travelers rave about this inviting oasis, marked by two gleaming white domes on the slopes of Cerro Calvario, with stupendous lake views. The rooms are pretty basic – and the beds will be too soft for some – but we love the gardens, hammocks, shared kitchen and friendly atmosphere. The helpful staff speak several languages. Best to reserve ahead.

Hostal Flores del Lago   HOTEL $

(📞862-2117; www.taypibolivia.com; Jáuregui; s/d/tr B$80/120/180; 📶) This large four-story hotel on the north side of the harbor is a top-tier budget option. The clean rooms are slightly damp, but you'll love the views and the friendly lobby area.

Ecolodge del Lago   LODGE $$

(📞862-2500; www.ecocopacabana.com; s/d/tr B$180/320/480) Situated 20 minutes on foot along the Costañera (or a quick taxi ride), this ecofriendly place, right on the lake in a wonderful nature paradise, offers a tranquil experience. The quirky adobe rooms and self-equipped apartments are self-heated thanks to the mud bricks and have solar-powered water. The rambling garden of dahlias and gladioli affords great views of the lake.

Hostel Leyenda   HOTEL $

(📞7067-4097; hostel.leyenda@gmail.com; cnr Av Busch & Constañera; s/d incl breakfast B$80/120; 📶) A solid bet for budgeteers, with views of the water, a lush garden and 'Bolivian Boutique' rooms. The corner rooms have lots of space for the same price and the top-story suite (also the same price) has a *totora*-reed raft and its own terrace.

Hostal Sonia   HOTEL $
(☎862-2019; hostalsoniacopacabana@gmail.com; Murillo 256; s/d B$40/70; @☎) Well worth the extra B$10 more than other budget options charge, this lively spot has bright and cheery rooms, great views from the upstairs rooms and a top-floor terrace, making it one of the top budget bets in town.

Hostal Los Andes   HOTEL $
(☎862-2103; fvelazquez@entelnet.bo; Busch s/n; s/d incl breakfast B$100/140; ☎) Although nothing fancy, this top-notch budget choice is neat and clean, light and breezy, polished and professional. The top-floor rooms offer good views. There's cable TV and gas – yay, not electric – showers. We only wish there were better common areas.

Hostal Emperador   HOTEL $
(☎862-2083; Murillo 235; r per person B$30, without bathroom B$20) This budget travelers' favorite is a basic, albeit lively and colorful, joint with hot showers, a laundry service, a small shared kitchen and luggage storage. A newer wing at the back has brighter rooms with bathrooms and a sunny terrace, ideal for lounging and views.

Hotel Wendy Mar   HOTEL $
(☎862-2124; hotelwendymar01@hotmail.com; 16 de Julio; r B$70-90; ☎) Everything about this excellent budget option is neat and orderly, from the hospital corner sheets to the spotless floors.

Hotel Utama   HOTEL $$
(☎862-2013; www.utamahotel.com; cnr Michel Peréz & San Antonio; s/d incl breakfast B$105/175; P@☎) Set on the hill overlooking town, this clean reliable option has firm beds, a fun central terrace and sketchy electric showers. Try to get a room with a view. Free bag storage and a book exchange add to the mix.

Hostal 6 de Agosto   HOTEL $
(Av 6 de Agosto; r per person B$30) A rosy and very central place with a sunny outlook over a garden and clean, if standard, rooms at dirt-cheap prices.

Hotel Gloria   HOTEL $$$
(☎862-2094; www.hotelgloria.com.bo; 16 de Julio & Manuel Mejía; r incl breakfast B$450; @☎) While

it feels a bit like a hospital, this resort-style hotel is a decent (if slightly decaying) top-tier option.

Hotel Las Kantutas   HOTEL $$
(☎862-2093; hotelkantutas@entelnet.bo; Jáuregui, cnr Bolívar; incl breakfast s B$80-100, d B$140-160) This central option has slightly stinky rooms and stained bed spreads, but will do in a pinch come festival time when it's tough to find accommodation.

Hotel Chasqui del Sol   HOTEL $$
(☎7-359-4599; www.chasquidelsol.com; Costañera 55; s/d incl breakfast B$80/170; P☎) A lurking beachfront behemoth with basic rooms, dirty towels and pretty damned good views. For the price, you can probably do a little better.

Eating

The specialty is *trucha criolla* (rainbow trout) and *pejerrey* (king fish) from Lake Titicaca. The trout were introduced in 1939 to increase protein content in the local diet. Today, trout stocks are mainly grown in hatcheries; *pejerrey* stocks are seriously depleted. The catch of the day is served ad nauseam to varying degrees of taste – some resemble electrocuted sardines while others are worthy of a Michelin restaurant rating.

Some of the best trout is served at the **beachfront stalls** and can cost as little as B$20, though hygiene is questionable. The bargain basement is the market *comedor* (dining hall), where you can eat a generous meal of *trucha* or beef for a pittance, or an 'insulin shock' breakfast or afternoon tea of hot *api morado* (hot corn drink; B$2) and syrupy *buñuelos* (donuts or fritters; B$1).

A Groundhog Day horde of eateries lies along Av 6 de Agosto.

La Orilla   INTERNATIONAL $$
(☎862-2267; Av 6 de Agosto; mains B$25-45; ⏱4-9:30pm Mon-Sat; ☑) Some say this cozy maritime-themed restaurant is the best restaurant in town, with fresh, crunchy-from-the-vine vegetables, crispy and super savory pizzas and interesting trout creations that incorporate spinach and bacon (mmm, bacon). They might just be right.

La Cúpula Restaurant   INTERNATIONAL $$
(www.hotelcupula.com; Michel Pérez 1-3; mains B$20-50; ⏱closed lunch Tue; ☑) Inventive use of local ingredients make up an extensive international and local menu. The vegetarian range includes a tasty lasagna and there's

plenty for carnivores, too. Dip your way through the cheese fondue with authentic Gruyère cheese – it's to die for...which leaves the Bolivian chocolate fondue with fruit platter beyond description. The glassy surroundings admit lots of Altiplano light and maximize the fabulous view of the lake.

Kota Kahuaña INTERNATIONAL **$$**
(862-2141; Paredes at Costañera; mains B$25-55) This hotel restaurant has excellent views of the lake, great service and well-prepared international dishes. While it is one of the more expensive in town, it also has higher standards than some of its counterparts. Stuffed trout, an excellent salad bar, and satisfying main courses and Bolivian wines ensure a fine-dining experience.

Pueblo El Viejo INTERNATIONAL **$$**
(Av 6 de Agosto 684; mains B$35-50) Readers love this rustic, cozy and chilled cafe-bar, with its ethnic decor and laid-back atmosphere. It serves up a good burger and pizza, and is open until late. Service can be quite slow, so plan on being here a while.

Pensión Aransaya BOLIVIAN **$**
(Av 6 de Agosto 121; almuerzo B$15, mains B$25-40; lunch) Super-friendly local favorite for a tall, cold beer and trout heaped with all the trimmings. It's neat, clean, very traditional and popular with the locals.

Drinking

New nightspots come and go as frequently as tour boats. As well as Pueblo El Viejo, the following places are among the reliable options.

Waykys BAR
(Av 16 de Julio, at Busch) A friendly, warm den of a place with cozy corners, graffiti-covered walls and ceilings (you can add what you want), a billiards table, book exchange and range of music.

Nemos Bar BAR
(Av 6 de Agosto) This dimly lit, late-night hangout is a popular place for a tipple.

Shopping

Local specialties include handmade miniatures of *totora*-reed boats and unusual varieties of Andean potatoes. Massive bags of *pasankalla*, which is puffed *choclo* (corn) with caramel, the South American version of popcorn, abound. Dozens of stores sell llama- and alpaca-wool hats and sweaters; a

reasonable alpaca piece will cost about B$80. Vehicle adornments used in the *cha'lla*, miniatures and religious paraphernalia are sold at stalls in front of the cathedral.

Information

Dangers & Annoyances

There are continuing reports of nasty incidents involving travelers on illegal minibuses and taxis offering services from Copacabana and La Paz, especially on those that arrive in La Paz at night. Syndicates, posing as fellow passengers, kidnap and hold tourists bound and blindfolded for more than 24 hours while their bank accounts are depleted to the maximum amount permitted. The smaller minibuses are more dangerous – they tend to be packed with people and are prone to speed. Travelers are encouraged to take the formal tourist buses (or the larger buses) and schedule your trip to arrive by day.

Tourists should also be especially careful during festivals. Stand well back during fireworks displays, when explosive fun seems to take priority over crowd safety, and be wary of light-fingered revelers.

The thin air, characteristically brilliant sunshine and reflection off the water mean scorching levels of ultraviolet radiation. Wear a hat and sunscreen in this region, and drink lots of water to avoid dehydration.

Internet Access

Entel Internet alf@net (Av 6 de Agosto; per hr B$10; 9am-11pm) The best connection (and cheap video rentals and a book exchange) is available at this friendly place.

Entel Internet (Av 6 de Agosto; per hr B$10; 8:30am-11pm) A second, smaller branch.

Left Luggage

Most hotels will hold luggage free of charge for customers for a few days if you want to take a trip to Isla del Sol.

Medical Services

There is a basic hospital on the southern outskirts of town with medical and dental facilities, but for serious situations don't think twice – head straight to La Paz.

Money

Travelers beware: the ATMs in town often don't work. Av 6 de Agosto is the Wall Street of Copacabana and nearly every shop will exchange foreign currency (dollars are preferred over euros and must be clean – not ripped – bills). The **Banco Bisa ATM** (6 de Agosto & Pando) works on most international systems, if it works at all. You can buy Peruvian *soles* at most *artesanías* (stores selling handcrafted items), but you'll normally find better rates in Kasani at the Bolivian border, or Yuguyo, just beyond the Peruvian border.

Post
Post office (☺8:30am-noon & 2:30am-4pm Tue-Sun) On the north side of Plaza 2 de Febrero, but often closed or unattended.

Telephone
Entel, Cotel, Tigo and Viva *puntos* (privately run phone offices) are dotted along Av 6 de Agosto and around town.

Tourist Information
Centro de Información Turística (16 de Julio, near Plaza Sucre; ☺9am-1pm & 2-6pm Wed-Sun; 🖩) There is a helpful English-speaking attendant, although only rudimentary information is available.

Copacabana community tourism site (www.copacabana-bolivia.com) Has a good events calendar and updated info on community tourism projects. Run by tourism operator Turisbus.

❶ Getting There & Away

Bus
Most buses leave from near Plazas 2 de Febrero or Sucre. The more comfortable nonstop tour buses from La Paz to Copacabana – including

Milton Tours and Combi Tours – cost from about B$25 to B$30 and are well worth the investment as night-time hijackings are not uncommon on this route. They depart from La Paz at about 8am and leave Copacabana at 1:30pm (3½ hours). Tickets can be purchased from tour agencies. You will need to exit the bus at the Estrecho de Tiquina (Tiquina Straits), to cross via **ferry** (per person B$1.50 per car B$35-40, 5am-9pm) between the towns of San Pedro de Tiquina (should you need it, there's a tourist office on the main plaza) to San Pablo de Tiquina.

Buses to Peru, including Arequipa, Cuzco and Puno, depart and arrive in Copacabana from Av 6 de Agosto. You can also get to Puno by catching a public minibus from Plaza Sucre to the border at Kasani (B$3, 15 minutes). Across the border there's frequent, if crowded, onward transportation to Yunguyo (five minutes) and Puno (2½ hours).

BUS COSTS & DISTANCES

DESTINATION	COST (B$)	DURATION (HR)
Arequipa	120	8.5
Cuzco	110	15
La Paz	30	3.5
Puno	30	3-4

ENTERING OR LEAVING PERU

Most travelers enter/exit Peru via Copacabana (and the Tiquina Straits) or the scruffy town of Desaguadero (avoiding Copacabana altogether). Note that Peruvian time is one hour behind Bolivian time, and Bolivian border agents often charge an unofficial B$30 (collaboration fee) to use the border. Always keep your backpack with you when crossing the border.

Via Copacabana

Micros to the Kasani-Yunguyo border leave Copacabana's Plaza Sucre regularly, usually when full (B$3, 15 minutes). At Kasani you obtain your exit stamp at passport control and head on foot across the border. Sometimes the border agent will charge you a nominal fee for the crossing (about B$30). On the Peruvian side, *micros* and taxis will ferry you to Yunguyo (about 6 Peruvian soles, 15 minutes). From here, you can catch a bus heading to Puno. An efficient alternative is to catch a tourist bus from/to La Paz to Puno via Copacabana (from B$60); some allow you a couple of days' stay in Copacabana. Note, though, that even if you've bought a ticket to Cusco or elsewhere in Peru, you'll change buses in Puno. Buses to Cusco depart from Puno's international terminal, located about three blocks from the local terminal.

Via Desaguadero

A quicker, if less interesting, route is via Desaguadero on the southern side of the lake. Several bus companies head to/from this border from/to Peru. The crossing should be hassle-free: you obtain your exit stamp from the **Bolivian passport control** (possible fee of B$30; ☺8:30am-8:30pm), walk across a bridge and get an entry stamp at *migración* in Peru. Frequent buses head to Puno hourly (about 3½ hours).

Boat

Buy your tickets for boat tours to Isla de la Luna and Isla del Sol from agencies on Av 6 de Agosto or from beachfront kiosks. Traveling in a big group? Consider renting a private boat through one of the following operators for B$600 per day. Separate return services are available from both islands.

Asociación Unión Marines (Costañera; one-way B$20, round-trip B$25 ; ⊘departs Copacabana 8:30am & 1:30pm) Ferry service to the north and south of Isla del Sol, with a stop on the return at a floating island.

Titicaca Tours (Costañera; round-trip B$35; ⊘departs Copacabana 8:30am) Offers a round-trip boat tour that stops on Isla de la Luna for an hour, continuing to the southern end of Isla del Sol for a two-hour stop before heading back to Copacabana.

Copacabana to Yampupata

Hiking, biking or simply busing along the road from Copacabana to Yampupata, a small hamlet about 17km north of town, is a fun little adventure and an interesting alternative to the standard Copa–Isla tour. Along the way, you'll see ruins, stop at floating islands, get chased by dogs and pass through traditional communities.

MAIN ROUTE

If walking, this trek is road-bound, making it a fairly hot and hard slog (allow seven hours one way if you're stopping along the way). By bike the round-trip can be done in a day, while taxi or minibus trips will take under an hour one way. Take your own snacks; there's little, if anything, along the way.

From Copacabana, head northeast on the road that follows the shoreline. Just after the Baño del Inca turnoff the **Isla Flotante Kalakota** is a good spot to stop for a fresh-caught trout lunch (B$25). About 1½ hours into the journey, you arrive at the **Gruta de Lourdes** (aka Gruta de Fátima), a cave that for locals evokes images of its respective French and Portuguese namesakes. For a shortcut, turn right immediately after the small bridge leading to the Virgin and follow the Inca path. When the path peters out head directly uphill to rejoin the main road at the crest. To save an hour or so and avoid the flat and litter-strewn outskirts of town, you can catch a minibus (B$5) or taxi (one way/return B$40/70) from Copa to the cave (9km), from where the more picturesque hiking begins.

At the fork just below the crest of the hill bear left and descend to the shore and into the village of **Titicachi** where, if it's open, there's a basic *tienda* (shop) selling soft drinks. For die-hard archaeologists, in and around Titicachi are some pre-Inca walls and the abandoned **Tiahuanacota Inca cemetery**, but these are not obvious to the visitor. The community runs a couple of **floating islands** (B$10 per person per island) just off-shore.

At the next village, **Sicuani**, the Hostal Yampu offers very basic accommodations with bucket showers, but is not always in operation. Hikers can pop in for a beer or soft drink. Ask around town for trips around the bay in a *totora*-reed boat or via motorboat to the peninsula opposite (prices negotiable).

CONSTRUCTION OF A TOTORA-REED BOAT

The construction of *totora*-reed boats is an art form. Green reeds are gathered from the lake shallows and left to dry in the sun. Once free of moisture, they are organized into fat bundles and lashed together with strong grass. In former days, a sail of reeds was often added. These bloated little canoes don't last long as far as watercraft go; after several months of use they become waterlogged and begin to rot and sink. Traditionally, the canoes often would have been stored some distance away from the water to increase their life span. Now the boats are made and used mainly for tourism purposes.

In the early 1970s Dr Thor Heyerdahl, the Norwegian adventurer and ethnographer, solicited the help of the well-known shipbuilders from Lake Titicaca's Isla Suriqui, the Limachi brothers and Paulino Esteban, to design and construct his vessel *Ra II* to sail from Morocco to Barbados.

Dr Heyerdahl wanted to test his theory that migration and early contact occurred between the ancient peoples of North Africa and the Americas. He planned to show the feasibility of traveling great distances using the boats of the period, in this case, papyrus craft.

Yampupata

Yampupata

LAKE TITICACA ISLA DEL SOL

hotels. You can return on foot to Copacabana via the higher eastern route (four hours). Although this road doesn't pass through main villages, it affords magnificent views and a more nature-bound experience.

ⓘ Getting There & Away

Taxis from Copacabana to Yampupata cost about B$80. For those who don't want to walk or catch a taxi, the easiest way to travel between Yampupata and Copacabana is by minibus (B$10, 40 minutes). At the time of research, these were leaving Copacabana's 2 de Febrero Plaza, every two hours or so.

For those who want to spend the night in isolation, you can camp here.

Five to six hours from Copacabana you'll reach Yampupata, a collection of lakefront adobe houses. If you ask around, you'll find rooms for rent. Asociación Transport Yampu Tour Lacustre (p89) takes passengers across to the south of Isla del Sol for B$100 or to the north for B$200. B$200 will also get you to Isla de la Luna. A rowboat to Fuente del Inca (B$30) or Pilko Kaina (B$20) makes for an interesting journey to the southern end of Isla del Sol.

ALTERNATIVE ROUTES

An alternative hiking option, especially for those who don't want to head to Isla del Sol, is to catch a taxi (B$80) from Copacabana along the main road and stop at villages along the way. You finish at the beautiful and unspoiled cobblestone village of **Sampaya**, 5km from Yampupata, which has some basic

Isla del Sol

POP 2500 / ELEV 3808M

Easily the highlight of any Lake Titicaca excursion (and perhaps your entire Bolivia romp), Isla del Sol is a large island with several traditional communities, decent tourist infrastructure such as hotels and restaurants, a few worthwhile pre-Columbian ruins, amazing views, great hikes and, well, lots of sun.

The large 70 sq km island definitely merits a night or two – you can then devote a day each to the northern and southern ends. While the day tour gives you a decent introduction to the island (you can do a walking circuit of the main sights in a long day), whirlwind half-day tours are strictly for the been-there-done-that crowd.

The island's permanent residents – a mix of indigenous peoples and recent émigrés/escapers – are distributed between the main

Isla del Sol

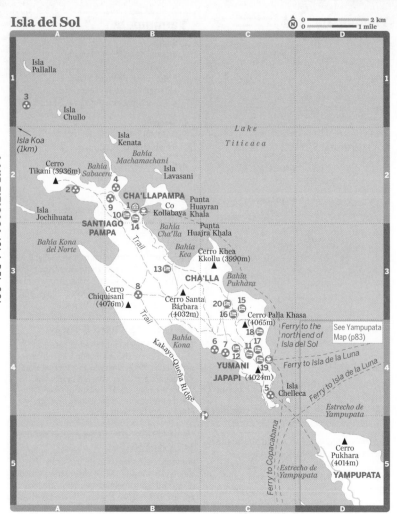

settlements of **Cha'llapampa**, near the island's northern end; **Cha'lla**, which backs onto a lovely sandy beach on the central east coast; and **Yumani**, which straddles the ridge above the Escalera del Inca in the south and is the biggest town on the island.

There are no vehicles on Isla del Sol, so visitors are limited to hiking along rocky trails (some are now paved in Inca style) or traveling by boat. The main ports are at Pilko Kaina, the Escalera del Inca in Yumani and near the Templo del Inca and Chincana ruins at Cha'llapampa. There's also a small port at Japapi on the southwest coast.

Extensive networks of walking tracks make exploration fairly easy, though the altitude and sun may take their toll. Hikers should carry lunch and ample water. The sun was born here and is still going strong; a good sunscreen is essential, particularly by the water.

History

The Island of the Sun was known to early inhabitants as Titi Khar'ka (Rock of the Puma), from which Lake Titicaca takes its name. This island has been identified as the birthplace of several revered entities, including

Isla del Sol

the sun itself. Legend has it that the bearded white god-king Viracocha and the first Incas, Manco Capac and his sister-wife Mama Ocllo, mystically appeared under direct orders from the sun. Most modern-day Aymará and Quechua peoples of Peru and Bolivia accept these legends as their creation story.

⊙ Sights & Activities

You'll need to walk everywhere, so allow plenty of time to explore the island. There's a B$5 fee to cross the island and each site exacts its own admission fees. These fees change regularly and are leveraged to maintain tourist infrastructure.

There are two major routes between the northern and southern ends of Isla del Sol. The lower route winds scenically through fields, hamlets and villages, and around the bays and headlands above the eastern coast. The most commonly used route follows the dramatic ridge path that runs between Cha'llapampa in the north and Yumani in the south. In the north, the Chincana ruins sit on top of an uninhabited ridge. The views down to both coasts of the island are nothing short of spectacular.

SOUTHERN ISLA DEL SOL
Fuente del Inca &
Escalera del Inca   GARDENS
(admission B$5) Just uphill from the ferry dock at the village of Yumani, this lovely hanging garden and rolling waterfall is most people's introduction to Isla del Sol. As you head up from the dock along the beautifully reconstructed Escalera del Inca (Inca stairway), you'll pass plenty of terraced

gardens, small shops and hotels. The road is crisscrossed by three artificial stone channels that start in the Fuente del Inca natural springs. It's a lung-buster that gains almost 200m in elevation over less than 1km, so take your time – or hire donkeys (B$30 to B$50) to carry your pack.

Early Spaniards believed Yumani's spring was a fountain of youth and for the Incas the three streams represented their national motto: *Ama sua, Ama llulla, Ama khella,* meaning 'Don't steal, don't lie and don't be lazy.' Today, the fountain is a crucial source of water for locals, who come daily to fetch and carry it up the steep trail.

Pay your admission fee at the dock for access to the stairway and village.

Yumani   VILLAGE
Yumani is the main village at the south end of the island. Most boats drop you at the village's dock, about 200m downhill along the Escalera Inca from the town proper. The village's small church, **Iglesia de San Antonio**, serves the southern half of the island. Nearby you'll find an exploding cluster of guesthouses and fabulous views over the water to Isla de la Luna. You can climb to the ridge for a view down to the deep sapphire-colored **Bahía Kona** on the western shore (about a half-hour hike along a well-worn trail). From the crest you'll also find routes leading downhill to the tiny pretty village of **Japapi** and north along the ridge to the Chincana ruins and Cha'llapampa.

With extra time you can make your way over the isthmus and up onto the prominent **Kakayo-Queña Ridge**, the island's southwestern extremity. The serene walk along the ridge to the **lighthouse** at the southern tip takes at least half a day (return) from Yumani.

Pilko Kaina   RUINS
(admission B$5) This prominent ruins complex near the southern tip of the island, about 30 minutes (2km) south by foot from Yumani, sits well camouflaged against a steep terraced slope. The best-known site is the two-level **Palacio del Inca**, thought to have been constructed by the Incan Emperor Tupac-Yupanq. The rectangular windows and doors taper upward from their sill and thresholds to narrower lintels that cover them on top. The arched roof vault was once covered with flagstone shingle and then reinforced with a layer of mud and straw.

Cha'lla   VILLAGE
(admission B$5) This agreeable little village stretches along a magnificent sandy beach that could be straight out of a holiday brochure for the Greek islands. The village is spread out – it extends over the hill to the south. There's a small kiosk and a guesthouse, Hostal Qhumphuri (p88). You have to pay an admission fee to pass along the trail into town.

In the pastoral flatlands over the low pass between Cha'lla and Yumani is the **Museo Étnico** (admission free with Cha'lla trail fee), with some dusty exhibits including Inca pots. It's an hour's walk (4km) north of Yumani along the lower path (or on the western route if coming from the north). It's worth it for the stunning bay and valley views; the museum itself is disappointing and you will have to ask around to be let in.

NORTHERN ISLA DEL SOL
Cha'llapampa   VILLAGE
(museum admission B$10 – includes Chicana Ruins entrance) Most boat tours visiting the northern ruins land at Cha'llapampa, a small village straddling a slender isthmus. The small **Cha'llapampa Museum** (admission B$10) contains artifacts excavated in 1992 from Marka Pampa, referred to by locals as La Ciudad Submergida (Sunken City). Among the dusty exhibits are anthropomorphic figurines, Tiwanaku-era artifacts, animal bones, skull parts, puma-shaped ceramic *koa* censers and cups resembling Monty Python's Holy Grail.

Piedra Sagrada & Templo del Inca   RUINS
From Cha'llapampa Village, the Chincana route continues parallel to the beach, climbing gently along an ancient route to the isthmus at **Santiago Pampa** (also known as Kasapata).

Immediately east of the trail is an odd carved boulder standing upright in a small field. This is known as the **Piedra Sagrada** (Sacred Stone). There are theories that it was used as an execution block for those convicted of wrongdoing.

Over the track and in a field, just southwest of the Piedra Sagrada, are the ancient walls of the complex known as the **Templo del Inca** (or Templo del Sol). Although little remains of this temple, built for an unknown purpose, it contains the only Bolivian examples of expert Inca stonework comparable to the renowned walls found in Cuzco.

Chincana Ruins   RUINS
(admission B$10) The island's most spectacular ruins complex, the Chincana ruins, lies near the island's northern tip. Its main feature is the **Palacio del Inca**, a maze of stone walls and tiny doorways, also known as El Laberinto (the Labyrinth) or by its Aymará name, Inkanakan Utapa. Within the labyrinth there is a small well, believed by Inca pilgrims to contain sacred water with which they would purify themselves.

About 150m southeast of the ruins is the **Mesa Ceremónica** (Ceremonial Table). It's thought to have been the site of human and animal sacrifices and makes for a damned good picnic spot in modern times. East of the table stretches the large rock known as Titicaca – or, more accurately, **Titi Khar'ka** (Rock of the Puma) – which is featured in the Inca creation legend. The name is likely to derive from its shape, which, when viewed from the southeast, resembles a crouching puma.

Three natural features on the rock's western face also figure in legend. Near the northern end is one dubbed the **Cara de Viracocha** (Face of Viracocha) – your guide will point it out with the help of a mirror (and some imagination). At the southern end are four distinctive elongated niches: the two on the right are locally called the **Refugio del Sol** (Refuge of the Sun); the ones on the left are called the **Refugio de la Luna** (Refuge of the Moon). According to tradition it was here during the Chamaj Pacha ('times of flood and darkness') that the sun made its first appearance, and later Manco Capac and Mama Ocllo appeared and founded the Inca Empire.

Immediately south of the rock you'll pass the **Huellas del Sol** (Footprints of the Sun).

A BOLIVIAN ATLANTIS?

At low tide an innocuous-looking column of rock peeps just a few centimeters above Lake Titicaca's surface, north of Isla del Sol. Most locals dismiss it as a natural stone column, similar to many others along the shoreline. In 1992 stone boxes containing artifacts (including several made of pure gold) were discovered at the underwater site known as **Marka Pampa** (aka La Ciudad Submergida). In 2000 and 2004 further excavations near the site revealed a massive stone temple, winding pathways and a surrounding wall, all about 8m underwater. Although it remains unclear who was responsible for the structures, it has been postulated that they could be as much as 6000 years old. Some even say they are the lost traces of Atlantis. Investigations – and conspiracy theories – are ongoing.

These natural markings resemble footprints and have inspired the notion that they were made by the sun after its birth on Titi Khar'ka.

If you've the energy, climb nearby **Cerro Uma Qolla** for a great view.

🛏 Sleeping

The most scenic place to stay is Yumani – high on the ridge – where guesthouses are growing faster than coca production. Cha'llapampa and Cha'lla have basic options. Hotels often close or shut down for weeks on end, so plan on being flexible. If camping, it's best to ask permission from the local authority and then set up away from villages, avoiding cultivated land (a nominal payment of B$10 should be offered).

With no cars and no roads, and just a wild series of walking paths, it can be difficult to find the hotel you are looking for. Ask around, and try to see a few before settling.

Water is a precious commodity. The island does not yet have access to water mains and supplies are carried by person or donkey. Bear this in mind; think twice before taking showers (after all, we're all in – and on! – the same boat).

Note that in high season (June to August and during festivals) prices listed here may double.

YUMANI

La Estancia Ecolodge   LODGE $$$
(☎2-244-2727; www.ecolodge-laketiticaca.com; s/d incl breakfast & dinner US$150/200) Magri Turismo's delightful adobe cottages are set above pre-Inca terraces facing snow-capped Illampu. They are authentically ecological with solar-powered showers, sun-powered hot-boxes for heaters and Aymará thatched roofs. La Estancia is a 15-minute walk from Yumani.

Palla Khasa   CABIN $$
(☎7321-1585; palla-khasa@hotmail.com; s/d incl breakfast B$150/250) About 300m north of Yumani proper, this top choice has lovely grounds, simple (but workable) rooms – we like *número* 3 the best – funky carved-wood bedstands and remarkably low ceilings. Work is underway to build new larger huts. The solar-heated water is good all night long. The restaurant is highly recommended.

Las Cabañas   CABIN $$
(s/d incl breakfast B$80/160) Perched on the hill leading into town from the dock, these simple adobe bungalows afford great views and have 24-hour hot water. The beds are nice and soft.

Hostal Puerta del Sol   HOTEL $
(☎7195-5101; s with/without bathroom B$150/40, cabin per person B$150, d B$200) On the promontory on top of the hill, this friendly option has good views from most rooms (number 14 is awesome), clean sheets and a nice terrace. The rooms with bathrooms are much better, and the Andean textiles add a nice touch. Passive solar heating in the cabins helps keep you warm at night. They have a serious bug problem in the garden areas.

Hotel Imperio del Sol   HOTEL $
(r per person with/without bathroom B$60/30) This peachy and central place on the hillside running into town is a good bet, with clean rooms and friendly, reliable service.

Hostal Illampu   HOTEL $
(r per person without bathroom B$25) Halfway up the hill into town, this budget option has excellent views and decent rooms – though the shared bathrooms are quite basic. The locks on the doors do not look very secure; single female travelers may wish to go elsewhere.

Hostal Templo del Sol HOTEL $

(☎7351-8970; r per person with/without bathroom B$80/30) This basic option at the top of the hill was being renovated at the time of visiting, but should have decent options.

Hostal Inti Wayra HOTEL $

(r per person from B$45) The amicable and rambling Inti Wayra affords great views from most rooms; these vary a great deal – some are larger and more open. This hotel isn't always open.

Inti Wasi Lodge HOSTEL $

(☎7196-0223; museo_templodelsol@yahoo.es; dm per person B$25, cabins per person incl breakfast B$70) Four basic but cozy cabins with en suites, smashing views and a recommended restaurant, Palacio de la Trucha, attached. To get here, turn right just before Hostal Illampu as you head up the hill.

Inka Pacha HOTEL $

(☎289-9160; hostellingbolivia@yahoo.com; r per person B$25, s/d/tr incl breakfast B$70/140/200) What this HI-affiliated place lacks in luxury (read: simple rooms), it makes up for in friendliness and service. The airy, communal area is a nice spot to meet fellow travelers.

Inti Kala Hostal HOTEL $

(☎7194-4013; javierintikala@hotmail.com; r per person incl breakfast B$80) This place has a massive deck and small, neat rooms. The terrace is a hit, but many complain about the service.

CHA'LLA

Hostal Qhumphuri HOTEL $

(☎7152-1188, La Paz 02-284-3534; hostalqhumphuri@hotmail.com; s/d B$20/40) Located on the hill behind the beach at Cha'lla is the simple family-run Hostal Qhumphuri, a mustard-colored construction that offers clean rooms and meals for a bit more.

CHA'LLAPAMPA

The neatest of a choice of very basic options is the flowery **Hostal San Francisco** (r per person B$30). It's to the left of the landing site. **Hostal Cultural** (☎7-190-0272; r per person B$35, without bathroom B$25) behind the beach is the only option with private bathrooms. Other budget options are on the beach behind the museum.

There are several restaurants in the village that serve good fish dishes.

Eating

There are more pizzerias in Yumani than Titicaca has *trucha*. We suggest you follow your nose and taste buds, plus fellow travelers' recommendations (see how far your feet can take you) and choose what appeals to you. Many midrange and top-end accommodation options have good eateries. Most restaurants are blessed with good views and those on the ridge are special for the sunset. Nearly all menus are identical; *almuerzos* and set dinners cost between B$25 and B$30.

❶ Getting There & Around

Boat

You can reach Isla del Sol by ferry from either Copacabana or Yampupata, or with a guided tour.

Ferry tickets may be purchased at the ticket kiosks on the beach or from Copacabana agencies. Boats to the northern end of the island land at Cha'llapampa, while those going to the southern end land at either Pilko Kaina or the Escalera del Inca near Yumani.

Launches embark from Copacabana beach around 8:30am and 1:30pm daily. Depending on the season and the company, you may get to choose if you get dropped at the island's north or south (check with the agency). Return trips leave Yampupata at 10:30am and 4pm (one way B$20) and Cha'llapampa at 1pm (B$20).

Most full-day trips go directly north to Cha'llapampa (two to 2½ hours). Boats anchor for 1½ hours only – you'll have just enough time to hike up to the Chincana ruins and back again to catch the boat at 1pm to the Escalera del Inca and Pilko Kaina in the island's south. Here, you'll spend around two hours before departing for Copa.

Half-day trips generally go to the south of Isla del Sol only.

Those who wish to hike the length of the island can get off at Cha'llapampa in the morning and walk south to the Escalera del Inca for the return boat in the afternoon.

Alternatively, you can opt to stay overnight or longer on the island (highly recommended), then buy a one-way ticket to Copacabana with any of the boat companies. Asociación Unión Marines (p82) and Titicaca Tours (p82) run trips here.

Walking

A more adventurous alternative is to walk to Yampupata (four to seven hours), just across the strait, and hire a boat to the north or south of the island.

Isla de la Luna (Koati)

POP 120 / ELEV 3808M

Legend has it that the small Island of the Moon was where Viracocha commanded the moon to rise into the sky. The island offers an interesting alternative (or add on) to your Titicaca odyssey. It's way smaller, way drier and way less touristed than its solar counterpart, and if you only have a day, you are better off heading to the Isla del Sol. This said, for slightly more adventurous experiences this is a good option and it's easy enough to tack a half-day here onto your Isla del Sol trip.

Most boats arrive on the eastern side of the island, where you'll find a visitor center, a hostel and artisan stands – all of which may or may not be open. On the other side of the hill, the island's main settlement has basic hotels, a store, a soccer field and a small chapel.

◉ Sights & Activities

Templo de las Vírgenes   RUIN
(admission B$10) The ruins of an Inca nunnery and temple dedicated to the Virgins of the Sun – also known as Acllahuasi or Iñak Uyu – occupy an amphitheaterlike valley on the northeast shore where most ferries drop you. It's constructed of well-worked stone set in adobe mortar and was where chosen girls (believed to be around eight years old) were presented as an offering to the sun and moon. Half of the site has been reconstructed.

Interpretive Trail   HIKING
A walk up to the eucalyptus grove at the summit where shepherds graze their flocks is rewarded by a spectacular vista of aquamarine waters, Cerro Illampu and the entire snow-covered Cordillera Real. Signs along the trail recount local legends (in Spanish).

⊨ Sleeping & Eating

There are three hostels in the main settlement on the east side of the island, with ultra-basic rooms going for about B$15 to B$25 per person. Food in town will cost about B$25 a meal. Ask around. The hotel on the east-side tourist dock costs B$20 per person, but you miss out on the interactions of being in the main community.

❶ Getting There & Away

Asociación Transport Yampu Tour Lacustre
(☏7-525-4675; Yampupata) runs trips to Isla de la Luna from Yampupata.

Huatajata

This little lakefront pueblo on the road from La Paz to Copacabana is a good kick-off point for trips to Islas Kalahuta and Pariti. Get here on the Copacabana–La Paz bus line.

The cheapest lodging in town is the **Hostal Inti Karka** (r B$60). The owner can take you to the neighboring islands. **Inca Utama Hotel & Spa** (☏233-7533; www.crillontourstiticaca.com; s/d/ste incl breakfast B$320/400/650; ☎), run by Crillon Tours (p76), offers surprisingly luxurious resort-style rooms, guided trips to the rest of the lake and four onsite museums.

Islas de Wiñaymarka

Lago de Wiñaymarka's most frequented islands, Kalahuta and Pariti, are easily visited in a half-day trip. Tourism has become an economic mainstay, but it has not been entirely beneficial to the Kalahuta people who reside on the islands. Behave sensitively; ask permission before taking photos and refuse requests for money or gifts.

It's possible to camp overnight, particularly on sparsely populated Pariti; however, camping is not recommended on Kalahuta – you will probably attract some criticism from locals, who believe in night spirits.

ISLA KALAHUTA

When lake levels are low, Kalahuta ('stone houses' in Aymará) is a peninsula. Its shallow shores are lined with *totora* reed, the versatile building material for which Titicaca is famous. By day fisherfolk ply the main bay in their wooden boats; a few years ago you'd also have seen the *totora*-reed boats and men paddling around to gather the reeds to build them, but they are no longer used.

During Inca times the island served as a cemetery and it is still dotted with stone *chullpas* (funerary towers) and abandoned stone houses. Legends abound about the horrible fate that will befall anyone who desecrates the cemetery and locals have long refused to live in the area surrounding the island's only village, Queguaya.

ISLA PARITI

This tiny island, surrounded by *totora*-reed marshes, made world news in 2004 when a team of Bolivian and Finnish archaeologists discovered ancient Tiwanaku ceramics here in a small circular pit. While the American archaeologist Wendell Bennet was the first to excavate the island in 1934, the more recent

WORTH A TRIP

CULTURAL EXPERIENCES AT SANTIAGO DE OKOLA

For an extremely genuine cultural experience, don't miss an overnight stay at **Santiago de Okola** (☑7154-3918; www.santiagodeokola.com; r per person all-inclusive B$160), a tiny traditional fishing and farming community on the shores of Lake Titicaca, approximately three hours from La Paz on the road to Apolobamba. With the support of external funding bodies, Okola has formed a community-based agro-tourism company to conserve its rich agricultural heritage and generate income for members. Visitors stay with families in basic but specially designated rooms and participate in daily life. Great beaches, walks and hikes abound, including a short climb to the crest of a magnificent rocky outcrop behind the village with spectacular lake views known as the Sleeping Dragon. Other activities include weaving classes, a medicinal plant walk, mountain-bike trips and Andean cooking classes (at extra cost).

finds uncovered some extraordinary shards and ceramics, believed to be ritualistic offerings, and many of which are intact. Today, many of these stunning pots and *ch'alladores* (vases) are displayed in the **Museo de Pariti** (admission B$15), while the remainder are displayed in the Museo Nacional de Arqueología in La Paz. These stunning exhibits reflect the high artistic achievements of Tiwanaku potters. Don't miss the *Señor de los patos*. For that matter, don't miss a visit here.

❶ Getting There & Around

Many tour agencies in La Paz offer day tours to the islands (see p46 for more information). For a more local option, try the Spanish-speaking **Maximo Catari** (☑7197-8959; Hostal Inti Karka) based in Huatajata. He runs informative day visits to Isla Suriqui (B$200) and Isla Pariti (B$350), including a stop at a floating island. Balsa Tours (p76) and Crillon Tours (p76) also run trips in the area.

Around Lake Titicaca

HUARINA

This nondescript but pleasant little village, midway between Copacabana and La Paz, serves as a road junction, particularly for the town of Sorata. If you're traveling between Sorata and Copacabana, you'll have to get off at the intersection with the main road (500m from the town itself) and wait here to flag down the next bus, usually from La Paz, going in your direction.

ESTRECHO DE TIQUINA

The narrow Tiquina Straits separate the main body of Lake Titicaca from the smaller Lago de Wiñaymarka. Flanking the western and eastern shores respectively are the twin villages of San Pedro and San Pablo. Vehicles are shuttled across the straits on *balsas* (rafts), while passengers travel across in small launches (per person B$1.50, per car B$35 to B$40, 5am to 9pm). It seems unlikely that a bridge will be built as the ferries ensure that locals remain in business. Bus travelers should carry all valuables onto the launch with them.

Small restaurants and food stalls on both sides serve people caught up in the bottleneck of traffic. Note that, occasionally, foreigners traveling in either direction may have to present their passports for inspection at San Pedro, which is home to Bolivia's largest naval base.

The Cordilleras & Yungas

Best Places to Eat

» Café Illampu (p111)
» Back-Stube Konditorei (p99)

Best Places to Stay

» Hotel Sol y Luna (p97)
» Altai Oasis (p110)
» Huayna Potosi Refugio (p117)

Why Go?

Caught between the Andes and the Amazon, this rugged transition zone has just about everything you could ask for from your Bolivian adventure.

For the vertically inspired, there are glacier-capped 6000m peaks and adrenaline-charged mountain-bike descents. Nature lovers will appreciate the cloud forests and hillside semi-tropical Yungas towns of Chulumani, Coroico and Sorata, where you can hike to nearby waterfalls, start your river trip into the Amazon, go mountain biking, or simply enjoy the breeze from a mountain hideaway.

Far off the tourist trail, the areas around the Quimsa Cruz and Cordillera Apolobamba offer large swaths of wilderness, a few lost ruins and great opportunities for adventure.

Everywhere in between there are treks into the past along preserved Inca trails, wildlife watching aplenty, warm weather, cool breezes and a pervading air of hard-won tranquility.

When to Go
Coroico

| °C/°F **Temp** | | | | | | | | | | | | Rainfall inches/mm |

May–Sep Climbing season means dry weather and good visibility.

May–Oct Trekking season is longer. In shoulder months your feet might get wet.

Jan–May Cheaper hotels, less people and high rivers. Remote travel can be tough.

The Cordilleras & Yungas Highlights

1 Travel in the path of the Inca on the inspiring **El Choro trek** (p100)

2 Treat yourself to a few days of warm weather, a hammock and poolside drink in **Coroico** (p94)

3 Swing over to **Sorata** (p108) for less-traveled climbing, hiking and biking opportunities

4 Meet delicate wild vicuñas and the renowned Kallawaya healers in the remote **Cordillera Apolobamba** (p120)

5 Strap on your crampons and swing your ice ax to climb one of the fabulous peaks of the **Cordillera Real** (p116)

6 Leave the tourist trail behind for out-of-this-world adventures in the rugged **Cordillera Quimsa Cruz** (p126)

7 Suck some dust on your mountain-bike descent around **Coroico** (p94) or **Sorata** (p108)

8 Explore lost ruins at **Iskanwaya** (p115)

9 Settle down for a long journey into the Amazon from the jungle outpost of **Guanay** (p115)

10 Marvel at the views and discover far-removed Andean cultures along the **Takesi trek** (p102)

History

With its steep mountains, plunging valleys and rugged terrain, the Yungas and Cordillera region has been slow to develop. Boom-and-bust cycles kept the region a political backwater until the end of the first decade of the 2000s when new emphasis on coca production brought it to the forefront of national discourse.

The first settlers to the Yungas were inspired by economic opportunity. In the days of the Inca Empire, gold was discovered in the Tipuani and Mapiri valleys, and the gold-crazed Spanish immediately got in on the act. To enrich the royal treasury, they forced locals to labor for them, and the region became one of the continent's most prolific producers of gold. Later, the fertile valleys were used as the agricultural breadbasket to fuel mining operations in the Altiplano. Today the rivers of the lower Yungas are ravaged by hordes of wildcat prospectors and bigger mining outfits.

Coca – and cocaine – have also played a central role in the development of the region's modern economy. The Yungas' coca has been cultivated since pre-Columbian times, and much of Bolivia's legal production (up to 12,000 hectares) takes place here. In the early days of Morales' presidency, national coca production grew from 24,500 hectares in 2006 to around 31,000 hectares in 2010. In the early 2010s, coca production was down, however, according to US government reports. Nevertheless, using new refining processes, Bolivia was actually able to increase its cocaine output during the same period.

All this has meant new political weight for the coca growers of the region. However, they have been unable to find a united voice, with two main factions forming: *Las Proteccionistas*, the more established highland farmers who want to defend the localized economy, and the more numerous *Nacionalistas*, from newly colonized lower altitude areas who seek to expand the coca economy. *Las Proteccionistas* claim that coca is the only viable crop at the altitudes at which they live and that Morales' policies – he supports alternative legalized uses of coca in medicines, foods and drinks – actually threaten their livelihoods by opening coca cultivation up to the multitudes.

During October 2003 – the dying days of President Sánchez de Lozada's government – the Yungas was the scene of roadblocks and violent clashes between police, the military and *campesino* (subsistence farmer) protestors angry at the selling of the nation's natural resources (principally gas) and the mistreatment of the indigenous population. More than 100 tourists found themselves trapped in the town of Sorata for over a week during the demonstrations, until a military mission was launched to 'rescue' them, sparking violent clashes that left six people dead. The fall-out from the violence and the mismanagement of the situation led to the resignation of Sánchez de Lozada and ultimately to the election of Evo Morales, a former coca farmer.

Climate

The Yungas' physical beauty is astonishing, and although the hot, humid and rainy climate may induce lethargy, it's nevertheless more agreeable to most people than the chilly Altiplano. Winter rains are gentle, and the heavy rains occur mainly between November and March. The average year-round temperature hovers in the vicinity of 18°C, but summer daytime temperatures in the 30s aren't uncommon. As a result, the region provides a balmy retreat for chilled highlanders, and is a favorite R&R hangout for foreign travelers. The mountains of the Cordilleras, on the other hand, are serious, lofty beasts and conditions can be extreme, with warm days and nights that drop well below zero.

ℹ Getting There & Around

Access is entirely overland and the region's unpaved roads can get mucky and washed out in the rainy season. Scheduled public transportation to many trekking and mountaineering base camps is infrequent, so chartered private transportation from La Paz is used more often here than in other regions of the country.

If you are scared of heights, or just don't have much faith in Bolivian bus drivers, ask for an aisle seat. Roads are narrow, drops are steep and some of the routes, such as the one to Chulumani, are particularly hairy.

Traveling between towns in the region often necessitates backtracking to La Paz, a frustrating business.

THE YUNGAS

The Yungas – the transition zone between dry highlands and humid lowlands – is where the Andes fall away into the Amazon Basin. Above the steaming, forested depths rise the near-vertical slopes of the Cordillera Real and the Cordillera Quimsa Cruz, which halt Altiplano-bound clouds, causing them to deposit bounteous rainfall. Vegetation is abundant and tropical fruit, coffee, coca, cacao and tobacco grow with minimal tending. The Yungas is composed of two provinces in La Paz department, Nor and Sud Yungas (oddly, most of Sud Yungas lies well to the north of Nor Yungas), as well as bits of other provinces. Coroico and Chulumani are the main population centers. Most people here claim Aymará descent but there is also a noticeable afro-Bolivian population. Visitors often find the locals to be more friendly here than in the colder Altiplano (must be the heat).

Coroico

📖 2 / POP 2360 / ELEV 1750M (5741FT)

With warm weather, spectacular views, good resort-style hotels for all budgets and an infectious laid-back air, Coroico is the most visited tourist town in the Yungas. Perched eyrie-like on the shoulder of Cerro Uchumachi, the village commands a far-ranging view across forested canyons, cloud-wreathed mountain peaks, patchwork agricultural lands, citrus orchards, coffee plantations and dozens of small settlements. When the weather clears, the view stretches to the snow-covered summits of Mururata, Huayna Potosí and Tiquimani, high in the Cordillera Real.

Coroico is derived from the Quechua word *coryguayco* meaning 'golden hill.' The town's biggest attraction is its slow pace, which allows plenty of time for swimming, sunbathing and hammock-swinging. The hill-walking around here is more strolling than trekking, which appeals to stiff-legged hikers from the Choro trail or those nursing bruised bottoms after the hectic mountain-bike descent from La Paz.

Coroico is relatively warm year-round, but summer storms bring some mighty downpours. Because of its ridge-top position, fog is common, especially in the afternoon when it rises from the deep valleys and swirls through the streets and over the rooftops. The town festival is on October 20, and Saturday and Sunday are market days. On Monday much of the town closes down, with most stores and restaurants reopening Tuesday morning.

The village of Yolosa is located about 7km from Coroico along the World's Most Dangerous Road. There are a few cool hangouts, an animal refuge, and a steady stream of dust-caked Dangerous Road bikers who generally end their rides here.

🏃 Activities

Hiking

The **Choro trek** ends near Coroico. You can always do the trail backwards, and just take a day hike.

It can get extremely hot while hiking, so carry plenty of water. You should also bring bug spray, and consider wearing long sleeves and pants, as well as bringing a headlamp along. Single travelers – especially women – should check with their hotels about the security situation before heading out.

Cerro Uchumachi Walk   HIKING
For pretty views head uphill toward Hotel Esmeralda and on up to **El Calvario**, an easy 20-minute hike. At El Calvario the **Stations of the Cross** lead to a grassy knoll and chapel. There are two good trailheads from El Calvario. The one to the left leads to the **cascadas**, a trio of waterfalls 5km (or two hours' walk) beyond the chapel – bring a guide or travel in a group as assaults have occurred on this trail. The trail to the right leads to **Cerro Uchumachi**, which affords terrific valley views.

El Vagante   WALKING, SWIMMING
A good day's walk will take you to and from El Vagante, an area of natural stone swimming holes in the **Río Santa Bárbara**. Follow the road toward Coripata for about two hours. Turn left at a fork in the road and head steeply downhill past Hacienda Miraflores; at the second fork, bear right (the left fork goes to Santa Ana). After two hours along this route, which features a stretch with some **pre-Columbian terraces**, you'll reach a cement bridge. Turn right before the bridge and follow the river downstream for 20 minutes to a series of swimming holes and waterfalls. The water isn't drinkable, so carry water or purification tablets – and bear in mind that the return route is uphill all the way!

Mountain Biking

La Paz agencies take you down the World's Most Dangerous Road (see boxed text, p46) to Coroico. In town you can rent bikes from most hotels to take you to some of the nearby attractions.

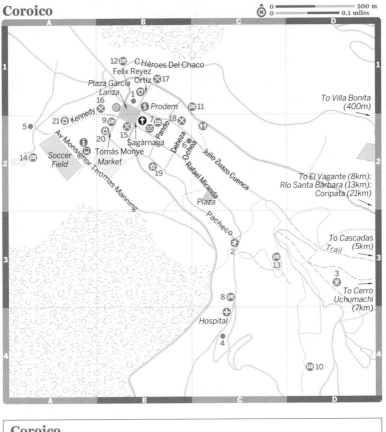

Coroico

Coroico

Activities, Courses & Tours
1 Asociación de Guias Turismo
 Local de Coroico B1
2 Cross Country Coroico C3
3 El Calvario D3
4 El Rincón Pichilemino C4
5 Siria León A2
6 Tours 4x4 .... B2

Sleeping
7 Hostal 1866 .... B2
8 Hostal El Cafetal C3
9 Hostal Kory B2
10 Hostal Sol y Luna D4
11 Hostal Tunqui Eye C1
12 Hotel Bella Vista B1
13 Hotel Esmeralda C3

14 Hotel Gloria Coroico A2

Eating
15 Arco Irís B2
16 Back-Stube Konditorei B1
17 Bamboo's Café B1
 El Cafetal .... (see 8)
 Luna Llena .... (see 10)
18 Restaurant La Casa B2

Entertainment
19 Murcielaguitos B2

Shopping
20 Blue Pine Farm B2
21 Madres de Clarisa Convent A2

THREE GREAT DAY TRIPS FROM COROICO

Coroico is a good launching point for day trips or longer excursions into the neighboring countryside. By staying the night out of town, you are doing your small part to spread your tourist dollars and support local businesses.

La Senda Verde Refugio Natural (☏7472-2825; www.sendaverde.com; Yolosa; admission B$49, reservations required, children under 10 not admitted; ☉10am-12:30pm) This 12-hectare animal refuge is located just 500m south of Yolosa (about 7km from Coroico). You can volunteer here (two-week minimum) for B$1050 per week, including three meals, or head over for the day for an hour-long tour. The refuge provides a sanctuary for animals that have been rescued from illegal traffickers. Approximately 50,000 exotic animals are illegally exported from Bolivia each year, with around 6000 being trafficked annually within the country, according to Animales SOS. Just one out of every 10 animals survives the ordeal. At the Senda Verde refuge, the monkeys are the indisputable stars of the show, and most are free to wander about the grounds, jump on you, steal your wallet (you'll need to check your wallet, watch and glasses before you enter the monkey area) and generally get up to lots of monkey business. There are over 70 monkeys in the refuge, including spider, squirrel, capuchin, red howler and nocturnal varieties. Toucans, caimans, Andean bears (only overnight guests get to see the bears; see the resort (p98) for more information), ocelots and margay are among the other wild residents. There's a nice buffet-style **restaurant** (Reyes Ortíz; snacks B$5) on site.

Zip the Flying Fox (☏2231-3849; www.ziplinebolivia.com; Yolosa; one trip B$255; ☉9-11am & 1-5pm) Three zipline sections take you flying through the forest canopy near Yolosa at speeds of up to 85km per hour. The 1500m zipline can be combined with trips down the World's Most Dangerous Road. Book your ticket at a La Paz or Coroico agency.

Poza Esmeralda y Turquesa Book a trip with a Coroico agency for an afternoon swim in this 'secret' spot.

Cross Country Coroico   MOUNTAIN BIKING (☏7157-3015; www.cxccoroico.lobopages.com; Pacheco 2058) The area around Coroico is great for mountain biking. Friendly Cross Country Coroico offers day trips to attractions in the region for all levels of rider from B$280 per person, including a guide and packed lunch. The office is sometimes closed and, according to readers, service can be a bit disorganized.

White-Water Rafting

About three hours north from Coroico is the **Río Coroico**, which flows through the Nor Yungas. This is the country's most popular commercially rafted river, and is the most convenient to La Paz. The river features well over 30 rapids, great surfing holes, dramatic drops and challenging technical maneuvers (most of these can be scouted from the river and from several bridges). It alternates between calm pools and 50m to 900m rapids, with sharp bends, boils, mean holes, undercurrents, sharp rocks and rather treacherous undercuts.

The white water normally ranges from Class II to IV, but may approach Class V during periods of high water (when it becomes too dangerous to raft). There are few spots to take out and rest, so stay focused and be prepared for surprises.

Access is from the highway between Yolosa and Caranavi; the best put-ins are a 20-minute drive north of Yolosa and near the confluence with the Río Santa Bárbara, a 50-minute drive north of Yolosa. Just look for any track that winds down from the road toward the river and find one that provides suitable access. Trips average three to five hours. For the take-out, look on the right side of the river for a devastated steel bridge (destroyed in a 1998 flood) across a normally diminutive creek. Don't miss it because after this the climb to the road up the steep jungled slopes is practically impossible, and it's a long, long way to the next possible exit.

The **Río Huarinilla** flows from Huayna Potosí and Tiquimani down into the Yungas to meet the Río Coroico near Yolosa, and is best accessed from Chairo, at the end of El Choro trek. Although it's normally Class II and III, high water can swell it into a much more challenging Class IV to V. The full-day trip is best suited to kayaks and narrow paddle rafts. The new Yungas Hwy passes right by the take-out at the confluence of the Ríos Huarinilla and Coroico.

The white water is great, but unfortunately the high tourist season coincides with the dry season. Several agencies in La Paz and around Coroico's plaza offer day-long rafting trips for B$250 to B$350 per person. Check out the **Downhill Madness** (Map p38; ☑231-2628, 239-1810; www.madness-bolivia.com; Sagárnaga 339; ☺8am-8pm) website for information on a recently launched kayaking school.

☞ Tours

Asociación de Guias Turismo Local de Coroico
GUIDED TOUR

(☑7-306-9888; Plaza García Lanza; ☺8am-noon & 2:30-7:30pm) Stop here for good tourist info or to hire a guide to local attractions. Guide services including transit cost B$280 to B$320 (for up to four people) for local day-trip attractions.

Tours 4x4
GUIDED TOUR

(☑7-371-9251; cosingis@hotmail.com; Cuenca 22) As well as offering 4WD tours, it also has fun trips to a zipline (B$170), remote swimming holes (B$70) and waterfalls.

☜ Courses

Siria León
LANGUAGE COURSE

(☑7-195-5431; siria_leon@yahoo.com; private lesson per hr B$40) Coroico is a relaxed place to learn Spanish. A recommended teacher is Siria León. Call or email to book your class.

El Rincón Pichilemino
LANGUAGE COURSE

(☑7-190-7301; www.spanishschoolcoroico.com; 200m past the hospital) This well-publicized school also has accommodations.

☷ Sleeping

On weekends from June to August hotels are often booked out. It's possible to make advance reservations, but there's no guarantee that all hotels will honor them. On holiday weekends prices may increase by as much as 100%. Around the tiny village of Yolosa (about 7km from Coroico) there are several ecolodges worth checking out.

COROICO

Hostal Sol y Luna
RESORT $

(☑7373-1232, in La Paz 2-244-0588; www.solyluna-bolivia.com; campsite B$30, s/d B$120/200, without bathroom B$70/100, d apt or cabañas B$260-300; � ☀) Set on a jungle-covered hill, this inspiring spot offers appealingly rustic accommodations in a variety of *cabañas* (cab-

ins), simple dorms and camping spots. The rambling six-hectare grounds includes two pools, a small hot tub, a children's play area, secluded bungalows and enchanted forests. Many cabins come with their own kitchens, and there's also a top-tier onsite restaurant. It's a bit out of town, making this a better bet for the non-party crowd. Yoga and massage are also available. It's a 20-minute uphill walk from town, or a B$15 taxi gets you to and from the main plaza.

Hotel Esmeralda
RESORT $

(☑213-6017; www.hotelesmeralda.com; Julio Suazo s/n; s/d B$216/360, dm/s/d without bathroom B$75/120/200; @☞☀) A top pick for backpackers and the party set, this resort-style hotel on the hillside overlooking town has amazing grounds, tremendous views, and a swimming pool and a fun traveler scene. There's a room for all tastes, from cheap dorms to larger digs with balconies and private bathrooms. The rooms with shared bathrooms can be a bit dark. A book exchange and onsite restaurant mean you may never leave the hotel.

Hostal Kory
HOTEL $

(☑7156-4050; Kennedy s/n; r per person with/without bathroom B$140/70; ☀) Right in the center of town, this is one of your best budget bets. There are fabulous views of the valley and Cordillera peaks from the large pools or rooms in the rambling six-story complex. The rooms have older sheets, but are clean. They can be a bit musty at first. Check to see if the pool is open to nonguests.

Hotel Bella Vista
HOTEL $$

(☑213-6059; coroicohotelbellavista@hotmail.com; Héroes del Chaco s/n; r per person without bathroom B$65, s/d incl breakfast B$125/205; ☞) The views truly are something to behold, and while the sheets are getting a little thin, you'll love the bright colors, firm mattresses (an oddity in Coroico), cast-iron furniture, and... oh yeah, the views!

Hotel El Viejo Molino
RESORT $$$

(☑279-7329; www.hotelviejomolino.com; s/d/tr/q incl breakfast B$300/420/550/650; ☀) Coroico's most luxurious option is a 15-minute downhill walk northeast of town on the road toward the Río Santa Bárbara. All the carbon-copy resort-style rooms have firm beds, clean lines and plenty of space. The pool has wonderful views, as do many rooms, but you are a little secluded from town.

THE COCA CONTROVERSY

The government estimates that as many as 1.2 million kilos of coca leaf are consumed monthly in Bolivia for traditional uses such as chewing the leaf, drinking it in *mate* and using it in religious ceremonies. In fact, its mild alkaloids are said to provide an essential barrier against altitude sickness and fatigue for farm workers and miners in the highlands.

In the new constitution, Evo Morales declared coca an intrinsic part of Bolivia's heritage and Andean culture. Following the expulsion of the US ambassador in September 2008, the US State Department placed Bolivia on its 'drug blacklist' for their unwillingness to cooperate on the drug trafficking problem. In retaliation, Morales suspended the activities of the US Drug Enforcement Agency in Bolivia. At a UN meeting in March 2009 he announced that Bolivia would start the process to remove the coca leaf from the 1961 Single Convention that prohibits the traditional chewing of coca leaf. Evo has been hard at work attempting to establish a new industry of legal coca-based by-products such as tea, medicines and cosmetics, in hopes of creating a growing market and boosting the income of coca growers. Some see this as opting out of the war on drugs. But, using the motto 'coca yes, cocaine no', Morales has cracked down on illegal drugs; in April 2009, a new anti-corruption unit was established in Bolivia mainly to fight drug trafficking and related crime.

Hostal Tunqui Eye   HOTEL $
(☏7490-6666; coroico_eye@yahoo.com; Iturralde 4043; r per person with/without bathroom B$40/30; 🛜) In the ultra-budget spectrum, this recent entrant has newer beds, clean(ish) sheets and good views from the terrace. A small tiki bar adds to the ambience.

Hostal El Cafetal   HOTEL $
(☏7193-3979; Miranda s/n; r per person with/without bathroom B$70/50; 🏊) Out of town by the hospital, this hotel has a lot of potential – with tremendous views, a nice pool and large grounds. We just wish it were a little better maintained. The rooms with private baths are worth the price, while those without have soft beds and are slightly unkempt. French is spoken.

Hostal 1866   HOTEL $
(☏259-6440; www.hostal1866.net; Cuenca s/n; r per person with/without bathroom B$65/45) Just up from the plaza, this architecturally impossible building – a hybrid of medieval and Moorish style with turret-like corner rooms – is a solid option for the budget set. The interior rooms are windowless and dingy, but the rooms with bathroom are spacious, light and breezy, especially on the higher floors. A rooftop terrace adds to the appeal.

Hotel Gloria Coroico   RESORT $$
(☏240-8090; www.hotelgloria.com.bo; d/tr incl breakfast B$388/464; @🛜🏊) At the bottom of town, this aging resort hotel has a likeable colonial ambience, with its spacious lounges, high ceilings and grandiose halls. The rooms are cramped and simple, but definitely passable. Make sure you get a room on the pool/valley side, rather than the car-park side.

YOLOSA & AROUND

🌿 La Senda Verde Resort   LODGE $
(☏7472-2825; www.sendaverde.com; r per person incl breakfast B$120-150; 🏊) This delightful spot is accessed from the Yolosa–La Paz road, a short walk from town (500m south of Yolosa). It has a verdant setting on the banks of two rivers and is a great spot to relax. The duplex *cabañas* are excellent, as is the Tarzan-meet-Jane tree house. This is a wildlife refuge (p96) with animals running free. Children under 10 are not allowed (for their own safety). Overnight visitors get to see the Andean bear, while day visitors mostly hang out with the 70-plus monkeys that have the run of the place.

Río Selva Resort   RESORT $$
(☏241-1818; r/ste/apt/cabin B$350/400/630/700; @🏊) About 5km from the end of the Choro trek in Pacollo is this posh five-star riverside retreat that can be a welcome deal for larger groups. Peripheral amenities include racquetball courts, a sauna and swimming pool. There's a range of accommodations, from double rooms to cabins sleeping up to six. The owners can arrange transportation

from La Paz, but it's much cheaper to head to Coroico or Yolosa and get a taxi from there.

El Jiri Ecolodge LODGE $$$
(☎7067-7115; www.jiribolivia.com; 2-day & 1-night program per person B$468; ⌧) Near Charobamba, across the valley from Coroico, this lodge is a fun spot to stay, with hanging bridges, a zipline tour, a pool and meals under a thatched roof. You're kept busy with walks in Parque Nacional Cotapata and plenty of activities. Ask to see the ruins of an old Jewish settlement nearby. Book ahead.

✖ Eating

The plaza is ringed by a number of inexpensive local cafes and pizzerias; all have ordinary menus, acceptable fare and a typically tropical sense of urgency and service.

Back-Stube Konditorei GERMAN $$
(Kennedy s/n; mains B$30-50; ⊙9:30am-2:30pm & 6:30-10pm Wed-Fri, 9:30am-10pm Sat & Sun) One of the best places to eat in town, this welcoming bakery/restaurant has excellent breakfasts, tempting cakes and pastries as well as pasta, vegetarian plates and memorable *sauerbraten* (marinated pot-roast beef) with *spätzle* (German dough noodles). There's also a great terraced area and a book exchange.

El Cafetal INTERNATIONAL $$
(Miranda s/n; mains B$15-40) This secluded hotel restaurant has unbeatable views, as well as cane chairs and slate-topped tables where you can enjoy some of the Yungas' finest food. There's a large range of dishes prepared with a French touch. The menu includes sweet and savory crepes, soufflés, steaks, sandwiches, curries, vegetarian lasagna and regular specials that might include llama goulash. It's near the hospital, a 15-minute walk uphill from the plaza.

Luna Llena INTERNATIONAL $$
(Hostal Sol y Luna; mains B$20-40; ✍) The small outdoor restaurant at the Hostal Sol y Luna has a well-priced, tasty menu of Bolivian and European dishes including vegetarian options. It's a bit of a walk from town, but a worthwhile afternoon excursion.

Bamboo's Café MEXICAN $$
(Iturralde 1047; mains B$20-40) This friendly candlelit Mexican restaurant has pretty authentic guacamole, tacos, burritos and refried beans. It's a fun spot for a drink or two later on.

Arco Irís CAFE $
(Plaza García Lanza; B$5-10) For the best pastries in town, hit up this little spot on the plaza. It also sells decent *artesanía* (locally handcrafted items).

Villa Bonita INTERNATIONAL $
(☎7192-2917; Héroes del Chaco s/n; mains B$12-30; ⊙10am-6pm) This delightfully peaceful garden cafe is 600m from town but feels a world away. The relaxed, personable owners offer delicious homemade ice creams and sorbets bursting with fresh fruit, tasty sundaes with unusual local liqueurs, and an eclectic range of vegetarian dishes. Meals are served outside where you can appreciate the valley views.

Restaurant La Casa FONDUE $$
(Cuenca s/n; mains B$40-50; ⊙6:30-11pm) While not quite what it was in its glory days, this home-style, candlelit restaurant is still a good choice for its friendly management and selection of fondue and à la carte meals. It also offers small but tasty steaks, pasta dishes and a range of scrumptious pancakes. For those with a sweet tooth there is a sinful chocolate fondue.

Drinking & Entertainment

Most people start their night with happy-hour drinks in the town's restaurants. If you don't find what you're looking for there, head on for a party at one of the bars in town. Ask around for the latest.

Murcielaguitos DANCE
(Pacheco s/n; ⊙Fri & Sat night) After midnight, when the restaurant bars shut, it's time for Murcielaguitos, in the Residencial 20 de Octubre, where students from the agricultural college join others to dance to loud Latin music and sing karaoke.

🛍 Shopping

Blue Pine Farm FOOD & DRINK
(Tomás Monye) For natural and organic produce, snacks and other goodies.

Madres de Clarisa Convent FOOD & DRINK
(⊙8am-8pm) The Madres de Clarisa Convent sells homemade brownies, orange cakes, creatively flavored biscuits, and ridiculously sweet wines. You'll find it down the steps off the southwest corner of the plaza; ring the bell to get into the shop area.

ℹ Information

There's a basic regional hospital near Hostal El Cafetal, but for serious medical treatment you'll be better off in La Paz. There are no foreign-card-accepting ATMs in Coroico, and not all hotels accept credit cards. For tourist information online try www.coroico-info.com. Hotels offer laundry services at a decent price, and most have book exchanges.

Prodem (☑213-6009; Plaza García Lanza; ⊙8:30am-12:30pm & 2:30-6pm Wed-Fri) Changes dollars at a fair rate and does cash advances for 5% commission.

Tourist office (Bus Terminal; ⊙8am-8pm) There's also a small information kiosk at the bus terminal.

Únete (Plaza García Lanza; per hr B$3; ⊙10am-10pm) Offers the most reliable internet access in town.

ℹ Getting There & Away

The La Paz–Coroico road is now open, replacing the World's Most Dangerous Road as the town's access route. It's asphalted along its whole length, but in the short time it's been open several landslides have cut up some sections. Buses and *micros* from La Paz arrive at the bus terminal on Av Manning. It's a steep walk uphill to the plaza, or hop in a taxi (B$5). **Turbus Totaí** (☑2289-5573) runs comfortable taxi services to La Paz from the terminal, leaving when full (B$25, two hours).

Bicycle

An exhilarating, adrenaline-filled option is to descend by mountain bike from La Paz to Coroico (see boxed text, p46). The thrilling one-day descent from the top at El Cumbre is a memorable experience, but not for the fainthearted. An ever-increasing number of operators run the trip. Choose carefully – if your company cuts corners, it's a long way down. There have been many fatalities on this route, the vast majority caused by over-eager bikers going too fast. However, if you're sensible and follow instructions, there's no great risk.

Bus

From the Villa Fátima area in La Paz, buses and *micros* leave for Coroico (B$25, 3½ hours) at least hourly from 7:30am to 8:30pm, with extra runs on weekends and holidays. En route they stop in Yolosita, a dusty crossroads where you can connect with buses and *camiones* (flatbed trucks) heading north to Rurrenabaque (B$100, 15 to 18 hours) and further into the Bolivian Amazon.

For Chulumani, the quickest route is to backtrack to La Paz. Although the junction for the Chulumani road is at Unduavi, few passing *micros* have spare seats at this point.

The road to Caranavi was only open 3pm to 6am at the time of writing. Buses from the Coroico terminal will take you there (and on to other Amazon destinations) for B$30.

El Choro Trek

The La Cumbre to Coroico (El Choro) trek, which traverses the Cordillera Real and Parque Nacional Cotopata, is one of Bolivia's premier hikes. It begins at La Cumbre (4725m), the highest point on the La Paz–Coroico highway, and climbs to 4859m before descending 3250m into the humid Yungas and the village of Chairo (where most end up taking a taxi down to Coroico). Along the 57km route (which is in the best condition during the April to September dry season), you'll note a rapid change in climate, vegetation and wildlife as you leave the Altiplano and plunge into the forest.

Energetic hikers can finish the trek in two days, but it's a demanding walk more comfortably done in three days. Many people allow even more time, or organize a stay of a few days in the *albergue* (basic accommodation) at Sandillani.

Prepare for a range of climates. It can be pretty cold, even snowy, on the first day, but you'll soon be in sweatier climes. For the lower trail, light cotton trousers will protect your legs from sharp vegetation and biting insects. The Inca paving can be pretty slippery, so make sure you've got shoes with grip and consider using trekking poles.

Dangers & Annoyances

Travelers have occasionally been robbed doing this trek solo, with most thefts reported below Choro village. Though these appear to be isolated incidents, it's a better idea to go in a group or with a guide. Camp out of sight if possible and do not leave anything outside your tent.

Access

Once you find the trailhead, the trail is easy to access and follow. From Villa Fátima (p63) in La Paz, catch any Yungas-bound transportation and ask to be dropped at **La Cumbre**, marked by a **statue of Christ**, where the trek begins.

The road climbs steeply out of Villa Fátima, and La Cumbre is less than an hour out of La Paz, at the 4725m crest of the La Paz–Yungas road. For the best chance of good clear views of the stunning scenery, start as

El Choro Trek

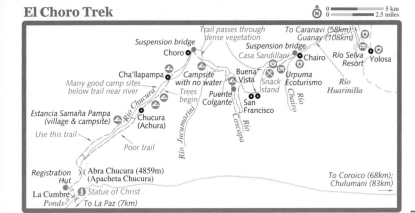

early as possible, before the mist rises out of the Yungas.

You can also take a taxi to the trail (30 minutes). One advantage of this is that they can take you up the first bit to the pass at **Abra Chucura**, thus avoiding the initial climb if you think it might cause you altitude problems.

The Route

At the **statue of Christ** is a park registration office where you should sign in. Traditionally this is also the place to perform the ritual *cha'lla*, which asks for blessing from the gods and good luck for your journey. In former times it was an Aymará sanctuary, which was replaced with the Christ monument in the colonial era. In August, *yatiris* (traditional Aymará medicine men) set up tents here to bless people coming from La Paz for benedictions from the *achachillas* (mountain spirits). From here, follow the well-defined track to your left for 1km then turn off onto the smaller track that turns right and passes between two small **ponds** (one often dry). Follow it up the hill until it curves to the left and begins to descend.

At this point follow the light track leading up the gravelly hill to your right and toward an obvious notch in the barren hill before you. This is **Abra Chucura** (4859m), and from here the trail runs downhill all the way to its end at Chairo. At the high point is a pile of stones called **Apacheta Chucura**. For centuries travelers have marked their passing by tossing a stone atop it (preferably one that has been carried from a lower elevation) as an offering to the mountain *apus*

(sacred places). An hour below Abra Chucura lies the remains of a **tambo** (wayside inn) dating from Inca times.

One hour below the *tambo* is the hamlet of **Estancia Samaña Pampa**, where there's a store selling water, a grassy campsite, a shelter and another registration hut.

A short way further on, basic supplies are available at the village of **Chucura** (Achura; 3600m). Here you pay a toll of B$10 for maintenance of the trail – you will notice the difference it makes as you head on. An hour's walk from here leads to some **campsites** (per person B$10), which are found along the river. The sites are nice, but you might wish to push on down the beautifully paved Inca road to **Cha'llapampa** (2825m), a lovely village with a roofed campsite and simple shelters approximately seven hours from the trail's start point. There are toilets, and water is available from a convenient stream below a bridge close to town.

After two hours following beautiful but slippery stretches of pre-Columbian paving, you'll reach a **suspension bridge** across the Río Chucura at **Choro** (2200m). The track continues descending steadily along the true left (west) side of the Río Chucura, where there are some small **campsites** (per person B$10) and a store providing drinks and snacks.

From the ridge above Choro, the trail alternately plunges and climbs from sunny hillsides to vegetation-choked valleys, crossing streams and waterfalls. You'll have to ford the **Río Jucumarini**, which can be rather intimidating in the wet season. Further along, the trail crosses the deep gorge of the **Río Coscapa** via the relatively sturdy Puente Colgante suspension bridge.

The trail continues through some tiny hamlets, including **San Francisco** and **Buena Vista**, which are separated by the stiff ascent and descent of the **Subida del Diablo**. Some five to six hours from Choro is the remarkable **Casa Sandillani** (2050m), a home surrounded by beautifully manicured Japanese gardens with a view. You can camp here and nearby there's also a new community project lodge, **Urpuma Ecoturismo** (☎7258-4359; urpuma@yahoo.com; dm B$80, s/d B$100/200); it's best to book ahead. Built from natural resources available in the area, the atmospheric wattle and thatch rooms are comfortable. Rates include breakfast as well as a guided walk, and dinner is also available. Even if you're not staying, you can use the toilets for a nominal fee. There are also several snack and soft-drink stalls, and a clear water supply is provided by a pipe located diagonally opposite Casa Sandillani (to the right, 20m along the main trail).

From Casa Sandillani it's an easy 2½ hours downhill to **Chairo**, where camping is possible in a small, flat, grassed area with no facilities, near the bridge above town.

It's possible to walk the relatively level 12km past the Río Selva Resort or take transportation from Chairo to **Yolosa** (16km) and then catch an onward service the 7km to **Coroico**. A few private vehicles head to Yolosa and Coroico on most days, but beware of being charged scandalous prices. Don't pay more than B$170 – you could call a cab in Coroico to pick you up for less than that. Infrequent minibuses also run the route, or you can arrange transport with an agency in La Paz prior to departure.

 Tours

A growing number of La Paz outfits (see p46) offer organized El Choro treks. Most include meals, guides and camping equipment; some include the services of porters.

Takesi Trek

Also known as the Inca Trail, the Takesi trek is one of the most popular and impressive walks in the Andes. The route was used as a highway by the early Aymará, the Inca and the Spanish, and it still serves as a major route to the humid Yungas over a relatively low pass in the Cordillera Real. The 45km trail still conserves expertly engineered pre-Inca paving, more like a highway than a walking track. It has been suggested that this paved section was part of a long road that linked the La Paz area with the Alto Beni region.

The walk itself is demanding and takes two days, but plan on longer because of transportation uncertainties to and from the trailheads. On the first day you ascend to 4650m, so spend a few days acclimatizing in La Paz before heading off. The trail is hiked by about 5000 people annually, more than half of whom are Bolivians, and suffers from a litter problem due to its growing popularity.

The May to October dry season is best for this trip. In the rainy season the wet and cold, combined with ankle-deep mud, may contribute to a less-than-optimal experience. Since the trail's end is in the Yungas, plan on some rain year-round.

The entire route appears on a single 1:50,000 IGM topo sheet: *Chojlla – 6044-IV*. A good source of information is **Fundación Pueblo** (☎212-4413; www.fundacionpueblo.org; Casilla 9564, La Paz), an NGO that supports rural development projects that encourage local self-sufficiency. The group has done a lot of work with villagers along the trail to improve facilities. The foundation can organize a package that includes transportation to and from the trailheads, meals, accommodations and a guide for B$500 to B$700 per person.

With a fully serviced lodge two-thirds of the way along the route, the hike is easily done with just a daypack, but agencies and Fundación Pueblo can arrange guides and mules if you want them.

Access

If you're traveling by public transportation, your first destination will be **Ventilla**. *Micros* leave from La Paz (B$12, three hours) hourly from 7am until noon from the market area above Calle Sagárnaga, at the corner of Calles Rodríguez and Luis Lara. Another option for groups is to charter a taxi (around B$350 for up to four people) to the **Choquekhota trailhead**. Most La Paz tour agencies can organize this for you or contact Fundación Pueblo (p102).

You can also take an urban *micro* or *trufi* (collective minibus that follows a set route) from La Paz to Chasquipampa or Ovejuyo, then trek through the beautiful Palca Canyon (and the Valle de las Ánimas) to Palca and then to Ventilla. This will add at least one extra day to the trip, but will be a fitting prelude to the longer trek.

Transportation between Ventilla and the **San Francisco mine trailhead** is sparse. You will probably have to pay for a taxi, or hike two or three hours uphill to the trailhead.

The Route

About 150m beyond Ventilla, turn left and take the road uphill, following the Río Palca. After climbing for 60 to 90 minutes, you'll reach the village of **Choquekhota**. You'll come to the access road to the **San Francisco mine** after a further hour or two of uphill hiking; after crossing a stream, you'll see the signpost indicating the trailhead. The mine route veers left here, but hikers should continue along the signposted track where the original pre-Columbian trail begins.

After an hour of climbing you'll begin switchbacking for 30 minutes for the final ascent, partly on superb precolonial paving, to the 4700m **Apacheta** (Abra Takesi) pass. There, you'll find the *apacheta* (shrine of stones) and a spectacular view of Nevado Mururata (5868m) to the right and the plunging valleys of the Yungas far below. Just beyond the pass you'll see an abandoned **Mina David tunnel**; wolfram and tin are mined around here. Entry is not advisable.

From the pass the trail begins to descend sharply into the valley, passing a series of abandoned mining camps and high glacial lakes. If daylight is on your side, look for another lake, **Laguna Jiskha Huara Huarani**, to the left of the trail midway between the pass and Takesi. The trail from here contains some of Bolivia's finest examples of Inca paving. A little later the trail widens to between 6m and 8m and you will reach **Inka Tambo**. With five rooms, it's a good place to spend the night. If you prefer to push on, you'll next reach the ancient-looking thatched village of **Takesi** where there's a hut and campsite; you may also find villagers who can prepare simple meals of potatoes and local trout. It is at this point that you will begin to experience the sudden change to Yungas' cloud forest vegetation.

Beyond Takesi the increasingly muddy trail winds downhill until it crosses a bridge over the **Río Takesi** then follows the beautifully churning river before it moves upwards and makes a long traverse around the **Loma Palli Palli**, where you're protected from steep drop-offs by a pre-Columbian wall. Shortly after passing a particularly impressive *mirador* (lookout), you'll enter the village of **Kacapi**, the heart of the former colonial *estancia* (ranch) that once controlled the entire Takesi valley. Most of the overseers' dwellings have been reclaimed by vegetation, but you can still see the ruins of the chapel, **Capilla de las Nieves**. Kacapi's 10-bed **Albergue Turístico** (dm B$30) and campsite are equipped with solar-powered showers. Basic meals are also available.

After Kacapi the track drops sharply to a bridge over the **Río Quimsa Chata** (which suffers varying degrees of damage each rainy season), then climbs past a soccer field on the left to a pass at the hamlet of **Chojlla**. From there the route descends to the final crossing of the Río Takesi via a concrete bridge, marking the end of the pre-Columbian trail. It's then a 1½-hour trudge along an **aqueduct** to the ramshackle mining settlement of **Mina Chojlla** (2280m), where there is a cheap *alojamiento* (basic accommodations) and food stalls.

From Mina Chojlla, crowded buses leave for Yanacachi (B$3, 30 minutes) and La Paz (B$12, three hours) at 5:30am and 1pm daily – buy your ticket on arrival. If you can't endure a night in Mina Chojlla (and few people can), keep walking about one hour down the road past the headquarters of the hydroelectric power project to the more pleasant village of **Yanacachi**.

Yunga Cruz Trek

This is a relatively little-trodden trek between the village of Chuñavi and the Sud Yungas' provincial capital, Chulumani. Declared a national monument in 1992, it preserves good stretches of pre-Columbian footpaths and archaeological remains dating from the Tiwanaku and Inca periods. This is one of your best bets for wildlife watching, as there's less traffic here than on other treks. Keep your eyes peeled for Andean foxes, condors, and plenty of birds and butterflies.

There are a couple of variations to the standard trek, including a pass over the northern shoulder of Illimani to get you started, as well as an alternative – and considerably more spectacular – route over Cerro Khala Ciudad, which begins beyond Lambate. Some guides even offer the trek backwards, starting at Chulumani, but that's

Takesi Trek

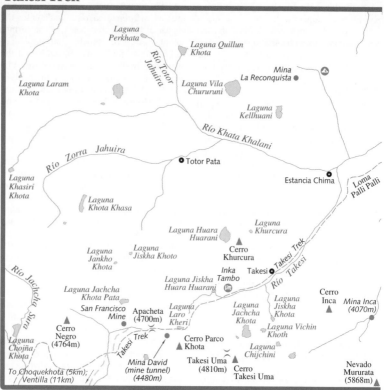

THE CORDILLERAS & YUNGAS CHULUMANI

a fairly punishing alternative. Crossing several passes at over 5000m, it's easily the most demanding of the Inca trails and usually takes five or six days. There are no official campsites along the route, although there are plenty of spots along the way to set up camp.

If you are going to attempt this trek you'll need to carry the 1:50,000 topo sheets *Palca – 6044-I*, *Lambate – 6044-II* and *Chulumani – 6044-III* or, even better, arrange a guide (highly recommended). Many agencies in La Paz offer this trek, with guides, cook and pack animals.

Note that there is no water available on the last day, so stock up ahead of time.

Access

There's a good case for hiring a 4WD to take you to the trailhead at Lambate. Otherwise you can go straight to Chuñavi (five hours) or Lambate (six hours) by *micro* from La Paz, with departures from Calle Venancio Burgoa, near Plaza Líbano, leaving daily at 7am.

The return to La Paz from Chulumani and Irupana is straightforward: catch one of the many daily buses or *camiones* from the *tranca* (police post) in Chulumani.

Chulumani

⬛2 / POP 2950 / ELEV 1700M (5577FT)

Perched scenically on the side of a hill, this peaceful little town is the capital of the Sud Yungas. It's a lot like Coroico, with a friendly town square, bustling market and tropical attitude, but receives next to no international visitation.

The town was founded because of the supposed healing qualities of the mineral streams in the vicinity. However, when its fertile soils provided bumper crops of coca (the country's best for chewing), citruses,

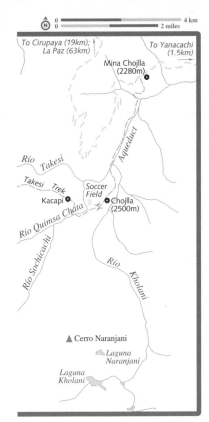

To Cirupaya (19km);
La Paz (63km)

To Yanacachi
(1.5km)

Mina Chojlla
(2280m)

Río Takesi

Takesi Trek

Kacapi

Soccer
Field

Chojlla
(2500m)

Río Quimsa Chata

Aqueduct

Río Sochicachi

Río Kholani

▲ Cerro Naranjani

Laguna
Naranjani

Laguna
Kholani

bananas, coffee and cacao, Chulumani soon became more important as a trade center for the nearby farming communities. The area is also a paradise for birds and butterflies – there are clouds of the latter, and several endemic species of the former. At a tropically warm and often wet altitude, Chulumani is a great trekking base camp and a relaxing weekend retreat with a great view. The only time its pervasive tranquility is interrupted is during the week following August 24, when Chulumani stages the riotous **Fiesta de San Bartolomé**.

Sights & Activities

Chulumani sees few visitors, but it is a good base for several worthwhile excursions.

There are some lovely walks in the Chulumani area. A five-hour (one-way) downhill hike through clouds of butterflies will take you from Chulumani to the Río Solacama; you can easily get a bus or *micro* back. In

three to four hours you can also walk to Ocabaya. Other walks take you from the higher village of Villa Remedios to the lower one, or from Chicaloma down to Ocabaya. Another beautiful hike is the four-hour walk from Chulumani to Chirca, where there's the church of a revered local virgin.

Apa-Apa Reserva Ecológica WILDLIFE RESERVE
(☑7254-7770; apapayungas@hotmail.com) An interesting day trip is to the Apa-Apa Reserva Ecológica, 8km from Chulumani. The private 500-hectare property has dry forest and one of the last remnants of primary cloud forest in the Yungas, and is rich in trees, orchids, butterflies and birds. The reserve runs four-hour **guided forest walks** (per person B$50 with a B$200 minimum) and has a cafe serving meals and homemade ice cream. A taxi from Chulumani to the reserve costs B$15.

Sleeping

Country House HOTEL $
(Tolopata 13; r per person incl breakfast B$70; ☒)
Probably your best bet in town, this welcoming country home is 10 minutes west of the plaza by the basketball court and the lookout Mirador La Ladera. The rooms, decorated in an attractively rustic style, are spotless, and have hot-water bathrooms and fresh flowers. Great breakfasts, abundant birdlife, a pool table and an extensive movie collection are other highlights, as are the delicious home-cooked dinners and relaxing mineral pool. Owner Javier can organize all sorts of local excursions including inner-tubing on local rivers.

Apa-Apa Reserva Ecológica LODGE $
(☑7254-7770; apapayungas@hotmail.com; r per person B$50, campsites B$70 plus per person per night B$15; ☒) This beautiful old adobe hacienda makes a good place to stay. It's set in elegant grounds, and the cordial owners maintain the property with care and thought. There's an excellent grassy camping area with palm-thatched tables, barbecues and good bathroom facilities, as well as five rooms, a cafe-restaurant and a lovely pool. It's 8km from Chulumani.

Hostal Dion HOTEL $
(☑289-6034; hostaldion@hotmail.com; Bolívar s/n; r per person with/without bathroom incl breakfast B$70/50) Half a block south of Plaza Libertad, this is the best of the central options. The homey setting includes extremely

clean rooms, cable TV, electric showers and sparkling tile floors.

Hotel Monarca   HOTEL **$**

(✆7726-2112; r per person B$75; ☒) Like most ex-prefectural holiday camps, the Monarca is a bit run-down and lacks character, but it's managed by nice people and is good value. The enormous pool is open to nonguests for B$15. It's about a five-minute walk downhill southwest from the plaza; ask for directions.

Parque Ecológico Hotel El Castillo del Loro   LODGE **$$**

(✆235-9881; www.hotelcastillodelloro.com; r per person incl breakfast B$200; ☒) Located along the Chulumani road (20km beyond Unduavi) at 1934m, this unique riverfront castle is a real surprise; it is a very unexpected sight in the Yungas. It functions as a hotel and restaurant, offers access to a 100-hectare ecopark, and is only a couple of hours from La Paz. Its swimming pool, waterfalls and subtropical climate makes for an appealing weekend getaway.

✖ Eating

Food choices are limited in most cases to *almuerzos* (set lunches) and it's a case of first come first served. After 2pm you'll be hard pressed to find anything decent to eat. For cheap and cheerful fried chicken, **Restaurant Rinconcito Chulameño** on the plaza is a friendly choice – the second-story balcony offers a bird's-eye view over the action on the plaza. **Snack San Bartolomé** is another decent option on the plaza. There are also basic *comedores* (dining halls) near the *tranca*.

If you are looking for something more adventurous, the Country House (p105) and Apa-Apa Reserva Ecológica (p105) do tasty dinners with a few hours' notice.

ⓘ Information

Chulumani's tourist office is in a kiosk on the main plaza, but if you are thinking of exploring the region it is worth seeking out hotel owners such as English-speaking Javier Sarabia at the Country House. There's no ATM in Chulumani; Banco Fie on the main plaza may do credit card advances for 5% commission. Prodem (two blocks west of the Plaza on Pando) changes US dollars and gives cash advances on credit cards (5% commission). The Cotel office on Plaza Libertad is one of several central phone offices. Internet connections are sporadic; when there is a connection, head to **Enternet** (Sucre s/n).

ⓘ Getting There & Away

Since the closure of the original La Paz–Coroico road to traffic, the nail-biting route from La Paz to Chulumani, which extends on to Irupana, has claimed the title of 'The World's Most Dangerous Road.' If you can keep your nerves in check, it is actually an exceptionally beautiful route, though it's hard to appreciate when your bus is reversing round a blind, muddy bend in search of a section wide enough to let oncoming traffic past.

Yunga Cruz (p103) trekkers finish in Chulumani. The town is also readily accessed from Yanacachi at the end of the Takesi trek (p102). From Yanacachi, walk down to the main road and wait for transportation headed downhill; it's about 1½ hours to Chulumani.

From Villa Fátima in La Paz, around the corner of Calles San Borja and 15 de Abril, different companies depart when full for Chulumani (B$20, four hours) from 8am to 4pm. From Chulumani, La Paz–bound buses wait around the *tranca*. Theoretically, there are several departures before 10am and after 4pm, but in reality services are frequently cancelled due to lack of interest. Buy your ticket in advance; even if your company doesn't depart it will be valid for one of those that does.

If you're coming from Coroico, get off at Unduavi and wait for another vehicle. It will likely be standing-room only; if a seat is a priority, you'll have to go all the way back to La Paz.

It's also possible to go to Coroico via Coripata; take a La Paz–bound bus and get off at the crossroads just after Puente Villa at Km 93. Here, wait for a bus or *camión* to Coripata and then change again for a lift to Coroico. It's a long and dusty but worthwhile trip. An easier option is to hire a taxi; expect to pay B$300 for the trip to Coroico for up to four people.

Around Chulumani

The area around Chulumani is a beautiful, fertile zone with patches of intact cloud forest and plenty of farms producing coca, coffee, bananas and citrus fruits. Walking, biking or busing your way between the small colonial-era towns of the region is an interesting experience.

An intriguing circuit takes you from Chulumani past the Apa-Apa Reserva Ecológica (p105) toward the humble fruit-farming hamlets of **Villa Remedios**. There are two villages, a higher and a lower one; the latter has a pretty little church. Look out for coca leaves being harvested and dried (and remember that while much coca production in the region is legal, farmers may be sensitive about pictures or lots of questions).

BOLIVIA'S INVISIBLE MINORITY

The hill villages of the Chulumani region are home to a high proportion of the country's Afro-Bolivian people. There are an estimated 35,000 Bolivians descended from African slaves who were brought to Bolivia to work in the Potosí silver mines (where an astronomical number of them died working 12-hour shifts and living underground for up to four months continuously). Because of the high death rate, slaves were three times more expensive than local labor by the time they reached Potosí, and it wasn't long before the Spaniards transferred them to domestic labor and farm work.

Simón Bolívar's original Bolivian constitution technically ended the practice of slavery, but slaves were still indebted to their owners, and it wasn't until 1851 that they became 'free'. After the abolishment of slavery, many Afro-Bolivians settled (or were forcibly settled) in the Yungas region, where they worked in a hacienda system. They could not own land, and were virtually enslaved under a sharecropper-style system for another 100 years. While Afro-Bolivians were never fully assimilated into local culture – and have always been one of Bolivia's most marginalized communities both economically and politically – they did pick up the Aymará language and Afro-Bolivian women adopted the traditional dress of the Aymará. They are recognized by Bolivia's new constitution, but still lack a voice on the national stage.

In their haunting *saya* music (a hybrid of African, Aymará and Spanish styles) and distinct funerary rites, you will see distinct African overtones. See a documentary on how Afro-Bolivian's are using *saya* music as a form of social protest at www.solidarityinsaya.com.

One of the traditional Bolivian dances, the *morenada,* has its roots in a portrayal of an African slave train arriving at the mines. More information about Afro-Bolivians can be found on the websites for Fundación Activos Culturales Afro (www.programaacua.org, in Spanish) and Fundación Praia (www.fundapraia.org, in Spanish).

The main road winds its way down to the **Río Solacama**, whose banks are populated by numerous butterflies; it's a lovely spot to bathe on a hot day. Just after the bridge, a left turn heads away from the main road up a steep hill to **Laza**. A *via crucis* (Stations of the Cross) leads up to the pretty square and its church, where there's an appealing dark-wood and gold altarpiece and baldachin. The much-revered statue of Christ, *El Señor de la Exaltación*, is the destination for an important *romería* (pilgrimage-fiesta) on September 14.

The main settlement over this side of the river is **Irupana**, an attractive, sleepy colonial town founded in the 18th century on one of the few bits of flat ground in the area. It became an important fortress, just as the nearby ruins of **Pasto Grande** had once been in Tiwanaku and Inca times.

From Irupana, you can head back to Chulumani a different way, fording the Río Puri and passing through the principal Afro-Bolivian town, dusty **Chicaloma** – known for its annual town festival on May 27, which features lots of traditional *saya* music (a hybrid of African, Aymará and Spanish styles) – before crossing the Río Solacama again. On the way back, you pass through tiny, post-card-pretty **Ocabaya**, which has one of the oldest churches in Bolivia, fronted by a liberty bell and a memorial to two local martyrs of the struggle for *campesino* (subsistence farmer) rights. Locals may well offer food in their homes here.

Javier Sarabia at the Country House in Chulumani will happily give walking information (even for nonguests) and can help arrange taxi drop-offs or pick-ups.

🏃 Activities

The road to Chulumani follows part of another good river for white-water rafting, the **Río Unduavi**. The upper section ranges from essentially unnavigable Class V to Class VI, with steep chutes, powerful currents, large boulder gardens, blind corners and waterfalls. Beyond this section it mellows out into some challenging Class IV white water followed by Class II and III rapids. Access is limited, but the Chulumani road does offer several put-ins and take-outs. The best access points have been left by construction crews who've mined the riverbanks for sand and gravel. A good take-out point is Puente Villa, which is three to four hours below the best put-ins. La Paz tour operators (see p46) can help arrange a guided trip.

🛌 Sleeping

In addition to a few cheap *alojamientos* (basic lodgings) – Sarita on Irupana's main street is the cleanest – Irupana has a couple of interesting options for accommodations.

Posada Nirvana Inn LODGE **$$**
(📞213-6154; www.posadanirvanainn.com; cabañas per person incl breakfast B$180; 🏊) One of the most memorable places to stay in the Yungas is Posada Nirvana Inn in the barrio of Chiriaca at the top of Irupana (go past the soccer field and turn right). It consists of five sublime *cabañas* (cabins) in an immaculate hillside garden full of orange and mandarin trees with top views over the valley. It's run by considerate hosts, and the rooms are well looked after – comfortable and romantic with a log fire – and there are optional kitchen facilities. There's also a swimming pool and sauna. Staff can arrange forest walks.

Hotel Bougainvillea HOTEL **$**
(📞213-6155; Sucre 243; r per person B$70; 🏊) The Hotel Bougainvillea is an attractive, modernized, whitewashed building built around a pool. Its rooms are clean and appealing, although management is not overly welcoming.

ℹ️ Getting There & Away

Regular buses drive the 31km from Chulumani to Irupana (B$3, one hour) and there are also some direct connections to Irupana from La Paz. *Micros* run to the smaller villages from Chulumani and Irupana.

One of the most comfortable ways to see the places in this region is to hire a taxi from Chulumani (although not in the rainy season, December to February). For the whole circuit, expect to pay around B$200 to B$300 for a day's hire. It's worth getting hold of a driver who can also act as a guide; ask Javier Sarabia at the Country House in Chulumani for a recommendation.

Sorata

📞2 / POP 18,932 / ELEV 2670M (8759FT)

Sorata is the town that tourism forgot. Once rivaling Coroico for weekend visitors, this picturesque colonial village perched on a hillside beneath the towering snow-capped peaks of Illampu and Ancohuma is slowly falling into decay. Restaurants and hotels are going out of business, tour operators are jumping ship and trash isn't getting picked up. Every day it's becoming less touristy and, well... more Bolivian.

And while it doesn't have the shiny digs of its arch nemesis Coroico, this semi-tropical village sitting high above a verdant agricultural valley does offer great weather, access to some of Bolivia's best treks, kick-ass downhill mountain biking and an atavistic air that may just become intoxicating.

In colonial days Sorata provided a link to the Alto Beni's goldfields and rubber plantations, and a gateway to the Amazon Basin. In 1791 it was the site of a distinctly unorthodox siege by indigenous leader Andrés Tupac Amaru and his 16,000 soldiers. They constructed dykes above the town, and when these had filled with runoff from the slopes of Illampu, they opened the floodgates and the town was washed away.

So why the decline? In September 2003, Sorata hit the national headlines. A blockade further up the La Paz road – expression of an overwhelming wave of *campesino* dissatisfaction that eventually led to the downfall of the government – trapped hundreds of Bolivian and foreign tourists in Sorata. In a show of force, the army busted them out, killing a *campesino* and inducing a riot. Tourism dropped off in the wake of this, and the town hasn't been able to recover. These days, mining and coca production (and it's value-added industries) seem to be the main sources of employment in and around Sorata.

⊙ Sights

There isn't much of specific interest in Sorata itself – its main attractions are its historic ambience and maze of steep stairways and narrow cobbled lanes.

Casa Günther HISTORIC BUILDING
(northeast of the plaza) It's worth taking a look at Casa Günther, a rambling, historic mansion that now houses the Residencial Sorata. It was built in 1895 as the home of the Richters, a quinine-trading family, and was later taken over by the Günthers, who were involved in rubber extraction until 1955.

Plaza General Enrique Peñaranda PLAZA
The main square, Plaza General Enrique Peñaranda, is Sorata's showcase. With the town's best view of the *nevados* (snow-capped

mountain peaks), it's graced by towering date palms and immaculate gardens.

Gruta de San Pedro
CAVE

(San Pedro Cave; admission B$15; ☺8am-5pm) Although it's not the most spectacular of caves, Gruta de San Pedro makes for a popular excursion. The cave is approximately 400m deep with an enclosed lagoon, and though it is no longer possible to swim in it, the lagoon can be crossed in pedal boats.

It's a scenic 6km hike to the cave along a dirt road (two hours each way). Taxis will do the return trip for around B$30, including waiting time. The local community has also set up two simple *albergues* (basic accommodations) to overnight in. There are a total of four rooms with a single bed in each and prices are negotiable. Remember that all proceeds go to help the community, so be generous.

🏃 Activities

Hiking

Sorata is best known as a convenient base for hikers and climbers pursuing some of Bolivia's finest high-mountain landscapes. The peak hiking season is May to September.

The most popular walk is the hike to **Laguna Chillata**, a pretty spot with great views of the surrounding sierra and Lake Titicaca. It's a fairly stiff five-hour climb, ascending some 1500m, and, while you can get there and back in a day, it's a pleasant and popular spot to camp. It's worthwhile taking a guide, as it's easy to get lost. If you're going to overnight there, a beast of burden is a sound investment; let the mule do the carrying while you enjoy the views.

An optional third day can be built into this hike. Leaving the tent and your gear at Laguna Chillata (it'll get nicked if you haven't brought a guide, who can detail someone to watch over it), a steep ascent takes you up to **Laguna Glacial**, a top spot where you can watch big chunks of ice cracking off into the water. It's at 5100m, so take it easy; the altitude can make it a tough climb.

Ambitious adventurers can do the seven-day **El Camino del Oro trek** (p112), an ancient trading route between the Altiplano and the Río Tipuani goldfields. Otherwise there's the challenging five-day **Mapiri trail** (p114) or the seven-day **Illampu circuit**.

The ultimate hardcore challenge is the 20-day **Trans Cordillera route**: eight days gets you from Sorata to Lago Sistaña, with possible four-day (to Huayna Potosí) and eight-day (to Illimani) extensions.

Basic information on climbing some of the region's peaks is included under Cordillera Real. Hikers should carry the *Alpenvereinskarte Cordillera Real Nord* (Illampu) 1:50,000 map, available online or maybe at Buho's Internet & Café (p112) in town.

While it's possible to hike independently, it is best to hook up with a guide, mainly because of the need to be aware of local sensibilities and the difficulty of finding passable routes.

The most economical, authorized option is to hire an independent, Spanish-speaking guide from the **Asociación de Guías de Sorata** (Sorata Guides & Porters Association; ☎213-6672; guiasorata@hotmail.com; Sucre 302), which also rents equipment of varying quality and arranges many different treks. Expect to pay around B$300 to B$400 per day for a guide (and mule to carry your equipment). Cooking equipment is included in these prices, but food is extra. Clients are expected to pay for the guide's food.

WARNING: HIKING NEAR SORATA

With Sorata's economy turning from tourism to mining and farming, there are fewer guides offering services here, and fewer pack animals for hire. Reports indicate that this could be a dangerous area for trekking and many agencies are no longer offering treks in the region. The El Camino de Oro trek is reportedly seeing little traffic these days, meaning you'll have to clear the trail with a machete and may face some tough locals along the way. The Mapiri trek has an even rougher record, with increased reports of robberies. The villages along the way are now charging passage fees and are said to have become quite aggressive with those who do not pay.

To stay safe, check with the guide service, your local hotel and fellow travelers before heading out. In this region and the Cordillera Apolobamba, it is recommended that you travel in groups and with a guide.

Sorata

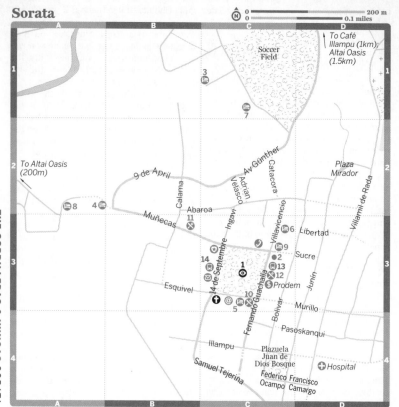

Mountain Biking

The Sorata area, with its thrillingly steep descents and spectacular mountain scenery, makes it a top two-wheel destination. The **Jach'a Avalancha (Grand Avalanche) Mountain Bike race** takes place in Sorata each year. This is the biggest downhill race course in South America based on the Mega Avalanche format. It is a 2000m descent using a mass start and draws riders from across Bolivia and the world. One of the best trips around is the descent into the town from the mountains astride Lake Titicaca. From La Paz, take a Sorata-bound bus to the pass north of Achacachi and then choose either the main road or any of the downhill routes along unpaved roads. Most routes eventually lead to Sorata – or come at least in view of it (but as some don't it's wise to have a map). Throughout the ride you're presented with superb views of towering snow-capped peaks, plunging valleys and tiny rural villages. The Reggae House may have bikes for rent.

Andean Epics MOUNTAIN BIKING

(☑7127-6685; www.andeanepics.com) This La Paz–based operator is your best bet for rides near Sorata. Its signature trip combines two days of riding with three days on motorized dugout canoes from Sorata to Rurrenabaque (B$2500 per person, all inclusive). It was moving at the time of writing, so check the website for the new location.

🛏 Sleeping

TOP CHOICE **Altai Oasis** LODGE **$$**

(☑7151-9856; www.altaioasis.lobopages.com; campsites B$30, s/d B$245/315, dm/s/d without bathroom B$84/125/250, cabin B$500-800; ☎🐕) This really does feel like an oasis, with a lush garden, hammocks, caged macaws, a pretty balcony cafe-restaurant and a range of accom-

Sorata

◉ **Sights**

modations options. The beautiful riverside retreat offers grassy campsites, comfortable rooms, and romantic accommodations in appealingly rustic *cabañas,* each one intricately and fancifully painted. We only wish they'd update their slumping mattresses. To get there, follow the downhill track past the soccer field to the river, climb back up to the road and turn left before reaching Café Illampu.

Hotel Santa Lucia
HOTEL $

(☏7151-3812; r per person with/without bathroom B$50/40) Located near the soccer field, this is the cleanest, neatest option in town. The bright yellow hotel does have a slightly institutional feel, but in return you get excellent mattresses (by Sorata standards), crisp lines and tidy shared facilities. The owner is as friendly as it gets.

Hostal Las Piedras
HOTEL $

(☏7191-6341; laspiedras2002@yahoo.de; Ascarrunz s/n; s/d/tr B$100/140/180, s/d without bathroom B$50/80) This German-owned joint has amazing views from most rooms, a cool vibe, shared kitchen and fun common area. The sheets are clean, but the mattresses and pillows are paper-thin. The optional breakfast

includes homemade wholemeal bread and yogurt.

Hostal Paraíso
HOTEL $

(☏7302-3447; Villavicencio s/n; r per person B$40) This central spot has a bright, flowery patio, a series of roof terraces with nice views, new beds and old carpets, and decent rooms with private bathrooms and circumspect electrical wiring on the showers.

Residencial Sorata
HOTEL $

(☏2213-6672; r per person with/without bathroom B$35/25) On the northeast corner of the plaza, this ultra-characterful colonial-style mansion makes a romantic place to stay. Do your eyes a favor and ask to see the old-style rooms; do your back a favor and ask to stay in one of the new ones (with private bathroom). There's a restaurant, laundry service, wild garden and a friendly welcome. This is a good spot to gather info on local hikes.

Hostal Panchita
HOTEL $

(☏7120-5651; r per person without bathroom B$30) Built around a clean and sunny courtyard on the south side of the plaza, the Panchita has dark cell-like rooms with shared baths. At least the management is friendly, there's hot water, and you are right on the plaza.

Hostal Mirador
HOTEL $

(☏2878-5078; Muñecas 400; r per person with/without bathroom B$60/30) If you've got OCD, head somewhere else, fast! This place is quite cluttered. That said, there's a tremendous terrace, shared kitchen and decent rooms with caved-in beds. The atmosphere can be a little unfriendly.

Reggae House
HOTEL $

(☏7323-8327; Muñecas s/n; r per person B$20-25) There's a definite relaxed vibe at the aptly named Reggae House. Sorata-farians will love the wonderful terrace for guitar jams and drum circles, while the tiny rooms with single beds leave something to be desired. The whole place is rather dirty, but, hey, that's part of the deal, right? It also has a shared kitchen, and staff can sometimes arrange bike or horse trips.

✕ Eating

TOP
CHOICE **Café Illampu**
BAKERY $

(snacks B$20-35; ⊙9am-6:30pm Wed-Mon) A 15-minute down-and-up walk from town, this lovely relaxing spot is en route to the Gruta de San Pedro. Stop in on the return journey – if you stop on the way to the cave, you might not make it as Café Illampu is exceedingly tranquil with views, a garden and llamas. It also offers good coffee, sandwiches on homemade bread and great cakes – the Swiss owner is a master baker. You can camp here for B$18.

Altai Oasis INTERNATIONAL $$
(mains B$20-50; ☑) The peaceful balcony restaurant at this lovely retreat, 15 minutes' walk from town, serves coffee, drinks and a range of vegetarian dishes. There are also T-bone steaks and, for an Eastern European touch, Polish borscht and tasty goulash. It's a great place to just sit with a drink too, with views over the valley and the tinkle of wind chimes.

Mercado MARKET $
(Muñecas s/n; mains B$5-20) Head to the market to grab the goods for a picnic lunch. There's some food stands here, too.

La Casa del Turista INTERNATIONAL $$
(Plaza Enrique Peñaranda s/n; mains B$25-35) This friendly eatery offers the best pizza on the plaza, traditional international favorites like pasta and tacos, along with a few tried-and-true Bolivian treats like *pique macho* (beef chunks and sausages over French fries with lettuce, tomatoes, onions and spicy locoto peppers). It's cleaner than most restaurants in town.

Restaurant Jalisco MEXICAN $
(mains B$25-30; ☑) On the east side of the plaza, Jalisco delivers an ambitious menu of pizzas, Bolivian fare, pasta and creditable attempts at Mexican food such as tacos and burritos. There's quite a few vegetarian options.

🍷 Drinking & Entertainment

Not a lot goes on in Sorata at night. The restaurants on the plaza are your best bet.

❶ Information

Sunday is market day, and Tuesday, when many businesses are closed, is considered *domingo sorateño* (Sorata's Sunday). There's no tourist information center or ATM.

Buho's Internet & Café (per hr B$12) For slow and expensive internet access; on the south side of the plaza. It also sells a small selection of local arts and crafts.

Prodem (Plaza Enrique Peñaranda 136; ⊘8:30am-12:30pm & 2:30-6pm Tue-Fri, 8am-3pm Sat) Changes US dollars and does credit card cash advances for a 5% commission.

❶ Getting There & Away

Sorata is a long way from the other Yungas towns, and there's no road connecting it directly with Coroico, so you must go through La Paz via a paved road.

From near La Paz' cemetery, buses leave hourly between 4am and 5:30pm (B$17, three hours). From the plaza in Sorata, La Paz–bound *micros* depart when full and *flotas* (long-distance buses) leave on the hour between 4am and 5pm. **Sindicato de Transportes Unificada Sorata** (Plaza Enrique Peñaranda s/n) has a daily service to Copacabana (9am, B$40), Coroico (9am, B$36), Achacachi (no set time, B$12), and Haurina (hourly, B$15). For Copacabana you can also get off at the junction town of Huarina and wait for another, probably packed, bus. Similarly, for Charazani you should change at Achacachi, but you'll need to start out from Sorata very early.

Sindicato de Transportes Unificada Sorata also services the towns on the rough 4WD track to the gold mining settlement of Mapiri, including Quiabaya (10:30am and noon, B$15), Tacacoma (10:30am, B$15) and Constata (9am, B$70), with no continuing service to Mapiri. The biggest drawbacks are the horrendous mud, the road construction and some river crossings that are passable only with a 4WD.

Camionetas (pickup trucks) leave Sorata sporadically for the grueling journey to Consata (seven hours) and on to the Sorata Limitada mine (10 hours). From Sorata Limitada you'll find *camionetas* to Mapiri, which is another hour away.

El Camino del Oro (Gold Digger's Trail)

For nearly 1000 years this Inca road has been used as a commerce and trade link between the Altiplano and the lowland goldfields. Indeed, the Tipuani and Mapiri valleys were major sources of the gold that once adorned the Inca capital, Cuzco.

Today, however, the fields are worked primarily by bulldozers and dredgers owned by mining cooperatives. They scour and scrape the landscape and dump the detritus, which is picked over by out-of-work Aymará refugees from the highlands. Fortunately, the upper part of the route remains magnificent, and almost everything between Ancoma and Chusi has been left alone, including some wonderfully exhausting Inca staircases and dilapidated ancient highway engineering.

This trek is more challenging than the Takesi and El Choro routes; if you want to get the most from it, plan on six or seven days to walk between Sorata and Llipi, less if you opt for a 4WD to Ancoma. At Llipi, find transportation to Tipuani or Guanay to avoid a walking-pace tour through the worst of the destruction.

Word of warning: this is a rough part of Bolivia, and not many people are taking this trek at the moment. With wildcat (illegal) miners in the area, it can be quite dangerous. Also, now that there is less regular traffic on the trail, you'll need to clear parts of it with machetes. If you decide to go, it's highly recommended that you travel with a local guide.

Access

Nearly everyone does the route from Sorata down the valley to Tipuani and Guanay, simply because it's generally downhill. If you don't mind a climb, however, you might prefer to do it in reverse, thus leaving the prettiest bits to last. Whatever you choose to do, it is best with a guide.

There are three options for the route between Sorata and Ancoma. First, you can rent a 4WD in Sorata and cut two days off the trek. You'll have to bargain but expect to pay at least B$400. A challenging alternative is the steep route that begins near the cemetery in Sorata. The route roughly follows the Río Challasuyo, passing through the village of Chillkani and winding up on the road just below the Abra Chuchu (4658m) – this is also the access to the Mapiri trail, a four-hour walk from Ancoma. The third option, which is shorter and more scenic, is to follow the route through the village of Lakathiya and over the Abra de Illampu (4741m) to meet up with the road about 1½ hours above Ancoma. Foreigners are charged B$10 per person to camp anywhere in the vicinity of Ancoma or you can ask about lodging in the school room. There is also a B$3 charge for crossing the bridge. Alternatively, continue a few kilometers on to Tushuaia where there is a flat terrace that makes for excellent camping.

The Route

Once you're in Ancoma, the route is fairly straightforward. Leave the 4WD track and follow the southern bank of the Río Quillapituni (which eventually becomes the Río Tipuani). At a wide spot called Llallajta, 4½ hours from Ancoma, the route crosses a bridge and briefly follows the north bank before recrossing the river and heading toward Sumata. Another Inca-engineered diversion to the north bank has been destroyed by bridge washouts, forcing a spontaneously constructed, but thankfully brief, detour above the southern bank.

Just past the detour is the village of **Sumata**; just beyond, a trail turns off to the north across the river and heads for **Yani**, which is the start of the Mapiri trail. A short distance further along from the trail junction is **Ocara**. From here, the path goes up the slope – don't follow the river. After 1½ hours you'll reach **Lambromani**, where a local may ask you to pay B$3 per person to pass. You can camp here in the schoolyard.

An hour past Lambromani you'll reach **Wainapata**, where the vegetation grows thicker and more lush. Here, the route splits (to rejoin at Pampa Quillapituni); the upper route is very steep and dangerous, so the lower one is preferable. A short distance along, the lower route passes through an interesting tunnel drilled through the rock. There's a popular myth that it dates from Inca times, but it was actually made with dynamite and likely blasted out early in the 20th century by the Aramayo mining company to improve the access to the Tipuani goldfields. At **Pampa Quillapituni**, 30 minutes beyond, is a favorable campsite. Just east of this, a trail branches off to the right toward Calzada Pass, several days away on the Illampu circuit.

Four hours after crossing the swinging bridge at the **Río Coocó**, you'll reach the little settlement of **Mina Yuna**, where you can pick up basic supplies, and it's possible to camp on the soccer field.

An hour further down is **Chusi**, which is four hours before your first encounter with the road. There's no place to camp here, but you can stay in the school. **Puente Nairapi**, over the Río Grande de Yavia, is a good place for a swim to take the edge off the increasing heat.

Once you reach the road, the scene grows increasingly depressing. For a final look at relatively unaffected landscape, follow the shortcut trail, which begins with a steep **Inca staircase** and winds up at **Baja Llipi** and the **Puente de Tora** toll bridge (B$2) over the **Río Santa Ana**.

After crossing the bridge, climb up the hill and hope for a *camioneta* or 4WD to take you to **Tipuani** and **Guanay**. *Camionetas* from the Río Santa Ana bridge to **Unutuluni** cost B\$5 per person; to continue on to Tipuani or Guanay costs an additional B\$15.

You can pick up basic supplies at Ancoma, Wainapata, Mina Yuna, Chusi and Llipi, as well as at all the lower settlements along the road. Spartan accommodations may be found in Unutuluni, Chima (rough-and-ready and not recommended), Tipuani and Guanay, all of which are along the road.

Mapiri Trail

A longer, more adventurous alternative to El Camino del Oro trek is the six- to seven-day precolonial Mapiri trail, which was upgraded 100 years ago by the Richter family in Sorata to connect their headquarters with the *cinchona* (quinine) plantations of the upper Amazon Basin. The trek is now considered dangerous, and you should check to see if conditions have changed before heading out.

It's a tough, demanding trek which requires a lot of physical exertion beyond mere walking – expect to clamber over and under logs, hack at vegetation with a machete, get assaulted by insects and destroy formerly decent clothing! That said, it's an amazing experience; the nature is unspoiled, and for the large part you are out on your own miles from any roads or villages.

An excellent side-trip before you get started will take you from Ingenio up to the lovely medieval, cloud-wrapped village of **Yani**, where there's a basic *alojamiento*. Bolivia doesn't get much enigmatic than this and adventurers won't regret a visit.

No maps are available for this route, due to government sensitivity on mining issues, and landslides often cause changes to the paths, which in some parts are heavily overgrown – a machete will be necessary. Therefore, it is strongly recommended to take a guide from Sorata. Guides for this trek charge around B\$350 to B\$400 per day, and porters are about B\$500 each. You'll thank yourself for every kilo you're not carrying if you opt for the porter.

Access

The Mapiri trail begins at the village of Ingenio, which has basic *alojamientos*. It can be reached either by 4WD from Sorata (around B\$500 for five people, three to four hours) or on foot over Abra Chuchu (4658m). For the latter, start at the cemetery

in Sorata and follow the track up past the tiny settlements of Manzanani and Huaca Milluni to the larger village of Chillkani, about three hours beyond Sorata. From there you have five hours of fairly relentless climbing through semiforested slopes to Abra Chuchu. You'll meet up with the road twisting 4km below the pass.

Shortly after the crest, take the left turn down toward a small lake – the route straight on leads to Ancoma and El Camino del Oro trek. This route will take you over Paso Lechasani (4750m) and down past Mina Suerte to Ingenio and the start of the Mapiri trail at 3550m.

The Route

Past Ingenio you'll cross the **Río Yani**. Here the trail starts downstream, but half an hour later it cuts uphill along a side stream; there's a good campsite where the trail crosses the stream. The path then twists uphill for 1½ hours over a 4000m pass. In the next two hours you'll cross three more ridges, then descend past **Cueva Cóndor**, a cave that is also a good campsite, to a small lake. From the lake the route ascends to **Paso Apacheta Nacional** (3940m), then twists down **El Tornillo**, a corkscrew-like track that drops 150m. In under an hour you'll cross the **Río Mamarani**, where a good campsite is protected by large rocks.

The next campsite lies three hours further along, beside a stream crossing at the foot of the next big ascent. There is another campsite 30 minutes after this one, near the next stream (collect water here). Here the trail climbs a long staircase, then descends into a valley before climbing to the next pass, **Abra Nasacara** (4000m). At this stage you're on the ridge that dominates most of the Mapiri trail route, with great views of the Illampu massif. For the next three days, you'll follow this ridge up and down, slowly losing altitude and passing through mostly lush jungle vegetation; fill your water bottles at every opportunity. The first water along this stretch is at **Tolapampa**, which also makes a good campsite.

The trail then passes through thick forest and you may need to do a bit of bush bashing with a machete; plan on getting good and wet from mud and the soaked vegetation. Six hours beyond Abra Nasacara is a very pleasant ridge-top campsite, **Koka Punku**, with water in a shallow pond 50m away. About three hours further on, just before a prominent landslide, look out for the water 3m off the track to the right. Four hours and three crests later is the last permanent water source and campsite at **Lagunillas**. An hour later you'll find good (but dry) campsites on the hill, **Alto Palmar**.

From Alto Palmar, the trail tunnels through dense vegetation along the **Cuesta de Amargura** (Bitterness Ridge). After three hours the jungle gives way to merely thick bush. Six hours later you'll reach **Pararaní** (1900m), where there's water (which needs to be purified) in a small pond near the ruins of an old house. An hour later there's a semi-permanent lake, and just beyond it the trail leaves the dense vegetation and issues onto a grassy ridge flanked by thick forest. It's then 4½ hours to **Incapampa**, with a semi-permanent marsh and a campsite. Along this stretch, wildlife is rife – mainly in the form of bees, ants, ticks, flies and mosquitoes, as well as plenty of butterflies.

About three hours beyond Incapampa you'll reach the hamlet of **San José** (1400m), where there's a campsite and a view over the village of Santiago. Water can sometimes be found 300m down to the right of the route. After an open area that's actually an old cemetery, the left fork provides the faster track to Mapiri.

Four to five hours of walking from San José brings you to **Mapiri**, which is visible 1½ hours before you arrive. Here you'll find several decent *alojamientos* and motorized canoes that race the 80km downstream to **Guanay** (B$25, three hours), which will seem like a city after a week of isolation. Boats leave around 9am, but get there an hour earlier to get a place. Alternatively, catch a *camioneta* along the 4WD track first to Santa Rosa (don't attempt to walk as there are two large river crossings), which has a decent *hostal* with a swimming pool, and then 175km uphill back to Sorata (B$45, 12 hours).

Guanay

POP 11,528 / ELEV 500M (1640FT)

Isolated Guanay makes a good base for visits to the gold-mining operations along the Ríos Mapiri and Tipuani. Chatting with the down-to-earth miners and *barranquilleros* (panners) can make for a particularly interesting experience. This area and other spots upriver are frontier territory that are reminiscent of the USA's legendary Old West, and a bit of caution is advised.

A block downhill from the plaza, **Hotel Pahuichi** (r per person B$30) is fairly primitive but probably offers the best value in town. It also boasts Guanay's best and most popular restaurant.

A good alternative to Hotel Pahuichi (and right next door) is **Hotel Minero** (r per person B$30).

ℹ Getting There & Away

For detailed information on walking routes from Sorata, see El Camino del Oro and Mapiri trek descriptions.

Boat

Access to the mining areas is by 4WD along the Llipi road, or by motorized dugout canoes up the Río Mapiri. Boats to Mapiri leave daily at 9am (B$30, four hours) from Puerto Mapiri when the river is high enough. The exhilarating three-hour downstream run back to Guanay costs B$25. Charter boats take travelers to Rurre, but these are pricey (B$2500 for a 10- to 15-person boat, 10 hours). Stock up on equipment and food. Some agencies in La Paz offer this trip.

Bus

The bus offices are all around the plaza, but buses actually depart from a block away toward the river. Four companies offer daily runs to and from La Paz via Caranavi and Yolosita (B$5, 10 hours). Departures in La Paz are from along Av Las Americas daily at 9am, 10:30am and 1:30pm (noon on Sunday). For Coroico, get off at Yolosita and catch a lift up the hill.

Aucapata & Iskanwaya

♪2 / POP 4,146 / ELEV 2850M (9350FT)

The tiny, remote village of Aucapata is about as far off the beaten track as most people will get. Perched on a ledge, on the shoulder of a dramatic peak, it's a great place to hole up for a couple of days' reading, hiking and relaxing. While most of Aucapata's very few visitors want to see Iskanwaya – somewhat optimistically dubbed 'Bolivia's Machu Picchu' – they may well take one look at the 1500m descent to the ruins (and the corresponding climb back up) and seek out the small Iskanwaya **museum** in the village itself, which contains artifacts from the site. Admission is free but donations are expected.

The major but near-forgotten ruins of Iskanwaya, on the western slopes of the Cordillera Real, sit in a cactus-filled canyon, perched 250m above the Río Llica. Thought to date from between 1145 and 1425, the site is attributed to the Mollu culture.

While Iskanwaya isn't exactly another Machu Picchu, the 13-hectare site is outwardly more impressive than Tiwanaku. This large citadel was built on two platforms and flanked by agricultural terraces and networks of irrigation canals. It contains more than 70 buildings, plus delicate walls, narrow streets, small plazas, storerooms, burial sites and niches.

For more information ask around Acuapata for Señor Jorge Albarracín, who is passionate about the area and the Iskanwaya ruins, or Marcelo Calamani, who can guide you to the ruins and speaks a little English. You can get in touch with them on the village telephone (☑213-5519). For background reading, *Iskanwaya: La Ciudadela que Sólo Vivía de Noche,* by Hugo Boero Roja (1992), contains photos, maps and diagrams of the site, plus information on nearby villages.

🛏 Sleeping & Eating

There's a small **alojamiento** (r per person B$15) behind the church. For meals there's only a small eatery on the corner of the plaza where you'll get whatever happens to be available. Be sure to bring small change or you're likely to clean out the town.

Hotel Iskanwaya   HOTEL **$**
(☑2-213-5519; r per person B$35) Aucapata's smart-looking hotel has clean rooms and hot showers.

ℹ Getting There & Away

Aucapata lies about 20km northeast of Quiabaya and 50km northwest of Sorata, but is most easily reached from La Paz. A **Trans Provincia del Norte** (☑238-2239) bus departs at 5am from Reyes Cardona in the cemetery district of La Paz every Tuesday and Friday (B$35, 10 hours). You might have better luck getting transportation from more accessible Charazani, or getting off a Charazani–bound bus at the *cruce* (turnoff) for Aucapata, but don't bank on it.

There's also rather difficult access from Sorata, which involves a four-day trek via Payayunga. Guides are available in Sorata. One other access route, which is quite challenging but very interesting, is a little-known trek from the village of Amarete, in the Cordillera Apolobamba. A guide is essential; you may be able to hire one by asking around Amarete, Curva or Charazani. Note that there's no accurate map of the area, and in the rainy season hiking is dangerous on the exposed routes in the region and not recommended.

Caranavi

☑2 / POP 51,000 / ELEV 976M (3202FT)

All buses between La Paz and the lowlands pass through uninspiring Caranavi, a bare-brick town midway between Coroico and Guanay that could do with a lick of paint. Travelers love to knock this place, but it doesn't deserve their scorn. If you're passing time here, take a look at the **Untucala suspension bridge**, which spans a crossing used since Inca times.

Caranavi has several inexpensive hotels, all near the highway. **Hotel Landivar** (☑823-2052; Calama 15; r per person B$50; ☒) is one of the better ones and has a pleasant pool. More sophisticated is the recommended **Hostal Caturra Inn** (☑823-2209; s/d US$120/180; ☒), which has hot showers, fans, lovely gardens, a good restaurant and a clean pool – a really unexpected treat if you've just climbed out of a dusty bus.

The road between here and Coroico is only open at night.

CORDILLERA REAL

Bolivia's Royal Range has more than 600 peaks over 5000m, most of which are relatively accessible and many of which are just a few hours' drive from the nation's capital. They're also still free of the growing bureaucracy attached to climbing and trekking in the Himalayas. The following section is a rundown of the more popular climbs in the Cordillera Real – there are also fun treks, bikes and hikes here for non-climbers – but it is by no means an exhaustive list. There are many other peaks to entice the experienced climber, and whether you choose one of those described here or one of the lesser known, climbing in the Bolivian Andes is always an adventure.

The best season for climbing in the Cordillera Real is May to September. Note that most of the climbs described here are technical and require climbing experience, a reputable climbing guide and proper technical equipment. You should be fully acclimatized to the altitude before attempting any of these ascents.

CLIMBING RESOURCES

Call the new rescue group **Socorro Andino Bolivia** (☏7197-1147, 7158-1118; www.socorro andino.org) if you get in a jam. It does technical mountain rescues and charges around US$100 per day, per person on the rescue.

The Andes: A Guide for Climbers (2005, John Biggar) Has basic descriptions and decent maps from the area.

Bolivia: Guía de Trekking y Ascenciones (2012, David Taurá) A new Spanish-language guide to Bolivia's hikes and climbs.

Andes Handbook (www.andeshandbook.com) A good website to consult, it offers route information on several of the peaks in the Cordillera Real in Spanish.

Bolivia: A Climbing Guide (1999, Yossi Brain) Now out of print, but available online, this has lots of info on climbs in the Cordillera Real.

Nuestras Montañas A Spanish-language resource written by local mountaineering guides, available at InfoTur (p61) in La Paz.

Guides & Equipment

By far the easiest way of tackling these mountains is to go on a guided climb. Several La Paz agencies offer trips that include transportation, *refugio* (mountain hut) accommodations, equipment hire and a guide. Some of the same agencies will rent you equipment on its own if you want to tackle the peaks without taking the tour but this option should only be considered by those with extensive mountaineering experience at similar altitudes. Prices start at around B$900 for an ascent of Huayna Potosí, but are significantly higher for the more technical climbs – around B$3000-plus for Illimani, for example. Several agencies and foreign climbing-tour agents offer packages that combine ascents of several of the Cordillera Real peaks. Choose your tour agent carefully; cheaper does not mean better.

You can also contract a guide independently. The **Asociación de Guías de Montaña** (www.agmtb.org) is an association of registered mountain guides. If you are in a group, it's worth paying extra to make sure that there are two guides accompanying you, so that if one member of the group succumbs to altitude sickness the ascent isn't compromised.

Huayna Potosí

This is Bolivia's most popular major peak because of its imposing beauty and ease of access, as well as the fact that it's 88m over the magic 6000m figure (but 26ft under the magic 20,000ft figure). While most people come here to climb, you can also stay at the mountain lodge, and head out for some fun hikes or mountain bikes.

There are a number of routes to the top; the one described here is the North Peak route, the most popular with visitors and tour companies. It's appealing because it can be climbed by beginners with a competent guide and technical equipment. Beginners yes, but fit beginners; it's quite steep toward the end and it's a tough climb. Though some people attempt to climb Huayna Potosí in one day, it is not recommended. You're better off attempting the climb in two or three days (three days is best for newbies to ensure you properly acclimatize and learn the ropes before you hit higher sections). Guided trips cost between B$900 and B$1100.

There are five *refugios* in the Paso Zongo area; the better-equipped is **Huayna Potosí Refugio** (☏in La Paz 2-245-6717; www.huayna-potosi.com; dm incl breakfast B$175, dinner B$50). Run by a La Paz tour company, it's a comfortable, heated spot and a fine place to acclimatize – there's pretty walking to be done hereabouts and plenty of advice and good cheer. Reserve ahead. **Refugio San Calixto** (Casa Blanca; dm B$40) is right by the La Paz–Zongo road (buses will let you off outside) and is a simpler but very hospitable spot. You can also camp here. Transportation to the *refugios*, guides, rations and porters can be arranged through most La Paz tour agencies.

Mountain Biking

La Paz mountain-bike outfits take advanced riders here for the descent from the base of spectacular mountain, past Zongo Dam, and then along a dramatic 40km, 3600m descent into the lush and humid Yungas. This is a dead-end road that lacks a great destination at its finish, but there's little vehicular traffic, so you tend to have the road to yourself and can open up the throttle a little more.

Access

A 4WD from La Paz to the trailhead at Paso Zongo costs around B$500 one way for up to five people. A taxi should be a bit less with haggling (aim for B$250 one way and make sure your driver knows the way). Daily Trans Zongo buses leave at 6am from Plaza Ballivián in El Alto (B$13, two hours).

As Huayna Potosí is so popular, lots of climbers are headed out that way during the climbing season. If you only want a lift, check with specialist climbing agencies. Someone will probably have a 4WD going on the day you want, and you can share costs for the trip.

The Route

From the **Huayna Potosí Refugio**, cross the dam and follow the aqueduct until you reach the third path on your left signed 'Glacier Huayna Potosí.' Take this path to a glacial stream then through and across the rocks to reach the ridge of a moraine. Near the end of the moraine – where you'll pay B$10 to climb the mountain at a small rock hut – descend slightly to your right and then ascend the steep scree gullies. At the top, bear left and follow the cairns to reach the **Campo Rocas Glacier** (5200m). There's a hut to sleep in, and dry places to camp. Most tours stop here for the night, before commencing the ascent at around 2am.

The glacier is crevassed, especially after July, so rope up while crossing it. Ascend the initial slopes then follow a long, gradually ascending traverse to the right, before turning left and climbing steeply to a flat area between 5500m and 5700m known as **Campo Argentino** (a seldom-used alternate sleeping spot). It will take you about two to three hours to reach this point. Camp on the right of the path, but note that the area further to the right is heavily crevassed, especially later in the season.

The following morning you should leave from here between 4am and 6am. Follow the path/trench out of Campo Argentino, and head uphill to your right until you join a ridge. Turn left here and cross a flat stretch to reach the steep and exposed **Polish Ridge** (named in honor of the Pole who fell off it

and died while soloing in 1994). Here you cross a series of rolling glacial hills and crevasses to arrive below the summit face. Either climb straight up the face to the summit or cross along the base of it to join the ridge that rises to the left. This ridge provides thrilling views down the 1000m-high west face. Either route will bring you to the summit in five to seven hours from Campo Argentino.

The descent to Campo Argentino from the summit takes a couple of hours; from there, it's another one or two hours back to the *refugio* at Paso Zongo.

Illimani

Illimani, the 6438m giant overlooking La Paz, was first climbed in 1898 by a party led by WM Conway, a pioneer 19th-century alpinist. Although it's not a difficult climb technically, the combination of altitude and ice conditions warrants serious consideration and caution. Technical equipment is essential above the snow line; caution is especially needed on the exposed section immediately above Nido de Cóndores where several climbers have perished.

Access

The easiest way to reach the first Illimani camp, **Puente Roto**, is via Pinaya, a three-hour trip by 4WD from La Paz (about B$850). From there, it's two to three hours' walk to Puente Roto. At Pinaya you can hire porters (B$120) and mules (B$120) to carry your gear to Puente Roto or to the high camp at Nido de Cóndores. This is a wise investment.

For those on the cheap, a daily 5am bus (B$10) goes from near La Paz' Mercado Rodríguez to the village of Quilihuaya, from where you'll have a three-hour slog to Pinaya – complete with a 400m elevation gain. Buses return from Quilihuaya to La Paz several days a week at around 8:30am, but if you're relying on public transportation you should carry extra food just in case.

An alternative route to the base camp is via Cohoni. Buses and *camiones* leave La Paz for Cohoni (B$30, five hours) in the early afternoon Monday to Saturday from the corner of General Luis Lara and Calle Boquerón. They leave Cohoni to return to La Paz around 8:30am and may take anywhere from five hours to all day depending on which route is followed.

The Route

The normal route to Pico Sur, the highest of Illimani's five summits, is straightforward but heavily crevassed. If you don't have technical glacier experience, hire a competent professional guide.

The route to **Nido de Cóndores** (5400m), a rock platform beside the glacier, is a four- to six-hour slog up a rock ridge from Puente Roto. There's no water at Nido de Cóndores, so you'll have to melt snow – bring sufficient stove fuel.

From Nido de Cóndores you need to set off at about 2am. Follow the path in the snow leading uphill from the camp; the path grows narrower and steeper, then flattens out a bit before becoming steeper again. It then crosses a series of crevasses before ascending to the right to reach a level section. From here, aim for the large break in the skyline to the left of the summit, taking care to avoid the two major crevasses, and cross one steep section that is iced over from July onwards. After you pass through the skyline break, turn right and continue up onto the summit ridge. The final three vertical meters involve walking 400m along the ridge at over 6400m elevation.

Plan on six to 10 hours for the climb from Nido de Cóndores to the summit and three to four hours to descend back to camp.

If possible continue down from Nido de Cóndores to Puente Roto on the same day. The 1000m descent is not appealing after a long day, but your body will thank you the following day and will recover more quickly at the lower altitude. You'll also avoid having to melt snow for a second night.

On the fourth day you can walk from Puente Roto back out to Pinaya in about two hours.

Condoriri Massif

The massif known as Condoriri is actually a cluster of 13 peaks ranging in height from 5100m to 5648m. The highest of these is **Cabeza del Cóndor** (Head of the Condor), which has twin winglike ridges flowing from either side of the summit. Known as Las Alas (The Wings), these ridges cause the peak to resemble a condor lifting its wings on takeoff. According to local legend, the massif is the last refuge of the biggest and most ferocious condors in the Andes, which kidnap children and educate them to be-

come 'man-condors' and then return them to the human population to bring terror and death.

Cabeza del Cóndor is a challenging climb following an exposed ridge, and should be attempted only by experienced climbers. However, a number of other peaks in the Condoriri Massif, including the beautiful Pequeño Alpamayo (5370m), can be attempted by beginners with a competent guide.

The hike to the glacier is fun for non-climbers.

Access

There is no public transportation from La Paz to Condoriri. A 4WD to the start of the walk-in at the dam at **Laguna Tuni** costs around B$550. If you don't want to use a 4WD transfer, you can trek the 24km from Milluni to the Laguna Tuni dam on the road to Paso Zongo. Take everything you will need with you as there is nowhere to buy provisions once you begin the trek.

It isn't possible to drive beyond the dam because there's a locked gate across the road. Some drivers know a way around it, but if you need to hire pack animals you'll have to do so before you reach the dam. Locals charge B$70 per day for mules, and a bit less for llamas, which can carry less. You also might have to sign into the Parque Nacional Condoriri.

From Laguna Tuni, a rough road circles south around the lake and continues up a drainage trending north. Once you're in this valley, you'll have a view of the Cabeza del Cóndor and Las Alas.

From the end of the road, follow the obvious paths up along the right side of the valley until you reach a large lake, **Chiar Khota**. Follow the right shore of the lake to arrive at the base camp, which is an easy three hours from Laguna Tuni. There are toilet facilities here and the community will charge you B$20 to stay the night.

The Route

Leave base camp at about 3am and follow the path up the east-trending valley through boulders, passing some lakes on your left. Keep heading up the main trail, on the right-hand side of the valley, until you reach the glacier. You should reach this point in about 1½ hours from base camp.

Here you should rope up and put on crampons. Head left across the glacier before rising to the *col* (lowest point of the ridge), taking care to avoid the crevasses. Climb to the right up the rock-topped summit **Tarija** (5240m), which affords impressive views of Pequeño Alpamayo, before dropping down (100m) a scree and rock slope to rejoin a glacier on the other side. From there, follow the main ridge to the summit. The ridge has some exposure.

Ancohuma

Ancohuma is the highest peak in the Sorata Massif, towering on the remote northern edge of the Cordillera Real. It was not climbed until 1919 and remains a challenging climb.

For a long time, various sources put Ancohuma at around 7000m, which would have made it higher than Argentina's Aconcagua, but in 2002 an American student lugged GPS equipment to the top and determined that its true height is 6427m, a few meters short of Bolivia's highest mountain, Sajama. Most climb the peak in two days.

Access

The peak is accessed via Sorata from where it is possible to rent a 4WD for the long traverse to Cocoyo or up to **Laguna Chilate** (4200m). More convenient is hiring a 4WD all the way from La Paz to Cocoyo, but it is also considerably more expensive. If you have a serious amount of gear, you can rent a mule train to carry it from Sorata to base camp, which is in the lake basin east of the peaks at about 4500m. Plan on at least two days for these various transportation arrangements to get you to the lakes. Ancohuma is most often climbed from the west, using Laguna Glacial as a base camp. Further advice and information is available in Sorata.

The Route

If you have opted for the more easily accessed western route, hike from Sorata to the base camp at **Laguna Glacial**. From here the route climbs the obvious moraine and then ascends the glacier, over fields of extremely dangerous crevasses. Most make a high camp at 5400m or 5800m. It then climbs to the *bergschrund* (crevasse) and across a relatively level ice plateau to the summit pyramid. This is most easily climbed via the north ridge; the first part is quite steep and icy, but then gets easier toward the summit.

CORDILLERA APOLOBAMBA

The remote Cordillera Apolobamba, flush against the Peruvian border north of Lake Titicaca, is becoming a popular hiking, trekking and climbing destination. Mountaineers in particular will find a wonderland of tempting peaks, first ascents and new routes to discover, and the trek from Lagunillas to Agua Blanca – with magnificent Andean landscapes – was one of the most memorable in the country. Recent reports from tour operators of robberies and assaults indicate this area could be dangerous for trekking.

While access is improving, it must be emphasized that this is an isolated region, and far from set up for tourism. There are few services, transportation isn't reliable and the people maintain a fragile traditional lifestyle. Comparatively few locals – mostly men – speak more than rudimentary Spanish. Sensitivity to the local sentiments of this highly traditional Aymará- and Quechua-speaking area will help keep its distinctive character intact.

Mining is on the rise in the region. Pollution from mining operations has caused some conflicts with the largely agrarian communities here, and you should check on the political situation before visiting.

Every town and village in the region holds an annual festival, most of which fall between June and September. The **Fiesta de La Virgen de las Nieves**, one of the best, takes place in Italaque, northeast of Escoma, around August 5. It features a potpourri of traditional Andean dances.

Charazani

POP 9161 / ELEV 3250M (10,662FT)

Charazani is the administrative and commercial center and transportation axis of Bautista Saavedra province, and by far the largest town in the area. You can hike from here to the trailhead for the Lagunillas–Agua Blanca trek. Services in Charazani have increased exponentially in recent years, and several NGOs are working in the area on sustainable development projects, including solar power, textile production and the promotion of responsible tourism. It's a relaxed spot to visit, and weary hikers will enjoy the hot springs.

THE KALLAWAYA

Originating in six villages around **Curva** in the Apolobamba region, the Kallawaya are a group of healers who pass ancient traditions down the generations, usually from father to son. Around a quarter of the inhabitants of these villages become involved in the healing tradition, although there are many more people throughout the Andes that pass themselves off as authentic Kallawaya when they are nothing of the kind.

The origins and age of the Kallawaya tradition are unknown, although some Kallawaya claim to be descended from the vanished people of Tiwanaku. The Kallawaya language, Machaj Juyai, used exclusively for healing, is derived from Quechua, the language of the Incas. With only 100 to 200 Kallawaya speakers left in the world, the language is at risk of extinction – globally around half of the 7000 languages spoken on earth may disappear in the next 100 years. Check out www.livingtongues.org to hear recordings of Kallawaya and learn more about language preservation initiatives.

For the Kallawaya, language, knowledge and skills are passed down through generations, although it's sometimes possible for aspiring healers to study under acknowledged masters.

The early Kallawaya were known for their wanderings and traveled all over the continent in search of medicinal herbs. The most capable of today's practitioners will have memorized the properties and uses of 600 to 1000 different healing herbs, but their practices also involve magic and charms. They believe that sickness and disease are the result of a displaced or imbalanced *ajallu* (life force). The incantations and amulets are intended to encourage it back into a state of equilibrium within the body.

A hallmark of the Kallawaya is the *alforja* (medicine pouch), which is carried by the men. While women don't become healers, they still play an important part in the gathering of herbs.

In Lagunillas, there's a small exhibition about the Kallawaya in the Museo Interpretativo Center. The Kallawaya's legacy has also been recorded by several anthropologists and medical professionals; German university psychiatrist Ina Rössing has produced an immense four-volume work called *El Mundo de los Kallahuaya* about her ongoing research, and Frenchman Louis Girault has compiled an encyclopedia of herbal remedies employed by the Kallawaya, entitled *Kallahuaya, Curanderos Itinerantes de los Andes*.

Two fiestas are held in Charazani; the biggest takes place around July 16 and the smaller one around August 6. There's also a wonderful children's dance festival (around November 16) in honor of the Virgen del Carmen, an invocation of the Virgin Mary.

◎ Sights & Activities

Termas de Charazani Phutina   HOT SPRINGS
(admission B$5; ☉7am-9pm, closed Mon to 2pm for cleaning) Along the river, about 10 minutes' walk upstream from town, you'll pass the Termas de Charazani Phutina, a hotsprings complex where you can bathe and enjoy a hot shower. Other natural **thermal baths**, complete with a steaming hot waterfall, can be found a two-hour hike away. Head down the valley from Charazani along the Apolo road alongside the Río Kamata. It's a lovely spot.

Chari   VILLAGE
The traditional Kallawaya village of Chari, 1½ hours' walk from Charazani, is a blend of terraces, flowers and vegetable gardens. A German anthropologist started the Tuwans textile project, which is designed to market the local hand-dyed weavings. The town is also home to a **Kallawaya cultural museum**, a stone and thatch structure with exhibits pertaining to medicinal plants and textile arts.

Pre-Incan Ruins   RUINS
About an hour's walk outside Chari are some pre-Incan ruins, reached by walking through town and turning left at the enormous boulder that creates a small cave. Follow this path to the cemetery, keep left until you gain the ridge, then continue 200m up to the ruins. To avoid suspicion it's best to advise locals where you're headed before setting off.

Cordillera Apolobamba

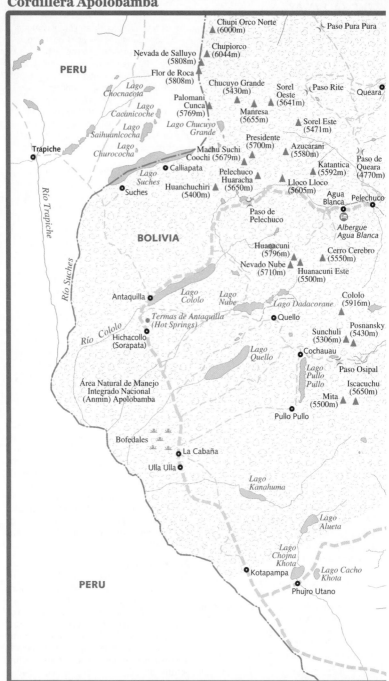

🛏 Sleeping & Eating

Several *pensiones* around the plaza offer soup, a main course and bad coffee for under B$10.

Essentials can be purchased at *tiendas* (small, family-run shops) surrounding the plaza. Trekkers, however, are advised to bring their supplies from La Paz.

Accommodations are basic no matter where you look. These are relatively comfortable options.

Residencial Charazani   HOTEL $
(r per person B$20) Just off the plaza on the Curva road, this nine-room hotel is on your right. It's fairly basic but offers a fabulous view over the valley and, crucially, access to doña Sofia's fine Bolivian cooking.

Hotel Akhamani   HOTEL $
(r per person B$20, apt B$40) A block below the plaza, Hotel Akhamani has the highest standards and the widest variety of options, including a four-bed mini-apartment with a private bathroom and small kitchen.

Residencial Inti Wasi   HOTEL $
(r per person B$25) Arranged around a traditional cobbled courtyard that provides a pleasant atmosphere, this place can be found a block below the plaza.

ℹ Information

There are telephones at the **Transportes Altiplano** (☑213-7439) office on the plaza and in the **alcaldía** (Town Hall; ☑213-7282), a block below the plaza. There is no ATM in town; ask at your hotel for local moneychangers. If you happen to find it open, the public Nawiriywasi Library has books on medicinal plants and the Kallawaya culture, and maps and information for hikers, trekkers and climbers. Market day is Sunday.

ℹ Getting There & Away

From La Paz (B$25), **Trans Provincia del Norte** (☑in La Paz 2-238-2239) and the more reliable **Trans Altiplano** (☑in La Paz 2-238-0859) depart daily at 6am from Calle Reyes Cardona in the cemetery district. The services take six to eight hours and return from Charazani daily at 6pm. Book tickets in advance.

From Charazani, a 4WD route winds down to the Yungas village of Apolo at the edge of the Amazon Basin, where you can stay overnight at the monastery. The route is frequently negotiated by *camiones* during the dry season, but several serious stream crossings and landslide risks mean it's best suited to mountain bikes or foot traffic in the wet.

Área Natural de Manejo Integrado Nacional Apolobamba

In the late 1990s the Reserva Nacional de Fauna Ulla Ulla was renamed the Área Natural de Manejo Integrado Nacional (Anmin) Apolobamba and was expanded by nearly 300,000 hectares to 484,000 hectares. It now includes the entire Cordillera Apolobamba and most of the renowned Lagunillas to Agua Blanca trek along the range's eastern slopes. At its northern end it abuts Parque Nacional Madidi to form one of the western hemisphere's most extensive protected areas.

The original park – a loosely defined vicuña reserve along the Peruvian border – was established in 1972, and was upgraded in 1997 in Unesco's 'Man and Biosphere Reserve Program.' Later that same year the Instituto Nacional de Fomento Lanero (Infol) was created to represent wool producers and was charged with researching, monitoring and preventing habitat degradation of the reserve's camelids. Infol morphed into the Instituto Boliviano de Tecnología Agropecuaria (IBTA), which focuses more on agricultural development and social services.

The modern park is home to several thousand alpacas and vicuñas, and also to Bolivia's densest condor population. In addition to the popular hiking routes, you'll find excellent wild trekking around Lagos Cololo, Nube, Quello, Kanahuma and Pullo Pullo, all of which enjoy snow-covered backdrops and rich waterbird populations, including flamingos and several species of Andean geese.

🍴 Sleeping & Eating

Noncampers can normally find accommodations in local homes for B$20 per person – just ask around. The biggest *tienda* is in Ulla Ulla. At La Cabaña, 5km from Ulla Ulla village, IBTA has a small hostel where you may be able to stay, but it's suggested that you reserve via SERNAP in La Paz.

The best accommodations in the area are two associated *albergues* at **Lagunillas** (🖉213-37439; per person B$25) and **Agua Blanca** (🖉872-0140; per person B$25, with meals B$65). They offer dorm beds, hot showers, kitchen facilities and a fireplace in a modern building. Reserve ahead, or hunt around to find the keeper of the keys. There are ranger stations at Antaquilla, Charazani, Curva, Ko-

tapampa, Pelechuco, Pullo Pullo, Suches and Hichacollo; the last three were designed by a La Paz architect and blend adobe construction, domed thatched roofs and passive solar walls to reflect both modern and traditional styles.

Hikers can camp at any of these sites or stay inside – sufficient space and your Spanish skills permitting.

ℹ️ Information

A team of park rangers roams between several far-flung Casas de Guardaparques, which are all linked via radio communication but infrequently staffed during the day. For pre-departure information contact Servicio Nacional de Áreas Protegidas (SERNAP) in La Paz. In an emergency contact them by radio on frequency 8335 USB.

The village of Curva (3780m) has a few basic stores, and at nearby Lagunillas is the Museo Interpretativo Center, which provides limited local information and an exhibition on the Kallawaya traditions. As part of the same project, Agua Blanca has a small museum and weaving workshop. Curva's main festival is a colorful affair that takes place on June 29.

Lagunillas to Agua Blanca (Curva to Pelechuco) Trek

This fantastic four- to five-day hike (45km) passes through splendid and largely uninhabited wilderness. Recent reports indicate that safety is a concern here, as are pollution and the lack of support services along the way. Check around before you head out.

The track stays mostly above 4000m and includes five high passes. There's arguably no better scenery in the Andes, and along the way you're sure to see llamas and alpacas, as well as more elusive Andean wildlife, such as viscachas, vicuñas, condors and perhaps even a spectacled bear.

The trek may be done in either direction, as both ends have relatively reliable – albeit limited – public transportation links with La Paz. Most people do the route from south to north, but starting in Agua Blanca would mean an additional day of downhill walking and could include a grand finale at Charazani's hot springs. The trail is pre-Columbian and built on a stone platform; some areas still have cobbled paving up to 2m wide.

It is strongly recommended that you hire a guide and pack animals for the trek – no reliable maps of the region exist. Clients must often carry their own food and stove, and are also often expected to provide meals for their guides, porters and muleteers. Bring enough food for a week, preferably from La Paz, as Curva and Pelechuco have only basics at inflated prices.

Access

Trans Altiplano (☑in La Paz 2-238-0859) runs daily buses to Lagunillas from La Paz. They leave from Reyes Cardona in the cemetery district in the early hours of the morning. **Trans Norte** (☑in La Paz 2-238-2239) runs a daily service to Agua Blanca and Pelechuco from El Alto (at the ex-*tranca* Río Seco) at 6am (B\$35, 12 hours). The bus may stop en route – depending on the driver's mood – at the market in Huancasaya on the Peruvian border, before continuing to Ulla Ulla, Agua Blanca and Pelechuco. Buses return at odd hours so check the schedules before leaving La Paz, as they change often. At the time of writing, the return from Agua Blanca departed between 3am and 4am.

A more expensive but considerably easier and more comfortable way to go is by 4WD. A vehicle and driver from La Paz to Lagunillas (B\$2100, seven hours) or Agua Blanca (B\$2500, 10 hours) may be worthwhile because it allows daylight travel through the incomparable scenery. Alternatively, you can pay to leave the logistics to someone else and do the trek with an agency.

The Route

Because most people do the trek from south to north – from Lagunillas (also known as Tilinhuaya) to Agua Blanca – that's how it's described here. If you want to start from **Charazani**, you can either follow the long and winding road for four to five hours or take the 3½ to four-hour shortcut. Cross the river at the thermal baths, then climb the other bank and head back to the road. After about an hour you should follow a path that climbs to a white-and-yellow church on your left. Beyond the church, descend the other side of the hill, to just above the community of **Niñocorín**. After a short distance you'll strike an obvious path; turn left onto it and follow it as it contours through the fields and then descends to cross a river, where it starts the steep climb into Curva.

Most people choose to start in **Lagunillas**, with its pretty lake bristling with waterbirds. The *albergue* here can arrange beasts of burden and guides. From here, it's a short walk to the village of **Curva**, center of the Kallawaya community. From Curva, head toward the cross on the hill north of the village and skirt around the right side of the hill. About an hour out of Curva, you'll go across a stream. Continue uphill along the right bank of the stream. At a cultivated patch about 200m before the valley descending from the right flank of the snowy peak, cross the stream to join a well-defined path entering from your left. If you continue along this path, you'll reach an excellent flat, streamside campsite. Alternatively, keep following this trail for another 1½ hours to an ideal campsite at **Jatunpampa** (4200m).

From Jatunpampa, head up the valley and across a small plain to the *col* (saddle between two peaks) with a cairn, about two hours along. Known as the **Cumbre Tambillo**, this 4700m pass offers fabulous views of Akamani off to the northwest. One to two hours further along you'll arrive at a good campsite (4100m) near the **Incacancha** (aka Incachani) waterfall.

The following morning's zig-zag ascent of the **Akamani Sacred Hill** looks a bit daunting, but it isn't that bad. Cross the bridge below the waterfall and follow the switchbacks up the scree gully. As you ascend, enjoy distant views of Ancohuma and Illampu. After two hours or so you'll reach **Mil Curvas** (4800m), another high pass.

From the pass, traverse gently uphill to the left until you gain the ridge, which affords great views of the Cordillera Real to the south and Cuchillo II to the north. At this point the obvious trail descends past a small lake before arriving at a larger lake with a good view of Akamani.

Climb up to the next ridge before descending an hour to the small mining settlement of **Viscachani**, where you'll strike the 4WD track toward Hilo Hilo (aka Illo Illo). In another hour this road ascends to the **Cumbre Viscachani** pass (4900m), which also provides superb views of the Cordillera Real to the south and the Sunchulli Valley to the north and west.

At the pass the road drops into the valley; at the point where it bears right, look for a path turning off to the left. This will take you to a point above the **Sunchulli gold mine**. From Sunchulli, follow a contour line above the aqueduct for about an hour, until you see an idyllic **campsite** (4600m) below Cuchillo I.

The fourth day of the hike is probably the finest, as it includes sections that have been used for centuries by miners and *campesinos*.

From the campsite, the road ascends for about two hours via a series of switchbacks to the **Cumbre Sunchulli** (5100m) pass. From the pass, you can scramble up to a cairn above the road for excellent views dominated by **Colocolo** (5916m), the southern Cordillera Apolobamba's highest peak.

Descend along the road for a few minutes, then jog right down a steep but obvious path that crosses a stream opposite the glacier lake below Cuchillo II before descending to the valley floor. If you follow the valley floor, you'll rejoin the road a couple of minutes above the picturesque stone-and-thatch village of **Piedra Grande**, three hours from the pass. Camping is possible here.

Follow the road for about an hour, then join the precolonial road turning off downhill to your right. After you cross a bridge, you should follow the obvious path to the right, leading you up into the village of **Hilo Hilo** in about an hour. Here you'll find small stores selling the basics and it may even be possible to rent a room for the night.

When leaving Hilo Hilo don't be tempted onto the path to the left, which leads west to Ulla Ulla (although this is also a viable trek). The correct route is to the right, leaving the village above the school between the public facilities and the cemetery. From there, cross the llama pastures until the path becomes clear again. After crossing a bridge (about an hour out of town) and beginning up the **Palca Valley** with a sharp rock peak at its head (if it's too overcast to see the rock, look for several small houses on your left and turn there), you'll stumble onto an ideal campsite set in a bend in the valley, where there are a number of large fallen rocks.

From the campsite, head up the valley for about 1½ hours until you reach a bridge over the stream. At this point the route begins to ascend to the **Cumbre Kiayansani** pass (4900m), which you should reach in another 1½ hours. From the pass, descend past a lake, crossing pastures full of llamas, and follow some pre-Columbian paving as well as stone steps cut into the rock that date from the same period. In less than two hours you'll arrive in **Pelechuco**, a quaint colonial village founded by Jesuits in 1560.

There are a couple of simple *alojamientos* in Pelechuco, but a 30-minute walk further, passing two intriguing pre-Columbian settlements, takes you to the mining village of **Agua Blanca**, where there's an *albergue*, for a well-deserved rest.

CORDILLERA QUIMSA CRUZ

The Cordillera Quimsa Cruz, although close to La Paz, is a largely undiscovered wilderness of 5000m-plus peaks, some of which have only been climbed for the first time in the last few years. Basque climbing magazine *Pyrenaica* once labeled it a 'South American Karakoram.' In 1999, near the summit of Santa Veracruz, the Spaniard Javier Sánchez discovered the remains of an 800-year-old ceremonial burial site with ancient artifacts and weavings.

The Quimsa Cruz is not a large range – it's only some 50km from end to end – and the peaks are lower than in other Bolivian ranges. The highest peak, Jacha Cuno Collo, rises to 5800m, and the other glaciated peaks range from 4500m to 5300m. Granite peaks, glaciers and lakeside camping make the Quimsa Cruz an unforgettable, untouristed Andean experience. It lies to the southeast of Illimani, separated from the Cordillera Real by the Río La Paz, and geologically speaking it's actually a southern outlier of that range.

The Quimsa Cruz lies at the northern end of Bolivia's tin belt, and tin reserves have been exploited here since the late 1800s. While Bolivia's tin industry has gone through numerous boom-and-bust cycles, with international prices up miners are returning to the region, and many of the major mines that were closed during the price drops of the 1980s are now open for business.

🏃 Activities

The Quimsa Cruz offers some of the finest adventure climbing in all of Bolivia, and in every valley mining roads provide access to the impressively glaciated peaks. Although all of the *nevados* of the Quimsa Cruz have now been climbed, there are still plenty of unclimbed routes, and expeditions are likely to have the mountains to themselves. If you have no previous climbing experience you should take a guide from a La Paz agency who really knows the area.

Trekking is also possible throughout the range, which is covered by IGM mapping. The main route is the two- to three-day **Mina Viloco to Mina Caracoles trek**, which crosses the range from west to east. Of interest along this route is the renowned site of a 1971 airplane crash, which had already been stripped by local miners before rescue teams arrived at the scene two days later. Mina Viloco is 70km southeast of La Paz, and is centered on a major tin mine. Mina Caracoles is still worked by cooperatives, and is 13km northwest of Quime.

Staples are available in both Mina Viloco and Quime, but it's still best to carry everything you'll need (food, fuel and other supplies) from La Paz.

① Getting There & Away

Road access is relatively easy because of the number of mines in the area, and it's possible to drive to within 30 minutes' walk of some glaciers. Others, however, are up to a four-hour hike from the nearest road. The easiest access

is provided by **Flota Trans-Inquisivi** (⌨ in La Paz 2-228-4050), which leaves daily in the early morning from La Paz' main bus terminal for the eastern side of the range (to Quime, Inquisivi, Cajuata, Circuato, Suri, Mina Caracoles, and, less often, Yacopampa and Frutillani). **Trans Araca** (⌨ in La Paz 2-228-4050) serves the communities and mines on the western side of the range from its office on Av Francisco Carvajal, in Barrio Villa Dolores, El Alto. To Mina Viloco, Araca or Cairoma, a bus departs daily at 7am taking seven to 10 hours.

Those with a bit more ready cash can rent a 4WD and driver for the five- to seven-hour journey from La Paz (expect to pay at least B\$2000); any of the services used by mountaineers and trekkers can organize the trip.

Southern Altiplano

Includes »

Best Places to Eat

» Minuteman Revolutionary Pizza (p150)

» Mercado Campero (p137)

» Milan Center (p163)

Best Places to Stay

» Hotel Tayka de Sal (p154)

» Hostal Kory Wara (p140)

» Hotel Mitru (p161)

Why Go?

The harsh and at times almost primeval geography of the southern Altiplano will tug at the heartstrings of visitors with a deep love of bleak and solitary places. Stretching southward from La Paz, this high-plains wilderness is framed by majestic volcanic peaks, swathes of treeless wilderness and the white emptiness of the eerie *salares* (salt deserts), which are almost devoid of life. At night the stargazing is spectacular, and it's as cold as you could ever imagine.

The area around Parque Nacional Sajama offers an amazing wilderness to explore, while revelers may wish to hit up Carnaval celebrations in the gritty, straight-talking mining city of Oruro. Further south the Salar de Uyuni is the star attraction, and a three-day jeep tour of the region is at the top of most travelers' itineraries. From here, you can head to the warmer cactus-studded valleys around Tupiza for horseback riding and mountain biking.

When to Go
Uyuni

Aug-Oct The best time for salt-flat and wilderness trips.

Oct-Nov Good deals on *salar* tours and the chance to see the salt flat flooded.

Jan-Mar Amazing Carnaval costumes and a huge water-balloon fight.

History

The prehistoric lakes Minchín and Tauca once covered most of this highland plateau. They evaporated around 10,000 years ago, leaving behind a parched landscape of brackish puddles and salt deserts. Pre-Columbian civilizations didn't leave much of a mark on the region; some time in the mid-15th century an Inca ruler sent his son Tupac-Yupanqui southward to conquer all the lands he encountered. Tupac-Yupanqui and his gang marched on across the wastelands to the northern bank of Chile's Río Maule, where a fierce band of Araucanian people inspired them to stake out the southern boundary of the Inca empire and turn back toward Cuzco.

These days, outside the major towns and cities, most people cluster around mining camps. During the late 1980s a mining crisis devastated the industry, sending miners fleeing to lower elevations. But with commodity prices up and the world's largest stash of lithium just waiting to be extracted, mining is back and, with it, controversy. In fact, much of Bolivia's social conflict now centers around contamination from mines, and the nationalization and management of the industry. Climate change and desertification is affecting the region's natural and social landscape in a major way as well, making it easier to sow lucrative quinoa crops at higher elevations and triggering a ten-fold spike in land prices.

National Parks

Parque Nacional Sajama, Bolivia's first national park, is a region of magnificent peaks, plains and wildlife habitat. It is also home to the world's highest forest and some of South America's loftiest hot springs. Even if you're not into hardcore mountaineering, an evening dip in the clear springs at the base of Volcán Sajama in the company of a few camelids is worth the trek. The Reserva Nacional de Fauna Andina Eduardo Avaroa is a highlight of Southwest Circuit tours and the gateway to Chile for those headed to San Pedro de Atacama.

ⓘ Getting There & Away

From La Paz, the southern Altiplano is easily accessed by bus, although off the paved main roads the ride can be long and bumpy. The route from the central highland cities of Potosí and Sucre is fairly easy, with new paved roads taking you to both Tupiza and Oruro. The overland route from Chile is a scenic mountain traverse on a good road from Arica, and Villazón has an easy border crossing with Argentina.

The train between Oruro and Villazón, which stops in Uyuni and Tupiza, provides a fine overland alternative to grueling bus travel.

ORURO

🎵 2 / POP 201,000 / ELEV 3706M (12,158FT)

Oruro is dirty, crowded, the food sucks and there's not much to do outside of Carnaval season. Yet, there's something about this place – the largest berg in the region, a miners' city that takes no slack from anyone – that endears it to visitors, making for an oddly atavistic experience that some may find intoxicating.

In many ways Oruro (which means 'where the sun is born') is the most 'Bolivian' of Bolivia's nine provincial capitals and an intriguing place where 90% of the inhabitants are of indigenous heritage. *Orureños* (Oruro locals) are salty, hard-working and upfront people who have had it tough over the years. Locals refer to themselves as *quirquinchos* (armadillos), after the carapaces used in their *charangos* (traditional Bolivian ukulele-like instruments).

The town sits against a range of low mineral-rich hills at the northern end of the salty lakes Uru Uru and Poopó. Record-high mineral prices are creating a boom in the city – and construction is on the rise. While many visitors skip Oruro altogether, it's got decent museums and there's plenty to see in the surrounding area. It's also culturally very colorful, with a rich dance and musical heritage that culminates in the riotous Carnaval celebrations, famous throughout South America for the lavish costumes and elaborate traditions on display.

History

Founded in the early 17th century, Oruro owes its existence to the mineral-rich 10-sq-km range of hills rising 350m behind the city. Chock-full of copper, silver and tin, these hills still form the city's economic backbone.

By the 1920s Bolivia's thriving tin-mining industry rested in the hands of three powerful capitalists. The most renowned was Simón Patiño, a mestizo from the Cochabamba valley who became one of the world's wealthiest men. In 1897 Patiño purchased La Salvadora mine near the village of Uncia, east of Oruro, which eventually became the

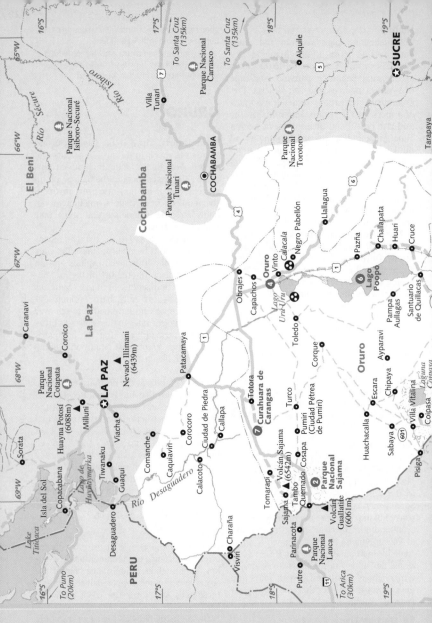

Southern Altiplano Highlights

1 Gorge your senses on the almost extraterrestrial landscapes of the **Los Lípez** (p155) region in the country's far southwest

2 Explore **Parque Nacional Sajama** (p142) with its towering snow-topped volcano, Bolivia's loftiest peak

3 Strap on some sunglasses and wonder at the salty expanse of the **Salar de Uyuni** (p152)

4 Marvel at the stunning costumes of Oruro's boisterous **Carnaval** (p136)

5 Whistle the theme from your favorite Western as you guide your horse up the narrow gullies around **Tupiza** (p158)

⑥ Travel in nomad style on a do-it-yourself adventure around **Lago Poopó** (p152) near Salar de Uyuni

⑦ Sample llama jerky and learn about llama-herding traditions from Aymará pastoralists in **Curahuara de Carangas** (p140)

⑧ Cross the border to the Chilean desert oasis of **San Pedro de Atacama** (p157)

Oruro

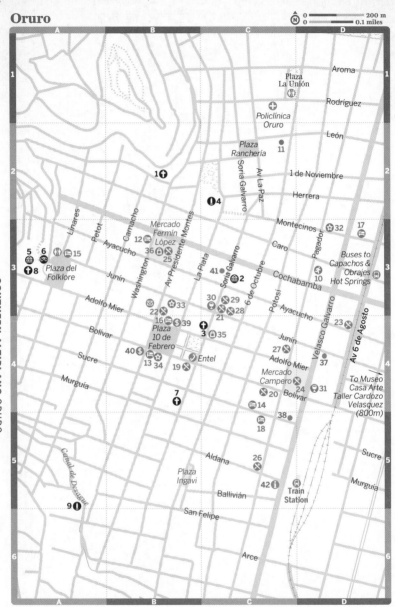

world's most productive tin source. Patiño's fortunes snowballed and by 1924 he had gained control of about 50% of the nation's tin output.

Once secure in his wealth, Patiño emigrated from Bolivia to Britain, where he started buying up European and North American smelters and tin interests. As a consequence, Bolivia found itself exporting both its precious metal and its profits. Public outcry launched a series of labor uprisings, and set the stage for nationalization of the

Oruro

mines in 1952 and the subsequent creation of the government-run Corporación Minera de Bolivia (Comibol).

Decades of government inefficiency, corruption and low global tin prices preceded the push for *capitalización* (a variation on privatization), which eventually brought about the dissolution of Comibol in the mid-1980s. When the last mine closed in Oruro, it was a hard hit for the city.

The price of tin went back up in the early 1990s and a handful of local cooperative mines reopened. Then in 2008 the price of tin dropped to US$7 per pound and salaries plummeted. Things have slowly started to look up since with more than 7% annual income growth in the area, and high mineral and metal prices worldwide.

Orureños are extremely proud that current president Evo Morales is from their province; he was born in Isallavi, a tiny Aymará village on the western side of Lake Poopó, and went to secondary school in Oruro.

Dangers & Annoyances
The region has been mined since preColumbian times and there is an estimated 2 million tons of mining waste sitting on the hillsides outside of town. This waste contaminates the water, the air and the general environment, and clashes between mining and agricultural interests are on the rise.

⊙ Sights
The action around town tends to center on the Plaza 10 de Febrero and Plaza del Folklore. Bolívar is the main commercial drag and a fun people-watching walk in the evening.

Santuario de la Virgen del Socavón CHURCH
(Plaza del Folklore s/n) Miners began worshiping the Virgen de Candelaria (the patron of Oruro miners) on this site in the 16th century.

CHULLPA TOMBS

A *chullpa* is a funerary tower or mausoleum that various Aymará groups built to house the mummified remains of some members of their society, presumably people of high rank or esteem within the community. The Oruro department is particularly rich in *chullpas*, especially along the shores of **Lago Poopó** and around the **Sajama** area. A *chullpa* was constructed of stone or adobe, and typically had a beehive-shaped opening, which nearly always faced east toward the rising sun. The body was placed in the fetal position along with various possessions. Some communities would ritually open the *chullpas* on feast days and make offerings to the mummified ancestors; the Chipaya still do. Most of the tombs, however, have been looted, apart from some bones here and there, and the mummies can now be found in museums, such as the Museo Antropológico Eduardo López Rivas (p134) in Oruro. The biggest concentration is found along the road from Patacamaya to Chile. There are also between 18 and 25 *chullpas* along the Lauca circuit (p142).

The present church, which is a 19th-century reconstruction of the 1781 original, figures prominently in Oruro's Carnaval as the site where good ultimately defeats evil.

Museo Sacro, Folklórico, Arqueológico y Minero
MUSEUM
(Plaza del Folklore s/n; admission both museums B$10, camera/video use B$3/20; ⊙9-11:15am & 3:15-5:30pm) This is an excellent double museum attached to the Santuario de la Virgen del Socavón. Access is by guided tour only. The tour descends from the church down to an old mining tunnel with various tools from both colonial and modern mining eras as well as representations of the devilish El Tío, spirit of the underground. The tour then goes upstairs to the other part of the museum, which has a variety of exhibits, from Wankarani-period stone llama heads to Diablada (Dance of the Devils) costumes. Guides are knowledgeable but they often don't speak English – some exhibits have bilingual explanations.

Cathedral
CHURCH
(Sorria Galvarro s/n) Just east of Plaza 10 Febrero, the cathedral has fine stained glass above the altar. The adjacent tower was constructed by the Jesuits as part of a church built before Oruro was founded. When the Jesuits were expelled, it was designated as the cathedral of the Oruro bishopric. In 1994, the original baroque entrance was moved and reconstructed at the Santuario de la Virgen del Socavón, which presents a grand city view.

Plaza del Folklore Stairway
LOOKOUT
(Plaza del Folklore) Just up from the Plaza del Folklore there's a stairway that takes you huffing and puffing to a handful of interesting murals and a dangerous-looking three-story slide.

Capilla de Serrato
CHURCH
Capilla de Serrato, a steep climb from the end of Calle Washington, offers impressive city views.

Casa de la Cultura Simón Patiño
MUSEUM
(S Galvarro 5755; admission B$8; ⊙8:30-11:30am & 2:30-6pm Mon-Fri, 9am-2:30pm Sat) The former residence of tin baron Simón Patiño includes his furniture, personal bric-a-brac, fine toys (you're not allowed to play with them though) and an ornate art nouveau stairway. Visiting exhibitions are featured in the downstairs lobby; the permanent collection is on the upper level. Entry is by guided tour only.

Portada del Beaterio
CHURCH
(Soria Galvarro s/n) A couple of blocks southeast of Plaza 10 de Febrero, it's worth checking out the Portada del Beaterio, the facade of a convent church carved with ornate vegetal and bird motifs.

Museo Antropológico Eduardo López Rivas
MUSEUM
(España s/n; admission B$3; ⊙8am-noon & 2-6pm Mon-Fri, 10am-6pm Sat & Sun) At the south end of town adjacent to the zoo, the Museo Antropológico Eduardo López Rivas is an anthropological and archaeological museum well worth a visit. The fascinating hodgepodge of exhibits includes mastodons, Carnaval costumes, stone-carved llama heads, mummies from the *chullpares* (funerary towers) that dot the region and skulls exhibiting the horrific cranial deformations once practiced on children. Take any *micro* (half-

sized bus) marked 'Sud' from the northwest corner of Plaza 10 de Febrero or opposite the train station and get off just beyond the old tin-foundry compound.

Museo Mineralógico
MUSEUM

(Ciudad Universitaria; admission B$10; ☺8:30am-noon & 2:30-6pm Mon-Fri, weekends by appointment) On the university campus south of town, the Museo Mineralógico houses a remarkable collection of more than 5200 minerals, precious stones, fossils and crystals from around the world, housed in wooden cabinets amid a series of stairways, exposed bricks and glass. Hop on minibus 102 or 2 or any *micro* marked 'Sud' or 'Ciudad Universitaria' from opposite the train station or Plaza 10 de Febrero.

Museo Casa Arte Taller Cardozo Velasquez
MUSEUM

(☎527-5245; juegueoruro@hotmail.com; Junín 738; admission B$8; ☺no specific hours, call ahead) A family of seven artists – Gonzalo (sculptor), his wife María (potter) and their five daughters – open their whimsical little house and art studio to visitors. The tour includes a peek into their workshop, the many nooks and crannies with artsy bric-a-brac and a leafy patio with Gonzalo's fascinating sculptures – check out the one in the middle, devoted to Pachamama (Mother Earth). If you're lucky, you may even get a tea made with medicinal herbs from their courtyard garden. On Sunday mornings, the family goes out to the streets to paint with children. Every first Friday of the month, they hold a *k'oa* ceremony, an Andean ritual that pays respect to Pachamama, which you are welcome to join if you announce yourself.

Faro de Conchupata
MONUMENT

(Montechinos s/n) On November 17, 1851 Bolivia's red, gold and green flag was first raised at Faro de Conchupata: red for the courage of the Bolivian army, gold for the country's mineral wealth and green for its agricultural wealth. The spot is now marked by a platform and column topped by an enormous glass globe, illuminated at night. It provides a fine vista over the town.

Mina San José
MINE

There are numerous mines in the Oruro area, many operated by *cooperativos* (small groups of miners who purchase temporary rights). One of the most important is Mina San José, which has been in operation for over 450 years. Now run by six *cooperativos*,

they have opened a part of the mine to tourists. The tour, which is available in Spanish only, lasts about three hours and costs B$50. English tours are available through Charlie Tours (p135) for B$250, with transport and guide. To get there, you can take a yellow *micro* (marked 'D' or 'San José') or the light-blue mini (B$5) from the northwest corner of Plaza 10 de Febrero.

🏃 Activities

Club de Montañismo Halcones
ROCK CLIMBING

(cmh_oruro@yahoo.com) Rumi Campana (Bell Rock), named after an unusual acoustic phenomenon, is a climber's playground just 2km northwest of town. On weekends you can practice your skills with the friendly local climbing club, Club de Montañismo Halcones. There's a range of routes with protection already in place. Try your hand at the challenging overhanging routes of the Angel sector. For softer routes, try the Vieja Palestra sector.

🎓 Courses

Centro de Aprendizaje de Lenguas Modernas
LANGUAGE COURSE

(☎528-7676; Pagador 5635; per hr $B40) Drop by for Quechua or Spanish classes.

🔗 Tours

There's a wealth of things to explore in the wild reaches of Oruro department. Tour operators can arrange custom excursions or simpler trips to nearby sites such as Calacala (p142) or the Termas de Obrajes hot springs (p142).

Charlie Tours
GUIDED TOUR

(☎524-0666; charlietours@yahoo.com) Run by the knowledgeable Juan Carlos Vargas, Charlie Tours is a real specialist in the region. In addition to city tours, mine visits and excursions to nearby attractions such as Calacala and Termas de Obrajes, it offers trips to places further afield, including the Chipaya, Salar de Coipasa and Sajama. The offices are outside of town, so call or email.

🛏 Sleeping

Accommodations are often booked solid during Carnaval, when there's also a three-night minimum stay. It's wise to reserve well ahead of time or ask the tourist office about rooms in local homes. Expect to pay up to five or six times the normal price for a room.

A DEVIL OF A GOOD TIME

Oruro's **Carnaval** has become Bolivia's largest and most renowned annual celebration. There are two sides to this party of all parties. For the angels in all of us, there are processions, dances and religious pageantry; for our inner devil, there's plenty of drinking and debauchery in what is one of the biggest water fights the world has ever seen.

In a broad sense, these festivities can be described as reenactments of the triumph of good over evil, but the festival is so interlaced with threads of Christian and indigenous myths, fables, deities and traditions that it would be inaccurate to oversimplify it this way.

The origins of a similar festival may be traced back to the medieval kingdom of Aragón, although *orureños* (Oruro locals) maintain that it commemorates an event that occurred during the early days of their own fair city. Legend has it that one night a thief called Chiruchiru was seriously wounded by a traveler he'd attempted to rob. Taking pity on the wrongdoer, the Virgen de Candelaria gently helped him reach his home near the mine at the base of Cerro Pié del Gallo and succored him until he died. When the miners found him there, an image of the Virgin hung over his head. Today, the mine is known as the **Socavón de la Virgen** (Grotto of the Virgin), and a large church, the **Santuario de la Virgen del Socavón**, has been built over it to house the Virgin, the patron saint of the city. Above the Canal de Desagüe, a massive **statue of the Virgen del Socavón** (Virgin of the Grotto) is being built; it should be completed by the time you read this.

This legend is combined with the ancient Uru tale of Huari and the struggle of Archangel Michael (San Miguel) against the seven deadly sins.

Ceremonies begin several weeks before Carnaval itself, there are various candlelit processions, and dance groups practice boisterously in the city's streets.

Hotel Virgen del Socavón HOTEL **$$**
(☎528-2184; www.hotelvirgendelsocavon.com; Junín 1179; s/d/ste incl breakfast B$280/380/480; P wi-fi) One of the best hotels in town, this modern option has rooms looking right onto the Plaza del Folklore, making it the most sought-after in town at Carnaval time when prices spike tenfold. Outside Carnaval season, it's a good option, with new bedspreads, modernish decor (with plastic chairs) and excellent balconies overlooking the plaza.

Plaza Flores Hotel HOTEL **$$**
(☎525-2561; www.floresplazahotel.com; Mier 735; s/d/tr incl breakfast B$210/300/460; P @ wi-fi) A top midrange choice right on the main plaza, this eight-story, three-star hotel offers recently renovated rooms, good city views and friendly management. Request a room on a higher floor for better views.

Residencial 21 de Abril HOSTEL **$**
(☎527-9205; simon21deabril@bolivia.com; Montecinos 198; d B$50, dm/r per person without bathroom B$40/50; P wi-fi) Probably your best budget bet, this friendly family-run spot is a short walk from the center with bright and tidy rooms, TV and hot water available all day. There's a sauna for guests' use.

Hotel Sumaj Wasi HOTEL **$$**
(☎527-6737; www.hotelessamaywasi.com; Brasil 232; s/d B$160/220; P wi-fi) This attractive business-style hotel near the bus terminal has large rooms offering tiled floors, decent bathrooms with plenty of hot water and cable TV. There is a lingering smell of detergent but, hey, at least you know it's clean. Ask for a room with a patio view.

Hotel Briggs HOTEL **$$$**
(☎525-1724; www.s-hotelbriggs.com.bo; Washington 1206; s/d/tr/ste incl breakfast B$320/480/600/800; P @ wi-fi) Centrally located across Mercado Fermín López, this slightly overpriced option has comfortable, smallish rooms. Some have a private terrace and Jacuzzi, and all have toasty heating.

Hotel Eden BUSINESS HOTEL **$$$**
(☎521-0671; www.hoteleden.com; cnr Bolívar and Presidente Montes; s/d/tr/ste incl breakfast B$560/840/952/980; P wi-fi pool) If you're looking for a business-style hotel, this is it. Big beds (check), flat-screen TVs (check), clean and modern bathrooms, pool, onsite restaurant and casino (check, check, check and check). What's missing is a bit of soul. But who needs soul when you've got cable TV?

As well as traditional Bolivian dance groups, such as the Caporales, Llameradas, Morenadas and Tinkus, Oruro's Carnaval features La Diablada (Dance of the Devils).

The main event kicks off on the Saturday before Ash Wednesday with the spectacular *entrada* (entrance procession) led by the brightly costumed San Miguel character. Behind him, dancing and marching, come the famous devils and a host of bears and condors. The procession is followed by vehicles adorned with jewels (in commemoration of the *achura* rites in which the Inca offered their treasures to Inti, the sun, in the festival of Inti Raymi), and the miners offer the year's highest-quality mineral to El Tío, the demonic owner of all underground minerals and precious metals.

When the archangel and the devils arrive at the soccer stadium, they engage in a series of dances that tell the story of the ultimate battle between good and evil. After it becomes apparent that good has triumphed over evil, the dancers retire to the Santuario de la Virgen del Socavón at dawn on the Sunday, and a Mass is held in honor of the Virgen, who pronounces that good has prevailed.

There's another, less spectacular *entrada* on the Sunday afternoon, and more dance displays on the Monday. The next day, Shrove Tuesday, is marked by family reunions and *cha'lla* libations, in which alcohol is sprinkled over worldly goods to invoke a blessing. The following day people make their way into the surrounding countryside where four rock formations – the Toad, the Viper, the Condor and the Lizard – are also subjected to *cha'lla* as an offering to Pachamama.

Tickets typically cost between B$80 and B$230 for the seats along Av 6 de Agosto. On the main plaza, prime seats cost between B$320 and $450.

Hotel Bernal HOTEL **$**
(☎527-9468; Brasil 701; s/d/tr B$85/130/170) Opposite the bus terminal, this budget option has soft beds, limpid pillows and slightly dirty sheets. The baths are tight, but have a good supply of hot water.

Hotel Repostero HOTEL **$**
(☎525-8001; ph_tania@hotmail.com; Sucre 370; s/d/tr incl breakfast B$150/200/230; P🛜) You'll love the sign at this faded but likeable old place. It has a variety of ever so slightly smoky rooms in two wings, all with cable TV and pretty nice hot showers. The third-story rooms are the best.

Residencial San Miguel HOTEL **$**
(☎527-2132; Sucre 331; s/d without bathroom B$30/50) The cheapest place in town is handy for both the train station and the center, but it's pretty rock bottom in terms of comfort. Hot water is sporadic and rooms are tiny. But at least the threadbare sheets seem to be clean.

✗ Eating

Local specialties include *thimpu de cordero* (a mutton-and-vegetable concoction smothered with *llajua,* a hot tomato-based sauce) and *charquekan* (sun-dried llama meat with corn, potatoes, eggs and cheese).

Note that most restaurants are closed on Sunday evening, except the fast-food places along the main plaza.

Mercado Campero MARKET **$**
(food B$5-15; ⊘6am-8pm) There are rows of lunch spots at this market, as well as drinks stalls serving *mate* (a herbal infusion of coca, chamomile or similar), *api* (a local drink made of maize) and coffee. You will find similar offerings at **Mercado Fermín López** (food B$5-15; ⊘6am-8pm).

Restaurant Ardentia INTERNATIONAL **$**
(S Galvarro; mains B$17-27; ⊘6:30-11pm Mon-Sat) We don't know how Halle Berry would feel about the restaurant using her likeness for its publicity, but copyright infringement issues aside, this is probably one of the best restaurants in town. It has a thoughtfully prepared lasagna, simple but savory chicken and beef dishes, and familiar standards such as hamburgers. Surely Halle would approve.

Nayjama BOLIVIAN **$$**
(cnr Aldana & Pagador; mains B$30-55; ⊘closed for dinner Sun) This appealing choice serves high-quality traditional *oreño* food with a dash of innovation. The servings are huge, so ask for half a portion of anything you order.

ANDEAN CAMELIDS

There's nothing like them on earth – playful, elegant, independent, ecological and cute as hell – the camelids of the Andes are the species that define a continent.

Unlike the Old World, the western hemisphere had few grazing mammals after the Pleistocene era, when mammoths, horses and other large herbivores disappeared from North and South America. For millennia, the Andean people relied on the New World camelids – the wild guanaco and vicuña, and the domesticated llama and alpaca – for food, fiber and companionship.

Both of the domesticated varieties are highly ecological, friendly animals. Cross the Altiplano and you are likely to see perfect circles of llama poop. Yes, in order to fulfill their Darwinian obligations, llamas and alpacas all poop in the same place, protecting the delicate Andean high plains from turning into a veritable desert. They also emit less noxious gas than other livestock – not insignificant considering that 18% of the world's CO_2 emissions come from livestock according to the Food and Agricultural Organization, and most of that comes from the 1.5 billion cows now living on our little blue planet. Don't want to become a vegan just yet? No worries, the low CO_2-emitting llamas also have low-fat, zero-cholesterol meat. And it tastes great – somewhere between beef and lamb – whether in a stew, steak or jerky.

Until just recently, many Bolivian pastoralists had fairly large llama herds, but they kept them more as pets and pack animals, only sacrificing animals on occasion for big feasts. This asset-rich, cash-poor scenario – llamas are worth about $100 each, and most high-plains ranchers have herds of around 80 head – prompted the Bolivian government to invest heavily in camelids through projects like Proyecto Vale (www.proyectovale.com, in Spanish) that look to protect the environment, reduce desertification and provide new uses for camelids throughout the high plains. Now, with demand rising on international markets for llama meat and alpaca and vicuña wool, many Bolivian ranchers are also turning back to their Inca roots and getting rid of their sheep and cattle herds in favor of alpacas and llamas.

Lamb is the specialty, as is *cabeza* (sheep's head served with salad and dehydrated potatoes). The English menu is slightly more expensive so ask for the Spanish one.

La Casona
ITALIAN $

(Montes 5969; pizzas from B$20) Straight-out-of-the-oven *salteñas* (meat and vegetable pasties), quick sandwiches for lunch, and pizza and pasta for dinner keep this little place buzzing, especially at night when it gets really busy and warm.

Las Delicias
BOLIVIAN $$

(6 de Agosto 1284; almuerzo B$13-25, mains B$28-50) Of the several *churrasquerías* (grilled meat restaurants) on this long street, Las Delicias is the best, with attentive service, sizzling tableside *parrilladas* (plates of mixed grilled meats), great *almuerzos* (set lunches) and a pleasant covered patio.

El Fogon
BOLIVIAN $

(Brasil 5021; mains B$25) One of your best bets in town for *charquekan*, this glossy diner-style eatery may feel like a chain, but locals love it.

Irupana
SELF-CATERING $

(S Galvarro 5891) This health-food chain has a great selection of nutritious snacks – but not a Nacho Cheese Dorito in sight.

Pagador
BOLIVIAN $

(Pagador 1440; almuerzo B$15, mains B$25-45) This no-frills restaurant is deservedly popular with locals. The fixed lunch is especially good on the covered patio outside.

Pastelería Dumbo
BAKERY $

(Junín, near 6 de Octubre; almuerzo B$9; ⊘closed Sat & Sun) A decent quick stop for cakes, empanadas, *salteñas*, hot drinks and *helados* (ice creams).

El Huerto
CAFE $

(Bolívar near Pagador; almuerzo B$10; ⊘closed Sat) Tasty cakes, snacks and cooked-to-order vegetarian lunches are served at this friendly hole-in-the-wall.

Bravo's Pizza
PIZZERIA $

(cnr Bolívar & S Galvarro; pizzas B$19-30, pastas B$28-45) Bright, with big windows overlooking the square and a light ambience, this 2nd-floor eatery has 20 varieties of pizza,

Species at a Glance

Vicuña (Vicugna vicugna) Nearly hunted to extinction for their fine wool – once reserved exclusively for Inca emperors – the delicate rusty-orange vicuña are rebounding throughout the Andes. Innovative catch-and-shear programs and increased patrols have cut down on poaching, and there are now around 350,000 vicuña across Argentina, Bolivia, Chile, Ecuador and Peru. Bolivia has around 60,000, and the populations are on the rise. You are likely to see them in Parque Nacional Sajama, Reserva Nacional de Fauna Andina Eduardo Avaroa, Área Natural de Manejo Integrado Nacional Apolobamba and in other wild areas above 4000m. Ongoing threats to the vicuña include a lack of continuous protected areas, degraded land and poaching (vicuña blood is believed to cure all kinds of ailments, and the wool is worth US$400 on local markets and up to US$2000 on international markets per pound).

Guanaco (Lama guanicoe) These wily brownish animals are rarely seen in Bolivia, even though they will inhabit a much wider range than their wild vicuña cousins: from sea level up to 4000m or higher. They are sometimes seen in the highland plains of the Reserva Nacional de Fauna Andina Eduardo Avaroa.

Alpaca (Vicugna pacos) These domesticated animals are prized for their fine wool, used to make shawls, sweaters and scarves. Smaller and more delicate than their llama brethren, alpacas require well-watered grasslands and are more common in lower elevations.

Llama (L glama) The taller, rangier and hardier llama has relatively coarse wool that is used for blankets, ropes and other household goods. It also works as a pack animal, but thanks to the introduction of the camión (flatbed truck), llama trains are increasingly rare in Bolivia. Llamas can survive in dry, poor pastures, making them ideal for the harsh Altiplano.

SOUTHERN ALTIPLANO ORURO

including a spicy one with dried llama meat, plus hamburgers, sandwiches, burritos and breakfasts (B$20).

🍷 Drinking & Entertainment

Bar Huari BAR
(Junín 608, cnr S Galvarro) Not much seems to have changed in this traditional bar since the 1930s – locals still while away the evenings playing games and drinking beer in its series of high-ceilinged rooms. There are cheap *almuerzos* (B$10) and dinner options.

Dali CAFE
(Plaza 10 de Febrero, 2nd floor; ◷10am-2am) About as hoity-toity as you can get in Oruro, this stylish and popular cafe caters to Oruro's young set. Come for the drinks – not the food.

Fruit Juice Stalls JUICE BAR
(V Galvarro) On hot days, locals flock to the row of excellent fruit juice stalls opposite the Mercado Campero.

Club Social Arabe LIVE MUSIC
(Junín 729; ◷closed Sun) A slice of old-fashioned Oruro, this 2nd-floor spot hosts occasional live music on weekends.

Metro DANCE
(Plaza 10 de Febrero, basement) This subterranean nightclub caters to Oruro's youngsters. Expect a lot of boom, boom, boom.

Bravo Bravo KARAOKE
(Montecinos near Pagador) The best karaoke in town is run by the owners of Bravo's Pizza.

Palais Concert Cinema CINEMA
(Plaza 10 de Febrero) Housed in an opulent baroque-style, colonial-era concert hall, this no-name cinema was closed for renovations at the time of writing, but should screen first-run films nightly.

🛍 Shopping

The design, creation and production of artistic Diablada (Dance of the Devil) masks and costumes is the main focus of retail in Oruro. Av La Paz, between León and Villarroel, is lined with small workshops offering devil masks, headdresses, costumes and other devilish things.

Hawkers sell cheap *zampoñas* (pan flutes made of hollow reeds), *charangos* and other indigenous musical instruments near the train station.

A street market takes over the streets surrounding Mercado Fermín López on Wednesday and Saturday.

Mercado Tradicional MARKET
(middle row, Mercado Fermín López) The impressive Mercado Tradicional has more dried llama fetuses and flamingo wings than a voodoo master has pins. The affable vendors are more than happy to explain the usage of their wares, but make sure to ask if you want to take a photo.

For more herbal remedies and witchcraft items, head to Calle Junín between V Galvarro and 6 de Agosto.

ARAO Artesanías Oruro ARTS & CRAFTS
(Mier 5999) This place offers an excellent selection of high-quality, cooperatively produced handicrafts from four communities in the Oruro department.

Information

Emergency

Tourist police (☎528-7774) Round-the-clock operation at the bus terminal; shares the kiosk with the tourist info point and gives out maps.

Immigration

Migración (☎527-0239; S Galvarro, btwn Ayacucho & Cochabamba; ⊗8:30am-12:30pm & 2:30-6:30pm Mon-Fri) Extend your stay here – it's the last door on the left.

Internet Access

There are plenty of places to get online in Oruro (for about B$3 per hour). Many also offer cheap international calls.

Laundry

Andes Dry Cleaners (Sucre 240, at Pagador; per kg B$10) Offers a 24-hour service.

Medical Services

Policlínica Oruro (☎524-2871; Rodríguez, btwn La Paz & 6 de Octubre) Near Plaza la Unión, this is Oruro's best hospital.

Money

There are several banks with ATMs in town (as well as change kiosks at the bus and train stations), which will change several currencies, including euros (at a pretty poor rate). There are several Western Union offices.

Banco Bisa (Plaza 10 de Febrero) Cashes Amex traveler's checks into bolivianos without commission (for US dollars, there's a US$6 fee).

Banco de Crédito (Plaza 10 de Febrero) ATM issues US dollars or bolivianos.

WORTH A TRIP

CURAHUARA DE CARANGAS

This scenic village halfway between Oruro and Sajama has a lovely adobe-and-thatch church, a community hostel, and plenty of hiking and adventure opportunities nearby. Attractions worth visiting include the following:

Sistine Chapel of the Altiplano This lovely adobe-and-thatch church (admission B$30, inquire at the hostel for entrance) contains a wealth of lovely naive 17th-century frescoes depicting typical mestizo-style themes. There are plenty of Biblical scenes as well as, plus some interesting artifacts in a small room behind the altar.

Palestra Calachua Just 2km from town, this climbing spot has interesting natural formations, and makes for a good afternoon jaunt.

Monterani Get up early to hit the summit of this nearby mountain, which has been revered by local indigenous communities for centuries.

Pukara de Pichaca Ask around for directions to this nearby Aymará fortress.

Accommodations options include the community-run **Hostal Kory Wara** (☎6708-5005; hkorywara@hotmail.com; near the entrance to town; r per person incl breakfast B$50), which offers cozy rooms, friendly service, a fun common area draped with Andean textiles, as well as plenty of tips on trips to the nearby countryside. There are heaters in the rooms, but it's still good to bring a sleeping bag if you've got one.

To get here, inquire at **Trans Sajama** (☎7407-1385; Plaza) for the regular service to Patacamaya (B$10, 2½ hours). You can also grab an Arica-bound bus from La Paz and ask to be dropped at the *cruce* (crossroads), where you can hump it the 5km into town or get a taxi (B$25).

Post

Post office (Av Presidente Montes) The main post office is just north of Plaza 10 de Febrero. Parcels must first be inspected by the Aduana Nacional (Customs; Velasco Galvarro at Junín), which is located where the city's fort once stood.

Telephone

Entel (Calle Bolívar, Plaza 10 de Febrero area) The modern Entel office is west of the corner of Soña Galvarro and Bolívar; there are numerous other call centers around town. There's also a Punto Entel and last-minute postal kiosk downstairs at the bus terminal.

Tourist Information

Tourist information office (Caseta de Información Turística; across from bus terminal and train station) These booths give out city maps and leaflets – tourist police are occasionally on hand.

ⓘ Getting There & Away

Bus

All long-distance buses use the **bus terminal** (☎527-9535; terminal fee B$1.50), a 15-minute walk or short cab ride northeast of Oruro's center. To get here, head north on S de Agosto until you hit Aroma, then turn left and continue walking for a few blocks. There's a *casa de cambio* (money-changing office) on the upper level, luggage storage (B$5) on the ground floor and a sporadically open tourist info kiosk, which provides maps.

Buses to La Paz depart every half-hour, and there are several departures for Cochabamba, Potosí and Sucre. For Santa Cruz, you must make a connection in Cochabamba. Night buses to Uyuni leave between 7pm and 8pm – they are freezing cold, so bring a sleeping bag.

There is daily service to Arica, Calama and Iquique in Chile, which generally departs in the evening.

BUS COSTS & DISTANCES

DESTINATION	COST (B$)	DURATION (HR)
Arica (Chile)	100	10
Calama (Chile)	130	20
Cochabamba	20	4
Iquique (Chile)	80	8
La Paz	20	3
Potosí	25	5
Sucre	80	8
Tarija	70	20
Tupiza	60	12
Uyuni	30–35	8

Train

Trains run south from Oruro to Villazón on the border with Argentina, passing through Uyuni, Atocha and Tupiza along the way. The Expreso del Sur is slightly more luxurious, departing Oruro on Tuesdays and Fridays. Cheaper service is had on the Wara Wara line, leaving Oruro on Wednesdays and Sundays. There is return service from Villazón on Mondays, Wednesdays, Thursdays and Saturdays. From Uyuni, you can get slow trains to Calama in Chile.

Buy tickets at least a day ahead from the **train station** (☎527-4605; www.fca.com.bo; ⏰8:15-11:30am & 2:30-6pm Mon & Thu, 8:15am-6pm Tue & Fri, 8:15am-noon & 2:30-7pm Wed, 8:15-11:30am & 3-7pm Sun). Don't forget to bring your passport. On train days, there's a left-luggage kiosk here. Watch your belongings on the train, and bring a sleeping bag.

EXPRESO DEL SUR

RUN	COST (COACH/1ST)	FROM ORURO TUE & FRI
Oruro–Uyuni	B$56/112	3:30-10:20pm
Uyuni–Atocha	B$77/168	10:40pm-12:45am
Atocha–Tupiza	B$101/224	12:55-4am
Tupiza–Villazón	B$119/261	4:10-7:05am

WARA WARA

RUN	COST (NORMAL/ COACH/1ST)	FROM ORURO WED & SUN
Oruro–Uyuni	B$32/44/95	7pm-2:20am
Uyuni–Atocha	B$42/57/126	2:50-5am
Atocha–Tupiza	B$56/75/170	5:20-8:35am
Tupiza–Villazón	B$67/94/205	9:05am-12:05pm

ⓘ Getting Around

Micros (half-sized buses; B$0.80 to B$1.50) and minibuses (B$1) connect the city center with outlying areas. Their routes are designated by their letters, colors and signs (and in the case of minibuses, numbers). It's a fairly confusing system so check with the driver before boarding. Note that micros and minibuses are small and crowded so, if possible, avoid carrying luggage aboard.

Taxis around the center, including to and from the terminals, cost a non-negotiable B$3. **Radio taxis** (☎527-7775) cost around B$4.

AROUND ORURO

There's plenty to see around Oruro, particularly along the road south toward Uyuni, where bleak and epic scenery surrounds old mines and the remnants of ancient lakeside cultures. These areas can be visited by bus from Oruro or on a tour.

The **Termas de Obrajes hot springs** (admission B$10), 25km northeast of town, is a popular destination. It's a well-run complex, with a pool and a private rooms with tubs that you can rent by the half-hour. There's an unspectacular restaurant adjacent to a modest hotel. From the corner of Caro and Av 6 de Agosto, catch an Obrajes *micro* (B$7, 30 minutes) from 7:30am to 5pm daily, which passes the grungier **Capachos hot springs** (admission B$3), 10km east of town. The last *micro* to Oruro departs at 4pm.

The atmospheric **Calacala** (admission B$40) makes a worthwhile trip from Oruro. The site consists of a series of rock paintings of llamas and humans in red and orange tones, presumably dating from the first millennium BC. It's located under an overhang 2.5km beyond the village of Calacala, which is 26km east of Oruro. Stop in the village to locate the guard who has the keys and collects the fee; she can often be found in the small cafe marked by a rusted Pepsi sign. The site itself is a 30-minute walk past the village, near the old brewery. The views from the site of the exceptionally beautiful valley, which provides some of Oruro's water, are spectacular. There's no public transport unless it's the feast day of Señor de la Laguna (Lord of the Lake) on September 14; a taxi there and back will cost you B$120.

Poopó, a tough mining town halfway between Oruro and Uyuni, offers authentic glimpses of Andean life, plus hot springs and a resort-style hotel. There are mining ruins at the entry to town that are haunting to say the least.

PARQUE NACIONAL SAJAMA

Bolivia's first national park occupies 1000 sq km abutting the Chilean border. The park offers expansive high-plains views, geyser fields, hot springs, and climbing and hiking opportunities aplenty.

Parque Nacional Sajama was created on November 5, 1945 for the protection of the rare wildlife that inhabit this northern extension of the Atacama Desert. Unfortunately, depredation has already eliminated several species. With increased protection, however, vicuña populations are on the rise – they were nearly hunted to extinction for their highly prized wool. You may also spot condors, flamingos, rheas and armadillos.

The world's highest forest covers the foothills flanking the awe-inspiring Volcán Sajama which, at 6542m, is Bolivia's highest peak. The forest consists of dwarf queñua trees, an endemic and ancient Altiplano species. But while technically a forest, it's a little underwhelming – the 'trees' look more like little bushes!

◉ Sights & Activities

The best map of the park is the glossy 1:50,000 *Nevado Sajama* published by Walter Guzmán Córdova; it can be found in better La Paz bookstores.

Volcán Sajama   VOLCANO
The volcano is a popular mountain to climb, especially between May and September; there are also some hikes on its lower slopes. Although it's a relatively straightforward climb, Sajama's altitude and icy conditions make the peak more challenging than it initially appears. Quite a few La Paz agencies offer organized climbs of Sajama. Only consider going without a guide if you have experience with high-altitude climbing, but

---

WORTH A TRIP

LAUCA

This growing tourist circuit near Parque Nacional Sajama is slowly attracting visitors. It's organized between three communities – Macaya, Julo and Sacabaya – that are trying to promote the area and boost their income. Highlights include several lagoons with flamingos and about 25 painted *chullpas* (funerary towers) that were erected between 1470 and 1540. The area is difficult to visit independently so your best bet is to go with Bolivia Millenaria (p347); the tour can be done in about four hours from Sajama National Park and costs B$425, with jeep transportation, entrance fee and lunch. You can ask to be dropped off in Tambo Quemado if continuing on to Chile.

Parque Nacional Sajama

prepare for extremely cold and icy conditions and carry lots of water close to your body (otherwise it will freeze). Do not try to climb the volcano in the rainy season; the electrical storms make this a dangerous time to ascend.

Hot Springs
SWIMMING

(B$30) For a relaxing warm soak, there are four lovely 35°C hot springs 8km northwest of Sajama village, an easy 45-minute walk; look for the bright orange house to the left of the road. Ask at your hotel about other undeveloped hot springs in the area – there are several.

Geyser Field
GEYSER

About 7km (1½ hours on foot) due west of Sajama is an interesting spouting geyser field. You could potentially combine this with a two- or three-day trekking circuit that takes you from the village of Sajama past the Lagunas Khasira, Sora and Chiar Khota.

Laguna Huañakota
LAKE

About 12km north of the village of Sajama, this lake is worth a day trip.

🛏️ Sleeping & Eating

Most people stay in the village of **Sajama** (4250m). Camping is fine just about anywhere in this sparsely populated region, so a tent and a good cold-weather sleeping bag are recommended. You can also contact the **tourism office** (☏513-5526; tatasajama@ hotmail.com; SERNAP headquarters) in Sajama village about **homestays** (per person B$35-55) with local families. There are numerous hotels in town, each serving breakfast (B$16), lunch (B$20) and dinner (B$20).

Hostal Sajama
LODGE $

(☏7150-9185; eliseosajama@hotmail.com; southern entrance to Sajama village; r per person B$70) With traditional-style thatched-roof huts, firm beds, clean sheets and electric heaters (nice!), this is your best bet in town. The arched ceilings give a feeling of openness to the otherwise tight rooms, with Andean textiles adding to the overall charm. Even with the electric heat, you may wish to bring a sleeping bag. Meals are B$16 to B$20.

ⓟ Albergue Ecoturístico
Tomarapi   LODGE $$$
(⌨in La Paz 2-241-4753; www.millenariantours.com/tours/eco-hostels; s/d B$400/550) Albergue Ecoturístico Tomarapi, on the northern border of the park, 12km beyond Sajama, is an enticing community-run 35-bed ecolodge, which offers the area's most comfortable accommodations. It has been widely cited as an ideal model for community involvement in tourism projects, with about 31 families from the nearby village of Caripe working at the lodge on a rotational basis. Occupying a lovely thatched building, styled along traditional local architectural lines, it boasts simple, comfortable rooms with private baths and hot water and a very welcome log fire. It also offers excellent food, featuring lots of alpaca meat. Rates include two meals per day. A two-day program from La Paz is available for B$1020 per person, including three meals per day, private transportation, a bilingual guide and visits to attractions in Sajama National Park.

❶ Information

Park admission (B$30, for which you are also provided with a small map) is payable at the Servicio Nacional de Areas Protegidas (SERNAP) headquarters in the sleepy Sajama village, 18km north of the Arica–La Paz highway. The fee applies to all foreigners, including those just visiting the village. SERNAP will help climbing expeditions organize mules and porters to carry equipment to the base camp; guides cost around B$560 per day, porters about B$140 for the climb.

❶ Getting There & Away

There is a daily bus from the town of Patacamaya to Sajama village (B$25, 12pm, 3½ hours); a return bus departs Sajama village at 6am. Patacamaya is easily reached on most buses from La Paz to Cochabamba, Oruro and Arica. La Paz–Arica buses pass through Parque Nacional Sajama – the border crossing between Tambo Quemado (Bolivia) and Chungará (Chile) 12km away is straightforward and open from 8am till 8pm. You could conceivably ask the bus driver to drop you at the park entrance and walk the 11km into Sajama village, or call the Hostal Sajama and ask for a lift.

UYUNI & THE SOUTHWEST CIRCUIT

Bolivia's southwestern corner is an awe-inspiring collection of diverse landscapes ranging from the blinding white Salar de Uyuni salt flat to the geothermal hotbed of Los Lípez, one of the world's harshest wilderness regions and an important refuge for many Andean wildlife species. The ground here literally boils with minerals, and the spectrum of color is extraordinary. A circuit from Uyuni takes you through absolutely unforgettable, literally breathtaking landscapes and is the highlight of many people's visit to Bolivia.

Although it gets plenty of visitors, in many ways Bolivia's southwest is still a remote wilderness, with rough dirt roads, scattered mining settlements, quinoa-producing villages and little public transportation. The main town, Uyuni, is a military outpost with a real frontier feel; at times you expect the harsh temperatures and biting winds to do away with it altogether. It's the launching point for expeditions into the region, from the desolate expanses of the *salares* to the craggy hills of Los Lípez, which rise into the high Andean peaks along the Chilean frontier. Way south, Tupiza has a pleasant climate, and plenty of hiking, biking and horseback riding adventures.

Much of the region is nominally protected in the Reserva Nacional de Fauna Andina Eduardo Avaroa, which was created in 1973, covers an area of 7150 sq km and receives in excess of 50,000 visitors annually. Its emphasis is on preserving the vicuña and the yareta plant, both of which are threatened in Bolivia, as well as other endemic species and unique ecosystems.

Most people visit the attractions that are part of the Southwest Circuit on an organized trip from Uyuni or Tupiza. Apart from a couple of Entel points, there are no phones out in the Southwest Circuit – all communication is by radio. Any phone numbers listed in this section are for offices located in Uyuni. Note that the toilet facilities in most stops along the way cost B$5.

Uyuni

POP 18,700 / ELEV 3669M (12,037FT)

Seemingly built in defiance of the desert-like landscape, Uyuni stands desolate yet undaunted in Bolivia's southwestern corner.

UYUNI DAY TRIPPER

If you have a few more days in Uyuni, consider heading out to explore some of the forgotten towns and sites around the area.

Pulcayo This semi-ghost town, 22km northeast of Uyuni, has some interesting architecture – including the mansion of Bolivia's 22nd President, Aniceto Arce Ruíz. There are decaying locomotives from the area's 18th-century heyday, cooperative mines, cool rock formations and the potential to do low-fi mine tours with a local guide. A bus (B$5) leaves for here from in front of Uyuni's post office.

Colchani Sometimes included on the *salar* tours, this town has a small **museum** (B$5) dedicated to the salt trade and a few interesting cooperative salt extraction cooperatives. If you are doing the salt flat on your own, this is the kick-off spot.

Mention Uyuni to a Bolivian and they will whistle and emphasize *harto frío* (extreme cold). Yet despite the icy conditions, Uyuni's got a cheerful buzz about it with hundreds of travelers passing through every week to kick off their tour of the Salar de Uyuni or the Southwest Circuit.

Although there's not much to see here, and the wind chill can strip your soul bare as you pace the wide streets, Uyuni's isolated position and outlook elicit an affectionate respect from both Bolivians and foreign travelers.

Founded in 1889 by Bolivian president Aniceto Arce, Uyuni remains an important military base. Tourism and mining are the other major sources of employment in the town. The world's largest lithium reserve – about 100 million tons – lies beneath the neighboring salt flat, and could potentially fuel all the iPods and electric cars the world could build over the next century. While work on building extraction and processing facilities has been slow going, expect more and more mining activity near Uyuni in coming years.

◎ Sights

FREE **Cementerio de Trenes**   HISTORIC SITE
The only real tourist attraction in Uyuni itself is the Cementerio de Trenes (Train Cemetery), a large collection of historic steam locomotives and rail cars dating back to the 18th century, when there was a rail-car factory in Uyuni. Today they sit decaying in the yards about 3km southwest of the modern-day station along Av Ferroviaria. They're fun to climb on, and it's a nice walk from town to keep you warm. Many tours visit the train cemetery as a first or last stop on the three-day *salar* circuit.

Museo Arqueología y Antropológico de los Andes Meridionales   MUSEUM
(Arce at Colón; admission B$5; ◎8am-noon & 2:20-6:30pm Mon-Fri) The Museo Arqueología y Antropológico de los Andes Meridionales is a small affair featuring mummies, long skulls, fossils, ceramics and textiles. There are also Spanish descriptions of the practices of mummification and cranial deformation.

Markets   MARKET
(◎Sun & Thu) The big market day in Uyuni is Thursday when Avenida Potosí gets taken over by stalls selling anything from arts and crafts to television sets; Sunday is a smaller market day.

⛟ Tours

While you can theoretically visit the Salar de Uyuni and the attractions of the Southwest Circuit independently, it is extremely challenging due to unreliable transport and the remoteness of the area. The vast majority of people take an organized tour from either Uyuni or Tupiza. From the end of December to the end of March, the salt flat floods and many agencies shut down, and you can travel just 10km into the salt flat.

Costs
Tours cost B$700 to B$800 for three days at a standard agency, and B$800 to B$1000 at a high-end operation. Four-day and custom trips will cost B$800 and up. The tours include a driver (who also serves as your guide, mechanic and cook, but probably doesn't speak English), two nights accommodation (quality varies depending on the agency), three meals a day and transit. You'll also need to pay a B$30 entrance fee to Isla Incahuasi and a B$150 fee to enter the Reserva

Uyuni

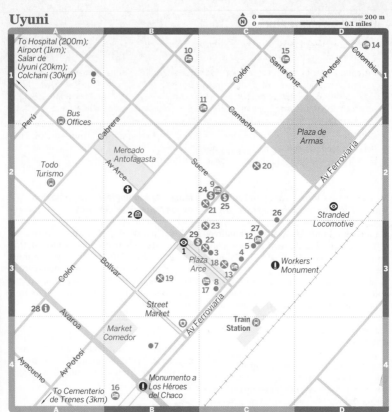

To Hospital (200m);
Airport (1km);
Salar de
Uyuni (20km);
Colchani (30km)

Perú

Bus
Offices

Cabrera

Av Arce

Mercado
Antofagasta

Todo
Turismo

Colón

Santa Cruz

Av Potosi

Colombia

Camacho

Sucre

Plaza de
Armas

Av Ferroviaria

Stranded
Locomotive

Bolívar

Colón

Plaza
Arce

Avaroa

Av Potosi

Ayacucho

Market
Comedor

Street
Market

Av Ferroviaria

Workers'
Monument

Train
Station

To Cementerio
de Trenes (3km)

Monumento a
Los Héroes
del Chaco

SOUTHERN ALTIPLANO UYUNI

Nacional de Fauna Andina Eduardo Avaroa (p155). Those traveling on to Chile will need B$21 to B$50 for the border crossing. Many agencies don't accept credit cards.

What to Bring

You'll want to bring a couple liters of water, snacks, headlamp, sunscreen, sunglasses, sunhat, warm clothes (gloves, stocking cap, waterproof/windproof jacket, wool socks, long underwear, sweater), cards or a game to play at the hotels, camera and chargers. A sleeping bag is also highly recommended. Ask your operator to include a free sleeping bag rental in your fee. Otherwise, they cost about B$50 to rent and are really worth it.

Choosing an Agency

Generally, it doesn't matter which agency you book with (other than the high-end ones), as most agencies share drivers and tend to sort travelers into groups of five or six people. This means that while you may

book with Agency A, you may end up in a car with a driver from Agency Z.

This said, you do have some power here. Talk to returning travelers, multiple agencies and use your judgment to pick a good operator. If you are custom-building an itinerary, have the agency put it in writing. If you can make your own group (try the pub), you'll be better off. The high-end agencies have better hotels, can customize tours and have more reliable cars.

A number of travelers have died on this trip, mostly in drunk-driving accidents – unscrupulous tour operations are not uncommon. Ask to see the car you will be traveling in (Toyota Landcruisers are the best) and to meet the driver ahead of time. If the agency tries to switch drivers or cars on you, call them on it. Along the way, make sure your driver is not drinking alcohol (and demand to switch cars if he is). It's also a good idea to ask to see photos of the hotel where you will be staying.

Uyuni

Standard Tours
The most popular tour is the three-day circuit taking in the **Salar de Uyuni**, **Laguna Colorada**, **Sol de Mañana**, **Laguna Verde** and points in between. There are probably 20 to 50 people a day doing this trip.

You can also book a day trip for B$200 to **Isla Incahuasi**, but really, you've come all this way, so you might as well go on with the rest of the pilgrims.

Your driver is generally your cook, and the quality of food varies. Vegetarians should make arrangements with the operator ahead of time (and bring plenty of snacks just in case). Higher-end operators offer nicer hotels – with heaters and down comforters – and better food.

Custom Tours
Check with the agency about reversing the standard circuit. That way you will arrive at the *salar* early in the morning on the third day, when the lighting is at its best.

If you have the time and cash to customize a trip, consider creating a four-day custom tour that includes a volcano climb, a visit to local communities and a possible final drop off in Tupiza.

Another option offered by a variety of agencies is to do the three-day circuit and then connect at Laguna Verde with an onward transfer to the pretty town of San Pedro de Atacama in northeast Chile. This is now a popular means of crossing between Bolivia and Chile. When booking, check that the price of the transfer to San Pedro is included.

Tour Agencies
There are around 80 agencies in town. Here are some recommended options.

Andrea Tours   GUIDED TOUR
(☑693-2638; www.salar-andreatours.com; Arce 27) Another office is at Peru 200, behind the bus terminal.

Cordillera Tours   GUIDED TOUR
(☑693-3304; www.cordilleratraveller.com; Ferroviaria 314) Good choice for transfers to Chile.

Fremen Tours   GUIDED TOUR
(☑693-3543; www.andes-amazonia.com; Sucre 325) This upmarket option focuses on community-based tourism, and has accommodation agreements with the Tayka Hotels on the Salar Tour. It also offers a few 'alternative routes' like a visit to a cave at Chiquini or a day with llama herders in San Pedro de Quimes.

WARNING: SALAR TOURS

Operators are piled high in Uyuni: there are currently more than 80 agencies offering trips to the *salar* (salt plain). Most offer Spanish-speaking drivers who take you on an identical three-day trip. While the competition may mean more choice, it also means lowered quality as many dodgy operators try to make a fast buck. It's your right to negotiate but remember that cost-cutting leads to operators cutting corners – at the expense of your safety and the environment! Common exploits include trying to cram an extra body into the jeep (six people should be the maximum).

The results of this have included deadly accidents. At least 21 people, including 17 tourists, have been killed in jeep accidents on the Salar de Uyuni salt plains since May 2008. There have been alarming reports of ill-equipped vehicles without seatbelts, speeding tour operators, a lack of emergency equipment, breakdowns, drunk drivers, poor food and service, and disregard for the once-pristine environment of the *salar*.

See Choosing an Agency on p146 for tips on picking a safe and reliable operator.

Hidalgo Tours   GUIDED TOUR
(☑693-2989; www.salardeuyuni.net; Potosí 113, Hotel Jardines de Uyuni) This upscale agency owns a couple of salt hotels.

Toñito Tours   GUIDED TOURS
(☑693-2094; www.bolivianexpeditions.com; Ferroviaria 152) More upmarket.

Other options include **Expediciones Empexsa** (☑693-2348; expedicion_empexsa@hotmail.com; Ferroviaria s/n) and **Turismo El Desierto** (☑693-3087; Ferroviaria s/n).

★ Festivals & Events

Annual Festival   PARADES
Uyuni's big annual festival falls on July 11 and marks the founding of the town. Celebrations involve parades, speeches, dancing, music and, naturally, lots of drinking.

🛏 Sleeping

The best of the bunch fill up fast in the high season so reservations are recommended, especially if you're chugging in on a late-night train. Only better hotels offer heating – and you should bring a sleeping bag if you have one. This is the frontier, and even the best hotels have heaters that fail, hot water that doesn't work and electricity that turns off. In the rainy season, prices are slightly lower and it's not as cold at night. Note that there are water rations in Uyuni year-round. Do not sleep with a propane heater in your room – you can die from the carbon monoxide.

UYUNI

Los Girasoles Hotel   HOTEL $$
(☑693-3323; girasoleshotel@hotmail.com; Santa Cruz 155; s/d/tr B$280/480/600) This spacious and handsome hotel has helpful service and attractive rooms with big comfortable beds, a TV, cactus-wood paneling and gas-heated bathrooms. It also offers a generous buffet breakfast, bike rental (per hour B$65) and laundry service (per kilo B$20).

Jardines de Uyuni   HACIENDA $$$
(☑693-2989; www.hotelesrusticosjardines.com; Potosí 113; s/d/tr incl breakfast B$420/525/700; @🦮🏊) Built around a courtyard in a delightful rustic style, this adobe hotel has the best common areas and overall panache in town. The rooms are on the small side and can be a bit dark, but all are well appointed with tasteful decorations and comfy beds. Needless to say, it's a popular choice for high-end tour groups, so book ahead. Other pluses include a pretty bar area, hammocks, a sauna and an indoor pool (only open on occasion).

Hostal Aymará   HACIENDA $$
(☑693-2227; www.tamboaymara.com; Camacho s/n; s/d/ste incl breakfast B$280/380/420; ℗) This stylish hacienda-style option has terrific common areas. The rooms have local touches including Bolivian textiles. There are also flannel sheets and electric heaters to you keep you warm. Some rooms are a bit dark but there's reliable hot water and the service is friendly.

Hostal La Magia de Uyuni   HOTEL $$
(☑693-2541; www.hostalmagiauyuni.com; Colón 432; r incl new section B$140, s/d in new section incl breakfast B$210/350; @🛜) One of the pioneers of Uyuni tourism, this choice Hacienda-inspired hotel is a solid midrange choice. The rooms in the older wing have bowed beds and less creature comforts, while the

newer rooms have nice antique furniture, new beds, thick comforters and heaters.

Piedra Blanca Backpackers Hostel
HOSTEL $

(☎693-2517; piedrablanca_hostel@hotmail.com; Arce 27; dm B$55, r with/without bathroom per person incl breakfast B$200/150) This upstart hostel has fun common areas in a cool building that wraps around an interior courtyard. There are three dorm rooms that sleep six to 18 people, plus a handful of private rooms with or without attached bathrooms. The dorms are worth it, with large pine bunks, heat (yes!), comfy mattresses and thick comforters. You can leave your luggage here for B$3 per day. Waiting for a train? Stop by for a hot shower (B$20) before heading on your way.

Hotel Avenida
HOTEL $

(☎693-2078; Ferroviaria 11; s/d B$50/100, s/d/tr without bathroom B$30/60/90) Near the train station, this place is popular for its clean, renovated rooms, friendly staff, laundry sinks and hot showers (available 7am to 9pm, in theory). It's good value for the price, but it doesn't have heating, so bring a sleeping bag (or sleeping buddy).

HI-Salar de Uyuni
HOSTEL $

(☎693-2228; cnr Potosí & Sucre; dm B$45, r per person with/without bathroom B$100/50) This Hostelling International (HI) affiliate offers good beds (no bunks) and all the typical hostel amenities. It's on the dark side and the rooms vary significantly so do check out a few. There is a TV room, a clean shared kitchen, laundry service (per kilo B$10) and

hot water (between 8:30am and 6pm, with a shower limit of 10 minutes per day). It can get cold in the rooms at night.

Hotel Julia
HOTEL $$

(☎693-2134; juliahotel5@hotmail.com; Ferroviaria at Arce; s/d/tr/q incl breakfast B$100/200/270/370, s/d without bathroom B$80/140; @) This neat and tidy option right in the center of town has heated rooms and piping hot showers. It's worth paying more for a room with bathroom, as these have more light.

Toñito Hotel
HOTEL $$

(☎693-3186; www.bolivianexpeditions.com; Ferroviaria 60; s/d B$200/300; P 🛜) An appealing choice built around a covered central courtyard that warms up nicely during the day, the Toñito has a set of pleasant rooms with spacious beds and electric showers. It's a bit overpriced, but remains a consistent top pick among tour groups, so book ahead.

Urkupiña El Cactu
HOTEL $

(☎693-2032; Arce 46; r B$160, s/d without bathroom B$40/70) A bit dirty and unorganized in the common areas, this budget spot earns points for the clean rooms (staff put in heaters before you go to bed, but don't sleep with them on – you could suffocate). The mattresses are a bit lumpy, and you'll probably be pretty cold by the AM. You gotta feel bad for their pet parrot who must be miserable in the cold.

SOUTHWEST CIRCUIT

On the standard tour, you will stay in a hotel made of salt the first night (just on the edge of the salt flat). They are all basically

SOUTHERN ALTIPLANO UYUNI

SALT HOTELS JUST OUTSIDE UYUNI

There are several hotels not far from Uyuni around the *salar* that are built of salt. These are unique and comfortable places to stay, where nearly everything is constructed of blocks of salt (with a few obvious exceptions).

Right on the edge of the salt, the **Hotel Palacio de Sal** (☎622-9512; www.palacio desal.com; s/d B$1190/1400; 🛋) is a luxurious complex built almost completely out of the white condiment. The first such hotel opened in the region, it boasts all sorts of facilities ranging from a pool and sauna to a salt golf course (don't bring your favorite white balls). Breakfast and dinner are included in the rates. The hotel is booked through Hidalgo Tours in Potosí or at the Jardines de Uyuni hotel; it comes cheaper as part of a package.

Another salty option is **Luna Salada Hotel** (☎278-5438; www.lunasaladahotel.com.bo; s/d B$600/775), an award-winning place, 7km from Colchani, with 23 stylish rooms and a panoramic restaurant.

It's illegal to stay in the salt hotel on the way to Isla Incahuasi. While people still bribe their way into the hotel, human habitation here – including the waste you generate – can be very hard on the environment.

the same, with salt furniture, crushed salt floors and rough mattresses. The next night, you'll stay in a basic lodge. None have heaters, some have hot showers (for B$10 extra), and you will be cold! They generally put your whole group in one room (sometimes couples can ask for a private room). If you are doing it yourself, these basic hotels cost about B$30 per night.

Tayka Hoteles (☑7202-0069; www.tayka hoteles.com) has four hotels along the Southwest Circuit: Hotel Tayka de Piedra (p155), del Desierto (p155), de Los Volcanes (p157) and de Sal (p154). They cost about US$100 a night, with much of the money going directly to the community, making this a top choice for green travelers. All the Tayka hotels offer plenty of perks, such as comfortable beds with feather duvets, heaters and solar-powered hot water in the rooms, as well as restaurants serving tasty meals (such as llama steaks with quinoa and dehydrated potatoes). Hotel staff can organize intriguing local excursions to little-known points of interest.

You could theoretically camp along the way. Note that it's illegal to camp on the salt flat, and illegal to stay in the salt hotel on the way to Isla Incahuasi.

🍴 Eating & Drinking

For quick eats, cheap meals are on offer at the market comedor (dining hall) and nearby street-food stalls. A fast-food kiosk next to the clock tower has a few tables outside and cheap bites like sandwiches and hamburgers (B$8 to B$35). Nearly every restaurant doubles as a pub.

TOP CHOICE / Minuteman

Revolutionary Pizza PIZZERIA $$
(Ferroviaria 60; pizzas B$30-40; ☺breakfast & dinner) This convivial spot, inside the Toñito Hotel, run by Chris from Boston and his Bolivian wife Sussy, is a deserved travelers' favorite with the best pizzas in town, tasty alternatives like salads, pastas and sandwiches, and fantastic desserts. It's also a cozy spot for a beer or candlelit glass of Tarija wine, or a hearty breakfast (B$20 to B$30) with all you can drink coffee or tea.

Lithium Club BOLIVIAN $$
(Potosí; mains B$45-70) This upper-end choice has horrible service and great food. The international takes on traditional Bolivian dishes like charque de llama (llama jerky) and

pailita de llama (llama stew) bring together authentic flavor combinations with a smidge of European styling. The high-roofed colonial dining room is made only better by the '80s rock anthems that play in the background.

Restaurant 16 de Julio INTERNATIONAL $$
(Arce; almuerzo B$18, mains B$18-45) Right along the main strip, this is a pleasant and friendly place, with a full spectrum of international and Bolivian dishes. Expect to wait a while to get served, especially at lunchtime when locals flock here.

La Loco INTERNATIONAL $$
(Potosí, btwn Sucre & Camacho; snacks B$9, mains B$25-30; ☺4pm-2am, closed in low season) This friendly French-run restaurant and pub is in a barnlike space that's lit low and furnished with comfortingly chunky wooden furniture around a log fire. There are plenty of drinks and a short menu that offers a variety of dishes from Mexico, France, Italy and even Bolivia.

Wiphala Pub PUB $$
(Potosí 325; mains B$25-50) Named after the multicolored Aymará flag, this place has a welcoming feel with its wooden tables, earthy vibe and board games. It serves tasty Bolivian dishes, specializing in llama meat and quinoa, and has quinoa beer.

Ristorante Italia ITALIAN $$
(Arce, btwn Potosí & Ferroviaria; mains B$18-25, pizza B$30-40) Service can be painfully slow at this buzzing place with bamboo decor and plenty of travelers. The menu features sandwiches and a wide selection of pizzas. You can wash your meal down with a beer or cocktail.

Arco Iris PIZZERIA $$
(Arce 27; pizzas B$30-35) Something of an Uyuni classic for pizza and drinks, this place with wooden benches and Bolivian indigenous decor is friendly and popular. It's a great place to socialize and link up with other travelers.

Extreme Fun Pub PUB $$
(Potosí 9; mains B$35-45) This relaxed spot is a very enticing place for a tea or coffee, a meal or sociable cocktail – try a Sexy Llama Bitch. It has salt floors, friendly service, a book exchange and beautiful salar photos. It's also a good place to learn classic Bolivian dice games.

ℹ Information

Dangers & Annoyances

Watch your cash, especially around the train and bus stations. Readers have reported groups of young men pretending to help buy tickets or transfer luggage to a bus, and then taking off with backpacks. Carnaval is a godsend for competent pickpockets, bag-slashers and con artists.

Emergency

Police station (cnr Ferroviaria & Bolívar) If you happen to get mugged, head here to fill out a report.

Immigration

Migración (Ferroviaria btwn Arce & Sucre; ☺8:30am-noon & 2:30-6pm Mon-Fri, 8:30am-noon Sat & Sun) For visa needs. If traveling to Chile, you are better off getting your exit stamp at the border.

Internet Access

There are several internet places in town but most have painfully slow connections; an hour costs between B$4 and B$5.

Laundry

Most hotels offer some sort of laundry service, costing between B$8 and B$20 per kilo. **Lavarap** (cnr Ferroviaria & Sucre; ☺7am-10pm) charges B$15 per kilo.

Medical Services

Hospital (☑693-2025) Along Arce on the edge of town; does good work and accepts most travel insurance.

Money

There are cash machines in town, but they don't always work. Banco Nacional de Bolivia and Banco Union both have ATMs. **Prodem** (Plaza Arce) and several similar places also change dollars and give cash advances for 5%. Several places on Potosí between Arce and Bolívar buy Chilean and Argentine pesos.

Tourist Information

Dirección de Turismo (direccionturismouyuni @hotmail.com; Potosí cnr Arce; ☺8:30am-noon & 2-6:30pm Mon-Fri) Inside the clock tower, this tourism office has sporadic hours and, theoretically, distributes information about Uyuni and the rest of Bolivia.

Office of Reserva Nacional de Fauna Andina Eduardo Avaroa (REA; www.boliviarea.com; Colón, at Avaroa; ☺8:30am-12:30pm & 2:30-6:30pm Mon-Fri) Somewhat helpful administrative office for the park of the same name. You can buy your park entry (B$150) here if going under your own steam.

ℹ Getting There & Away

You can get to Uyuni by bus, plane or train. Buy your bus ticket the day before and your train ticket as far in advance as you can.

Air

The easiest way to get to town is by flying direct from La Paz to Uyuni International Airport (1km north of Uyuni). **Amazonas** (☑222-0848; www.amaszonas.com; Potosí s/n) has Uyuni–La Paz flights Monday, Wednesday and Friday at 9am. La Paz–Uyuni flights leave Tuesday, Thursday, Saturday and Sunday at 7am (and possibly 1:40pm). Schedules change frequently. Tickets cost B$869 to B$975 one way.

Bus

All buses leave from the west end of Av Arce (where you'll also find the ticketing office), a couple of minutes' walk from Plaza Arce. There's a choice of companies to most destinations, so ask around to get the best price, time and service. Potosí buses leave at 9:30am and 6:30pm; Sucre buses leave at 9:30am, noon and 7:30pm.

The safest and most comfortable terrestrial transport to La Paz is with **Todo Turismo** (☑693-3337; www.todoturismo.bo; Cabrera 158, btwn Bolívar & Arce; B$230 one-way), which runs a heated bus service with friendly staff and an onboard meal, departing daily at 8pm. Other regular destinations from Uyuni include the following:

Atocha, Tupiza and Villazón Buses leave at 6am and 8pm.

Calama, Chile Buses depart at 3:30am on Monday and Thursday and at 5am on Sunday and Wednesday (B$100, nine hours) in Chile. You will have to change buses in Avaroa at the Chilean border; there are sometimes waits of up to two hours.

Oruro and La Paz Buses generally leave around 7pm or 8pm.

BUS COSTS & DISTANCES

DESTINATION	COST (B$)	DURATION (HR)
Atocha	30	4
Cochabamba	72-155	12
La Paz	71-230	10-12
Oruro	43-117	7-8
Potosí	30	6
Sucre	60-70	9
Tupiza	50	7-8
Villazón	60	10

Car

An alternative route to Chile is with an organized tour, which will leave you in San Pedro de

Atacama. Some of the tour companies, including Cordillera Tours (p147), offer direct jeep transfers to San Pedro, which cost around B$300 per person. The jeeps typically leave at 4pm, there's a sleepover in Villa Mar, and you arrive in San Pedro at noon the next day. From San Pedro, buses to Salta, Argentina, depart three times weekly (Tuesday, Friday and Saturday) at 10:30am. You can also get to Argentina via Villazón.

Train

Uyuni has a modern, well-organized **train station** (☑693-2320; www.fca.com.bo; Ferroviaria s/n). Trains take you north to Oruro, south to Villazón and east to Calama, Chile. Seats often sell out so buy your ticket several days in advance or get an agency to do it for you. There are numerous reports of slow trains, cancelled trains and large gaps in service – but that's all part of the adventure.

Depending on size, you may have to check your backpack/case into the luggage compartment. Look out for snatch thieves on the train just before it pulls out.

Expreso del Sur is the slightly more luxurious line, departing Uyuni for Oruro on Thursday and Sunday at 12:05am (1st/coach B$112/56); it departs for Atocha, Tupiza and Villazón on Wednesday and Saturday at 12:45am.

Wara Wara offers a cheaper service and leaves Uyuni Tuesday and Friday at 1:45am for Oruro (1st/coach/normal B$95/44/32); it heads south to Atocha, Tupiza and Villazón on Thursday and Monday at 2:50am.

A train for Avaroa on the Chilean border departs on Monday at 3am (B$32, five hours). From here you cross to Ollagüe and may have to wait a few hours to clear Chilean customs. Another train then continues to Calama (B$91 from Uyuni, six hours from Ollagüe). The whole trip can take up to 24 hours but it's a spectacular, if uncomfortable, journey. Taking a bus to Calama is more reliable.

Salar de Uyuni

An evocative and eerie sight, the world's largest salt flat (12,106 sq km) sits at 3653m (11,984ft). When the surface is dry, the *salar* is a pure white expanse of the greatest nothing imaginable – just blue sky, white ground and you. When there's a little water, the surface perfectly reflects the clouds and the blue Altiplano sky, and the horizon disappears. If you're driving across the surface at such times, the effect is positively surreal, and it's hard to believe that you're not actually flying through the clouds.

The Salar de Uyuni is now a center of salt extraction and processing, particularly around the settlement of Colchani (p145). The estimated annual output of the Colchani operation is nearly 20,000 tons, 18,000 tons of which is for human consumption while the rest is for livestock. And beneath the surface, massive lithium deposits should fuel Bolivia's economy (and your iPod) for the next 100 years.

Formation

Between 40,000 and 25,000 years ago, Lago Minchín, whose highest level reached 3760m, occupied much of southwestern Bolivia. When it evaporated, the area lay dry for 14,000 years before the appearance of short-lived Lago Tauca, which lasted for only about 1000 years and rose to 3720m.

BOLIVIA: SET TO BECOME THE SAUDI ARABIA OF LITHIUM?

Bolivia holds the key to an environmentally sustainable future – 50% of the world's lithium deposits, a mineral essential for hybrid and electric vehicles, is found in the salt flats of Uyuni.

Several major players in the global auto industry have their eyes set on this untapped potential. And while Bolivia's previous governments would have happily sold off its lithium reserves to foreign companies, it's not going to happen under Evo Morales. Faithful to his anti-capitalist rhetoric, he has continually rejected bids from international mining companies and, so far, successfully warded off outside involvement in this precious mineral. With an investment of US$6 million, Comibol, the state agency that oversees mining projects, is currently constructing a pilot plant in the salt flats. The project has seen numerous setbacks, but continues slowly forward.

Car manufacturers predict that the world will need 500 kilotonnes per year to service a niche market, with that figure to rise if electric cars become the norm. If the demand for eco-vehicles does rise, the world's existing supply of lithium will be outstripped by 2015. Critics claim that Bolivia doesn't have the technology to extract lithium quickly and efficiently enough, which may thwart its plans to become the Saudi Arabia of lithium.

Salares de Uyuni & Coipasa

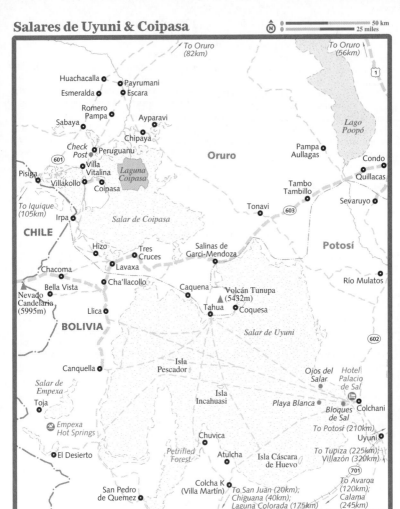

When it dried up, it left two large puddles, Lagos Poopó and Uru Uru, and two major salt concentrations, the Salares de Uyuni and Coipasa.

This part of the Altiplano is drained internally, with no outlet to the sea; the salt deposits are the result of the minerals leached from the mountains and deposited at the lowest available point.

ISLA INCAHUASI

After stopping in the Cementerio de Trenes (p145) and Colchani (p145) salt extraction areas, you can visit a **Salt Hotel** (admission B$25) where, although it is now closed to overnight visitors (see boxed text, p149), you can still stop to check out the salt sculptures inside. From here, your tour will continue on to the spectacular Isla Incahuasi, better known as Isla del Pescado, in the heart of the *salar* 80km west of Colchani. This hilly outpost is covered in Trichoreus cacti and surrounded by a flat white sea of hexagonal salt tiles. It was once a remarkably lonely, other-worldly place but since the advent of *salar* tours, it has become overrun with tourists. All the tour groups arrive at the same time (noon) and swarm over the hiking trails chasing the perfect photo of cacti and salt.

It's a 15-minute walk to the top of the island, with a trail that loops back.

At the base of the island, the Museo Ritual has some interesting Spanish-language displays on Aymará rituals, beliefs and cultures.

Most groups have their lunch here. There's also a **cafe-restaurant** (nyc0079@hotmail.com; mains B$14-48, set lunch B$40; ☺lunch Jul-Oct) run by La Paz–based Mongo's – reserve ahead. Altogether an industrialized tourist experience, it's still a beautiful sight if you forget the crowds.

VOLCÁN TUNUPA

A rounded promontory juts into the Salar de Uyuni diagonally opposite Colchani, and on it rises **Volcán Tunupa** (5432m). Altitude aside, this hulking yellow mountain is a relatively easy climb. One legend linking it to the origins of the salt flat states that 16th-century Inca ruler Atahualpa slashed the breast of a woman called Tunupa on the mountain's slopes, and the milk that spilled out formed the *salar*. Another story tells that back in ancient days, mountains were men and women. Right after giving birth to their baby, Tunupa learned her man was living with another woman. Devastated, she wept and wept, spilling her salty tears over her breast milk, and creating this vast area of sadness and beauty that is now the *salar*.

COQUESA

On custom tours, you can stop at the village of Coquesa, taking time to explore the several **ruined ancient villages** and **burial grounds** nearby. Ceramic, gold and copper artifacts and articles of clothing have been discovered at some of the sites, indicating the presence of an advanced but little-known culture. Unfortunately, the sites' remoteness has left them vulnerable to amateur treasure hunters who have plundered several items of archaeological value. Ask at the hotel for keys to the **Museo Coquesa** (admission per 4WD B$20), which has a collection of ceramics and mummies. You can also arrange a nighttime visit to the nearby **observatory**, to really appreciate the starry skies.

The **Maya Hostal de Sal** (r per person B$35) in Coquesa is run by a local Aymará family. The beds are built on salt blocks, the doors and windows of cactus wood, and the dining room has salt tables with a splendid view over the *salar*. At night, a camp fire and candlelight illuminate the place.

In the nearby village of Tahua, **Hotel Tayka de Sal** (☎7202-0069; www.taykahoteles.com; s/d US$88/95) is built entirely of locally

---

CLIMBING VOLCANOES

There are plenty of opportunities for getting out of the 4WD and doing something active throughout the Southwest Circuit. One of the most popular activities is volcano climbing, with guides easily available in the region's settlements. The challenging aspect of most of the climbs is the altitude rather than technical difficulty. Taking a guide is a good idea and contributes something to the local communities, which are so often bypassed by the Uyuni-based tours.

The most frequently climbed is the **Volcán Licancabur** (5960m); it takes about eight hours to climb to the summit, and two to get down. Several Uyuni and Tupiza agencies are happy to include a guided climb of the volcano in a Southwest Circuit route, adding an extra day to the trip. You can normally find a guide somewhere around Laguna Verde – they tend to charge about B$300 for an ascent of the mountain, which has a beautiful lagoon at the top. The climb can be done comfortably (if you handle the altitude) in one day. As the volcano is sacred to the locals, the guides usually perform a ritual for Pachamama, asking the earth goddess her permission to climb.

Nevado Candelaria (5995m), southwest of the Salar de Coipasa, is also an exhilarating climb. The active **Volcán Ollagüe** (5865m) on the Chilean border southwest of San Pedro de Quemez is another interesting option, with spectacular views – you can get pretty close to the summit with a jeep and then hike the remaining 400m to the top. Another volcano to climb is the hulking **Tunupa** (5400m), which you can approach from two sides – the village of Coquesa (10 hours there and back, including a visit to the caves with pre-Incan mummies) or the village of Jirira (four hours there and back).

It's also possible to climb **Uturuncu** (6020m), which is an active volcano; jeeps can drive up to just 1km below the summit and you can hike to the top – an easy way to say you've climbed a 6000m-high volcano!

extracted salt, apart from the thatched roof and the black-stone bathrooms. These hotels come with heating. Reservations required.

CHUVICA

Many tours spend the first night in the handful of salt hotels around the village of Chuvica that sits on the eastern edge of the salt flat. A signed **trail** (1km) just south of the village takes you up the hillside to a small cavern (make sure you get down before sunset). There's a basic store here. The **salt hotels** (☏7441-7357; r per person B$30) in town are nearly identical, with salt floors, furniture and walls, and common dining rooms where you can eat dinner (and shiver). The hotels have no heating, but an extra B$10 gets you a hot shower.

At the southwestern tip of the *salar*, off the beaten track, is **Hotel Takya de Piedra** (www.taykahoteles.com; s/d/tr US$88/95/115). Built of rugged local stone, it lies near the village of **San Pedro de Quemez**, near the burned-down ruins of a pre-Columbian settlement.

Los Lípez

Entering the remote and beautiful region of Los Lípez on the second day of the standard Southwest Circuit, many tours pass through a military checkpoint at the village of **Colcha K** (*col*-cha *kah*), where there's a pleasant **adobe church** and a series of fairly rudimentary dormitory accommodations.

About 15km further along is the quinoa-growing village of **San Juan** (elevation 3660m). It has a population of 1000, a lovely **adobe church**, and several **volcanic-rock tombs** and burial **chullpas** (funerary towers) in its vicinity. The community-run **Museo Kausay Wasi** (donation B$5) displays regional archaeological finds.

At this point the route turns west and starts across the borax-producing **Salar de Chiguana**, where the landscape opens up and snowcapped **Ollagüe** (5865m), an active volcano straddling the Chilean border, appears in the distance.

The route then turns south and climbs into high and increasingly wild terrain, past several mineral-rich lakes filled with flamingos and backed by hills. After approximately 170km of rough bumping through marvelous landscapes, the road winds down to the much-photographed **Árbol de Piedra** (Stone Tree) in the **Desierto Siloli**, 18km

north of Laguna Colorada. At the entrance to the lake, the **Reserva Nacional de Fauna Andina Eduardo Avaroa** (REA; www.bolivia -rea.com; admission B$150) has a station where you can pick up informative materials, pay your fee, and learn more about local flora and fauna.

The next attraction, **Laguna Colorada** is a rusty-burnt-orange-hued lake (4278m) that covers approximately 60 sq km and reaches a depth of just 80cm. The rich red coloration on the lake is derived from algae and plankton that thrive in the mineral-rich water, and the shoreline is fringed with brilliant white deposits of sodium, magnesium, borax and gypsum. The lake sediments are also rich in diatoms (tiny microfossils used in the production of fertilizer, paint, toothpaste and plastics, and as a filtering agent for oil, pharmaceuticals, aviation fuel, beer and wine). More apparent are the flamingos that breed here; all three South American species are present. The clear air is bitterly cold and winter nighttime temperatures can drop below -20°C.

Many tour groups end up spending the night not far from here in the village of **Huayajara**, where basic hotels (sorry, no more salt ones) cost about B$30 per night. This is the coldest night on the trip, as you're sleeping at around 4600m.

Hotel Tayka del Desierto (☏7202-0069; www.taykahoteles.com; s/d US$100/110) is a sumptuous offering not far from Laguna de Colorado.

On day three of the standard tour, you wake at dawn to visit the large geyser field dubbed **Sol de Mañana**. This 4850m-high geyser basin has bubbling mud pots, hellish fumaroles and a thick and nauseating aroma of sulfur fumes. Approach the site cautiously; any damp or cracked earth is potentially dangerous and cave-ins do occur, sometimes causing serious burns.

At the foot of **Cerro Polques** lies the **Termas de Polques**, a small 29.4°C hot-spring pool, and an absolute paradise after the chilly *salar* nights. Although they're not boiling by any means, they're suitable for bathing, and the mineral-rich waters are thought to relieve the symptoms of arthritis and rheumatism. There's a restaurant here, and changing sheds with toilet facilities.

The stunning blue-green **Laguna Verde** (4400m) is tucked into the southwestern corner of Bolivian territory, 52km south of Sol de Mañana. The incredible green color comes from high concentrations of lead, sulfur, arsenic and calcium carbonates. In this exposed position, an icy wind blows almost incessantly, whipping the water into a brilliant green-and-white froth. This surface agitation, combined with the high mineral content, means that it can remain liquid at temperatures as low as -21.2°C.

Behind the lake rises the cone of **Volcán Licancabur** (5960m), whose summit is said to have once sheltered an ancient Inca **crypt**. Some tours include an ascent of Licancabur, and although it presents no technical difficulties, the wind, temperature, altitude and ball-bearing volcanic pumice underfoot make it quite grueling.

Where the route splits about 20km south of Sol de Mañana, the more scenic left fork climbs up and over a 5000m pass, then up a stark hillside dotted with the enormous **Rocas de Dalí**, which appear to have been meticulously placed by the surrealist master Salvador himself.

Around Salar de Uyuni

Some of the tour agencies are increasingly offering alternative tours of the Southwest Circuit. These customized trips are usually pricier than typical three-day jaunts but involve visits to some less-visited attractions in Los Lípez and a real sense of discovery. This region is a land of bizarre lava formations, active volcanoes, abandoned villages,

badlands, salt flats, pre-Incan cave cemeteries, lone quinoa fields, flying condors, multicolored lagoons and sulfur lakes. We've listed some of the places where you won't be surrounded by packs of jeeps and other travelers, where the feel of the last frontier is true and real.

ISLA CÁSCARA DE HUEVO

The small 'Eggshell Island' was named for the broken shells of birds' eggs that litter it. It lies near the southern end of the Salar de Uyuni and is visited mainly to see the strange patterns of salt crystallization in the area, some of which resemble roses.

AQUAQUIZA

Some agencies now offer a side trip to Aquaquiza, a quinoa-producing village in Nor Lípez where there's *alojamiento* (basic accommodation; B$20). The area's attraction, **Gruta de las Galaxias**, lies 8km away. Discovered in 2003, Gruta de las Galaxias is a small two-level grotto full of beautiful petrified algae and corals from the ancient lake. Part of the same complex is **Cueva del Diablo**, a cave sacred to the locals with a pre-Incan cemetery scattered with small *chullpas*. Note the cross as you enter the cave, marking where a shepherd girl was found mysteriously dead after seeking protection from a storm inside the cave. There's a viewpoint at the top to admire the spectacularly desolate scenery and the petrified cacti.

FROZEN FLAMINGOS

Three species of flamingo breed in the bleak high country of southwestern Bolivia, and once you've seen these posers strutting through icy mineral lagoons at 5000m elevation, you'll abandon time-worn associations between flamingos, coconut palms and the steamy tropics. The sight of these pinky-white birds with their black bills and tails adds yet another color to the already spectacular palette hereabouts.

Flamingos have a complicated and sophisticated system for filtering the foodstuffs from highly alkaline brackish lakes. They filter algae and diatoms from the water by sucking in and vigorously expelling water from the bill several times per second. The minute particles are caught on fine hairlike protrusions that line the inside of the mandibles. The suction is created by the thick fleshy tongue, which rests in a groove in the lower mandible and pumps back and forth like a piston.

The Chilean flamingo reaches heights of just over 1m and has a black-tipped white bill, dirty blue legs, red knees and salmon-colored plumage. The James flamingo is the smallest of the three species and has dark-red legs and a yellow-and-black bill. It's locally known as *jututu*. The Andean flamingo is the largest of the three and has pink plumage, yellow legs and a yellow-and-black bill.

Environmentalists have been particularly concerned for the birds in recent years, as tourism has affected the flamingos' breeding. Don't try to creep up to them to get a better photo; above all don't put them to flight or encourage any guide that suggests doing this.

CROSSING THE BORDER TO CHILE

Most tour agencies now offer cross-border connections to San Pedro de Atacama by arrangement with Chilean operators. You'll make the connection not long after the Laguna Verde. Arrange this ahead of time with your operator. It may be wise to stop by Migración (p151) in Uyuni before doing this. The Hito Cajón border post is much more reliable than it used to be. They charge an exit tax of B$15 to B$30 here (B$21 is the standard), and supposedly operate 24 hours a day. Try to be there before 6pm just to be on the safe side.

Between March and December, a B$10 admission is charged for the complex; otherwise it's free but there's nobody to show you around.

SALAR DE COIPASA

This great 2218-sq-km remote salt desert, northwest of the Salar de Uyuni at an elevation of 3786m, was part of the same system of prehistoric lakes as the Salar de Uyuni – a system that covered the area over 10,000 years ago. The 4WD-only road to the Salar de Coipasa is extremely poor and the salt is thin so it's easy to get stuck, especially during the rainy season. If you go, make sure the vehicle and the driver are reliable. The salt-mining village of Coipasa, which (not surprisingly) is constructed mainly of salt, occupies an island in the middle of the *salar*. You can also reach the Salar de Coipasa from Oruro department.

LÍPEZ LAKES

The blue lake of **Laguna Celeste** or, more romantically, 'heaven lake', is still very much a peripheral trip for most Uyuni agencies, but it's gaining popularity with adventurous travelers as a one-day detour. A local legend suggests the presence of a submerged ruin, possibly a *chullpa,* in the lake. Behind the lake, a road winds its way up **Volcán Uturuncu** (6020m) to the **Uturuncu sulfur mine**, in a 5900m pass between the mountain's twin cones. That means it's more than 200m higher than the road over the Khardung La in Ladakh, India, making it quite possibly the highest motorable pass in the world.

In the vast eastern reaches of Sud Lípez are numerous other fascinating mineral-rich lakes that are informally named for their odd coloration and have so far escaped much attention. Various milky-looking lakes are known as **Laguna Blanca** (White Lake), sulfur-colored lakes are **Laguna Amarilla** (Yellow Lake) and wine-colored ones are

known as **Laguna Guinda** (Cherry Lake). **Laguna Cañapa** and **Laguna Hedionda** are also part of some circuits. You can negotiate to add any of these to a tailored circuit.

QUETENA CHICO & AROUND

About 120km northeast of Laguna Verde and 30km southwest of Laguna Celeste is the small mining settlement of Quetena Chico, which has a few basic services and supplies, a military post and a couple of simple *albergues* (hostels). It also has the **Centro de Ecología Ch'aska**, where you can see an exhibition about the geology and biology of the Los Lípez region, and the lives of the local llama herders.

Just 6km southeast from here is the picturesque abandoned village of **Barrancas**, which nestles against a craggy cliff.

To the northeast, and well off the standard circuit (although visited by some of the tours from Tupiza), the village of **San Pablo de Lípez** offers the latest Tayka Hoteles (p150) property, **Hotel Tayka de Los Volcanes** (☎7202-0069; www.taykahoteles.com; s/d US$100/110), a high-end option near the Argentinian border.

Heading back toward Uyuni, the village of **Villa Mar** has an interesting *mercado artesanal* (craft market) that's worth a visit. Stretch your legs by strolling the 4km to some of the area's most spectacular *pinturas rupestres* (rock paintings), with impressive human figures wearing headdresses, and incised animals. There are several simple *albergues* in **Mallku**, and also the upmarket **Mallku Cueva Lodge** (☎622-9512; www.salardeuyuni.net; s/d B$283/495) run by Hidalgo Tours (p148).

VALLES DE ROCAS & SAN CRISTÓBAL

In the midst of high, lonesome country stretch several valleys of bizarre eroded rock formations known as Valles de Rocas. These strangely shaped badlands are perfect for a wander and snapping some great photos.

CHIPAYA

Immediately north of the Salar de Coipasa, on the Río Sabaya delta, live the Chipaya people. They occupy two main desert villages (Santa Ana de Chipaya and Ayparavi) of unique circular mud huts known as *khuyas* or *putucus*, which have doors made from cactus wood and always face east. Chipayas are best recognized by their earth-colored clothing and the women's unique hairstyle, which is plaited into 60 small braids. These are, in turn, joined into two large braids and decorated with a *laurake* (barrette) at each temple.

Some researchers believe the Chipaya were the Altiplano's first inhabitants, and that they may in fact be a remnant of the lost Tiwanaku civilization. Much of this speculation is based on the fact that their language is vastly different from both Quechua and Aymará, and is probably a surviving form of Uru.

Chipaya tradition maintains that their people came into the world when it was still dark, and that they are descended from the 'Men of Water' – perhaps the Uru. Their religion, which is nature-based, is complex and symbolic, deifying phallic images, stones, rivers, mountains, animal carcasses and ancestors. The village church tower is worshipped as a demon – one of 40 named demons who represent hate, ire, vengeance, gluttony and other evils. These are believed to inhabit the whitewashed mud cones that exist within a 15km radius of the village, where they're appeased with libations, sacrifices and rituals to prevent their evil from invading the village.

The reverent commemoration of dead ancestors culminates on November 2, **Día de los Muertos** (Day of the Dead), when bodies are disinterred from *chullpas* (funerary towers). They're feted with a feast, copious drink and coca leaves, and informed about recent village events and the needs of the living. Those who were chiefs, healers and other luminaries are carried to the church where they're honored with animal sacrifices.

From the dusty village of **Alota** nearby, it's a six-hour jostle back to Uyuni through a string of 'authentic villages,' the most picturesque of which, **Culpina K**, has colorful little houses and a cafe.

The mining village of San Cristóbal is worth a stop for the lovely 350-year-old church. The entire village, including the church and the cemetery, was moved from its original location next to the mine by the American–Japanese mining project that took over the area digging for lead, zinc and silver. The **Hotel San Cristóbal** (dm B$80, s B$140, d B$210-280) offers electricity, sporadically hot solar-powered showers and a restaurant. There's a bus from Uyuni at 2pm; the return bus departs San Cristobal at 6am the following day (B$15).

TUPIZA

POP 22,300 / ELEV 2950M (9678FT)

The pace of things in tranquil Tupiza seems a few beats slower than in other Bolivian towns, making this a great place to relax for a few days, head out for a rip-romping cowboy adventure like Butch Cassidy and Sundance did 100 years ago, or trundle off on the back road to the Salar de Uyuni.

Set in a spectacular 'Wild West' countryside, the capital of the southern Chichas region is cornered in the Río Tupiza Valley, surrounded by rugged scenery – cactus-studded slopes and eroded rainbow-colored rocks cut by gravelly *quebradas* (ravines, usually dry).

The climate is mild year-round, with most of the rain falling between November and March. From June to August, days are hot, dry and clear, but at nighttime the temperatures can drop to below freezing.

Economically, the town depends on agriculture and mining. A refinery south of town provides employment, and the country's only antimony (a flame-retardant metallic element) smelter operates sporadically.

History

The tribe that originally inhabited the region called themselves Chichas and left some archaeological evidence of their existence. Despite this, little is known about their culture or language, and it's assumed these were distinct from those of the tribes in neighboring areas of southern Bolivia and northern Argentina.

Officially, Tupiza was founded on June 4, 1574, by Captain Luis de Fuentes (who was also the founder of Tarija). From Tupiza's

The Río Lauca, on which the Chipaya have depended for thousands of years, is not only heavily polluted but has also been drying out due to global warming. A lot of the Chipaya have emigrated to Chile and the ones left in the community are facing extinction. In the main settlement, Santa Ana de Chipaya, the traditional way of life is slowly vanishing. It's rare to see the circular houses, also known as *huayllichas*, and the original dress unless you go to Ayparavi or the rural areas.

Visiting the Chipaya

In general, tourists aren't especially welcome, and are expected to pay a fee for entering the Chipaya 'nation' (visitors have been charged anything from US$50 to US$100 per person; you'll pay a lot less if you don't turn up in a 4WD). The Chipayas don't like to be photographed but some will do so for a fee (expect to be charged between B$20 and B$100 per photo). There's simple *alojamiento* (basic accommodations) in Chipaya village and a small shop.

From Oruro, buses leave daily for Huachacalla; there you'll have to arrange onward transportation to Chipaya, 30km beyond. From Sabaya, it takes about an hour to get there. Ask for Jaime Soruco, who is the owner of the restaurant and hotel in the village, and who will be willing to help visitors. It costs about B$400 to get there and back, with a wait of two to three hours. Alternatively, you can reach Sabaya or Huachacalla on any bus between Oruro and Iquique along a bumpy road.

In addition, a few tour companies organize visits to the village; check with Charlie Tours (p135) in Oruro. Note that visiting the Chipaya in the rainy season is practically impossible, as the roads get washed away.

inception through the War of Independence, its Spanish population grew steadily, lured by the favorable climate and suitable agricultural lands. Later, the discovery of minerals attracted even more settlers. More recently, *campesinos* (subsistence farmers) have drifted in from the countryside and many unemployed miners have settled here.

◉ Sights & Activities

Tupiza's main attraction is the surrounding countryside, best seen on foot or horseback. The short hike up **Cerro Corazón de Jesús**, flanked by the Stations of the Cross, is a pleasant morning or evening outing when the low sun brings out the fiery reds of the surrounding countryside.

Mercado Negro　　　MARKET
(Junín, btwn Av Santa Cruz & Chichas) The ironically permanent *mercado negro* (black market) has a mishmash of consumer goods, and occupies an entire block between Av Santa Cruz and Chichas.

Street Markets　　　MARKET
Lively street markets convene Thursday and Saturday mornings near the train station. A kilometer south of town, the Mercado

Campesino features more of the same on Monday, Thursday and Saturday.

Mercado de Ferias　　　MARKET
The central Mercado de Ferias has lots of produce stalls and *comedores* upstairs.

Hotel Mitru Pool　　　SWIMMING
(Chichas 187; per half-day B$20) Nonguests can enjoy Hotel Mitru's solar-heated swimming pool. In the high season it has a snack bar with drinks, sandwiches and pizzas.

☞ Tours

There's an ever-increasing number of operators in Tupiza offering trips through the Southwest Circuit ending in Uyuni or back in Tupiza (or, in some cases, San Pedro de Atacama in Chile). Tupiza is a great place to do this trip from, as you get to explore the lesser-known wild lands of Sud Lípez as well as seeing the well-established highlights at different times to the large convoys of 4WDs that visit them out of Uyuni.

The downside is that you may have to wait a while in Tupiza to get a group together (although the larger outfits have departures almost daily). Expect to pay between B$1200 and B$1350 per person for the standard four-day trip, based on four

Tupiza

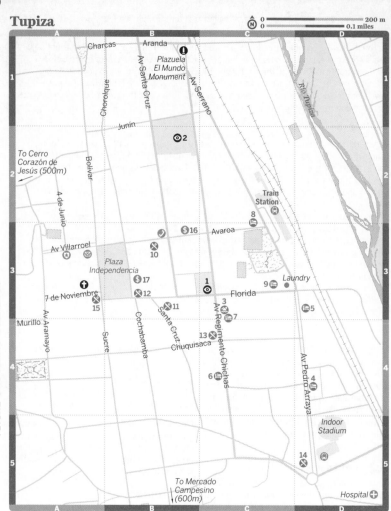

0   200 m
0   0.1 miles

people in a jeep during the high season. This price typically includes all meals, transport and basic accommodations, but does not include the B$150 entrance to the Reserva Nacional de Fauna Andina Eduardo Avaroa (p155), snacks, sleeping-bag rental (yes, do it!) or bottled water. Customized trips, many including climbing options, will cost a bit more but they're worth the surcharge.

While most tour operators display enthusiastic comments from satisfied customers, the truth is that standards vary widely. Many people end up choosing the agency based on their accommodations' choice, but it's well worth getting out there and chatting to a few different operators. Professionalism, honesty and flexibility are the things to look for, rather than willingness to haggle on the price. The same safety precautions apply as in Uyuni when looking for the right tour operator for you.

All agencies offer **horseback riding** (per 3/5/7 hr B$105/175/245, per 2/4 days B$380-480). Longer rides include a sleepover in basic accommodations in the villages of Espicaya or Quiriza. Also on offer by all the agencies is the **triathlon** (per person incl lunch B$200-300, based on 4 people), an active full-

Tupiza

day tour of the surrounding area by jeep, horseback and mountain bike. You can also arrange a **jeep tour** (per day B$450-600) or a **guided trek** (per half-day B$100-150). Note that in low season, you'll often find the rates negotiable but don't haggle too much, as the quality is also likely to go down.

These tours and activities are offered by the following agencies:

La Torre Tours   GUIDED TOUR
(☏694-2633; www.latorretours-tupiza.com; Chichas 220, Hotel La Torre) Run by a friendly couple, this agency offers personalized tours of Tupiza's surroundings and into the *salar*. During the dry season it rents bikes for B$70 per day.

Tupiza Tours   GUIDED TOUR
(☏694-3003; www.tupizatours.com; Chichas 187, Hotel Mitru) This outfit pioneered many of the Tupiza-area routes now also offered by competitors. While the agency is well run and has daily departures to the *salar*, there have been mixed reports about the quality of its tours that apparently lack a personal touch (it uses 12-person minivans). Their two-day **Butch and Sundance tour** (B$600, based on 4 people) is popular, and it includes an overnight stay in the hamlet of **Tatasi** as well as a visit to the abandoned mining village of **Portugalete**.

Valle Hermoso Tours   GUIDED TOUR
(☏694-4344; www.vallehermosatours.com; Arraya 478, Hostal Valle Hermoso) The agency inside Hostal Valle Hermoso gets mixed reviews and the owners tend to be pushy.

🛏 Sleeping

You'll often be quoted cheaper rates for rooms in the hope that you'll then take a tour with the hotel's agency. The cheapest options are several basic *residenciales* (simple accommodations) opposite the train station.

TOP CHOICE **Hotel Mitru**   HOTEL $
(☏694-3001; www.hotelmitru.com; Chichas 187; r per person without bathroom B$60, s with bathroom B$180-220, d with bathroom B$200-300; 🛜🏊) The best and most reliable hotel in town, the busy Mitru has been run by the same family for generations and is a relaxing choice built around a swimming pool that's just the ticket after a dusty day out on horseback. It has a variety of rooms in two sections: the older 'garden' part and the newer 'cactus' area. The suites with a fridge and minibar are particularly appealing, and the rooms with shared bathrooms are top value in the budget range.

Hotel La Torre   HOTEL $
(☏694-2633; www.latorretours-tupiza.com; Chichas 220; s/d incl breakfast B$70/140, r per person without bathroom B$50) This sound, central choice run by a retired nurse and doctor offers clean rooms with good beds and clean bathrooms. Rooms at the front of the rambling colonial-era home are much lighter but chillier, and the beds can be a bit lumpy. Guests have use of a kitchen, roof terrace and TV lounge – a good place to meet other travelers.

Hotel Mitru Anexo   HOTEL $
(☏694-3002; www.hotelmitru.com; Avaroa at Serrano; r with/without bathroom B$160/100; 🛜) A marginally cheaper offshoot of Hotel Mitru

SOUTHERN ALTIPLANO TUPIZA

THE LAST DAYS OF BUTCH CASSIDY & THE SUNDANCE KID

Butch and Sundance (real names Robert LeRoy Parker and Harry Alonzo Longabaugh) came to southern Bolivia in August 1908 and took up residence with the Briton AG Francis, who was transporting a gold dredge on the Río San Juan del Oro. While casing banks to finance their retirement, the outlaws learned of an even sweeter target: a poorly guarded US$480,000 mine-company payroll to be hauled by mule from Tupiza to Quechisla.

On November 3, 1908, manager Carlos Peró picked up a packet of cash from Aramayo, Francke & Compañía in Tupiza and headed north with his 10-year-old son and a servant, but they were discreetly tailed by Butch and Sundance. Peró's party stayed overnight in Salo, then set off again at dawn. As the trio ascended the hill called Huaca Huañusca, the bandits watched from above with binoculars. In a rugged spot on the far side of the hill, they relieved Peró of a handsome mule and the remittance, which turned out to be a mere US$90,000 – the prized payroll had been slated for shipment the following week.

Dispirited, Butch and Sundance returned to Francis' headquarters at Tomahuaico. The following day, Francis guided them to Estarca, where they spent the night. On the morning of November 6, the bandits bade farewell to Francis and headed west to San Vicente.

Meanwhile, Peró had sounded the alarm, and posses were scouring southern Bolivia. A four-man contingent from Uyuni reached San Vicente that afternoon. Butch and Sundance arrived at dusk, rented a room from Bonifacio Casasola and sent him to fetch supper. The posse came to investigate and had scarcely entered the courtyard when Butch shot and killed a soldier. During the brief gunfight that ensued, Sundance was badly wounded. Realizing that escape was impossible, Butch ended Sundance's misery with a shot between the eyes, then fired a bullet into his own temple.

At the inquest, Carlos Peró identified the corpses as those of the men who had robbed him. Although buried as *desconocidos* (unknowns) in the cemetery, the outlaws fit descriptions of Butch and Sundance, and a mountain of circumstantial evidence points to their having met their doom in San Vicente. For example, Santiago Lowe, Butch's well-known alias, was recently found among the hotel guest list published in the Tupiza newspaper just a few days before the Aramayo holdup, which confirms eyewitness accounts that he was there. Nonetheless, rumors of their return to the USA have made their fate one of the great mysteries of the American West.

In 1991 a team led by forensic anthropologist Clyde Snow attempted to settle the question by excavating the bandits' grave. No one in the village had any knowledge of its location, except one elderly – and as it turned out, imaginative – gentleman, who led them to a specific tombstone. The grave's sole occupant turned out to be a German miner named Gustav Zimmer.

Anne Meadows (the author of Digging Up Butch and Sundance, University of Nebraska Press, 2003) & Daniel Buck

with a similar vibe but no pool (you can use the Mitru's for free), this place offers good value. The solid rooms sport cable TVs, phones and hot water. The bathrooms are modern, and guests have use of a kitchen and terraces.

Hostal Valle Hermoso HOSTEL $
(694-4344; www.vallehermosotours.com; Arraya 478; s/d B$60/120, dm/r per person without bathroom B$40/40;) Set in two separate buildings a block apart, this is an old-school hostel with a book exchange, roof terrace and plenty of social space. It's HI-affiliated (members get a 10% discount), clean and convenient. **Annex Valle Hermoso** (Arraya

505) is nearer the bus station and more up-to-date, with rooms featuring more space, light and cable TVs.

Tupiza Hostal HOTEL $
(694-5240; Florida 10; r per person without bathroom B$30) Budget seekers should check out this hostel. The rooms are a bit dark and the beds are pretty poor quality, but the sheets are clean and the courtyard is a great spot to hang out with fellow travelers. It offers use of a communal shower and a shared kitchen.

 Eating

The upstairs section of the central market is the best place to fill up at lunch, for between B$10 and B$15. For a real morning treat, head for Mercado Negro after 8am for *charque*-filled *tamales* (cornmeal dough filled with jerky; B$1.50).

TOP CHOICE **Milan Center** PIZZERIA **$$**
(cnr Chichas & Chuquisaca; mains B$30-50, pizza B$27-30; ☺8am-10pm) For the best pizza in town, head over to Milan Center, which serves up crispy thin-crust pizzas and an amazing variety of topping options. The covered back patio is a wonderful break from the streets of Tupiza, and the service very friendly.

Il Bambino BOLIVIAN **$**
(Florida & Santa Cruz; almuerzo B$12) This friendly corner eatery offers excellent *salteñas* (B$3) in the morning and is a popular spot with locals. The *almuerzo* (set lunch) is thought to be one of the best in town, and is an excellent value in terms of kilo-per-Boliviano.

Tú Pizza PIZZERIA **$**
(Plaza Independencia s/n; mains B$16-30) This stylish little eatery on the main plaza has a rustic feel, high ceilings, nice artwork and good service. The food runs the usual gamut of pizzas, pastas and lasagna as well as mains with local goat cheese and quinoa. Try the sweet pizza with chocolate and *dulce de leche* (super-sweet caramelized milk).

Alamo MEXICAN **$**
(Avaroa & Santa Cruz; snacks B$4-9, mains B$9-15) A green light outside marks this popular saloon-style spot where locals and tourists mingle in the funky two-story space with a Mexican vibe and lots of knickknacks. The menu features mainly meat dishes, like *pique macho* (beef chunks and sausages over french fries with lettuce, tomatoes, onions and spicy *locoto* peppers), and comes in huge tasty portions.

Italiana INTERNATIONAL **$$**
(Florida near Plaza Independencia; mains B$18-35) Despite its name, Italiana also serves a variety of international dishes from China, the US and, yes, Italy. It's one of the better tourist-oriented restaurants in town and a good spot for a cocktail, glass of wine or beer.

Rinconcito Quilmes ARGENTINIAN **$$**
(Suipacha 14; almuerzo B$10, mains B$25-35) You'll see few other tourists in this little spot known for cheap, filling lunches served in a spacious dining room and a couple of outside tables. It's popular on weekends for its *asados* (barbecues) with quality meat from Argentina.

ℹ Information

Internet Access & Telephone
There are several internet places on the plaza that charge B$3 per hour, as does **Entel** (cnr Avaroa & Santa Cruz), where you can also make calls.

Laundry
All accommodations can do a load of washing for you. There's a **laundry** (☺Mon-Sat) on Florida that charges B$10 per kilo.

Maps
Most agencies distribute small maps of the town and the surroundings.

Money
Banco Union (cnr 7 de Noviembre & Sucre) has an ATM that accepts international cards. Try Prodem for cash advances. **Latin America Cambio** (Avaroa 160) accepts several currencies but not at the best rates.

Tourist Information
With no official tourist office, the hotels and agencies are your main source of information.

ℹ Getting There & Away

Bus
The **bus station** (Pedro Arraya) has buses to most major destinations or hubs in the region. There are multiple trips per day down to Villazón. Buses to other destinations tend to leave either in the morning or evening. Schedules change often so check ahead.

BUS COSTS & DISTANCES

DESTINATION	COST (B$)	DURATION (HR)
Cochabamba	80	16-18
La Paz	70	13-15
Oruro	60	11
Potosí	50	6
Tarija	50	6-8
Villazón	15-22	3

Train
Unfortunately, if you travel by train you miss most of the brilliant scenery on the route to Uyuni, so you might consider the less comfortable bus service. The ticket window at the **train station** (☎694-2527) opens irregularly on days when there's a train, so it can be easier to have an agency buy your tickets for a small surcharge.

RUN	COST (B$ 1ST/COACH)	SCHEDULE
Villazón–Tupiza	37/18	3:30-6:15pm
Tupiza–Atocha	56/24	6:25-9:30pm
Atocha–Uyuni	93/42	9:45-11:50pm
Uyuni–Oruro	224/101	12:05-7am

WARA WARA – VILLAZÓN TO ORURO MONDAYS & THURSDAYS

RUN	COST (B$ 1ST/ COACH/NORMAL)	SCHEDULE
Villazón–Tupiza	35/19/11	3:30-6:15pm
Tupiza–Atocha	44/18/15	7:05-10:45pm
Atocha–Uyuni	75/31/24	9:45-11:50pm
Uyuni–Oruro	170/75/56	1:45-9:10am

* Prices one-way from Tupiza.

Around Tupiza

Much of Tupiza's appeal lies in the surrounding landscape, a visually stunning wilderness of *quebradas* (ravines), thirsty riverbeds and thriving cacti that'll have you whistling a Western theme tune in no time. It's great hiking country and also perfect for exploration on horseback or 4WD – several Tupiza operators offer these excursions.

If you're hiking without a guide, it's not easy to get lost, but take a map anyway – you can get them from various tour agencies. Carry at least 3L of water per day in this dry desert climate. It's wise to wear shoes that can withstand assault by prickly desert vegetation, and to carry a compass or GPS if you're venturing away from the tracks. Flash flooding is also a danger, particularly in the summer months; avoid camping in the *quebradas* or entering the canyons, especially if it looks like rain.

El Cañón del Duende   CANYON
This canyon can be reached from Tupiza on a great half-day stroll; ask any of the agencies for a map and directions. You can also enter the canyon on foot for a scenic 20-minute hike through its towering red rock formations. **El Cañón del Inca** is also part of most itineraries.

El Angosto   LOOKOUT
This scenic spot near Tupiza is a spectacular tunnel of a road carved into the mountain – great for photographs.

QUEBRADA DE PALALA
Just northwest of Tupiza is Quebrada de Palala, a broad wash lined with some very impressive red formations known as fins. During the rainy season it becomes a tributary of the Río Tupiza, but in the winter months it serves as a highway into the back country and part of the salt route from the Salar de Uyuni to Tarija. Beyond the dramatic red rocks, the wash rises very gently into hills colored greenish-blue and violet by lead and other mineral deposits.

To get here, head north on Tupiza's Av La Paz from **Plazuela El Mundo** past the giant slide; 2km ahead, along the railroad line, you'll see the mouth of the *quebrada*. About 5km further along, the route passes some obvious fin formations and continues up the broad *quebrada* into increasingly lonely country, past scrub brush and cacti stands.

EL SILLAR
El Sillar (The Saddle), 15km from Tupiza, is where a road straddles a narrow ridge between two peaks and two valleys. Throughout this area, rugged amphitheaters have been gouged out of the mountainsides and eroded into spires that resemble a stone forest. The road continues on to San Vicente, of Butch and Sundance fame. This entire route is part of a centuries-old trade route. From May to early July you may see a trickle of llama, alpaca and donkey trains – or nowadays more likely *camiones* (pickup trucks) – humping salt blocks 300km from the Salar de Uyuni to trade in Tarija.

QUEBRADA PALMIRA
Between Tupiza and Quebrada Seca lies Quebrada Palmira, a wonderful, normally dry wash flanked by tall and precarious fin formations. The right fork of the wash is rather comically known as Valle de los Machos (Valley of Males) or Valle de los Penes (Valley of Penises). The names stem from the clusters of exceptionally phallic pedestal formations.

HUACA HUAÑUSCA & SAN VICENTE
On November 4, 1908, Robert LeRoy Parker (Butch Cassidy) and Harry Alonzo Longabaugh (the Sundance Kid) pulled off the last robbery of their careers when they politely

CROSSING THE BORDER TO ARGENTINA

The Bolivian side of the main border crossing to Argentina in the town of **Villazón** is a sprawling, dusty, chaotic sort of place. The frontier and bus station are always busy as numerous Bolivians work in Argentina. Watch out for the usual scammers who tend to congregate at borders; dodgy banknotes and petty theft are not unknown.

The **Argentine consulate** (☎597-2011; Plaza 6 de Agosto 123; ⏰10am-1pm Mon-Fri) is on the main square. Numerous *casas de cambio* (money changers) near the bridge along Av República Argentina offer reasonable rates of exchange for US dollars and Argentine pesos, less for bolivianos. **Banco Mercantil** (JM Deheza 423) changes cash and has an ATM dispensing US dollars and bolivianos.

All northbound buses depart from the **Villazón bus terminal** (fee B$2). All except those bound for Tarija pass through Tupiza (B$15 to B$22, 2½ hours); it's a beautiful trip, so try to go in the daylight and grab a window seat – at night the speed, turns and bumps can make it a very scary ride. Regular bus services also head to La Paz (B$140 to B$170, 21 hours) via Potosí (B$80 to B$120, 11 hours) and Oruro (B$140 to B$160, 17 hours). Daily evening buses along the rough but amazing route to Tarija (B$40, seven to eight hours) continue to Bermejo (there are four onward departures per day).

Argentine bus companies have ticket offices opposite Villazón's terminal, but all Argentine buses leave from the La Quiaca bus terminal, across the border. You'll be hassled by ticket sellers for both Argentine and Bolivian bus services; don't be rushed into buying a ticket, as there may be a service leaving sooner. You can easily bargain down the price on longer routes; conversely, the sellers may try and overcharge you on shorter journeys.

The Villazón train station is 1.5km north of the border crossing – a taxi costs B$5.

To just visit La Quiaca briefly there's no need to visit immigration; just walk straight across the bridge. Crossing the border is usually no problem, but avoid the line of traders getting their goods searched or it may take you hours to clear customs.

On the north side of the international bridge, **Bolivian customs & immigration** (⏰24hr) issues exit and entry stamps (the latter normally only for 30 days). There is no official charge for these services, but a B$21 to B$50 'service fee' is sometimes leveraged. Argentine immigration and Argentine customs are open from 7am to 11pm. Formalities are minimal but the wait and exhaustive custom searches can be very long. In addition, those entering Argentina may be held up at several control points further south of the border by more customs searches.

and peacefully relieved Carlos Peró of the Aramayo company payroll, which amounted to US$90,000, at the foot of a hill called Huaca Huañusca (Dead Cow). The name was apparently applied because of the hill's resemblance to a fallen bovine. From an obvious pass on the ridge, a walking track descends the steep slopes to the west for about 2km to the river, where there's a small meadow, a tiny cave and some rugged rocky outcrops where the bandits probably holed up while waiting for the payroll to pass. Several Tupiza agencies offer jeep trips to Huaca Huañusca.

San Vicente is a remote one-mule village that wouldn't even rate a mention were it not the legendary spot where the outlaws met their untimely demise. The mine in San Vicente is now closed and the place has declined to little more than a ghost town. Most of those remaining are military people, mine security guards and their families. To be honest, even hardcore Butch and Sundance fans are sometimes a little disappointed by the place, a dusty spot with a tiny **museum** (admission B$20) and little tourist infrastructure. The museum is often closed and the key-holder difficult to track down. Bring your imagination: you can still see the adobe house where the bandits holed up and eventually died, and the cemetery where they were buried.

There's no regular public transportation between Tupiza and San Vicente; occasionally, a *camión* (flatbed truck) departs for San Vicente early on Thursday morning from Tupiza's Plazuela El Mundo (p164). The easiest way to go is with an agency from Tupiza. While the one-day trips to San Vicente and back are a long, expensive slog, some of the agencies offer a more interesting two-day excursion, taking in Huaca Huañusca en route.

Central Highlands

Best Places to Eat

» El Huerto (p196)
» Malpartida (p215)
» Tentaciones (p196)
» Kabbab (p175)
» Tunari (p176)

Best Places to Stay

» Casa Verde (p194)
» Samary Boutique Hotel (p194)
» Hacienda Cayara (p219)
» Villa Etelvina (p186)
» Hotel Aranjuez (p174)

Why Go?

The Central Highlands are located at the heart of the country and for many represent the heart of the nation. Gorgeous whitewashed Sucre, with elegant patioed houses and noble churches, is where independence was declared in 1825. Potosí, on the other hand, is a powerful symbol of the natural wealth of the country, built on the silver deposits extracted from nearby Cerro Rico. At a much lower altitude, Cochabamba is one of Bolivia's most pleasant cities, with a perfect climate and modern vibe.

But it's not all about cities here. Throughout the region there are lovely, little-known colonial towns gently crumbling with age. It's well worth eschewing the city-to-city mode of travel to explore them. A more distant past is evoked by the Inca ruins in the Cochabamba valley, but Parque Nacional Torotoro has the last laugh on the age front; it's bristling with dinosaur footprints and fossils, some of which date back 300 million years.

When to Go
Potosí

Mar Indigenous festival Pujllay bursts into life on the third Sunday in March.

Aug Catch merry-making at the Fiesta de la Virgen de Urkupiña.

Oct–Mar Target the summer months to avoid the worst of Potosí's chills.

History

Prior to Spanish domination, the town of Charcas (nowadays Sucre) was the indigenous capital of the valley of Choque-Chaca. As the residence of local religious, military and political leaders, its jurisdiction extended to several thousand inhabitants. When the Spanish arrived, the area from southern Peru to the Río de la Plata in present-day Argentina came to be known as Charcas.

In the early 1530s Francisco Pizarro, the conquistador who felled the Inca empire, sent his brother Gonzalo to the Charcas region to oversee indigenous mining activities that might prove to be valuable to the Spanish realm. He was not interested in the Altiplano and concentrated on the highlands east of the main Andean cordilleras. As a direct result, in 1538 a new Spanish capital of the Charcas was founded. Following in the

CENTRAL HIGHLANDS

Central Highlands Highlights

① Admire the churches of **Potosí** (p205), filled with evocative religious artworks

② Goggle at the colonial beauty of **Sucre** (p187), Bolivia's most attractive city

③ Pack on the pounds or party hard in **Cochabamba** (p168), which boasts

some of the country's best restaurants and bars

④ Home in on remote and wild **Parque Nacional Torotoro** (p184), stomping ground of dinosaurs

⑤ Roam the **Cordillera de los Frailes** (p200),

with its intriguing Jal'qa weaving culture

⑥ Take in one of the whacky festivals at little **Tiquipaya** (p180)

⑦ Visit Bolivia's version of Machu Picchu, the mystical ruins of **Incallajta** (p182)

conquered population's footsteps, he chose the warm, fertile valley of Choque-Chaca for its site. The city, later to become Sucre, was named La Plata – silver was god in those days.

Whereas previously all territories in the region had been governed from Lima, in 1559 King Felipe II created the Audiencia (Royal Court) of Charcas, with its headquarters in the young city, to help administer the eastern territories. Governmental subdivisions within the district came under the jurisdiction of royal officers known as *corregidores*.

In 1776 a new Viceroyalty was established in what is now Buenos Aires and the Charcas came under its control. The city became known as Chuquisaca (a Spanish corruption of Choque-Chaca), as there were too many La Platas around for comfort.

The city had received an Archbishopric in 1609, according it theological autonomy. That, along with the establishment of the University of San Xavier in 1622 and the 1681 opening of the Academía Carolina law school, fostered continued development of liberal and revolutionary ideas and set the stage for 'the first cry of Independence in the Americas' on May 25, 1809. The minirevolution set off the alarm throughout Spanish America and, like ninepins, the northwestern South American republics were liberated by the armies of the military genius Simón Bolívar.

After the definitive liberation of Peru at the battles of Junín and Ayacucho, on August 6 and December 9, 1824, Alto Peru (historically tied to the Lima government) was technically free of Spanish rule. In practice, however, it had been administered from Buenos Aires and disputes arose about what to do with the territory.

On February 9, 1825, Bolívar's second-in-command, General Antonio José de Sucre, drafted and delivered a declaration that rejected the authority of Buenos Aires and suggested the political future of the region should be determined by the provinces themselves.

Bolívar, unhappy with this unauthorized act of sovereignty, rejected the idea but de Sucre stood his ground, convinced that there was sufficient separatist sentiment in Alto Peru to back him up. As he expected, the people of the region staunchly refused to wait for a decision from the new congress, which was to be installed in Lima the following year, and also rejected subsequent invitations to join the Buenos Aires government.

On August 6, the first anniversary of the Battle of Junín, independence was declared in the Casa de la Libertad at Chuquisaca and the new republic was christened Bolivia, after its liberator. On August 11 the city's name was changed for the final time to Sucre, in honor of the general who'd promoted the independence movement.

National Parks

The region's protected areas include the remote Parque Nacional Torotoro (p184), peppered with thousands of dinosaur footprints, and Parque Nacional Tunari (p179), easily accessible from the city of Cochabamba.

❶ Getting There & Away

The Central Highlands' major population centers are well served by intercity buses; timetables for the major cities can be consulted online at www.boliviaentusmanos.com/terminal. Getting between towns in the region is a bit more of a challenge if venturing beyond the Potosí–Sucre paved highway; the route between Cochabamba and Sucre is a particularly slow one.

Cochabamba has the busiest airport, but for Potosí you should fly into Sucre as it's only about 162km away.

COCHABAMBA

✈ 4 / POP 517,000 / ELEV 2553M

Busy, buzzy Cochabamba is one of Bolivia's boom cities and has a distinct, almost Mediterranean, vitality that perhaps owes something to its clement climate. While much of the city's population is typically poor, parts of town have a notably prosperous feel. The spacious new-town avenues have a wide choice of restaurants, eagerly grazed by the food-crazy *cochabambinos*, and the bar scene is lively, driven by students and young professionals. Despite this, Cochabamba remains a very affordable city, with prices far below those in Sucre or La Paz. You could easily find yourself staying a lot longer than you planned.

The city's name is derived from the Quechua *khocha pampa*, meaning 'swampy plain'. Cochabamba lies in a fertile green bowl, 25km long by 10km wide, set in a landscape of fields and low hills. To the northwest rises Cerro Tunari (5035m), the highest peak in central Bolivia. Cochabamba is famous for its *chicha*, a fermented corn drink that is the locals' favorite tipple.

History

Cochabamba was founded in January 1574 by Sebastián Barba de Padilla. It was originally named Villa de Oropeza in honor of the Count and Countess of Oropeza, parents of Viceroy Francisco de Toledo, who promoted its settlement.

During the height of Potosí's silver boom, the Cochabamba Valley developed into the primary source of food for the miners in agriculturally unproductive Potosí. Thanks to its maize and wheat production, Cochabamba became known as the 'breadbasket of Bolivia'. As Potosí's importance declined during the early 18th century, so did Cochabamba's and grain production in the Chuquisaca (Sucre) area, much closer to Potosí, was sufficient to supply the decreasing demand.

By the mid-19th century, however, the city had reassumed its position as the nation's granary. Elite landowners in the valley grew wealthy and began investing in highland mining ventures. Before long, the Altiplano mines were attracting international capital, and the focus of Bolivian mining shifted from Potosí to southwestern Bolivia. Cochabamba again thrived and its European-mestizo population gained a reputation for affluence and prosperity.

In 2000 the eyes of the world turned to Cochabamba as its citizens protested against rises in water rates. The World Bank had forced the Bolivian government to sell off its water company to US giant Bechtel in order to provide financing for a tunnel that would bring water from the other side of the mountains. The resultant price rise brought hundreds of thousands of citizens out in protest, eventually driving Bechtel out.

Politically, Cochabamba is suspended somewhere between the pro-Morales Altiplano and the pro-autonomous lowlands. In January 2007 pro-Morales trade unionists and coca growers set up a parallel local government that demanded the resignation of the pro-autonomy governor. The resultant clashes left two people dead.

◉ Sights

Cochabamba is Bolivia's biggest market town and shopping and gastronomy are what draw in the locals. The town is also blessed with a couple of interesting museums and a number of attractive churches, though the latter are usually open only during mass. A convenient **tourist bus** (☑450-8920; per person B\$25) leaves from Plaza Colón at 10am and 3pm and visits all the city sights.

Convento de Santa Teresa CONVENT

(Baptista & Ecuador; admission B\$20; ⊙tours hourly 9-11am & 2:30-4:30pm Mon-Fri, 2:30-4:30pm Sat) The most interesting building in town is the noble, timeworn Convento de Santa Teresa. Visits to this gracefully decaying complex are by guided tour only and provide a snapshot of the extraordinary lives led by the cloistered nuns that inhabit it. You see the peaceful cloister, fine altarpieces and sculptures (from Spanish and Potosí schools), the convent church and even get to ascend to the roof for a glorious view over the city. The convent was founded in 1760 and then destroyed in an earthquake. A new church was built with an excess of ambition, but was too big to be domed. The existing church was built inside it in 1790. There's still a Carmelite community here, but its handful of nuns are now housed in more comfortable modern quarters next door. It's a fascinating visit; pacing the convent's corridors, you could be in a Gabriel García Márquez novel.

Palacio Portales PALACE

(Potosí 1450; admission incl guide B\$10; ⊙gardens 3-6:30pm Tue-Fri, 9am-noon Sat & Sun, English tours 4pm & 5pm Mon-Fri, 10:30am & 11:30am Sat, 11:30am Sun) The Palacio Portales in the barrio of Queru Queru provides evidence of the extravagance of tin baron Simón Patiño. Patiño's tastes were strongly influenced by European styles and though he never actually occupied this opulent mansion it was stocked with the finest imported materials available at the time – Carrara marble, French wood, Italian tapestries and delicate silks. The European influence is obvious as you venture through the building; the gardens and exterior were inspired by the palace at Versailles, the games room is an imitation of Granada's Alhambra and the main hall takes its design inspiration from the Vatican City. Construction began in 1915 and was completed in 1927. Today it is used as an arts and cultural complex and as a teaching center.

Take *micro E* north from east of Av San Martín.

FREE Museo de Historia Natural Alcide d'Orbigny MUSEUM

(Potosí 1458; admission free but donations welcomed; ⊙9am-noon & 3-6pm Mon-Fri, 9am-12:30pm Sat)

Cochabamba

N
0 _____ 400 m
0 _____ 0.2 miles

To SERNAP
(4.5km)

Portales

Av Portales

🏛 Palacio
🏛 Portales
7

To IC Norte (150m);
Sudamericana Rent-a-Car
(150m); Puka Killa Bed
& Breakfast (500m)

P Blanco

To Hotel
Aranjuez (50m);
TAM (50m);
Kropl's Bierhaus
(200m)

Beni

31

Sejas
Paseo de la
Recoleta

✪ 52

3 14
🕀

Av Aniceto Padilla

68

Stadium

Potosí

33   51

Av Uyuni

Av Oblitas

49

Av del Ejército

60

Av Ramón Rivero

Plaza
Quintanilla

Oruro

24

🗙 34

Lanza

La Paz

Antezana

30

Av Oquendo

Vázquez

Migración

11

Baptista

41
37

Chuquisaca

35

21

Salamanca

65

57

56
42

38

27

Paccieri

Centro Medico
Boliviano Belga

Hospital
Viedma

26

54

Plaza
Colón

63

Venezuela

Av Aniceto Arce

México

46
16

32 47

22

9

Iglesia del
Hospicio

Ecuador

To Apart Hotel
Concordia (800m)

19

Mayor Rocha

Convento
de Santa
Teresa

36

8   28

12

Colombia

10

44

Templo
Santa
Clara

40

Av de las Heroínas

To Cristo
de la
Concordia
(600m)

17

España

50

29

Plaza
Busch

18 39

62   25
55

2

Bolívar

64

58

43

48

Sucre

To Escuela
Runawasi
(4.5km)

Achá

67

59

Market

23

Santiváñez

53 45
13

1
66

Jordán

6

4

69

Calama

Pasaje
Catedral

Ladislao Cabrera

Plaza
San
Sebastián

Uruguay

To Airport
(4km)

20

Av Aroma

To Mercado
de Ferias
(100m)

To Main
Bus Terminal
(250m)

61

Brasil

5

Av República

Cochabamba

Adjacent to the Palacio Portales is the city's rather more low-key natural history museum. With its creaky wooden floors and array of stuffed birds and mammals, this is a good way to kill half an hour while waiting for your Palacio Portales tour to begin. You can also take a look at the small geological collection.

Museo Arqueológico   MUSEUM
(Jordán E-199 cnr Aguirre; admission B$25; ⊙8:30am-6pm Mon-Fri, 8am-noon Sat) The Museo

THE NUNS OF SANTA TERESA

The Santa Teresa convent in Cochabamba houses what remains of an order of cloistered Carmelite nuns. A strict Catholic order with a strong devotion to the Virgin Mary, the Carmelites are thought to have been founded in the 12th century on Mt Carmel (hence the name). The order believes strongly in the power of contemplative prayer and shuns the excesses of society.

In recent times, and with local families believing that a daughter in the convent guaranteed the entire family a place in heaven, there was strong pressure on the first daughter of every *cochabambino* family to enter into the convent. Such was the demand to get some real estate in heaven that there was even a waiting list set up when no vacancies were available. An elderly nun had to pass on before a new young nun was allowed in.

Life inside was tough and a rigid class system operated. Those who paid a considerable dowry (equivalent to more than US$150,000 in modern money) earned themselves a *velo negro* (black veil) and a place on the council under the control of the Mother Superior. The council was responsible for all the decisions in the convent. As the elite members of the order, *velos negros* were blessed with a private stone room with a single window, where they spent most of their day in prayer, religious study and other acceptable activities such as sewing tapestries.

Each *velo negro* was attended by members of the *velo blanco* (white veil), second-class nuns whose family paid a dowry but could not afford the full cost of a *velo negro*. *Velo blanco* nuns spent part of their day in prayer and the rest in the personal service of the

Arqueológico provides an excellent overview of Bolivia's various indigenous cultures. The collection is split into three sections: the archaeological collection, the ethnographic collection and the paleontological collection. The first deals primarily with indigenous culture from the Cochabamba region. Look out for the Tiwanaku section; their shamans used to snort lines of hallucinogenic powder through elegant bone tubes. The ethnographic collection provides material from Amazonian and Chaco cultures including examples of nonalphabetized writing, which is from the 18th century and was used to bring Christianity to the illiterate Indians. The paleontological collection deals with fossilized remains of the various creatures that once prowled the countryside. There's good information in Spanish and an English-speaking guide is sometimes around in the afternoons.

Cristo de la Concordia   LANDMARK

This immense Christ statue standing atop Cerro de San Pedro behind Cochabamba is the second largest of its kind in the world. Its 44cm higher than the famous *Cristo Redentor* in Rio de Janeiro, which stands 33m high, or 1m for each year of Christ's life. *Cochabambinos* justify the one-upmanship by claiming that Christ actually lived '33 *años y un poquito*' (33 years and a bit).

There's a footpath from the base of the mountain (1250 steps), near the eastern end of Avenida de los Heroinas, but several robberies have been reported here and signs along the route warn you of the dangers, not-so-subtly suggesting that you should take the **teleférico** (Cable Car; return B$8; ⊘closed Mon). On Sunday you can climb right to the top of the statue (B$2) for a Christ's-eye view of the city.

The closest public-transport access is on *micro E* from San Martín and Sucre. Taxis charge B$40 for the round trip to the top, including a half-hour wait while you look around.

Cathedral   CHURCH

(Plaza 14 de Septiembre; ⊘8am-noon & 2-7pm Mon-Fri, 8am-noon Sat & Sun) On the arcaded Plaza 14 de Septiembre, Cochabamba's cathedral is the valley's oldest religious structure, begun in 1571. Later additions and renovations have removed some character, but a fine eastern portal has been preserved. Inside it is light and airy, with various mediocre ceiling paintings. There are statues of several saints, a gilded altarpiece and a grotto for the ever-popular Inmaculada (Virgin of the Immaculate Conception).

La Cancha   MARKET

(Av Aroma) The main market is the enormous La Cancha, which is one of the most crowd-

velo negro. Daughters of poor families who could not afford any kind of dowry became *sin velos* (without veils). These nuns were employed in the roughest chores of the convent, cooking, cleaning and attending to the needs of the *velo blanco*. They slept in communal quarters.

The rules inside the convent were strict. Personal effects were not permitted and communication with other nuns was allowed for only one hour a day – the rest was spent in total silence. Meals were eaten without speaking and contact with the outside world was almost completely prohibited. Once a month each nun was allowed a brief visit from their family, but this took place behind bars and with a black curtain preventing them from seeing and touching each other. Visits were supervised to ensure that no rules were broken and no goods changed hands. The only other contact with the city was through the sale of candles and foodstuffs, which was performed via a revolving door so that the vendor and the client were kept apart. Such transactions were the sole source of income for the nuns who were otherwise completely self-sufficient.

In the 1960s the Vatican declared that such conditions were inhuman and offered all cloistered nuns the world over the opportunity to change to a more modern way of life. Many of the nuns in Santa Teresa rejected the offer, having spent the better part of their life in the convent and knowing no different. Today most of the few remaining nuns are of advancing years and while the rules are no longer as strict as they once were, the practices have changed little. These days the cloistered lifestyle is understandably less attractive to young girls in an age where their families permit them to exercise their own free will.

ed, chaotic, claustrophobic and exhilarating spots in the country. Around the markets you'll find just about everything imaginable, including pickpockets.

The largest and most accessible area is **Mercado Cancha Calatayud**, which sprawls across a wide area along Av Aroma and south toward the former railway station. Here is your best opportunity to see **local dress**, which differs strikingly from that of the Altiplano.

The **Mercado de Ferias** spills out around the old railway station. *Artesanías* (stores selling locally handcrafted items) are concentrated along the alleys near the junction of Tarata and Arce, at the southern end of the market area. The fruit and vegetable section is on the shore of Laguna Alalay in the southeast of town.

Iglesia & Convento de San Francisco
CHURCH

(Calles 25 de Mayo & Bolívar) Constructed in 1581, the Iglesia & Convento de San Francisco is Cochabamba's second-oldest church. Major revisions and renovation occurred in 1782 and 1925, however, and little of the original structure remains. The attached convent and cloister were added in the 1600s. The cloister was constructed of wood rather than the stone that was customary at the time. The pulpit displays good examples of mestizo design and there's a fine gold-framed altarpiece.

Iglesia de Santo Domingo
CHURCH

(Santivañez & Ayacucho) The rococo Iglesia de Santo Domingo was founded in 1612 construction only began in 1778. Its intriguing main facade is made of stone, with anthropomorphic columns. The interior, with a much-revered Trinity, is less interesting.

Iglesia de la Recoleta
CHURCH

(Plazuela de la Recoleta) North of the river, the baroque Iglesia de la Recoleta was started in 1654. It houses the attractive wooden Cristo de la Recoleta.

🎓 Courses

Cochabamba is a popular place to hole up for a few weeks of Spanish or Quechua lessons. Cultural centers offer courses for about B$50 per hour.

Centro Boliviano Americano
LANGUAGE COURSE

(☑422-1288; 25 de Mayo N-365) Can recommend private language teachers.

Escuela Runawasi
CULTURAL COURSE

(☑424-8923; www.runawasi.org; Blanco Galindo km 4.5, Villa Juan XXIII) The Escuela Runawasi offers a recommended program that involves linguistic and cultural immersion from B$1200 per week. It also includes a trip to a relaxing Chapare rainforest hideout.

Instituto Cultural
Boliviano Alemán   LANGUAGE COURSE
(ICBA; ☑412-2323; www.icbacbba.org; Lanza 727) Offers group Spanish lessons.

☞ Tours

Various agents run a number of activities, particularly excursions to spots of interest in the province. The following are recommended:

Bolivia Cultura   OUTDOORS
(☑452-7272; www.boliviacultura.com; España 301) Professional trips to Parque Nacional Torotoro and other regional attractions.

Fremen Tours   OUTDOORS
(☑425-9392; www.andes-amazonia.com; Tumusla N-245) Organizes local excursions and high-quality trips to the Chapare, Amazon and Salar de Uyuni.

Villa Etelvina   OUTDOORS
(☑7073-7807; www.villaetelvina.com; Juan de la Rosa 908) A good local operator specializing in trips to Torotoro National Park.

✵ Festivals & Events

Heroínas de la Coronilla   MEMORIAL
A major annual event is the Heroínas de la Coronilla (May 27), a solemn commemoration in honor of the women and children who defended the city in the battle of 1812.

Santa Veracruz Tatala   RELIGIOUS
At the fiesta of Santa Veracruz Tatala (May 2), farmers gather at a chapel 7km down the Sucre road to pray for fertile soil during the coming season. Their petitions are accompanied by folk music, dancing and lots of merrymaking.

🛏 Sleeping

Don't be tempted by the rock-bottom prices for accommodation in the market areas and around the bus station. It's cheap for a reason: the area is dangerous after dark and it is in your best interests to stay somewhere north of Calle Sucre.

TOP CHOICE **Hotel Aranjuez**   HOTEL $$$
(☑424-0158; www.hotelaranjuez.com; Buenos Aires E-563; s/d B$460/530, ste B$665-910; ❄@☎) In the wealthy Recoleta district north of the center, this place is making a name for itself at the top end of the scale for getting the price-to-luxury ratio spot on. As you walk

around the wonderfully decorated salons you could be forgiven for thinking that you were staying in one of Patiño's palaces. The place has even been used as a film set.

Gran Hotel
Cochabamba   BOUTIQUE HOTEL $$$
(☑448-9520; www.granhotelcochabamba.com; Plaza Ubaldo Anze N-415; s/d B$700/793, ste B$885-1695; ❄@☎) Officially Cochabamba's top hotel, this five-star beauty is a stone's throw from Iglesia de la Recoleta and is housed in the same historic building that once housed the city's first hotel. It's classy, elegant, has a wonderful patio and yet manages to provide friendly, informal service that most hotels in this category lack.

Puka Killa Bed & Breakfast   HOSTEL $$
(☑445-9444; www.pukakilla.com; Av Circunvalacion II 946, cnr Av Pando; s/d/tr B$154/230/310) Meaning 'red moon' in Quechua (not cockney!), this is a great new Italian-run guesthouse in a spacious family house. You get a home-from-home welcome here and the fact that it is quite a distance from the center is more than compensated for by value for money.

City Hotel   HOTEL $$
(☑422-2993; www.cityhotelbolivia.com; Jordán E-341; s/d/f incl breakfast B$150/200/250; @) This spotless, friendly and central hotel is an excellent choice. Rooms are bright and well equipped, and the beds are firm and enticing. There's a laundry service and cable TV. It's close to the best value in town.

Hostal Sauna
Internacional Inn   HOTEL $
(☑452-5382; Junín near México; s/d B$70/140) HSII (it's much easier to say it like that!) is great value for basic but comfortable rooms with cable TV. Your boliviano goes a bit further here than in other nearby hotels and, despite being a slightly odd addition to the services on offer, the weekend sauna (3pm to 6pm) may be an added bonus for some people.

Hostal Gina's   HOSTEL $$
(☑422-2925; www.ginashostal.web.bo; México 346 nr España; s/d/tr B$130/240/300) Above Gina's beauty parlor, this is a modern, bright and freshly furnished hotel. Don't be put off by the reception (OTT with the lilac, perhaps?); this is a great place and the larger rooms, equipped with kitchen and living room, are good value.

Hotel Diplomat HOTEL **$$$**
(☑425-0687; www.hdiplomat.com; Ballivián 611; s/d B$470/540; @) Though the Diplomat, an up-market business hotel, is clinically efficient in its service, it has a snobbish atmosphere that some might feel verges on the unfriendly. There are great views from some of the well-appointed rooms and it has a good location on Av Ballivián, known as 'El Prado' – a center for shopping or barhopping. Free airport transfer.

Monserrat Hotel HOTEL **$$**
(☑452-1011; www.hotelmonserrat.com; España N-342; s/d B$180/300; @) In a renovated historic building at the heart of the eating and cafe scene. The rooms are elegant and comfortable, though some are a bit dark. Great views of the *Cristo* from the 2nd floor.

Residencial Familiar PENSION **$**
(☑422-7988; Sucre E-554; s/d B$130/160, without bathroom B$50/100) Set in a lovely old building, this budget place has plenty of character. It's built around a secluded patio, complete with a nude sculpture in the fountain, and is a real haven from the hustle and bustle of the street outside.

Apart Hotel Concordia APARTMENT **$**
(☑422-1518; Aniceto Arce 690; apt d/tr B$200/250; ☒) This fading but likable place is family-run and family-oriented. Two- and three-person apartments include a bath, kitchenette (dishes available on request) and phone. Guests have access to the pool and laundry service. It's north of town near the university (so often booked up with students) and accessible on *micro B*.

Hotel Americana HOTEL **$$$**
(☑425-0552; Aniceto Arce S-788; s/d/ste B$490/700/910) This friendly three-star option is a sound choice. The service is good and the spotless rooms have plenty of natural light and pleasing facilities, including cable TV. Only the location leaves a little to be desired.

Hostal Jardín PENSION **$$**
(☑452-5356; Hamiraya N-248; s/d B$100/200, without bathroom B$70/140) In a quiet part of town, this long-time favorite is centered around a likably chaotic garden with an enormous starfruit tree.

Hostal La Fontaine HOTEL **$**
(☑425-2838; Hamiraya N-181; s/d B$95/160; @) Decent value, though it could do with a lick of paint and the religious images adorning the stairwells are slightly unnerving. Rooms are spacious, with cable TV and minibar, but those on the ground floor are too dark.

Hostal Colonial PENSION **$**
(☑458-3791; Junín N-134; s/d B$60/120, without bathroom B$50/100) A travelers' favorite, but somewhat overrated considering the facilities and the other options in this price tier. Rooms are a bit rundown; the best are upstairs overlooking the leafy courtyard gardens.

✖ Eating

Cochabambinos pride themselves on being the most food-loving of Bolivians and there is a dazzling array of local specialties for foodies to try, including *lomo borracho* (beef with egg in a beer soup) and *picante de pollo* (chicken in spicy sauce). Ask at the **tourist office** (☑425-8030; Plaza 14 de Septiembre; ◔8am-noon & 2:30-6:30pm Mon-Fri) for its *Cochabamba Gastronòmica* leaflet.

There's tasty street food and snacks all over Cochabamba, with the *papas rellenas* (potatoes filled with meat or cheese) at the corner of Achá and Villazón particularly delicious. Great *salteñas* (filled pastry shells) and empanadas are ubiquitous; for the latter, try **Los Castores** (Ballivián 790; empanadas B$6), which has a range of delicious fillings both savory and sweet. Locals swear by the *anticuchos* (beef-heart shish kebabs) that sizzle all night at the corner of Avs Villaroel and América.

The jumbo-size **Dumbo** (Ballivián 55 or Av de las Heroínas E-345; mains B$10-79) and **Cristal** (Heroínas E-352; mains B$18-47) serve a range of foods throughout the day, from pancakes to bland-but-decent burgers and main dishes, and are particularly popular for a late-afternoon *helado* (ice cream) and coffee. A similar place that's a real fun-palace for children is **Globo's** (Plaza Colón or Santa Cruz btwn Beni & P Blanco; mains B$27-79). Balloons, ice creams, juices and kid-friendly meals – it's got the lot.

TOP CHOICE **Kabbab** ARABIC **$$**
(Potosí N-1392; mains B$30-60; ◔dinner) About thousand-and-one variations on Persian kebabs served in an intimate space adjacent to the Palacio Portales. Highlights include clay-oven flatbread, Turkish coffee and decent baklava.

Tunari
LATIN AMERICAN $$$

(Ballivián 676; mains B$30-70) With the distinction of being the oldest restaurant in the city, this local favorite specializes in the sort of things you either love or hate: grilled kidneys (a patent local hangover cure), tripe and tasty chorizo. But if innards aren't your thing, there are other typical Cochabamba plates.

Páprika
INTERNATIONAL $$$

(Chuquisaca; mains B$27-80) One of the 'in' spots, this is a swish restaurant-bar popular for its food, both Bolivian and international, including tasty baked potatoes and fondues, and more unusual plates such as ostrich and llama. After dark it becomes a trendy spot for a late drink and is also a good place to meet up with young bolivianos.

La Estancia
ARGENTINE $$$

(Uyuni E-786 nr Pasaje de la Recoleta; mains B$38-70) One of a knot of spacious restaurants across the river in Recoleta, this Argentine-style grill is a fine place. There are thick, juicy steaks (it's worth upgrading to the Argentine meat), ribs and kidneys, as well as fish and chicken, all sizzled on the blazing grill in the middle. There's also a decent salad bar and very good service.

La Cantonata
ITALIAN $$$

(España & Mayor Rocha; mains B$45-70; ☺noon-2:30pm & 6:30-11:30pm Tue-Sat) This classy Italian place is one of the city's most reputable places to eat. The cozy interior has a roaring fire, candlelit tables and waistcoated waiters. Pizza and pasta are top notch but pricey.

Casa de Campo
LATIN AMERICAN $$$

(Pasaje de la Recoleta 618; mains B$43-67) A Cochabamba classic, this loud and cheerful partly open-air restaurant is a traditional spot to meet, eat, and play *cacho* (dice). There's a big range of Bolivian dishes and grilled meats; the food is fine (and piled high on the plates) but the lively, unpretentious atmosphere is better.

Búfalo's Rodizio
BRAZILIAN $$$

(Oquendo N-654, 2nd fl Torres Sofer; buffet B$69; ☺noon-11pm Tue-Sat, lunch only Sun, dinner only Mon) This all-you-can-eat Brazilian-style grill has smart waiters bringing huge hunks of delicious meat to your table faster than you can pick up your fork. There's a large salad bar but, let's face it, it's designed for the carnivore.

Savarín
LATIN AMERICAN $

(Ballivián 626; almuerzo B$19) Despite lacklustre service this is a popular, well-established barn on Ballivián with a wide streetside terrace where people congregate at lunchime for filling *almuerzos* (set lunches) and, in the evening, for a beer or three.

Vicunqui
ARGENTINE $$$

(www.vicunqui.com; Plazuela Barba de Padilla 277, Acera Norte; mains B$30-70; ☺noon-11pm Tue-Sat, lunch only Sun, closed Mon) Top marks for the prime rib and a 'must try harder' for atmosphere. The pre-1950s music played on vinyl records is something you will either love or hate.

Sucremanta
LATIN AMERICAN $

(Ballivián 510; mains from B$18; ☺lunch) A chain of *restaurantes típicos* with two more branches on **Hamiraya** (Hamiraya 126) and **Arce** (Arce 340). Here you can sample dependable local dishes, including *mondongo* (pork ribs) and *menudito* (pork, chicken and beef stew).

HWA
ASIAN $$

(Salamanca 868; mains B$23-60, almuerzo B$25) If you like Asian food, you're in for a treat. Korean and Japanese dishes are on offer and the food is good.

Gopal
VEGETARIAN $$

(España N-250; mains B$20-40, buffet B$18; ☺lunch daily, dinner Mon-Fri) Half-decent vegetarian dishes, including soy-based versions of Bolivian dishes and a few curries.

Picasso's
MEXICAN $$

(España & Mayor Rocha; mains B$12-49) As with many of the places along España, Picasso's blurs the boundaries between cafe, restaurant and bar, metamorphosing from one to the next depending on the time of day. It's worth a look for its informal atmosphere and Mexican food.

Gopinath Uno's
VEGETARIAN $

(Av de las Heroínas 562 cnr San Martín; almuerzo B$15; ☺8am-4pm Mon-Sat) Tasty and remarkably cheap, with vegetarian-buffet fare served on plastic prison-style trays. It also does good fruit salads and soy burgers, but there's no alcohol served. Blink and you'll miss it, though – there's no sign outside and it's barely larger than a walk-in closet.

Self-Catering

IC Norte
SUPERMARKET $

(América at Pando) This is a well-stocked US-style supermarket with imported and unique export-quality Bolivian products.

Super Haas SUPERMARKET
(Av de las Heroínas E-585) Convenient if expensive mini-market with a deli and snack
counter.

 Drinking

There's plenty of drinking action along
El Prado (Av Ballivián) and the scene also
flourishes along España, home to an ever-
changing parade of appealing bohemian
cafe–bars.

Kropl's Bierhaus BEER HALL
(Av América E-992) Home-brew beer, a lively
atmosphere and Tex-Mex bar snacks make
this a happening place to hang out.

Cerebritos BAR
(España N-251; ⊙6pm-late) A grungy, likable
bar with cable drums for tables and loud
rock and hip-hop music. The house special
is a mixed platter of colorful shooters; local
students down them as *cacho* (dice) forfeits.

Oásis de Dali BAR
(España N-428) An interesting and popular
boliche (nightclub) that successfully mixes
alcohol consumption with an appreciation
for art. Regular exhibitions and live-music
performances make it worth staying a while.

Prikafé CAFE
(España & Mayor Rocha; ⊙5:30pm-midnight) This
cozy corner spot is an intimate, candlelit
place popular with romancing couples. It's
better for drinks – coffee, wine, cocktails –
than the tasty but calorie-laden food.

Espresso Café Bar CAFE
(Arce 340; ⊙8am-10pm Mon-Sat) Just behind
the Cathedral, this wins the 'best coffee in
town' award. It's an attractive, traditional-
looking place with pleasant staff. It also
serves good juices. A word of advice – don't
order a 'large' espresso unless caffeine is
more of a compulsion than a pleasure.

Café Paris CAFE
(España cnr Bolívar; ⊙8am-10pm Mon-Sat) Walls
lined with Parisian street scenes, newspapers on racks and a variety of crepes for
every day of the week. This is a popular, if
slightly pretentious, cafe that plays a little
too much on the faux-*Francais*.

 Entertainment

The huge cinema multiplex **Cine Center**
(Ramón Rivero s/n) has several screens; more
atmospheric are the bright **Cine Heroínas**

(Av de las Heroínas s/n) and the smaller **Cine
Astor** (Sucre & 25 de Mayo). For information
about what's on, see the newspaper entertainment listings.

Many of the bars along España and Ballivián turn into minidiscos after midnight
throughout the week, but at weekends the
in-crowd head to La Recoleta and Av Pando to trendy places like **Levoa** (Paseo de la
Recoleta). Expect to pay more than B$30 to
get in. Elsewhere, popular dancing spots
include **Lujo's Discoteca y Karaoke** (Beni
E-330; ⊙8pm-late Wed-Sun), which, when the
clientele don't take the music into their own
hands, plays salsa and pop.

 Shopping

Locally made woollens are available at a few
outlets. Try the expensive but reliable **Asarti**
(Edificio Colón No 5, Paccieri at 25 de Mayo), which
makes export-quality alpaca clothing, and
the cooperative **Arte Andino** (www.artesandi
nos.com; Pasaje Catedral s/n). Cheaper alpaca-
and llama-wool *chompas* (sweaters) are
found in the markets. For inexpensive souvenirs, scour the *artesanía* stalls behind the
main post office.

Decent bookstores include **Los Amigos
del Libro** (España cnr Bolívar) and the **Spitting Llama** (España 615), both of which stock
Lonely Planet books.

ⓘ Information

Cochabamba addresses are measured relative
to the crossroads of two main avenues, Heroínas (running east–west) and Ayacucho
(north–south). Streets crossing Heroínas to
the north are preceded by 'N' *(norte)* and to the
south by 'S' *(sud)*. Those that cross Ayacucho
are preceded by 'E' *(este)* to the east or 'O'
(oeste) to the west. The number immediately
after the letter tells you how many blocks away
from these division streets the address falls.

Dangers & Annoyances

According to locals the streets south of Av
Aroma are best avoided and are positively
dangerous at night. The bus station is around
here, so don't be surprised if, when arriving
in the early hours of the morning, you are not
allowed off the bus until sunrise. Pickpocketing
and petty theft are common in the markets;
don't carry any more than you are likely to
need. The parkland areas Colina San Sebastián
and Coronilla Hill near the bus station are both
extremely dangerous throughout the day –
avoid them!

Emergency

Tourist police (☑450-3880, 120; Plaza 14 de Septiembre)

Immigration

Migración (☑452-4625; La Paz cnr Ballivián; ⊗8:30am-4pm Mon-Fri) For visa and length-of-stay extensions.

Internet Access

If you happen to spot a city block that does not have an internet place let us know; they are everywhere. Most of them charge B$3 to B$4 per hour.

Laundry

Most hotels offer laundry services, but for commercial *lavanderías* try **Brillante** (Ayacucho 923; ⊗closed Sun) and **Lavaya** (Salamanca cnr Antezana; ⊗closed Sun), which charge about B$12 per kilo.

Medical Services

Ambulance (☑181)

Centro Medico Boliviano Belga (☑422-9407; Antezana N-455) Private clinic.

Hospital Viedma (☑453-3240; Venezuela) Full-service public hospital.

Money

Moneychangers gather along Av de las Heroínas and near the market at 25 de Mayo. Their rates are competitive but some only accept US cash. There are numerous ATMs and cash advances are available at major banks; a handy cluster of ATMs is at the corner of Heroínas and Ayacucho. **Banco Unión** (25 de Mayo cnr Sucre) has one of several Western Union offices.

Post

The **main post** (Ayacucho cnr Heroínas; ⊗6:30am-10pm) and Entel offices are together in a large complex. The postal service from Cochabamba is reliable and the facilities are among the country's finest. Downstairs from the main lobby is an express post office. In the alleyway behind, the customs office is a good place for sending packages; it stamps them so that they won't be opened later and offers a cheaper rate than the post office itself.

Telephone

You'll have no problem making phone calls. Entel and Punto Viva offices are scattered around the city and there are also large numbers of private telephone cabinas.

Tourist Information

Cochabamba has a superb website for visitors (www.cochabamba-online.net). This site also has details and information about places of interest, links to flight information, hotel listings, photos and local events.

Infotur (☑466-2277; Plaza Colón; ⊗8am-noon & 2:30-6:30pm Mon-Fri) Very welcoming and hands out good city material. There are several information kiosks, including at the bus station and airport, which also open Saturday mornings.

Instituto Geográfico Militar (IGM; ☑425-5563; 16 de Julio S-237) For topographic maps (useful for walkers) of Cochabamba department.

SERNAP Office (Servicio Nacional de Areas Protegidas; Atahuallpa 2367; ⊗8:30am-12:30pm & 2:30-6:30pm Mon-Fri) Has limited information about national parks. Private tour companies are usually better equipped to answer questions.

❶ Getting There & Away

Air

The flight between La Paz and Cochabamba's **Jorge Wilstermann International Airport** (CBB; domestic/international departure tax B$14/170) must be one of the world's most incredible (sit on the left coming from La Paz, the right from Cochabamba), with fabulous views of the dramatic Cordillera Quimsa Cruz and a (disconcertingly) close-up view of the peak of Illimani. Most flights between Santa Cruz and La Paz touch down briefly at Cochabamba and the city also connects them with flights to Sucre. It is a good idea to book your flights in advance.

TAM (☑441-1545; Potosí cnr Buenos Aires) runs two or three daily flights between Santa Cruz and La Paz via Cochabamba and a couple of daily flights to Sucre. Except on Thursdays, there is a daily flight to Trinidad and Tarija, the latter continuing on to Yacuiba on Tuesday and Saturday mornings. **Aerocon** (☑448-9177; Aniceto Padilla 755) has a couple of daily flights to Trinidad with onward connections to the Amazon region, but places are limited. **BoA** (☑414-0873; Jordan 202) flies to the same destinations as TAM but prices are slightly higher and so they usually fill up more slowly.

Bus

Cochabamba's **main bus terminal** (☑423-4600; Ayacucho nr Tarata; terminal fee B$4) has an information kiosk, a branch of the tourist police, ATMs, luggage storage and a *cambio* (money-exchange bureau).

Trufis (collective taxis) and *micros* to eastern Cochabamba Valley villages leave from along Av República at the corners of Barrientos or 6 de Agosto. Torotoro *micros* (B$25) depart daily at 6pm except Thursday, with an additional 6am service on Thursday and Sunday. Services to the western part of the valley leave from the corner of Ayacucho and Aroma. For Villa Tunari, *micros* leave from the corner of Av República and Oquendo.

DESTINATION	COST (B$)	DURATION (HR)
Buenos Aires	550	72
La Paz	45-100	20
Oruro	25	4
Potosí	52-120	15
Santa Cruz	old road 54-110, new road 66-120	8-10
Sucre	50-70	12
Villa Tunari	bus 15, trufi 35	bus 4, trufi 3

ⓘ Getting Around

To/From the Airport

Micro B (B$2) shuttles between the airport and the main plaza. Taxis to or from the center cost B$25.

Bus

Convenient lettered *micros* and *trufis* display their destinations and run to all corners of the city (B$1.80).

Car

Most rental companies have offices at the airport. **Sudamericana Rent-a-Car** (☑428-3132; www.sudamericanarentacar.com; Pando 1187) is a reliable, long-established option.

Taxi

The taxi fare around the center of Cochabamba is B$6 per person. An extra boliviano is charged if you cross the river or go far to the south. For a radio taxi, ring **Señor Taxi** (☑458-0058).

AROUND COCHABAMBA

Parque Nacional Tunari

This easily accessible 3090-sq-km park was created in 1962 to protect the forested slopes above Cochabamba, as well as the wild summit of Cerro Tunari. It encompasses a wide diversity of habitats from dry inter-Andean valleys to the more humid and highly endangered *Polylepis* forests of the Cordillera Tunari.

The SERNAP office in Cochabamba may have simple walking maps of the park, but often doesn't have visitor material. A series of small identification guides to the wildlife of the park have been produced by the Centro de Biodiversidad y Genética at the Universidad Mayor de San Simón and can be bought on campus in Cochabamba.

Cochabamba Area

A good dirt road zigzags its way from the park gate (open until 4pm) up the steep mountain face. About 3km after the gate, you'll reach a **picnic site** with barbecues and a playground. Beyond here is a *sendero ecológico* (nature trail). Don't expect too much in the way of *ecología,* but it's a well-made path that gains altitude rapidly, winding into thickening mature woodland. The views are tremendous, with Cochabamba spread out below, and in the opposite direction, Cerro Tunari and the Cordillera. With an early start and plenty of water you should be able to make it up to some of the nearer peaks on a long day hike.

Coming from town take *micro F2* or *trufi 35* from Av San Martín, which will drop you three minutes from the park entrance, at a big wooden archway with a fire-risk indicator. You may have to show ID and sign into the park. From the gate turn right, then left after 100m; the road winds up past the playground to the lakes.

Cerro Tunari Area

Snow-dusted Cerro Tunari (5035m) is the highest peak in central Bolivia (it's the second peak from the left on the Taquiña beer label). Its flanks are 25km west of Cochabamba along the road to Independencia. This spectacular area offers excellent hiking and camping, but access is less than straightforward. For climbs, pick up the 1:50,000 map *Cordillera de Tunari* (sheet 6342III) from the IGM.

From Quillacollo it's a complicated four-to five-hour ascent to the summit, with some sections requiring technical equipment. Experienced climbers can manage the round-trip in a long day, but the high-altitude ascent will be more pleasant if you allow two days and camp overnight. You'll need a guide to find the best route.

An easier route ascends from Estancia Chaqueri or Tawa Cruz, 12km beyond Cruce Liriuni (which has lodgings at the village school) at 4200m. *Micros* and *camiones* (flatbed trucks) toward Morochata leave on Monday, Thursday and Saturday at 7am from three blocks off the main plaza in Quillacollo; they return to Cochabamba in the afternoon on Tuesday, Friday and Sunday.

The relatively easy path, which takes around five hours, ascends the north face of the peak.

Another option is Fremen Tours (p174). It leads all-inclusive two-day excursions using the northern route.

WESTERN COCHABAMBA VALLEY

Quillacollo

Besides Cochabamba itself, Quillacollo (13km west of Cochabamba) is the Cochabamba Valley's most commercially important community, although it has lost much of its independent feel in recent years as Cochabamba's growth has more or less absorbed it as a suburb. Apart from the **Sunday market** and the **pre-Inca burial mound** discovered beneath Plaza Bolívar, the main attraction is the revered Virgen de Urkupiña in its church.

Tradition has it that long ago, the Virgin Mary appeared several times to a shepherd girl at the foot of the hill known as Calvario. The visits were later witnessed by the girl's parents and a crowd of villagers when she shouted *'Orkopiña'* (There on the hill!) as the Virgin was seen ascending heavenwards. At the summit of the hill, the townspeople discovered the stone image of the Virgin, which now stands in the church to the right of the altar, surrounded by votive offerings and commemorative plaques giving thanks for blessings received.

One thing to do here is to sample *garapiña*, a deceptively strong blend of *chicha* (fermented corn), cinnamon, coconut and *ayrampo*, which is a local mystery ingredient from a cactus that colors the drink red.

✯ Festivals & Events

Fiesta de la Virgen de Urkupiña   RELIGIOUS
From August 14 to 18 is the Fiesta de la Virgen de Urkupiña, the biggest annual celebration in Cochabamba department. Folkloric musicians and dancers come from around Bolivia to perform and the *chicha* flows for three days. It can be a fairly chaotic scene, with more attention paid to hitting the bottle than on reverence. It's also very crowded.

🛏 Sleeping & Eating

Eco-Hotel Planeta de Luz   RESORT $$
(✆426-1234; www.planetadeluz.com; camping per person B$20, full board dm/s/d/tr B$70/200/280/350, 5-person cabins B$525; ☀) At Estancia Marquina, 5km north of Quillacollo, is the HI-affiliated Eco-Hotel Planeta de Luz, a curious place with Gaudíesque architecture, spa treatments, a sauna, wandering domestic animals and a kooky New Age vibe. The variety of different accommodation options is as wide as your imagination, from round huts with circular beds to posh suites. To get here take the Bella Vista *trufi* (B$1.20) from Quillacollo.

❶ Getting There & Away

Micros and *trufis* to Quillacollo (B$2.20, 45 minutes) leave frequently from Oquendo, Av de las Heroínas, the corner of Ayacucho and Aroma, and the corner of Circunvalación and América in Cochabamba. In Quillacollo, the *trufi* stop is on Plaza Bolívar.

Tiquipaya

The town of Tiquipaya, whose name means 'Place of Flowers', is located 11km northwest of Cochabamba. It is known for its **Sunday market** and its array of unusual festivals. In late April or early May there's an annual **Chicha Festival**; in July there is a **Potato Festival**; the second week in September sees the **Trout Festival**; around September 24 is the **Flower Festival**; and in the first week of November there's the **Festival de la Wallunk'a**, which attracts colorful, traditionally dressed women from around the Cochabamba department.

The classy **Cabañas Tolavi** (✆431-6834; www.cabanastolavi.com; s/d/tr with breakfast buffet B$280/360/420, cabañas B$390-650; ☀) has chalet-style *cabañas* constructed of perfumed wood, which occupy a gardenlike setting among the trees. Nonguests can enjoy German-style meals, including a buffet breakfast. It's 500m downhill from the *trufi* stop in Tiquipaya.

Micros leave half-hourly from the corner of Avs Ladislao Cabrera and Oquendo in Cochabamba. A taxi costs about B$140.

Villa Albina

If you haven't already had your fill of Simón Patiño's legacy in Oruro and Cochabamba, you can visit Villa Albina in the village of

Pairumani and tour the home the tin baron occupied. This enormous white mansion, which could have inspired the TV home of the Beverly Hillbillies, was named after his wife. Albina was presumably as fussy as her husband when it came to the finer things in life and the elegant French décor of the main house and the Carrara-marble mausoleum seem fit for royalty anywhere in the world. There's a formal garden, complete with topiary, and the family mausoleum in which the don and his wife were finally laid to rest.

To get there, take a Pairumani *trufi* from the Plaza Bolívar in Quillacollo and get off at Villa Albina. It's only 18km from Cochabamba, but the trip can take a couple of hours so you might consider a taxi.

Inca-Rakay & Sipe Sipe

The ruins of Inca-Rakay, in the Serranía de Tarhuani, are the most readily accessible ruins in the Cochabmaba Valley, but they are mostly crumbling stone walls these days and you'll need some imagination to conjure up their former glory. It has been postulated that Inca-Rakay served as an Inca administrative outpost that oversaw agricultural colonies in the fertile Cochabamba Valley. That seems unlikely, however, given its lofty position and the difficulty of access. The rare Spanish-language book *Inkallajta & Inkaraqay,* by Jesús Lara, contains good site maps and theories about its origins and purposes.

The site includes the remains of several hefty buildings and a large open plaza overlooking the valley. One odd rock outcrop resembles the head of a condor, with a natural passageway inside leading to the top. Just off the plaza area is a cave that may be explored with a flashlight. Legend has it that this cave is the remnant of another of those apocryphal Inca tunnels – this one linking Inca-Rakay with faraway Cuzco. If you're there on a smog-free day, the plaza affords a spectacular view over the valley.

Do not camp or spend the night at the unattended ruins. Several readers have reported serious violent incidents while camping here. The access town for the ruins is the quiet and friendly village of Sipe Sipe, 27km southwest of Cochabamba.

If you're in Sipe Sipe on a Sunday between February and May, try to sample the local specialty – a sweet grape liquor known as *guarapo.*

❶ Getting There & Away

From Cochamabamba take a *micro* to Plaza Bolívar in Quillacollo and there jump on a *trufi* or a *micro* to Sipe Sipe. Inca-Rakay is accessed on foot from Sipe Sipe. Since staying overnight is not a safe option, you must get an early start out of Cochabamba; the trip takes the better part of a day and you'll need time to explore the ruins.

It's a 5km, 2½-hour cross-country (but well-signed) walk up a steep hill from Sipe Sipe to the site. From the southwest corner of Sipe Sipe's main plaza, follow the road past the secondary school. From there the road narrows into a path and crosses a small ditch. Across the ditch, turn left onto the wider road. Starting several hundred meters up the road from town, follow a water pipeline uphill to the first major ridge; there'll be a large ravine on your left. From there, bear to the right and follow the ridge until you see a smaller ravine on the right. At this point you're actually able to see Inca-Rakay atop a reddish hill in the distance, but from so far away it's hard to distinguish.

Cross the small ravine and follow it until you can see a couple of adobe houses on the other side. In front there'll be a little hill with some minor ruins at the top. Climb the hill, cross the large flat area and then climb up two more false ridges until you see Inca-Rakay.

EASTERN COCHABAMBA VALLEY

La Angostura

This village stands on the shores of the artificial lake of the same name and is a popular spot for *cochabambinos* to head to fill up on fish. It's on the route to Tarata, 18km from Cochabamba. There are many places to eat along the lake shore, which fill you up with enormous plates of *trucha* (trout) or *pejerrey* (king fish) with rice, salad and potato. There are also places to hire rowboats and kayaks at weekends. From the corner of Barrientos and Manuripi in Cochabamba, take any *micro* toward Tarata or Cliza and get off at the Angostura bridge; if you see the dam on your right, you've gone too far (just). Nearby, on the highway, is the famous open-air **Las Carmelitas**, where Señora Carmen López bakes delicious cheese and onion empanadas (B$3) in a large beehive oven.

Tarata & Huayculli

Tarata, 29km southeast of Cochabamba, is one of the region's loveliest towns; a picturesque but decaying beauty that's well worth a visit for its noble buildings, cobbled streets and gorgeous plaza, filled with palm trees and jacarandas. The town's name is derived from the abundant *tara* trees, whose fruit is used in curing leather. Tarata is famous as the birthplace of the mad president General Mariano Melgarejo, who held office from 1866 to 1871 and whose remains now lie in the town church. While the citizens aren't necessarily proud of his achievements, they're pretty proud of producing presidents (populist military leader René Barrientos, who ruled from 1964 to 1969, was also born here), and there's a huge horseback statue of him on the main road.

The enormous neoclassical **Iglesia de San Pedro** was constructed in 1788 and restored between 1983 and 1985; several of the interior panels include mestizo-style details carved in cedar. The 1792 **Franciscan Convent of San José**, which contains lovely colonial furniture and an 8000-volume library, was founded as a missionary training school. It now operates as a museum and contains the ashes of San Severino, Tarata's patron saint, whose feast day is celebrated on the last Sunday in November.

The village also has several other **historic buildings**: the Palacio Consistorial (government palace) of President Melgarejo (built in 1872) and the homes of President Melgarejo, General don Esteban Arce and General René Barrientos.

Huayculli, 7km from Tarata, is a village of potters and glaziers. The air is thick with the scent of eucalyptus being burned in cylindrical firing kilns. The local style and technique

CHICHA IN PUNATA

This small market town 50km east of Cochabamba is said to produce Bolivia's finest *chicha*. Tuesday is **market day** and May 18 is the riotous **town festival**. Access from Cochabamba is via *micros* (B$6, one hour) and taxis (B$10) that depart when full from Plaza Villa Bella at the corner of República (the southern extension of Antezana) and Av 6 de Agosto between 5am and 8pm.

are passed down from generation to generation and remain unique.

From Cochabamba, taxis (B$6, 30 minutes) leave when full and *micros* (B$5, 45 minutes) leave every 15 minutes between 5am and 8pm from Avs Barrientos and Magdalena. There are no *micros* to Huayculli, but minibuses running between Tarata and Anzaldo can drop you here.

Incallajta

The nearest thing Bolivia has to Peru's Machu Picchu is the remote and rarely visited site of Incallajta (meaning 'Land of the Inca'), situated 132km east of Cochabamba on a flat mountain spur above the Río Machajmarka. This was the easternmost outpost of the Inca empire and after Tiwanaku it's the country's most significant archaeological site. The most prominent feature is the immense stone fortification that sprawls across alluvial terraces above the river, but at least 50 other structures are also scattered around the 12-hectare site.

Incallajta was probably founded by Inca Emperor Tupac-Yupanqui, the commander who had previously marched into present-day Chile to demarcate the southern limits of the Inca empire. It's estimated that Incallajta was constructed in the 1460s as a measure of protection against attack by the Chiriguanos to the southeast. In 1525, the last year of Emperor Huayna Capac's rule, the outpost was abandoned. This may have been due to a Chiriguano attack, but was more likely the result of increasing Spanish pressure and the unraveling of the empire, which fell seven years later.

The site is on a monumental scale; some researchers believe that, as well as serving a defensive purpose, it was designed as a sort of ceremonial replica of Cuzco, the Inca capital. The site's most significant building, the *kallanka*, measures a colossal 80m by 25m. The roof was supported by immense columns. Outside it is a large boulder, probably a speakers' platform. At the western end of the site is a curious six-sided tower, perhaps used for astronomical observation. On the hilltop, a huge zigzag defensive wall has a baffled defensive entrance.

The ruins were made known to the world in 1914 by Swedish zoologist and ethnologist Ernest Nordenskiöld, who spent a week at the ruins measuring and mapping them. However, they were largely ignored – except by ruthless treasure hunters – for the next 50 years, until the University of San Simón in Cochabamba launched its investigations.

At Pocona, 17km from the ruins, there's an information center and a small exhibition of archaeological finds from the site.

Tours

Cochabamba agencies run day trips to Incallajta when they have a group large enough to make it worthwhile. Fremen Tours (p174) is recommended. Beware of tours that seem suspiciously cheap or that involve 'trekking'. That usually means getting a cab to the *cruce* (turnoff) and walking up to the site – you can do that yourself.

Sleeping & Eating

Without your own transportation, visiting Incallajta will prove inconvenient at best. Additionally, if you can't arrange lodging in private homes, you'll probably have to camp for two or three nights so be sure to take plenty of water, food, warm clothing and camping gear. Camping and basic shelters are available at the Centro de Investigaciones in Pocona.

Getting There & Away

Taxis (B$18, three hours) and *micros* (B$20, five hours) to Pocona leave Cochabamba when full between 5am and 6pm from the corner of República and Manuripi. Get off at the turnoff for the site at Collpa. From here it's an 8km uphill walk. If you'd rather not walk, Pocona is a further 9km past Collpa and you can strike a deal with a taxi driver there.

Totora

Totora, 142km east of Cochabamba, huddles in a valley at the foot of Cerro Sutuchira. It is on the main route between Cochabamba and Sucre, but few travelers ever see it because most buses pass through at night. Nevertheless it is a lovely colonial village, built around a postcard-pretty plaza with colorful buildings and arcades. In May 1998 the town was struck by an earthquake measuring 6.7 on the Richter scale. While there's still plenty of damage visible, much of the town has since been lovingly restored.

The annual **town festival** on February 2 features bullfights. There's a **piano festival** at the end of September, but Totora's most charming and famous festival is that of **San Andrés**. On November 2, giant swings are erected on the streets and throughout the month young women who are hoping for marriage are swung high on them. The women on the swings are also believed to be helping the wandering souls, who descended to earth on All Souls' Day, return to heaven.

The **Hotel Municipal** (Plaza Ladislao Cabrera s/n; r per person B$50) is an attractive reconstruction of what was once the town's hospital and is one of two good hotels in town. It's got spacious, comfortable rooms in an old-fashioned style. There's also a couple of simple *alojamientos* (cheap guesthouses).

Micros (B$20, three hours) destined for Aiquile leave daily for Totora at 6.30am, 11.30am and 5pm from the corner of Avs 6 de Agosto and República in Cochabamba.

Mizque

This pretty colonial village enjoys a lovely pastoral setting on the Río Mizque. Founded as the *Villa de Salinas del Río Pisuerga* in 1549, it soon came to be known as the *Ciudad de las 500 Quitasoles* (City of 500 Parasols), after the sun shields used by the locals. It makes a great escape from the cities and main tourist sights and the few visitors who pass through on trips between Sucre and Cochabamba are impressed by the beauty of the Mizque and Tucuna Valleys, where flocks of macaws squawk in the early morning.

Sights & Activities

There's a small archaeological and historical **museum**.

Iglesia Matríz   CHURCH
The lovely, restored Iglesia Matríz, which was slightly damaged in a 1998 earthquake, once served as the seat of the Santa Cruz Bishopric (until the seat was shifted to Arani in 1767).

Tours

With the help of Peace Corps volunteers, the *alcaldía* (town hall; on the north side of the plaza) organizes **self-guided hiking circuits** and **guided trips** to several local sites of natural and historic interest. Moises Cardozo at the Entel office or Restaurant Plaza can arrange an interesting visit to his **apiary** just outside of town.

Festivals

Besides its cheese and honey, Mizque is best known for its **Fería de la Fruta** (April 19), which coincides with the *chirimoya* (custard apple) harvest and **Semana Santa**. From September 8 to 14, Mizque holds the lively **Fiesta del Señor de Burgos**, which features much revelry and bull- and cockfighting. Monday is **market day**.

Sleeping & Eating

Mizque has a few cheap Taquiña-sponsored *alojamientos* that serve typical Bolivian meals. They're all within a block of the plaza. Alternatively, you can eat at the street stalls beside the church.

Hotel Bolivia   HOTEL $
(☑434-2158; r per person B$50, without bathroom B$30) Next to the *campesino* (subsistence farmer) market on the road to the river, Hotel Bolivia has firm beds and is probably the nicest place in town.

Hostal Graciela   PENSION $
(☑413-5616; r per person B$50) A good option with rooms that have decks; it's affiliated with the also-recommended Restaurant Plaza.

Residencial Mizque   PENSION $
(☑420-0224; r per person B$40) Set amid gardens, this clean place is the easiest to find if you arrive at night – look for the Prodem sign.

Getting There & Away

Three daily *micros* (B$20, four hours) leave Cochabamba from the corner of Avs 6 de Agosto and República at 8am, noon and 6pm; from Mizque they depart for Cochabamba at 8am, 10am and noon, and for Aiquile at 3pm daily. Occasional *micros* travel between here and Totora – 31km on a rough road.

Parque Nacional Torotoro

One of Bolivia's most memorable national parks, Torotoro at times can seem like a practical demonstration of geology on an awe-inspiring scale. Beds of sedimentary mudstone, sandstone and limestone, bristling with marine fossils and – from drier periods – dinosaur footprints, have been muscled and twisted into the sharp, inhospitable hillscapes of the Serranías de Huayllas and de Cóndor Khaka. In places, the immensity of geological time is showcased, with exposed layers revealing fossils below a hundred meters or more of sedimentary strata.

Amid it all the characterful, impoverished colonial village of **Torotoro** itself (2720m) is one of the region's most remote settlements (although road access is steadily improving).

Sights & Activities

Dinosaur Tracks   ARCHAEOLOGICAL SITE
Most visitors to Torotoro come for the paleontology. The village, which sits in a wide section of a 20km-long valley at an elevation of 2600m, is flanked by enormous, inclined mudstone rock formations bearing bipedal and quadrupedal dinosaur tracks from the Cretaceous period (spanning 145 million to 65 million years ago).

There are numerous tracks *(huellas)* all over the place and much work remains to be done on their interpretation. Many different dinosaur species are represented, both herbivorous and carnivorous.

The closest tracks are just at the entrance to the village, on the other side of the river. Above the water but below the road are the area's largest tracks, made by an enormous quadruped dinosaur (diplodocus or similar), and they measure 35cm wide, 50cm long and 20cm deep. Near here, just above the road, the angled plane of rock reveals a multitude of different tracks, including a long set from a heavy quadrupedal dinosaur that some have posited are those of the armadillo-like ankylosaurus.

Along the route to Umajalanta cave, the flat area known as the Carreras Pampa site has several excellent sets of footprints (on both sides of the path). These were made by three-toed bipedal dinosaurs, both herbivores (with rounded toes) and carnivores (pointed toes, sometimes with the claw visible).

All the tracks in the Torotoro area were made in soft mud, which then solidified into mudstone. They were later lifted and tilted by tectonic forces. For that reason, many of the tracks appear to lead uphill. Many local guides, however, incorrectly believe that the footprints were made in lava as the dinosaurs fled a volcanic eruption.

Sea Fossils   ARCHAEOLOGICAL SITE
In a small side gully, an hour's walk southwest of Torotoro on the Cerro de las Siete Vueltas (Mountain of Seven Turns – so called because the trail twists seven times before reaching the peak), is a major sea-fossil deposit. At the base of the ravine you may see petrified shark teeth, while higher up the limestone and sedimentary layers are

CENTRAL HIGHLANDS PARQUE NACIONAL TOROTORO

AIQUILE

Aiquile is known for some of Bolivia's finest *charangos* (traditional Bolivian ukulele-type instruments) and in late November plays host to the **Fería del Charango**. The small **Museo del Charango** (admission B$10) has some archaeological pieces and holds a collection of the instruments, including ones that have won prizes at the festival.

Aiquile lies on the main route between Cochabamba and Sucre, but most intercity buses pass in the wee hours of the night. Buses to Aiquile (B$20, six hours) depart daily at noon and 5pm from Av 6 de Agosto between Barrientos and República in Cochabamba. It's about two hours between Aiquile and Mizque. There are a couple of *micros* a day, or you can readily thumb a ride on passing *camiones*, but be prepared for a real dust bath.

set with fossils of ancient trilobites, echinoderms, gastropods, arthropods, cephalopods and brachiopods. The site is thought to date back about 350 million years. There's another significant sea-fossil site in the **Quebrada Thajo Khasa**, southeast of Torotoro.

Pachamama Wasi   MUSEUM
(Sucre s/n; admission B$5) This amazing and beautiful house-museum is the quirky home of a man who has spent years of his life pacing the *cerros* with a rockhound's eye. The house is like a botanic garden, but made of stones: fossils, geological quirks and unusually shaped rocks form a unique, soothing ensemble. It's uphill from the main street but only open when the owner or his family are at home.

Cañón de Torotoro & El Vergel   CANYON
Three kilometers from Torotoro, the ground suddenly drops away into an immense and spectacularly beautiful canyon, more than 250m deep. From the *mirador* (viewpoint) at the top you can gaze along it, watching vultures wheeling. The cliffside here is also home to the rare *paraba frente roja* (Redfronted macaw), which you have a good chance of seeing, or at least hearing.

From here, following the diminishing canyon along to the left, you come to a flight of 800 stairs that lead down to El Vergel (also called Huacasenq'a, meaning 'cow's nostrils' in Quechua), which always has water and is filled with incongruous moss, vines and other tropical vegetation. At the bottom a crystal-clear river tumbles down through cascades and waterfalls, forming idyllic swimming pools.

Batea Q'ocha Rock
Paintings   ARCHAEOLOGICAL SITE
Above the third bend of the Río Torotoro, 1.5km downstream from the village, are several panels of ancient rock paintings collectively called Batea Q'ocha because the pools below them resemble troughs for pounding laundry. The paintings were executed in red pigments and depict anthropomorphic and geometric designs as well as fanciful representations of serpents, turtles and other creatures.

Gruta de Umajalanta   CAVE
The Río Umajalanta, which disappears beneath a layer of limestone approximately 22m thick, has formed the impressive Umajalanta Cavern, of which 4.5km of passages have been explored.

The exciting descent is moderately physical and you must expect to get both wet and dirty; there are several parts where you need to crawl and wriggle to get through and a couple of short roped descents. Make sure you have good nonslip shoes on.

Inside are some spectacular stalagmite and stalactite formations, as well as a resident population of vampire bats that have produced an impressively large pile of steaming guano over the years. You eventually descend to an underground lake and river, which is populated by small white, completely blind, catfish. The ascent from here is fairly easy, as it takes a more direct route.

The 8km one-way walk to the cavern entrance takes two hours from the village, with plenty of dinosaur footprints to inspect on the way.

There are numerous other caverns in the area, most of which are virtually unexplored.

Llama Chaqui   RUINS
A challenging 19km hike around the Cerro Huayllas Orkho from Torotoro will take you to the ruins known as the Llama Chaqui (Llama's Foot). The multilevel complex, which dates from Inca times, rambles over distinctive terraces and includes a maze of

rectangular and semicircular walls, plus a fairly well-preserved watchtower. Given its strategic vantage point, it probably served as a military fortification and may have been somehow related to Incallajta, further north.

Tours

The team at Villa Etelvina are experts in the Torotoro area and passionate about the national park and the local community. They arrange comfortable 4WD transfers from Cochabamba and put visitors up in their excellent lodge in Torotoro village. A few Cochabamba agencies (p174) run trips, including visits to the major sights.

Festivals & Events

Fiesta del Señor Santiago   RELIGIOUS
From July 24 to 27, the village stages the Fiesta del Señor Santiago, which features sheep sacrifices, dynamite explosions, colorful costumes, much *chicha* and some light *tinku* (traditional Bolivian fighting). This is an interesting time to visit – and there's much more public transportation than usual – but the natural attractions are very crowded.

Sleeping & Eating

There are several downmarket *residenciales* in Torotoro, but few that are much more than huts with signs. One that's substantially better is **Hostal Las Hermanas** (r per person B$40), which is simple but clean and comfortable, with hot water; it's on the street that enters the village, on the left.

If you wish to camp, locals will expect you to pay. It's important to set a mutually agreeable price and pay only the family in control of the land.

Villa Etelvina   RESORT **$$**
(7073-7807; www.villaetelvina.com; Sucre s/n; per person B$150, d without bathroom B$100) The best option in town, this is a comfortable and welcoming oasis. As well as having extremely comfortable and stylish accommodation, it puts on some of the most delicious home cooking you're likely to find on your travels in Bolivia. Vegetarian fare is available on request and is particularly good. The owners can organise transfers from Cochabamba and professional tours of nearby attractions. Book ahead; they need notice to accommodate guests.

Information

Information about the park is sometimes available from the SERNAP office (p178) in Cochabamba, but don't bank on it. You may have more luck at one of the tour companies or online at www.tororoto-bolivia.com.bo (in Spanish). On the main street in the village of Torotoro, the **tourist office** (Charcas s/n; ⊙daily) is housed in the entrance of the *alcaldía*.

Registration & Guides

In order to protect the park's geological wonders, it is compulsory to take a guide on any excursion outside the village. Guides are contracted at the *alcaldía* where you also buy your entry ticket (B$20). Hang on to your ticket at all times as it will be inspected by park rangers. Guides are unlikely to speak English, but their knowledge of the surroundings greatly enhances your visit and contributes positively to the local community.

The going rate for a guide is about B$40 per person for a half-day excursion for groups of 10 to 15 people, more for a visit to the Gruta de Umajalanta. For dinosaur footprints, it can be very helpful if the guide has a brush (otherwise buy one) to whisk the dust out of the hollows. If you are going to the cave, the guide should have head-lanterns and rope.

Getting There & Away

Parque Nacional Torotoro is 135km southeast of Cochabamba in Potosí department. The road has been improved in recent years, and works are continuing, but more than half the distance is still a mud road and access in the rainy season (November to February) can be problematic. Flying is the best way to arrive.

Air

No air services are scheduled to Torotoro, but you can charter a plane for about B$1000 per person for up to five passengers return. It takes 30 minutes. Contact **Misión Sueca** (424-6289) for details.

Bus

Buses (B$25, four to seven hours) depart Cochabamba at 6pm from the corner of Avs República and Barrientos every day except Thursday, with an additional 6am service on Thursday and Sunday. They return from near the plaza in Torotoro.

Car & Motorcycle

The most comfortable terrestrial way to get to Torotoro is by 4WD or motorbike. Tour agencies arrange transfers from Cochabamba; the journey takes about five hours, depending on road conditions.

You can rent 4WDs in Cochabamba (p179), where you should fill the tank as there's no place to buy petrol in Torotoro itself. To reach Torotoro, head out on the old Santa Cruz road. Once you see the signs advertising La Angostura, take the uphill right turn that follows the lake above the village. If you reach the Angostura dam on your right, you have gone too far by a couple of hundred meters.

Follow this road via Caluyo until you reach the town of Tarata (35km from the La Angostura turnoff). Cross one bridge, then take a right turn immediately before a second bridge. About 500m along this road, you need to cut across the riverbed to your left; on the other side, a good cobblestone road starts and soon reaches the potters' village of Huaycullí. Continue on this road past the town of Anzaldo; this is the last possible refueling place. About 10km beyond here, you turn left onto a dirt road that is signposted, but easy to miss. This spectacular road descends into a river valley and finally makes a precipitous switchback ascent to Torotoro itself.

SUCRE

🏳4 / POP 215,000 / ELEV 2750M

Proud, genteel Sucre is Bolivia's most beautiful city and the symbolic heart of the nation. It was here that independence was proclaimed and while La Paz is now the seat of government and treasury, Sucre is recognized in the constitution as the nation's capital. A glorious ensemble of whitewashed buildings sheltering pretty patios, it's a spruce place that preserves a wealth of colonial architecture. Sensibly, there are strict controls on development, which have ensured Sucre remains a real showpiece of Bolivia. It was declared a Unesco World Heritage Site in 1991.

Set in a valley surrounded by low mountains, Sucre enjoys a mild and comfortable climate. It's still a center of learning and both the city and its university enjoy reputations as focal points of progressive thought within the country.

With a selection of excellent accommodations, a wealth of churches and museums, and plenty to see and do in the surrounding area, it's no surprise that visitors end up spending much longer in Sucre than they bargained on.

☉ Sights

Sucre is positively overflowing with impressive museums, colonial buildings and ornate churches. For the best view in town, inquire about climbing the cupula at the national police office inside the **Prefectura de Chuquisaca** (State Government Building), next to the cathedral. Note the murals depicting the struggle for Bolivian independence as you go upstairs.

Casa de la Libertad MUSEUM
(www.casadelalibertad.org.bo; Plaza 25 de Mayo 11; admission incl optional guided tour B$15; ☉9am-noon & 2:30-6:30pm Tue-Sat, 9am-noon Sun) For a dose of Bolivian history, it's hard to beat this museum where the Bolivian declaration of independence was signed on August 6, 1825. It has been designated a national memorial and is considered the birthplace of the nation.

The first score of Bolivian congresses were held in the Salón de la Independencia, originally a Jesuit chapel. Doctoral candidates were also examined here. Behind the pulpit hang portraits of Simón Bolívar, Hugo Ballivián and Antonio José de Sucre. Bolívar claimed that this portrait, by Peruvian artist José Gil de Castro, was the most lifelike representation ever done of him. The charter of independence takes pride of place, mounted on a granite plinth. A fine inlaid wooden ceiling and elaborate choir stalls are also noteworthy.

Museo de Arte Indígena MUSEUM
(www.asur.org.bo; Pasaje Iturricha 314; admission B$22; ☉8:30am-noon & 2:30-6pm daily) This superb museum of indigenous arts is a must for anyone interested in the indigenous groups of the Sucre area, focusing particularly on the woven textiles of the Jal'qa and Candelaria (Tarabuco) cultures. It's a fascinating display and has an interesting subtext: the rediscovery of forgotten ancestral weaving practices has contributed to increased community pride and revitalization.

Information in English is available and you can observe the weavers patiently at work. The contiguous store markets ceramics and weavings, but it's a more satisfying experience to buy them direct from the villages where they are made.

Museo de Etnografía y Folklore MUSEUM
(www.musef.org.bo; España 74; admission B$15; ☉9:30am-12:30pm & 2:30-6:30pm Mon-Fri, 9:30am-12:30pm Sat) Known locally as Musef and housed in the impressive former Banco Nacional building, this new museum brings together a series of fascinating displays that vividly illustrate the great diversity of Bolivia's ethnic cultures. On the ground floor is

Sucre

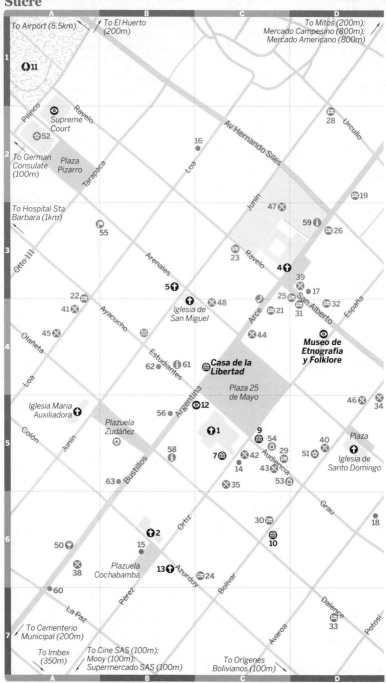

To Airport (5.5km)

To El Huerto (200m)

To Mitos (200m);
Mercado Campesino (800m);
Mercado Americano (800m)

11

Pilinco

Ravelo

Supreme Court

52

28

Ureullo

Av Hernando Siles

To German Consulate (100m)

Plaza Pizarro

Tarapaca

16

Loa

19

To Hospital Sta Barbara (1km)

Junín

47

59

26

55

Otto 111

Arenales

23

Ravelo

4

39

17

25

San Alberto

32

5

22

41

Ayacucho

48

31

España

45

Olañeta

Iglesia de San Miguel

Arce

21

44

Loa

Estudiantes

61

62

Casa de la Libertad

Museo de Etnografía y Folklore

Iglesia Maria Auxiliadora

Colón

Junín

Plazuela Zudáñez

56

Argentina

12

Plaza 25 de Mayo

46

34

1

9

54

58

7

42

29

14

43

51

40

Plaza

Iglesia de Santo Domingo

63

Bustillos

35

53

Audiencia

Grau

30

18

50

15

2

Ortiz

10

38

Plazuela Cochabamba

13

Azurduy

24

Bolívar

60

Pérez

Dalence

33

Avaroa

Potosí

La Paz

To Cementerio Municipal (200m)

To Imbex (350m)

To Cine SAS (100m);
Mooy (100m);
Supermercado SAS (100m)

To Orígenes Bolivianos (100m)

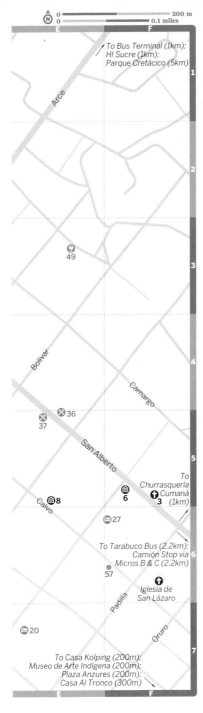

a professionally presented display of masks with more than 50 original examples, some of which you wouldn't want to bump into in a dark alleyway. The other permanent display deals with the Uru-Chipaya culture, with reconstructions of village life and exhibitions of everyday artifacts.

Parque Cretácico (Cal Orck'o)
ARCHAEOLOGICAL SITE

(Cretaceous Park; www.parquecretacicosucre.com; admission B$30; ☉9am-5pm Mon-Fri, 10am-3pm Sat, 10am-5pm Sun) It seems that 65 million years ago the site of Sucre's Fancesa (Fabrica Nacional de Cemento SA) cement quarry, 5km north of the center, was the place to be for large, scaly types. When the grounds were being cleared in 1994, plant employees uncovered a nearly vertical mudstone face bearing about 5000 tracks of at least eight different species of dinosaur – the largest collection of dinosaur footprints in the world.

Though you can see some of the prints from outside, entering the family-friendly Cretaceous Park gives a better panorama; the best light for photographs is during the afternoon. This slick theme park has a number of life-size models of dinosaurs, as well as an audio-visual display, optional guided tours and a restaurant. From the terrace, you can examine the tracks on the rock face opposite with binoculars, though the exposed prints are increasingly eroded with every passing winter.

Micro 4 (B$1.50) runs from the center past the site, tell the driver where you want to get off.

Templo Nuestra Señora de la Merced
CHURCH

(Pérez 1; admission B$5; ☉2-5pm Mon-Fri) Contrary to its ordinary exterior, this church is blessed with the most beautiful interior of any church in Sucre and possibly in Bolivia. Because the order of La Merced left Sucre for Cuzco in 1826, taking its records with it, the church's founding date is uncertain, but it's believed to be sometime in the 1540s.

The baroque-style altar and carved mestizo pulpit are decorated with filigree and gold inlay. Several paintings by the esteemed artist Melchor Pérez de Holguín are on display – notably *El Nacimiento de Jesús, El Nacimiento de María* and a self-portrait of the artist rising from the depths of purgatory. The views from the bell tower are splendid.

Sucre

Catedral CHURCH
(Plaza 25 de Mayo; ☉Sun) Sucre's cathedral dates from the middle of the 16th century and is a harmonious blend of Renaissance architecture with later baroque additions. It's a noble structure, with a bell tower that is a local landmark. Inside, the white single-naved space has a series of oil paintings of the apostles, as well as an ornate altarpiece and pulpit. The cathedral opens on Sundays;

otherwise you can enter as part of a visit to the Museo de la Catedral next door.

Museo de la Catedral   MUSEUM
(Ortiz 31; admission B$20; ⊘10am-noon & 3:30-5pm Mon-Fri) Next door to Sucre's Cathedral, this museum holds one of Bolivia's best collections of religious relics. There are four sections, ritually unlocked as your visit progresses. In the entry room is a series of fine religious paintings from the colonial era. Next, a chapel has relics of saints, and fine gold and silver chalices. The highlight, however, comes in the **Capilla de la Virgen de Guadalupe**, which was completed in 1625. Encased in the altar is a painting of the Virgin, the city's patron. She was originally painted by Fray Diego de Ocaña in 1601, but the work was subsequently coated with highlights of gold and silver and adorned with robes encrusted with diamonds, amethysts, pearls, rubies and emeralds donated by wealthy colonial parishioners. The jewels alone are worth millions of dollars, making it the richest Virgin in the Americas.

Museo de la Recoleta   MUSEUM
(Plaza Anzures; admission B$10; ⊘9-11:30am & 2:30-4:30pm Mon-Fri, 3-5pm Sat) Overlooking the city of Sucre from the top of Calle Polanco, La Recoleta was established by the Franciscan Order in 1601. It has served not only as a convent and museum but also as a barracks and prison. The highlight is the church choir and its magnificent wooden carvings dating back to the 1870s, each one intricate and unique, representing the martyrs who were crucified in 1595 in Nagasaki. The museum is worthwhile for its anonymous sculptures and paintings from the 16th to 20th centuries, including numerous interpretations of St Francis of Assisi.

Outside are courtyard gardens brimming with color and the renowned *Cedro Milenario* (Ancient Cedar), a huge tree that is one of the few survivors of the cedars that were once abundant around Sucre.

Museo de Santa Clara   MUSEUM
(Calvo 212; admission B$10; ⊘2-6pm Mon-Fri, to 5:30pm Sat) Located in the Santa Clara Convent, this museum of religious art, founded in 1639, contains several works by Bolivian master Melchor Pérez de Holguín and his Italian instructor, Bernardo de Bitti. In 1985 it was robbed and several paintings and gold ornaments were taken. One of the canvases, however, was apparently deemed too large to carry away, so the thieves sliced a big chunk out of the middle and left the rest hanging. The painting has been restored but you can still see evidence of the damage. Guides may also demonstrate the still-functional pipe organ, which was made in 1664.

Convento de Santa Teresa   CHURCH
(San Alberto; ⊘10am-noon) The brilliant-white Convento de Santa Teresa belongs to an order of cloistered nuns. They sell homemade candied oranges, apples, figs and limes daily by way of a miniature revolving door. The adjacent **Callejón de Santa Teresa**, a lantern-lit alleyway, was once partially paved with cow knee bones laid out in the shape of a cross, a local good luck symbol known as *tabas*. The alley was considered to be a haunted place, inhabited by a variety of local ghouls including a baby with a moustache and teeth, and the cow knees were thought to be the most reliable way of protecting passersby. In the 1960s it was repaved with the cobbles you see today.

Convento de San Felipe Neri   CHURCH
(Ortíz 165, entry via the school; admission B$10; ⊘2:30-6pm Mon-Sat) The view from the bell tower and tiled rooftop of the San Felipe Neri convent more than explains Sucre's nickname of the 'White City of the Americas'. In the days when the building served as a monastery (it is now a parochial school), asceticism didn't prevent the monks from appreciating the view while meditating; you can still see the stone seats on the roof terraces. The church was originally constructed of stone but was later covered with a layer of stucco. Poinsettias and roses fill the courtyard, an interesting painting of the Last Supper hangs at the entrance and the stairwell is lined with paintings that prepared the monks for confession.

Iglesia de San Francisco   CHURCH
(Ravelo 1 at Arce; ⊘7-9am & 4-7pm Mon-Fri) The Iglesia de San Francisco was established in 1538 soon after the founding of the city, but was turned over to the military in 1809. The soldiers weren't big on maintenance and it fell into disrepair before eventually being reconsecrated in 1925. Its most interesting features are its *mudéjar* (Moorish) paneled ceiling and the Campana de la Libertad, Bolivia's Liberty Bell, which called patriots to revolution in 1825.

THE LIBERATOR – SIMÓN BOLÍVAR

Born in Caracas in 1783, Bolívar, greatest of the Libertadores (the liberators) of South America, was sent to Europe as a 15-year-old to be educated. There the works of Rousseau and Voltaire awakened notions of progressive liberalism that would change his life and the destiny of a continent.

Bolívar married a Spaniard in 1802, but she succumbed to yellow fever in Caracas shortly afterwards. Although he had many lovers, he could never again marry. The death of his wife marked a drastic shift in Bolívar's destiny. He returned to France, where he met with the leaders of the French Revolution and then traveled to the USA to inspect the new order after the American Revolution. By the time he returned to Caracas in 1807, he had developed his own revolutionary theories.

In South America disillusionment with Spanish rule was already close to breaking into open revolt. On April 19, 1810, the Junta Suprema was installed in Caracas and on July 5, 1811, the Congress declared independence. This marked the beginning of a long and bitter war, most of which would be orchestrated by Bolívar.

His military career began with command of the Venezuelan independence movement. Battle followed battle with astonishing frequency until 1824. The independence forces won 35 battles personally directed by Bolívar, including a few key ones: the Battle of Boyacá (August 7, 1819) secured the independence of Colombia; the Battle of Carabobo (June 24, 1821) brought freedom to Venezuela; and the Battle of Pichincha (May 24, 1822) liberated Ecuador.

In September 1822 the Argentine liberator General José de San Martín, who had occupied Lima, abandoned the city to the Spanish and Bolívar took over the task of winning in Peru. On August 6, 1824, his army was victorious at the Battle of Junín and on December 9, 1824, General Antonio José de Sucre inflicted a final defeat at the Battle of Ayacucho. Peru, which included Alto Perú, had been liberated and the war was over. On August 6, 1825, the

Iglesia de Santa Mónica   CHURCH
(cnr Junín 601 & Arenales) The Iglesia de Santa Mónica was begun in 1574 and was originally intended to serve as a monastery for the Ermitañas de San Agustín. However, the order ran into financial difficulties in the early 1590s, resulting in its conversion into a Jesuit school. The interior is adorned with mestizo carvings and the courtyard is one of the city's finest. The church now serves as a civic auditorium and is only open to the public during special events.

Museos Universitarios   MUSEUM
(Bolívar 698; admission B$15; ⏰8:30am-noon & 2:30-6pm Mon-Fri, 9am-noon & 3-6pm Sat) The Museos Universitarios are three separate halls housing colonial relics, anthropological artifacts and modern art.

Museo Gutiérrez Valenzuela   MUSEUM
(Plaza 25 de Mayo; admission B$8; ⏰8.30am-noon & 2.30-6pm Mon-Fri) Run by the university, the Museo Gutiérrez Valenzuela is an old aristocrat's house with 19th-century decor and a small natural-history museum.

Parque Bolívar   PARK
A short walk north of Plaza Pizarro, the elongated Parque Bolívar is sandwiched between two avenues flanked with trees and overlooked by handsomely imposing government buildings. It's a pleasant place for a quiet stroll and its strongly European style is highlighted by the presence of a miniature replica of the Eiffel Tower; remarkably, it was built by the same hand as the original in 1906. The French influence is further seen in an archway that looks suspiciously like the Arc de Triomphe.

Cementerio Municipal   CEMETERY
(entrance on Calle José Manuel Linares; ⏰8:30am-noon & 2-5:30pm) The enthusiasm surrounding Sucre's cemetery seems disproportionate to what's there. There are some arches carved from poplar trees, as well as picturesque palm trees and the mausoleums of wealthy colonial families. At weekends it's jam-packed with families. You can walk the eight blocks from Plaza 25 de Mayo south along Junín, or take a taxi or *micro A*.

🍃 Courses

Sucre is a popular place to learn Spanish and a number of group and individual programs are available for all levels.

first anniversary of the Battle of Junín, Alto Perú declared independence from Peru at Chuquisaca (Sucre) and the new republic was named Bolivia in his honor.

But, as Bolívar well knew, freedom means just that and, although he had grand dreams for a unified state in the north of South America, they would prove difficult to realize. 'I fear peace more than war,' he wrote perceptively in a letter.

Establishing Gran Colombia (which comprised modern-day Venezuela, Colombia, Panamá and Ecuador) was easy, but holding it together proved impossible. Clinging stubbornly to his dream of the union, as it rapidly slipped from his hands, he lost influence, and his glory and appeal faded. Still seeing himself (perhaps correctly) as the best steward of the young nations, he then tried to set up a dictatorship, saying 'Our America can only be ruled through a well-managed, shrewd despotism'. After surviving an assassination attempt in Bogotá, he resigned in 1830, disillusioned and in poor health. Almost at once, his Gran Colombia dissolved.

Venezuela seceded in 1830, approved a new congress and banned Bolívar from his homeland. A month later, Antonio José de Sucre, Bolívar's closest friend, was assassinated in Colombia. These two news items reached Bolívar just as he was about to sail for France. Depressed and ill, he accepted the invitation of a Spaniard, Joaquín de Mier, to stay in his home in Santa Marta, Colombia.

Bolívar died alone on December 17, 1830, of pulmonary tuberculosis. De Mier donated one of his shirts to dress the body, as there had been none among Bolívar's humble belongings. Perhaps the most important figure in the history of the South American continent had died. 'There have been three great fools in history: Jesus, Don Quixote and I,' he said shortly before his death.

One of the final remarks in Bolívar's diary reads, 'My name now belongs to history. It will do me justice.' It has.

Instituto Cultural Boliviano
Alemán LANGUAGE COURSE
(ICBA; ☎645-2091; www.icba-sucre.edu.bo; Avaroa 326) Offers recommended Spanish lessons with homestay options and also runs Quechua classes. ICBA has a German-language library and listings of rooms for rent. It is affiliated to Kulturcafé Berlin (p196), just down the road.

Fox Language Academy LANGUAGE COURSE
(☎644-0688; www.foxacademysucre.com; San Alberto 30) Fox Language Academy runs volunteer schemes and learning Spanish or Quechua there subsidizes English classes for underprivileged local kids. The academy is inside the Instituto Médico building.

👉 Tours

While Sucre traditionally has been visited for its sublime colonial architecture and wealth of museums, there's an increasing amount on offer in the surrounding area, whether you are interested in indigenous culture or adrenaline-fueled adventure.

There are numerous agencies in town and nearly all offer trips to Tarabuco (about B$40 per person) for the Sunday market, including Candelaria Tours (p347); many ho-tels and *hostales* can also arrange this trip. Many also offer day-trips to the Cordillera de los Frailes, but you will contribute more to the local communities by going for longer.

Some readers have complained about overcharging by Sucre agencies when they booked in advance. Make a point of comparing prices before you sign on the dotted line.

Condor Trekkers HIKING
(☎7289-1740; www.condortrekkers.org; Loa 457) Highly recommended, nonprofit tour agency, with all earnings going towards social development projects. Organizes a series of multiday hikes and volunteer opportunities in local communities.

Joy Ride Bolivia OUTDOORS
(☎642-5544; www.joyridebol.com; Ortiz 14) Popular hikes, bikes and horses, with groups leaving almost daily. Also offers paragliding; both tandem jumps and courses. Bookings and inquiries can be made at the cafe of the same name.

Locot's Aventura OUTDOORS
(☎691-2504; Bolívar 465) Hiking, biking, horseback riding and paragliding. Based at the bar-restaurant of the same name.

Off Road Bolivia
MOUNTAIN BIKING

(☎7033-8123; www.offroadbolivia.com; Ortiz 30) Sharing an office with tour agency Bolivia Specialist (p347), these are the safest and best-quality quad-biking tours in Sucre.

★彡 Festivals & Events

Sucre celebrates its birthday on May 24 to 25 and this usually involves a visit by the President.

Fiesta de la Virgen
de Guadalupe
RELIGIOUS

On the weekend closest to September 8, people from all over the country flock to join local *campesinos* in a celebration of the Fiesta de la Virgen de Guadalupe with songs, traditional dances and poetry recitations. The following day, they dress in colorful costumes and parade around Plaza 25 de Mayo carrying religious images and silver arches.

Todos Santos
RELIGIOUS

On November 2 Todos Santos (All Saints' Day) is celebrated with much fervor.

🛏 Sleeping

Accommodations in Sucre are among the country's most expensive. On the upside, most of the choices are in typical, attractive whitewashed colonial buildings built around pretty central courtyards and offer good value for money. For an authentic Bolivian experience ask at Candelaria Tours (p347) about homestay options (minimum five nights).

The cheapest places cluster near the market (p197) and along Ravelo and San Alberto.

Casa Verde
B&B $$

(☎645-8291; www.hotelsucrebedandbreakfast.com; Potosí 374; s/d/ste B$120/195/245, s/d without bathroom B$70/80; @🐾) Treading the thin line between hotel and top-end hostel, the immaculate Casa Verde is a real home from home. Deservedly popular and frankly underpriced for the quality of service, Belgian owner Rene almost bends over backwards to be helpful and readers quite rightly sing his praises. Rooms are named after Rene's children and grandchildren and are arranged around a small courtyard with a pool. If you visit in winter you'll be thankful for the thick duvets.

Samary Boutique Hotel
BOUTIQUE HOTEL $$$

(☎642-5088; www.samaryhotel.com; Dalence 349; s/d B$450/520; ❄@🐾) Samary has an ambitious concept, reproducing a traditional Chuquisaca village in hotel form, and it

pulls it off surprisingly well. There's a plaza, a chapel and even a *chichería* selling authentic homebrew liquor. Rooms are of the highest standard, adorned with Yaluparaez textiles and replica rock carvings. Attention to detail is king here. Even the bread is baked fresh every morning in a traditional oven on the breakfast terrace.

Hostal de Su Merced
BOUTIQUE HOTEL $$$

(☎645-1355; www.desumerced.com; Azurduy 16; s/d/tr B$300/450/570) In true Sucre style, this charming and beautiful hotel is decorated with antiques and paintings, with rooms set around an intimate, tiled courtyard. Room No 7 is particularly nice and the view from the rooftop terrace is stunning. The helpful staff speak English and there's also a restaurant.

La Dolce Vita
GUESTHOUSE $

(☎691-2014; www.dolcevitasucre.com; Urcullo 342; s/d/tr B$90/140/195; s/d without bathroom B$55/100; @) A delightfully friendly and spacious guesthouse, offering a variety of comfortable honey-colored rooms for all budgets. Guests can use the kitchen, or catch some sun on the terraces and if you stay more than five nights a discount is offered.

Parador Santa
María la Real
HISTORIC HOTEL $$$

(☎643-9592; www.parador.com.bo; Bolívar 625; s/d B$515/590, ste B$635-850; @) Swish, stylish and refined, this five-star hotel is magnificently elegant. It boasts an arcaded courtyard, antique furniture, a communal spa bath with a view and a curious historic underground section.

Casa Al Tronco
GUESTHOUSE $

(☎642-3195; Topater 57; s/d B$80/150) This charming guesthouse in the Recoleta district has just three rooms, so book in advance. Glorious views of the city from two terraces, use of a kitchen and a welcoming reception might make you stay longer than planned. Stay more than five nights and there is a price reduction.

HI Sucre
HOSTEL $$

(☎644-0471; www.hostellingbolivia.org; Loayza 119; dm/s/d B$40/140/200, s/d without bathroom B$50/100; @) Set in a building with attractive original features, Sucre's HI hostel is one of Bolivia's few purpose-built hostels and thus has excellent amenities. It's clean and friendly and has a shared kitchen and even some private rooms with spa baths and cable TV. It is very handy for the bus station too (from the terminal, cross the street, head left then take the first right).

Hostal Charcas
PENSION $

(☑645-3972; Ravelo 62; s/d B$70/130, without bathroom B$40/80) In a central location opposite the market, this is a travelers' favorite. Laundry service, 24-hour hot water and simple but clean and attractive rooms mean it's a reliable bet and more than the sum of its parts. Breakfast is available.

Grand Hotel
HOTEL $$

(☑645-2461; Arce 61; s/d B$130/180; @) With a central location, excellent staff and tastefully decorated rooms, this really is a grand hotel and a deserved favorite among travelers of all budgets. There's a popular restaurant here, a beautiful plant-filled courtyard and some of the spacious rooms have their own separate lounge area.

Premier Hotel
HOTEL $$

(☑645-3510; San Alberto 43; s/d/ste B$150/250/450; @) A handsome modern option catering for the local business-traveler market, this has a central courtyard and is sparklingly clean, with leather armchairs, and rooms with inviting beds and minibars. It's in the heart of town but pretty quiet.

Gringo's Rincón
HOSTEL $

(Loa 743; dm B$50) A bit improvised (without a phone so far!), this is a new dorm-only hostel for young party-loving backpackers interested in meeting up with a like-minded crowd. It's clean, spacious and friendly, but can get noisy.

Casa Kolping
HOTEL $$

(☑642-3812; www.grupo-casas-kolping.net; Pasaje Iturricha 265; s/d B$190/280; @) High on a hill by Plaza Anzures, with great views over town, this excellent hotel caters mostly for conferences but is an appealing place to stay. As well as efficient service and a good restaurant, it boasts clean, well-equipped rooms that are on the smallish side but very comfortable. It's also a good place for kids, with family apartments, plenty of space and a ping-pong table.

La Posada
BOUTIQUE HOTEL $$

(☑646-0101; www.hotellaposada.com.bo; Audiencia 92; s/d/ste B$250/380/500; @) This comfortable and classy place has spacious, uncluttered rooms with a very appealing colonial ambience and wooden trimmings. There are views over town, a stylish and intimate feel, and a good family suite. The courtyard restaurant is also a recommended spot. Excellent service adds to the package.

Hotel Real Audiencia
HOTEL $$

(☑643-1712; www.hotelrealaudiencia.net; Potosí 142; s/d/ste B$315/385/525; @☀) This welcoming place in an appealing part of Sucre has a mixture of old and new. It's attractively set out, with a pool area and Mediterranean-style balustrades. Rooms are spacious and have cable TV, but the 'executive' suites in a more modern wing are significantly better, with beautiful furniture and a minibar, for not much more cash.

Hostal Las Torres
HOSTEL $$

(☑644-2888; www.lastorreshostal.com; San Alberto 19; s/d incl breakfast B$140/220) Light and pleasant, this attractive hostel is entered down a little alleyway. The rooms have comfy beds with cutesy frilly coverings, cable TV and good bathrooms. Breakfast is served in an elegant dining room.

Hostal San Francisco
PENSION $

(☑645-2117; Arce 191; s/d B$70/120) With a stunning entry hall and eye-catchingly ornamental staircase, this place belongs in a higher price bracket, but while the rooms don't quite live up to the initial impression, you won't feel you've wasted your bolivianos.

Casa de Huéspedes San Marcos
PENSION $

(☑646-2087; Arce 233; s/d B$50/100, without bathroom B$40/80) This place gets a good rap from travelers, who appreciate its friendly owners and clean, quiet rooms as well as kitchen and laundry access.

Residencial Bolivia
PENSION $

(☑645-4346; San Alberto 42; s/d B$80/150, without bathroom B$55/100) Good location with rooms set around a triple courtyard, some of which are markedly nicer than others – ask to see a selection before making your choice if you want value for money.

✖ Eating

The cosmopolitan population in Sucre ensures a pleasing variety of quality restaurants and keeps prices competitive. It's a great place to spend time lolling around cafes while observing Bolivian university life.

Good *salteñerías* (specializing in *salteñas*) include **El Patio** (San Alberto 18; ◔9am-12:30pm) and **El Paso de los Abuelos** (Bustillos 216); get there early as they sell out fast. Thanks to Sucre's status as Bolivia's chocolate capital, there are plenty of stores that cater to those with a sweet tooth along Arenales.

TOP CHOICE Tentaciones INTERNATIONAL $$
(Arenales 11; mains B$20-40) Although the gourmet pizza and pasta are advertised as the main draw here, this stylish contemporary cafe-restaurant is worth a visit if only to sample the fantastically inventive nonalcoholic fruit juice cocktails.

El Huerto INTERNATIONAL $$
(645-1538; Cabrera 86; mains B$25-40) Set in a lovely secluded garden, this is a favorite spot for Sucre's people in the know. It's got the atmosphere of a classy lawn party, with sunshades and grass underfoot; there's great service and stylishly presented traditional plates (especially the chorizo) that don't come much better anywhere in the country.

Florín INTERNATIONAL $$
(Bolívar 567; mains B$35-45) One of the places to be seen in Sucre, this atmospheric bar-restaurant serves a mixture of typical Bolivian food and international dishes, including a 'Full English' breakfast. Popular with locals and gringos alike, who line up along the enormous 13m-long bar (surely the biggest in Bolivia?) at night to swill down the beers.

Churrasquería Cumaná ARGENTINE $$$
(Plaza Cumaná, Barrio Petrolero; mains B$40-70; ⊙dinner only Tue-Thu, 11:30am-10:30pm Fri-Sun) A Sucre secret, this carnivore's delight is in the Barrio Petrolero, a cab ride east from the center. The full portions of exquisitely grilled meat can comfortably feed two; the courtyard is also a pleasant place to drink wine or cocktails.

Joy Ride Café INTERNATIONAL $$
(Ortiz 14; mains B$25-50; ⊙7:30am-2am Mon-Fri, 9am-2am Sat & Sun) 'Probably the Best Bar in Town,' or so the promotion will have you believe. This wildly popular gringo-tastic cafe, restaurant and bar has everything, from dawn espressos to midnight vodkas and nightly movies to weekend table-dancing. It's spacious, friendly, well run and you'll need an hour just to read through the menu.

La Taverne FRENCH $$
(Arce 35; mains B$20-48) With a quiet sophisticated atmosphere, the restaurant of the Alliance Française is a delight to visit. The short, select menu has a French touch and there are excellent daily specials. There's live music every Friday night and film screenings several times a week.

Locot's INTERNATIONAL $$
(Bolívar 465; mains B$20-42; ⊙8am-late) Relaxed and attractive, this bar-restaurant is in an interesting old building, with original art on the walls. It offers a wide choice of Bolivian, Mexican and international food, including vegetarian, and a gringo-friendly vibe.

Amsterdam INTERNATIONAL $
(Bolívar 426; sandwiches B$15-25) Founded with the intention of supporting the Centro Educativo Ñanta (a charity for street children), having a snack or two in Amsterdam gives something back to the community. Dutch owned, but you guessed that already didn't you?

Chifa New Hong Kong CHINESE $$
(San Alberto 242; mains B$30-50) Good-value Chinese food with huge portions. Watch your head on the ceiling upstairs though!

Bibliocafé LATIN AMERICAN $$
(Ortiz 42 & 50; mains B$20-40; ⊙11am-3am) With two adjacent locations, this has something for everyone; one side is dark and cozy, the other a little smarter. There's good service, a menu of pasta and Mexican-Bolivian food and drinks until late in a cheerful and unpretentious atmosphere, plus regular live music.

La Patisserie BAKERY $
(Audiencia 17; snacks B$10-25; ⊙8:30am-12:30pm & 3:30-8:30pm Mon-Fri) An elegant French-style tearoom and bakery, specializing in crepes, quiches and desserts in the evening and offering fullsome breakfasts in the morning.

Café Gourmet Mirador CAFE $
(Plaza Anzures; mains B$15-25; ⊙9am-7pm) Enjoy the best view in town from this friendly little cafe. The menu is simple with a selection of sandwiches, pasta and desserts, but after climbing the steps to Antunes you are more likely to be wooed by the fruit juice selection. A percentage of profits goes to a local children's home. Ask staff whether the adjacent Museo Tanga Tanga has reopened yet.

Kulturcafé Berlin INTERNATIONAL $$
(Avaroa 334; mains B$29-35; ⊙closed Sun) This quiet spot is affiliated with the ICBA and offers German-language newspapers and magazines, a book exchange and filling dishes; try the *papas rellenas* (spicy filled potatoes).

CENTRAL HIGHLANDS SUCRE

It's also a good bet for an evening beer, with some German choices.

Las Bajos
CHORIZO $$
(Loa 759; mains B$25-50) One of the oldest and most typical of the *choricerías* (restaurants specializing in chorizo) in Sucre, though it's not just sausage on the menu. The owner is a Beatles fanatic and downstairs is a miniature recreation of Liverpool's Cavern Club, the walls adorned with posters, album covers and other Fab Four memorabilia. On Saturday night it metamorphoses into a hard-rock bar.

La Posada
INTERNATIONAL $$$
(Audiencia 92; mains B$30-60; ⊘closed Sun dinner) This comfortable hotel also has one of Sucre's most appealing spots for a meal or a drink, offering elegant indoor and outdoor seating around its stone-flagged courtyard. There are tasty fish and meat dishes, pastas and salads, set meals and good-natured service.

Freya
VEGETARIAN $
(Loa 751; almuerzo B$20; ⊘noon-2pm Mon-Sat; ♪) Part of the Freya Gym, this likable place serves tasty vegetarian *almuerzos*, though the choice is very limited.

El Germen
INTERNATIONAL $$
(San Alberto 237; mains B$25-40, vegetarian almuerzo B$20; ♪) This simply decorated, peaceful spot is a favorite for its tasty vegetarian dishes; it also does decent goulash and roast meat, as well as cracking curries and tempting cakes. There's a book exchange too.

Self-Catering
Market
MARKET
(⊘7am-7:30pm Mon-Sat, breakfast only Sun) The central market is home to some gastronomic highlights. Don't miss the fresh juices and fruit salads – they are among the best in the country. The vendors and their blenders always come up with something indescribably delicious; try *jugo de tumbo* (unripe passion-fruit juice).

Supermercado SAS
SUPERMARKET
(Pérez 331; ⊘8am-10pm daily) A megalithic reply to all your shopping cries for help.

 ## Drinking

Many of the places mentioned in the Eating section, such as Joy Ride, Amsterdam, Locot's, Bibliocafé and Florín, are popular spots for a drink too, and get pretty lively –

especially during their respective happy hours.

For *discotecas* (weekends only) you'll need to head north of the center; it's easiest by taxi.

Mooy
DISCO
(Pérez 331, inside Supermercado SAS; admission B$20-60) An upmarket disco-bar for young ravers with cash to splash. There is frequent live music and it attracts the top bands and DJs from across the country.

Mitos
DISCO
(Cerro s/n; admission women/men B$5/10) Mitos is a spacious basement spot a 15-minute walk north of the center. It really fills up around 1am and plays well-loved local and international hits.

La Vitriola
KARAOKE
(Urcullo) End point for the organized bar crawls, this is a lively karaoke bar for those who like the sound of their own voice, even if others don't.

Salfari
PUB
(Bustillos 237; ⊘8pm-3am) This little gem of a pub has friendly service, a loyal local crowd and lively games of poker and *cacho* (dice) usually going on. Try its tasty but potent homemade fruit shots.

☆ Entertainment

Southeast of the center, the **Teatro al Aire Libre** is a wonderful outdoor venue for musical and other performances. **Teatro Gran Mariscal de Ayacucho** (Plazuela Libertad) is an opulent old opera house. The tourist office (p198) and the Casa de la Cultura both distribute a monthly calendar of events. **Cine SAS** (Pérez 331, inside Supermercado SAS) has three screens showing the latest Hollywood film releases.

Centro Cultural los Masis
PERFORMING ARTS
(☎645-3403; Bolívar 561; ⊘10am-noon & 3:30-9pm Mon-Fri) The Centro Cultural los Masis hosts concerts and other cultural events. It also has a small museum of local musical instruments and offers Quechua classes.

Orígenes Bolivianos
FOLKLORE
(☎645-7091; Azurduy 473; ⊘7-11pm Tue-Sat) Runs a highly entertaining twice-weekly Bolivian folklore show including dances, music and costumes from across the country. Tickets available in advance from Candelaria Tours (p347).

Cultural Centers

There's a monthly brochure detailing Sucre's cultural events; look for it at tourist offices or in bars and restaurants. Besides the Instituto Cultural Boliviano Alemán (p193), the following establishments can provide language assistance and host cultural events.

Alliance Française CULTURAL CENTER
(645-3599; www.afbolivia.org; Arce 35) French-language library and foreign films; also home to the La Taverne restaurant.

Casa de la Cultura CULTURAL CENTER
(645-1083; Argentina 65) Hosts art and *artesanía* exhibitions as well as music recitals and the public library.

Centro Boliviano-Americano CULTURAL CENTER
(644-1608; www.cba.com.bo; Calvo 301) English-language library. Also referrals for Spanish-language tutors and homestay courses.

Shopping

The best place to learn about traditional local weavings is the Museo de Arte Indígena, but to buy them you are best off going direct to the villages. Prices are steep by Bolivian standards, but the items are high quality.

A trip to the **Mercado Americano**, around the junction of Mujía and Reyes, will keep clothes-junkies busy for hours, while nearby on Aguirre the **Mercado Campesino** is a fascinating traditional food market with a really authentic feel. Take *micro 7* or *G* northbound from the center.

Inca Pallay ARTS & CRAFTS
(646-1936; www.incapallay.org; Audiencia 97) This weavers and artisans cooperative has an impressive array of high-quality handmade crafts, not all from the Sucre area. Prices are high, but this store returns the highest percentage to the weavers themselves. You can sometimes see weavers at work in the patio.

Pacha Mama ARTS & CRAFTS
(Audiencia 76) A new store with the biggest and best selection of local *artesanías* in town. Aymará owner Sayda Quispe offers some of his own jewellery and clothing designs. It's also a sales point for Lonely Planet books.

Information

Emergency

Tourist police (648-0467; Plazuela Zudáñez) Sucre has long enjoyed a reputation as one of Bolivia's safest towns, but occasion-ally visitors are harassed by bogus police or 'fake tourists.' If you have a problem, report it to the tourist police.

Immigration

Migración (645-3647; Bustillos 284; 8:30am-4:30pm Mon-Fri) A no-fuss place to extend visas and lengths of stay.

Laundry

Lavandería LG (Loa 407; per kg B$12; daily) Delivers to hotels.
Limpecable (Pérez 331, in Supermercado SAS; per kg B$12; daily)
Superlimp (Estudiantes 26; per kg B$12 ; 8:30am-8pm Mon-Sat)

Medical Services

Hospital Santa Bárbara (646-0133; cnr Ayacucho & René Moreno) Good hospital.

Money

ATMs are located all around the city center but not at the bus station. Businesses with *'Compro Dólares'* signs only change cash. Street money changers, who operate outside the market along Av Hernando Siles, are handy on weekends when banks are closed but check rates beforehand.

Internet Access, Post & Telephone

The **main post office** (cnr Estudiantes & Junín) has an *aduana* (customs) office downstairs for *encomiendas* (parcels). It doesn't close for lunch and is open late. There are many **Entel** (España & Urcullo, Main branch; opens 8am) and **Punto Viva** (Arce) centers around, charging competitive rates for international calls, and most have internet access (B$3 to B$4 per hour).

Tourist Information

In addition to the following, there are tourist information booths at the airport, bus terminal and Plazuela Libertad.
Infotur (645-5983; Dalence 1; 8am-noon & 4-6pm Mon-Sat, 9am-noon & 2:30-6pm Sat & Sun) Up the stairs behind the Prefectura de Chuquisaca. Can help with information about the Chuquisaca region.
Instituto Geográfico Militar (645-5514; Arce) Topographic maps of Chuquisaca department.
Oficina Universitaria de Turismo (644-7644; Estudiantes 49; 4-7pm Mon-Sat, 2-7pm Sun) Information office run by university students. Sometimes offers guides for city tours.

Getting There & Away

Air

The domestic departure tax is B$11. Sucre has daily flights to Tarija and Cochabamba with **TAM** (646-0944; Bustillos) and **Aerocon** (645-0007; Juana Azurduy Airport). Flights to Cochabamba connect with La Paz and Santa Cruz so they fill up fast and you will need to book ahead. **Juana Azurduy Airport** (☎645-4445) is frequently shut in bad weather, so check with the airline before heading out there.

Bus & Shared Taxi

The **Bus Terminal** (☎644-1292) is a 15-minute walk uphill from the center and most easily accessed by *micros A* or *3* (B$1.50) from along Ravelo, or by taxi (as the *micros* are too crowded for lots of luggage). Unless you're headed for Potosí, it's wise to book long-distance buses a day in advance in order to reserve a seat. There's a terminal tax of B$2.50; services include an information kiosk but no ATM. To save the trip to the bus station many central travel agents also sell tickets on selected services for a small commission.

If you are headed to Tarija, Villazón or Uyuni, you'll have more luck going to Potosí; the quickest and comfiest (if not the cheapest) way to get there is in a shared taxi (B$50, two hours), which can be arranged through your hotel or by calling direct. Try **Turismo Global** (☎642-5125), **Cielito Lindo** (☎644-1014) or **Infinito del Sur** (☎642-2277).

DESTINATION	COST (B$)	DURATION (HR)
Camiri	100	14
Cochabamba	50-70	12
La Paz	70-135	14-16
Oruro	50-60	10
Potosí	15-0	3
Santa Cruz	94-105	15-20

❶ Getting Around

To/From the Airport

The airport, 9km northwest of town, is accessed by *micros 1* or *F* (allow an hour to be safe) from Av Hernando Siles, by the *banderita blanca* taxi from Av España, or by taxi (fixed tariff B$25).

Bus & Micro

Lots of buses and *micros* (B$1.50) ply circuitous routes around the city's one-way streets and all seem to congregate at or near the market between runs. They're usually crowded, but fortunately Sucre is a town of short distances. The most useful routes are *micros 7, C* and *G* that climb the steep Av Grau hill to La Recoleta, and *micro A*, which serves the main bus terminal.

Rental Car

Imbex (☎646-1222; Serrano 165 btwn Bolívar and Potosí) 4WDs from B$350 a day.

Taxi

The city center is small enough to walk to most places, but **taxis** (day/night per person B$4/5)

are available if you want to go further afield or can't face the hills.

AROUND SUCRE

Tarabuco

☎4 / POP 19,500 / ELEV 3200M

This small, predominantly indigenous village 65km southeast of Sucre is famous for its textiles, among the most renowned in all of Bolivia. To travelers though, Tarabuco is best known for its **Sunday market**, a popular day trip from Sucre, and for its annual **Pujllay** celebrations in March.

Tarabuco's colorful, sprawling market, which features high-quality *artesanías* (pullovers, *charangos*, coca pouches, ponchos and weavings that feature geometric and zoomorphic designs), is one of Bolivia's most popular. By any standards, it's pretty touristy, which has meant the inevitable arrival of higher prices and lots of articles from well outside the local area. While there is some very high-quality work here, there's also a lot of generic stuff and few bargains to be had.

On market days, the **Centro Artesanal Inca Pallay** (Murillo 25) sells an array of local weavings and serves meals in its touristfriendly restaurant. Several places put on exhibitions of *pujllay* dancing while the market is on, for a small charge.

✸ Festivals & Events

Pujllay TRADITIONAL

On March 12, 1816, Tarabuco was the site of the Battle of Jumbati, in which the villagers defended themselves under the leadership of a woman, doña Juana Azurduy de Padilla, and liberated the town from Spanish forces. In commemoration of the event the village stages Pujllay ('play' in Quechua) on the third Sunday in March, when more than 60 surrounding communities turn up in local costume. The celebration begins with a Quechua mass and procession followed by the **Pukara ceremony**, a Bolivian version of Thanksgiving. Folk dancers and musicians perform throughout the two-day weekend fiesta. It's one of Bolivia's largest festivals and is great fun.

🛏 Sleeping & Eating

During Pujllay accommodations fill up quickly, so you may want to hedge your bets and carry camping gear. Alternatively you

ICLA

With Tarabuco becoming a bit of a tourist trap these days, more adventurous travelers will no doubt be in search of an alternative destination that is really off the beaten track. Icla, 120km from Sucre, just about fits the bill. Set in an imposing canyon dripping with waterfalls and riddled with caves, this remote area is of extreme natural beauty and you won't see another tourist for miles. Scores of dinosaur footprints surround the area and you may be able to convince locals to show you the geological formations and cave paintings in some of the more accessible caves.

To get here you'll need to take *micro 14* or *B* from Calle Ravelo in Sucre to the town of Pokonas, from where you can organise a ride on to Icla. It's definitely worth the trip.

can speak to the tourist office in Sucre about the possibilities of lodging with a local family (B$20 per person).

The plaza and nearby streets have a handful of basic restaurants. Meals of *chorizo*, soup and *charquekan* (dried llama meat served with potatoes and corn) are available from street stalls during market hours.

HI Centro Ecológico Juvenil HOSTEL $
(☎644-0471; r per person B$60) The nicest digs are at Centro Ecológico Juvenil, which is signposted from the plaza. The Centro is a member of Hostelling International and has brand spanking new rooms arranged around a little courtyard. They can also arrange meals if you are peckish.

Maliki LATIN AMERICAN $$
(just off the plaza; mains B$25-60) About the best place to eat in town and a notable step up in quality from the street stalls. Meats and chicken predominate, served in an attractive, sunny courtyard.

❶ Getting There & Away

The easiest way to get to Tarabuco is by charter bus (B$40 round-trip, two hours each way) from Sucre, which leaves from outside Hostal Charcas (p195) on Ravelo around 8:30am. Tickets must be bought in advance from bigger hotels or any travel agent. From Tarabuco, the buses return to Sucre any time between 1pm and 3pm.

Alternatively, *micros* (B$10, two hours) leave when full from Av de las Américas in Sucre on Sunday between 6:30am and 9:30am. Returns to Sucre leave between 11am and 3:30pm.

Candelaria

The Sunday market in Tarabuco is fairly touristy these days, so to get a better idea of the regional culture and textiles you could visit the appealingly rustic indigenous village of Candelaria, which produces many of the finest handweavings – blankets, rugs, ponchos and bags – in the local style. There's a very traditional way of life here and it's far removed from the bustle of Sucre or Tarabuco. The community has established a weaving association, which owns a **museum** (admission B$5) and textile store that explain the intricate weavings with displays depicting their culture rendered in vividly colored yarns. The store contains a large selection of the same high-quality weaving found in Sucre but at lower prices, with 100% of the profits going back into the small fair-trade association.

Some Sucre operators (p193) run tours leaving for Candelaria on Saturday, staying the night and proceeding to Tarabuco's market on Sunday morning. Candelaria Tours (p347) runs a highly recommended excursion, overnighting in a beautiful colonial hacienda. The weaving association can also arrange stays in private homes but this is best arranged in advance through an agency in Sucre. Do not arrive in town without an arrangement for accommodation, as there are no formal hotels.

There are buses from Sucre to Candelaria at 4pm on Tuesday, Thursday and Saturday. They are run by **Flota Charcas** and leave from the clock tower on Av Mendoza (the ring road). Several *camiones* pass through Candelaria daily, heading for Sucre.

Cordillera de los Frailes

The imposing serrated ridge forming Sucre's backdrop creates a formidable barrier between the departments of Chuquisaca and Potosí. It's home to the Jal'qa people and offers a rich selection of scenery, activities and intriguing options for getting to know the Jal'qa culture.

◎ Sights & Activities

The best way to see this region is on foot. A highly recommended three- or four-day circuit taking in several Cordillera highlights and the villages at the heart of the community tourism project begins at Chataquila, on the ridge above Punilla, 35km northwest of Sucre. From here (with an optional side trip to the abstract red, white and black man-animal rock paintings at Incamachay and Pumamachay) you descend to Chaunaca, then head to the Cráter de Maragua, before ending with the spectacular six- to seven-hour walk – via *chullpa* (funerary towers) and with a short diversion to see the dinosaur footprints at Niñu Mayu – to Potolo. At Potolo there is daily transportation back to Sucre.

We strongly recommend taking a guide to increase your enjoyment of the region and communicate with the Quechua-speaking *campesinos*. A responsible guide will help you avoid local hostility, minimize your impact and help you get a better feel for the local culture.

There are numerous walking routes through the Cordillera de los Frailes, some of which are marked on the 1:50,000 topo sheets *Sucre,* sheet 6536IV, and *Estancia Chaunaca,* sheet 6537III. You can get them at the Instituto Geográfico Militar (p198) in Sucre.

CHATAQUILA TO CHAUNACA

On the rocky ridgetop at Chataquila is a lovely stone chapel dedicated to the Virgen de Chataquila, a Virgin-shaped stone dressed in a gown and placed on the altar. The chapel was built from the local rock and blends in seamlessly with its surroundings.

From Chataquila look around on the south side of the road for an obvious notch in the rock, which leads into a lovely pre-Hispanic route that descends steeply for 6km (three hours) to the village of Chaunaca, 41km from Sucre. Lots of good paved sections remain and it's easy to follow.

Chaunaca is home to a school, a tiny church and an interpretation and information center on the Jal'qa region. Beds are available in the information center, but you'll have to find your own food. There's also a campsite and the renovated colonial hacienda, **Samay Huasi** (☎645-4129; per

---

THE JAL'QA COMMUNITIES

The Cordillera de los Frailes is home to the Quechua-speaking Jal'qa people, of whom there are some 10,000 in the area around Potolo and Maragua. They have traditionally made a living from farming potatoes, wheat and barley, and herding sheep and goats. The weaving of elaborately patterned *aqsus* (an apron-like skirt) is an important craft tradition and these Escher-like red-and-black garments are instantly recognizable, being patterned with inventive depictions of *khurus* – strange, demon-like figures.

In 2001 the Jal'qa decided that they wanted to embrace tourism, but in a sustainable form that would benefit the community without destroying its traditions. They have developed a series of accommodations, cultural centers and guiding services, all involving maximal community participation. The villages receive 100% of profits.

Accommodations and restaurant services have been set up in the villages of **Maragua** and **Potolo**. Sets of attractive thatched *cabañas* have been constructed using traditional methods and materials; they boast comfortable beds, hot water and attractive wooden furniture, and are decorated with local textiles. The cost is B$60 per person per night; for B$100 per person, meals and cultural displays are included. The villages also have good camping areas. In **Chaunaca** there's a camping area and some beds set up in the information center, but no restaurant service. The villages are well placed for hiking.

On the way, you will eat traditional Bolivian *campesino* meals – such as *kala purca,* a maize soup cooked by immersing hot stones in it. Cultural activities that can be organized include demonstrations of *pujllay* dancing or traditional medicine. Weaving workshops can be found in all the villages mentioned, as well as some others, while Chaunaca has an interpretation center and Potolo a museum of indigenous healing. Note that the Jal'qa aren't fond of being photographed.

To book the Maragua *cabañas,* call ☎644-5341. For Potolo call ☎693-8204. Alternatively, ask at the Museo de Arte Indígena (p187) in Sucre.

Cordillera de los Frailes

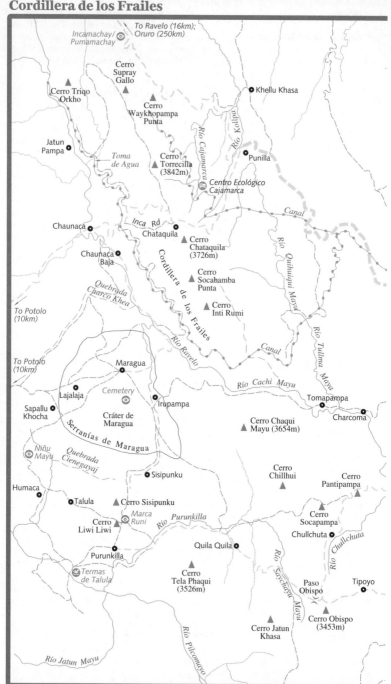

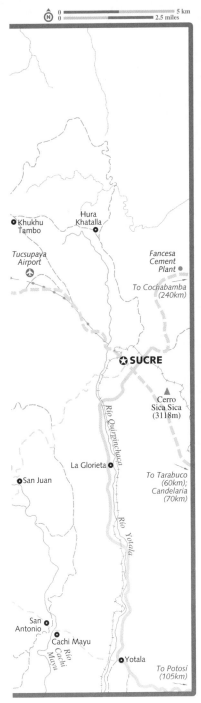

person B$300), which offers pricey but high-quality accommodation. The cost includes three meals a day and transportation can be arranged for a small fee. Slightly higher prices may apply if there are fewer than three people – ring to check.

For a head start, *camiones* run the route from Sucre to Chaunaca and Chataquila, departing from Av Juana Azurduy de Padilla. From Chaunaca you have the option of continuing west 15km direct to Potolo, or taking the very rewarding detour south via Maragua and Humaca. The latter will add an extra day to your hike but takes in some sites of real geological and paleontological interest.

INCAMACHAY & PUMAMACHAY

A worthwhile side trip from Chataquila or Chaunaca leads to two fascinating sets of ancient rock paintings estimated to be up to 2000 years old. At the first major curve on the road west of Chataquila, a rugged track heads north along the ridge. For much of its length the route is flanked by rugged rock formations, but it's relatively easygoing until you've almost reached the paintings, where you face a bit of a scramble. The first set, Pumamachay, lies well ensconced inside a rock cleft between two stone slabs. The pictographs here depict humans and geometric shapes in monochrome black. A more impressive panel, Incamachay, is 15 minutes further along beneath a rock overhang that contains anthropomorphic, zoomorphic and geometric motifs painted in red and white. Guides at the entrance charge B$10. You will need one to find the paintings.

From Incamachay, you can continue downhill for a couple of hours until you hit the road at the **Toma de Agua** aqueduct, where there's drinking water and a good campsite. From there take the road 6km to the Chataquila–Chaunaca road, where you can either ascend to Chataquila or descend to Chaunaca from where you can find transportation back to Sucre.

CRÁTER DE MARAGUA

This unearthly natural formation, sometimes called the Ombligo de Chuquisaca (Chuquisaca's Belly Button), features surreal settlements scattered across an 8km-wide red-and-violet crater floor, and bizarre slopes that culminate in the gracefully symmetrical pale green arches of the Serranías de Maragua. These scallop-shaped cliff faces make it one of the most visually striking

CENTRAL HIGHLANDS CORDILLERA DE LOS FRAILES

places in Bolivia. There's plenty to see: waterfalls, caves and a picturesque cemetery in the middle of the crater that dates from pre-Hispanic times.

The village of **Maragua** is an active weaving center. The weavers have set up a store and will take visitors into their homes to show them the creation of the textiles. Maragua has three *cabañas* and a campsite. A kilometer from the village, in **Irupampa**, the villagers started up a lovely little **hostel** (☑693-8088; r per person B$25), with running water, a cold shower next door and an appealing little garden. You can also camp here.

Maragua is an easy three-hour walk along the road from Chaunaca. If you'd prefer a lift, ask about shared 4WD taxis at one of the Sucre tourist agencies.

MARAGUA TO POTOLO

From Maragua, it's a spectacular walk to Potolo. You can get there in five hours, but there's plenty to see on the way to slow you down. In the area around **Humaca** you will find *chullpa* and a paleontological deposit where embedded fossils are clearly visible in the rocks. Additionally, dinosaur footprints at **Niñu Mayu** can be visited if you are prepared to add an extra hour or so to your hike. All of these can be found most easily with a local guide. Ask around in the villages and negotiate a price that is fair to the community.

Another side trip from Humaca could take you to the **Termas de Talula**, 5km away. You'll need to ford the Río Pilcomayo twice. The Talula hot springs issue into rock pools that have temperatures up to 46°C. Camping is possible anywhere in the vicinity.

From Talula it's 500m to the constricted passage that conducts the Río Pilcomayo between the steep walls of the Punkurani gorge. When the river is low, you can cross over to the Potosí shore and see the many rock-painting sites above the opposite bank.

POTOLO

The village of Potolo has some typically stunning weaving going on in the workshops and also has a museum of traditional medicine, which demonstrates vernacular healing practices and other aspects of the culture. There are three *cabañas* here, a store and a campsite.

Camiones run infrequently to Potolo from Av Juana Azurduy de Padilla in Sucre

via Chaunaca and Chataquila. They return to Sucre from Potolo when full.

QUILA QUILA

Another worthwhile destination is the beautiful village of Quila Quila, three hours south of Maragua by foot. It's a formerly deserted village of largely mud buildings that is being slowly repopulated. The tower of the elegant **colonial church** dominates the skyline and adjacent to it are buried the remains of the revered 18th-century indigenous leader Tomás Katari, who was murdered at the chapel in Chataquila in 1781. In 1777 Katari walked to Buenos Aires to confront colonial leaders and claim rights for the Aymará and returned triumphantly with a document signed by the viceroy ceding to his demands and recognizing him as *cacique* (chieftain). Upon his return to Bolivia he was imprisoned, sparking a widespread uprising that eventually led to his death. A kilometer away are the **Marca Runi** monoliths with pictographs. The area is rich in pre-Columbian archaeological artifacts.

Daily *camiones* to Talula via Quila Quila (B$8, three to four hours) depart at 6:30am from Calle Osvaldo Molina in Sucre, returning the afternoon of the same day. Alternatively negotiate with a taxi driver. In recent times some visitors have reported an unpleasant reception by villagers and it is strongly recommended that you check the current situation before setting out or, even better, go with a guide.

☞ Tours

To get the most out of the region it is essential to visit with a guide. Several Sucre travel agencies offer quick jaunts into the Cordillera – for example, a two-day circuit from Chataquila to Incamachay and Chaunaca. It's important to go with a responsible operator committed to giving something to the region. Exploitative day trips have created an atmosphere of hostility towards visitors in some communities and it is up to you to ensure that your visit does not exacerbate the problem.

Private guides can usually be arranged through the tourist offices in Sucre or one of the agencies, but if possible pick one that is local, has links to the communities and gives something back to them. Avoid guides who do not spend money locally or bring all their supplies from Sucre. Local guide **Pablo Ávila-Cruz** (☑7-711-4517; from B$200 per day) knows the region like the back of his hand

and comes highly recommended. He can be contacted through the Oficina Universitaria de Turismo (p198) in Sucre.

POTOSÍ

♩2 / POP 145,000 / ELEV 4070M

I am rich Potosí,
The treasure of the world...
And the envy of kings.

The conquistadors never found El Dorado, the legendary city of gold, but they did get their hands on Potosí and its Cerro Rico, a 'Rich Hill' full of silver. This quote, from the city's first coat of arms, sums it up. The city was founded in 1545 as soon as the ore was discovered and pretty soon the silver extracted here was bankrolling the Spanish empire. Even today, something very lucrative is said to *vale un Potosí* (be worth a Potosí).

Potosí's story is wholly tied to its silver. During the boom years, when the metal must have seemed inexhaustible, it became the largest and wealthiest city of the Americas. Once the silver more or less dried up, however, the city went into decline and its citizens slipped into poverty. The ore is still being extracted by miners in some of the most abysmal conditions imaginable – a visit to see today's miners at work provokes disbelief at just how appalling the job is. But the rest of Potosí – its grand churches, ornate colonial architecture and down-to-earth, friendly inhabitants – is a real delight.

History

No one is certain how much silver has been extracted from Cerro Rico over its four centuries of productivity, but a popular boast was that the Spanish could have constructed a silver bridge to Spain and still had silver left to carry across it. The Spanish monarchy, mortgaged to the hilt by foreign bankers, came to rely completely on the yearly treasure fleets, which brought the Potosí silver. On the rare occasions when they were intercepted by storms or pirates, it was a national disaster.

Although the tale of Potosí's origins probably takes a few liberties with the facts, it's a good story. It begins in 1544 when a local Inca, Diego Huallpa, searching for an escaped llama, stopped to build a fire at the foot of the mountain known in Quechua as 'Potojsi' (meaning 'thunder' or 'explosion', although it might also have stemmed from *potoj*, 'the springs'). The fire grew so hot that the very earth beneath it started to melt and shiny liquid oozed from the ground.

Diego immediately realized he had run across a commodity for which the Spanish conquerors had an insatiable appetite. Perhaps he also remembered the Inca legend associated with the mountain, in which Inca Huayna Capac had been instructed by a booming voice not to dig in the hill of Potojsi, but to leave the metal alone, because it was intended for others.

Whatever the truth of this, the Spanish eventually learned of the enormous wealth buried in the mountain of Potojsi and determined that it warranted immediate attention. On April 1, 1545, the Villa Imperial de Carlos V was founded at the foot of Cerro Rico and large-scale excavation began. In the time it takes to say 'Get down there and dig,' thousands of indigenous slaves were pressed into service and the first of the silver was already headed for Spain.

The work was dangerous, however, and so many workers died of accidents and silicosis pneumonia that the Spanish imported millions of African slaves to augment the labor force. The descendants of the very few to survive mainly live in the Yungas.

In order to increase productivity, in 1572 the Viceroy of Toledo instituted the *Ley de la Mita*, which required all indigenous and African slaves over the age of 18 to work shifts of 12 hours. They would remain underground without seeing daylight for four months at a time, eating, sleeping and working in the mines. When they emerged from a 'shift', their eyes were covered to prevent damage from the bright sunlight.

Naturally these miners, who came to be known as *mitayos*, didn't last long. Heavy losses were also incurred among those who worked in the *ingenios* (smelting mills), as the silver-smelting process involved contact with deadly mercury. In all, it's estimated that over the three centuries of colonial rule (1545 to 1825) as many as eight million Africans and indigenous Bolivians died in these appalling conditions.

In 1672 a mint was established to coin the silver, reservoirs were constructed to provide water for the growing population and exotic European consumer goods found their way up the llama trails from Arica and Callao. Amid the mania, more than 80 churches

Potosí

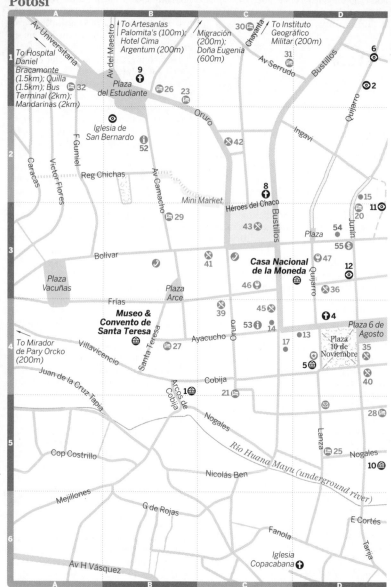

To Artesanías
Palomita's (100m);
Hotel Cima
Argentum (200m)

Migración
(200m);
Doña Eugenia
(600m)

To Instituto
Geográfico
Militar (200m)

Av Universitaria

Av del Maestro

To Hospital
Daniel
Bracamonte
(1.5km); Quilla
(1.5km); Bus
Terminal (2km);
Mandarinas (2km)

Plaza
del Estudiante

Iglesia de
San Bernardo

Caracas

F Gumiel

Victor Flores

Reg Chichas

Av Camacho

Mini Market

Plaza
Vacuñas

Bolívar

Plaza
Arce

Frías

Museo &
Convento de
Santa Teresa

To Mirador
de Pary Orcko
(200m)

Villavicencio

Santa Teresa

Juan de la Cruz Tapia

Cop Costrillo

Mejillones

G de Rojas

Av H Vásquez

Oruro

Av Serrudo

Bustillos

Ingavi

Quijarro

Héroes del Chaco

Bustillos

Plaza

Casa Nacional
de la Moneda

Quijarro

Oruro

Ayacucho

Plaza 6 de
Agosto

Plaza
10 de
Noviembre

Cobija

Arcos de
Cobija

Nogales

Río Huana Mayu (underground river)

Nicolás Ben

Fanola

Iglesia
Copacabana

E Cortés

Tarija

Lanza

Nogales

Junín

CENTRAL HIGHLANDS POTOSÍ

were constructed and Potosí's population grew to nearly 200,000, making it one of the largest cities in the world. As one politician of the period put it: 'Potosí was raised in the pandemonium of greed, at the foot of riches discovered by accident.'

As with most boom towns, Potosí's glory was not to last. The mines' output began to decline in the early 19th century and the city was looted during the independence struggles in Alto Perú. The population dropped to less than 10,000 and the mid-19th-century

Bolivia's major metallic exports but silver extraction continues on a small scale and reminders of the city's grand colonial past are still evident.

Most of the operations in Cerro Rico today are in the control of miner-owned cooperatives, which operate under conditions that have changed shamefully little from the colonial period. There's little prospect of change in sight, as the miners barely extract enough ore to keep themselves in bread. The dream of the lucky strike (there are still a few) keeps them going, although the number of miners is steadily dwindling.

⊙ Sights

In 1987 Unesco named Potosí a World Heritage Site in recognition of its rich and tragic history and its wealth of colonial architecture.

Casa Nacional de la Moneda MUSEUM
(Ayacucho at Bustillos; admission by mandatory 2hr guided tour B$40, camera B$20; ⊙9am, 10:30am, 2:30pm & 4:30pm Tue-Sat, 9am & 10:30am Sun) The National Mint is Potosí's star attraction and one of South America's finest museums. Potosí's first mint was constructed on the present site of the Casa de Justicia in 1572 under orders from the Viceroy of Toledo. This, its replacement, is a vast and strikingly beautiful building that takes up a whole city block. It was built between 1753 and 1773 to control the minting of colonial coins; legend has it that when the king of Spain saw the bill for its construction, he exclaimed 'that building must be made of silver' (expletive presumably deleted). These coins, which bore the mint mark 'P', were known as *potosís*.

The building has walls that are more than a meter thick and it has not only functioned as a mint but also done spells as a prison, a fortress and, during the Chaco War, the headquarters of the Bolivian army. As visitors are ushered into a courtyard from the entrance, they're greeted by the sight of a stone fountain and a freaky mask of Bacchus, hung there in 1865 by Frenchman Eugenio Martin Moulon for reasons known only to him. In fact, this aberration looks more like an escapee from a children's funfair, but it has become a town icon (known as the *mascarón*).

Apart from the beauty of the building itself, there's a host of historical treasures. They include a fine selection of religious paintings from the Potosí school, culminating in *La Virgen del Cerro,* a famous

drop in silver prices dealt a blow from which Potosí has never completely recovered.

In the present century only the demand for tin has rescued Potosí from obscurity and brought a slow but steady recovery. Zinc and lead have now taken over from tin as

Potosí

anonymous work from the 18th century, as well as the immense assemblies of mule-driven wooden cogs that served to beat the silver to the width required for the coining. These were replaced by steam-powered machines in the 19th century. The last coins were minted here in 1953.

The guided tour is long and the temperatures inside the building are chilly, so rug up. Although there are English and French tours available on request, the quality of the Spanish one is higher and the visit more comprehensive, so it's worth doing even if your levels are fairly limited.

Cooperative Mines   MINES

A visit to the cooperative mines will almost certainly be one of the most memorable experiences you'll have in Bolivia, providing an opportunity to witness working conditions that are among the most grueling imaginable. We urge you not to underestimate the dangers involved in going into the mines and to consider the voyeuristic factor involved in seeing other people's suffering. You may be left stunned and/or ill.

Dozens of Potosí operators offer guided tours through the mines. The best tour guides tend to be ex-miners, who know the conditions and are friendly with the men at work. The safety standards are hit-and-miss; you really are going down at your own risk.

Mine visits aren't easy and the low ceilings and steep, muddy passageways are best visited in your worst clothes. You'll feel both cold and hot at times, there will likely be a bit of crawling through narrow shafts and the altitude can be extremely taxing. On some tours, you'll end up walking 3km or 4km inside the mountain. You'll be exposed to noxious chemicals and gases, including silica dust (the cause of silicosis), arsenic gas and acetylene vapors, as well as asbestos deposits. Anyone with doubts or medical problems should avoid these tours. The plus side is that you can speak with the friendly miners, who will share their insights and opinions about their difficult lot. The miners are proud of their work in such tough conditions and generally happy for visitors to observe their toil.

Tours begin with a visit to the miners' market, where miners stock up on acetylene rocks, dynamite, cigarettes and other essentials. In the past, gifts weren't expected, but with the growing number of tourists, you'd be very unpopular if you didn't supply a handful of coca leaves and a few cigarettes – luxuries for which the miners' meager earnings are scarcely sufficient. Photography is permitted. Avoid taking plastic bags into the mine; accumulation of garbage is a growing problem.

The tours then generally visit an *ingenio*, before heading up to Cerro Rico itself. Note that since January 2011 it is now illegal for tour companies to give demonstrations of dynamite explosions, which destabilise the mountain and potentially threaten lives. Some companies continue to flout these regulations, however. Ask your tour company vendor if a dynamite explosion is included. If they say yes, choose another operator. It is unlikely to be the only corner they are cutting.

Tours run in the morning or afternoon and last from four to five hours. The standard charge is between B$100 and B$150 per person; slightly lower rates may be available during the low season. This price includes a guide, transportation from town

and equipment (jacket, helmet, boots and lamp). Note the claim that '15% of profits donated to miners' is a well-known marketing scam; all companies pay the same fee for entry into the mines and it is considerably less than 15%. If you want to help the miners, choose a company run by miners. Wear sturdy clothing, carry plenty of water and have a handkerchief/headscarf handy to filter some of the noxious substances you'll encounter. There is less activity in the mines on Sundays.

For more information about entering the mines, see boxed texts on p212 and p210.

Los Ingenios   HISTORICAL BUILDING
On the banks of the Río Huana Mayu, in the upper Potosí barrios of Cantumarca and San Antonio, are some fine ruined examples of the *ingenios*. These were formerly used to extract silver from the ore hauled out of Cerro Rico. There were originally 82 *ingenios* along 15km of the stream. Some remaining ones date back to the 1570s and were in use until the mid-1800s. Most tours of the Cerro Rico mines include a stop at a working *ingenio* as part of the trip.

Each *ingenio* consists of a floor penetrated by shallow wells *(buitrones)* where the ore was mixed with mercury and salt. The ore was then ground by millstones that were powered by water that was impounded in the 32 artificial Lagunas de Kari Kari.

Museo & Convento de
Santa Teresa   MUSEUM
(cnr Santa Teresa & Ayacucho; admission by guided tour B$21, photo permit B$10; ⊙9am-12:30pm & 2:30-6:30pm Mon-Sat, 9am-11am & 3-5pm Sun, last tours 11am & 5pm Mon-Sat) The fascinating Santa Teresa Convent was founded in 1685 and is still home to a small community of Carmelite nuns. One of them is an architect and has directed a superb restoration project that has converted part of the sizable building into a museum.

The excellent guided tour (in Spanish and English) explains how girls of 15 from wealthy families entered the convent, getting their last glimpse of parents and loved ones at the door. Entry was a privilege, paid for with a sizable dowry; a good portion of these offerings are on display in the form of religious artwork.

There are numerous fine pieces, including a superb Madonna by Castilian sculptor Alonso Cano, several canvases by Melchor Pérez de Holguín, Bolivia's most famous

THE JOB FROM HELL

In the cooperative mines on Cerro Rico, all work is done with mostly primitive tools and underground temperatures vary from below freezing – the altitude is more than 4200m – to a stifling 115°F on the 4th and 5th levels. Miners, exposed to all sorts of noxious chemicals and gases, normally die of silicosis pneumonia within 10 to 15 years of entering the mines.

Women are admitted to many cooperative mines but only five are allowed to be in the mine's interior at any one time. That's because quite a few miners hang on to the tradition that women underground invite bad luck and, in many cases, the taboo applies only to miners' wives, whose presence in the mines would invite jealousy from Pachamama (Mother Earth). At any rate, lots of Quechua women are consigned to stay right outside the mines picking through the tailings, gleaning small amounts of minerals that may have been missed.

Since cooperative mines are owned by the miners themselves, they must produce the goods in order to scrape a living. The majority of the work is done by hand with explosives and tools they must purchase themselves, including the acetylene lamps used to detect pockets of deadly carbon monoxide gas.

Miners prepare for their workday by socializing and chewing coca for several hours, beginning work at about 10am. They work until lunch at 2pm, when they rest and chew more coca. For those who don't spend the night working, the day usually ends at 7pm. On the weekend, each miner (or a group of miners) sells his week's production to the buyer for as high a price as he can negotiate.

painter, and a room of painted wooden Christs. Some of the artworks verge on the macabre, as does the skull sitting in a bowl of dust in the middle of the dining room and a display of wire whisks that some of the nuns used for self-flagellation.

The building itself is as impressive as the works of art on show, with two pretty cloisters housing numerous cacti and a venerable apple tree. It provides a glimpse into a cloistered world that only really changed character in the 1960s, with the reforms of the Second Vatican Council.

The guided tour lasts almost two hours; note that some of the rooms are particularly chilly. There's also a cafe and store, where you can buy almond and peanut sweets made by the nuns.

Museo & Convento de
San Francisco   MUSEUM
(cnr Tarija & Nogales; admission B$15; ☺9am-noon & 2:30-6pm Mon-Fri, 9am-noon Sat) The San Francisco Convent was founded in 1547 by Fray Gaspar de Valverde, making it the oldest monastery in Bolivia. Owing to its inadequate size, it was demolished in 1707 and reconstructed over the following 19 years. A gold-covered altar from this building is now housed in the Casa Nacional de la Moneda. The statue of Christ that graces the present altar features hair that is said to grow miraculously.

The museum has examples of religious art, including various paintings from the Potosí school, such as *The Erection of the Cross* by Melchor Pérez de Holguín, various mid-19th-century works by Juan de la Cruz Tapia and 25 scenes from the life of St Francis of Assisi.

The highlight of the obligatory tour (ask for an English-speaking guide), which has no real schedule and lasts about 1½ hours, comes at the end, when you're ushered up the tower and onto the roof for a grand view of Potosí. You also visit the catacombs, which have a smattering of human bones and a subterranean river running nearby.

Torre de la Compañía de Jesús   CHURCH
(Ayacucho nr Bustillos; mirador admission B$10; ☺8-11:30am & 2-5:30pm Mon-Fri, 8am-noon Sat) The ornate and beautiful bell tower, on what remains of the former Jesuit church, was completed in 1707 after the collapse of the original church. Both the tower and the doorway are adorned with examples of mestizo baroque ornamentation.

Cathedral   CHURCH
(Plaza 10 de Noviembre) Construction of Potosí's cathedral was initiated in 1564 and finally completed around 1600. The original

When miners first enter the mine, they offer propitiation at the shrine of the miners' god Tata Kaj'chu, whom they hope will afford them protection in the harsh underground world. Deeper in the mine, visitors will undoubtedly see a devilish figure occupying a small niche somewhere along the passageways. As most of the miners believe in a god in heaven, they deduce that there must also be a devil beneath the earth in a place where it's hot and uncomfortable. Since hell (according to the traditional description of the place) must not be far from the environment in which they work, they reason that the devil himself must own the minerals they're dynamiting and digging out of the earth. In order to appease this character, whom they call Tío (Uncle) or Supay – never Diablo – they set up a little ceramic figurine in a place of honor.

On Friday nights a *cha'lla* (offering) is made to invoke his goodwill and protection. A little alcohol is poured on the ground before the statue, lighted cigarettes are placed in his mouth and coca leaves are laid out within easy reach. Once formalities have been dispensed with, the miners smoke, chew coca and proceed to drink themselves unconscious. While this is all taken very seriously, it also provides a bit of diversion from an extremely harsh existence. It's interesting that offerings to Jesus Christ are only made at the point where the miners can first see the outside daylight.

In most cooperative operations there is a minimal medical plan in case of accidents or silicosis (which is inevitable after seven to 10 years working underground) and a pension of about US$15 a month for those so incapacitated. Once a miner has lost 50% of his lung capacity to silicosis, he may retire, if he so wishes. In case of death, a miner's widow and children collect this pension.

building lasted until the early 19th century, when it mostly collapsed. Most of what is now visible is the neoclassical construction and the building's elegant lines represent one of Bolivia's best exemplars of that style. The interior decor represents some of the finest in Potosí. You can visit the **bell tower** (admission B$10; ☉8am-noon & 2-6pm Mon-Fri) for nice views of the city.

La Capilla de Nuestra Señora de Jerusalén
CHURCH
(Plaza del Estudiante; ☉open for mass) La Capilla de Nuestra Señora de Jerusalén is a little-known Potosí gem. Originally built as a humble chapel in honor of the Virgen de Candelaria, it was rebuilt more lavishly in the 18th century. It houses a fine gilt baroque *retablo* (portable boxes with depictions of religious and historical events) – the Virgin has pride of place – and a magnificent series of paintings of Biblical scenes by anonymous artists of the Potosí school. The impressive pulpit has small paintings by Melchor Pérez de Holguín.

Iglesia de San Lorenzo de Carangas
CHURCH
(cnr Héroes del Chaco & Bustillos; ☉open for mass) The ornate mestizo baroque portal of Iglesia de San Lorenzo de Carangas is probably one of the most photographed subjects in Bolivia. It was carved in stone by master indigenous artisans in the 16th century, but the main structure wasn't completed until the bell towers were added in 1744. Inside are two Melchor Pérez de Holguín paintings and handcrafted silverwork on the altar. The church was renovated in 1987.

Iglesia de la Merced
CHURCH
(cnr Hoyos & Millares; ☉open for mass) Constructed between 1555 and 1687, the restored Iglesia de la Merced has a carved pulpit, a gorgeous wooden ceiling and a beautiful 18th-century silver arch over the altarpiece.

Iglesia de San Martín
CHURCH
(☎622-3682; cnr Hoyos & Almagro; admission B$10; ☉10am-noon & 3-6pm Mon-Sat) The rather ordinary-looking Iglesia de San Martín was built in the 1600s and is today run by the French Redemptionist Fathers. Inside is an art museum, with at least 30 paintings beneath the choir depicting the Virgin Mary and the 12 Apostles. The Virgin on the altarpiece wears clothing woven from silver threads. San Martín is outside the center and is sometimes closed, so phone before traipsing out here.

Historic Buildings
ARCHITECTURE
Potosí's elaborate colonial architecture merits a stroll around the narrow streets to

CENTRAL HIGHLANDS POTOSÍ

take in the ornate doorways and facades, as well as the covered wooden balconies that overhang the streets. Architecturally notable homes and monuments include the mustard-colored **El Cabildo** (Town Hall; Plaza 10 de Noviembre), the pretty **Casa de las Tres Portadas** (Bolívar 1052) and the **Arcos de Cobija** (Arches of Cobija) on the street of the same name.

On Calle Junín, between Matos and Bolívar, is an especially lovely and elaborate **Portón Mestizo** (Junín), a doorway flanked by twisted columns. It once graced the home of the Marqués de Otavi, but now ushers patrons into the Banco Nacional.

Calle Quijarro   ARCHITECTURE
North of the Iglesia de San Agustín, Calle Quijarro narrows as it winds between a wealth of colonial buildings, many with doorways graced by old family crests. It's thought that the bends in this street were an intentional attempt to inhibit the cold winds that would otherwise whistle through and chill everything in their path. This concept is carried to extremes on the **Pasaje de Siete Vueltas** (Passage of Seven Turns), which is an extension of Calle Ingavi, east of Junín. During colonial times Quijarro was the street of potters, but it's now known for its hat makers. The intersection of Quijarro and Modesto Omiste, further north, has been dubbed the **Esquina de las Cuatro Portadas** because of its four colonial doorways.

☞ Tours

In addition to mine tours, there are a variety of guided tours offered by the huge number of local agencies, including a three-hour city tour (B$70 to B$100, not including entry fees) of the museums and monuments. Other popular options include Tarapaya (B$50 to B$100); guided trekking trips around the Lagunas de Kari Kari (B$160 to B$280); and tours of colonial haciendas around Potosí (B$150). Agencies, offering all of these, include the following:

Altiplano Tours   MINE TOUR, TINKU
(622-5353; Ayacucho 19) At the end of its mine tours, you can try some of the work yourself. This company also offers *tinku* excursions.

Big Deal Tours   MINE TOUR
(623-0478; www.bigdealtours.blogspot.com; Bustillos 1092) A new company specializing in mine tours run by current and ex-miners. One of the best ways to make sure your visit has a positive impact.

Greengo Tours   MINE TOUR
(623-1362; www.greengotours.com.bo; Junín) This agency has been getting good reader reviews for its responsible mine tours and has a small cafe in its office. The passionate owner, ex-miner Julio Zambrana, is actively fighting to improve conditions for miners.

Hidalgo Tours   TOUR
(622-9512; www.salardeuyuni.net; cnr La Paz & Matos) One of the better upmarket options.

Sin Fronteras   TOUR
(622-4058; Bustillos) Not really designed for walk-ins, these are mostly private tours that are pricier but of a higher quality. Worth booking in advance.

★ Festivals & Events

Fiesta del Espíritu   SPIRITUAL
Potosí's most unusual event happens on the last three Saturdays of June and the first Saturday of August. It's dedicated to Pachamama (Mother Earth), whom the miners regard as the mother of all bolivianos.

WARNING!

The cooperatives are not museums but working mines that are fairly nightmarish places. Anyone planning to take a tour needs to realize that there are risks involved. People with medical problems – especially claustrophobia, asthma and other respiratory conditions – should avoid them. While medical experts including the NHS note that limited exposure from a tour lasting a few hours is extremely unlikely to cause any lasting health impacts, if you have any concerns whatsoever about exposure to asbestos or silica dust, you should not enter the mines. Accidents can also happen – explosions, falling rocks, runaway trolleys etc. For these reasons, all tour companies make visitors sign a disclaimer absolving them completely from any responsibility for injury, illness or death. If your tour operator does not, choose another. Visiting the mines is a serious decision. If you're undeterred, you'll have an eye-opening and unforgettable experience.

Campesinos bring their finest llamas to the base of Cerro Rico to sell to the miners for sacrifice. The ritual is conducted to a meticulous schedule. At 10am one miner from each mine purchases a llama and their families gather for the celebrations. At 11am everyone moves to the entrance of their respective mine. The miners chew coca and drink alcohol from 11am until precisely 11:45am, when they prepare the llama for Pachamama by tying its feet and offering it coca and alcohol. At noon the llama meets its maker. As its throat is slit, the miners petition Pachamama for luck, protection and an abundance of minerals. The blood of the llama is splashed around the mouth of the mine to ensure Pachamama's attention, cooperation and blessing.

For the next three hours the men chew coca and drink while the women prepare a plate of grilled llama. The meat is served traditionally with potatoes baked along with *habas* (fava beans) in a small adobe oven. When the oven reaches the right temperature, it is smashed in on the food, which is baked beneath the hot shards. The stomach, feet and head of the llama are buried in a 3m hole as a further offering to Pachamama, then the music and dancing begin. In the evening, celebrants are taken home in transportation provided by the miner who bought his mine's llama.

Fiesta de San Bartolomé (Chu'tillos)
TRADITIONAL

This rollicking celebration takes place on the final weekend of August or the first weekend of September and is marked by processions, student exhibitions, traditional costumes and folk dancing from all over the continent. In recent years it has even extended overseas and featured musical groups and dance troupes from as far away as China and the USA. Given all the practicing during the week leading up to the festival, you'd be forgiven for assuming it actually started a week earlier. Booking accommodations for this period is essential.

Exaltación de la Santa Vera Cruz
RELIGIOUS

This festival, which falls on September 14, honors Santo Cristo de la Vera Cruz. Activities occur around the Iglesia de San Lorenzo Carangas and the railway station. Silver cutlery features prominently, as do parades, dueling brass bands, dancing, costumed children and, of course, lots of alcohol.

🛏 Sleeping

If you are arriving in Potosí from Sucre you'll doubtless be pretty disappointed by what you get for your money in terms of accommodations. It gets very cold in winter so choose where you stay carefully. Usually only the top-end hotels have heating and they sometimes need to be persuaded to use it, despite what they tell you when they are trying to sell you a room. There may be blanket shortages in the cheapies, so you'll want a sleeping bag.

TOP CHOICE **Hostal Carlos V Imperial** HOTEL **$**

(☎623-1010; Linares 42; d/ste B$180/B$200, s/d without bathroom B$70/140) In terms of value for money this is about your best bet in town, though the rooms with shared bathroom are a little cramped. The same can't be said for en suite rooms though, and the extra is money well spent. Tastefully decorated, professionally run and with a bargain suite the match of any hotel in a higher price range, you can't go wrong.

Hotel Cima Argentum HOTEL **$$**

(☎622-9538; www.hca-potosi.com; Villazón 239; s/d B$310/350, ste B$440-470; @) This well-run place with a light-flooded patio is a handsome, slightly stuffy choice with decent facilities, including safes and minibars in every room and off-street parking. The suites are a good choice for families and all the rooms have good bathrooms, heating and wi-fi. The international restaurant offers room service.

Hotel Coloso Potosí HOTEL **$$$**

(☎622-2627; www.potosihotel.com; Bolívar 965; s/d/tr B$530/670/920, ste B$707-884; @≋) Potosí's latest five-star option, it has all the perks of a luxury hotel – spick-and-span rooms with minibars, heating and wi-fi – but suffers from a stuffy formal atmosphere. There's a pool, a restaurant, a sauna and room service. Some rooms come with great city views.

Hostal María Victoria HOSTAL **$**

(☎622-2132; Chuquisaca 148; s/d B$70/90, without bathroom B$40/70) This attractive hostel occupies an old colonial home at the end of a quiet lane. The rooms surround a classic whitewashed and tree-shaded courtyard; there's also a roof terrace with views. A small breakfast is included and there's a tour agency on site. Note there's an eight-minute shower limit.

Hostal San José
PENSION **$$**

(☎622-4394; Oruro 171; s/d B$90/180, without bathroom B$70/140) This cheap place has a cheery welcome and decent location; a 3rd floor was going up at research time. Ground-floor rooms are pokey with low ceilings so it's worth paying the extra for a better room, which will give you more warmth, an electric socket and a bigger bed with a less lumpy mattress.

Hostal Colonial
HOTEL **$$**

(☎622-4265; www.hostalcolonialpotosi.com; Hoyos 8; s/d/tr B$280/360/400; ☻) In a well-kept colonial building near the main plaza, this warm whitewashed retreat has smallish rooms with windows onto a central courtyard; all have minibars and cable TV, and some have bathtubs. It's a longstanding favorite with midrange travelers and boasts very helpful English-speaking staff and a great location.

Hotel Santa Teresa
HOTEL **$$**

(☎622-5270; www.hotelsantateresa.com.bo; Ayacucho 43; s/d/tr B$220/380/480; ☻) This well-appointed hotel is by the convent of the same name, in a quiet part of central Potosí. It has smallish but pleasant, and occasionally overly green, rooms; the upstairs units have more light. The courtyard restaurant, Rosicler, is one of the city's best. It's a somewhat formal dining experience that can be enjoyed in your room with less fuss.

Hostal Las Tres Portadas
HOTEL **$**

(☎622-8919; www.tresportadas.com; Bolívar 1092; s/d/t/ste B$90/150/200/300, s without bathroom B$70; ☻) Situated in one of Potosí's most characterful buildings (p212) and based around two pretty patios, this blue-colored hotel is well run and adequately heated. New owners have added a nice touch, decorating the courtyards like little town plazas and naming them after important historic figures, and more importantly they have cut the price substantially for an improved level of service. Note that a name change may soon be on the cards.

Hostal Patrimonio
HOSTEL **$$**

(☎622-2659; www.hostalpatrimonio.com; Matos 62; s B$294, d B$420-460) Fairly standard hotel with rooms opening on to a central atrium. That said, the friendly service and reliable hot water make up for the lack of character and it is better than most options in this price range in Potosí. Avoid the rooms at the front, especially on weekends, as it is opposite a disco.

Hotel Jerusalén
HOTEL **$$**

(☎622-4633; Oruro 143; s/d/tr B$150/250/330; ☻) Popular with visiting groups, this vast hotel is a dependable choice. Nobody would really claim that it's great value for money, but comfort counts; the staff can arrange all sorts of tours and the rooms have quality gas showers and cable TV. There's a lively bar next door.

Macuquina Dora Hotel
HOTEL **$$**

(☎623-0257; Camacho 243; s/d/tr B$160/260/340; ☻) A modern but fading hotel in a handy central location. There's cordial service and a bunch of extras such as a sauna and gym, but the rooms with their frilly bedspreads may have seen better days. Try to bag one of the front rooms (Nos 301 to 303); they have miles more light and space than the others.

Hostal Felimar
HOSTEL **$**

(☎622-4357; Junín 14; s/d/tr B$100/140/170, s/d without bathroom B$60/90) This pleasant and centrally located hostel has some low-ceilinged rooms and some nicer upstairs rooms with balconies affording views over the colonial street below. A small breakfast is included and there's a great suite on the top floor.

Hotel El Turista
HOTEL **$$**

(☎622-2492; Lanza 19; s/d/tr B$140/240/330) The oldest functioning hotel in town that, despite a makeover, still shows its age in places. Rooms are spacious and fairly comfortable with creaky heating, electric showers, TVs and superb views from the top floor. It's fair value, with an airy feel, nice wooden floors and a vibrantly colored patio.

Residencial 10 de Noviembre
PENSION **$**

(☎622-3253; Serrudo 181; d B$120, r per person without bathroom B$40) In a tall white building, with fresh paint outside and in. Rooms are perfectly decent, with impeccable shared bathrooms, reliable hot water and a pleasant covered terrace.

Residencial Felcar
PENSION **$**

(☎622-4966; Serrudo 345; s/d B$70/140, without bathroom B$30/60) This friendly place makes a sound choice with its clean, simple rooms (you'll want a sleeping bag in the cheaper ones). Newer rooms with bathrooms are attractive, with typical Latin American furniture, TVs and heaters. There are reliable hot showers throughout and a nice terrace. On Sunday, they offer a traditional lunch of barbecued llama for B$25.

Residencial Sumaj   PENSION $

(☎622-3336; Gumiel 12; s/d/tr without bathroom B$45/80/120) This longtime budget standby has small rooms with shared bathroom. It's only worth staying on the top floor, which is lit by skylights; those downstairs are dreadfully dingy. There's an adequate kitchen for guests, but you have to pay B$15 per day for the privilege.

La Casona Hostal   HOSTEL $$

(☎623-0523; www.hotelpotosi.com; Chuquisaca 460; s/d/tr/q B$125/170/230/300, without bathroom B$65/90/135/180) An 18th-century colonial house in the center of town, with rooms set around a yellow atrium that is beginning to fall apart. It's popular with backpackers but gets mixed reviews and the state of the shared bathrooms is an issue. There's also a money exchange, a shared kitchen, a small cinema (B$3 per film) and some internet terminals (B$2).

✕ Eating

Though you don't get the culinary diversity you may see in Sucre, there are a few appealing restaurants in Potosí that are good spots to ward off the nighttime chill with a hearty meal.

Stalls in the **market** (Oruro; ⊙6am-7pm daily) *comedor* (dining hall) serve inexpensive breakfasts of bread, pastries and coffee. Downstairs there are some excellent juice stands. Cheese or meat empanadas are sold around the market until early afternoon and in the evening, street vendors sell *humitas* (cornmeal filled with cheese, onion, egg and spices, baked in the oven or boiled).

⬛TOP⬛CHOICE **Malpartida**   SALTENERIA $

(Bolívar 644; salteñas B$5; ⊙morning only) Most Bolivians acknowledge, when pushed, that Potosí does the best *salteñas* – juicy, spicy and oh-so-tasty. In Potosí, if you ask around town where you can get the best *salteñas* this is where you'll be sent, presumably making it the best of the best.

Pizzeria El Maná   PIZZA $

(Bustillos 1080; almuerzo B$15, pizza B$14-26) You can't beat this family-style locals' favorite right opposite Casa Nacional de la Moneda for its great-value lunches. This yellow-painted spot is simple both in decor and cuisine. At night, it serves pizzas only.

Phishqa Warmis   INTERNATIONAL $$

(Sucre 56; meals B$20-50, almuerzo B$25) A pleasingly cozy little restaurant lounge with colored walls and a vaulted ceiling. The pub-style à la carte food gets mixed reviews, but the buffet *almuerzo* is better. Attentive service and a refined but friendly atmosphere make it worth a try.

El Mesón   FRENCH $$

(cnr Tarija & Linares; mains B$28-50) The air at this vaulted restaurant on a corner of the plaza is heavy with smells of warm garlic. The elaborate menu is somewhat French, with food (steak, pasta, salads) that is a tad overpriced but nonetheless excellent. The attractive ambience adds to the experience.

4060   INTERNATIONAL $$$

(www.cafepub4060.com.bo; Hoyos 1; mains B$20-75; ⊙4pm-midnight) This spacious contemporary cafe-bar has earned plenty of plaudits for its pizzas, burgers and Mexican food (and paella, if you order it in advance) as well as being a sociable spot for a drink. There's a good beer selection.

Doña Eugenia   LATIN AMERICAN $$

(cnr Santa Cruz & Ortega; dishes B$10-40; ⊙9.30am-12.30pm, closed Wed) Potosí residents swear by this convivial local restaurant at the northern end of town. Head there early (around 10am is best) to make sure you get some of the legendary *kala purca* (thick maize soup with a hot rock in it). Other specialties include a hearty *fricasé* (pork stew) only served on Sunday.

Manzana Mágica   VEGETARIAN $

(Oruro 239; mains B$12-25; ⊙8:30am-3pm & 5:30-10pm Mon-Sat; ✎) This is a worthwhile, strictly vegetarian spot known for its breakfast – muesli, juice, eggs, brown bread and tasty soy steaks. The *almuerzo* (B$15) is ultra-healthy and the generous portions of the à la carte dinners are assertively spiced.

El Fogón   INTERNATIONAL $$$

(www.elfogon.com.bo; cnr Oruro & Frías; almuerzo B$25, mains B$22-70; ⊙noon-11pm) This spacious, colorful and brightly lit central restaurant is popular for its range of international and Bolivian food, including llama steaks. In truth, though, it trades a bit on its past reputation – portions aren't huge and the service leaves much to be desired. Check out the English translations on the menu!

TINKU – THE ART OF RITUAL MAYHEM

Native to the northern part of Potosí department, *tinku* (ritual fighting), which takes place on May 3, ranks as one of the few Bolivian traditions that has yet to be commercialized. This bizarre practice lies deeply rooted in indigenous tradition and is thus often misunderstood by outsiders, who can make little sense of the violent and often grisly spectacle.

Tinku may be best interpreted as a type of ritualized means of discharging tensions between different indigenous communities. Festivities begin with singing and dancing, but participants eventually drink themselves into a stupor. As a result, celebrations soon erupt into drunken mayhem and frequently violence, as alcohol-charged emotions are unleashed in hostile encounters.

A *tinku* usually lasts two or three days, when men and women in brightly colored traditional dress hike in from surrounding communities. The hats worn by the men strongly resemble those originally worn by the Spanish conquistadores, but are topped, Robin Hood–style, with one long iridescent feather.

On the first evening, the communities parade through town to the accompaniment of *charangos* and *zampoñas* (a type of pan pipe). Periodically, the revelers halt and form two concentric circles, with women on the inside and the men in the outer circle. The women begin singing a typically repetitious and cacophonous chant while the men run in a circle around them. Suddenly, everyone stops and launches into a powerful stomping dance. Each group is headed by at least one person – usually a man – who uses a whip to ensure slackers keep up with the rhythm and the pace.

This routine may seem harmless enough, except that alcohol plays a significant and controlling role. Most people carry bottles filled with *puro* (rubbing alcohol), which is the drink of choice, if the intent is to quickly become totally plastered. By nightfall, each participating community retreats to a designated house to drink *chicha* until they pass out.

Mirador de Pary Orcko INTERNATIONAL $$
(Cerro Pary Orcko; mains B$20-45) At 4100m this is officially the world's highest revolving restaurant, offering a fabulous panorama of the city and surrounding sierras. It takes 45 minutes to complete a single revolution, but the view is better than the food.

Cherry's Salon de Té CAFE $
(Padilla 8; mains B$9-22; ⊙8am-10pm) This cafe makes a nice but very slow pit stop while you're out exploring the town. The apple strudel, chocolate cake and lemon meringue pie are superb. It also offers light meals and breakfasts.

Café de la Merced CAFE $
(Iglesia de la Merced; Hoyos s/n; light meals B$15; ⊙11am-12:30pm & 2-6pm) You couldn't ask for a better location than this rooftop cafe: atop the Iglesia de la Merced, right by the bells, with stellar city views. It serves very tasty juices, acceptable coffee, delicious cakes and light meals; you may have to wait for a table, though, as it's a small space.

Confitería Capricornio FAST FOOD $
(Paseo Blvd 11; mains B$7-18; ⊙9am-9pm) Packed with students in the evening, this quick-bite eatery with a funky old-school vibe serves soup, fast food, pizza, sandwiches, spaghetti, coffee and juices, all of which are cheap as chips.

Café Cultural Kaypichu VEGETARIAN $
(Millares 14; mains B$12-35, breakfasts B$13-21; ⊙7:30am-10pm Tue-Sun; ✐) A peaceful and relaxed, mainly vegetarian, spot that is good at any time of day, starting with healthy breakfasts (10 different varieties) and heading through sandwiches to pasta and pizza dinners. It has regular nighttime entertainment of folk music on weekends (admission B$10).

Café la Plata CAFE $$
(Plaza 10 de Noviembre; mains B$14-35; ⊙10am-11pm Tue-Sat, 1:30-11pm Mon) This handsome place is comfortable and chic in a restored sort of way, and a good place to hang out. There are rich espressos, magazines to read and wine served by the glass. Pastas, cakes, salads, sandwiches – it's all pretty tasty.

Chaplin Café CAFE $
(Matos cnr Quijarro; meals B$10-20; ⊙7am-2pm) Friendly and comfortable, this place serves mostly Bolivian fare with a few international, including Mexican, dishes. It does decent breakfasts too.

This excessive imbibing inevitably results in social disorder and by the second day the drunk participants can grow increasingly aggressive. Roaming the streets, individuals encounter people from other communities with whom they may have some quarrel, either real or imagined, and may challenge them to fight.

The situation rapidly progresses past yelling and cursing to pushing and shoving, before it turns into an unusual – almost choreographed – form of warfare. Seemingly rhythmically, men strike each other's heads and upper bodies with extended arms. This has been immortalized in the *tinku* dance, which is frequently performed during Carnaval in highly traditional Oruro. To augment the hand-to-hand combat, the fighters may also throw rocks at their opponents, occasionally causing serious injury or death. Any fatalities, however, are considered a blood offering to Pachamama in lieu of a llama sacrifice for the same purpose.

The best known and arguably most violent *tinku* takes place in the village of Macha during the first couple of weeks of May, while the villages of Ocurí and Toracarí, among others, also host *tinkus*.

As you'd imagine, few foreigners aspire to witness this private and often violent tradition, which categorically cannot be thought of as a tourist attraction; many people who have attended insist they'd never do it again. For the terminally curious, however, Altiplano Tours in Potosí conducts culturally sensitive – and patently less-than-comfortable – visits to several of the main *tinku* festivities. Note, however, that if you do go it will be at your own risk. Keep a safe distance from the participants and always remain on the side of the street to avoid being trapped in the crowd. When walking around the village, maintain a low profile, speak in soft tones and ignore any taunting cries of 'gringo'. Also, bear in mind that these traditional people most definitely do not want hordes of foreign tourists gawking at them and snapping photos; avoid photographing individuals without their express permission and do not participate.

Drinking

The disco of choice for the Potosí youth right now is **Mandarinas** (Av Murillo; admission B$20-30), which plays a mixture of salsa, kumbia and reggaeton. Alternatively try **Quilla** (Av Murillo; admission B$15), on the same road, which is aimed squarely at a local crowd.

La Casona Pub　　　　　　　　PUB
(Frías 41; ☺6pm-midnight Mon-Sat) The atmospheric La Casona Pub is tucked away in the historic 1775 home of the royal envoy sent to administer the mint. It's a memorable, friendly watering hole with pub grub. On Friday it stages live music performances.

Sumaj Orcko　　　　　　　　　BAR
(Quijarro 46; ☺10am-10pm) A popular restaurant with a low-lit comfortable bar on the corner for a quiet drink.

☆ Entertainment

Ask around at the bars, cafes and restaurants for live music. Several occasionally host acoustic *peñas*.

Potosí has two cinemas, the **Multicine Universal** (☎622-6133; Padilla 31) and the **Cine Universitario** (☎622-3049; Bolívar 893),

which both screen relatively recent releases, though the latter was undergoing repairs at the time of writing. They both charge B$40 per screening.

Real Potosí, the local soccer team, is one of Bolivia's most successful and play at the town stadium on the hilariously named Calle Highland Players.

Shopping

Favored Potosí souvenirs include silver and tin articles available from stands near the market entrance on Calle Oruro. Many of these were produced in the village of Caiza, 80km south of Potosí, which now has its own co-op store featuring naturally dyed wool items. Small dangly earrings, hoop earrings, spoons and platters cost between B$10 and B$40.

Arte Nativo　　　　　　　ARTS & CRAFTS
(Sucre 30) Sells ecologically sound, indigenous handiwork, improving the economic condition of rural women who weave with the naturally dyed wool of sheep, llamas and alpacas.

Artesanías Palomita's　　　ARTS & CRAFTS
(Museo Etno-Indumentario; Serrudo 148-152; ☺9am-noon & 2:30-6pm Mon-Fri, 9am-noon Sat) Half

shop, half museum and has costumes and weavings from each of the 16 provinces of Potosí department.

🛈 Information

Emergency

Tourist police (Plaza 10 de Noviembre) Helpful; on the ground floor of the Gobernación building. At the time of writing there was talk that the tourist police may move to the ex-Hotel IV Centenario building on Plaza del Estudiante.

Immigration

Migración (☑622-5989; Calama 188) For visa extensions.

Internet Access

There are numerous places to get online, mostly charging between B$3 and B$4 per hour, including **Café Internet Candelaria** (Ayacucho 5), where the first 15 minutes is free with breakfast.

Laundry

Most hotels can organize laundry services for their guests. Failing that, try **Janus Limpieza** (Bolívar 773; per kg B$9; ⊘8am-8:30pm Mon-Sat).

Medical Services

If you need an English-speaking doctor, visit the **Hospital Daniel Bracamonte** (☑624-4960; Italia s/n).

Money

ATMs are common in the center of town. Lots of businesses along Bolívar, Sucre and in the market change US dollars at reasonable rates; stalls along Héroes del Chaco also change euros and Chilean and Argentine pesos. Cash advances are available at **Banco de Crédito** (cnr Bolívar & Sucre) and **Prodem** (cnr Bolívar & Junín), which also change US dollars.

Post & Telephone

The **central post office** (cnr Lanza & Chuquisaca; ⊘8am-8pm Mon-Fri, 8am-5:30pm Sat, 9-11:30am Sun) is close to the main square. There are lots of cheap international telecom centers.

Tourist Information

Potosí has an in-depth tourist information website, www.potosy.com.bo.
Instituto Geográfico Militar (Chayanta at 1 de Abril) Sells topographic sheets of all areas of Potosí department.
Infotur (☑623-1021; Ayacucho nr Bustillos; ⊘8am-noon & 2-6pm Mon-Fri) Quite helpful

and making a big effort to improve the standard of Potosí's services. At the time of writing there were unconfirmed rumors that the office may move to the ex-Hotel del IV Centenario building on Plaza del Estudiante.

🛈 Getting There & Away

Timetables and contact details for all transport operators can be found online at www.potosy.com.bo.

Air

Potosí boasts the world's highest commercial airport, Aeropuerto Capitán Rojas. In the early 1990s the runway was extended to 4000m to accommodate larger planes. At present, however, no scheduled services fly in or out of Potosí and Sucre is the closest airport.

Bus & Shared Taxi

All road routes into Potosí are quite scenic and arriving by day will always provide a dramatic introduction to the city. The new bus terminal is about 2km north of the center on Av Las Banderas and nearly all *flotas* (long-distance buses) now depart from here. *Micros* I or A run between the bus terminal and the cathedral.

There are direct *flotas* to La Paz but in many cases it can be quicker to look for a connection in Oruro. Similarly for Sucre shared taxis (B$50, two hours) are pricier than the *flotas*, but are faster and more comfortable and can pick you up at your hotel. Try **Cielito Express** (☑624-6040), **Infinito** (☑624-5040) or **Correcaminos** (☑624-3383), but expect speed.

For Uyuni (B$40, six hours) buses depart irregularly from the old terminal 15 minutes downhill on foot from the center. The rugged route to Uyuni is quite breathtaking.

DESTINATION	COST (B$)	DURATION (HR)
Cochabamba	52-120	15
La Paz	52-135	8
Oruro	30-40	6
Sucre	15-30	3
Tarija	60-70	12-15
Tupiza	60-100	7
Villazón	60-80	9

🛈 Getting Around

Micros and minibuses (B$1.30) shuttle between the center and the Cerro Rico mines, as well as to the bus terminal. Taxis charge B$4 per person around the center, slightly more at night, and B$10 to the bus terminal.

HACIENDA CAYARA

For a peaceful retreat or some comfortable hill walking, visit **Hacienda Cayara** (☑622-6380; www.hotelmuseocayara.com.bo; lunch & dinner B\$50, tea B\$20; r per person B\$180), which lies 25km down the valley northwest of Potosí. Set amid lovely hills at 3550m, this beautiful working farm produces vegetables and milk for the city and as a place to stay is streets ahead of anywhere in town. It dates back to colonial times and these days it's owned by the English Aitken family, who converted it into a hostel in 1992. The hacienda is part hotel and part museum: an opulent colonial mansion furnished with original paintings and period furniture. Guests have use of the fireplace and extensive library, which includes works dating from the 17th century.

Around Potosí

The **Lagunas de Kari Kari** are artificial lakes constructed in the late 16th and early 17th centuries by 20,000 indigenous slaves to provide water for the city and for hydropower to run the city's 82 *ingenios*. Of the 32 original lakes only 25 remain and all have been abandoned – except by waterfowl, which appreciate the incongruous surface water in this otherwise stark region.

The easiest way to visit Lagunas de Kari Kari is with a Potosí tour agency, which charge about B\$180 per person per day based on a group of three. If you prefer to strike out on your own, carry food, water and warm clothing. In a long day, you can have a good look around the *lagunas* and the fringes of the Cordillera de Kari Kari, but it may also be rewarding to camp overnight in the mountains. Access is fairly easy, with public transport from Potosí. Inquire with one of the agencies in town and make sure you get a good map of the area. The Cordillera de Kari Kari is included on the IGM topo sheet *Potosí (East)* – sheet 6435.

Belief in the curative powers of **Tarapaya** (3600m), the most frequently visited **hotsprings** area around Potosí, dates back to Inca times. It even served as the holiday destination for Inca Huayna Capac, who would come all the way from Cuzco (now in Peru) to bathe. The most interesting sight is the 30°C **Ojo del Inca**, a perfectly round, green lake in a low volcanic crater, 100m in diameter. Along the river below the crater are several *balnearios* (resorts) with medicinal thermal pools utilizing water from the lake, but be aware that *remolinos* (whirlpools) make bathing here a hazardous affair. *Camiones* leave for Tarapaya (B\$4, 30 minutes) from Plaza Chuquimia near the old bus terminal in Potosí roughly every half-hour from 7am to 7pm. Taxis cost about B\$50 one way. The last *micro* from Tarapaya back to Potosi leaves between 5pm and 6pm.

South Central Bolivia & the Chaco

Includes »

Best Places to Eat

» Pizza Pazza (p227)

» Taberna Gattopardo (p227)

» La Floresta (p228)

» Churrasquería El Rodeo (p228)

Best Places to Stay

» Resort Hotel Los Parrales (p226)

» Hostal del Sol (p227)

» Victoria Plaza Hotel (p227)

» Hotel El Rancho Olivo (p235)

» Residencial Gran Chaco (p235)

Why Go?

Famed for its dances, wines and an almost Mediterranean character, the isolated department of Tarija is a Bolivia that not many travelers know.

The culture here gravitates towards neighboring Argentina and dreams of being closer to faraway Andalucía. The references to the region's resemblance to the south of Spain were started by Tarija's founder, Luis de Fuentes, who was seemingly anxious to lend a bit of home to a foreign land. He thus named the river flowing past the city of Tarija the Guadalquivir (after Andalucía's biggest river), and left the *chapacos* – as *tarijeños* (Tarija locals) are otherwise known – with a lilting dialect of European Spanish.

Tarija's far eastern regions are full of petroleum-rich scrublands, backed by stark highlands and the red earth of the Gran Chaco. This is where you'll find Bolivia's hottest town, Villamontes, and a series of savage, impenetrable reserves where wildlife abounds and few people dare to tread.

When to Go
Tarija

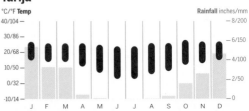

Late Mar Rosillas goes cow crazy during the Fiesta de Leche y Queso.

Aug The coolest time of year to visit blistering Villamontes is during the fishing festival.

Sep Honor the lepers in Tarija's colorful Fiesta de San Roque, on the first Sunday in September.

History

Prior to the 1932–35 Chaco War, Bolivia had long claimed rights to the Chaco, an inhospitable region beneath which rich oil fields were mooted to lie. The disputed area of about 240,680 sq km stretched northeast of the Paraguay and Pilcomayo Rivers in Paraguay, and included the 168,765 sq km chunk of Argentina north of the Río Bermejo. With political turmoil in Paraguay causing a distraction and economic hardship in Bolivia providing a stimulus, the Bolivians saw their opportunity and began to slowly advance into Paraguayan territory.

After losing the War of the Pacific in 1884, Bolivia was desperate to have the Chaco as an outlet to the Atlantic via the Río Paraguay. Hoping that physical possession would be interpreted as official sovereignty, the Bolivian army set up a fort at Piquirenda on the Río Pilcomayo and then refused to relinquish rights to Fuerte Vanguardia, its only port on the Paraguay river (and not in Bolivian territory). In 1928 Paraguay responded by sending its army to seize the fort. Although things got heated, both sides maintained a conciliatory attitude, hoping that a peaceful solution might be possible.

Things, however, didn't go as planned. During settlement talks in Washington and under orders from Bolivian President Daniel Salamanca, the Bolivian army tried to seize land without authorization, triggering full-scale warfare. Bolivia was widely seen as the aggressor in diplomatic circles and its case generated little support.

As the war progressed the Bolivians were driven back beyond their existing borders, though they continued to fight, with their most successful battle in the town of Villamontes in 1934. The hot, dry climate made access to fresh water a decisive factor in the war, with capturing and keeping access to wells a key strategy. Conditions were miserable, soldiers were ill-equipped and disease was rife. As a result, casualties on both sides were heavy.

Though no decisive victory was reached in the war, both nations had grown weary of fighting and peace negotiations held four years later awarded most of the disputed territory to Paraguay. To date, no oil has ever been found in the Chaco, though prospectors are still searching and ironically the smaller area of Chaco awarded to the Bolivians harbors gas reserves that have boosted the Bolivian economy and are the envy of the Paraguayans on the other side of the border.

Climate

This is the area of Bolivia where you most feel the country's proximity to the equator and its distance from the sea. Tarija's Mediterranean climate quickly disappears as soon as you head downhill, where it is replaced by scorching aridity and a merciless sun. The dry season in the region lasts from April to November.

National Parks & Reserves

Remote, wild and off the beaten track, South Central Bolivia's parks and reserves are perfect for hardcore adventure seekers. Infrastructure is almost nonexistent, but a visit to any of the reserves will make a lasting impression. Those covered in this chapter include the Reserva Biológica Cordillera de Sama, Reserva Nacional de Flora y Fauna Tariquía, Parque Nacional y Área Natural de Manejo Integrado Aguaragüe and the Reserva Privada de Patrimonio Natural de Corbalán.

ℹ Getting There & Around

Most people visit Bolivia's far south on the way to or from somewhere else. Overland connections from Argentina, Paraguay and other regions within Bolivia involve long bus rides. Tarija has the biggest airport in the area and scheduled flights to La Paz, Sucre and other major towns go several times a week.

Public transportation runs frequently between towns, but you'll need a 4WD to get almost anywhere else. Few roads are paved so prepare yourself for hauls that take longer than they should.

SOUTH CENTRAL BOLIVIA

Tarija

☑ 4 / POP 153,500 / ELEV 1905M

Tarija's biggest drawcard is the vineyards on its doorstep, and the city makes a great base for visiting the surrounding wineries in El Valle de la Concepción (p230), home to the world's highest wines and the throat-tingling *singani* (distilled grape spirit).

There's not much else to do in Tarija, but it has some interesting colonial architecture and grows on those who stay a while to enjoy the pleasantly mild climate and take in the chilled atmosphere; the little

South Central Bolivia & the Chaco Highlights

① Sample the world's highest-grown wines in **El Valle de la Concepción** (p231)

② Stroll around the colonial streets of tranquil **Tarija** (p221)

③ Get revolutionary on the **Che Trail** (p236) in Camiri

④ Hike the fascinating **Inca Trail** (p232) in the Reserva Biológica Cordillera de Sama

⑤ Discover spectacular **Chaco wildlife** in the region's many parks and reserves

⑥ Get down and party Tarija-style at the **Fiesta de San Roque** (p225)

⑦ Snack on some fresh fish in scorching **Villamontes** (p234)

city is as laid-back as they get, with palm-lined squares, sizzling Argentine barbecues, sprawling bar and cafe terraces, and tight streets with narrow pavements.

Despite the fact that many Bolivians from bigger cities regard South Central Bolivia as a half-civilized backwater and that '*chapaco*' is the butt of tasteless jokes told in La Paz, Tarija is a worthy stop off on your way to Argentina or Paraguay.

History

Tarija was founded as La Villa de San Bernardo de Tarixa by don Luis de Fuentes y Vargas on July 4, 1574, under the orders of Viceroy don Francisco de Toledo. In 1810 the region declared independence from Spanish rule. Although the breakaways weren't taken seriously by the Spanish, the situation erupted into armed warfare on April 15, 1817. At the Batalla de la Tablada, the *chapacos* won a major victory over the Spanish forces.

In the early 19th century, Tarija actively supported Bolivia's struggle for independence. Although Argentina wanted to annex the agriculturally favorable area, Tarija opted to join the Bolivian Republic when it was established in 1825.

⊙ Sights

You can see everything Tarija has to offer in an afternoon. Wander around the narrow streets and imbibe the colonial architecture before rounding off your day with a glass of the local *vino* on one of the plazas.

Casa Dorada MUSEUM
(Ingavi O-370; guided tour B$5; ☉9-11am & 3-5pm Mon-Fri, 9-11am Sat, guided visits only on the hour) The Gilded House dates back to 1930, when it was one of several properties owned by the wealthy Tarija landowner and merchant Moisés Navajas (often described as Bolivia's Teddy Roosevelt) and his wife, Esperanza Morales. The building, with its roof topped with a row of liberating angels, appears imposing and impressive on tourist brochures, but in reality the exterior is sloppily splashed with gold and silver paint.

The museum is on the upper floor, displaying original family furniture and examples of the bits and bobs that they imported from Europe. Perhaps the most worthwhile relic is the *funola*, an early type of piano that produced music by forcing air through a strip of perforated paper. The building now belongs to the university and houses the **Casa de la Cultura**.

FREE Museo de Arqueología y Paleontología MUSEUM
(cnr Lema & Trigo; ☉8am-noon & 3-6pm Mon-Sat) The university-run Archaeology & Paleontology Museum provides a glimpse of the prehistoric creatures and lives of the early peoples that once inhabited the Tarija area. Downstairs you'll see the well-preserved remains of several animals: *megatherium,* a giant ground sloth that was the size of an elephant; *glyptodon,* a prehistoric armadillo-like creature about the size of a Volkswagen Beetle; *lestodon,* another ground sloth that resembled a giant-clawed aardvark; *scelidotherium,* a small ground sloth; *smilodon,* the saber-toothed tiger; and *Cuvierionius tarijensi,* a fossil elephant that was discovered close to the city by the great French zoologist Georges Cuvier.

Upstairs the focus is on history, geology and anthropology, with displays of old household implements, weapons, ceramics and various prehistoric hunting tools, including a formidable cudgel known as a *rompecabezas* (head-breaker). Look for the desiccated mummified corpse of a man from the Pampagrande area, which shrunk via natural processes to measure just 35cm long.

Iglesia de San Roque CHURCH
Architecturally, Tarija's most unusual church and major landmark is the bright, white 1887 Iglesia de San Roque. Dedicated to the city's patron saint, the church sits on the hill at the end of Trigo, lording it over the town. Its balcony once served as a lookout post.

Basílica de San Francisco CHURCH
(cnr Campos & La Madrid; ☉museum 8am-6pm Mon-Fri) The Basílica de San Francisco was founded in 1606 and is now a national monument. The 16th-century convent library and archives, which may conjure up images reminiscent of *The Name of the Rose,* can be used only by researchers who have been granted permission by the Franciscan order. Inside the basilica, the free **Museo Franciscano Frey Francisco Miguel Mari** displays ecumenical paintings, sculptures and artifacts.

Iglesia de San Juan CHURCH
(Bolívar) The Iglesia de San Juan was constructed in 1632 and it was here that the Spanish signed their surrender to the liberation army after the Batalla de la Tablada. The garden serves as a *mirador* (lookout) over Tarija and its dramatic backdrop of brown mountains.

Tarija

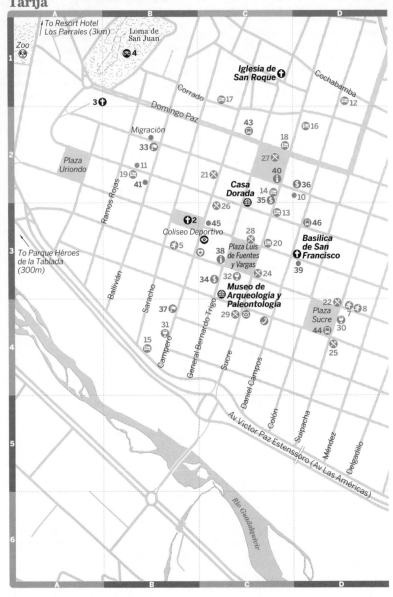

Mirador Loma de San Juan   LOOKOUT
This park area above the tree-covered slopes of the Loma de San Juan provides a grand city view and makes it a favorite with smooching students. Climb uphill to the end of Calle Bolívar, then turn right behind the hill and follow the footpath up the slope that faces away from the city.

Castillo de Moisés Navajas   NOTABLE BUILDING
(Bolívar E-644) The exterior of this oddly prominent and deteriorating private man-

Cathedral
CHURCH

(cnr Campero & La Madrid) This rather dull-looking cathedral contains the remains of prominent *chapacos,* including Tarija's founder, don Luis de Fuentes y Vargas. It was constructed in 1611 and has some interesting stained glass depicting harvest scenes.

Tours

Standard packages offered by operators include tours to the wineries from B$150 for a half-day or B$200 for a full day, the latter also including a city tour and visits to other sights in El Valle de la Concepción. For more information about the wineries of Valle de la Concepcion, see p231.

Viva Tours
WINE, ECOTOUR

(☑663-8325; Bolívar 251, 2nd fl) For wine tours and adventurous ecotrips to Tarija's hinterlands – including four nearby national reserves – it's tough to beat Viva Tours.

VTB Tours
TOUR

(☑664-4341; Ingavi 0-784) One of the city's longest established agencies with a reliable reputation.

Festivals & Events

Tarija is one of Bolivia's most festive towns, especially around **Carnaval**. Ask around about the **arts fair** in October and about the **Serrano Ham & Cheese Festival**.

Rodeo Chapaco
RODEO

(⊙Ap 15-21) In keeping with its gaucho heritage, Tarija stages an annual rodeo in **Parque Héroes de la Tablada**, beginning on the departmental holiday. Rodeo Chapaco includes all the standard cowboy events. To get there, take *micro C* from the center.

Fiesta de San Roque
RELIGIOUS

(⊙Aug 16) Tarija's well-known Fiesta de San Roque gives thanks to the saint whose appearance supposedly marked the end of the plague and leprosy in the area. The main celebration, however, doesn't begin until the first Sunday of September and then continues for eight days. It features traditional musical performances and a colorful *Chuncho* (an indigenous tribe) procession in which the participants wear 'cover-all' clothes traditionally worn by lepers. A statue of the saint is carried, his clothes being changed daily during the festival, and believers line the streets asking him to cure their family's ills.

sion is worth a look for its garish blue-and-white striped 'bananas in pyjamas' extravagance. It's still inhabited and is occasionally open for informal tours – check at the tourist office (p229).

Tarija

Fiesta de las Flores RELIGIOUS
(◉2nd Sun in Oct) The annual Fiesta de las Flores is a religious celebration dedicated to the Virgin of Rosario. It begins with a procession, which sets off from the Iglesia de San Juan. Along the route, spectators shower participants with petals. The highlight of the day is a colorful fair and bazaar in which the faithful spend lavishly for the benefit of the Church.

🛏 Sleeping

Budget accommodation is found mainly north of Bolívar, though most places in this price tier do not have heating and you may need it in winter. The cheapest rooms have shared bathroom; higher rates get you a private bathroom and cable TV. Midrange and upmarket options are south of Bolívar. Bus services arriving from Villamontes get into town during the early hours of the morning, so many hotels offer half rates if you book in advance.

TOP
CHOICE **Resort Hotel**

Los Parrales LUXURY HOTEL **$$$**
(☑664-8444; www.losparraleshotel.com; Urbanización Carmén de Aranjuez; s/d B$800/975; ❄@❄) In a relaxed setting 3.5km from the center, Tarija's only five-star option offers you a complimentary cocktail when you arrive and has a spa, a giant Jacuzzi and a lovely open-air dining area overlooking the countryside. The rooms are colonial-style luxury, with very comfy beds. Significant discounts (up to 45%) are available for stays of more than one night during the low season.

Hostal del Sol HOTEL $$
(☎666-5259; www.hoteldelsol.com.bo; Sucre N-782; s/d B$250/350; ❄@) Among the nicest in town, Hostal del Sol has coffee-colored walls, flat-screen TVs, marble floors and a bright, modern design. Friendly service, good breakfasts and free internet make this a great place to stay.

Victoria Plaza Hotel HOTEL $$$
(☎664-2600; www.victoriaplazahoteltarija.com; cnr La Madrid & Sucre; s/d B$300/450; ❄@) A charming, four-star place just off the main plaza, with lovely 1950s rooms decked with gleaming wooden floors, comfy beds and old-school furnishings. All rooms are en suite (though the bathrooms are a bit dated) and have cable TV. A stylish cafe-bar, La Bella Epoca, is downstairs.

Grand Hotel Tarija HOTEL $$
(☎664-2684; Sucre N-770; s B$160, s/d with cable TV B$210/300; ❄@) One of the town oldies that's busy for lunch when locals flood to the hotel's restaurant. The spacious, ocher-colored rooms are comfortable and central, though some are aging more gracefully than others. Avoid the patio-facing rooms or you'll have your curtains drawn all day.

Hostal La Costañera HOTEL $$
(☎664-2851; cnr Victor Paz Estenssoro & Saracho; s/d incl breakfast B$200/300; ❄@) Rooms here are elegant and decorated in caramels and sandy shades, with spacious bathrooms and great showers. There are phones, mini-bar, heaters (upon request) and parking, plus the staff is super friendly.

Hotel Luz Palace HOTEL $$
(☎663-5700; Sucre N-921; s/d/t B$180/300/420; ❄@) Recently refurbished, this huge colonial hotel-cum-shopping-mall offers great value with its modern, spacious rooms.

Hostal Zeballos HOSTAL $
(☎664-2068; Sucre N-966; s/d B$120/160, without bathroom B$60/120) Superficially the most attractive budget option, with dozens of potted plants and climbers giving the place a fresh, spring feel. However, make sure you see the room before you commit: the basement ones are grim and dark; go for something upstairs.

Gran Hotel Londres HOTEL $
(☎664-2369; Daniel Campos 1072; s/d B$80/120, without bathroom B$45/80) This kind of retro style may once have looked very grand in London (or maybe not!), but these days

wood-paneled walls and dated tourism posters might best be described as quirky.

Residencial El Rosario PENSION $
(☎664-2942; Ingavi 777; s/d B$40/80, with cable TV B$45/90) It's rare to find a budget place that is so well tended, with freshly painted and clean (though rather small) rooms that look onto a quiet patio. There are reliable gas-heated showers, laundry sinks and a common room with cable TV.

Hostería España PENSION $
(☎666-5003; Corrado O-546; s/d B$80/120, without bathroom B$50/90) A decent budget option, but the slightly overpriced rooms are pretty cold in winter. The hot showers and a pleasant flowery patio keep it popular with long-term university student residents and there is plenty of tourist information at reception.

✖ Eating

Chapaco cuisine is unique and Tarija's restaurants pay it due homage. You'll need to be brave to try *ranga ranga* (tripe with onion, tomato and chili) and *chan faina* (lamb guts with greens), but even delicate stomachs will enjoy *sopa de mani* (peanut soup) or *saice* (diced meat and vegetables). Don't forget to sample the desserts too – *dulce de lacayote* (caramelized squash), *pepitas de leche* (cinnamon fudge) and *tojori* (pancakes with cloves and aniseed) are all favorites. Get a copy of the *Guía Gastronomica* from the tourist office for more mouthwatering ideas.

TOP CHOICE ▷ Pizza Pazza PIZZERIA $$$
(Carlos Lazcano, cnr Belgrano y Pino; pizza B$40-110) Exuberant hostess Edith Paz Zamora has put together a really unique blend of art and, you guessed it, pizza. The walls are splashed with colorful paintings (many featuring giraffe-necked, bug-eyed women!) and those with a creative ilk take over on Thursdays (art night) and Fridays (Bohemian night), when folklore, music and dancing are added to the tasty menu. Ring the bell to get in!

Taberna Gattopardo INTERNATIONAL $$
(Plaza Luis de Fuentes y Vargas; mains B$22-50) This welcoming European-run tavern is one of Tarija's most popular hangouts. There are good espressos and cappuccinos in the morning, well-prepared salads, burgers, pizzas and *ceviche* (Peruvian dish of raw seafood marinated in lime juice) at midday, and chicken fillets and fondue bourguignonne in the evening.

THE CHAPACO CARNAVAL

Tarija is Bolivia's music and dance region, famous for its unique traditions and loud, colorful festivals, especially during Carnaval (www.carnaval.tarija.gov.bo, in Spanish), when all *chapacos* (Tarija locals) come out to dance, sing and party the days away. If you find yourself in the region during a fiesta, here's what to expect.

The folk music of Tarija features unusual woodwind instruments, such as the *erque* and *quenilla*, the *caña* and the *camacheña*. The song that accompanies the music is called a *copla* – a direct import from Spain – with comic verses, sung in a duet. The dance that tops it all off is the traditional *Chuncho*; dancers wear colorful outfits, feathered headgear and masks, symbolizing the Chiriguano tribes and their long-term resistance against the conquerors.

Tarija's Carnaval is one of the most animated in Bolivia and brilliant fun. To launch the festivities, two Thursdays before Carnaval Tarija celebrates the **Fiesta de Compadres**. This unique fiesta is Tarija's largest pre-Carnaval festival. It's assumed that the celebration, originating in the village of Pola de Siero, in the northern Spanish region of Asturias, was inspired by the wives of Spanish colonial authorities and soldiers, who saw to it that social customs and morals were strictly followed. It was eventually adopted by the local indigenous population and is now celebrated by the entire community with music, dancing and special basket tableaux constructed of bread known as *bollus preñaus*. Flowers, fruits, tubers, small cakes and other gifts are passed between female friends and relatives.

Throughout the Carnaval season, the streets fill with dancing, original *chapaco* music and colorfully costumed country folk who turn up in town for the event. There's a Grand Ball in the main plaza after the celebration and the entire town comes out for the dancing and performances by folk groups, bands and orchestras. Beware: water balloons figure prominently in the festivities.

On the Sunday after Carnaval, the neighborhood near the cemetery enacts a 'funeral' in which the devil is burned and buried in preparation for Lent. Paid mourners (actors pretending to mourn the death of the devil) lend the ritual a morose air – although we suspect they're actually lamenting that they must now remain vice free for the 40 days until Easter.

La Floresta BUFFET **$$**
(Carretera a San Jacinto, Barrio Germán Busch; buffet B$45-60; ⊘Fri-Sun) A great place for pitchers of fresh lemonade and all-you-can-eat buffets of pork, chicken and salads served in a lovely, leafy garden with a large swimming pool. It's a bit out of town, so you should get a taxi here – the staff will call you one for the return journey.

Churrasquería El Rodeo BARBECUE **$$$**
(Oruro E-749; mains B$40-70) With Argentina so close, it's not surprising that big slabs of red meat are popular in Tarija, and that forms the basis of what you get here. This sparkling and classy choice also has a salad bar, but really it is a place for those who like their steak.

Club Social Tarija BARBECUE **$$**
(Calle 15 de Abril E-271; almuerzo B$25-40, mains B$40-70) The Club Social has gone upmarket, but its lunch menu is still good value. At

night it metamorphoses into a stylish grill restaurant, with prices to boot.

Café Mokka SANDWICHES **$$**
(Plaza Sucre; mains B$16-42, cocktails B$18-22; 🛜) A stylish place with a pavement terrace and wi-fi access, overlooking the square. It serves average coffee, but decent cocktails and good, light grub. Tables are decorated with weird arrangements of peanuts and coffee beans.

Café Campero SANDWICHES **$**
(Campero near Bolívar; mains B$10-30; ⊘dinner Tue-Sun) Dive into the fabulous range of breads, cakes and pastries, including French-style baguettes, chocolate cake and *cuñapes* (cassava and cheese rolls). And if you prefer to have yours to go, pop into the Palacio de las Masas next door, which is open in the morning.

Heladería Napoli ICE CREAM **$$**
(Campero N-630; per kg B$50; ⊘10am-8pm) Serves simply divine scoops of ice cream.

Mercado Central MARKET $

(Sucre & Domingo Paz) At the northeast corner of the market, street vendors sell snacks and pastries unavailable in other parts of Bolivia, including delicious crêpe-like *panqueques*. Breakfast is served out the back, other cheap meals are upstairs and you'll find fresh juices in the produce section. Don't miss the huge bakery and sweets section off Bolívar.

Self-Catering

Ecosol HEALTH FOOD

(Plaza Sucre) Pick up organic and ecofriendly foodstuffs from this interesting little corner shop.

Todo Natural HEALTH FOOD

(Sucre 397) Snacks and more for those who like to keep in trim.

Drinking & Entertainment

Tarija's bar and cafe scene is vibrant and many of the popular lunch spots during the day transform into drinking dens after dark. Plaza Sucre is the hub of activity for the younger generation. Keep an eye out for flyers advertising *peñas* (folk-music programs), usually held at restaurants on weekends.

La Candela BAR

(Plaza Sucre; ⊙9am-midnight Mon-Fri, 9am-2am Sat & Sun) French-owned, this thriving little bar-cafe has a bohemian atmosphere, a great snack menu as well as live music at weekends.

Xoxo BAR

(Calle 15 de Abril; ⊙8am-midnight Mon-Sun) Retro rock chic is the go at this bar-cafe. Walls are adorned with pop art and drinks cans from across the globe.

La Cava de Strocco BAR

(Calle 15 de Abril; ⊙noon-3pm & 7pm-midnight) This is a refined restaurant-bar with courtyard seating.

❶ Information

Street numbers are preceded by O (*oeste* – west) for those addresses west of Colón, and E (*este* – east) for those east of Colón; addresses north of Victor Paz Estenssoro (Av Las Américas) take an N.

Between 1pm and 4pm Tarija becomes a virtual ghost town. Conduct all your business in the morning or you'll have to wait until after the siesta.

Emergency

Hospital San Juan de Dios (☎664-5555; Santa Cruz s/n)

Police (☎664-2222; cnr Campero & Calle 15 de Abril)

Immigration

Migración (☎664-3594; Ingavi 789) For entry/exit stamps or to extend your stay.

Laundry

Out of hours at the *lavandería*, ask at larger hotels. Expect to pay B$2 to B$3 per item.

Lavandería La Esmeralda (☎664-2043; La Madrid O-157; ⊙8:30am-12:30pm & 3-7:30pm Mon-Fri, 8am-1pm Sat) Does a quick machine-wash-and-dry service for B$12 per kilo.

Money

There are numerous ATMs around the plaza and at the airport. **Casas de Cambio** (Bolívar) changes US dollars and Argentine pesos. **Banco Bisa** (Trigo) and **Banco Nacional** (Sucre) will change traveler's checks.

Post Office

Post office (cnr Sucre & Virginio Lema)

Telephone & Internet Access

Internet places are ten a penny and usually have phone cabins incorporated as well. Try along Bolívar for decent connections (per hour B$3 to B$4).

Tourist Information

Bus terminal tourist kiosk (☎663-7701; Av Victor Paz Estenssoro) Often open when the main tourist offices are closed.

Infotur (☎667-2633; cnr 15 de Abril & Trigo; ⊙8am-noon & 2:30-6:30pm Mon-Fri, 9am-noon & 4-7pm Sat & Sun) Distributes basic town maps and is reasonably helpful with queries regarding sites in and around town.

Local tourist office (☎663-3581; cnr Bolívar & Sucre; ⊙2.30-6.30pm Mon-Fri) Not much material or information, but friendly staff.

❶ Getting There & Away

Air

The **Oriel Lea Plaza Airport** (☎664-2195) is 3km east of town off Av Victor Paz Estenssoro. **TAM** (☎664-2734; La Madrid O-470) has flights to Santa Cruz (B$558) every day except Thursday and regular flights to Sucre (B$477) with connections to La Paz (B$783) and Cochabamba (B$519). The short hop to Yacuiba (B$308) leaves daily except Tuesday and Thursday. **Aerocon** (☎665-8634; Ballivián 525) flies daily between Yacuiba and Santa Cruz (B$880) via Tarija.

SAN LORENZO

San Lorenzo (population 21,400), 15km north of Tarija along the Tupiza road, is a quaint colonial village with cobbled streets, carved balconies, a church built in 1709 and a flowery plaza. It's best known, however, as the home of José Eustaquio 'Moto' Méndez, the hero of the Batalla de la Tablada, whose former house is now the **Museo Moto Méndez** (admission free; ☺9am-12:30pm & 3-5pm Mon-Sat, 10am-noon Sun). The popular **Fiesta de San Lorenzo** takes place here on August 10 and features *chapaco* musical instruments and dancing.

After seeing the museum, head 2km north to the former Méndez family chapel, **Capilla de Lajas**, which is delicate, exquisitely proportioned and a fine example of colonial architecture. Just to the north is the **former home of ex-president Jaime Paz Zamora**, with an adjacent billboard paying homage to him.

Micros and *trufis* (B$3, 30 minutes) to San Lorenzo leave from the corner of Domingo Paz and Saracho in Tarija approximately every 20 minutes during the day.

Bus

The **bus terminal** (☎663-6508) is at the east end of town, a 20-minute walk from the center along Victor Paz Estenssoro. Annoyingly, if you are looking for a quick getaway, almost all services leave in the afternoon between 4:30pm and 8:30pm. Services to Santa Cruz pass through Villamontes from where there are connections to Yacuiba and Asunción in Paraguay, though frustratingly the latter pass through in the early hours of the morning meaning you'll have to wait almost 20 hours for your onward ride.

DESTINATION	COST (B$)	DURATION (HR)
Cochabamba	90-115	26
Oruro	90	20
Potosí	60-70	12-15
Sucre	70-90	18
Santa Cruz	90-115	24
Villamontes	40-50	9

ℹ Getting Around

To/From the Airport

Syndicate taxis from the airport to the center cost about B$20, but if you walk 100m past the airport gate (visible from outside the terminal), you'll pay as little as B$12 per person for a normal taxi. Otherwise, cross the main road and take a passing *micro A* or *trufi*, which runs by the bus terminal and the Mercado Central.

Bus

City *micros* and *trufis* cost B$2.50 per ride. Routes are clearly marked on the front windows of the vehicles.

Car & Bike Hire

Barron's Rent-a-Car (☎663-6853; Ingavi E-339)

Taxi

Although you can walk just about anywhere in Tarija (including to the airport), taxis cost B$5/8 per person for day/night trips around the center, including to the bus terminal.

San Jacinto Reservoir

If you're hot in Tarija and after some aquatic refreshment, go to the 17-sq-km reservoir, 7km southwest of town. There's a tourist complex with little *cabañas* (cabins), a restaurant serving *dorado* (a delicious local fish) and a place to rent canoes or, if you feel the need for speed, jet skis. Those who prefer more tranquil ways to enjoy themselves will delight in the nice walks along the shore and surrounding ridges. Though billed as one of the region's biggest attractions, it's not – but it does make for a pleasant day trip and is popular with *chapacos* on Sunday afternoons. *Trufis* run to San Jacinto (B$3, 10 minutes) every 20 minutes from the corner of Ingavi and Campos (outside the Palacio de la Justicia) in Tarija.

El Valle de la Concepción

📍4 / ELEV 1900-2100M

The Concepción Valley, or simply 'El Valle,' is the heart of Bolivian wine and *singani* production. The village of La Concepción still bears many picturesque colonial elements and the plaza sports some lovely endemic flowering ceibo trees, but there is no reason to stay here – it is much more conveniently visited on a day trip from Tarija.

The **Fiesta de la Uva** (Grape Festival), held here for three days in March, coincides with the grape harvest.

Wineries

The Tarija region claims to be home to the 'world's highest wines'. The grapevines, first brought to the region by 17th-century missionaries, grow at a staggering 1900m and 2100m and are only 22 degrees south of the equator. They ripen quicker than their sea-level cousins and the wine is given a head start in the maturing process, making rich reserves easier to produce. The grapes grown here are a mix of muscat of Alexandria and Californian, but with a crisp taste all their own.

Most bodegas also produce *singani,* a distilled grape spirit (40%) of varying quality. *Mi Socio,* the cheapest and harshest, is marked by a blue-label; the red-label *Special de Oro* is of medium price and quality; the best, *Colección Privada,* is a flowery, fresh, fragrant spirit and has a black label. The cheaper types are usually drunk mixed with soda and lemon. All offices sell bottles at factory prices (B$15 to B$100).

Bodega La Concepción WINERY
(Map p224; ☎664-5040; www.bodegaslaconcepcion.com; office O'Connor N-642, Tarija) Considered the region's best winery, it promotes its vintages as the 'world's highest wines'. It's found 25km south of Tarija, just before the village of Concepción.

Bodega Casa Vieja WINERY
(Map p224; ☎666-2605; www.lacasavieja.info; office 15 de Abril & Saracho, Tarija) Home to the best *patero* (foot-trodden) wine, this atmospheric winery has a lovely restaurant (lunch B$25). It's in the village of Concepción, about 30km from Tarija.

Campos de Solana/Casa Real WINERY
(Map p224; ☎664-8481; www.casa-real.com; office 15 de Abril E-259, Tarija) Modern winery with big vaults of wine, in the Santa Ana area, 17km southwest of Tarija.

Tarija's Wine Country

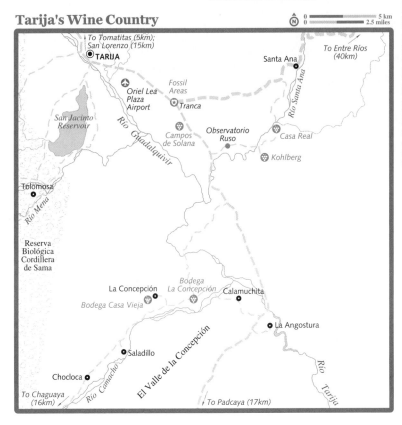

LA FIESTA DE LECHE Y QUESO

Tiny **Rosillas** (population 1000), a satellite town located to the west of Padcaya, is the host of an off-the-wall celebration dedicated to the products provided by our uddered amiga, the humble moo-cow. Taking place during the last week of March, the Fiesta de Leche y Queso is a cheesy celebration that the locals milk for all it's worth. It's a slightly weird affair, with something resembling a bovine beauty pageant, bull-fighting and plenty of music. It concludes with the local ranchers asking Pachamama (Mother Earth) for a bountiful harvest so they can do it all again the following year.

Kohlberg   WINERY
(Map p224; ☑663-6366; www.bodegaskohlberg.com; office 15 de Abril E-275, Tarija) The area's oldest winery and also the most popular.

❶ Getting There & Away

For a guided visit to the valley's wineries, contact Viva Tours (p225) or VTB Tours (p225) or the winery offices in Tarija. If you prefer to visit under your own steam, El Valle lies off the route toward Bermejo; take the right fork at the *tranca* (police post) east of Tarija. Taxis and *micro V* leave when full (B\$5, 30 minutes) from the corner of Corrado and Trigo.

Padcaya & Chaguaya

Visiting Padcaya, south of Tarija, brings full meaning to the old saying that 'it's better to travel than to arrive', with the route twisting its way through 45km of lovely mountainous desert and green river valleys. The town itself has a few old colonial buildings and is located in an area rich in fossils, meaning you are more likely to bump into a paleontologist than another tourist.

Chaguaya, 68km south of Tarija, is home to the pilgrimage shrine Santuario de la Virgen de Chaguaya. The **Fiesta de la Virgen de Chaguaya** begins on August 15; celebrations follow on the subsequent Sunday. Alcohol is forbidden at this time. Pilgrims from all over Bolivia arrive during the following month, some making the trip on foot (including an annual procession from Tarija).

Micros (B\$7, 90 minutes) from Tarija to Padcaya depart every 20 minutes from the Parada del Chaco. Less frequent services run to Chaguaya from the same place, leaving midafternoon.

Reserva Biológica Cordillera de Sama

The Sama Biological Reserve protects representative samples of both the Altiplano and inter-Andean valley ecosystems. In the highland portion of the reserve (3400m above sea level), one can visit the Tajzara lakes, a RAMSAR site of international importance for aquatic birds. Temperatures in the highlands stay quite chilly year-round but are slightly more comfortable in the drier winter months (May to August). The best time to visit the lower elevations is in the summer, when it's warm enough to swim.

The reserve is administered by Servicio Nacional de Áreas Protegidas (SERNAP), which has an office opposite the bus terminal (p230) in Tarija. Entry to the reserve costs US\$15 and the fee is not included in the prices offered by tour companies.

TAJZARA SECTION

The area known as Tajzara lies high on the cold and windy *puna* (high open grasslands) of western Tarija department. Here, several shallow flamingo-filled lagoons appear like jewels in the harsh Altiplano, vegetated only by *thola* (a small desert bush) and *paja brava* (spiky grass of the high Altiplano). Tarija's New Agers consider Tajzara to be a natural power site while the locals claim that the lakes are haunted by nocturnal spirit voices and woe betide anybody that stays out after dark. The night air does produce some eerie voicelike cries, but unimaginative people ascribe the phenomenon to winds rushing through the *thola*.

Along the eastern shores of the lagoons, the wind has heaped up large *arenales* (sand dunes). An interesting climb takes you to the symmetrical peak of **Muyuloma**, which rises about 1000m above the plain. The summit affords views across the lagoons and beyond to the endless expanses of the southern Altiplano. The return climb takes the better part of a day.

An *albergue* (basic guesthouse) near the Tajzara visitors center was out of action at the time of writing, but contact SERNAP for the latest information. The observatory here is a favorite with bird-watchers in search of three of the world's six flamingo species, and the rare horned and giant coots. Hikers can spend a very enjoyable six to eight hours on the wonderful **Inca Trail** as it descends 2000m to the valley below. With luck, you may see vicuñas, condors or mysterious petroglyphs of unknown origin.

INTER-ANDEAN VALLEYS

During the summertime, there are several places in the valley to go swimming in the rivers, including Tomatitas, Coimata and Chorros de Jurina.

Tomatitas, with its natural swimming holes, three lovely rivers (the Sella, Guadalquivir and Erquis) and happy little eateries, is popular with day-trippers from Tarija. The best swimming is immediately below the footbridge, where there's also a park with a campground and barbecue sites. From here you can walk or hitch the 9km to **Coimata**. From Tarija, turn left off the main San Lorenzo road. After less than 1km, you'll pass a cemetery on the left, which is full of flowers and brightly colored crosses. Just beyond it, bear right towards Coimata. Once there, turn left at the soccer field and continue to the end of the road. Here you'll find a small cascade of water and a **swimming hole** that makes a great escape, as lots of Tarijeño families can attest. There's also a choice of small restaurants serving *misquinchitos* and *doraditos* (fried local fish with white corn), as well as *cangrejitos* (small freshwater crabs). From this point, you can follow a walking track 40 minutes upstream to the base of the two-tiered **Coimata Falls**, which has a total drop of about 60m.

Another swimming hole and waterfall are found at **Rincón de la Victoria**, 6km southwest of Tomatitas in a green plantationlike setting. Instead of bearing right beyond the colorful cemetery, as you would for Coimata, follow the route to the left. From the fork, it's 5km to Rincón de la Victoria.

The twin 40m waterfalls at **Chorros de Jurina**, 26km from Tarija, also make an agreeable destination for a day trip. Set in a beautiful but unusual landscape, one waterfall cascades over white stone while the other pours over black stone. In late winter, however, they may diminish to a mere trickle or dry up completely.

The route from Tarija to Jurina passes through some impressive rural landscapes. From near the flowery plaza in San Lorenzo, follow the Jurina road, which turns off be-

side the Casa de Moto Méndez. After 6km, you'll pass a school on the left. Turn left 200m beyond the school and follow that road another 2.5km to the waterfalls. From the end of the road, it's a five-minute walk to the base of either waterfall. The one on the left is reached by following the river upstream; for the other, follow the track that leads from behind a small house.

❶ Getting There & Away

Tour companies in Tarija organize overnight trips to the most accessible areas of Sama, but require a minimum of three people and an advance booking. Buses to Villazón depart between 8pm and 9pm and pass through Tajzara approximately five hours later. The Tajzara visitors center is a 20-minute walk from the road.

Micros A and *B* to Tomatitas leave every 20 minutes from the corner of Domingo Paz and Saracho in Tarija (B$1.50), some continuing on to Jurina (B$5) via San Lorenzo. Get off near the school and then walk the rest of the way. For Coimata, similarly frequent departures leave from the corner of Campesino and Comercio (B$3) in Tarija.

Reserva Nacional de Flora y Fauna Tariquía

The lovely and little-known 2470-sq-km Tariquía Flora & Fauna Reserve (created in 1989) protects a large portion of cloud forest and a smaller area of *polylepis* woodland on the eastern slopes of the department of Tarija's mountains. Ranging in altitude from 400m to 1500m, it houses rare animals such as the spectacled bear, as well as hundreds of bird species including the threatened rufous-throated dipper and the spectacular military macaw.

Access to this largely wild reserve is extremely complicated and there are no formal tours. Hiking is possible but extremely challenging in this remote area and should not be attempted without a guide. The best time to visit Tariquía is during the dry winter months (May to September) when the climate is mild and river crossings are possible.

Prometa   TOUR

(Map p224; ☑663-3873; www.prometa.org.bo; Alejandro del Carpio E-659, Tarija; albergue r per person B$100-150) Prometa operates seven camps in Tariquía, including a simple *albergue* with camping and cooking facilities – the Tariquía Community Center in the heart of the reserve. From the road it's a two-day hike to the center, but allow six days to fully explore the area on foot. You'll need to bring camping gear. Contact Prometa's office for details of how to visit.

THE CHACO

Flat and sparsely populated, the Chaco is a vast expanse of thorn scrub where dispersed ranchers, isolated indigenous villages and Mennonite communities farm plots of land – it's also dotted by police and military troops, guarding their posts. This silent flatland covers most of southeastern Bolivia and western Paraguay and stretches into neighboring Argentina.

Wildlife abounds in the undisturbed wilderness of the Chaco. With humans a relatively rare species, animals are bolder and more visible here than in the Amazon and this is one of the best places in South America to see large mammals like the tapir, jaguar and puma. Plant life amazes with a series of bizarre (and often spiny) adaptations to the xeric environment. Apart from being prickled by various species of cacti, you'll be surprised by brilliant flowering bushes and trees, such as the yellow *carnival* bush; the white-and-yellow *huevo* (egg) tree; the pink or white thorny bottle tree, locally known as the *toboroche* or *palo borracho* (drunken tree); and the red-flowering, hard *quebracho* (axe-breaker) tree whose wood, too heavy to float, is one of the Chaco's main exports.

Yacuiba

📍4 / POP 83,500

There's only one reason to visit Yacuiba: to cross the border between Argentina and Bolivia. Tiny **Pocitos**, 5km south, is the easternmost Bolivia–Argentina border crossing.

🛌 Sleeping & Eating

The only thing Yacuiba has going for it is that there are lots of hotels. The best of the limited eating options are around the plaza.

Gran Residencial Victoria PENSION $
(📞682-3752; San Martín 639; s/d B$40/60, d with bathroom & cable TV B$90; ❄) Hyperbolic name? Well yes, but this is the best of the motley selection of *residenciales* in front of the bus terminal; useful if you have an early bus to catch (or indeed a late one) and

are looking for somewhere to rest your head for a few hours. Even the cheap rooms have air-con.

Hotel Paris HOTEL $$
(📞682-2182; Comercio at Campero; s/d B$180/225; ❄) Two blocks from the plaza, this is an upmarket hotel decked out in hardwoods that give it a classical feel. All rooms have TV and air-conditioning and there's a pleasant courtyard restaurant for meals.

ℹ Getting There & Around

Yacuiba's bus terminal is about 10 blocks from the plaza on Av San Martín. Buses for Tarija (B$40 to B$60, 12 hours) leave before 9am and after 6pm. Numerous *flotas* leave every evening for Santa Cruz (B$51 to B$110, 15 hours) via Villamontes and Camiri, and *trufis* (B$20, 1½ hours) depart for Villamontes throughout the day when full. There is a B$2 terminal fee payable on boarding any bus.

Yacuiba's **railway station** (📞682-2308) ticket window opens in the morning on the day of departure; line up early. A single service runs to Santa Cruz (B$47, 16½ hours) via Villamontes (B$11, 2½ hours) on Friday at 5pm.

Flights to Tarija depart with TAM on Tuesday and Saturday (B$390) if there is enough demand, and Aerocon flies daily to Santa Cruz (B$880) via Tarija (B$522).

If you are unfortunate enough to get stuck in town and are looking for something to do, check the town's online information portal (www.yacuiba.com, in Spanish) for ideas or event schedules.

Villamontes

📍4 / POP 23,800 / ELEV 383M

As the temperature soars and the hot, dry winds coat everything with a thick layer of dust, you can see the pride rising in the residents of Villamontes almost as fast as the mercury, for this is officially Bolivia's hottest town. Despite the heat, it is a welcoming place and the majority-indigenous-Guaraní population means that lovely woven baskets and furniture made from natural Chaco materials can be found at the town's market. Villamontes' biggest employer is the local gas plant, which is responsible for an influx of migrant workers from across the border in Paraguay. The 6pm whistle that rings out across town indicates the end of the working day.

The best time to visit is during the annual **fishing festival** on the Río Pilcomayo in August, the fishy obsession being exemplified

BORDER CROSSINGS INTO ARGENTINA

The two main border crossings to Argentina are at Yacuiba and Bermejo, the former being the most accessible from Santa Cruz and the latter from Tarija. *Casas de cambio* (exchange houses) are abundant in both border towns. It is in your best interest to get rid of your extra bolivianos before crossing the border – rates in Argentina are not favorable. Note that Argentina is one hour ahead of Bolivia.

Shared taxis (B$10 per person) shuttle between the terminal at Yacuiba and Argentine immigration at Pocitos. After crossing the border on foot, onward bus services to Tartagal and Embarcación leave every couple of hours, where you can make connections to Salta, Jujuy and Buenos Aires.

Crossing to Argentina from Bermejo is slightly more complicated as the border is only open from 8am to 5pm. *Chalanas* (ferries) over the river (B$3) leave every few minutes. Be sure to pick up an exit stamp before crossing.

Bermejo's bus terminal is eight blocks southeast of the main plaza. Buses leave every couple of hours from Tarija to Bermejo (B$20, three hours) between 7:30am and 9pm, but you'll need to get a morning service (last departure 10:30am) if you want to cross the border the same day. From Agua Blanca, Argentine buses to Orán (US$2, one hour) depart hourly from the terminal opposite the immigration office. From Orán, you can connect to Argentina's Salta, Jujuy and Tucumán.

by the pride with which locals give directions that invariably reference the location in relation to the **El Pescadito** statue, the town's only landmark.

🛏 Sleeping & Eating

Villamontes is known for its fish restaurants, shacklike structures clustered at the base of the bridge on the road to Yacuiba, which serve freshly caught *surubí* among other local scalies. You'll be given the option to have your fish cooked *a la parilla* (grilled) or *frito* (fried). Pick the former unless you want the only moisture in it to be cooking oil.

The town center is 12 blocks west of El Pescadito, but there is no real reason to head there unless it is to stock up for your journey at the humungus **market** at the corners of Arcos Mendes and Av Ingavi. There are a couple of *churrasquerías* near the plaza that also serve *almuerzos*, but none are up to much.

TOP CHOICE **Hotel El Rancho Olivo**   HOTEL **$$**
(✆684-2049; www.elranchoolivo.com; Av Méndez Arcos; s/d B$250/330; ❈@❈) Opposite the railway station this is Villamontes' best hotel by a long shot. Rooms try hard to aim for moderate luxury, with their stained wooden furniture and decorative lamps, but the 4WD vehicles that line up in the car park are enough to confirm that this is the place of choice in Villamontes for those with a bit

of money to spend. A pleasant but pricey restaurant sits by the side.

Residencial El Gran Chaco   PENSION **$**
(✆672-4620; main road a block south of El Pescadito; r per person B$80; ❈) Brand spanking new, this tastefully presented *residencial* is superb value for money if you are just passing through because of its perfect location near El Pescadito and spick-and-span bathrooms. The owners are friendly and helpful, despite their grumpy dog.

Residencial El Pescadito   PENSION **$**
(✆672-2896; r per person with/without bathroom B$80/60; ❈) Budget option on the main road opposite El Pescadito and close to the bus offices for departures to Paraguay.

❶ Getting There & Away

Buses run to Tarija (B$50, nine hours) and Santa Cruz (B$120, eight hours) after 6pm from the terminal two blocks west of El Pescadito. *Trufis* for Camiri (B$30, two hours) leave when full from the main road a block north of El Pescadito and for Yacuiba (B$20, 1½ hours) from three blocks south.

The main reason for stopping in Villamontes, however, is to catch a bus connection to Asunción in Paraguay (B$300, 15 hours) via the border crossing at Infante Rivarole before continuing on to the Trans-Chaco Road. All companies have their offices on the main road close to the El Pescadito statue and buses pass through in the early hours of the morning. You should buy your ticket in advance, but you will be allocated to a bus irrespective of which company sold you the ticket. Unfortunately, the quality of service varies considerably between companies and which one you get is pot luck.

The train to Yacuiba (B$11, 2½ hours) passes through on Friday morning at 5am and returns to Santa Cruz (B$38, 14 hours) on Friday evening at 7:45pm, but the route is painfully slow.

Parque Nacional y Área Natural de Manejo Integrado Aguaragüe

The long and narrow 1080-sq-km Aguaragüe National Park takes in much of the mountains of **Serranía de Aguaragüe**, which divide the vast Gran Chaco and the highlands of the department of Tarija. Right in the center of the region known for being the hottest in Bolivia, it is best visited in the cooler winter months (May to October).

Although it lacks visitor facilities, the Cañón del Pilcomayo is easily accessible from Villamontes. The name of the park comes from Guaraní, meaning 'the lair of the jaguar', because the range is famous for being home to this lovely spotty (and scary) cat. Foxes, tapirs, anteaters, assorted parrots, numerous plant species and 70% of the region's potable water sources can also be found here. Viva Tours (p225) conducts guided hikes and visits, or negotiate with a taxi driver in Villamontes.

CAÑÓN DEL PILCOMAYO

In the beautiful Pilcomayo Canyon at **El Chorro Grande** waterfall, fish are prevented from swimming further upstream. Abundant *surubí, sábalo* and *dorado* are easily caught, making the area a favorite with anglers from all over the country. The predatory *dorado* is prized by game fishermen because of its legendary fight; it's particularly interesting because it has an odd hinge at the front of its jawbone that allows its mouth to open wide horizontally.

There are great views from the restaurants 7km to 10km west of town where you can sample local fish dishes.

To reach the gorge, you can take any Tarija-bound transportation, or taxi to the *tranca* and hitch or walk from there (as usual, weekends are the best time to hitchhike). Where the road forks, bear right and continue another 2km to the mouth of the gorge.

Camiri

⊿3 / POP 31,000 / ELEV 825M

This town is the most southerly point on the vaguely defined 'Che Trail', which ends in Vallegrande. However, Camiri's real revolution occurred not when Che passed through but in the 1990s, when this town of cobblestoned streets became the center for the production of petroleum and gas for the national oil company, YPFB (known more simply as 'Yacimientos'). The town is so proud of its oily role that it bills itself as the Capital Petrolífero de Bolivia (Oil Capital of Bolivia).

CROSSING THE BORDER INTO PARAGUAY

Crossing the border into Paraguay has never been easier. The infamous Ruta Trans-Chaco is paved along its entire length on the Paraguay side, though it takes a slight detour away from the original Trans-Chaco at La Patria, crossing into Bolivia at the military checkpoint of Infante Rivarola. Several bus services from Santa Cruz via Villamontes now run this route to Asunción on a daily basis.

Bolivian customs formalities take place at Ibibobo. You will need to present your passport and visa to both customs and military representatives. Buses typically pass here around 4am or 5am, so don't expect a tranquil night's sleep. From here the Paraguayan border point, Infante Rivarola, is another hour or so away but Paraguayan customs formalities are not carried out until you are well beyond here, at the domineering *aduana* (customs office) in Mariscal Estigarribia. Buses typically arrive here around 7am or 8am.

This is a notorious smuggling route so expect to be lined up with your bags as customs officials and sniffer dogs rifle through your private possessions. Once you are given the OK to proceed, you get your entry stamp from the small immigration office just outside the main compound. There is a service station here that sells food if you're peckish and, provided you are not carrying anything you shouldn't be, it is as simple as that!

⚫ Sights & Activities

Cuartel-Museo   MUSEUM
(⊙9am-noon & 2-6pm Mon-Fri) Camiri was the site where the French intellectual Régis Debray and Argentine artist Ciro Bustos, members of Che Guevarás guerilla group, were held and tortured following their capture. Debray spilled the beans on Guevara's operation and Bustos sketched the group members for his captors. The site of their imprisonment was this museum, then the local military barracks. Bustos's original images are displayed in the Cuartel's 'Casino' – the site where, bizarrely enough, Debray was married, receiving a two-hour 'permission' for his nuptials before returning to his cell. The two were tried and found guilty (what a surprise!) in the local library.

YPFB Plant   LANDMARK
Camiri is damn proud of its YPFB plant. There's no formal tour, but if you're keen to visit get up at the crack of dawn and roll up at 8am and they might let you look around. Don't miss the **Petrolero (Oil Worker) monument** in the middle of Av Petrolero.

🛏 Sleeping & Eating

All the places listed here are within two blocks of the main plaza.

Hotel JR   HOTEL $$
(☎952-2200; Sánchez 247; s/d B$210/330; ❋) If you fancy hanging out with oil barons check out the friendly JR, possibly named after the *Dallas* soap character. All rooms have telephones, heating and cable TV, and there's a bright sitting area with fine views.

Hotel Premier   HOTEL $
(☎952-2204; Busch 60; s/d B$120/150) A block from the plaza, this is a nice modern hotel with small rooms, each with cable TV and hot shower. Particularly nice are the bright and spacious upstairs rooms that open onto a leafy patio.

Cupesi   INTERNATIONAL $$$
(Sánchez 247; mains B$45-70) Under the Hotel JR, this is arguably the best food in town. The extensive menu contains meat, chicken and fish dishes that are not cheap, but if

RESERVA PRIVADA DE PATRIMONIO NATURAL DE CORBALÁN

This private 18-sq-km reserve on the Paraguayan border was established in 1996 to protect a choice piece of Gran Chaco. Jaguars, pumas, tapirs, giant anteaters and giant armadillos are found here, though you'll more likely see Azara's fox, the three-banded armadillo and birds such as the blue-fronted Amazon parrot and Chaco chachalaca. The only access route is a poor road from Villamontes, which takes at least four hours with a good vehicle. If you plan to visit, accommodations are limited to a simple **park rangers' camp**, and you need to bring your own food, water and other supplies. The only commercial access is with Viva Tours (p225) and Prometa (p233).

you are in town for more than a few days it's worth the extra bolivianos to avoid succumbing to a monotonous diet of junk food.

Membiray   CHINESE $$
(Plaza Principal; mains B$25-50) A brave attempt to introduce Chinese and vegetarian dishes to the conservative town residents. Portions are large, well cooked and the surroundings are pleasant – though there is nothing Oriental about them.

ℹ Information

There is no official tourist information office, but local resident **doña Karen** (☎952-4792) gives information by phone if you speak Spanish.

ℹ Getting There & Away

Camirí's new bus terminal is outside of town on the road to Santa Cruz in Barrio La Williams. *Flotas* leave every two hours or so to Santa Cruz (B$30, five hours). If you are heading to Tarija, Yacuiba or Paraguay, the quickest way to get there is to take a *trufi* to Villamontes (B$30, three hours) and get a connection there. Andesbus and Emperador alternate for a daily service to Sucre (B$100, 14 hours).

Santa Cruz & Gran Chiquitania

Includes »

Best Places to Eat

» Taj Mahal (p246)
» Yorimichi (p246)
» Naïs (p246)
» Latina Café (p259)
» La Casa del Telegrafista (p262)

Best Places to Stay

» El Pueblito (p258)
» Senses Boutique Hotel (p245)
» La Posada del Sol (p258)
» Gran Hotel Concepción (p265)
» Los Aventureros (p245)

Why Go?

The Bolivian Oriente is not what you generally see in Bolivian tourist brochures. This tropical region, the country's most prosperous, has a palpable desire to differentiate itself from Bolivia's traditional highland image. The region's agriculture boom in recent years brought about a rise in income and a standard of living unequalled by any other Bolivian province.

Though Santa Cruz is Bolivia's most populous city, it retains a small-town atmosphere despite its cosmopolitan population. From here visit the charming Jesuit mission towns with the country's loveliest examples of Jesuit architecture. Pre-Inca ruins hide near the small town of Samaipata; revolutionaries make a pilgrimage to where Che Guevara met his maker on the Che Trail around Vallegrande; and there are miles of trekking and tons of wildlife at the little-disturbed Parque Nacional Amboró. If you want a look into a part of Bolivia that defies the stereotype, this is the place to be.

When to Go
Santa Cruz

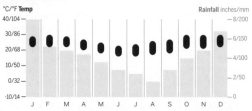

Jan Give in to desire at the Buena Vista Chocolate Festival on the last Sunday in January.

May–Aug The best time to visit lowland Chiquitania to avoid the worst of the heat.

Oct Join the faithful at Vallegrande's Che Festival, in memory of the legendary revolutionary.

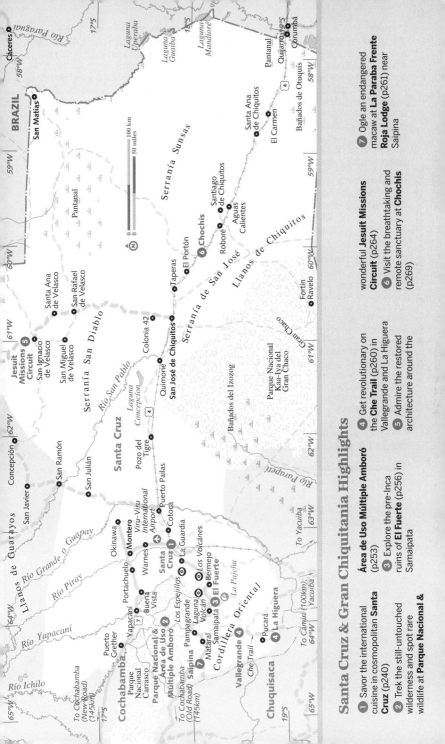

Santa Cruz & Gran Chiquitania Highlights

1 Savor the international cuisine in cosmopolitan **Santa Cruz** (p240)

2 Trek the still-untouched wilderness and spot rare wildlife at **Parque Nacional & Área de Uso Múltiple Amboró** (p253)

3 Explore the pre-Inca ruins of **El Fuerte** (p256) in Samaipata

4 Get revolutionary on the **Che Trail** (p260) in Vallegrande and La Higuera

5 Admire the restored architecture around the wonderful **Jesuit Missions Circuit** (p264)

6 Visit the breathtaking and remote sanctuary at **Chochis** (p269)

7 Ogle an endangered macaw at **La Paraba Frente Roja Lodge** (p261) near Saipina

Climate

The Oriente's climate is tropical but, because it occupies the transition zone between the Amazon rainforest, the highlands and the dry Chaco plains, Santa Cruz enjoys more sun and less stifling temperatures than the humid Amazon Basin. Winter rainfall means little more than 10-minute downpours, but a single summer deluge can last for days. At times during winter, *surazos* (chilly winds) blow in from Patagonia and the Argentine pampas and the temperature plummets.

National Parks

Parque Nacional Amboró is an unquestionable highlight of the region. The remote Parque Nacional Kaa-Iya del Gran Chaco is Latin America's largest park but is largely inaccessible.

ℹ️ Getting There & Away

Santa Cruz is the country's most connected city. Many flights from Europe and neighboring countries come direct to Santa Cruz and are worth considering if you're arriving from sea level and don't want to spend days acclimatizing in La Paz. Direct flights depart daily for Asunción, Buenos Aires, Miami, São Paulo and Rio de Janeiro, as well as a comprehensive network of domestic destinations.

Trains trundle south to Argentina and east to the Brazilian Pantanal, and there are long-distance buses running along paved roads to the west and south.

SANTA CRUZ & AROUND

Santa Cruz

📍3 / POP 1.13 MILLION / ELEV 417M (1368FT)

Santa Cruz may surprise you with its small-town feeling, lack of high-rise blocks and a lightly buzzing, relaxed tropical atmosphere. Bolivia's largest city oozes modernity yet clings stubbornly to tradition. The city center is vibrant and thriving, its narrow streets crowded with suited businessmen sipping *chicha* (fermented corn drink) at street stalls, while taxis jostle with horses and carts for pole position at traffic lights. Locals still lounge on the main square listening to *camba* (Eastern Lowlands) music, restaurants close for siesta and little stores line the porch-fronted houses selling cheap, local products.

This is not the Bolivia that you see on postcards, but this is the place with the largest population diversity in the country – from the overall-wearing Mennonites strolling the streets past local Goth kids, to a Japanese community, Altiplano (High Plateau) immigrants, Cuban doctors, Brazilian settlers, bearded Russians and fashionable *cruceños* (Santa Cruz locals) cruising the tight streets in their SUVs. To help filter the ever increasing traffic away from the center, the city is laid out in a series of concentric circular avenues *(anillos)* that are joined by spoke-like thoroughfares *(radiales)*.

It's worth spending a few days here, wandering the streets, eating at the many international restaurants and checking out the rich kids' play area, Equipetrol, where nightlife is rife with naughtiness. Alternatively, join the locals and chill out on the town square.

History

Santa Cruz de la Sierra was founded in 1561 by Ñuflo de Chávez, a Spaniard who hailed from present-day Paraguay. The town originated 220km east of its current location, but in 1621, by order of the King of Spain, it moved to its present position, 50km east of the Cordillera Oriental foothills. The original location had proved too vulnerable to attack from local tribes. Ñuflo himself was killed in 1568 at the hands of the mestizo Itatine tribe made up of indigenous and Spanish settlers.

The city's main purpose was to supply the rest of the colony with products such as rice, cotton, sugar and fruit. Its prosperity lasted until the late 1800s, when transportation routes opened up between La Paz and the Peruvian coast, making imported goods cheaper than those hauled from Santa Cruz over mule trails.

During the period leading up to Bolivia's independence in 1825, the eastern regions of the Spanish colonies were largely ignored. Although agriculture was thriving around Santa Cruz, the Spanish remained intent upon extracting every scrap of mineral wealth that could be squeezed from the rich and more hospitable highlands.

In 1954 a highway linking Santa Cruz with other major centers was completed and the city sprang back from its 100-year economic lull. The completion of the railway line to Brazil in the mid-1950s opened trade routes to the east, after which time tropical agriculture boomed and the city grew as prosperously as crops such as oranges, sugar cane, bananas and coffee. That growth continues to the present day.

The *cruceños* are an independent lot who feel little affinity for their government in La Paz and are well aware of their city's stock value as the country's trade and transport center. Support for President Morales is thin on the ground here and *cruceños* voiced their overwhelming desire for the region's autonomy in 2006. Though they lost that battle following a national referendum, calls for independence continue to be the main source of inspiration for the city's graffiti artists.

⊙ Sights & Activities

Santa Cruz is not the richest town when it comes to sightseeing. You'll probably spend most of your time here strolling around and sipping coffee in one of the city's many cafes.

Plaza 24 de Septiembre   PLAZA
The city's main plaza serves as a lush tropical space where you'll see locals lounging on benches or strolling, *camba* bands banging out their tropical rhythms and families bringing their kids to play. Once there were resident jaywalking sloths here, but they were relocated to the zoo in an effort to protect them from electrocution and increasing traffic hazards in the city center.

Basílica Menor de San Lorenzo   CHURCH
(bell tower admission B$3; ⊙bell tower 8am-noon & 3-6pm Mon-Fri, 8am-noon Sat) Although the original cathedral on Plaza 24 de Septiembre was founded in 1605, the present structure dates from 1845 and wasn't consecrated until 1915. Inside, the decorative woodwork on the ceiling and silver plating around the altar are worth a look. There are good views of the city from the **bell tower**.

Museo de Arte Sagrado   MUSEUM
(Basílica Menor de San Lorenzo, Plaza 24 de Septiembre; admission B$10; ⊙8:30am-noon & 2:30am-6pm Mon-Fri) The Museum of Holy Art, inside the cathedral, displays a collection of religious icons, vestments and medallions. More interesting are the many gold and silver relics from the Jesuit Guarayos missions. Look out for one of the world's smallest books, a thumbnail-sized volume containing the Lord's Prayer in several languages.

Parque El Arenal   PARK
Locals relax around the lagoon at Parque El Arenal, but it's best not to dawdle here at night. On an island in the lagoon, a bas-relief mural by renowned Bolivian artist

DON'T MISS

BIOCENTRO GÜEMBE

A great place for a day out of Santa Cruz, **Biocentro Güembe** (☑370-0700; www.biocentroguembe.com; Km 5, Camino Porongo, Zona Urubó; adult/child B$90/50) has a butterfly farm, orchid exhibitions, 15 natural pools, sports facilities and you can go fishing and trekking in the surrounding forest. There's a restaurant with international cuisine, so you won't go hungry, and cabins or camping if you wish to stay the night. Its a rough road out there, so the best way to get here is by taxi from Santa Cruz; expect to pay around B$40. If it's a hot day get there early, the place fills up fast!

Lorgio Vaca depicts historic and modern-day aspects of Santa Cruz.

FREE **Museo Etno-Folklórico**   MUSEUM
(☑342-9939; admission free; ⊙8am-noon & 2:30am-6:30pm Mon-Fri) Located at the entrance to the Parque El Arenal on Beni and 6 de Agosto is the Museo Etno-Folklórico, which has a small collection of traditional art and artifacts from several *camba* cultures including Guaraní, Mojeño, Ayoreo and Chiquitano.

Jardín Zoológico   ZOO
(☑342-9939; adult/child B$10/5; ⊙9am-6:30pm) Santa Cruz' zoo has a collection of native birds, mammals and reptiles kept in pleasingly humane conditions, although the llamas are a bit overdressed for the climate. If you're not into going to the jungle, this is a good place to see spectacular species such as tapirs, pumas, jaguars and spectacled bears. Keep your eyes open for free-ranging sloths and squirrel monkeys in the trees.

Take *micro* (minibus) *55* from Calle Vallegrande, 76 from Calle Santa Bárbara or anything marked 'Zoológico'. Taxis for up to four people cost around B$15 from the center.

Museo Guaraní   MUSEUM
(admission B$5; ⊙8am-4pm Mon-Fri) A small but fascinating and professionally presented exhibition of Guaraní culture. Look for the animal masks and *tinajas* (huge clay pots) used for making *chicha*. You'll need to knock on the gate for entry.

Take *micro 55* from Calle Vallegrande or 76 from Calle Santa Bárbara.

Santa Cruz

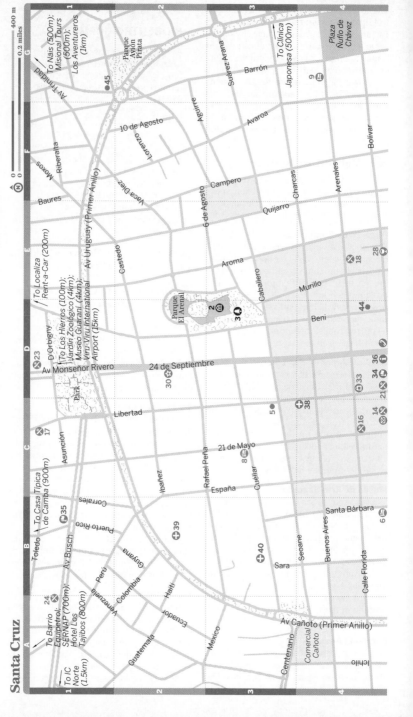

400 m
0.2 miles
N

G
F
E
D
C
B
A

1
2
3
4

To Naís (500m);
Misional Tours
(500m);
Los Aventureros
(1km)

Av Trinidad

Parque
Avión Pirata

●45

Parque
Avión Pirata

Suárez Arana

Aguirre

Barrón

Avaroa

To Clínica
Japonesa (500m)

Plaza
Nuflo de
Chávez

9

Bolívar

Arenales

10 de Agosto

Lorenzo

Vaca Díez

Campero

6 de Agosto

Charcas

Quijarro

Moxos

Riberalta

Baures

Av Uruguay (Primer Anillo)

Castedo

Aroma

Caballero

Murillo

18
28

To Localiza
Rent-a-Car (200m)

D'Orbigny

To Los Hierros (100m);
Jardín Zoológico (4km);
Museo Guaraní (4km);
Viru-Viru International
Airport (15km)

Parque
El Arenal

2
3
4

Beni

44

23

Av Monseñor Rivero

Park

24 de Septiembre

30

Libertad

Asunción

17

To Casa Típica
de Camba (900m)

35

Corrales

Puerto Rico

Guyana

21 de Mayo

8

Rafael Peña

Ibañez

España

Cuéllar

5
38

16

14

33
34
36

21

Santa Bárbara

6

To Barrio
Equipetrol-
SERNAP (700m);
Hotel Los
Tajibos (800m)

24

Toledo

Av Busch

Perú

Colombia

Venezuela

Haití

Ecuador

39

40

Seoane

Sara

Buenos Aires

Calle Florida

México

Centenario

Av Cañoto (Primer Anillo)

Comercial
Cañoto

Ichilo

To IC
Norte
(1.5km)

Guatemala

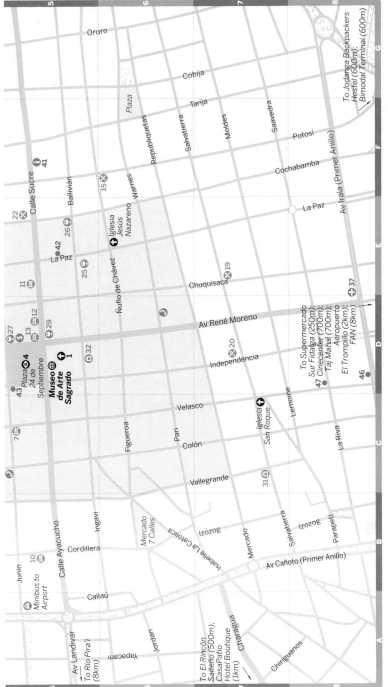

Santa Cruz

Aqualand SWIMMING
(half day B$35-50, full day B$50-70; ☻10am-6pm Thu-Sun May-Sep) For a real splash, dive into this water park near Viru-Viru airport, north of the city center. It can provide a welcome relief from the stifling muggy heat in the city. The best way to get here is by taxi (around B$30).

☞ Tours

Numerous companies offer organized tours, but it's hard to vouch for quality, particularly for those with cheap rates. Those listed below all have excellent reputations.

Amboró Tours TOUR
(☎339-0600; www.amborotours.com; Libertad 417, 2nd fl) Trips to Amboró national park and Jesuit missions.

Bird Bolivia BIRDWATCHING
(☎356-3636; www.birdbolivia.com) Professional birding and wildlife tours with expert guides for those with a special interest in nature.

Misional Tours TOUR
(☎360-1985; www.misionaltours.com; Los Motojobobos 2515) One of the city's best-organized and reliable operators, specializing in the Mission Circuit but just as good for other attractions across Bolivia.

🎇 Festivals & Events

If you're in Santa Cruz during **Carnaval**, you should most certainly head for the paintball-plagued streets and join in the collective chaos. Carnaval occurs annually in February or March, one week before Lent begins.

International Theater Festival THEATER
Theater groups from all over the world perform in venues around the city. Held from April 14 to 24 (odd-numbered years only), it's a great time to be in Santa Cruz.

**International Festival of
Baroque Music** MUSIC
A 10-day festival, held from the end of April to the beginning of May, with concerts in Santa Cruz and the Jesuit mission towns.

ExpoCruz COMMERCIAL
(www.fexpocruz.com.bo) Every year in mid- to late September, Santa Cruz hosts this enormous two-week fair where you can buy anything from a toothbrush or clothing to a new house, a combine harvester or a 20-ton truck.

🛏 Sleeping

Santa Cruz has a growing number of mid-range hotels, all with private bathrooms but many of the central places are fading ungracefully and are overpriced. Many of Santa Cruz' luxury options are away from the center and are more like resorts than hotels.

TOP CHOICE **Senses Boutique
Hotel** BOUTIQUE HOTEL $$$
(343-4793; www.sensesboutiquehotel.com; 24 de Septiembre cnr Sucre; s/d/ste B$840/980/1330; ✳@) Four restaurants and two bars may be overkill, but you should prepare yourself for sensory overload at this ultramodern boutique hotel. From the reception area with its half-ball chairs and TVs in picture frames, right down to the luxurious rooms with king-size beds and walk-in closets, the owners have come up with a concept designed to challenge your idea of luxury by giving it a decidedly modern twist.

Los Aventureros HOSTEL $$
(343-4793; www.losaventureros.net; Pedro Rivera Méndez btwn Beni & Alemania; dm B$60, s/d B$120/200; ✳@≋) Run by a couple of ex-*mochilleros* (backpackers) from Sucre who have combined the experience of their own world wanderings to create the ultimate hostel for the adventurous independent traveler. A cool place to stay, this is a new breed of hostel offering great-value rooms and little quirks such as Arabian tents for those who like to sleep under the stars.

CasaPatio Hotel Boutique BOUTIQUE HOTEL $$$
(333-1728; www.casapatio-hotelboutique.com; Av Ibérica Calle 5, Las Palmas; s/d B$400/580; ✳@)

This affordable boutique hotel is worth every boliviano. The rooms have a delicate, understated appeal, as well as quirky names such as the '*No se lo digas a nadie habitación matrimonial*' ('Don't tell anybody matrimonial suite'). It offers use of a kitchen, which is handy for the budget-minded traveler and of course the patio is exquisite.

Hotel Los Tajibos HOTEL $$$
(342-1000; www.lostajiboshotel.com; San Martín 455, Barrio Equipetrol; s/d/ste B$1200/1350/2500; ✳@≋) The facilities at Los Tajibos are top class with rooms set in lush tropical gardens. Enjoy the nightclub, racquetball courts and pool then relax with a massage in the health club.

Residencial Ikandire HOTEL $$
(339-3975; www.residencialikandire.com; Sucre 51; s/d/tr B$160/200/270, without bathroom B$110/160/240; ✳) A converted colonial house that retains a number of quaint original features, though the nausea-inducing bedspreads in some rooms are not among them. That said, this new place is excellent value and one of the best options in the center, being located just half a block from the main plaza.

Residencial Bolívar HOSTEL $$
(334-2500; Sucre 131; s/d B$200/240, without bathroom dm/s/d B$80/110/170) It's been in business since 1905 and is reputedly the city's oldest hotel. There are leafy tropical patios, a toucan snoozing on a branch and clean, if small, rooms. You can laze in the hammocks or read in the courtyard. Spanish lessons are available for guests and there is a kitchen for guests to use.

Jodanga Backpackers Hostel HOSTEL $$
(312-0033; www.jodanga.com; El Fuerte 1380, Zona Parque Urbano; dm B$70-85, d B$220, without bathroom B$180; ✳@≋) The 'in' place for Santa Cruz backpackers, this superbly equipped hostel has a pool, jacuzzi, pool table, free internet and seriously groovy, air-conditioned rooms, as well as a party atmosphere inspired by its own bar. It also organizes great value Spanish classes.

Hotel Rio Magdalena HOTEL $$
(339-3011; www.hotelriomagdalena.com; Arenales 653; dm B$90, s/d B$140/180; ✳≋) A former Peace Corps hangout, this is a top-notch midrange option with comfortable rooms, an inviting pool and a roof terrace with glorious views of the city.

Hotel Lido
HOTEL $$

(☎336-3555; www.lido-hotel.com; 21 de Mayo 527; s/d/tr B$315/385/490; ❄@) A nice but relatively simple upmarket choice in the center, above a Chinese restaurant, the Lido has comfortable rooms with TVs, and access to laundry facilities. There's also a weight-lifting gym for guests on the ground floor.

Hotel Copacabana
HOTEL $$

(☎336-2770; Junín 217; s/d/tr with air-con B$239/305/382, without air-con B$175/275/330; ❄) A strange sort of retro joint that will appeal to some but be a turn-off for others. Dated, wood-paneled rooms with modern bathrooms and cable TV compound the mixed messages sent by this place. It's about the best of the otherwise similarly uninspiring options along this strip.

Hotel Sarah
HOTEL $$

(☎332-2425; Sara 85; s/d B$125/190; ❄) Sarah has let herself go in recent years, but is still fair value compared to some of the other hotels in this area. Walls are adorned with jungle scenes to prepare you for any Amazonian adventures that may lie ahead, but pick your room carefully as some are falling to pieces.

Alojamiento Santa Bárbara
PENSION $

(☎332-1817; Santa Bárbara 151; s/d B$40/60) This is a low-key place with a courtyard and bare rooms with hospital-like beds. It's much loved by backpackers and young Bolivians for being cheap and central.

✗ Eating

The international population has rolled up its sleeves and opened some fine restaurants, so what the city lacks in sightseeing it makes up in gastronomic offerings.

Av Monseñor Rivero is lined with snazzy cafes and coffee shops that seem to get trendier, or at least more expensive, the further along you walk from the center of the city.

⎡TOP CHOICE⎦ Taj Mahal
INDIAN $$$

(Bumberque 365; mains B$55-110) Hallelujah! It's pretty hard to find an Indian restaurant in South America, and even harder to find a good one, but this upmarket curry house is a cut above the rest. Bangladeshi-owned (despite the Taj Mahal images on the wall), the shrimp, chicken and lamb dishes are mouth-wateringly good and portions are generous. It's on a side street behind Cinecenter.

Naïs
INTERNATIONAL $$

(Av Alemania; mains B$23-49) This Chilean-owned place serves a bit of everything, from juicy grills with notable racks of ribs, to saucy chicken and fine fish dishes. The food is reasonably priced and tasty, but what really sets this place apart is the superbly attentive service, effective without ever being overbearing.

Yorimichi
JAPANESE $$$

(Av Busch 548; mains B$50-90; ⏱11:30am-2:30pm & 6-11pm) A swish Japanese restaurant with bamboo screens separating eating spaces and traditional music tinkling from the speakers, this is the place to come for brilliant sushi, sashimi, tempura and heart-warming sips of sake. It's a favorite of upmarket *cruceños*.

La Casona
INTERNATIONAL $$$

(www.bistrolacasona.com; Arenales 222; mains B$44-120; ⏱Mon-Sat) This German-run splash of California gourmet has seating in a shady courtyard or inside amid the colorful indigenous art that adorns the walls. The food is diverse, with a variety of salads, German dishes or pasta in a spicy, palate-tingling *arrabiatta* (spicy tomato sauce), but portions are small.

Los Hierros
ARGENTINE $$$

(Av Monseñor Rivero; mains B$40-80) Argentinian-style *churrasquería* (grilled meat restaurant) that, according to locals, serves the best T-bone steak in the country. Hanging on the wall is a rifle that supposedly once belonged to Butch Cassidy.

Y Se Llama Peru
SEAFOOD $$$

(Av Monseñor Rivero; mains B$50-95) Adventurous seafood restaurant with a huge variety of imaginative fish and shellfish dishes. Try the *picante de mariscos* if you like your shellfish to come with a nip.

Ichiban
SUSHI $$$

(Libertad 899; mains B$35-70, sushi B$60-290) A Japanese-Peruvian sushi bar where you can get a decent feed for a decent price. It takes the bar part quite literally too, with an expansive wine list and dance music to accompany your meal.

El Aljibe
BOLIVIAN $$

(Ñuflo de Chávez; mains B$35-45; ⏱noon-3am & 7-11:30pm Mon-Sat) An atmospheric little restaurant in a cluttered old colonial house. It specializes in *comida típica* (typical food) which is increasingly difficult to find in cosmopolitan Santa Cruz.

Casa Típica de Camba
BOLIVIAN **$$**

(www.casadelcamba.com; Mendoza 539; mains B$25-55) You are likely to end up at this lively, sprawling landmark if you ask Bolivian friends where to find the 'most typical' *cruceño/camba* experience. Juicy meat comes sizzling off the grill while live singers holler traditional tunes and straw-hatted waiters attend to your every need. Take *micro 35* or *75* from the center.

Pizzería Marguerita
PIZZA **$$$**

(north side of Plaza 24 de Septiembre; mains B$38-70) Long known for its high-quality pizza, pasta and salads, and always popular with foreigners, this well-located place on the north side of the plaza is good for a casual meal though it gets a bit smoky inside.

Michelangelo's
ITALIAN **$$$**

(Chuquisaca 502; mains B$50-80) Located in a classy house, complete with fireplaces and marble floors, this is a good choice for a romantic evening or a little Italian self-indulgence.

Vegetarian Center Cuerpomonte
VEGETARIAN **$**

(Aroma 64; buffet per kg B$25; ⊙9am-6pm Mon-Sat; 🖋) This place has a buffet selection of basic and simple food including quinoa cake, mashed sweet potato, salad bar goodies, veggie soups and lots of other wholesome, healthy treats.

Alexander
INTERNATIONAL **$$**

(Junín; mains B$22-35) This is a haven for delicious breakfasts and good coffee. Part of a chain, Alexander is excellent for sampling local Madidi coffee and any range of breakfasts, including *huevos rancheros* (spicy scrambled eggs) and gigantic fruit salads served with yogurt and honey.

Self-Catering

For a good variety of (relatively expensive) fixings to prepare meals yourself, try minimart **Hipermaxi** (cnr 21 de Mayo & Florida). **Supermercado Sur Fidalga** (Plaza Blacutt) is the cheapest option for groceries, but **IC Norte** (Av Busch at third anillo) is the biggest and best supermarket in the city, selling all those foods you miss from home as well as having an extensive food court. **Naturalia** (www.naturalia.com.bo; Independencia 452) organic grocery store has a wide selection of locally produced healthy goodies and a small café.

Drinking

The hippest nightspots are along Av San Martin, between the second and third *anillos* (rings) in **Barrio Equipetrol**, a B$10 to $B15 taxi ride from the center. Hot spots change frequently so it's best to dress to impress, cruise the *piranhar* (strip; literally 'to go piranha fishing') and see what catches your fancy. Cover charges run from B$20 to B$70 and drinks are expensive; most places start selling drinks between 6pm and 9pm but don't warm up until 11pm; they then continue until sunrise.

If you don't want to pay entry fees to the discos, at weekends a young beach crowd gathers with their cars at Río Pira'i during the day, banging out unbelievably loud music from their gigantic car-boot speakers, while drinking beer, dancing and chatting till late. The area is potentially unsafe at other times though. Near the university, Av Busch is lined with places catering to more serious, mostly male, drinkers with less ready cash.

Irish Pub
IRISH PUB

(Plaza 24 de Septiembre) On the east side of the plaza this place is something of a second home to travelers in Santa Cruz, and has pricey beers, delicious soups and comfort food plus tasty local specialties. It serves breakfast, lunch and dinner, though most people while away the hours away drinking beer, relaxing and watching the goings-on in the plaza below.

Lorca
BAR

(Moreno 20; ⊙8am-late) A meeting place for the city's arty crowd and those loving diversity, Lorca is one of the most innovative and happening places in town. It's perfect for a chilled caipirinha or mojito while you enjoy the live music (B$20 cover). Before the music starts, short films are screened. There is also an art gallery in the back, right next to the little theater.

Clapton's Blues Bar
THEME BAR

(cnr Ballivián & Cochabamba; admission B$20; ⊙Sat & Sun) A dark jazz-and-blues bar with local bands playing till very late to a sparse drinking audience. There can be good jazz here (and very bad rock), so check what's playing by asking at the bar.

Bar El Tapekuá
LOUNGE

(cnr La Paz & Ballivián; ⊙from 7:30pm Wed-Sat) This casual yet upscale Swiss- and Bolivian-owned place serves good, earthy food and has live music most nights (B$15 to B$20 cover).

Kiwi's
BAR

(Bolívar 208; snacks B$28-46) A laid-back place where you can sip on *bebidas extremas* served in 2L receptacles, or puff away on *shisha* (Arabic flavored-tobacco pipes). Great snacks and sandwiches, too, all served with their trademark *papas kiwi.*

☆ Entertainment

For movie schedules and other venues, see the daily newspapers *El Mundo* and *El Deber.*

Cinecenter
CINEMA

(☑free phone 900-770077; cinema admission B$30-50) Modern mall with a food court, trendy shops and a 12-screen US-style cinema that shows all the latest Hollywood releases. This place has rapidly become the place to be seen in Santa Cruz, to the detriment of a number of smaller cinemas and art-houses that have closed as a result.

Eleguá
PERFORMING ARTS

(Libertad 651) During the week this is a Cuban cultural-center-cum-bar-cum-dance-school (it depends which day you visit!). At weekends it metamorphoses into a groovy Latino disco where you can swing your thing to the latest samba sounds.

El Rincón Salteño
TRADITIONAL MUSIC

(26 de Febrero, at Charagua; ⊙from 10pm Fri-Sun) Traditional *peñas* (folk-music programs) are scarce in modern Santa Cruz, but this is an excellent choice. Positioned on the second *anillo,* there's a great variety of musical styles, from Argentine guitarists to Cuban village drummers, local singers and dancers in costume.

🔒 Shopping

Wood carvings made from the tropical hardwoods *morado* and the more expensive *guayacán* (from B$150 for a nice piece) are unique to the Santa Cruz area. Relief carvings on *tari* nuts are also interesting and make good, portable souvenirs. Locals also make beautiful macramé *llicas* (root-fiber bags).

Av René Moreno is a good place for souvenir shopping. Be aware that prices are much higher here than in La Paz for llama and alpaca wool goods.

Artecampo
ARTS & CRAFTS

(Salvatierra 407; ⊙9am-12:30pm & 3:30-7pm Mon-Sat, 9am-12:30pm Sun) The best place to find fine *artesanías* (locally handcrafted items), this store provides an outlet for the work of 1000 rural *cruceña* women and their families. The truly inspired and innovative pieces include leatherwork, hammocks, weavings, handmade paper, greeting cards and lovely natural-material lamp shades.

Paseo Artesanal La Recova
ARTS & CRAFTS

(Libertad; ⊙8am-8pm Mon-Sat) An alleyway packed with little stores selling both authentic and fabricated handicrafts at reasonable prices.

ℹ Information

Roughly oval in shape, Santa Cruz is laid out in *anillos* (rings), which form concentric circles around the city center, and *radiales* (spokes) that connect the rings. Radial 1, the road to Viru-Viru airport, runs roughly north–south; the *radiales* progress clockwise up to Radial 27.

Within the *primer anillo,* Junín is the street with the most banks, ATMs and internet cafes, and Av René Moreno is lined with souvenir stores and bars. To the northwest of the center, Av San Martin, otherwise known as Barrio Equipetrol, is the main area for the party crowd, being full of bars and clubs.

Dangers & Annoyances

Beware of bogus immigration officials and carefully check the credentials of anyone who demands to see your passport or other ID. No real police officer will ever ask to see your documents in the street; be especially wary of 'civilian' police who will most certainly turn out to be fraudsters.

Emergency

Tourist police (☑800-140099; north side of Plaza 24 de Septiembre)

Immigration

Migración (☑333-2136; ⊙8:30am-4:30pm Mon-Fri) Migración is north of the center, opposite the zoo entrance. Visa extensions are available here. The most reliable office is at Viru-Viru airport.

Internet Access

There are numerous internet places along Junín and wi-fi in all but the very cheapest *residenciales* (simple accommodations), so you will have no problem getting online.

Laundry

Efficient wash-and-dry places offer same-day service (with drop-off before noon) for around B$12 per kilo including **Lavandería La Paz** (La Paz 42; ⊙Mon-Sat).

Medical Services

Clínica Foianini (☑336-2211; Av Irala 468) Hospital used by embassies, but be aware that some travelers have reported unnecessary tests and being required to stay for longer than is strictly necessary.

Clínica Japonesa (☑346-2038) On the third *anillo,* east side; recommended for inexpensive and professional medical treatment.

Farmacia América (Libertad 345) A good pharmacy; efficient and inexpensive.

Money

Cash advances are available at most major banks, and ATMs line Junín and most major intersections. The easiest place to change cash or traveler's checks (2% to 3% commission) is **Casa de Cambio Alemán** (east side of Plaza 24 de Septiembre). Street money changers shout *'¡Dolares!'* in your face on the main plaza, but make sure you know the value of what you are changing.

Post Office

Main post office (Junín; ⊙8am-8pm Mon-Sat, 9-11:30am Sun)

Telephone

You can have fun using public telephone boxes which come in a variety of shapes – anything from toucans to jaguars suspended mid-growl. Better rates are found at phone centers, such as the main **Entel office** (Warnes 82), and internet telecom stores along Bolívar that offer cheap international calls. The **Punto Entel** (Bolívar) office near the plaza has landlines. Local cellphone rates are very cheap and chips already charged with credit can be bought at **Tonytel** (Junín 320).

Tourist Information

Online information about the city of Santa Cruz and the main attractions of the Oriente region can be found at www.santacruz-online.net.

Casa de Gobierno (☑333-3248; Palacio Prefectural, Plaza 24 de Septiembre; ⊙8am-8pm Mon-Fri) A small information kiosk on the north

---

TRANS-CHIQUITANO TRAIN

No longer the harrowing journey that earned this line the nickname 'Death Train,' the route from Santa Cruz to Quijarro via San José de Chiquitos and Roboré (for Santiago de Chiquitos) is now plied by three different types of train. It's a glorious journey through forest, scrub and Pantanal teeming with wildlife, though you might be advised to take mosquito repellent. Most operate *cama* (sleeper) and *semi-cama* classes with comfortable reclining seats.

The slowest and most frequent is the Tren Regional. It departs Santa Cruz Monday, Thursday and Saturday at 11:45am, passing through San José de Chiquitos (semi-cama/cama B$23/53; 6:28pm), Roboré (B$34/77; 11:06pm) and arriving at Quijarro (B$52/115; 6:20am) the following day. The return departs Quijarro on Monday, Wednesday and Friday at 11am, passing through Roboré (5:57pm), San José de Chiquitos (11:08am) and arrives at Santa Cruz at 6:38am.

Next in line in terms of quality is the Expreso Oriental which operates a single comfortable Super Pullman class. It departs Santa Cruz on Monday, Wednesday and Friday at 4pm, passing through San José de Chiquitos (B$58; 9:50pm), Roboré (B$85; 1:47am) and arriving at Quijarro (B$127; 8am) the following day. The return departs Quijarro on Tuesday, Thursday and Sunday at 4pm, passing through Roboré (9:11pm), San José de Chiquitos (1:53am) and arrives at Santa Cruz at 8am.

The fastest, comfiest and priciest is the Ferrobus. It departs Santa Cruz on Tuesday, Thursday and Sunday at 6:30pm, passing through San José de Chiquitos (B$205; 11:39am), Roboré (B$288; 2:58am) and arriving at Quijarro (B$257; 7:56am) the following day. The return departs Quijarro on Monday, Wednesday and Friday at 6:30pm, passing through Roboré (11:24pm), San José de Chiquitos (2:31am) and arrives at Santa Cruz at 7:55am.

There is rarely a problem getting a seat from Santa Cruz or Quijarro, but if joining the service midway along the line then tickets are best bought in advance – only a limited number of seats are allotted for these stations. Hot and cold food and drinks are available during daylight hours, and a constant stream of vendors pass through the carriages selling all manner of goods.

side of the plaza is good for quick inquiries, but has little or no printed information.

Fundación Amigos de la Naturaleza (FAN; ☑355-6800; www.fan-bo.org; Carretera a Samaipata, Km 7.5; ⊗8am-4:30pm Mon-Thu, 8am-2pm Fri) Though no longer in charge of the parks, FAN is still the best contact for national parks information. It's west of town (micro 44) off the old Cochabamba road.

Infotur (☑336-9681; Sucre; ⊗8am-noon & 3-7pm) Within the Museo de Arte Contemporáneo, this office is very well stocked with information for the whole region and the rest of the country.

SERNAP (Servicio Nacional de Áreas Protegidas; www.sernap.gob.bo; Calle 9 Oeste, Barrio Equipetrol) For information on national parks.

❶ Getting There & Away

Air

Viru-Viru International Airport (VVI; ☑338-5000), 15km north of the center, handles some domestic and most international flights. The smaller **Aeropuerto El Trompillo** (☑351-1010), in the southeast of the city, receives the majority of the domestic flights.

TAM (☑353-2639) flies direct to La Paz daily, stopping en route in Cochabamba from where there are connections to Sucre. Flights to Tarija leave most days if there is sufficient demand and morning flights to Trinidad depart four times a week. **TAM Mercosur** (☑339-1999; cnr of La Riva & Velasco) flies to Asunción every day with connections to Buenos Aires, Santiago de Chile and several Brazilian cities. **Aerocon** (☑351-1200; Aeropuerto El Trompillo) flies several times daily to Trinidad with onward connections to Cobija and Riberalta from El Trompillo airport.

American Airlines (☑334-1314; Beni 167) flies direct daily to Miami in the morning, with a second evening flight from Thursday to Sunday. **Aerolíneas Argentinas** (☑333-9776; Junín 22) flies several times a week to Buenos Aires.

Bus, Micro & Shared Taxi

The full-service **bimodal terminal** (☑348-8482; terminal fee B$3), the combined long-distance bus and train station, is 1.5km east of the center, just before the third anillo at the end of Av Brasil.

The main part of the terminal is for flotas (long-distance buses) and the train; on the other side of the tunnel is the micro (minibus) terminal for regional services. International routes have offices at the left-hand end of the main terminal as you enter. Most flotas leave in the morning before 10am and in the evening after 6pm. Taking a series of connecting micros or taxis can be a faster, if more complicated way, of reaching your destination, rather than waiting all day for an evening flota.

To the Jesuit missions and Chiquitania, flotas leave in the morning and early evening (7pm to 9pm). Micros run throughout the day, every two hours or so, but only go as far as Concepción.

Smaller micros and trufis (collective taxis or minibuses that follow a set route) to regional destinations in Santa Cruz department leave regularly from outside the old bus terminal and less regularly from the micro platforms at the bimodal terminal. To Buena Vista (B$23, two hours), they wait on Izozog (Isoso), near the old bus terminal. To Samaipata (B$30, three hours), trufis leave on the opposite side of Av Cañoto, about two blocks from the old bus terminal. To Vallegrande (B$60, six hours) trufi departures are from the Plazuela Oruro on the third anillo.

DESTINATION	COST (B$)	DURATION (HR)
Camiri	30	5-6
Cochabamba	old road 54-110; new road 66-120	8-10
Concepción	35	7
La Paz	old road 85-170; new road 95-180	15-23
Quijarro	70	12
San Javier	30	6
San José de Chiquitos	50	5
San Matías	150	20
Sucre	80-110	15-25
Tarija	90-115	24
Trinidad	53-125	8-10
Vallegrande	35	7-8
Yacuiba	51-110	15

Train

Trains depart from the bimodal terminal bound for Quijarro and Yacuiba. For access to the platform you need to buy a platform ticket and show your passport to the platform guard.

The rail service to Yacuiba on the Argentine border (via Villamontes; the connection point for buses to Paraguay) departs at 3:30pm on Thursday (B$47, 16½ hours) and returns on Friday at 5pm.

❶ Getting Around

To/From the Airport

Handy minibuses leave Viru-Viru for the center (B$3, 30 minutes) when flights arrive, or take micros 40, 41, 42 and 55, which run between the airport and the center. Micros to the airport leave every 20 minutes starting at 5:30am from Av Cañoto at stops along the first anillo. Taxis for up to four people cost B$70 from Viru-Viru or B$30 from the more central El Trompillo.

To/From the Bus & Train Station

The bimodal bus-train station is beyond easy walking distance but *micros 2, 4, 11, 41* and *85* run between the terminal and the center. Expect to pay B$10 per person for a taxi.

Bus

Santa Cruz' system of city *micros* (B$1.70) connects the transportation terminals and all the *anillos* with the center. *Micros 17* and *18* circulate around the first *anillo*. To reach Av San Martin in Barrio Equipetrol, take *micro 23* from anywhere on Vallegrande. A *Guía de Micros* documenting all the city routes is available from bookstores and kiosks (B$25 to B$50).

Car

Most rent-a-car companies also have offices at the airport.

American Rent-a-Car (☏333-7376; Av Suárez Arana 3230)

Avis Rent-a-Car (☏343-3939; www.avis.com.bo; Carretera al Norte, Km 3.5)

Barron's Rent-a-Car (☏342-1060; www.rentacarbolivia.com; Av Alemana 50)

Localiza Rent-a-Car (☏341-4343; www.localiza bolivia.com; second anillo cnr Beni)

Taxi

Taxis are very cheap but there is no rigid price structure. Typically the price is higher if you are in a group, are carrying lots of luggage or wish to travel after 10pm, and drivers will quote a fee that they consider fair for the journey. If you think it is too much refuse and try the next one: there are plenty to choose from. Typically a trip for one person within the first *anillo* during the day is about B$10, rising to B$15 if you stray to the second *anillo*. Agree on your price in advance to avoid arguments.

Buena Vista

☏3 / POP 13,300

Despite the presence of two hulking cellphone masts overlooking the plaza, Buena Vista is a nice little town two hours (103km) northwest of Santa Cruz, serving as an ideal staging point for trips into Parque Nacional Amboró's forested lowland section. Though most foreigners prefer Samaipata for national park exploration, Buena Vista has some of the best places to view wildlife, observe birds and see local traditions. The downside is a sweatier, more humid climate.

◉ Sights & Activities

Iglesia de los Santos Desposorios   CHURCH
Buena Vista's Jesuit mission was founded in 1694 as the fifth mission in the Viceroyalty of Peru, but in its current form dates from 1767. When the Jesuits were expelled from Bolivia later that year, the administration of the church passed to the bishop of Santa Cruz. Although the building is deteriorating, it has a lovely classic form, but you'd have to be a brave soul to scale the precarious ladder to the bell tower for views of the plaza.

Río Surutú & El Cairo   OUTDOORS
Río Surutú is a popular excursion for locals, and there's a pleasant sandy beach ideal for picnics, swimming and camping during the dry season. From Buena Vista it's an easy 3km walk to the river bend nearest town. The opposite bank is the boundary of Parque Nacional Amboró.

An even better swimming hole is near **El Cairo**, which is an hour's walk from town. To get there, head downhill from the plaza past the *alcaldía* (town hall) and follow the unpaved road as it curves to the right. About 2km from town, take the left fork and cross over a bridge. After passing El Cairo, on your right, keep going until you reach the river.

✸ Festivals & Events

The local fiesta, **Día de los Santos Desposorios** (26 November), features bullfights, food stalls and general merrymaking. Culinary festivals include the **Chocolate Festival** (last Sunday in January), the **Coffee Festival** (third Sunday in April) and the **Rice Festival** (early May) after the harvest.

🛏 Sleeping

Hotel Flora & Fauna   CABIN $$$
(☏7104-3706; amboroadventures@hotmail.com; s/d all-inclusive B$490/980) British ornithologist/entomologist Robin Clarke runs this modern, utilitarian collection of cabins. Pluses include wildlife-viewing platforms, an extensive book exchange and guided walks (for guests only) from B$70. Access is by car/moto-taxi (B$20/15) from Buena Vista. Book in advance.

Buena Vista Hotel   RESORT $$
(☏339-1080; www.buenavistahotel.com.bo; s/d/ste B$300/350/450; ✳@☒) A glorious range of suites, cabins and rooms set in gorgeous gardens around a refreshing pool. There is something for everyone in this, the best hotel within walking distance of the center. The restaurant is top class, too.

Parque Nacional Amboró (Buena Vista Section)

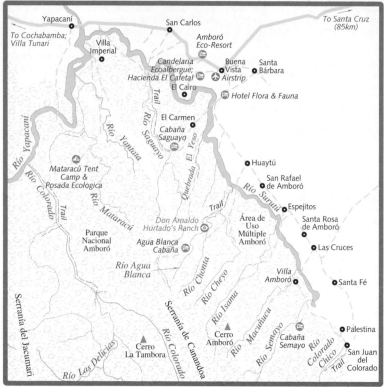

Amboró Eco-Resort
RESORT $$

(☎932-2048, in Santa Cruz 3-342-2372; s/d/ste B$210/280/600; ❋ ☎) A 20-minute walk outside of town, this resort is surrounded by its own tropical forest, complete with walking paths and fenced-in forest animals. Amenities include a swim-up bar, a sauna and a disco. It's not the world's quietest place, but it's fun if you're with children. The resort also operates Mataracú Tent Camp.

La Casona
PENSION $

(☎932-2083; western cnr of plaza; s/d B$70/120, without bathroom per person B$50) This is a colorful place on the plaza, with a friendly owner and a nice patio with sagging hammocks. The rooms are decked out in pastel shades, have good beds and a floor fan.

Residencial Nadia
PENSION $

(☎932-2049; Sevilla 186; s/d B$60/100) Just off the main square, the spacious rooms at this family home surround a patio. There are firm beds and the owner is a good source of park information. All rooms have fans.

✖ Eating

A few places are dotted around the plaza, but given the proximity to the national park you should boycott anything that offers wild game.

La Plaza
INTERNATIONAL $$$

(north side of plaza; mains B$38-80; ⊙closed Mon) By far the best eating in town, La Plaza serves a variety of beef, fish and chicken dishes in rustic, ranch house–style surroundings. This is a good place to pig out if you are back from roughing it in the park.

La Cantina Tex Mex
MEXICAN $$$

(north side of plaza; mains B$15-65) With its tacos and tequilas, this wannabe Mexican bar is a little out of place in lazy Buena Vista, but the food isn't bad at all. There is a nightly happy hour from 7pm to 8pm but don't expect dancing on the tables.

ℹ Information

There is no tourist office at the time of writing but there is an extremely useful online resource, www.buenavista.com.bo. For information on Parque Nacional Amboró, visit **SERNAP** (☏932-2055; www.sernap.gob.bo; ⊘7am-7pm), a block south of the plaza, where you can pick up an entry permit and inquire about current park regulations and accommodations options if you are lucky enough to find it manned.

There's no bank or ATM here, so bring cash from elsewhere. If you are desperate, a **Moneygram office** (⊘8:30am-noon & 2:30-6pm Mon-Fri, 8:30am-noon Sat) on the street corner one block north of the plaza can wire money from abroad. An acceptable internet connection is available at **Punto Viva** (per hr B$4; ⊘8am-10pm) just off the southwest corner of the plaza.

ℹ Getting There & Away

From Santa Cruz, shared taxis (B$23, two hours) leave for Yapacaní from the *micro* side of the bimodal terminal and behind the old long-distance bus terminal. Make it clear that you want to get off at Buena Vista. Returning taxis cruise around the plaza with horns blaring in search of passengers.

Parque Nacional & Área de Uso Múltiple Amboró

This 430,000-hectare park lies in a unique geographical position at the confluence of three distinct ecosystems: the Amazon Basin, the Chaco and the Andes.

The park was originally created in 1973 as the Reserva de Vida Silvestre Germán Busch, with an area of 180,000 hectares. In 1984, due to the efforts of British zoologist Robin Clarke and Bolivian biologist Noel Kempff Mercado, it was given national park status and in 1990 was expanded to 630,000 hectares. In late 1995, however, amid controversy surrounding *campesino* (subsistence farmer) colonization inside park boundaries, it was pared down to its current size.

The park's range of habitats means that both highland and lowland species are found here. Mammals include elusive spectacled bears, jaguars, tapirs, peccaries and various monkeys, while more than 800 species of birds have been documented. The park is the stronghold of the endangered horned curassow, known as the unicorn bird.

BUENA VISTA AREA

Access to the eastern part of the reserve requires crossing over the Río Surutú, either in a vehicle or on foot. Depending on the rainfall and weather, the river may be anywhere from knee- to waist-deep. Inexperienced hikers should not attempt any of the treks in the park without a guide.

RÍO MACUÑUCU

The Río Macuñucu route is the most popular into the Área de Uso Múltiple Amboró and begins at **Las Cruces**, 35km southeast of Buena Vista (taxi B$30). From there it's 7km to the Río Surutú, which you must drive or wade across; just beyond the opposite bank you'll reach **Villa Amboró**, where there is a community-run **campsite** (☏Adrian Rodríguez 7368-6784, Hugo Rojas 7368-6784; per person B$150) with good facilities. Villagers may charge an entrance fee to any tourist who passes their community en route to Macuñucu, regardless of whether you intend to stay there or not – avoid unpleasantness and pay.

From here a popular trek runs to the banks of the **Río Macuñucu** and follows its course through thick forest. After four hours or so you pass through a narrow canyon, which confines hikers to the river, and a little later you'll reach a large rock overhang accommodating up to 10 campers. Beyond here the trek becomes increasingly difficult and the terrain more rugged as you head toward some beautiful waterfalls and a second campsite. Take a guide if doing the full hike.

RÍO ISAMA & CERRO AMBORÓ

The Río Isama route turns off at the village of **Espejitos**, 28km southeast of Buena Vista, and provides access to the base of 1300m Cerro Amboró, the bulbous peak for which the park is named. It's possible to climb to the summit, but it is a difficult trek and a guide is essential.

MATARACÚ

From near Yapacaní, on the main Cochabamba road, a 4WD track heads south across the Río Yapacaní into the northern reaches of the Área de Uso Múltiple Amboró and, after a rough 18km, rolls up to Amboró Eco-Resort's **Mataracú Tent Camp** (☏932-2048, in Santa Cruz 3-342-2372; per person incl breakfast & lunch B$700), which has palm huts capped by thatched roofs, and *cabañas* on stilts. There is also the community-run **Posada Ecológica** (☏7167-4582; dm B$35, d B$50), which offers all-you-can-eat meals (breakfast/lunch

AMBORÓ COMMUNITY PROJECTS

The location of Parque Nacional Amboró is a mixed blessing; although it's conveniently accessible to visitors, it also lies practically within spitting distance of Santa Cruz and squarely between the old and new Cochabamba–Santa Cruz highways. Considering that even the remote parks of the Amazon Basin are coming under threat, Amboró feels 'people pressure' more than most.

When Parque Nacional Amboró was created in 1973, its charter included a clause forbidding settlement and resource exploitation. Unfortunately for naturalists and conservationists, hunters, loggers and *campesino* (subsistence farmer) settlers continued to pour in – many of them displaced from the Chapare region by the US Drug Enforcement Agency. By 1996, with conflicts increasing over the park, it was redesignated as the Área de Uso Múltiple Amboró, which effectively opened it up for settlement.

This reducing of the park's protection status necessitated a change in tactics by local NGOs and conservation groups keen to avoid the complete destruction of the natural treasures of the region, but also fully aware of the needs of the human population. As a result, a number of responsible and sustainable 'community projects' have sprung up in the area, using tourism as a means of generating income for locals without them having to exploit their natural resources. The following are some of the more interesting of these projects:

Candelaria Ecoalbergue (☎7100-6869; per person B$150) In the community of Candelaria 3km south of Buena Vista, this place manages comfortable four-person cabins and offers forest walks in the surrounding area. Perhaps more interesting is the opportunity to observe local craftsmen practicing the arts of weaving *jipijapa* and whittling *tacuara* (bamboo) into all manner of useful objects.

Hacienda El Cafetal (☎935-2067; s/d Mon-Fri B$150/200, s/d Sat & Sun B$250/300, 5-person cabañas B$500; ✹✹) Set up to support Bolivian coffee growers and their families; the accommodations are good, with stylish, self-catering *cabañas* (cabins) and suites, all with good views. You can go around the plantations and see how coffee is produced, taste different types of the strong black stuff, and then, caffeine-pumped, ride horses and go bird-watching.

Refugio Volcánes (☎337-2042; www.refugiovolcanes.net; per person B$500) Ecofriendly *cabañas* with hot showers in the breathtaking Los Volcánes region 4km off the Santa Cruz–Samaipata road at Bermejo. Transportation from the road is offered, as well as guided hikes through the wonderfully wild landscapes.

B$10/15) and can be booked through any agency in Buena Vista. This is the only SERNAP *cabaña* accessible by motor vehicle; however, crossing the Río Yapacaní may be a problem except in the driest part of the year.

SAMAIPATA AREA

Samaipata sits just outside the southern boundary of the Área de Uso Múltiple Amboró and provides the best access point for the Andean section of the park. There's no real infrastructure, or any public facilities, in this area.

The best guides to the region are available in Samaipata. The road uphill from there ends at a small cabin, and then it's a four-hour walk to a camping spot near the boundary between the primary forest, giant ferns and Andean cloud forest. From this point, you can continue an hour further into the park.

MAIRANA AREA

From Mairana, it's 7km uphill along a walking track (or take a taxi) to **La Yunga**, where there's a community-run guest hut and a FAN office. It's in a particularly lush region of the Área de Uso Múltiple Amboró, surrounded by tree ferns and other cloud-forest vegetation. From La Yunga, a 16km forest traverse connects with the main road near Samaipata.

To enter the park here, visit the guard post at the south end of the soccer field in La Yunga. Access to Mairana is by *micro* or taxi from Samaipata.

COMARAPA AREA

Northwest of Comarapa, 4km toward Cochabamba, is a little-used entrance to the Área de Uso Múltiple Amboró. After the road crosses a pass between a hill and a ridge with a telephone tower, look for the minor road turning off to the northeast at the settlement of **Khara Huasi**. This road leads uphill to verdant stands of cloud forest, which blanket the peaks.

Other worthwhile visits in this area include the 36-sided **Pukara de Tuquipaya**, a set of pre-Inca ruins on the summit of **Cerro Comanwara**, 1.5km outside of Comarapa; and the colonial village of **Pulquina Arriba**, several kilometers east of Comarapa.

🛏 Sleeping

Inside the park are five wilderness *cabañas* (around B$40 per person per day). For bookings and information, contact SERNAP. The *cabañas* are very basic, so you'll need your own sleeping bag, food and drinking water. The most popular and accessible *cabaña* is the one on the Río Macuñucu. It's 4km upstream, with a sleeping loft and rudimentary cooking facilities. Other *cabañas* can be found on the lower Río Semayo, above the Río Mataracú, on the Río Agua Blanca and on the lower Río Saguayo.

❶ Getting There & Away

By far the easiest and safest way to visit the park is by guided tour with one of the recommended tour agencies in Santa Cruz. To do it yourself, a *micro* heads south from Buena Vista through Huaytú, San Rafael de Amboró, Espejitos, Santa Rosa de Amboró, Las Cruces and Santa Fé. This boundary provides access to several rough routes and tracks that lead southwest into the interior, following tributaries of the Río Surutú. To really probe into the park though you will need a 4WD vehicle and a good deal of previous experience in jungle trekking. Note that all access to the park along this road will require a crossing of the Río Surutú.

Santa Cruz to Samaipata

The spectacular route from Santa Cruz to Samaipata passes a number of attractions that are worth a brief stop. Any *micro* or *trufi* running this route passes by the places of interest mentioned in this section.

Los Espejillos Community Project (admission B$5) has several waterfalls and natural swimming pools, with lovely, clean and refreshing water sparkling over the polished black rock that characterizes the area. It stands across the Río Pira'i 18km north of the highway. Get off just beyond San José and walk or hitch north along the 4WD

track, following the signposts. Basic accommodation is available at the **Tacuaracú community** (per person B$20), which oversees the project.

Bermejo, 85km southwest of Santa Cruz, is marked by a hulking slab of red rock known as **El Portón del Diablo**, which is flaking and chipping into nascent natural arches. A great place to stay here is the pleasant eco/agrotouristic organic farm **Ginger's Paradise** (☑6777-4772; www.gingers paradise.com; r per person, volunteer/full board B$70/100) surrounded by virgin forest and run by an ex-rockstar. It's a hit with birdwatchers, offers reductions for working volunteers and is famed for its home grown organic meals.

Laguna Volcán is an intriguing crater lake 6km up the hill north of Bermejo. A lovely **walking track** climbs from the lake to the crater rim; it begins at the point directly across the lake from the end of the road. The beautiful nearby region known as **Los Volcánes** features an otherworldly landscape of tropical sugarloaf hills.

A turnoff to the community of Bella Vista, 100km from Santa Cruz on the Samaipata road leads to the **Codo de los Andes**. In this dramatically beautiful area famed for its giant ferns and monkey-tail cacti, there is great trekking to be had, as well as an excellent community-run **lodge** (☑944-6293; per person B$90, incl meals B$120).

Just 20km short of Samaipata lies **Las Cuevas** (admission B$10). If you walk upstream on a clear path away from the road, you'll reach two lovely waterfalls that spill into eminently swimmable lagoons bordered by sandy beaches. About 100m beyond here is a third waterfall, the biggest of the set. You can also camp here for a small fee.

Samaipata

☑3 / POP 9750 / ELEV 1650M (5413FT)

Samaipata has developed into one of the top gringo-trail spots over the last few years. This sleepy village in the foothills of the Cordillera Oriental is brimming with foreign-run, stylish hostels and restaurants. Visitors flock to see the pre-Inca site of El Fuerte, some in search of a dose of the ancient site's supposed mystical energy, while increasingly it is the main jumping-off point for forays to Parque Nacional Amboró. But it's not just foreigners who come up here; Samaipata is a popular weekend

Samaipata

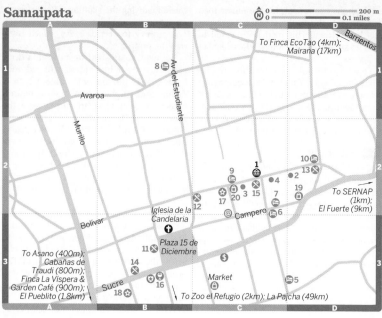

Samaipata

◉ Sights
1 Museo Arqueológico C2

✛ Activities, Courses & Tours
2 Jukumari Tours D2
3 Michael Blendinger
   Tours C2
4 Roadrunners C2

🛏 Sleeping
5 El Jardín D3
6 Hostal Andoriña C2
7 Hotel Siles C2
8 La Posada del Sol B1
9 Palacio del Ajedrez C2
10 Residencial Don
   Jorge D2

✕ Eating
11 La Chakana B3
12 La Ranita C2
13 Latina Café D2
14 Tierra Libre B3
15 Zentro Café Cultural C2

🍷 Drinking
16 La Boéme B3

✦ Entertainment
17 Disco Ché Wilson C2
18 Melody B3

🛍 Shopping
19 ASOPEC D2
20 Mucho Mundo C2

destination for *cruceños*, too. The Quechua name, meaning 'Rest in the Highlands,' could hardly be more appropriate.

◉ Sights

El Fuerte   RUINS
(admission B$50, guides per group of up to 6 B$75; ⊙9am-5pm) The mystical site of El Fuerte exudes such pulling power that visitors from all over the world make their way to

Samaipata just to climb the hill and see the remains of this pre-Inca site.

Designated in 1998 as a Unesco World Heritage site, El Fuerte occupies a hilltop about 10km from the village and offers breathtaking views across the rugged transition zone between the Andes and low-lying areas further east. There are two observation towers that allow visitors to view the ruins from above. Allow at least two hours to fully explore the complex, and take sunscreen and a hat with you. There is a kiosk with food and water next to the ticket office.

First occupied by diverse ethnic groups as early as 2000 BC, it wasn't until 1470 AD that the Incas, the most famous tenants, first arrived. By the time the Spanish came and looted the site in the 1600s it was already deserted. The purpose of El Fuerte has long been debated, and there are several theories. The conquistadors, in a distinctly combative frame of mind, assumed the site had been used for defense, hence its Spanish name, 'the fort.' In 1832 French naturalist Alcides d'Orbigny proclaimed that the pools and parallel canals had been used for washing gold. In 1936 German anthropologist Leo Pucher described it as an ancient temple to the serpent and the jaguar; his theory, incorporating worship of the sun and moon, is now the most accepted. Recently the place has gained a New Age following; some have claimed that it was a take-off and landing ramp for ancient spacecraft.

There are no standing buildings, but the remains of 500 dwellings have been discovered in the immediate vicinity and ongoing excavation reveals more every day. The main site, which is almost certainly of religious significance, is a 100m-long stone slab with a variety of sculpted features: seats, tables, a conference circle, troughs, tanks, conduits and *hornecinos* (niches), which are believed to have held idols. A total of seven steps leading up to the main temple represent the seven phases of the moon. Zoomorphic designs on the slab include raised reliefs of pumas and jaguars (representing power) and numerous serpents (representing fertility). *Chicha* and blood were poured into the snake designs as an offering to Pachamama (Mother Earth). Sadly, these designs are unprotected from the elements and erosion is making them harder to discern with every passing year.

About 300m down an obscure track behind the main ruin is **Chincana**, a sinister hole in the ground that appears all the more menacing by the concealing vegetation and sloping ground around it. It's almost certainly natural, but three theories have emerged about how it might have been used: that it served as a water-storage cistern; that it functioned as an escape-proof prison; and that it was part of a subterranean communication system between the main ruin and its immediate surroundings.

On the approach to the site look out for **La Cabeza del Inca**, apparently a natural rock formation that bears a startling resemblance to the head of an Inca Warrior, so much so that many insist it is a manmade project that was abandoned halfway through. Watch too for condors soaring on thermals overhead.

Taxis for the round-trip, including a two-hour stop at the ruins, charge B$80 for up to four people from Samaipata. Better yet, taxi up and walk back down. Gluttons for punishment who prefer to walk up should follow the main highway back toward Santa Cruz for 3.5km and turn right at the sign pointing uphill. From here it's a scenic 5km to the summit. Guided tours from Samaipata start from about B$100 per person.

Museo Arqueológico   MUSEUM
(Bolívar; admission B$5; ⊙8:30am-noon & 2-6pm Mon-Fri, 8:30am-4pm Sat-Sun) Samaipata's small archaeological museum makes an interesting visit, but offers little explanation of El Fuerte. It does have a few Tiwanaku artifacts and some local pottery. If you buy your admission to the ruins here you get into the museum for free.

Zoo el Refugio   ZOO
(☑944-6169; admission B$20; ⊙8am-6pm) This charming and responsible little zoo is actually a refuge for rescued animals. The zoo accepts volunteers who can lodge for free in exchange for their labor, and there is an attractive wooded camping area if you fancy spending a night among the animals. Horses are available for hire for B$25 per hour.

☞ Tours

Several agencies organize trips to nearby attractions and almost every hotel runs its own tours. Local taxi syndicates also run transportation to many of the local attractions and rates are very reasonable, though not up for negotiation.

Amboró Tours is the most established of the Santa Cruz–based agencies, but the Samaipata office is open only sporadically.

Michael Blendinger Tours   ECOTOUR
(☑944-6227; www.discoveringbolivia.com; Bolívar) The best for biologist-run orchid, birding and full-moon tours, offered in English and German.

Jukumari Tours   TOUR
(☑7262-7202; Bolívar) An excellent locally run agency; in addition to the local attractions

it offers packages to the Che Trail and the Jesuit Missions Circuit.

Roadrunners
GUIDED TOUR

(☎944-6294; Bolívar) Visit Olaf and Frank at German- and English-speaking Roadrunners for guided hikes to Amboró's waterfalls, cloud forests and El Fuerte.

🛏 Sleeping

You're spoiled for choice when it comes to accommodations in Samaipata. From basic dorms to lush campsites, rustic hostels and organic farms, it's all here. Excellent digs can be found in central hostels from around B$50 per person. For cabins outside town ask at Michael Blendinger Tours for a series of options to fit all budgets.

TOP CHOICE La Posada del Sol
HOTEL $

(☎7211-0628; www.laposadadelsol.net; Zona Barrio Nuevo; dm/s/d B$60/120/140; ❄) With hotel quality and hostel prices this is the best value in town. Modern, tastefully furnished en suite rooms have high-quality Egyptian cotton sheets on every bed. Rooms are set around attractive gardens and have spectacular views, and there's a great new restaurant, the **Luna Verde**. Owners Trent and Rosario have thought of everything, right down to the close personal attention they offer guests. Three blocks uphill north of the plaza.

El Pueblito
RESORT $$$

(☎944-6386; www.elpueblitoresort.com; s/d B$210/420; ❄) This four-star resort is arranged like a little village complete with its own church and plaza. Each room is uniquely styled after a village shop and positively dripping with creativity. There's a swimming pool (B$30 for nonguests), *artesanía* shops and the resort is set on a hillside with marvelous views of Samaipata in the valley below. There is even an excellent restaurant-bar, **El Cabildo** (☺Thu-Sun).

🍃 Finca EcoTao
RESORT $$

(☎7462-6871; www.ecoato.org; per person incl full board B$150) On a hillside 4km north of Samaipata, Finca EcoTao is a new ecotourism venture designed to bring man closer to nature. Besides offering delightful accommodation, it provides courses in skills as diverse as construction using natural materials, organic agriculture and yoga, as well as volunteer opportunities. Water filtration systems and solar panels ensure that your visit has a minimal impact on the environment.

🍃 Finca La Víspera
CABINS $

(☎944-6082; www.lavispera.org; campsite with/without own tent B$30/40, cabins per person B$55-80) This relaxing organic farm and retreat is a lovely place on the outskirts of Samaipata. The owners rent horses (B$60 per hour), run courses in esotericism and organize adventurous trips throughout the region. The attractive rooms with communal kitchens, and four self-contained guesthouses (for two to 12 people), enjoy commanding views across the valley. Campsite includes hot showers and kitchen facilities. It's an easy 15-minute walk southwest of the plaza.

Hostal Andoriña
HOSTEL $

(☎944-6333; www.andorinasamaipata.com; Campero; dm/s/d B$45/80/140) Cluttered but characterful, the house and rooms are painted in earthy colors, the beds are comfy and the breakfasts (included in the price) big and healthy. There's a communal room downstairs, with a roaring fire in winter and a *mirador* (lookout) on the top with great views of the valley, plus a decent movie collection to while away rainy days.

El Jardín
HOSTEL $

(☎7311-9461; campsite/per person B$20/35, cupola room B$130) Hippy-style hangout squirreled away in a wild garden in the southeast corner of town. Chilled music, basic digs and a relaxed scene for those who like to take it easy. There is a kitchen for guest use and a pair of unique cupola rooms if you can't abide the idea of a room with corners.

Palacio del Ajedrez
HOSTEL $

(☎944-6196; Bolívar; s/d B$80/140; ❄) Home of the chess club that has created Bolivia's national chess champions. The rooms are reminiscent of student halls, with modern furniture in oranges and blues, and there's a small swimming pool for guests to enjoy.

Cabañas de Traudi
CABINS $

(☎7263-1398; www.traudi.com; s/d B$70/140, cabins per person B$56-70; ❄) This amenable Austrian-run spread southwest of town has ample manicured grounds. It's set up for family-oriented recreation and the swimming pool is open to nonguests for B$25 per person.

Residencial Don Jorge
PENSION $

(☎944-6086; Bolívar 20; s/d/tr B$50/100/150, without bathroom B$40/80/120) Minimalist whitewashed rooms, some with private bathroom and cable TV, set around the standard shady courtyard liberally scattered with hanging oropendola bird nests. Just a short stagger across the road from the Latina Café.

Hotel Siles PENSION $
(944-6408; Campero; s/d B$40/80, without bathroom B$30/60) This neat and tidy little hostel even throws in a basic breakfast for the price. Rooms are simple but well kept and there is even the use of a communal kitchen for those who prefer to cook for themselves.

Eating & Drinking

The cosmopolitan crowd in Samaipata ensures that good eating is never far away. Besides the inventive and frequently excellent hotel restaurants such as Luna Verde at Posada del Sol (p258), El Cabildo at El Pueblito (p258) and the renowned vegan slow food at La Víspera's Garden Café (p258), the following are all good.

TOP CHOICE Latina Café INTERNATIONAL $$
(Bolívar 3; mains B$30-60; dinner Mon-Fri, lunch & dinner Sat & Sun) This bar-restaurant serves some of the best food in town: juicy steaks, saucy pastas, vegetarian delights and gorgeous brownies. The lighting is intimate and the sunsets beautiful. For a real treat try the steak in coca sauce. Happy hour is from 6pm to 7pm.

Tierra Libre INTERNATIONAL $$$
(Sucre 70; mains B$29-62) This place is loved by backpackers for its ample and affordable eats. Top-notch dishes from around the globe are served in a bohemian setting. Veggie meals and exotic Indian concoctions are among the treats on offer and you shouldn't miss the succulent *lomito* (steak sandwich) or tasty Lake Titicaca trout.

Zentro Café Cultural VEGETARIAN $
(Bolívar; mains B$15-30; 8am-2pm & 5-9pm Wed-Sun) Tasty meatless plates will set you up nicely for one of the activities in this cultural center, where you can partake in anything from reflexology and yoga, to dance classes or massage.

La Ranita TEAHOUSE $
(Estudiante; snacks B$6-18; 8am-12.30pm & 3.30-7pm Mon-Sat) Inventive breakfast combos and fresh bread and pastries are on offer in this superb, French-style teahouse.

Asano VEGETARIAN $
(lunch Tue-Sun) Along the road to Finca La Víspera, this Japanese religious sect sells organic vegetables fertilized with divine light. For under B$10 you can be blessed with the 'energy' of the Mahikari Luz Divina – go on, don't be shy.

La Chakana INTERNATIONAL $$$
(Plaza 15 de Diciembre; mains B$30-70) The long-established Chakana, on the west side of the plaza, serves reasonably priced breakfasts, sandwiches, vegetarian meals, excellent pizzas, homemade sweets, cocktails and European specialties. The drawback is the surly and lethargic service.

La Boéme BAR
(south side of plaza; 3pm-2am Wed-Mon) A bumping little bar on the corner of the plaza, this is just what Samaipata's nightlife has been lacking. There's a wide selection of intoxicating cocktails and, if you get the munchies, a chalkboard snack menu that changes daily.

Entertainment

A slice of Santa Cruz teenage nightlife is transported to Samaipata each weekend and revived at the popular **Disco Ché Wilson** (Bolívar). Alternatively try **Melody**, a block southwest from the plaza, which has regular live shows. At least once a month there is a live open-air disco at El Jardín, where rock and salsa play to a mixed, and largely inebriated, crowd.

Shopping

The market is open on Saturday and Sunday. **ASOPEC** (Asociación de Productoras Ecológicas; 2-6pm Mon-Fri) offers *artesanías*, produced and sold by Bolivian women from local communities, with all proceeds going to the makers. Wool, ceramics, soap, candles and even ice cream are on offer. **Mucho Mundo** (Bolívar) sells all kinds of bric-a-brac designed by a group of resident artists.

Information

There are no banks or ATMs in Samaipata so it's best to bring cash. Or draw cash on a credit card with your passport from the Co-operativa Merced just off the main plaza on Calle Sucre.

There is no official tourist office, though many tour companies and hostels can help you with information about the local sites. For reliably unbiased advice check out Samaipata's excellent tourist website www.samaipata.info. **SERNAP** (www.sernap.gob.bo) has an office 1km outside of town on the road to Santa Cruz.

The best internet connection is at **Anyi** (Campero; per hr B$4), one block east of the plaza.

ℹ Getting There & Around

Trufis run throughout the day when full between Santa Cruz and Samaipata (☑333-5067; B$30, three hours). From Santa Cruz, services leave from the corner of Av Omar Chavez Ortíz and Solis de Olguin a few blocks from the old terminal. From Sampaipata, services depart from the main plaza.

Finding a lift west to Vallegrande or Cochabamba is a bit trickier. For Vallegrande, buses pass the gas station on the main road at 11am and 4pm and typically have seats, while for Cochabamba services on the old road leave Mairana around 3pm on Tuesday, Friday and Sunday. To take the new road to Cochabamba it's easiest to just head back to Santa Cruz and catch a *flota* there.

Around Samaipata

LA PAJCHA

A series of three beautiful waterfalls on a turbid mountain river that plunge 45m into a dreamy tropical lagoon. La Pajcha has a sandy beach for swimming and some inviting campsites. It's 42km south of Samaipata, toward San Juan, where there is a turnoff that leads 7km to the falls. The site is privately owned and visitors are charged B$10 to visit and swim here. The easiest way to get here is in a shared taxi from the plaza in Samaipata (B$250, two hours).

EL NIDO DE LOS CONDORES

El Nido de los Condores (Condor Nest) is the end point of a hugely popular eight-hour hike that begins from the trailhead near La Pajcha. Here, as you might expect, you will find more than 25 condor nests perched precariously on the hillside and have the opportunity to admire these glorious birds at close quarters as they soar on thermals over the valley below. The site has been dubbed the best condor-watching place in South America.

Vallegrande

☑3 / POP 16,850 / ELEV 2100M (6890FT)

Vallegrande's claim to fame is that it was the spot where Che Guevara's emaciated corpse was exhibited before its burial, and it is the main base for the **Che Trail**, a community-based tourism project. Che's final movements are followed on the trail on foot, mule, bicycle and boat, with rustic accommodations available at encampments and with local families.

Most visitors to the town are passing through on a Che pilgrimage, but Vallegrande is also a nice spot to relax and walk in the hills. It's a quiet little town set in the Andean foothills and enjoys a lovely temperate climate.

◉ Sights

Museo Ruta del Che &
Museo Arqueológico   MUSEUM

(admission B$10; ⊗8am-noon & 2-6pm Mon-Sun) On the 2nd floor is a photo-documentary of events leading up to the capture of Che, featuring objects and artefacts that belonged to the guerrilla group. A small archaeological museum, mainly of ceramics, is on the ground floor.

Hospital Señor de la Malta   LANDMARK

After Che Guevara's execution in La Higuera, south of Vallegrande, his body was brought to the now-dilapidated hospital laundry here. The hospital still functions, but the laundry itself has now been cordoned off as a pilgrimage site, where graffiti pays homage to this controversial figure. To get here, head one block south of the plaza along Escalante, and then five blocks east along Malta.

El Mausoleo del Che   MUSEUM

In 1997, nearly 30 years after Che's death, one of the soldiers who carried out the burial revealed that his body lay beneath Vallegrande's airstrip. The Bolivian and Cuban governments called for his exhumation and Che was officially reburied in Santa Clara, Cuba, on October 17, 1997. The spot where he was originally buried is marked by a mausoleum adorned with the typical smiling image of Che that beams out across the valley. The interior can only be visited by guided tour, but the building is clearly visible from the bus station.

✪ Festivals & Events

The weekly *feria* (market) is held every Sunday. Around February 23 the town marks its anniversary with various sporting and cultural events.

Che Guevara Festival   FOLK

Since the bodies of Che and several of his comrades were recovered from the airport in 1997, the town has celebrated an annual Che Guevara festival in October, featuring folk art and cultural activities.

LA PARABA FRENTE ROJA

The endangered red-fronted macaw *(Ara rubrogenys)*, known locally as *la paraba frente roja*, reflects its Bolivian specialty status in its red, green and yellow plumage – the colors of the national flag. Found only in dry inter-Andean valleys in the Vallegrande area, this handsome bird has a world population of just 1000. Thanks to an extensive public awareness campaign, local conservation NGO Armonía was able to raise the funds to purchase a small reserve close to the town of **Saipina** that is dedicated to the conservation of the bird. It has now constructed a superb and comfortable **lodge** (incl full board B$490) as a means of sustainably supporting the reserve.

Visit the **Armonía office** (☑356-8808; www.armonia-bo.org; Lomas de Arenas 400; ☺8:30am-12:30pm & 2:30-6pm Mon-Fri) in Santa Cruz for more information about its conservation programs and how to visit the lodge. For a guided birding tour contact Bird Bolivia (p244).

🛏 Sleeping & Eating

Vallegrande has a fair number of basic, budget hostelries, so while you're unlikely to be without a bed, you are likely to be without a private bathroom. Budget options in the street around the plaza all charge around B$30 for very similar rooms with shared bathroom.

Plaza Pueblo Hotel　　　　HOTEL $
(☑942-2630; Virrey Mendoza 132; s/d B$80/160) Two and a half blocks uphill from the market, this brand-new hotel is surprisingly upmarket for the price. OK, at the time of writing it was still only half operational, but with spiffing bathrooms and an on-site restaurant it's already looking like the best value in town.

Hostal Juanita　　　　HOTEL $
(☑942-2231; Manuel María Caballero 123; s/d B$80/140) This is a clean, family-run hotel just two blocks from the main square where you get decent value for money and a flowery courtyard with fountain.

La Nueva China　　　　CHINESE $$$
(Florida; mains B$30-70) Somewhat less than authentic Chinese food picked from a menu that hangs on the wall. It's Bolivian-owned and while your food might not look or taste exactly as you expected, keep an open mind and you'll conclude that different doesn't necessarily mean bad!

El Mirador　　　　INTERNATIONAL $$$
(☑942-2341; El Pichacu; mains B$40-80) Literally the top spot in town, with excellent views, and good fish and meat dishes.

❶ Information

A tourist office next to the museum on the east side of the plaza provides information on the Che Trail as well as offering guided tours with local Che expert **Gonzalo Flores Guzmán** (☑7318-6354). Tours start from B$200 per person for a group of four, or B$450 for a single person for a full day. An interesting aspect of the tour is the chance to chat with people who actually met Che to get a first-hand account of events. There is also a decent Spanish language municipal website with tourist information: www.vivirenvallegrande.com.

❶ Getting There & Away

From Plazuela Oruro in Santa Cruz *trufis* leave for Vallegrande (B$60, five hours) when full. *Flotas* (B$35, seven hours) from the bimodal terminal leave mainly in the morning, From Samaipata, *micros* leave from the main road at 11am and 4pm (three hours), or if you are in a group you can haggle for a shared taxi; expect to pay around B$300 for a car load.

Vallegrande's bus terminal, 1km north of the center, looks impressive, but very few services actually run from there. There are *micros* to Santa Cruz at 8am and 1pm and several between 9pm and 10pm, and a 6pm service to Cochabamba. *Trufis* to Samaipata and Santa Cruz also leave from here when full, though it is frequently a long wait. The bus between Santa Cruz and Sucre passes through Vallegrande between 1pm and 4pm every day except Monday, continuing on to Pucará from where it's a pleasant 15km walk to La Higuera or else a good place to negotiate with a taxi driver. Taxis to La Higuera (B$300, three hours – try haggling) depart from the market, two blocks east of the main plaza along Sucre.

HASTA SIEMPRE, COMANDANTE

As you travel around Bolivia, the iconic image of Che – the revolutionary with a popularity status reached only by rock stars, and remembered in Cuban songs such as *'Hasta siempre, Comandante'* (Forever with You, Commander) – will be staring at you from various walls, paintings, posters and carvings. Bolivia is where Che went to his death and where his image is being fervently resurrected.

Fresh from revolutionary success in Cuba (and frustrating failure in the Congo), Ernesto 'Che' Guevara de la Serna was in search of a new project when he heard about the oppression of the working classes by dictator René Barrientos Ortuño's military government in Bolivia. Strategically located at the heart of South America, Bolivia seemed like the perfect place from which to launch the socialist revolution on the continent. Though Fidel Castro had required him to sign a letter of resignation upon leaving Cuba, thereby publically distancing the Cuban government from Guevara's activities, the two remained in close contact throughout the Bolivian escapade.

Che's Bolivian base was established in 1966 at the farm Ñancahuazú, 250km southwest of Santa Cruz. Initially his co-revolutionaries had no idea who he was, and only when his trademark beard began to grow back (he had shaved it off to arrive incognito in Bolivia) did they realize that they were in the presence of a living legend. Che hoped to convince the *campesinos* (subsistence farmers) that they were oppressed, and to inspire them to social rebellion, but was surprised to be met only with suspicion. In fact a cunning move by Ortuño to grant *campesinos* rights to their land had guaranteed their support and all but doomed Che's revolution to failure before it had even begun.

Bolivian Diary was written by Che during the final months of his life. Originally planned as a first-hand documentation of the revolution, it reads as a somewhat leisurely adventure.

La Higuera

The isolated town of La Higuera is where Che Guevara was held prisoner following his capture. An oversized bust of the revolutionary lords over the dusty **Plaza del Che**, while the **Boina del Che** monument is a replica of the famous star design that once adorned his beret. A full body cement **statue of Che** at twice life size completes the set. The schoolroom where Che was kept before being executed is just off the plaza with a star monument in front. It is now a **museum** (admission B$10), though the building has unfortunately been altered from its original design.

Sleeping & Eating

La Casa del Telegrafista PENSION **$**
(☎7493-7807; www.lacasadeltelegrafista.com; s/d B$50/100) Offers vegetarian lunches and rustic rooms in a historic house with all electricity provided by solar panels. It also arranges Che tours.

Los Amigos PENSION **$**
(☎7268-4879; s/d B$50/100; **P**) French-run pension has simple rooms with furniture made by the owners and a recommended restaurant (mains B$35-60) using vegetables grown in the garden.

GRAN CHIQUITANIA

The Gran Chiquitania is the area to the east of Santa Cruz where the hostile, thorny Chaco and the low, tropical savannas of the Amazon Basin have a stand-off. Watched by the foothills of the Cordillera Oriental to the west, the Llanos de Guarayos to the north and the international boundaries of Paraguay and Brazil to the south and east, these two vastly different landscapes stand together, never making peace.

The flat landscapes of the Chiquitania are broken and divided by long, low ridges and odd monolithic mountains. Much of the territory lies soaking under vast marshes, part of the magnificent Pantanal region. Bisected by the railway line, it's also the area of Jesuit mission towns with their wide-roofed churches and fascinating history.

The region takes its name from the indigenous Chiquitanos, one of several tribes that inhabit the area. The name Chiquitanos (meaning 'little people') was coined by the Spanish who were surprised by the low doorways to their dwellings.

Despite occasional minor setbacks Che considered things to be moving along nicely and in his last entry on October 7, 1967, 11 months after his arrival in Bolivia, he writes that the plan was proceeding 'without complications.'

The following day he was captured near La Higuera by CIA-trained Bolivian troops under the command of Capitán Gary Prado Salmón, receiving bullet wounds to the legs, neck and shoulder. He was taken to a schoolroom in La Higuera and, just after noon on October 9, he was executed in a flurry of bullets fired by Sergeant Mario Terán, who had asked for the job following the death of several of his close friends in gun fights with the guerillas. Once the deed was done the assassins were said to be perturbed by the open eyes and peaceful smile on the dead revolutionary's face.

The body was flown to Vallegrande, where it was displayed in the hospital laundry room to prove to the whole world that 'El Che' was finally dead. Local women noted an uncanny resemblance to the Catholic Christ and took locks of his hair as mementos, while the untimely deaths of many of those involved in his capture and assassination has led to widespread belief in the 'Curse of Che,' a sort of Tutankhamen-style beyond-the-grave retribution.

Almost 40 years later the socialist revolution finally arrived in Bolivia, via the ballot and not the bullet, with the election of Evo Morales Ayma. The country that executed Che now officially embraces him as a hero, and celebrated his time in Bolivia with the establishment of the Che Trail, a community-based tourism project that traces his last movements. Somewhat vaguely defined, the trail begins in distant Camiri (the southernmost point), though it's quite a trek on to the sites of real interest which are clustered in the area immediately around Vallegrande.

History

In the days before eastern Bolivia was surveyed, the Jesuits established an autonomous religious state in Paraguay in 1609. From there they fanned outward, founding missions in neighboring Argentina, Brazil and Bolivia and venturing into territories previously unexplored by other Europeans.

Keen to coexist with the numerous indigenous tribes of the region, the Jesuits established what they considered an ideal community hierarchy: each settlement, known as a *reducción,* was headed by two or three Jesuit priests, and a self-directed military unit was attached to each one, forming an autonomous theocracy. For a time the Jesuit armies were the strongest and best trained on the continent. This makeshift military force served as a shield for the area from both the Portuguese in Brazil and the Spanish to the west.

Politically, the *reducciones* were under the nominal control of the *audiencia* (judicial district) of Chacras, and ecclesiastically under the bishop of Santa Cruz, though their relative isolation meant that the *reducciones* basically ran themselves. Internally, the settlements were jointly administered by a few priests and a council of eight indigenous representatives of the specific tribes who met daily to monitor community progress. Though the indigenous population was supposedly free to choose whether it lived within the missionary communities, the reality was that those who chose not to were forced to live under the harsh *encomienda* (Spanish feudal system) or, worse still, in outright slavery.

The Jesuit settlements reached their peak under the untiring Swiss priest Father Martin Schmidt, who not only built the missions at San Xavier, Concepción and San Rafael de Velasco, but also designed many of the altars, created the musical instruments, acted as the chief composer for the *reducciones* and published a Spanish-Chiquitano dictionary. He was later expelled from the region and died in Europe in 1772.

By the mid-1700s, political strife in Europe had escalated into a power struggle between the Catholic Church and the governments of France, Spain and Portugal. When the Spanish realized the extent of Jesuit wealth and influence they decided to act. In 1767, swept up in a whirlwind of political babble and religious dogma, the missions were disbanded and King Carlos III signed the Order of Expulsion, which evicted the Jesuits from the continent. In the wake of the Jesuit departure the settlements fell into

SANTA CRUZ & GRAN CHIQUITANIA GRAN CHIQUITANIA

decline, their amazing churches standing as mute testimony to their achievements.

Jesuit Missions Circuit

The seven-town region of Las Misiones Jesuíticas hides some of Bolivia's richest cultural and historic accomplishments. Forgotten by the world for more than two centuries, the region and its history captivated the world's imagination when the 1986 Palme d'Or winner *The Mission* spectacularly replayed the last days of the Jesuit priests in the region (with Robert de Niro at the helm). The growing interest in the unique synthesis of Jesuit and native Chiquitano culture in the South American interior resulted in Unesco declaring the region a World Heritage site in 1991. Thanks to 25 years of painstaking restoration work, directed by the late architect Hans Roth, the centuries-old mission churches have been restored to their original splendor.

To travel through the entire circuit takes five or six days, but for those with an interest in architecture or history, it's a rewarding excursion. If you have less time on your hands, prioritize the two most accessible churches at San José de Chiquitos and Concépcion, which are also conveniently the most representative of the extremes of styles.

❶ Information

The major mission towns all now have well-stocked Infotur offices, but for online information about the Gran Chiquitania region and the mission circuits, see www.chiquitania.com.

❶ Getting There & Away

If you wish to travel the mission circuit on public transport, the bus schedules synchronize better going counterclockwise: that is starting the circuit at San José de Chiquitos. Traveling the opposite way, unsynchronized and irregular bus schedules make for a frustrating journey. A much less time-consuming way of doing it is by taking a guided tour from Santa Cruz, which costs around US$450 for a four-day package taking in all the major towns. Misional Tours is a recommended operator.

SAN JAVIER
📞3 / POP 11,300

The first (or last, depending on which way you travel) settlement on the circuit, San Javier, founded in 1691, is the oldest mission town in the region. It's also a favorite holiday destination for wealthy *cruceño*

families. Swiss priest Martin Schmidt arrived in 1730 and founded the region's first music school and a workshop to produce violins, harps and harpsichords. He also designed the present church, which was constructed between 1749 and 1752. It sits on a lovely forested ridge with a great view over the surrounding low hills and countryside. Restoration work was completed in 1992 to beautiful effect, and the newly restored building manages to appear pleasantly old and authentic.

San Javier has some inviting **hot springs** 13km northwest of town along a rough road (B$150 return in a taxi). A further 5km along is a natural pool and waterfall, **Los Tumbos de Suruquizo**, where you can enjoy a refreshing swim. There is also a small free **Museo Misional** (⊙9am-noon & 2-6pm Mon-Fri) with the emphasis on musical instruments, and on the northeast corner of the plaza the **Museo Casa Natal German Busch** (⊙9am-noon & 2-6pm Mon-Fri) is in the former home of the ex-Bolivian president and Chaco War hero who died in mysterious circumstances aged just 35.

🍴 Sleeping & Eating

The following are all on the main plaza or, like everything in town, just a stone's throw away.

Hotel Momoqui   HOTEL $$
(📞7603-1326; s/d/tr B$200/400/500; ❄️❄️) The choice of wealthy *cruceños* who enjoy the private pool and buffet restaurant, all a cut above the other options in town.

Residencial Amé-Tauná   PENSION $
(📞963-5018; dm B$50, s/d/tr B$100/150/210) A typical mission circuit lodging on the main plaza, with Chiquitano-ornamented rooms arranged around little green patios.

Residencial de Chiquitano   PENSION $
(📞963-5171; s/d B$65/120, s/d without cable TV or fan B$45/80; ❄️) On the main road a little way up from the bus stop this is a clean and bright hostel on two floors decorated with toucan and macaw motifs. Ask for room 16 or 17 for killer views of the surrounding hills, but don't even think of getting a room without a fan unless it's cold outside.

El Ganadero   BOLIVIAN $
(mains B$20-30) Half-decent home-cooked meals and a good-value *almuerzo* (set lunch, B$20), but the uncooperative service will have you rushing to finish.

Pascana   BOLIVIAN **$**
(mains B$20-25) The food is home cooked and good value and the family atmosphere and smiling waiters make all the difference.

ℹ Getting There & Away

All Santa Cruz–Concepción buses pass through San Javier (B$30, six hours), stopping on the main road a short walk from the main plaza. Connections to Concepción pass through every three hours or so from noon to midnight, along the way look out for the Piedras de Paquio rock formation on your right side at Km 322. Buses for San Ignacio de Velasco pass through around 4pm and 9:30pm, but the road is in a terrible state and it's a tiresome journey. For the return to Santa Cruz you can avoid the often overcrowded buses by taking a taxi (B$50, 4½ hours); these leave when full. Listen for them honking for passengers along the main road.

CONCEPCIÓN
📞3 / POP 14,500

Sleepy 'Conce' is a dusty village with a friendly, quiet atmosphere in the midst of an agricultural and cattle-ranching area. It stands 182km west of San Ignacio de Velasco and is the center for all the mission restoration projects. The town is the most visited of the missions, partly because of its accessibility (the asphalt road ends here), but also because its picture-perfect church is one of the most elaborate on the circuit.

◎ Sights

Buying a museum pass (B$25) from any of the town's main sights gets you entry to all the others.

Catedral de Concepción   CHURCH
(◷8am-noon & 2-6pm Mon-Sat, 10am-noon Sun) Built in 1709, this elaborately restored cathedral on the east of the plaza has an overhanging roof supported by 121 huge tree-trunk columns and a similar bell tower. It is decorated with golden baroque designs depicting flowers, angels and the Holy Virgin. The decor gives some idea of the former opulence of the village.

Restoration Workshops   MUSEUM
(◷7:30am-noon & 1:30am-5:45pm Mon-Fri) Architectural aficionados should visit the restoration workshops behind the mission, where many of the fine replicas and restored artworks are crafted.

Museo Misional   MUSEUM
(admission B$8; ◷8am-noon & 2-6pm Tue-Sat, 10am-noon Sun) Intricate art restoration work is performed in the Museo Misional

on the south side of the plaza which, apart from being the birthplace of the former Bolivian president Hugo Suárez, also has scale models of all the churches on the mission circuit.

🛏 Sleeping & Eating

There are plenty of places to stay in Conce, but you'll start to notice a recurring theme of flowery courtyards, Chiquitano wall paintings and very similar prices.

TOP CHOICE Gran Hotel Concepción   BOUTIQUE HOTEL **$$$**
(📞964-3031; s/d/tr B$225/405/450; ❄≋) The most upscale place to lay your head is this charming, unapologetically Jesuit-styled hotel with a pool, a quiet patio with a lush, pretty garden, and intricately carved wooden pillars. The laundry comes in handy if you are finishing the dusty mission circuit. It's on the west side of the plaza.

Hotel Oasis Chiquitano   HOTEL **$$**
(📞964-3223; s/d B$90/180, with air-con B$130/260; ❄≋) Well maintained with simple rooms and an orchid garden, it's one block north of the plaza. The price includes access to the Oasis Chiquitano pool complex (admission for nonguests B$15) next door.

La Casona   HOTEL **$**
(📞964-3064; s/d B$70/140; ❄) Though not exactly going out on a limb in terms of decor and layout (courtyard, wall paintings, you know the type!), the price here is slightly lower for very much the same level of quality, making it a wise choice for the thrifty, despite the lack of a pool.

El Buen Gusto   BUFFET **$**
(north side of plaza; almuerzo B$28) Good-value *almuerzos*, with salad bar, are served here – enjoy the leafy, quiet patio on the north side of the plaza. Locals insist it's the best place to eat in town.

Alpina   ICE CREAM **$**
(ice cream B$5) Top place to cool off with a *helado*. It's on the south side of the plaza.

ℹ Information

There is a very well-stocked **Infotur office** (◷8am-noon & 2-6pm Mon-Sat) a block north of the plaza with information on the entire mission circuit.

ℹ Getting There & Away

Micros (B$35, seven hours) from Santa Cruz to Concepción run every two or three hours from

7:30am till 8:30pm via San Javier and drop off on the main road, a 15-minute walk from the plaza or a B$3 moto-taxi ride away, or at the respective company offices. *Trufis* (B$60, five hours) to Santa Cruz leave when full from near the market. If you are thinking of visiting Concepción and continuing on to San Ignacio de Velasco on the same day, you need to leave Santa Cruz very early. The San Ignacio buses from Santa Cruz (B$60, 11 hours) pass through Concepción around 5:30pm and 11pm, stopping on the main road 1km from the plaza.

SAN IGNACIO DE VELASCO
3 / POP 41,400

The first mission church at San Ignacio de Velasco, founded in 1748, was once the largest and most elaborate of all the mission churches. It was demolished in the 1950s and replaced by a modern abomination. Realizing they'd made a hash of it, the architects razed the replacement and designed a reasonable facsimile of the original structure. The new version retains a beautiful altar and wooden pillars from the original church and overlooks an extensive and well-pruned plaza. Several attractive, large wooden crosses (a trademark of Jesuit mission towns and villages) stand at intersections just off the plaza.

Only 700m north of the church is the imposing **Laguna Guapomó**, where you can swim or rent a boat and putter around.

Festivals & Events
There's a big party celebrating the **election of Miss Litoral** during the last weekend in March. San Ignacio fetes its patron saint every July 31. Every summer, the Chiquitania hosts the **International Festival of Baroque Music**, which runs for several weeks and centers on San Ignacio de Velasco.

Sleeping
San Ignacio de Velasco is the commercial heart of the mission district, so there's a good choice of accommodations.

Hotel La Misión   BOUTIQUE HOTEL $$$
(962-2333; www.hotel-lamision.com; s/d B$400/470;) For a bit of luxury, neocolonial style, try this place on the east side of the plaza. It has chic rooms, a little pool and opulent suites and there's also a good upmarket restaurant serving an eclectic choice of dishes. Check out the wooden pillars in front, one is beautifully carved with the image of a group of Bolivian musicians.

Hotel Palace   HOTEL $
(962-2063; s/d B$80/160) 'Palace' is overdoing it a bit, but for budget travelers this simple hotel, in the shadow of the church on the west side of the plaza, couldn't be better placed. Rooms lack much in the way of imagination but this is still a cheap central option.

Casa Suiza   PENSION $
(7630-6798; Sucre; s/d B$35/70) The helpful proprietor here speaks German and Spanish, has a wonderful library and can organize horseback riding, fishing trips and visits to surrounding haciendas. Paying B$20 extra gets you a fantastic homemade breakfast.

Eating
Unfortunately, eating options are pretty poor here and on Sunday everything is closed; eat at your hotel if you can. If you are on a budget try the following, all on the plaza.

Club Social   INTERNATIONAL $$
(mains B$30-50) Arguably the best in town, at least at weekends, when it serves up juicy *churrasco* (steak) for all and sundry. Á la carte menu during the week. It's on the west side of the plaza.

Bar-Restaurant Renacer Princezinha   BOLIVIAN $$
(mains B$25-50) Fortunately, the name of this place isn't the only mouthful on offer here. Basic, filling fare will help you fuel your mission tour. On the south side of the plaza.

Information
The Casa de la Cultura on the southwest corner of the plaza houses a small **tourist office** (8am-noon & 2:30-6:30pm Mon-Fri). There is now an ATM in town.

Getting There & Away
Micros leave from their respective offices scattered inconveniently around the market district, a B$5 moto-taxi ride from the center. Cover your luggage to prevent it from arriving with a thick coating of red dust. An 11am service with 131 del Este runs to Santa Cruz (B$70, 11 hours) via San Javier and Concepción, and there is sometimes a second departure in the evening.

Several companies run an overly complicated timetable to San José via either San Miguel or Santa Ana (sometimes depending on the day of departure). Departure times change constantly and it is worth inquiring locally about your onward trip on arrival. It can be extremely frustrating if you intend to stop off briefly at San Miguel or Santa Ana en route – necessitating an overnight stay. Consider haggling with a taxi driver to visit these towns. A full-day round-trip should cost around B$300 if the roads are in good condition.

SAN MIGUEL DE VELASCO
♪3 / POP 10,300

Sleepy San Miguel hides in the scrub, 37km from San Ignacio. Its **church** was founded in 1721 and is, according to the late Hans Roth, the most accurately restored of all the Bolivian Jesuit missions. Its spiral pillars, carved wooden altar with a flying San Miguel, extravagant golden pulpit, religious artwork, toylike bell tower and elaborately painted facade are simply superb.

Although not designed by Martin Schmidt, the church does reflect his influence and is generally considered the most beautiful of Bolivia's Jesuit missions. A unique feature of San Miguel is the presence of no fewer than seven bells in the bell tower. When rung in combination they transmit a complicated code language to the populace. The largest bell rung in tandem with two others signals the departure of a dignitary, rung alone it's the baptism of a child, while a special bell calls the faithful to prayer. You might want to pray that you never hear the smallest bell in tandem with a medium-sized bell; it means a child has died.

🛏 Sleeping & Eating

If you'd like to camp, speak with the nuns at the church, who can direct you to a suitable site.

Alojamiento Pardo   PENSION $
(♪962-4209; Sucre; s/d B$70/120, without bathroom B$40/80) Just off the plaza, this is a simple and spartan option.

❶ Information

There is a **tourist office** (♪962-4222; Calle 29 de Septiembre) for information.

❶ Getting There & Away

A complicated system of *micros* runs the circuit between San Miguel, San Ignacio de Velasco and San Rafael de Velasco, with departures sometimes running clockwise and sometimes counterclockwise (according to the day, rain, driver's fancy etc). Typically they leave in the morning with an occasional additional mid-afternoon service, but timetables change constantly and locals recommend that you inquire about your onward travel on arrival. If necessary get a taxi to San Ignacio, but if the roads are bad expect to pay more.

SANTA ANA DE VELASCO

The mission at this tiny Chiquitano village, 24km north of San Rafael de Velasco, was established in 1755. The **church**, with its earthen floor and palm-frond roof, is more rustic than the others and recalls the first churches constructed by the Jesuit missionaries upon their arrival. In fact the building itself is post-Jesuit, but the interior contains exquisite religious carvings and paintings.

Given its age, the original structure was in remarkable condition and the church has been recently restored. During renovations a diatonic harp, more than 1.5m tall, was found; it's displayed in the church and is a lovely complement to the local children's music practice.

SAN RAFAEL DE VELASCO
♪3 / POP 5000

San Rafael de Velasco, 132km north of San José de Chiquitos, was founded in 1696. Its church was constructed between 1743 and 1747, the first of the mission churches to be completed in Bolivia. In the 1970s and 1980s

---

VISIT THE BAT CAVE

Bats may not be everybody's cup of tea, but if you have made the long slog to San Matías then you may want to take the time to pop in on the nearby bat cave, home of the golden spear-nosed bat *Lonchorrhina aurita*. Characterized by its golden fur and ridiculously long ears and nose-leaf, it is a charismatic creature that has only recently been rediscovered in Bolivia, having been last recorded in the 1930s.

A campaign by the **Programa para la Conservacion de Murcielagos de Bolivia** (PCMB; http://murcielagosdebolivia.com) has raised awareness of the importance of this cave for the conservation of the species, even making it the central character in a children's book that teaches the ecological benefits of its conservation. A community-led ecotourism project has been proposed to protect the habitat of the bat, though you can't enter the cave itself. The PCMB website has a wealth of bat-related information.

the building was restored, along with the churches in Concepción and San José de Chiquitos.

The interior is particularly beautiful, and the original paintings and woodwork remain intact. The pulpit is covered with a layer of lustrous mica, the ceiling is made of reeds and the spiral pillars were carved from *cuchi* (ironwood) logs. It's the only mission church to retain the original style, with cane sheathing. Most interesting are the lovely music-theme paintings in praise of God along the entrance wall, which include depictions of a harp, flute, bassoon, horn and maracas.

On the main road **Alojamiento Paradita** (☑962-4008; s/d B\$50/100, without bathroom B\$30/60) is good enough for a brief stay and has a basic *comedor* (dining hall).

The best place to wait for rides south to San José de Chiquitos (five to six hours) or north to Santa Ana, San Miguel or San Ignacio is on the main road. In the morning, buses run in both directions. Ask at the small **tourist office** (☑962-4022) in the municipal building for the latest timetables.

SAN JOSÉ DE CHIQUITOS

☑3 / POP 16,600

An atmospheric place, San José de Chiquitos has the appeal of an old Western film set. The frontier town, complete with dusty streets straight out of *High Noon* and footpaths shaded by pillar-supported roofs, is flanked on the south by a low escarpment and on the north by flat, soggy forest. With an enormous and handsome plaza shaded by *toboroche* (thorny bottle) trees, the most accessible Jesuit mission town is also arguably the nicest.

DON'T MISS

SANTIAGO DE CHIQUITOS

Set in the hills, the Jesuit mission at Santiago de Chiquitos, 20km from the militarized access town Roboré (on the railway line), provides a welcome break from the tropical heat of the lowlands. Its church is well worth a look, and there are some great excursions from Santiago, such as the restaurant El Mirador, a 15-minute walk from the village, with dizzy views of the Tucavaca valley. The round-trip taxi fare from Roboré is B\$120 for up to four people.

◉ Sights & Activities

Jesuit Mission Church CHURCH
(⊙8am-noon & 2-6pm Mon-Sat, 10am-noon Sun) San José has the only stone Jesuit mission church and merits a visit even if you miss all the others. Although the main altar is nearly identical to those in other nearby missions and has vague similarities to churches in Poland and Belgium, the reason behind its unusual exterior design remains unclear.

The church compound consists of four principal buildings arranged around the courtyard and occupying an entire city block. Construction began prior to 1731 with the bell tower finished in 1748, the *funerario* (death chapel) dated 1752 and the *parroquio* (living area) completed in 1754. It is believed, however, that only the facades were finished before the Jesuits were expelled in 1767. All construction work was done by the Chiquitano people under Jesuit direction.

Santa Cruz la Vieja Walk WALKING
Just south of town, an **archway** supported by *bañistas* (bathers) indicates your entry into the **Zona Balnéaria** where there are a number of open-air swimming options.

A few kilometers further along is the **Parque Histórico Santa Cruz la Vieja** (admission B\$10), site of the original city of Santa Cruz de la Sierra. The only thing left behind of the old city is an abandoned guardhouse. Just beyond here is a statue of town founder Ñuflo de Chávez next to a reconstructed *choza* – a typical Chiquitano dwelling with the characteristic low doorway used for defensive purposes.

Uphill from here there is a trek to the **Cataratas del Suton** waterfall and a stunning viewpoint, though it is easy to get lost and a guide is recommended. Ask at the tourist office.

⌷ Sleeping

Hotel Villa Chiquitana HOTEL \$\$
(☑7315-5803; s/d/tr B\$350/400/450; ⊛⊠) Set on the east side of the plaza this is the most attractive place to stay in town and is on a par with the best hotels on the circuit. OK, so the decor with its regional wall paintings is probably something you've seen before, but it's still nice, isn't it?

Hotel Turubó HOTEL \$
(☑972-2037; s B\$80-120, d B\$100-150; ⊛) A good, solid, budget choice, in which the more expensive rooms have air-con. On the west side of the plaza.

CHOCHIS

Tiny Chochis, 360km east of Santa Cruz on the railway line, sits at the base of the imposing red rock **Cerro de Chochis**. The main reason for visiting is to see the remarkable **Santuario Chochis**, a religious sanctuary and memorial built to commemorate the victims of a flood. Though relatively modern (the disaster occurred in 1979), the wood carvings that adorn the sanctuary are the rival of anything seen in the Jesuit missions and the site has a palpable sense of mourning that allows you to share in the grief of the townsfolk.

Today the town is trying to organize itself toward a sustainable community-led tourism project and there is a basic **eco-albergue** (per person B$50) built from local materials where you can spend the night. The surrounding countryside here is great for walking, and local guides can take you to waterfalls, stunning viewpoints and hidden natural pools. Contact **Probioma** (☏in Santa Cruz 343-1322; www.probioma.org.bo) for details on how to visit.

Hotel El Patriarca　　　　　HOTEL **$**
(☏972-2089; s B$60-70, d B$100; ❋) A standard but clean budget hotel situated on the main plaza that represents good value for money.

✖ Eating

El Cubanito　　　　INTERNATIONAL **$$**
(mains B$30-55) A mishmash of decorative styles gives this restaurant a somewhat unfinished look, but smiling straw-hatted waiters serving pastas and meats more than make up for it. It's located on the main plaza.

Sabor y Arte　　　　　ITALIAN **$$**
(mains B$29-60) There's a distinctly French ambience here, though the menu is Italian with mainly pizza and pasta. The paintings and *artesanías* that adorn the place are all for sale. Owner Pierre is a mine of local tourist information. Just off the main plaza.

❶ Information

There is no ATM in town but local banks will give cash advances on Visa and MasterCard. A useful **Infotur office** (☏972-2084) in the Alcaldía on the corner of the plaza has information about all the missions.

❶ Getting There & Away

The route between San Ignacio and San José (via San Rafael de Velasco and San Miguel de Velasco) suffers from a confused, irregular and frequently changing timetable. At the time of writing there was a single 7am or 2pm departure on alternate days between the two towns, but we recommend that you check locally for the latest departure times. Buses from Santa Cruz depart daily from the bimodal terminal between 4pm and 6pm (B$50, five hours), though the road is in a terrible state.

Easily the easiest and most comfortable way to travel between San José and Santa Cruz or Quijarro is by train. You'll need to show your passport on purchasing your ticket and again to access the platform.

FAR EASTERN BOLIVIA

East of San José de Chiquitos the railway line passes through a bizarre and beautiful wilderness region of hills and monoliths. Further east, along the Brazilian border, much of the landscape lies soaking beneath the wildlife-rich swamplands of the Pantanal.

Quijarro

☏3 / POP 12,900
The eastern terminus of the railway line has its home in Quijarro, a muddy collection of shacks and the border-crossing point between Bolivia and the city of Corumbá, Brazil. On a hill in the distance you will glimpse a wonderful preview of Corumbá, the gateway to the Brazilian Pantanal, a Unesco-recognized eco-region.

☞ Tours

Pantanal　　　　　ECOTOUR
Hotels in Quijarro can organize boat tours to the Pantanal but almost invariably they visit the Brazilian side and frequently go to the same areas as cheaper trips in Brazil do. A comfortable three-day excursion, including transportation, food and accommodations (on the boat), should cost around B$1200 per person.

🛌 Sleeping & Eating

There are *alojamientos* (basic accommodations) on the left as you exit from the railway

CROSSING THE BORDER TO BRAZIL

The main border crossing to Brazil is at Quijarro at the end of the train line, with a second, minor crossing at San Matías, the access point to the northern Brazilian Pantanal.

You'll more than likely arrive in Quijarro by train between 7am and 9am to be greeted by a line of taxi drivers offering to take you the 3km to the border (B$10). **Customs offices** (☺8am-11am & 2-5pm Mon-Fri, 9am-1pm Sat & Sun) are on opposing sides of the bridge. Bolivian officials have been known to unofficially charge for the exit stamp, but stand your ground politely. Crossing this border you are generally asked to show a yellow-fever vaccination certificate. No exceptions are granted and you will be whisked off to a vaccination clinic if you fail to produce it. On the Brazilian side of the border yellow *canarinhos* (city buses) will take you into Corumbá (R$2.50). Brazilian entry stamps are given at the border. Get your stamp as soon as possible to avoid later problems and make sure you have the necessary visas if you require them.

For a slightly more adventurous border crossing try San Matías. In the dry season, a Trans-Bolivia bus leaves at 7:45pm from Santa Cruz to Cáceres in Brazil (30 hours), via San Matías (B$150, 26 hours). Brazilian entry or exit stamps should be picked up from the Polícia Federal office at Rua Antônio João 160 in Cáceres; get your exit and entry stamps for Bolivia in Santa Cruz.

station. The Lonely Planet–reviewed options are better.

Tamengo HOSTEL **$$**
(☏978-3356; www.tamengo.com; Costa Rica 57; dm B$60-100, r B$360, r without bathroom B$240; ❋☎) A cracking HI hostel that is something of a mini-resort as there are a variety of minimalist rooms to suit a varied clientele. Though the bar may be a popular hangout for young backpackers, you are just as likely to run into families and even businessmen in this something-for-everyone option.

El Pantanal Hotel-Resort RESORT **$$$**
(☏978-2020; www.elpantanalhotel.com; s B$348-728, d B$446-992; ❋☎) This five-star place is in the beautiful Arroyo Concepción, 12km from Puerto Suárez and 7km from Corumbá. It offers wide-ranging luxury, 600 hectares of grounds and several restaurants, as well as a number of touristic packages exploring the Pantanal.

❶ Getting There & Away

Train services cross the Chiquitania en route from Quijarro to Santa Cruz, arriving at the border town between 6am and 8am each day. The ticket office opens around 7am and tickets sell out fast, so don't hang around. The bus station is two blocks from the train station. Services to Santa Cruz (B$70, 12 hours) via San José (B$60; seven hours) leave at 4pm.

Amazon Basin

Best Places to Eat

» Churrasqueria La Estancia
(p295)

» Los Farroles (p295)

» Tropical (p302)

» Jungle Bar Moskkito (p283)

» La Perla de Rurre (p282)

Best Places to Stay

» Sadiri (p286)

» Chalalan (p286)

» Los Lagos (p299)

» Hotel de Selva El Puente
(p276)

» Hostal Sirari (p293)

Why Go?

The Amazon Basin is one of Bolivia's largest and most mesmerizing regions. The rainforest is raucous with wildlife and spending a few days roaming the sweaty jungle is an experience you're unlikely to forget. But it's not only the forests that are enchanting: it's also the richness of the indigenous cultures, traditions and languages that exist throughout the region.

Mossy hills peak around the town of Rurrenabaque, most people's first point of entry into the region and the main base camp for visits to the fascinating Parque Nacional Madidi. This is home to a growing ethno-ecotourism industry that looks to help local communities. The village of San Ignacio de Moxos is famous for its wild July fiesta and Trinidad, the region's biggest settlement and an active cattle ranching center, is the transit point toward Santa Cruz. North of here the frontier towns of Riberalta and Cobija are in remote regions that few travelers dare to tread.

When to Go
Rurrenabaque

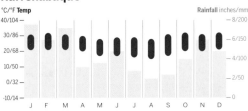

May-Oct Make travel a whole lot easier by avoiding the rain.

Mid-Jun Bull running and mayhem at the Fiesta de la Santísima Trinidad.

Jul The village goes wild during the San Ignacio de Moxos fiesta.

Amazon Basin Highlights

1 Glide down the long **Río Mamoré** (p294) on a boat trip between Trinidad and Guayaramerín

2 Probe the pampas on a tour from **Rurrenabaque** (p279)

3 Party with the locals at the Amazon's best village fiesta in **San Ignacio de Moxos** (p288)

4 Hike to the Cavernas del Repochón in **Parque Nacional Carrasco** (p278)

5 Boat off into the rainforest to the sustainable community-

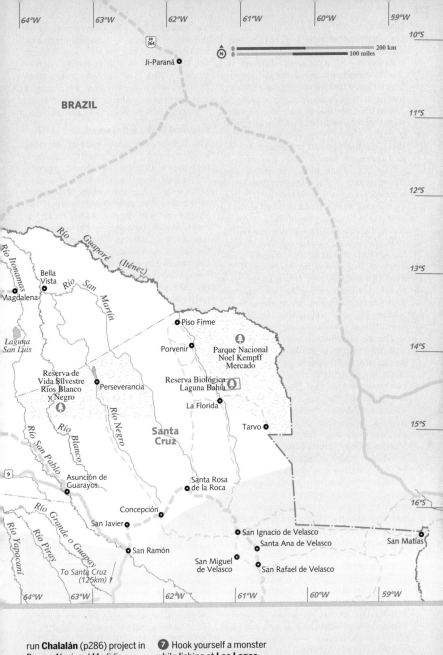

run **Chalalán** (p286) project in Parque Nacional Madidi

6 Taste the high life in the luxurious mountain forest at **Sadiri** (p286)

7 Hook yourself a monster while fishing at **Los Lagos** (p298)

History

The Bolivian Amazon has always oozed mystery. The Incas believed that a powerful civilization lived in the great rainforest, and tried to conquer the area in the 15th century. Legend has it that the indigenous peoples of the western Bolivian Amazon, mainly the Moxos tribe, are said to have offered such a mighty resistance to the invading army that, once they realized they were unable to beat them, the Incas sought an alliance and settled among the Moxos.

The tale of the Incas' experience fired the imagination of the Spanish conquerors a century later – they were chasing their own legend in search of a rich and powerful civilization in the depths of the Amazonian forest. The name of the kingdom was El Dorado (the Golden One) which they thought lay somewhere east of the Andean Cordillera, near the source of the Río Paraguay. The Spanish spent the entire 16th century trying to find the elusive kingdom, but, unfamiliar with the rainforest environment, found nothing but death and disease. By the 17th century they moved their search elsewhere.

Though the Spanish were disappointed with their search in the Moxos region, the Jesuits saw their opportunity to 'spread the word' to the highly spiritual *moxeños*. The hardy missionaries were the first Europeans to significantly venture into the lowlands. They founded their first mission at Loreto in 1675. While they imposed Christianity and European ways, the Jesuits also recognized the indigenous peoples' expertise in woodwork, which eventually produced the brilliant carvings now characteristic of the missions. They imported herds of cattle and horses to some of their remote outposts, and ranching remains today the region's main source of income. The region is now under increasing pressure from the expansion of the agricultural frontier, as vast tracts of forest are converted into ranch land.

Following the expulsion of the Jesuits in 1767, the Franciscan and Dominican missionaries, as well as the opportunistic settlers who followed, brought mainly slavery and disease. Otherwise, the vast, steamy forests and plains of northern Bolivia saw little activity for decades.

More recently finding a way to sustainably exploit the natural resources of the region has become an increasingly hot potato. A proposed road building project that would link Villa Tunari with San Ignacio de Moxos was canceled following demonstrations by indigenous groups and environmentalists who complained that the route would bisect the Tipnis Reserve. This inspired a counter march in 2012 by indigenous groups from the Moxos and Tunari areas who insisted that the road was vital for the economic development of their isolated homeland.

National Parks & Reserves

The Bolivian Amazon is part of the most biodiverse biome on earth, and the country's best-known national parks and reserves are located here. For bird-watchers, monkey lovers and jaguar seekers, this region is paradise. You can choose between the jungles and wild rivers of lush Parque Nacional Madidi, the less-frequented *cerrados* (savannas) of Reserva Biosférica del Beni, the Barba Azul Reserve, home to one of the world's rarest parrots, and the virtually unexplored 'lost world' of Parque Nacional Noel Kempff Mercado. **Conservation International** (www.conservation.org) is attempting to raise awareness of the need for protection of the headwaters of several major Amazon tributaries with its ambitious Vilcabamba-Amboró Conservation Corridor initiative, which aims to link Madidi with Manu National Park in Peru.

ℹ Getting There & Around

Rurrenabaque in the west and Trinidad in the east are the main access towns to the region. Though it's easy enough to get to Trinidad from Santa Cruz, delving deeper into the region either involves flying (if you are smart) or uncomfortably long bus rides on unpaved roads (get ready to push if it rains!). If there is even a hint of a shower you'll need a 4WD to get where you are going or, if you are lucky, bank on your bus taking at least twice as long as the ticket salesman tells you. Particularly tedious is the route from La Paz to Rurrenabaque. Many people decide to wing it (or take a faster 4WD) after surviving the initial bus ride.

The main airlines all fly to the region, with Aerocon and Amaszonas specializing in the more remote destinations. Though handy, flights are frequently canceled during inclement weather. When flying from La Paz to Rurrenabaque the low-flying planes afford great glimpses of Lake Titicaca after takeoff, before squeezing past Chacaltaya and soaring over the Yungas. Watch the landscape change from desolate, rugged highlands to lush, forested lowlands.

Boat travel is big here, especially in the rainy season, when it is usually the only viable option. Riverboat travel isn't for everyone: it's relaxing but slowgoing, and there are no real schedules.

While the scenery can be mesmerizing, it changes little, so you'll want to bring a couple of books along. Passenger comfort is the last thing cargo-boat builders have in mind, but Bolivian accommodations standards are still superior to those on the Brazilian 'cattle boats' that ply the Amazon proper.

CHAPARE REGION

The Chapare stretches out beyond the last peaks of the Andes into the dramatically different landscape of the upper Amazon Basin, where lush, moist rainforest replaces the dry, barren mountains. The contrast is breathtaking on the spectacular road between Cochabamba and Villa Tunari, where twists around the high peaks and mountain lakes drop steeply into deep, steaming tropical valleys.

The Chapare region is heavily populated with highland *campesinos* (subsistence farmers) who emigrated here in the 1970s and started growing the controversial coca leaf, turning the region into Bolivia's main source of coca grown for the manufacture of cocaine (as opposed to Yungas coca, which makes up the bulk of what Bolivians themselves chew, make into tea etc). Subsequent attempts by the US Drug Enforcement Agency (DEA) to eradicate coca have made the region unstable, with frequent messy confrontations between *cocaleros* (coca growers), the DEA and the Bolivian government. A former coca farmer himself, President Evo Morales has worked hard to protect the rights of those involved in the legal production of the plant while simultaneously targeting cocaine production and smuggling.

Villa Tunari

✔4 / POP 52,900 / ELEV 300M (984FT)

Strung out along the Cochabamba–Santa Cruz highway, Villa Tunari is a pleasant spot to relax, hike and swim in cool rivers, and is a relatively tame introduction to the wilder Amazon. Whether you are coming from the frozen highlands, or heading toward them, the hot, steamy, jungle air will make you grateful for the proximity of 'Las Pozas,' a series of natural swimming holes. As visitor numbers increase, the town is developing into something of a tourist trap and your bolivianos won't go as far here as they do further north in the Amazon. That said, the town is a great base for probing into the wonderful Parque Nacional Carrasco.

◉ Sights & Activities

A good, independent **hike** will take you to the friendly village of Majo Pampa. Follow the route toward Hotel de Selva El Puente and turn right onto the walking track about 150m before the hotel. After crossing the Arroyo Valería, it's 8km to the village.

Parque Machía   ZOO
(Inti Wara Yassi; ✔413-6572; www.intiwarayassi.org; admission B$6, photo or video permit B$10; ☾closed Mon) This 36-hectare wildlife refuge houses more than 200 free-range, poached or injured animals, and other abused critters. An international crew of volunteers tends to the animals' every need, but no attempts are made to reintroduce them into the wild (that means the animals, not the volunteers!).

Tours for wannabe volunteers are conducted daily at 10am. Volunteers must stay for a minimum of 15 days and can choose between rustic camping and the hostel, both of which cost B$1450 for the first two weeks, including food.

Orquidario Villa Tunari   GARDENS
(☾closed Mon) Lovingly tended by a group of German botanists, Villa Tunari's beautiful orchid nursery is home to more than 70 species of tropical orchids. There's also a small **museum** that is worth visiting, El Bosque restaurant and a couple of *cabañas* (cabins) available for rent. It's just north of the highway, 2km west of town near the *tranca* (police post).

Pozas   SWIMMING
Pozas (swimming holes) are the main source of fun in Villa Tunari. In addition to Hotel de Selva El Puente's Las Pozas, there are several free *pozas* in town along the Río San Mateo. Great opportunities for **fishing**, **kayaking** and **white-water rafting** abound in the surrounding rivers, but ask around to see what's safe before heading out into the forest on your own.

⌕ Tours

Fremen Tours   TOUR
Villa Tunari is the focus for Cochabamba-based Fremen Tours (p174), which organizes all-inclusive tours, accommodations, river trips and other activities at out-of-the-way sites. It also offers live-aboard

SACRED COCA?

Erythroxylum coca is the scientific name for coca, a plant of the family Erythroxylaceae, native to northwestern South America. A small tree growing to a height of 7ft to 10ft, the species is identified by its long, opaque leaves and clusters of yellowish-white flowers, which mature into red berries. In Bolivia the plant grows primarily in the Yungas, north of La Paz, and in the Chapare region.

But, unless you are a botanist, or have a strange taste in garden plants, you are likely to have heard of coca for other reasons – prince among them being its role in the production of the narcotic cocaine. To make the drug, leaves are dried, soaked in kerosene and mashed into a paste. Then they are treated with hydrochloric and sulfuric acids to form a foul-smelling brown base. Further treatment with petrol and other chemicals creates cocaine.

The leaf was first imported into Europe in the 16th century and by the end of the 19th century German scientists were investigating the potential medicinal applications of its analgesic and anaesthetic properties. It wasn't long before those same properties made it a popular vice though, with Sherlock Holmes even enjoying its recreational qualities. Recreational use was responsible for a five-fold increase in users between 1890 and 1903, and with the drug being linked to a supposed increase in criminality over the same period its widespread prohibition followed shortly afterwards

For most Bolivians, however, the white powder snorted by party-goers worldwide has nothing to do with their sacred plant, and they resent the suggestion that they should be held responsible for anyone else's misuse of it. President Evo Morales, a former *cocalero* (coca grower) himself, has vowed to continue the war against drug-trafficking, but not at the expense of the country's coca industry – according to his government, the two are very different animals. During an address to the UN in 2006, Morales held up a coca leaf to demonstrate that the leaf and cocaine are not the same.

riverboat cruises around Trinidad and adventure tours in Parque Nacional Isiboro-Sécure.

🎉 Festivals & Events

The festival of **San Antonio**, the town's patron saint, is celebrated in the first week of June. And for delicious and unique Amazonian fish dishes, be in town the first week of August for the **Feria Regional del Pescado**.

🛏 Sleeping

Villa Tunari has a huge selection of largely uninviting budget options, all of which are much of a muchness and charge around B$30/50 per person for rooms with shared/private bathrooms. However, note that many do not provide a fan, and you will need one. Those listed here are the ones that stand out.

TOP CHOICE **Hotel de Selva El Puente** RESORT **$$**
(☑458-0085; Integración; s/d/tr B$150/220/360; ☀) This gorgeous place is set in 22 hectares of rainforest 4km outside Villa Tunari, near the Ríos San Mateo and Espíritu Santo confluence. Handsome stone cabins gravitate around a courtyard and hammocks are on the top floor. The big attractions here are 'Las Pozas,' 14 idyllic natural swimming holes (B$10 for nonguests) deep in the forest. The hotel is run by Fremen Tours. Mototaxis will take you here from the center for B$8.

Los Tucanes CABINS **$$**
(☑413-6506; 4-person cabins B$677, s/d B$231/354; ☀☀) Luxurious *cabañas* with good beds, elegant decor and a pool to lounge around. Each room is individually decorated with its own unique wall painting and it's a great spot for total vacation surrender. It's at the Santa Cruz entrance to town opposite the turnoff for Hotel El Puente.

Hotel Los Cocos HOTEL **$**
(☑413-6578; s/d B$100/180, without bathroom B$70/120; ☀) Villa Tunari's top budget option, with well-tended rooms, modern bathrooms and a glorious pool to cool off in. Owner Ray Charles Paz is helpful, friendly and fortunately doesn't own a piano!

Hotel/Restaurant Las Palmas HOTEL **$$**
(☑7281-5695; south side of main road; s/d/tr B$300/400/480, cabins B$600; ☀☀) This is another tropical hotel with a refreshing swim-

So what else is coca used for?

Coca has formed a part of the religious rituals of the inhabitants of the Altiplano since the pre-Inca period as an offering to the Gods *Apus* (Mountains), *Inti* (Sun) and *Pachamama* (Mother Earth). It is drunk as a tea *(mate de coca)* or chewed to combat altitude sickness or overcome fatigue and hunger. To *picchar* (to chew coca, from the Aymará) involves masticating a pile of leaves stored as a bolus in the cheek. The bolus is added to continuously and saliva passed over the mass has a mild stimulant and anaesthetic effect on the user. Furthermore chewing coca also serves as a powerful symbol of religious and cultural identity.

During the conquest, the Spanish rulers were somewhat perturbed by these religious connotations. Seeing it as an obstacle to their evangelization of the masses, they were, however, aware that consumption greatly increased output by the labor force. This double-edged sword led King Philip II to permit its use as 'essential to the well-being of the Indians', but to discourage any religious association.

Outside Bolivia, most people know that cocaine was the original active ingredient in Coca-Cola, but few realize that the coca plant is still involved in its manufacture. Medical company Stepan is one of the very few to have a license permitting possession of the plant and its derivatives in the US, and it imports 100 tons of dried leaf annually, some of it for the manufacture of medicines, some of it for the production of the Coca-Cola flavoring agent.

Regardless of its status in Bolivia, coca is illegal in most of the world and travelers should not attempt to take any coca leaves home. Most countries consider the leaf and the narcotic as one and the same, and you could be charged with possession of a Class A drug for having even a single petiole in your pocket.

ming pool and enormous tiled rooms. The *cabañas* are a better bet for big groups. The open-air restaurant serves well-prepared locally caught fish, and there are superb views of the river and surrounding hills.

Hotel San Antonio HOTEL $
(☎7431-0200; Plaza Principal; d B$120, s/d without bathroom B$50/100; ☒) Despite a location on the main square, this budget place goes for an Amazonian-lodge feel and nearly achieves it. Rooms are basic but tidy, and those with shared bathrooms do not have fans. You can, however, cool off in the pool.

Hotel San Martín HOTEL $$
(☎413-6512; south side of main road; s/d/tr B$130/180/250; ☒) This welcoming place has a gorgeous garden with a pool.

Don Corsino Gran Hotel HOTEL $$
(☎413-6547; north side of main road; d/tr/q B$170/210/350) Despite being brand new, the unimaginatively plain rooms here are a little disappointing and air-conditioning would have been a welcome addition at this price. There are no single rooms and no breakfast, but the per person rate for triple and quadruple rooms works out quite favorably if you are in a group.

✕ Eating

With the influx of tourists over recent years, a few reasonable restaurants have sprung up around town. A rank of food stalls along the highway sells inexpensive tropical fare, but check hygiene levels before you buy.

Restaurant San Silvestre INTERNATIONAL $$$
(main road next to Las Palmas; mains B$28-63) If the jars of pickled snakes (not for consumption!) and animal skins hanging off the walls don't deter you, dig in to these huge portions big enough for two. Try the gargantuan *pique macho* (beef, sausage and chips dish) to really pig out, but avoid the wild game! The attached Café Mirador opens in the evening for drinks and has nice river views.

Mamma Titi INTERNATIONAL $$
(Beni; mains B$20-60) Great value on regional and local dishes, plus a wide selection of pastas and some vegetarian dishes; it's a in a wooden cabin, a block from the bridge over the Río Espíritu Santo.

❶ Information

There's an ATM at Banco Union and several telecom and internet places along the highway.

① Getting There & Away

Buses taking the new road between Cochabamba and Santa Cruz pass through Villa Tunari, though not all at convenient times. Those leaving in the morning are the best bet. Taxis and *micros* (minibuses) from Cochabamba leave from the corner of Avs Oquendo and República during the day when full (micro/taxi B$15/40, four/three hours).

Getting a taxi from Santa Cruz is much faster than the bus, but means several changes – this typically involving hopping out of one taxi and straight into the next. From the old bus terminal take a taxi to Yapacani (B$23, two hours), from there go to Bulo-Bulo (B$13, one hour), then on to Ivirgazama (B$13, one hour), then another to Shinahota (B$10, 45 minutes) and finally one to Villa Tunari (B$6, 30 minutes). It sounds more complicated than it really is and is a good way of avoiding waiting around for a bus, though you can expect more people to be piled into each cab than actually fit!

Parque Nacional Carrasco

Created in 1988, this 622,600-hectare park has some of Bolivia's most easily explored cloud forest. It skirts a large portion of the road between Cochabamba and Villa Tunari, and also includes a big lowland area of the Chapare region. The rainforest hides a vast variety of mammal species, together with a rainbow of birds, crawling reptiles, amphibians, fish and insects.

Tour programs include the highly recommended hike to the **Cavernas del Repechón** (Caves of the Night Birds), where you'll see the weird, nocturnal *guáchero* (oilbird) and six bat species. Access is from the village of Paractito, 8km west of Villa Tunari. This half-day excursion involves a short slog through the rainforest and a zippy crossing of the **Río San Mateo** in a cable-car contraption.

Another interesting option is the Conservation International–backed **Camino en las Nubes** (Walk in the Clouds) project, a three-day trek through the park's cloud forests, descending with local guides from 4000m to 300m along the old Cochabamba–Chapare road.

For more details on these tours contact Fremen Tours (p275).

Puerto Villarroel

📓4 / POP 40,800

This muddy, tropical port on the Río Ichilo is a small settlement with tin-roofed houses raised off the ground to defend them from the mud and wet-season floods. The population here is composed almost entirely of indigenous Yuqui and colonizing Quechua groups. The town has tried hard to promote tourism but hasn't had much success, as there isn't much to actually see – unless you're excited by a military installation, a petroleum plant and a loosely defined port area. However, if you fancy gliding down the river toward Trinidad, then a good place to start would be Puerto Villarroel, a vital transportation terminal and gateway to the Amazon lowlands.

🏃 Activities

Boat Trips   BOAT TOUR

Two types of boat run between Puerto Villarroel and Trinidad. The small family-run cargo boats that putter up and down the Ríos Ichilo and Mamoré normally only travel by day and reach Trinidad in around six days. Larger commercial crafts travel day and night and do the run in three or four days. Note that these boats are not specifically for tourists and so you should not expect any special treatment. Conditions are basic.

In Puerto Villarroel, the Capitanía del Puerto and other related portside offices can provide sketchy departure information on cargo transporters. Unless military exercises or labor strikes shut down cargo services, you shouldn't have more than a three- or four-day wait. Note that when the river is low you will have much more difficulty finding a boat.

The average fare to Trinidad on either type of boat is around B$250, including food, or a bit less without meals. The quality of food varies from boat to boat, but overall the repetitive shipboard diet consists of fish, dried meat, *masaco* (mashed yucca or plantain) and fruit. You should seriously consider bringing snacks to supplement your diet. Few boats along the Ichilo have cabins. Most passengers sleep in hammocks slung out in the main lounge, so a mosquito net is a wise investment.

If you are not up to the odyssey of a multiday river cruise, ask around at the port for owners of *lanchas* (small boats). For a negotiable fee they can organize day-long fishing or camping trips to nearby river beaches, as well as visits to nearby indigenous settlements. In the spirit of responsible tourism offer to pay what you consider a fair price; a gift of diesel is always welcome.

🛏 Sleeping & Eating

Accommodations options are extremely basic, with a bunch of run-down *residenciales* (simple accommodations) clustered around the central plaza; they charge around B$20 per person. Those who are using river transportation may be permitted to sleep on the boat.

Half a dozen restaurant shacks opposite the port captain's office serve up greasy fish and chicken dishes.

ℹ Getting There & Away

Micros from Cochabamba to Puerto Villarroel, marked 'Chapare' (B$25, seven hours), leave from the corner of Avs 9 de Abril and Oquendo, near Laguna Alalay. The first one sets off around 6:30am, and subsequent buses depart sporadically when full.

Alternatively, from the old bus terminal in Santa Cruz take a taxi to Yapacani (B$23, two hours), then another to Bulo-Bulo (B$13, one hour) and finally a third to Puerto Villaroel (B$10, one hour).

Note that transportation between Cochabamba and Santa Cruz doesn't stop at Puerto Villarroel.

WESTERN BOLIVIAN AMAZON

This is the Amazon as it's meant to be. Rich with wildlife, flora and indigenous culture, you may never want to leave. In the midst of the tropical lushness is the lovely town of Rurrenabaque, a major gringo trail hangout. Pampas, jungle and ethno-ecotourism options are innumerable but vary significantly in quality and price. Parque Nacional Madidi, one of South America's, and the world's most precious wilderness gems, sits on Rurrenabaque's doorstep.

Rurrenabaque

♫3 / POP 13,700 / ELEV 229M (751FT)

Relaxing 'Rurre' (pronounced 'zussay'), as the town is endearingly known, has a fabulous setting. Sliced by the deep Río Beni and surrounded by mossy green hills, the town's mesmerizing sunsets turn the sky a burned orange, and a dense fog sneaks down the river among the lush, moist trees. Once darkness falls, the surrounding rainforest comes alive, and croaks, barks, buzzes and roars can be heard from a distance.

Rurre is a major traveler base. Backpackers fill the streets, and restaurants, cafes and hotels cater mainly to Western tastes. Some travelers spend their days relaxing in the ubiquitous hammocks, but at some stage the majority go off on riverboat adventures into the rainforest or pampas.

The area's original people, the Tacana, were one of the few lowland tribes that resisted Christianity. They are responsible for the name 'Beni,' which means 'wind,' as well as the curious name of 'Rurrenabaque,' which is derived from 'Arroyo Inambaque,' the Hispanicized version of the Tacana name 'Suse-Inambaque,' the 'Ravine of Ducks.'

⊙ Sights & Activities

Though there isn't really that much to do in town, Rurrenabaque's appeal is in its surrounding natural beauty. It's easy to pass a day or three here while waiting to join a tour. Behind town is a low but steep *mirador* (lookout) that affords a view across the seemingly endless Beni lowlands; it's reached by climbing up the track at the southern end of Bolívar.

Butterfly Pool El Mirador SWIMMING
Near the *mirador* it is named after, this is a fabulous spot where you can swim and swoon over gobsmacking views of the Beni lowlands.

Hotel El Ambaibo
Swimming Pool SWIMMING
(nonguest B$20) If you prefer a tiled, chlorinated pool, try the Olympic-sized *piscina* at Hotel El Ambaibo on Santa Cruz.

BIGGEST CANOPY IN BOLIVIA

Community-run projects are well worthy of support as the profits go directly to the people who deserve them. A series of *tranquilo* (tranquil) community-run tourism projects operate in Parque Nacional Madidi but if you need more adrenaline, then try the unambiguously named Biggest Canopy in Bolivia. It's a forest canopy zipline in Villa Alcira, outside Rurrenabaque, which is aimed at those with a head for heights, a strong stomach and a need for speed. Book at the office in Rurre; the price includes transportation.

Rurrenabaque

AMAZON BASIN RURRENABAQUE

To Hotel
Safari (200m)

18 de Noviembre

Comercio

Avaroa

Junín

Bolivar

To San Buenaventura (250m);
SERNAP Parque Nacional
Madidi Office (500m)

Río Beni

Ferry

Aniceto Arce

21
23

16

Prodem

8

25

Ferries
to/from San
Buenaventura

Market

14

1

Moto-taxi
parada

22

Calle Pando

30
18

31

17
11

Banco
Union

28
5

20
13

Santa Cruz

12

26
2

3

29

24

19

Vaca Diez

27

7

6
15

4

Avaroa

Plaza 2
de Febrero

Campero

Bolivar

9

Templo de la
Virgen de la
Candelaria

Busch

Comercio

Camacho

Sucre

El Chorro SWIMMING
El Chorro, an idyllic waterfall and pool 1km upstream, makes for a pleasant excursion. On a rock roughly opposite El Chorro is an ancient **serpentine engraving**, which was intended as a warning to travelers: whenever the water reached serpent level, the Beni was considered unnavigable. You can only reach it by boat so inquire at the harbor and strike a deal.

coles, a comfortable pampas lodge on Río Yacumo and a forest lodge Tacuaral.

Fluvial Tours/Amazonia Adventures TOUR
(892-2372; Avaroa) This is Rurrenabaque's longest-running agency.

🛏 Sleeping

The sleeping scene in Rurrenabaque is ruled by one thing: the hammock. The sagging sack can be the sole factor in deciding whether a business does well here or not, so expect hammocks and enjoy the mandatory laziness.

Hotel Oriental HOTEL $
(892-2401; Plaza 2 de Febrero; s/d B$100/150) If you meet people who are staying at the Oriental, right on the plaza, they'll invariably be raving about what an excellent place it is – and it really is. Comfy rooms, great showers, garden hammocks for snoozing and big breakfasts are included in the price.

La Isla de los Tucanes CABINS $$$
(892-2127; www.islatucanes.com; Bolívar; s/d B$380/480, cabins min 3 people per person from B$240; ✷) An ecological cabin complex in the north of town with thatched Amazonian bungalows designed to make you feel further away from the town center than you really are. With pool tables, an international restaurant and several swimming pools there is no real reason to leave – unless of course you are going into the jungle proper.

Hostal Pahuichi HOSTEL $
(892-2558; Comercio; s/d/tr B$100/100/150) It's amazing what a good facelift can do to an ageing hotel. The newly renovated suites here are tasteful, colorful and dare we say it stylish (almost!), with sleek wooden furniture and sparklingly tiled private bathrooms. Only the reception left to fix now!

Hotel Safari HOTEL $$
(892-2210; Comercio; s/d B$250/330; ✷) Rurre's poshest option sits by the riverfront, away from the town center. It's a quiet, Korean-run place with simple but comfortable rooms with fans. Amenities, catering to tour groups, include a restaurant.

Hotel Los Tucanes de Rurre HOTEL $
(892-2039; Bolívar at Aniceto Arce; s/d B$80/100, without bathroom B$70/80) This big, thatched-roof house offers a sprawling garden, a roof terrace and sweeping views over the river. There are hammocks swinging on the patio, a pool table, and the clean and

👉 Tours

Most agencies have offices on Avaroa.

Bala Tours TOUR
(892-2527; www.visit-amazonia.com; Santa Cruz at Comercio) Has its own jungle camp, Cara-

AMAZON BASIN RURRENABAQUE

Rurrenabaque

simple rooms are painted in gentle colors. Breakfast is included.

Centro de Recreación del Ejército PENSION $
(☎892-2377; Plaza 2 de Febrero; r per person B$80, without bathroom B$30) If only all army barracks were like this they might not have so much trouble getting people to sign up! It's a strange concept, almost an officers club, but it's essentially a good, modern, budget hotel with a river terrace. Just remember to salute if somebody calls your name and expect disciplined reception staff!

Hostal Rurrenabaque HOSTEL $
(☎892-2481; Vaca Diez, near Bolívar 1490; s/d B$100/120, s without bathroom B$70; 🛜) A mustard-colored, porticoed edifice, with muted wood-floored rooms. There are no-frills here except for on the curtains, but the availability of a flaky wi-fi connection may give it the edge over its competitors.

Hostal Turístico Santa Ana PENSION $
(☎892-2614; Avaroa; s/d B$80/90, without bathroom B$40/70) Decent value, though some of the rooms with shared bathrooms are dingy and claustrophobic. As with most places there is the obligatory hammock garden.

La Perla Andina PENSION $
(☎7283-5792; 18 de Noviembre s/n; r per person B$35) A block from the bus station, this bottom-end budget option is useful if you're looking to catch an early bus. It's clean and an effort has been made to prettify the rooms despite the price.

🍴 Eating

Rurre's eating options are varied, from quick chicken and snacks to fresh river fish and decent international cooking. Several fish restaurants line the riverfront near the market: candlelit La Cabaña and Playa Azul grill or fry up the catch of the day for around B$40. In addition to the Beni standard, *masaco* (mashed yucca or plantains, served with dried meat, rice, noodles, thin soup and bananas), try the excellent *pescado hecho en taquara* (fish baked in a special local pan) or *pescado en dunucuabi* (fish wrapped in a rainforest leaf and baked over a wood fire).

 La Perla de Rurre SOUTH AMERICAN $$
(Bolívar at Vaca Diez; mains B$40-50) Everyone in Rurre will tell you that this is their favorite restaurant and 'The Pearl' does indeed serve up some mean fresh fish and chicken

dishes. The surroundings are simple but the service is excellent.

Casa de Campo
HEALTH FOOD **$$$**

(Vaca Diez at Avaroa; breakfast B$20-65; ☺8am-2pm & 6-10pm) Healthy food is the name of the game here, with all-day breakfasts, homemade pastries, vegetarian dishes, soups, salads, you name it. The friendly owner is keen to make her guests happy, but her breakfast is the priciest in town.

Restaurant Tacuaral
INTERNATIONAL **$$**

(Santa Cruz at Avaroa; mains B$18-38, sandwiches B$18) This open-air eatery with shaded sidewalk seating has an ambitious menu, covering breakfast to dinner. It's friendly and popular, especially for its lasagna. The Mexican dishes won't have you tossing your *sombrero* into the air, but the sandwiches are huge.

Café Piraña
INTERNATIONAL **$$**

(Santa Cruz nr Avaroa s/n; mains B$15-50) This Piraña has bite, with a great chill-out area, delicious vegetarian and meat dishes, yummy breakfasts, lovely fresh juices, a library and film screenings most nights upstairs.

Cherrie's Ice Cream Shop
ICE CREAM **$**

(Santa Cruz near Avaroa; ice cream B$6-25) Sometimes you just need one, don't you? This little kiosk has a variety of flavors, plus inventive sundaes and milkshakes to whet your appetite.

Drinking & Entertainment

Rurre is a lively town and there are several bars and discos. Most bars run along the same lines, following a very successful bamboo-walled, palm-roof model with pub meals served during the day and tropical cocktails at night. Ask about happy hour, they all have one!

Jungle Bar Moskkito
BAR

(www.moskkito.com; Vaca Diez) Peruvian-run, but English is spoken here. There's a positive vibe, cheery service and the foliage that hangs from the roof makes you feel like you are in the jungle, whether there are 'moskkitos' or not. Throw some darts, shoot some pool and choose your own music – the extensive menu of CDs is played by request.

Luna Lounge
BAR

(Avaroa, near Santa Cruz) Though it has moved from its original location, this is one of Rurre's longest standing bars with a bouncing atmosphere, good pizza and great cocktails.

Bungalow Café Lounge
BAR

(Comercio, near Santa Cruz) Another chip off the old stick of bamboo, though this takes a slightly harder rock angle in its music.

Banana Club
CLUB

(Comercio; admission incl 1 drink B$15) If you want to try salsa dancing or Bolivian-style grooving, this slightly sleazy club has Cuban doctors shaking their booties, locals getting drunk and gringos joining in.

Shopping

The cheap clothing stalls along Pando are a good place to pick up *hamacas* (hammocks; single/double B$150/250) and finely woven cotton and synthetic *mosquiteros* (mosquito nets; from B$80). **Pampas Supermercado** (Pando, cnr Comercio) is convenient for stocking up on sun block, repellent and other jungle necessities.

ⓘ Information

Immigration

Immigration (☏892-2241; Aniceto Arce, btwn Busch & Bolívar; ☺8.30am-12.30pm & 2.30-6.30pm Mon-Fri) For visa extensions.

Internet Access

Getting online is pricey (B$6 per hour) and often frustratingly slow.

Internet (Comercio; ☺9am-10pm) Conveniently located and open all day.

Laundry

A couple of 'per kilo' laundries offer a next day service (B$8 per kilo), a same day service (B$10 per kilo) and a four-hour service (B$12 per kilo) if you are in a hurry.

Laundry Service Rurrenabaque (Vaca Diez; ☺8am-8pm)

Laundry Number One (Avaroa; ☺8am-8pm)

Money

There is one ATM here, a block north of the plaza at **Banco Union** (Comercio), but it is wise to bring enough cash just in case it is out of order. For emergencies you can get cash advances at **Prodem** (Avaroa; ☺8am-6pm Mon-Fri, 8am-2pm Sat), but only on Visa and MasterCard (including Visa debit cards). It also does Western Union transfers and changes cash. Tours can usually be paid for with credit cards.

Post

The post office is on Arce.

Telephone

Entel (cnr Comercio & Santa Cruz; ☺7am-10pm)

CHOOSING A JUNGLE OR PAMPAS TOUR

Jungle and pampas tours are Rurrenabaque's bread and butter, but quality of service provided by the numerous tour agencies varies considerably and in the name of competition some operators are much less responsible than they ought to be. This is largely a result of over-demanding budget travelers expecting low prices with big results, bartering prices down and compromising their own safety and levels of service in the process. In the interests of responsible travel, consider the following carefully before you hand over your cash.

Not all companies provide the same level of service, and cheaper most definitely does not mean better. Local authorities have set minimum prices at B$900 for a three-day, two-night excursion; be suspicious of any company that undercuts those rates and do not barter for a lower price.

Every company uses the word 'ecofriendly' as a throwaway sales gimmick. Catch out the conmen by asking the vendor to explain how their company is ecofriendly.

There are no guarantees of spotting wildlife. Any company that offers them is likely to be breaking the rules. Guides are forbidden from feeding, handling or disturbing animals. If your guide offers to capture anacondas, caiman or other animals, object and tell him why.

Use only SERNAP-authorized operators as these are the only ones allowed to legally enter Parque Nacional Madidi.

Foreigners must be accompanied by a local guide, but not all speak good English. If this is likely to be a problem ask to meet your guide.

Talk to other travelers about their experiences and boycott companies that break the rules. Be responsible in your own expectations.

Tourist Information

Tourist office (☎7138-3684; Vaca Diez at Avaroa; ◷8am-noon & 2.30-6pm Mon-Fri) Happy to answer questions and keen to advise on responsible tourism, but short on material.

SERNAP Parque Nacional Madidi office (☎892-2246, 892-2540; Libertad behind the market; ◷7am-3pm Mon-Sun) Across the river in San Buenaventura. Access to the park costs B$125 but should be included in tour quotes.

❶ Getting There & Away

Air

Rurre's airport is a few kilometers north of town and there is a two-pronged terminal fee of B$15. Transfer in minibus to and from the airline offices costs an additional B$6. The brief flight to La Paz is an affordable way of avoiding the arduous 24-hour bus journey to the capital. Flights sell out fast but are frequently cancelled during bad weather. You will be refunded only 70% of the ticket value if your flight is cancelled and you're not prepared to wait around for the next one. Be sure to reconfirm your ticket the day before your flight otherwise you may find yourself without a seat. Irritatingly, if you wish to fly to Riberalta or Guayaramerín, you need to return to La Paz or Trinidad.

TAM (☎892-2398; Santa Cruz) flies between La Paz and Rurre (B$480, one hour) at least once a day, with additional services during peak periods. **Amaszonas** (☎892-2472; Comercio,

near Santa Cruz) has four daily flights to La Paz (B$650) and theoretically flies daily to Trinidad (B$581).

Boat

Thanks to the Guayaramerín road, there's little cargo transportation down the Río Beni to Riberalta these days and there's no traffic at all during periods of low water. You'll need a dose of luck to find something and will have to negotiate what you consider a fair price for the trip, which may take as long as 10 days.

Bus & Jeep

The bus terminal is a good 20-minute walk northeast of the center and all buses and shared taxis depart from here. Prices are standard and do not vary between companies.

Several daily services make the daunting trip from Rurrenabaque to La Paz (B$70, 18 to 24 hours), via Yolosita (B$65, 14 to 20 hours), the hop-off point for Coroico. If you find the narrow, twisting Andean roads and sheer drops a harrowing experience on a bus, another option is to bus it as far as Caranavi and take a shared taxi from there, the rest of the trip being the most scary, or picturesque, depending on your point of view.

The route to Trinidad (B$150, 17 to 30 hours) via San Borja (taxi/bus B$80/50, nine to 18 hours) and San Ignacio de Moxos (B$100, 12 hours) remains one of the worst in the country and is typically closed during the rainy season.

Better still, opt for one of the community-run ecotourism ventures, which, although more expensive, are definitely more worthwhile and aim to help sustain communities and preserve the richness of the rainforests for the generations to come.

Jungle Tours

The Bolivian rainforest is full of more interesting and unusual things than you could ever imagine. Local guides, most of whom have grown up in the area, can explain animals' habits and habitats and demonstrate the uses of some of the thousands of plant species, including the forest's natural remedies for colds, fever, cuts, insect bites (which come in handy!) and other ailments. Note that you are likely to see a lot more plants than animals.

Most trips are by canoe upstream along the Río Beni, and some continue up the Río Tuichi, camping and taking shore and jungle walks along the way, with plenty of swimming opportunities and hammock time. Accommodations are generally in agencies' private camps.

Rain, mud and *mariguí* (sandflies) make the wet season (especially January to March) unpleasant for jungle tours, but some agencies have camps set up for wildlife watching at this time.

Pampas Tours

It's easier to see wildlife in the wetland savannas northeast of town, but the sun is more oppressive, and the bugs can be worse, especially in the rainy season. Bring binoculars, a good flashlight, extra batteries and plenty of strong anti-bug juice. Highlights include playful pink river dolphins, horseback riding and night-time canoe trips to spot caiman.

Buses now run year-round to Riberalta (B$110, 17 to 40 hours) and Guayaramerín (B$120, 18 hours to three days), but you need a healthy dose of stamina, insect repellent and food if you're going to attempt it in the wet season.

ⓘ Getting Around

TAM and Amazonas *micros* (B$6, 10 minutes) shuttle between the airport and airline offices in town. Moto-taxis around town cost B$3 per ride; there is a convenient *parada* (taxi stand) at the corner of Comercio and Santa Cruz. The ferry across to San Buenaventura leaves from the port area every 20 minutes (B$1) or so from 6am to midnight, though services are less frequent after 6pm.

Parque Nacional Madidi

The Río Madidi watershed is one of South America's most intact ecosystems. Most of it is protected by the 1.8 million-hectare Parque Nacional Madidi, which takes in a range of habitats, from the steaming lowland rainforests to 5500m Andean peaks. This little-trodden utopia is home to an astonishing variety of Amazonian wildlife: 44% of all New World mammal species, 38% of neotropical amphibian species, almost 1000 species of bird and more threatened species than any park in the world.

The populated portions of the park along the Río Tuichi have been accorded a special Unesco designation permitting indigenous inhabitants to utilize traditional forest resources, but the park has also been considered for oil exploration and as a site for a major hydroelectric scheme in the past. In addition, illicit logging has affected several areas around the perimeter and there's been talk of a new road between Apolo and Ixiamas that would effectively bisect the park. Though the hydroelectric scheme has been abandoned, the debate continues over whether road building and oil exploration will be permitted, and most suspect that if it is, illegal loggers will be quick to capitalize on the improved access.

It is difficult to visit the park independently, but if you wish to do so the B$125 admission fee is payable at the SERNAP office in San Buenaventura – you must be accompanied by an authorized guide. By far the easiest and most responsible way to arrange access is by visiting one of the community projects listed following.

🛏 Sleeping

Providing a model for responsible, sustainable ecotourism in Bolivia, the community projects in Madidi preach a respect for culture, environment and wildlife; and benefit

SAN BUENAVENTURA

Sleepy San Buenaventura sits across the Río Beni, watching all the busy goings-on in Rurre, content with its own slower pace. If you're looking for fine Beni leather goods, visit the store of well-known leather artisan Manuel Pinto on the main street. Avoid purchasing anything made from wild rainforest species. The **Centro Cultural Tacana** (🖉892-2394; west side of plaza; admission B$5; ☉Sun-Thu) has a handicrafts store and celebrates the Tacana people's unique cosmovision.

local communities rather than private operators. You can choose from one-day tours to longer stays, incorporating walks in the rainforest with visits to indigenous communities, where you can peek into local lifestyles and traditions. Make sure you don't give sweets or presents to children, no matter how cute they look, as this builds unrealistic expectations. Booking offices for most of these community lodges are located in Rurrenabaque and prices include park access.

TOP CHOICE Chalalán Ecolodge
LODGE $$$

(🖉892-2419, in La Paz 2-231-1451; www.chalalan.com; 3 nights & 4 days all inclusive per person US$390) Bolivia's oldest and most successful community-based ecotourism project. Set up in the early 1990s by the inhabitants of remote San José de Uchupiamonas, it has become a lifeline for villagers, and has so far generated money for a school and a small clinic. Built entirely from natural rainforest materials by the enthusiastic San José youth, the lodge's simple and elegant huts surround the idyllic oxbow lake, Laguna Chalalán.

Chalalán provides the opportunity to amble through relatively untouched rainforest and appreciate the diversity of the native wildlife. While the flora and fauna are lovely, it's the sounds that provide the magic here: the incredible dawn bird chorus, the evening frog symphony, the collective whine of zillions of insects, the roar of bucketing tropical rainstorms and, in the early morning, the reverberating chorus of every howler monkey within a 100km radius.

Your trip (once you're in Rurre) starts with a six-hour canoe ride upstream on the misty Río Beni, and moves onto the smaller tributary, Río Tuichi. Once you're at Chalalán, you can go on long daytime treks or on nocturnal walks. Boat excursions on the lake are a delight and you can see different types of monkey who come to feed and drink water. Swimming in the lake among docile caimans is a must, especially at dusk when the light is heavenly. On nights prior to departures from the lodge, the guides throw parties, with windpipe playing, coca chewing and general merriment.

The village of San José is another three hours upstream by boat, and if you wish to visit it from Chalalán, though you'll need to arrange it in advance, it's especially rewarding during the week-long fiesta for the local patron saint around May 1.

Rates include transfers to and from the airport (if you're coming from La Paz), one night in Rurre, three great meals per day, a well-trained English-speaking guide, excursions, canoe trips on the lake, plus local taxes and a community levy. The **booking office** (🖉892-2419; www.chalalan.com; Comercio near Campero) is in Rurrenabaque.

TOP CHOICE Sadiri
LODGE $$$

(🖉6770-9087, in Santa Cruz 3-356-3636; full board including transfer & return to Rurrenabaque per person per day US$150) The newest kid on the community project block is wonderful Sadiri, a set of six luxury cabins in dense foothill rainforest in the Serranía Sadiri. The indigenous San José de Uchupiamonas community rejected the advances of the courting oil companies and with the assistance of local conservationists opted instead for a sustainable tourist project aimed at bringing long-term benefits to the area. With community members staffing the lodge and the best-trained wildlife guides in the Rurrenabaque area, this innovative lodge caters as much for serious bird-watchers and ecotravelers as it does to those who just revel in the beauty of natural areas.

What sets Sadiri apart from the other Madidi lodges is its highland location (between 500m and 950m), resulting in a much cooler temperature than the sweaty lowlands. This means that there is a whole new set of animals and birds to enjoy, including mixed flocks filled with dozens of species of glittering tanagers, each one like a feathered jewel. Bird Bolivia (p244) organizes recommended trips.

Traditional home-cooked meals are served on a terrace flanked with hummingbird feeders and looking out over Madidi with some of the most awe-inspiring views of the national park that you could ever imagine. Bookings are by phone only.

San Miguel del Bala — LODGE $$$

(892-2394; www.sanmigueldelbala.com; Comercio near Vaca Diez, Rurrenabaque; per person per day B$450) A glorious community ecolodge in its own patch of paradise right on Madidi's doorstep, 40 minutes upstream by boat from Rurre. This Tacana community consists of around 230 inhabitants who'll be happy to show you their traditional agricultural methods, weaving and wood-carving.

Accommodations are in cabins with mahogany wood floors, separate bathrooms and beds covered by silky mosquito nets. There are several guided walks, including a visit to the San Miguel community. What the guides lack in English, they make up for with their enthusiasm and knowledge.

The price includes transportation, accommodations, food and guided tours. If you go for the three-day/two-night arrangement, you can have a day's visit into Parque Nacional Madidi. Guests can also chill in hammocks in the communal hut. The **booking office** (892-2394; www.sanmigueldelbala.com; Comercio btwn Vaca Diez) is in Rurrenabaque.

San Borja

3 / POP 34,350

San Borja is pretty much just a bus- and truck-stop destination, though you can easily find yourself stuck here waiting for transportation to Trinidad or Rurrenabaque during the rainy season.

🛏 Sleeping

San Borja's hotels specialize in hard mattresses and turquoise walls. Listed are two that try to break the mold.

Hostal Jatata — HOSTEL $

(895-3212; s/d B$90/150) Two blocks off the plaza, pick of the bunch Jatata offers good, comfy rooms and a patio with drooping hammocks. There is a *palapa* roof and a half-decent restaurant.

Hotel San Borja — HOTEL $

(r per person B$50) Higher-end rooms cater to the choosier visitor; cheaper ones fall into the turquoise trap but provide a crash-pad for the night. Note that there is a 6am gospel wake-up call courtesy of the nearby Catholic church.

ℹ Getting There & Away

Amazonas (895-3185; Bolívar 157) supposedly has daily round-trip flights between La Paz, San Borja and Trinidad but they only stop here if there is demand.

The San Borja to Trinidad road is notoriously bad and can be closed for long periods during the wet season. It's frustrating for anybody wanting to travel between Rurrenabaque and Trinidad, and even more so when transportation that sets out from Rurre bound for Trinidad announces, after a little local consultation at San Borja, that they can go no further. In theory, more services to Trinidad depart from San Borja than from Rurre, so you may find yourself here whether you like it or not, either looking for a connection, or simply stranded and waiting.

In the dry season buses pull out several times daily from the bus terminal (3km south of the plaza; B$4 by moto-taxi) for the Reserva Biosférica del Beni (B$20, 1½ hours), San Ignacio de Moxos (B$40, five hours), Trinidad (B$50, eight to 12 hours) and Santa Cruz (B$100, 20 to 24 hours). During the wet season the trip to Trinidad is sometimes attempted by privately owned 4WD vehicles (per person B$100) commissioned by the bus companies, though whether they depart or not depends on the whim of the driver. There are frequent *micro* services to Rurrenabaque (B$50, nine hours), which depart when full, or in the wet season you'll need a 4WD taxi (B$80 per person).

If you're Trinidad-bound, note that the Río Mamoré *balsa* (raft) crossings close at 6pm, and you need five to six hours to reach them from San Borja. There are no accommodations on either side of the crossing, so give yourself plenty of time. Watch for pink river dolphins at river crossings.

Reserva Biosférica del Beni

Created by Conservation International in 1982 as a loosely protected natural area, the 334,200-hectare Beni Biosphere Reserve was recognized by Unesco in 1986 as a 'Man & the Biosphere Reserve,' and received official recognition the following year through a pioneering debt swap agreement with the Bolivian government.

The adjacent **Reserva Forestal Chimane**, a 1.15-million-hectare buffer zone and indigenous reserve, has been set aside for sustainable subsistence use by the 1200 Chimane people living there. The combined areas are home to at least 500 bird species as well as more than 100 mammals and myriad reptiles, amphibians and insects.

The Chimane reserve was threatened in 1990 when the government decided to open the area to loggers. Seven hundred Chimanes and representatives of other tribes staged a march from Trinidad to La Paz in protest at the decision that would amount to the wholesale destruction of their land. Logging concessions were changed but not altogether revoked, and the problems continue.

◎ Sights

The reserve headquarters, El Porvenir, is in the *cerrado* (savanna) and quite a distance from the rainforest. The station organizes everything in the reserve: accommodations, food, guides and horseback riding. The best way to observe wildlife is to hire a guide at the station and go for a hike, though the heat might be easier to take if you hire a horse.

Laguna Normandia   LAKE
This savanna lake, an hour's walk from El Porvenir, is the reserve's most popular destination. The sight of the world's largest population of crawling, rare black caimans – there are at least 400 of them – is truly astounding. The reptiles are the descendants of specimens originally destined to become unwilling members of the fashion industry, by providing shoe and bag material for a leather company. When the caiman breeder's business failed, the animals were left behind, and sadly the majority perished from neglect, crowding and hunger. The survivors were rescued by Bolivian authorities and airlifted to safety.

Fortunately, caimans have little interest in humans, so it's generally safe to observe them at close range while rowboating around with a guide. If you find them too scary to get up close and personal, climb the 11m **viewing tower**.

Totaizal & Reserva Forestal Chimane   PARK
A stone's throw from the road and a 40-minute walk from El Porvenir is Totaizal. This friendly and well-organized village of 140 people lies hidden in the forest of the Chimane reserve. The Chimane, traditionally a nomadic forest tribe, have in recent times faced expulsion from their ancestral lands by lumber companies and highland settlers. Skilled hunters, the Chimane people have a fascinating way of fishing, using natural poisons to kill their prey. They are also highly adept at collecting wild honey and avoiding ballistic bees. People living in the settlement of **Cero Ocho**, a four-hour walk from Totaizal, trudge into the village to sell bananas, while others provide guiding services for visitors. You can visit the village of Totaizal, but you'll have to make prior arrangements through El Porvenir.

☞ Tours

El Porvenir   WALKING TOUR, HORSEBACK RIDING
(cerrado hike per person B$120) Theoretically the El Porvenir station can organize a variety of tours with enough notice, though these are more difficult to arrange during the wet season. The most popular are the four-hour canoe trips to see the black caimans in **Laguna Normandia** (per person B$80); a four-hour **cerrado hike** to the monkey-rich

---

FIESTA DE MOXOS

Annually, 2pm on July 30 marks the first day of celebrations of the huge Fiesta del Santo Patrono de Moxos, held in honor of San Ignacio, the sacred protector of the Moxos. This is one of the best festivals in the Amazon and if you're in Bolivia during this time, you'd be crazy to miss it.

Strictly speaking, the festival begins on July 22 and gets off to a strange start. The small statue of Santiago from the church is paraded and worshipped each evening until July 25 (Día de la Fiesta de Santiago), after which point the same statue is then worshipped as an image of San Ignacio for the rest of the *fiesta*! During this time each family in the village brings an image of San Ignacio to the church and places it there in his honor. These solemn processions continue for another four days before the real festivities begin.

On July 30, a procession leaves from the church incorporating *macheteros* (local youths dressed in white with remarkable radial headdresses traditionally made from macaw feathers), *achus* (village elders with wooden masks and hats bearing fireworks) and musicians beating out the tunes of the unique Moxos music – using drums, enormous bamboo pan-pipes and flutes. One by one the procession visits every house in the village, returning the images of San Ignacio that had been deposited in the church and receiving food and drink

rainforest islands; and a full-day **Las Torres tour** (per person with food B$250) on horseback to three wildlife-viewing towers where you can observe both *cerrado* (savanna) and rainforest ecosystems, and also fish for piranhas for dinner.

If you're a bird fanatic, take the **Loro tour** (per person B$80) on foot or horseback to see the colorful spectacle of macaws and parakeets coming to roost – or you can check them out in the palms at El Porvenir, where they provide a natural 6am alarm clock.

The most interesting but also the most taxing option is the four-day **Tur Monitoreo** (per person without/with food B$600/700), during which visitors accompany park rangers on their wildlife monitoring rounds into the furthest reaches of the reserve. You will need your own camping gear for this and, of course, plenty of insect repellent, but you'll have a great shot at seeing monkeys, macaws and pink river dolphins.

To go into the rainforest beyond Laguna Normandia, you'll definitely need a guide. It's a four-hour walk from the lake to the edge of the secondary-growth rainforest. A further four hours' walk takes you into the primary forest. Along the way, a 6m viewing tower provides a vista over an island of rainforest, and a 4m tower along the Río Curiraba provides views over the forest and savanna in the remotest parts of the reserve.

🛏 Sleeping & Eating

El Porvenir   LODGE **$$**
(per person incl food dm/camping B$100/50) Accommodations at El Porvenirare are in airy bunk-bed rooms. Its fine when it's hot, but in cold weather you might wish you had brought your sleeping bag. Amenities include a library, a researchers' workshop, an interpretive center, and a small cultural and biological museum. There's plenty of drinkable water but consider bringing snacks and refreshments as there is nowhere to buy anything for miles around.

ℹ Information

The reserve is administered by SERNAP in La Paz in conjunction with a local committee of representatives. Admission to the biosphere reserve is B$35 per person. Horse rentals are available from around B$70 per eight-hour day.

The best months to visit the reserve are June and July, when there's little rain and the days are clear; bring warm clothing to protect against the occasional *surazo*. During the rainy season, days are hot, wet, muggy and miserable with mosquitoes, so bring plenty of repellent.

ℹ Getting There & Away

El Porvenir is 200m off the highway, 90 minutes east of San Borja, and is accessible via any *movilidad* (anything that moves) between Trinidad and San Borja or Rurrenabaque – ask your driver to drop you at the entrance. In the dry season Trinidad-bound buses mainly pass in the morning between 9am and 11am, those for San Borja usually in the late afternoon between 4pm and 7pm. Otherwise there's surprisingly little traffic. Note that this route is in a dismal state and often closed during the rainy season, so check the weather forecast before setting out to avoid getting stranded.

AMAZON BASIN RESERVA BIOSFÉRICA DEL BENI

in return. The winding route ends at the church, where they attend Mass, its close signifying the end of formalities and the beginning of festivities.

The evening of the first day of fiesta starts with huge fireworks let off by two rich local families outside the church, who 'compete' through the lavishness of their displays. Then it's over to the *achus*, men and women wearing large, high-topped leather hats with firecrackers fizzling on the top, who run through the crowd, while everyone shrieks and runs away, laughing and screaming – children have a particularly good time. Fresh river fish is eaten in abundance, plenty of drinking takes place (as you'll see by the number of booze-casualties sleeping in the streets) and local *artesanía* (handcrafted items) are displayed around the village.

On the morning of the second day another Mass is held. The small statue of San Ignacio is returned to the church and a larger statue of the same saint is extracted for the first time to lead a second procession, one that is this time accompanied by local politicians, religious authorities, invited dignitaries and others worthy of a bigger statue. Once the formalities are dispensed with, it's party time again. The second and third days are filled with lots of dancing and bull-teasing, when the (drunk) locals attempt to get the bulls' attention. A few days later, San Ignacio goes back to its quiet life, only to go wild again the following year.

San Ignacio de Moxos

📷3 / POP 20,500

San Ignacio de Moxos is a friendly, tranquil indigenous Moxos village, 92km west of Trinidad, that dedicates itself to agriculture and oozes an ambience quite distinct from any other Bolivian town. The people speak an indigenous dialect known locally as *ignaciano,* and their lifestyle, traditions and food are unique in the country. The best time to visit San Ignacio is during the annual festival on July 30 and 31. This is when the villagers let their hair down and get their feather headgear up, and don't stop drinking, dancing and letting off fireworks for three days.

The village was founded as San Ignacio de Loyola by the Jesuits in 1689. In 1749 it suffered pestilence and had to be shifted to its present location on healthier ground.

◉ Sights & Activities

Main Plaza   PLAZA
(museum B$10; ☺church 8am-7pm) In the main plaza is a **monument** to Chirípieru, El Machetero Ignaciano, with his crown of feathers and formidable-looking hatchet, a look that's re-created extensively during the village festival. The **church** on the plaza was restored and rebuilt from 1995 to 2003 and adopts the familiar Jesuit style with a wide roof supported by wooden columns, though they are noticeably smooth and without decoration in this example. If you get a small group together, one of the church workers will take you around for a small fee.

At the **museum** in the Casa Belén, near the northwest corner of the plaza, you'll see elements of both the Ignaciano and Moxos cultures, including the *bajones,* the immense flutes introduced by the Jesuits.

Laguna Isirere   LAKE
North of town at the large Laguna Isirere, you can go fishing and swimming, observe the profuse bird life and watch the gorgeous sunset. A statue on the shores depicts the local legend about the formation of the lake. A young boy named Isidoro was paddling in a small pool when he was swallowed up by the waters, the work of the mischievous water spirit Jichi who needed a human sacrifice in order to turn the pool into the lake it is today. It's accessible on a 30-minute walk or by hitchhiking from town.

The greater area also boasts a number of obscure – and hard-to-reach – places of interest: the **Lomas de Museruna,** several

archaeological ruins, and the ruins of the missions San José and San Luis Gonzaga.

🍴 Sleeping & Eating

Plenty of accommodations are available in town, though quality varies from rustic to 'only in an emergency'! Note that prices double during the fiesta, but visitors can camp at established sites just outside town during the festivities.

Plaza Hotel   PENSION $
(📷482-2032; per person B$70, without bathroom B$50) On the plaza, a cheery option with bright, spacious doubles with fans.

Residencial Don Joaquín   PENSION $
(📷482-8012; Montes; per person B$80, without bathroom B$50) At the corner of the plaza near the church, it offers a nice patio and clean, simple rooms.

Residencial 31 de Julio   PENSION $
(per person without bathroom B$30) A block off the plaza, this friendly place maintains clean and basic rooms.

Restaurante Moxos   INTERNATIONAL $$
(3 blocks north of plaza; mains B$30-40) The already functioning restaurant, of the soon to be functioning (maybe?) Hotel Ecoturístico Moxos. This is part of a Trinidad-run project to provide a more upscale service for visitors.

La Cabaña del Gordo   BOLIVIAN $
(St Esteban; mains B$20) A local favorite that specializes in traditional Moxos dishes.

❶ Getting There & Away

San Ignacio is located smack-bang in the middle of the notoriously poor Trinidad–San Borja road, which is impassable following periods of rain. From March to October, it's four hours from Trinidad to San Ignacio, including the *balsa* crossing of the Río Mamoré, but this route is often closed during the rainy season. If you're making your own way note that the *balsa* closes at 6pm (it may stay open later at times of heavy traffic) and there are no accommodations on either side, so check the timing before setting out.

By far the easiest access is from Trinidad, with *camionetas* (open-backed 4WDs) running when full from the *parada* at 1 de Mayo near Velarde (B$70, four hours). San Borja–bound bus services pass through San Ignacio in the early afternoon but take considerably longer (B$50, six hours). During intense periods of rain and during the festival, flights to Trinidad may be offered. The tiny Moxos airport is at the top end of Av Aeropuerto but you'll have to ask around for information.

From San Borja, several buses to San Ignacio (B\$40, five hours) theoretically leave daily. In the wet season *camionetas* (per person B\$100) replace the buses, but they're frequently canceled if the drivers don't need the work. Sporadic departures to Rurrenabaque leave during the dry season only, but it's usually easier to catch a lift to San Borja and take one of the more frequent *micros* from there.

EASTERN BOLIVIAN AMAZON

Trinidad, the Bolivian Amazon's main population center, is still very much a frontier settlement, though it's also an access point for dozens of smaller communities, wild rivers and remote jungle reserves. The eastern side of the Amazon hides spectacular wildernesses and reserves of difficult access that are a rewarding challenge for the intrepid ecotourist.

Trinidad

📞 3 / POP 80,000 / ELEV 235M (771FT)

Trinidad is the place you'll come to if you're after a trip down the long and deep Río Mamoré, or on your way between Santa Cruz and Rurrenabaque. Despite its colonial architecture and colonnaded streets, it's a modern town that is growing rapidly. Its most notable feature is the massive, green, tropical main square (Trinidad is only 14 degrees south of the equator), once home to a population of friendly sloths.

The city of La Santísima Trinidad (the Most Holy Trinity) was founded in 1686 by Padre Cipriano Barace as the second Jesuit mission in the flatlands of the southern Beni. It was originally constructed on the banks of the Río Mamoré, 14km from its present location, but floods and pestilence along the riverbanks necessitated relocation. In 1769 it was moved to the Arroyo de San Juan, which now divides the city in two.

THE AMAZONIAN EL DORADO

In the Llanos de Moxos, between San Ignacio de Moxos and Loreto, the heavily forested landscape is crossed with more than 100km of canals and causeways and dotted with hundreds of *lomas* (artificial mounds), embankments and fanciful prehistoric earthworks depicting people and animals. One anthropomorphic figure measures more than 2km from head to toe – a rainforest variation on Peru's famed Nazca Lines. The original purpose of the earthworks was probably to permit cultivation in a seasonally flooded area, but inside the mounds were buried figurines, pottery, ceramic stamps, human remains and even tools made from stone imported into the region.

The discovery of the *lomas* has caused scientists to look at the Beni region with entirely new eyes: what was previously considered to be a wilderness never touched by humans, save for a few dispersed tribes who inhabited the region, is now thought to have been an area where a vast, advanced civilization farmed, worked and lived in a highly structured society with sophisticated cities.

It is believed that the ceramic mounds came from the large numbers of people who lived on them and who ate and drank from pots, which were then destroyed and buried to improve soil stability. Archaeologists say that the sheer amount of pots indicates the complexity of this lost society.

Romantics associate the prehistoric structures of the Beni with the legendary Paititi tribe, and infer that this ancient Beni civilization was the source of the popular Spanish legends of the rainforest El Dorado known as Gran Paititi. The Patiti were said to be an Inca tribe associated with the cultural hero Inkarri who, after founding Cuzco, retired to the Amazon to found another great but mysterious civilization in an unknown location. Though some Inca fragments were found in northern Bolivia during excavations in 2003, the Inca origin of the Moxos sites remains doubtful, and the most accepted theory is that if Paititi even existed at all its most likely location is Peru.

Archaeologists continue their research into this fascinating part of history, but one thing is for sure: once you know what lies here in terms of world history, you'll never look at the forests of the Beni in the same way again.

Trinidad

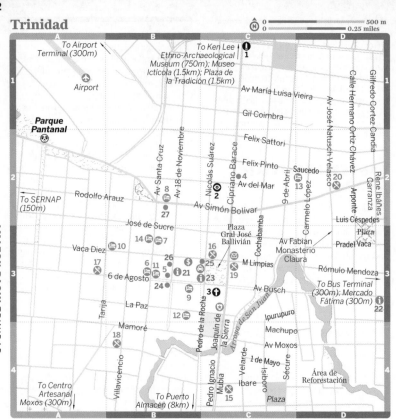

Trinidad

◉ Sights

Plaza Gral José Ballivián   PLAZA
Trinidad's loveliest feature is Plaza Gral José Ballivián, with its tall, tropical trees, lush gardens and community atmosphere. You can spend a pleasant evening eating ice cream and listening to the rhythmic drone of hundreds of motorcycles orbiting around the square. In the past, the traffic was refereed by a police officer who sat in a big wooden chair and conjured up red, yellow and green traffic lights by touching an electric wire against one of three nails. On the south side of the plaza, the **cathedral** (Plaza Gral José Ballivián; admission free), built on the site of an earlier Jesuit church, is an unimpressive building that doesn't even have its own bells – the on-the-hour bell ringing is played from a recording.

Ken Lee Ethno-Archaeological Museum   MUSEUM
(Av Ganadera; admission B$5; ⊙8am-noon & 3-6pm) This Spanish-funded museum north of the center is considered the city's top cultural attraction. It exhibits artefacts from the Trinidad region, including traditional instruments and tribal costumes.

Museo Ictícola   MUSEUM
(admission B$5; ⊙8am-noon & 3-6pm Mon-Fri) At the university 1.5km north of town along Cipriano Barace is the Museo Ictícola, an extensive aquarium featuring 400 species of Amazonian fish.

FREE Parque Pantanal   ZOO
(Av Laureano Villar; admission free; ⊙8am-6pm) On the road to the airport this wooded park is a nice place to while away a few hours while admiring the rehabilitated wildlife that roams free around you. There are several deer here and also some anacondas in the ponds, so watch your toes!

Plazuela Natuch   PLAZA
(Nicolás Suárez at Av del Mar) Worth a quick look for the colourful Beni wall murals and statues of native wildlife, including a prone jaguar and a family of capybara. There are usually some stalls selling local *artesanía*, as well as canoodling teenagers.

⌔ Tours

Several agencies run tours into the city's hinterlands.

Turismo Moxos   TOUR
(☑462-1141; turmoxos@entelnet.bo; 6 de Agosto 114) Turismo Moxos organizes three-day dolphin cruises on the Río Ibare, visits to Sirionó villages, four-day canoe safaris into the jungle and one-day horseback trips into remote areas.

Fremen Tours   BOAT TOUR
(☑462-2726; www.andes-amazonia.com; Cipriano Barace 332) Fremen Tours specializes in all-inclusive river cruises. Trips are booked through the offices in Cochabamba (p174).

★☆ Festivals & Events

Fiesta de la Santísima Trinidad   RELIGIOUS
The town's mid-June founding fiesta is a big, loud, drunken party at the Plaza de la Tradición, and features the climbing of greased poles for prizes and a *hocheadas de toros* (teasing of bulls).

⋐ Sleeping

Most hotels offer cheaper rooms with fan and more expensive rooms with air-conditioning. The latter is a wise investment.

TOP CHOICE Hostal Sirari   PENSION $
(☑462-4472; Santa Cruz 538; s/d B$100/160, with air-con B$160/200; ❉) A step up in quality without the step up in price. Rooms are whitewashed, sparkling new and in comparison to other Trinidad hostels worth more than what you pay. There is a small courtyard with tame toucans that beg for your breakfast scraps.

Hotel Jacarandá Suites   HOTEL $$
(☑462-2400; La Paz near Pedro de la Rocha; s/d B$300/420; ❉@⊛) For a long time taking the mantle of Trinidad's undisputed best hotel, this is a modern, smart place with an upscale clientele. All rooms are minisuites with air-conditioning, some of which have small balconies overlooking the leafy courtyard. Enjoy a cocktail in the Tropical Bar or cool off in the pool.

Hotel Campanario   HOTEL $$$
(☑462-4622; www.hotel-campanario.com; Av 6 de Agosto 80; s/d B$300/480, ste B$650-750; ❉@⊛) As the newest top-end hotel on the scene in Trinidad, Hotel Camapanario is aiming to capitalize on an increase in wealthy business travelers from Santa Cruz by offering a series of high-class rooms and suites. Suites are tastefully decorated and airy, with colorful bed spreads, and the pool

DOWN THE LAZY RIVER

River trips from Trinidad will carry you to the heart of the Bolivian Amazon along the Río Mamoré, where you'll experience the mystique and solitude for which the rainforests are renowned. For optimum enjoyment, visit during the dry season, which lasts roughly from May or June until some time in October.

Although the scenery along the northern rivers changes little, the diversity of plant and animal species along the shore picks up any slack in the pace of the journey. The longer your trip, the deeper you'll gaze into the forest darkness and the more closely you'll scan the riverbanks for signs of movement. Free of the pressures and demands of active travel, you'll have time to relax and savor the passing scene.

In general, the riverboat food is pretty good, but meals consist mainly of *masaco* (mashed yucca or plantains), served with *charque* (dried meat), rice, noodles, thin soup and bananas in every conceivable form. After a couple of days you'll probably start dreaming of pizza, so bring along some treats to supplement the daily fare. It's also wise to carry your own water or some form of water purification.

You'll need to be quite resourceful to organize your trip. Ask around at the *Capitanía* in Puerto Almacén (moto-taxi B$15) 8km southwest of Trinidad and be sure to discuss sleeping arrangements before setting out. Passengers must usually bring their own hammocks (available in Trinidad), but you may be allowed to sleep on deck or on the roof of the boat. You'll also need a sleeping bag or a blanket, especially in winter, when jungle nights can be surprisingly chilly. If you're fortunate enough to be on a boat that travels through the night, a mosquito net isn't necessary, but on boats that tie up at night, passengers without a mosquito net will find the experience ranges from utterly miserable to unbearable.

The Guayaramerín run takes up to a week (larger boats do it in three to four days) and costs around B$350 including food, B$250 without. South to Puerto Villarroel, smaller boats take five days and cost about B$250 including meals.

For a plusher river affair, get on Fremen Tours' posh hotel-boat *Flotel Reina de Enin*.

---

access and air-conditioning contribute toward what should be a pleasant stay.

Mi Residencia HOTEL $$
(☑462-1543; Felix Pinto 555; s/d B$250/400; ❋@❄) A flashy entrance through a wooden gate takes you into the smooth, glass-fronted reception here. The large rooms are decked out in loud, kitsch designs, and each has a TV and fridge. The hotel is a 10-minute walk from the main plaza.

Hotel Aguahí HOTEL $$
(☑462-5569; Bolívar at Santa Cruz; s/d/tr B$320/440/560; ❋@❄) The rooms are large, the beds comfortable and there is a large, figure-of-eight pool in the spacious, tropical garden.

Hostal El Tajibo HOTEL $
(☑462-2324; Santa Cruz 423; s/d B$100/150, with air-con B$200/250; ❋) One of Trinidad's better-value budget options, this hotel has attractive, almost stylish rooms and comfortable beds. Some rooms have balconies overlooking the street and breakfast is included with air-con rooms. Ask about reductions when it is quiet

Hotel Colonial HOTEL $
(☑462-2864; Vaca Diez 76; s/d B$100/150, with air-con B$200/250; ❋) If El Tajibo is full, the same owners run the carbon-copy Colonial a couple of blocks further on from the plaza. It's almost identical, from the decor right down to the price.

Hotel Gran Moxos/Palace VIP HOTEL $$
(☑462-8777; www.hotelmoxos.com.bo; 6 de Agosto 146; s/d B$140/240, with air-con B$240/360; ❋) Despite the shabby-looking reception, this isn't a bad hotel, though an attack of the hyperboles was obviously involved in its naming. Rooms are carpeted, comfortable and characterless, with breakfast included and served in the cafe downstairs.

Residencial Santa Cruz PENSION $
(☑462-0711; Santa Cruz 537; s/d B$80/140, s without bathroom B$60) A budget place that makes a real effort to cheer up its rooms with colorful decor, hand-painted wall hangings and

bright bedclothes. Rooms on the 1st floor are airier (and slightly pricier). All rooms have cable TV.

Eating & Drinking

For a city of its size, Trinidad disappoints with the quality of its restaurants and, despite being in the heart of Beni cattle country, it can be surprisingly difficult to get a decent steak.

 Churrasquería
La Estancia   BARBECUE $$$
(Ibare near Velarde; B$40-120) Ask anybody in Trinidad where to get a good bit of beef and you will be sent here. With its palm roof and coal-fire barbecue hamming up the ranchhouse setting, the succulent and juicy cuts will make you wonder how other restaurants even dare to call themselves *churrasquerías* (grilled meat restaurants).

Los Farroles   INTERNATIONAL $$$
(6 de Agosta, near 18 de Noviembre; almuerzo B$25, mains B$30-130) Don't fall out of your chair! They serve salads here! In fact this upmarket (by Trinidad standards) restaurant serves a bit of everything from pizza and steak to chicken and fish. It's the restaurant of the swish Hotel Campanario, but that doesn't stop them from offering a well-cooked and excellent value *almuerzo* (set lunch) as well.

El Tabano   SEAFOOD $$
(Villavicencio, near Mamoré; mains B$20-55) With cool beers and cocktails served in the courtyard, this grass-roofed resto-pub is a popular place with Trinidad's young crowd on account of its lively atmosphere and excellent food. The menu consists of a number of inventive variations on fish and caiman dishes.

El Balcón   INTERNATIONAL $$$
(6 de Agosta, near Tarija; mains B$35-70; ⊘dinner only) Named presumably for the cramped wooden balconies outside, this is one of the more popular eating spots for couples. It's hardly an experience in fine dining, but the meat and chicken dishes are well prepared.

La Choza del Pescador   SEAFOOD $$
(Bolívar at Velasco; mains B$40-55) There's not much on the menu here, just fish cooked in about five different ways, but if you are feeling fishy then this is a good place to drop anchor.

Club Social   BOLIVIAN $$$
(Suárez; almuerzo B$20, mains B$25-60) Right on the plaza, in a shady, breezy courtyard, the lovely social club is a local family favorite. The generous two-course lunch menu includes soup, meat, rice and veg. The dinner menu isn't such good value.

La Casona   INTERNATIONAL $$$
(east side of Plaza Gral José Ballivián; almuerzo B$15, mains B$25-100) Trinidad's most-famous restaurant unfortunately doesn't live up to the hype. Give the greasy and overpriced à la carte meals a miss and stick to the lunchtime *almuerzo*.

Shopping

Centro Artesanal Moxos   ARTS & CRAFTS
(⊘462-2751; Bopi) Local Beni crafts, including weavings, woodwork and ceramics, are sold at the Centro Artesanal Moxos, 300m southwest of town along the river. Look out for the *pifano*, an indigenous flute made from the wing bone of the Jabiru stork using a technique more than 1000 years old – it's the staple instrument of the unique Moxos music.

ℹ Information

Dangers & Annoyances
Use bottled water for everything in Trinidad except your shower. The town water supply is contaminated.

Immigration
Immigration office (⊘462-1449; Av Los Tajibos, near Ibañez Carranza) Top floor of the white building a block from the bus terminal.

Money
Several Enlace ATMs near the main plaza accept international cards – this is a good spot to get some cash before heading out to the Amazon proper. Moneychangers gather on Av 6 de Agosto between Suárez and Av 18 de Noviembre.
Prodem (Vaca Diez) Just off the plaza for cash advances.

Tourist information
Tourist office (⊘462-1322; Felix Pinto; ⊘8.30am-12.30pm & 2.30-6pm Mon-Fri)

Telephone & Internet
Telephone cabins and internet access (B$4 per hour) are on almost every block, with a

notable concentration along 6 de Agosto near the plaza.

❶ Getting There & Away

Air

Departing air travelers must pay B$7 for use of the Jorge Henrich Arauz airport, which is just outside the northwest corner of town along Av Laureano Villar (moto-taxi B$7).

Amazonas (☑462-2426; 18 de Noviembre 267) shuttles daily to La Paz, sometimes via San Borja and has regular flights to Cobija, Riberalta and Guayaramerín. **AeroCon** (☑462-4442; 18 de Noviembre, near 6 de Agosto) handles several daily flights to Santa Cruz, Riberalta and Cobija. **TAM** (☑462-2363; Bolívar at Santa Cruz) has a couple of flights a week to Cochabamba and La Paz.

Bus & Camioneta

The rambling bus terminal is a 10-minute walk east of the center. Several *flotas* depart nightly between 6pm and 10pm for Santa Cruz (normal/*bus cama* B$53/125, eight to 10 hours). A number of companies theoretically serve Rurrenabaque (B$130, 17 to 30 hours) daily via San Borja (B$50, eight to 12 hours), though from November to May these services are typically suspended. There are also daily dry-season departures to Riberalta (B$200, 17 to 30 hours) and Guayaramerín (B$240, 22 to 35 hours).

Camionetas (pickup trucks) run to San Ignacio de Moxos (B$70, four hours) when full from the *parada* at 1 de Mayo near Velarde. Buses (B$50, six hours) occasionally run from the terminal around 9am but departures are increasingly sporadic.

❶ Getting Around

To/From the Airport

Taxis to and from the airport charge around B$25, but if you don't have much luggage, moto-taxis are cheaper (B$10) – you'll be surprised how much luggage they can accommodate with a bit of creativity.

Motorcycle

Motorcycles are a great way to while the day away – for B$15 per hour or B$80 for a full day you can rent a bike and join the general public in whizzing around the square. Pick one up from **Alquiler de Motos** (Main Plaza; ⊗8am-6pm), or alternatively strike a private deal with a moto-taxi driver (though you can expect to be followed!). You'll need a regular driver's license from home.

Taxi

Moto-taxis around town cost B$3, while increasingly scarce car taxis charge B$10. For rides to outlying areas, phone **Radio Taxi German Busch** (☑462-0008), or look for one on the plaza. Bank on around B$40 per hour for up to four people, including waiting time.

Santuario Chuchini

The Santuario Chuchini (Jaguar's Lair), 14km northwest of Trinidad, is one of the few easily accessible 'Paititi' sites. This wildlife sanctuary sits on an 8-hectare *loma* (artificial mound), one of many dotted throughout the surrounding forest. From the camp, you can take short walks in the rainforest to lagoons with caimans, other large animals and profuse bird life.

The camp has shady, covered picnic sites, trees, children's swings, and a variety of native plants, birds and animals. There's also an **archaeological museum** displaying articles excavated from the *loma*, including bizarre statues as well as a piece that appears to be a female figure wearing a bikini (it's actually thought to be an identification of, and homage to, specific body areas rather than an article of clothing).

For a day visit, including admission, a three-hour cruise and a meal, the price is B$450; to stay overnight it's B$850. Package tours booked in Trinidad may work out a bit cheaper. Further information is available from **Lorena or Efrém Hinojoso** (☑462-1968), or travel agencies in Trinidad.

Unless you organize a tour, which will include transportation, you'll have to negotiate with a moto-taxi driver. The road isn't great, so you'll have to be very persuasive and expect to be charged a bit more than usual. It's also a good destination for those who've rented motorcycles. If you're not staying, exotic dishes are available in the restaurant; the food is good but pricey.

Reserva de Vida Silvestre Ríos Blanco y Negro

This 1.4-million-hectare reserve, created in 1990, occupies the heart of Bolivia's largest wilderness area and contains vast tracts of undisturbed rainforest and *cerrado* with myriad species of plants and animals. These include giant anteaters, peccaries, tapirs, jaguars, bush dogs, marmosets, river otters, capuchin monkeys, caimans, squirrel monkeys, deer and capybaras. The diverse bird life includes curassows, six varieties of macaw and hundreds of other bird species.

The area's only settlement, the privately owned *estancia* (ranch), **Perseverancia**, is 350km north of Santa Cruz. It started as a rubber production center in the 1920s, working until the last *seringueros* (rubber tappers) left in 1972. When the airstrip was completed, professional hunters went after nutrias and large cats. By 1986 the *estancia* had again been abandoned, and it remained so until tourism – albeit scanty – began to be promoted in 1989.

In the mid-1990s Moira logging concerns began encroaching on the eastern portion of the reserve and USAID recommended that loggers clear a section of the forest rather than cut selective trees. Things have calmed down in recent years, though it is the difficulty of access to most of the park that has been the reason for this, rather than a more effective program of protection.

❶ Getting There & Away

Perseverancia is most easily accessed by a 1½-hour charter flight from El Trompillo airport in Santa Cruz. For those with a solid backside there's a 100km 4WD track between Asunción de Guarayos and Perseverancia that's passable year-round – with considerable perseverance. Currently no tour companies run trips to the park.

NORTHERN BOLIVIAN AMAZON

The isolated, once-untouched rainforests of northern Bolivia's frontier attract only the intrepid, the renegade and the loggers. Fire, chainsaws and cattle are guzzling the wilderness at increasing speed, but the rare visitor in search of the unexplored and untamed will have their sense of adventure tickled. Facilities are scarce and travel is slow: perfect for those who really want to avoid the gringo trail.

Santa Ana de Yacuma

🛈 3 / POP 22,400

A real cowboy town (in the nicest possible way), populated by ranchers, farmhands and, of course, cows. Santa Ana is the main population center in this area of Beni and is proud to call itself the cattle capital of Bolivia, a title that has resulted in officially the highest standard of living in the Bolivian Amazon region.

Unless your visit coincides with the annual **town festival** (July 24), during which cattle-related activities unsurprisingly play a starring role, there isn't much to do in town and you are most likely to land here en route to Los Lagos or the Barba Azul Reserve.

PARQUE NACIONAL NOEL KEMPFF MERCADO

The wonderfully remote and globally important Noel Kempff Mercado National Park is home to a broad spectrum of Amazonian flora and fauna and has a wide range of dwindling habitats, from open *cerrado* to dense rainforest. The park lies in the northernmost reaches of Santa Cruz department, between the banks of the Ríos Verde, Guaporé (Río Iténez on Bolivian maps) and Paraguá. It encompasses more than 1.5 million hectares of the most dramatic scenery in northern Bolivia, including rivers, rainforests, waterfalls, plateaus and rugged 500m escarpments.

An attempt to generate a tourist trail to the park appears to have failed, and more recently loggers and ranchers have started to move into the region. The park still remains an exciting off-the-beaten-track option for adventurous independent travelers though, but a lack of infrastructure for visitors means that visiting is a challenge that should be taken seriously. Camps at La Florida, Flor de Oro and Los Fierros have not been maintained, but with a little local advice and some serious planning a fascinating frontier awaits. If you are really lucky you may be able to convince a Santa Cruz tour agency to take you, but expect conditions to be basic and costs to be high.

The park is administered by SERNAP and every prospective visitor to the park must first visit a park information office in La Paz or Santa Cruz to register their visit.

🛏 Sleeping & Eating

A variety of basic *residenciales* cluster in the streets around the plaza offering cheap accommodations to the needy.

Hotel Mamoré   HOTEL **$$**
(☑337-8294; Roca Suárez; s/d B$250/350; 🅷🅴) Out by the airstrip this four-star place is hands down the best in town. Bad news is that the ranchers know it too, so if you want a room you're best to book it in advance.

ℹ Getting There & Away

Land routes to and from Santa Ana de Yacuma operate in the dry season only, but because of the thriving local industry there are frequent *trufi* departures (B$150, four hours) from the landmark La Vaca y El Toro statue at the northern end of Cipriano Barace in Trinidad. Once in town onward transport to Los Lagos or the Barba Azul reserve needs to be negotiated locally or arranged in advance.

Barba Azul Reserve

Thanks to the efforts of the conservation NGO Armonía, the squawkily endangered blue-throated macaw or *barba azul* has become something of a regional celebrity in the Bolivian Amazon. Endemic to the unique Beni savannas, a fast-disappearing habitat found nowhere else on earth, a quarter of the world's minute population of this spectacular psittacid calls this 5000-hectare private reserve home. Unlike most of the surrounding savanna, the open grasslands here are completely ungrazed and the birds can be seen relatively easily along with a plethora of other threatened birds and mammals such as maned wolf, giant anteater and marsh deer.

Accommodations are at the fledgling research station, but logistics demand a minimum three-night stay. A memorable stay here costs US$150 per person per night, including food, access to a motorboat and horseback riding.

ℹ Getting There & Away

For most of the year by far the quickest and easiest way to get to the reserve is by chartering a plane from Trinidad or Santa Cruz. Ask around at the aircraft hangars in Trinidad or try **Aereos Magdalena** (☑346-2226). Bank on around US$250 per person per hour (based on four people) and at least an hour flight time from Trinidad in good conditions. In the dry season

(July to October) land transportation can be arranged in Santa Ana de Yacuma, but although it is only 80km, rough roads mean that the drive will take at least three hours.

Your visit should be arranged in advance at the **Armonía office** (☑3-462-8287; 18 de Noviembre 282; ⊙8.30am-12.30pm & 2.30-6pm Mon-Fri) in Trinidad and the staff may be able to help with transportation, or contact Bird Bolivia (p244) for a guided tour. Armonía can also sometimes arrange shared flights to the reserve to reduce transportation costs.

Los Lagos

North of Santa de Yacuma is a cluster of 11 wonderful natural lakes flanked by wild rainforest and linked together by a network of weed-choked streams which are known collectively as Los Lagos. The two largest lakes are Lagos Ginebra and Rogaguado, both vast enough to be mistaken for inland seas, but exploring the winding swampy creeks, where wildlife abounds and you must trade your outboard motor in for a paddle, is where the real fun is at. This unique and enchanting region has hardly been explored by foreign tourists because of its remoteness, but for anybody looking for Amazonian adventure it is a real treat. Whether you are an angler, a nature enthusiast, wanting to relax or just somebody who appreciates a damn good sunset, Los Lagos ticks all the right boxes.

🏃 Activities

Predictably, water-related activities are the main draw here and the area is nationally famous with sports anglers who come to hook the predatory *tunare* and the gigantic *general*, a catfish-like monster that can reach 200kg. The **fishing** is extremely easy, though most is done at night to avoid the constant harassment of piranhas.

Other aquatic activities can also be arranged from **jet-skiing** on the lake to **boat trips** through dense forested swamps inhabited by deer, howler monkeys, river dolphins and the comical hoatzin, a large, crested chicken-like bird whose flightless offspring hurl themselves into the water at your approach. Boat trips are usually combined with forest walks on specially prepared trails with occasional viewing towers that will give you a wonderful panorama of your breathtaking surroundings.

NATIONAL TREASURE: THE BARBA AZUL

With more than 1200 bird species inhabiting the country, Bolivia is a bird-watcher's paradise. But it's not just the sheer quantity of species that makes Bolivia such an attractive destination for bird lovers, it is the quality of the birds you can see.

Asociacíon Armonía, the Bolivian Birdlife International Partner, has developed a series of community-based conservation programs designed to protect the country's most threatened birds, principally by creating a feeling of pride among the locals.

The gorgeous blue-throated macaw *(Ara glaucogularis)*, endemic to the unique Beni savannas, numbers, according to the most optimistic of estimates, just 250 individuals. Known to the Bolivians as *barba azul* (blue beard), this charismatic bird has become a flagship species for Armonía, which runs a superb, community-orientated conservation program aimed squarely at making sure the bird is around for future generations to appreciate.

Threats to the species are numerous, but one of the most unusual is indiscriminate killing for the sole purpose of harvesting the tail feathers. This practice affects all macaws, but because of the species' similarity to the common blue-and-yellow macaw *(Ara ararauna)* and a lack of public awareness of its plight, this species has suffered at the hands of hunters who collect the tail plumes to adorn ceremonial headdresses for regional celebrations like the famous Moxos festival.

Armonía's response has been rapid, effective and ingenious. It has worked on an extensive public education campaign designed to teach locals how to distinguish between the two similar blue macaws that occur in the area and, crucially, to instil a sense of pride in the citizens of Beni for their emblematic bird. An agreement with local indigenous leaders not to hunt live macaws, but to instead fabricate artificial feathers for headdresses has not only been a huge success, but has led to the creation of a small and very lucrative local manufacturing industry. Perhaps most important of all has been the purchase of the small **Barba Azul Reserve** dedicated to the conservation of the bird.

Visit **Armonía** at its Santa Cruz office (p261) or its Trinidad office (p298) for more information on its innovative conservation programs.

🛏 Sleeping

TOP CHOICE Los Lagos Lodge   LODGE $$$
(☑337-8294; www.loslagoslodge.com; s/d US$100/ 150, 4-person cabins US$130-180; ❄❄) Situated on the shore of the crystalline Lago Agua Clara in the north of the Los Lagos region, this four-star hotel finds the perfect balance between luxury and nature. Offering a series of packages for visitors depending on their interests – fishing, wildlife watching, adrenalin adventures – and well-trained guides, it is a visually stunning hotel in a visually stunning region. It's a favorite retreat for Beni ranchers, but for most of the year you will have the place almost to yourself.

ℹ Getting There & Away

As with most places in this part of Beni, chartering a plane from Trinidad or Santa Cruz is your safest bet if you want to get here as painlessly as possible. **Aereos Magdalena** (☑346-2226) at the hangars in Trinidad airport are a good bet for an aero-taxi. The flight takes about an hour and costs around US$250 per person (based on four people). From July to November land transport can be arranged in Santa Ana de Yacuma. It's a spectacular six-hour drive.

Guayaramerín

☑3 / POP 40,450 / ELEV 130M (426FT)

Knocking on Brazil's back door, Guayaramerín is twinned with the Brazilian town of Guajará-Mirim on the other side of the Río Mamoré. This lively town thrives on all kinds of trade (legal and illegal) with Brazil, and its streets are full of dusty motorcycle tracks and markets heaving with synthetic garments. It is now the northern terminus for river transportation along the Río Mamoré.

👣 Tours

Mary's Tours   TOUR
(☑855-3882; Oruro) Mary's Tours conducts five-hour city tours of Guayaramerín and Guajará-Mirim, as well as La Ruta de la Goma (The Rubber Trail) to Cachuela Esperanza. You can

also arrange one-day cruises on the Río Yata or fishing trips to Rosario del Yata, plus it can help organize flights.

🛏 Sleeping

Hotel Balneario San Carlos HOTEL $$
(☑855-3555; San Carlos, near 6 de Agosto; s/d B$190/260; ❄️❄️) The choice for anyone here on business, this hotel has a restaurant, redundant sauna, pool room and 24-hour hot water.

Hotel Santa Ana HOTEL $
(☑855-3900; 25 de Mayo 611; s/d with fan B$70/140, d with air-con B$150; ❄️) The best of the cluster of hotels on this corner, with spacious, often air-conditioned rooms and some suites. Reasonable value, though be sure to avoid the windowless rooms.

Hotel Litoral PENSION $$
(☑855-3895; 25 de Mayo, near 16 de Julio; per person B$90, without bathroom B$20) Relax in the clean rooms of this budget place, or chill out in front of Brazilian soaps in its courtyard snack bar.

🍴 Eating & Drinking

Churrasquería Patujú BARBECUE $$
(6 de Agosto; mains B$30-50) This place serves up tasty, good-value steak-oriented meals. The best place for a decent feed in the town center.

Churrasquería Sujal BARBECUE $$
(mains B$35-55) This out-of-town steakhouse is a nice, quiet place, most readily accessible by moto-taxi (B$15).

Heladería Pato Roca ICE CREAM $
(main plaza; ice cream B$5-20) Renowned for its mountainous fruit and ice-cream creations.

Snack Bar Antonella FAST FOOD $
(main plaza; mains B$15-30) Pleasant place for a beer and a snack as you watch the world go round the plaza.

🔒 Shopping

Thanks to its designation as a duty-free zone (authorities couldn't fight the illicit trade, so they decided to sanction it), Guayaramerín is a shopper's mecca. There's nothing of exceptional interest, but there are lots of counterfeit brand-name shoes and clothes, and fake brand-name electronic goods. For *artesanía,* visit Caritas, near the airfield, which sells locally produced wooden carvings for reasonable prices.

ℹ️ Information

There is a slow internet connection at **Masas** (per hr B$5) just off the plaza. A block east of the plaza, the relatively efficient **Brazilian consulate** (☑855-3766; Beni & 24 de Septiembre; ⊙9am-5pm Mon-Sat) issues visas in three days. Money changers hanging around the port area deal in US dollars, Brazilian *reais* and bolivianos. **Prodem** on the corner of the plaza can give you cash advances on Visa and MasterCard.

ℹ️ Getting There & Away

Air

The airport is on the edge of town and the airline offices are on the nearby 16 de Julio, around the corner of 25 de Mayo. **AeroCon** (☑855-5025; 25 de Mayo, near Beni) runs daily flights to Trinidad with onward connections to other cities. **TAM** (☑855-3924; Av 16 de Julio) flies to Riberalta on Sunday mornings (B$130, 20 minutes) and has a daily flight to Trinidad (B$523, 50 minutes), except Tuesday and Thursday. Amaszonas connects Guayaramerín with Riberalta and Trinidad most days, though there is no office in town. Flights to Cobija via Riberalta (per person B$600) are by private rental *avionetta* (light aircraft) and must be full (five people) to depart. Call **Avionetta Ariel** (☑852-3774) or **El Capitán** (☑7686-2742) at least a day in advance.

Boat

Cargo boats up the Río Mamoré to Trinidad (around without/with food B$250/350) leave very irregularly and take six days. Ask at the port captain's office opposite the immigration office for information.

Bus, Camión & Taxi

The bus terminal is on the south end of town, beyond the market. Buses run to Riberalta (B$25, 2½ hours) several times daily. Foolhardy Vaca Diez departs daily in the morning for Rurrenabaque (B$120, 18 hours to three days) and La Paz (B$170, 30 to 60 hours) via Santa Rosa and Reyes. Do not contemplate either journey if there is even a hint of rain or else be prepared to help pull the bus out of muddy holes every couple of hours. There are daily buses to Cobija (B$70, 16 hours) and Trinidad (B$240, 22 to 35 hours). Be aware that if enough tickets aren't sold, any of these runs may be summarily canceled. Flying to either destination is your best option and you will not regret the extra expense. Shared taxis to Riberalta (B$50 per person, two hours) leave from the terminal when they have four passengers.

ℹ️ Getting Around

Guayaramerín is small enough to walk just about anywhere. Moto-taxis and auto rickshaws charge

CROSSING THE BORDER INTO BRAZIL

Crossing to Brazil from the northern Bolivian towns of Cobija and Guayaramerín involves crossings of the Ríos Acre and Mamoré respectively.

Popping into the Brazilian town of Guajará-Mirim for the day from Bolivian Guayaramerín is really easy. Day visits are encouraged, and you don't even need a visa. *Lanchas* (B$10) across the river leave from the port every half an hour from 6am to 6pm, and sporadically through the night. To travel further into Brazil or to enter Bolivia, you'll have to complete border formalities. The immigration offices in **Guajará-Mirim** (Av Quintina Bocaiúva; ⊙8am-noon & 2-6pm Mon-Fri) and **Guayaramerín** (Av Costanera) are in the respective port areas.

It's a long, hot slog across the bridge from Cobija to Brasiléia. Entry/exit stamps are available at immigration in Cobija at the Bolivian end of the bridge and from **Brasiléia's Polícia Federal** (Av Prefeito Moreira; ⊙8am-noon & 2-5pm). With some negotiation, taxis will take you to the Polícia Federal in Brasiléia, wait while you clear immigration, then take you on to the center or to the bus terminal. Alternatively, take the *lancha* (B$5) across the Río Acre; from there it's another 1.5km to the Polícia Federal.

Although officials don't always check, technically everyone needs to have a yellow-fever vaccination certificate to enter Brazil. If you don't have one, head for the convenient and relatively sanitary clinic at the port on the Brazilian side. For more information, check out Lonely Planet's *Brazil*.

B$5 to anywhere in town. To explore the area, you can rent motorcycles from the plaza for B$15 per hour or negotiate all-day rentals – figure B$70 for 24 hours.

Riberalta

🎵 3 / POP 76,000 / ELEV 115M (377FT)

Despite being a major town in Bolivia's northern frontier region, Riberalta has very little going for it, unless you count the exciting fact that this is one of the world's top Brazil-nut production sites. A crumbly place, it is pleasant enough, even if the only thing to do is to watch the orange sunsets and circling motorcycles as you enjoy a beer on the plaza. According to locals of both sexes, *las riberalteñas* are the most beautiful women in all of Bolivia – but they would say that, wouldn't they?

◎ Sights & Activities

Cathedral   CHURCH

Riberalta's cathedral is a wonderful structure in classic Missionary style, wide and elegant, built using red brick and cedar. It sits on the main square in the same spot as the old, less grandiose church and it cost more than half a million US dollars to build.

Tumichucuá   PARK

Tumichucuá is a small resort about 5km outside town toward 'El Triángulo' (the road junction to Cobija). There is a lake for swimming and a forested island with walking trails, plus basic cabins. Nobody is sure how far from Riberalta it is, as according to local legend the lake moves at night, sometimes coming to rest closer to the town, sometimes further away.

Parque Mirador La Costañera   PARK

This park, on Riberalta's river bluff, overlooks a broad, sweeping curve of the Río Beni and affords the standard Amazonian view over water and rainforest.

Puerto Beni-Mamoré   ARTS CENTER

At Puerto Beni-Mamoré, within walking distance of the center, you can watch the hand-carving and construction of small boats and dugouts by skilled artisans. About 2km east of the plaza along Ejército Nacional, you can visit an **old rubber plantation**, watch coffee beans being roasted and visit a **carpentry workshop**.

Club Náutico   SWIMMING

(2 blocks north of the plaza; admission B$10) In the paralyzing heat of the day, strenuous activity is suspended and you'll find yourself clambering into the nearest hammock. Cool down in the Club Náutico's sparkling riverside pool, a favorite local activity.

🛏 Sleeping

Riberalta doesn't see that many visitors so hotel prices are high and you should not expect value for money.

AMAZON BASIN RIBERALTA

Hotel Colonial   HOTEL $$

(852-3018; www.hotelcolonial.web.bo; Plácido Méndez 745; s/d B$180/250; ❄) Riberalta's most-expensive hotel is a renovated colonial home dotted with antique furniture and backed by a delightfully fresh garden where you can relax in a hammock. Unfortunately, the rooms themselves lack the same charm and some are just musty and old. Choose carefully.

Hotel Las Palmeras   B&B $$

(852-2354; Suárez 855; s B$150, s/d with air-con B$210/270; ❄) Salmon pinks shimmer in this quiet, family home-cum-B&B, 15 minutes' walk from the center. The rooms are cozy and have their own bathrooms. Rates include breakfast.

Residencial Los Reyes   PENSION $

(852-2628; s/d B$40/70) Close to the airport, this is a basic choice with a lovely, cool, garden courtyard. Iced water and hot coffee are always available.

Eating

Riberalta's specialty is its famous *nueces del Brasil* (Brazil nuts), which are roasted in sugar and cinnamon and sold at the bus terminals and airport for B$10 per packet. The classic Riberalta breakfast of *api* (a syrupy beverage made from sweet purple corn, lemon, cinnamon and lots of white sugar), juice and empanadas is sold in the market.

TOP CHOICE Tropical   INTERNATIONAL $$$

(near the airport; mains B$90-150) This is Riberalta's most upscale restaurant, leading the residents to nickname it Tropicarísimo (Very Expensive...). Gargantuan portions of meat, chicken and fish accompanied by salad, rice and fried manioc feed two or three normal-sized people, though the profusion of animal skins and stuffed wildlife hanging off the walls are a turn off.

Horno Camba   BARBECUE $$

(Dr Martínez; mains B$25-55) The best of the restaurants on the plaza serving fish, chicken and Beni beef. What's more, the sidewalk seating provides a front-row view of the nightly 'Kawasaki derby' round the plaza.

Club Social El Progreso   BOLIVIAN $

(Dr Martínez; almuerzo B$15) This place serves inexpensive *almuerzos*, good filtered coffee, drinks and fine desserts.

ℹ Information

Banco Ganadero on the plaza has an ATM. If it's not working you can get cash advances and change US dollars at **Prodem** (857-2212; Suárez 1880). The post office and Entel are near the main plaza and there is an **internet cafe** (per hr B$6) on the plaza itself. The town's municipal water supply is contaminated, so stick to bottled or thoroughly purified water.

ℹ Getting There & Away

Air

The airport is a 15-minute stroll south of the main plaza. Departing flights are subject to an airport tax of B$7. Flights to Cobija and most to Guayaramerín are by *avioneta* and must be full to depart. Call **Avioneta Ariel** (852-3774) or **El Capitán** (7686-2742) at least a day in advance. Bank on paying around B$600 per person.

TAM (852-2646; Chuquisaca 1146) flies to La Paz daily (B$949, two hours) except Monday and Friday, and has weekend flights to Guayaramerín (B$130, 20 minutes). Flights to Trinidad leave on Monday, Tuesday and Thursday (B$130, 20 minutes), but **AeroCon** (852-4679; airport) departures to Trinidad are much more frequent, with several flights each day. **Amazonas** (852-3933; Chuquisaca cr Sucre) also flies to Trinidad and has the most regular connections with Guayaramerín.

Boat

The Río Beni passes through countless twisting kilometers of virgin rainforest and provides Bolivia's longest single-river trip. Unfortunately, boats upriver to Rurrenabaque are now rare and, in any case, they normally only run during the wet season (November to mid-April). For information on departures ask at the Capitanía del Puerto at the northern end of town between Calles Ballivián and Sánchez. Budget on spending B$250 to B$350 (including meals and hammock space) for the five- to eight-day trip. Lucky Peru-bound travelers may also find cargo boats to the frontier at Puerto Heath, which has onward boats to Puerto Maldonado.

Bus

The bus terminal is 3km east of the center, along the Guayaramerín road. The road from Riberalta to Guayaramerín is a high-speed gravel track, and taxis (B$40, 1½ hours) ply the route, leaving when full from the bus terminal. Buses (B$25, 2½ hours) are cheaper but slower – they depart in the morning.

All *flotas* between Guayaramerín and Cobija (B$120, 12 to 16 hours), and the horrendously uncomfortable route via Rurrenabaque (B$110, 17 to 40 hours) to La Paz (B$180, 35 to 60 hours), stop at Riberalta. Several *flotas* also go to Trinidad (B$200, 17 to 30 hours) daily, though the road may be closed during the wet season – it's easier to fly.

ⓘ Getting Around

Moto-taxis (day/night B$3.50/5) will take you anywhere. With a driver's license from home, you can rent motorcycles (per hour/day B$15/80) from *taxistas* (taxi drivers) at the corner of Nicolás Suárez and Gabriel René Moreno.

Riberalta to Cobija

The much-improved road between Riberalta and Cobija connects the once-isolated Pando department with the rest of the country. Unfortunately, better access means more logging and the region has now been opened up to indiscriminate exploitation of its natural resources with large tracts of virgin rainforest being cleared at a frightening rate.

The journey requires two major *balsa* crossings, the first at Peña Amarilla, two hours outside Riberalta crossing the Río Beni. On the western bank, you can find stands selling empanadas and other snacks.

The most interesting crossing on the trip, however, traverses the Río Madre de Dios. From the eastern port, the 45-minute crossing begins with a 500m cruise along a backwater tributary onto the great river itself. Along the way listen for the intriguing jungle chorus that characterizes this part of the country.

The crossing of the Río Orthon, at Puerto Rico, is by bridge. From Puerto Rico to Cobija, development has been particularly rampant. The scene is one of charred giants, a forest of stumps and smouldering bush; when something is burning, the sun looks like an egg yolk through the dense smoke.

Cobija

POP 22.300 / ELEV 140M (459FT)

Capital of the Pando and Bolivia's wettest (1770mm of precipitation annually) and most humid spot, Cobija sits on a sharp bend of the Río Acre. Cobija means 'covering' and, with a climate that makes you feel as though you're being smothered with a soggy blanket, it certainly lives up to its name.

Cobija was founded in 1906 under the name 'Bahía,' and in the 1940s it boomed as a rubber-producing center. The town's fortunes dwindled with the shriveling of that industry and it has been reduced to little more than a forgotten village, albeit with a Japanese-funded hospital and a high-tech Brazil-nut processing plant.

★彡 Festivals

Feria de Muestras   ARTS
The Pando's biggest annual bash, the Feria de Muestras (August 18 to 27), showcases the work of local artisans and is held at the extreme western end of town, near the Río Acre.

◎ Sights & Activities

The town rambles over a series of hills, giving it a certain desultory charm. If you spend a day here, take a look at the remaining **tropical wooden buildings** in the center, and the lovely avenues of royal palms around the plaza.

Cathedral   CHURCH
The cathedral, on the main plaza, has a series of naive paintings from the life of Christ.

Natural History Museum   MUSEUM
(6 de Febrero; ◎8am-noon & 2-6pm Mon-Fri) A small natural history museum is filled with the usual collection of pickled animal bits.

🛏 Sleeping & Eating

Most of the best places to eat are along Molina, but none are up to much and prices are fairly high.

Hotel Nanijós   HOTEL **$$**
(📞842-2230; 6 de Agosto 147; s/d B$200/350; 🕸🖼) A large, modern hotel, with the best facilities in town. All rooms have tiled floors and cable TV, and the courtyard splash pool is very welcome in the sticky climate.

Esquina de la Abuela   INTERNATIONAL **$$$**
(Molina nr Sucre; mains B$40-65) This is Cobija's nicest eatery with alfresco tables and fresh, well-cooked chicken and meat dishes served under a gigantic *palapa* wigwam.

Hong Kong   CHINESE **$$**
(Molina; mains B$20-55) Standard Chinese fare in the usual big portions. There is an authentic Chinese bakery next door for snacks.

ⓘ Information

The **Brazilian consulate** (📞842-2110; Av René Barrientos; ◎8.30am-12.30pm Mon-Fri) grants visas. **Bolivian immigration** (◎9am-5pm Mon-Fri) is in the Prefectura building on the main plaza, with another branch at the airport.

In addition to giving cash advances on Visa and MasterCard and changing US dollars, **Prodem** (Plaza Principal 186) has an ATM; there are a bunch of other ATMs around the plaza. The post office is also on the plaza and a number of telephone places are nearby. Internet use is expensive (B$8 per hour) and to connect you'll need to head to Calle Mercado, predictably located next to the market.

ℹ Getting There & Away

Air

Flights arrive and depart from Aeropuerto Anibal Arab (CIJ), 5km from the center at the top end of Av 9 de Febrero. Amaszonas (no office in town) and **AeroCon** (☏842-4575; Leoncio Justiniano 43) between them have at least daily flights to Trinidad. **TAM** (☏842-4145; Av 9 de Febrero 59) flies daily to La Paz (B$746, two hours), except Sunday. Flights to Guayaramerín via Riberalta are in *avionetas*; ask at the airport or call (☏7621-0035). It pays to book your flights well in advance.

Bus & Camión

There is no bus terminal in Cobija, but buses pull into their respective offices on Av 9 de Febrero out toward the airport. Services to Riberalta and Guayaramerín (B$70, 16 hours) depart daily between 5am and 8am. There is one tortuous service to La Paz via Rurrenabaque run by **La Yungueña** (B$280, 35 to 60 hours), but if you are really smart, you'll take a flight.

ℹ Getting Around

Moto-taxis charge a set B$4 to anywhere in town, B$10 to the airport. Taxis charge B$20 to the international airport. A cheaper option is to hop on *micro A* (B$2.50), which shuttles between the airport and the market.

Understand
Bolivia

population per sq km

BOLIVIA   US   UK

 ≈ 9 people

Bolivia Today

In Bolivia crisis is the status quo. Protests, poverty, inequality, social change and slow economic progress are part of everyday life. At the center of it all is president Evo Morales and his new constitution, reforms, and policies that have marked the nation's revolutionary movement toward socialism. All of these political and social changes are now coming together to create what will certainly be one of the most interesting chapters in Bolivian history.

» Population:
10 million

» People living
on less than
US$2 per day:
2.5 million

» People below
national poverty
line: 5.1 million

» GDP per person: US$4100

» Gini Inequality Index: 58.2
(8th most unequal in the
world)

» Inflation:
6.9 %

» Literacy:
86.7%

» Fertility rate:
2.93

» Infant
mortality rate:
4.094/1000
live births

Economy

The nationalization of energy and mining interests was applauded by Bolivia's poor, but it has soured relations with foreign investors and some foreign governments. And despite sky-high commodity prices, the Bolivian economy hasn't grown as fast as it should have. The export of raw materials remains the nation's bread and butter, and with the world's largest lithium deposits, plenty of natural gas and minerals, Bolivia could very well continue to see moderate economic progress for the foreseeable future. The stumbling blocks will include environmental conditions (deforestation, desertification and climate change), depressed foreign markets, and the reluctance of foreign companies to invest money and expertise in a country with a growing track record of nationalizations.

Society

Despite modest economic growth, more than half of the population still lives in poverty, and the social programs outlined in the new constitution have made only minimal progress toward remedying poverty traps.

The new measures have succeeded, however, in reframing Bolivia's social structure. Despite practically no escape from poverty, there seems to be a spark of self-awareness and hope that's never been more evident

Dos & Don'ts

Kissing Greet members of the opposite sex with a kiss on one cheek in the north, both cheeks in the south. An empty-grip handshake followed by a distant two-arm embrace and another hand-grab are standard with Quechua and Aymará people.

Stealing Pictures If you can't touch your subject and haven't talked to them, you may be guilty of image theft.

Greetings Greet people with *Buenos días, Buenas tardes* and *Buenas noches*.

Politics Do express your views.

Top Artists

Kalamarka Contemporary Andean music at its best.
Mamani Mamani Aymará art made for the 21st century.
Los Kjarkas A top folk act featuring traditional Bolivian instruments.

language
(% of population)

61 Spanish

21 Quechua

15 Aymará

4 Other

if Bolivia were 100 people

30 would be Quechua
30 would be mixed white & Amerindian
25 would be Aymará
15 would be white

among the nation's indigenous majority. And indigenous people today, especially highlands groups, are playing a significant role in politics and policy. The role of women is also slowly evolving, as they step out of their traditional roles as mothers, wives and heads of private households, emerging as businesspeople and community leaders.

Politics

Conflict is on the rise. There are around 1000 standing conflicts across the nation over high food and energy prices, the use of natural resources, education, social inclusion, environmental degradation and more. People protest against poor working conditions, mining operations that contaminate rivers, and roads that displace communities and affect ecosystems. For example, a proposed Brazilian-financed road through the Amazon brought about major national protests in 2012 and was later rejected by Morales. Protests regularly shut down Bolivia's roads and are having a detrimental effect on the economy. Violence stemming from the ever-evolving drug trade is also building throughout the region.

Moves to redistribute land and wealth have met with strong opposition from Bolivia's resource-rich eastern region, where autonomy movements are ongoing. Despite this opposition and growing discontent over what many perceive as weak rule of law and widespread corruption, others still expect the numerous social entitlement programs sponsored by the government and funded with the growing income from mining, agriculture and gas exports to keep Morales' revolution moving forward.

Internationally, the Bolivian government is engaged in a political two-step that tries to balance foreign investment with national interests. At the heart of this is the desire to keep the wealth from Bolivia's natural resources in Bolivia.

Bolivia is the world's second or third biggest cocaine producer – up to 290 tons of the white stuff are produced here each year. Between 24,000 and 30,000 hectares of coca are cultivated nationally (legal production is capped at 12,000 hectares).

Marina Nuñez del Prado The legacy of Bolivia's beloved sculptor lives on.
Ukamau y Ké El Alto's hip-hop act is outrageous and intense.

Top Films

The Devil's Miner (2005) Documentary on a young boy working in Potosí's silver mine.
Cocalero (2007) Documentary on Morales' run for the presidency.
Amargo Mar (Bitter Sea; 1984) A look at the loss of Bolivia's coastline to Chile.

Top Books

Fat Man from La Paz: Contemporary Fiction from Bolivia (2003, Santos) Modern fiction.
Whispering in the Giant's Ear: A Frontline Chronicle from Bolivia's War on Globalization (2006, Powers) A look at battles over natural resources.

History

Bolivia's history is evident in every corner of daily life – in the country's pre-Hispanic ruins, colonial-era churches and in the museums, galleries and chaotic markets of the city centers. The cultural imprint that dates back more than 6000 years is seen in the language, dress, customs and traditions of indigenous peoples, and in the unique dual society that sorts Spanish descendants, recent immigrants and indigenous peoples into difficult-to-escape archetypes: a dominant paradigm that is only now being challenged with the rise of the country's first self-declared indigenous president.

From a purely economic standpoint, Bolivia is a country that never should have been. The country has vast natural resources but a small, sparse population, meaning that it primarily produces raw goods but lacks the industry required to turn these into more valuable products. Politically it has been pushed and pulled and bent out of shape by the stronger forces centering in Cuzco, Madrid, Lima, Buenos Aires and Washington. And while much of Bolivia's history follows the macro-trends of the rest of South America, the country's spirit, character and context have come together to form a complex and intricate story unique unto itself.

Prehistory

The great Altiplano (which literally means 'high plateau'), the largest expanse of arable land in the Andes, extends from present-day Bolivia into southern Peru, northwestern Argentina and northern Chile.

Cultural interchanges between the early Andean peoples occurred mostly through trade, usually between nomadic tribes in the lowlands, farmers in the Yungas, organized societies such as the Tiwanaku and Inca in the high plateau, and coastal traders in present-day Peru and Chile. These interchanges and geographic advantages around the Altiplano resulted in food surpluses and eventually led to the Andes' emergence as the cradle of South America's highest cultural achievements.

Top Historic Attractions

» Tiwanaku
» Iskanwaya
» Isla del Sol
» *chullpa* tombs
» Potosí
» Sucre
» Che Trail
» Choro trek
» Samaipata
» Jesuit Missions Circuit

TIMELINE

4000 BC	3200–800 BC	AD 500–900
The first settlers arrive and begin to domesticate crops and animals, adapting slowly to high-altitude living in the Altiplano. The tough conditions influence a sparse population distribution.	First traces of pottery shards in the Altiplano date from around 3200 BC, indicating the formation of more structured societies. On the Peruvian coast the Chavín culture rises.	There's a food surplus, and the ceremonial center of Tiwanaku, on the shores of Lake Titicaca, flourishes, developing into the religious and political capital of the Altiplano.

Advanced civilizations first developed along the Peruvian coast and in the valleys in the early AD period. Highland civilizations developed a little later. Some archaeologists define the prehistory of the Central Andes in terms of 'horizons' – Early, Middle and Late – each of which was characterized by distinct architectural and artistic trends.

Early & Middle Horizons

The so-called Early Horizon (1400–400 BC) was an era of architectural activity and innovation, most evident in the ruins of Chavín de Huantar, on the eastern slopes of the Andes in Peru. Chavín influences resounded far and wide, even after the decline of Chavín society, and spilled over into the Early Middle Horizon (400 BC–AD 500).

By 700 BC, Tiwanaku had developed into a thriving civilization. A highly advanced culture for the Andes, it had an extensive system of roads, irrigation canals and agricultural terraces. This system is believed to have supported a population of thousands of people in the 83-sq-km Tiwanaku Valley.

The Middle Horizon (AD 500–900) was marked by the imperial expansion of the Tiwanaku and Huari (of the Ayacucho Valley of present-day Peru) cultures. The Tiwanakans produced technically advanced work, most notably the city itself. They created impressive ceramics, gilded ornamentation, engraved pillars and slabs with calendar markings, and designs representing their bearded white leader and deity, Viracocha.

Tiwanaku was inhabited from 1500 BC until AD 1200, but its power in the region – based more on religious than economic factors – was strongest from AD 600 to around AD 900, when the civilization began the mysterious decline that lasted until the 1200s. One speculation is that Tiwanaku was uprooted by a drop in Lake Titicaca's water level, that left the lakeside settlement far from shore. Another theory postulates that it was attacked and its population massacred by the warlike Kollas (also known as the Aymará) from the west. When the Spanish arrived, they were told an Inca legend about a battle between the Kollas and 'bearded white men' on an island in Lake Titicaca. These men were presumably Tiwanakans, only a few of whom were able to escape. Some researchers believe that the displaced survivors migrated southward and developed into the Chipaya people of the western Oruro department.

The Inca spoke Runasimi (later called Quechua by the conquistadors). They lacked a writing system but did have advanced math systems, keeping track of accounts – and perhaps other information – with knotted collections of cords known as *quipus*.

Late Horizon – the Inca

The period between 900 and 1475 is known as the Late Intermediate Horizon. After the fall of Tiwanaku, regionalized city-states such as Chan Chan in Peru and the Aymará kingdoms around the southern shores of Lake Titicaca came to power. However, it was the rise and fall of the Inca empire that would truly define the pre-Columbian period.

1000–1200	1440s	1520s
Tiwanaku's power wanes, the population disperses and the ceremonial site is largely abandoned due to unknown reasons – possibly climate change (drought), an earthquake or a foreign invasion.	The Inca, based in Cuzco, extend their political boundaries by pushing eastward into Kollasuyo (present-day Bolivia) and imposing taxation, religion and the Quechua language on local tribes.	Internal rivalries herald the beginning of the end for the Inca empire, a political force for less than a century. In a brief civil war, Atahualpa defeats his half-brother, Huáscar, and assumes the emperor's throne.

JOHN ELK III/GETTY IMAGES ©

» Statue at Tiwanaku

DISEASES

The Inca inhabited the Cuzco region (in present-day Peru) from the 12th century. They were renowned for their great stone cities and their skill in working with gold and silver. The Inca set up a social welfare scheme, taxed up to two-thirds of produce and worked in a system primarily based on the communal ownership of property. Through the *mita* system (where short-term forced labor was used to build public projects) they were able to create a complex road network and communication system that defied the difficult terrain of their far-flung empire.

Around 1440 the Inca started to expand their political boundaries. The eighth Inca king, Viracocha (not to be confused with the Tiwanaku deity of the same name), believed the mandate from their sun god was not just to conquer, plunder and enslave, but to organize defeated tribes and absorb them into the realm of the benevolent sun god.

Between 1476 and 1534 the Inca civilization managed to extend its influence over the Aymará kingdoms around Lake Titicaca. They pushed their empire from its seat of power in Cuzco eastward into present-day Bolivia, southward to the northern reaches of modern Argentina and Chile, and northward through present-day Ecuador and southern Colombia.

The people of the Aymará kingdoms were permitted to keep their language and social traditions, and never truly accepted Inca rule. Today you can still see these linguistic and cultural splits in the Quechua, Aymará and myriad other indigenous groups of Bolivia.

By the late 1520s internal rivalries began to take their toll on the empire with the sons of Inca Huayna Capac – Atahualpa and Huáscar – fighting a bloody civil war after the death of their father. Atahualpa (who controlled the northern reaches of the empire) won the war. While he was traveling south to Cuzco to claim his throne, he ran into the conquistador Francisco Pizarro, who captured, ransomed and eventually beheaded him. This left a power vacuum, making it easy for the Spanish to conquer the lands and peoples of the Inca empire.

Smallpox and other European diseases killed off up to 90% of the indigenous population in some areas. These epidemics continued on 20-year cycles well into the 17th century.

Spanish Conquest

The Spanish conquest of South America was remarkably quick. The chaos left by the Inca civil war helped, as did the epidemics caused by European diseases. European mastery of metallurgy for war also played its part, and so did their horses (what strange beasts they must have seemed to the Inca people) and the myth that bearded men would some day be sent by the great Viracocha.

Within a year of their arrival in Ecuador in 1531, Francisco Pizarro, Diego de Almagro and their bands of conquistadors arrived in Cuzco.

Alto Perú (the area we now know as Bolivia) was aligned with the defeated Huáscar during the Inca civil war, making its conquest rather easy

1531	1544	1545	1780
The Spanish, led by conquistador Francisco Pizarro, arrive in Ecuador. After a quick-won fight with the Inca, they claim Alto Perú, which would later become Bolivia.	The wandering Indian Diego Huallpa discovers silver in Potosí's Cerro Rico (Rich Mountain), which leads to the development of the world's most prolific silver mine.	Potosí is founded as a mining town. Due to the incredible wealth, it grows rapidly and gains a mint, 86 churches and a population approaching 200,000 by 1672.	Tupac Amaru's revolt kicks off in Peru, extending later into Bolivia. The revolt is put down, and effectively dismantles the *cacique* (chieftain) structure of local indigenous government.

for Diego de Almagro. He was assassinated in 1538, then three years later Pizarro suffered the same fate at the hands of mutinous subordinates. But this didn't deter the Spanish, who kept exploring and settling their newly conquered land.

During these initial stages of conquest, infighting between Spanish factions was common and the fate of Bolivia – a political backwater until the discovery of silver – was tied to the interests of the more powerful political centers in Cuzco and Lima.

About 8 million people have died in the Potosí mine over the years. You can still visit the mine today, or go on other interesting mine tours near Oruro.

The Legacy of Potosí

By the time Diego Huallpa revealed his earth-shattering discovery of silver at Cerro Rico in Potosí in 1544, Spanish conquerors had already firmly implanted their customs on the remnants of the Inca empire. Taking a page from the Inca book, they left the local *cacique* (chieftain) leadership and *mita* structure in place within the indigenous communities. This provided a local system of governance and an ongoing labor supply. The best conquistadors were granted *encomiendas*, vast swaths of land and the peasant labor that went with it.

Potosí was officially founded in 1545, and in 1558 Alto Perú gained its autonomy from Lima with the placement of an Audiencia (Royal Court) in present-day Sucre. Transportation hubs, farming communities and other support centers sprung up, centered on Potosí. And while some other Bolivian cities such as La Paz and Sucre were coming to life, the focus in the region was on Potosí. Potosí's mine was the most prolific in the world and its silver underwrote Spain's international ambitions, enabling the country to conduct the counterreformation in Europe, and supporting the extravagance of its monarchy for at least two centuries. But not all wealth left the region, and cathedrals sprung up across the Altiplano, eventually giving rise to a local school of design, and later the establishment of Bolivia's place in the fields of arts, politics and literature.

HISTORY SPANISH CONQUEST

CONQUISTADORS – BRAVE EXPLORERS OR SOCIAL CLIMBERS?

It's important to note the circumstances that brought the conquistadors to the Americas. Most were not part of the landed Spanish elite, rather they were wealthy enough to make the crossing to the New World but lacked any prospects of upward mobility in Europe...the kind of person that has nothing to lose and everything to gain. Ironically, the riches they found in the Americas would never win the conquistadors (or early American settlers) a place in European society. This no-exit scenario led to the formation of local class structures and governments, the intermixing of languages and cultures, and eventually the independence movements.

1809
Bolivia proclaims its independence from Spain by establishing the first *juntas* (autonomist governments); first in Chuquisaca (later renamed Sucre), then in La Paz.

1822
General Simón Bolívar succeeds in liberating Venezuela, Ecuador, Colombia and Panama from Spanish rule. He is made president of a short-lived new nation, Gran Colombia (1819–31).

KRZYSZTOF DYDYNSKI/GETTY IMAGES ©

1825
General Sucre incites a declaration of independence for Alto Perú, and the new Republic of Bolivia is born, loosely modeled on the US, with legislative, executive and judicial branches of government.

» Portrait of Simón Bolívar

Missionaries showed up in the 18th and 19th centuries in the areas around Santa Cruz and Tarija, altering the cultural landscape of the region. Increased conflict between new Spanish arrivals and the elite of Potosí in the late 17th century triggered a broad economic decline in the 18th century.

Independence

The early part of the 19th century was a time of revolution and independence in Bolivia. Harvest failures and epidemics severely affected the Bolivian economy between 1803 and 1805, creating fertile ground for revolution. To top it off, with the French Revolution, Napoleon's wars in Europe and British support for Latin America's independence movements, the colonists of the Americas were finally able to perceive what a world without royalty would look like.

By May 1809, Latin America's first independence movement had gained momentum and was well underway in Chuquisaca (later renamed Sucre), with other cities quick to follow suit. This first revolutionary spark was quickly put down. Ironically, while the first shouts of revolution came from Bolivia, it would be the last country in South America to gain independence.

Here's how it played out. By the early 1820s General Simón Bolívar had succeeded in liberating both Venezuela and Colombia from Spanish domination. In 1822 he dispatched Mariscal (Field Marshall) Antonio José de Sucre to Ecuador to defeat the royalists at the battle of Pichincha. In 1824, after years of guerrilla action against the Spanish and the victories of Bolívar and Sucre in the battles of Junín (August 6) and Ayacucho (December 9), Peru won its independence. During this time, another independence leader coming from the Río de la Plata, José de San Martín, was busy fighting battles in eastern Bolivia and liberating much of the southern corner of the continent.

With both Argentina and Peru eyeing the prize of the Potosí mines, Sucre incited a declaration of independence from Peru and, in 1825, the Republic of Bolivia was born. Bolívar (yes, the country was named after him) and Sucre served as Bolivia's first and second presidents but, after a brief attempt by the third president Andrés Santa Cruz to form a confederation with Peru, things began to go awry. Chilean opposition eventually broke up this potentially powerful alliance, and Bolivia was relegated to a more secondary role in regional affairs with a period of *caudillo* rule dominating the national politics until the 1880s. Thereafter Bolivia was ruled by a civilian oligarchy divided into liberal and conservative groups until the 1930s, when the traditional political system again fell apart, leading to constant military intervention until the 1952 Revolution.

Between 1780 and 1782 an indigenous revolt led by Tupac Amaru extended from Peru into Bolivia. During this time, the indigenous nobility lost much of their power, creating the framework for complete domination by Spanish-descendent interests.

In 1865 General Mariano Melgarejo drunkenly set his army off on an overland march to aid France at the outset of the Franco-Prussian War. A sudden downpour sobered him up.

1879–84	1903	1932	1935–38
Bolivia loses its coastline to Chile in the War of the Pacific. The loss of this transit point continues to hobble the Bolivian economy to this day.	During the rubber boom, Brazil annexes the remote Acre area, which stretched from Bolivia's present Amazonian borders to halfway up Peru's eastern border.	Bolivia enters the Chaco War against Paraguay over a border dispute for control of the potentially huge deposits of oil eyed by rival foreign oil companies.	A ceasefire in the Chaco War is negotiated in 1935, at which time Paraguay controls much of the region. A 1938 truce awards Paraguay three-quarters of the Chaco.

Political & Economic Strife

During the 20th century wealthy tin barons and landowners controlled Bolivian farming and mining interests, while the peasantry was relegated to *pongueaje,* a feudal system of peonage. Civil unrest brewed, with the most significant development being the emergence of the Movimiento Nacionalista Revolucionario (MNR) political party. It united the masses behind the common cause of popular reform, sparking friction between peasant miners and absentee tin bosses. Under the leadership of Víctor Paz Estenssoro, the MNR prevailed in the 1951 elections, but a last-minute military coup prevented it from actually taking power. What ensued was a period of serious combat, which ended with the defeat of the military and Paz Estensorro's rise to power in what has been called the National Revolution of 1952. He immediately nationalized the mines,

SHRINKING TERRITORY

At the time of independence Bolivia's boundaries encompassed well over 2 million sq km. But its neighbors soon moved to acquire its territory, removing coastal access and much of the area covered by its ancient Amazonian rubber trees.

The coastal loss occurred during the War of the Pacific, fought against Chile between 1879 and 1884. Many Bolivians believe that Chile stole the Atacama Desert's copper- and nitrate-rich sands and 850km of coastline from Peru and Bolivia by invading during Carnaval. Chile did attempt to compensate for the loss by building a railroad from La Paz to the ocean and allowing Bolivia free port privileges in Antofagasta, but Bolivians have never forgotten this devastating *enclaustramiento* (landlocked status).

The next major loss was in 1903 during the rubber boom when Brazil hacked away at Bolivia's inland expanse. Both Brazil and Bolivia had been ransacking the forests of the Acre territory – it was so rich in rubber trees that Brazil engineered a dispute over sovereignty and sent in its army. Brazil then convinced the Acre region to secede from the Bolivian republic and promptly annexed it.

There were two separate territory losses to Argentina. First, Argentina annexed a large slice of the Chaco in 1862. Then, in 1883, the territory of Puna de Atacama also went to Argentina. It had been offered to both Chile and Argentina, the former in exchange for the return of the coastal areas, the latter in exchange for clarification over Bolivia's ownership of Tarija.

After losing the War of the Pacific, Bolivia was desperate to have the Chaco, an inhospitable region beneath which rich oil fields were mooted to lie, as an outlet to the Atlantic via the Río Paraguay. Between 1932 and 1935, a particularly brutal war was waged between Bolivia and Paraguay over the disputed territory (more than 80,000 lives were lost). Though no decisive victory was reached, both nations had grown weary of fighting, and peace negotiations in 1938 awarded most of the disputed territory to Paraguay.

1942	1952	1964	1967
Hundreds of trade-union laborers are shot down by government troops at a Catavi tin-mining complex while striking for better wages and conditions. The fight for labor rights is on.	A military coup provokes a popular armed revolt by the miners, known as the April Revolution. After heavy fighting the military is defeated and Víctor Paz Estenssoro takes power.	After trying and failing for 12 years to raise the standard of living, the MNR's popularity wanes, and Víctor Paz Estenssoro's government is finally forced out by a military junta.	Argentine revolutionary Ernesto 'Che' Guevara, having failed to foment a peasant revolt in Bolivia, is executed by a US-backed military squad in the hamlet of La Higuera.

evicted the tin barons, put an end to *pongueaje* and set up Comibol (Corporación Minera de Bolivia), the state entity in charge of mining interests. The MNR remained in power for 12 years but even with US support it was unable to raise the standard of living or increase food production substantially.

The '60s and '70s were decades of military coups, dictators, brutal regimes of torture, arrests and disappearances, as well as a marked increase in cocaine production and trafficking.

In 1982 Congress elected Hernán Siles Zuazo, the civilian left-wing leader of the Communist-supported Movimiento de la Izquierda Revolucionaria (MIR), which began one of the longest democratic periods in Bolivian history to date. His term was beleaguered by labor disputes, government overspending and huge monetary devaluation, resulting in a truly staggering inflation rate that at one point reached 35,000% annually.

When Siles Zuazo gave up after three years and called general elections, Paz Estenssoro returned to politics to become president for the fourth time. He immediately enacted harsh measures to revive the shattered economy including ousting labor unions, imposing a wage freeze and eliminating price subsidies, then deployed armed forces to keep the peace. Inflation was curtailed within weeks, but spiraling unemployment threatened the government's stability.

Economic Reforms Overshadowed

The early '90s were characterized by political apathy, party politics, and the struggle between *capitalización* (the opening of state companies to international investment) and populist models. The free market won with the election of Gonzalo 'Goni' Sánchez de Lozada, the MNR leader who had played a key role in the curtailing of inflation through 'shock therapy' during the Estenssoro government.

Economic reforms saw state-owned companies and mining interests open up to overseas investment in the hope that that privatization would bring stability and make the enterprises profitable. Overseas investors were offered 49% equity, total voting control, license to operate in Bolivia and up to 49% of the profits. The remaining 51% of the shares were distributed to Bolivians as pensions and through Participación Popular, a program meant to channel spending away from the cities and into rural schools, clinics and other local infrastructure.

In late 1995 reform issues were overshadowed by violence and unrest surrounding US-directed coca eradication in the Chapare. In the late '90s the government faced swelling public discontent with the coca eradication measures and protests in response to increasing gas prices, a serious water shortage and economic downturn in the department of Cochabamba.

To encourage the settlement of the Amazon, Paz Estenssoro promoted road building (with Japanese aid) in the wilderness and opened up vast indigenous lands and pristine rainforest to logging interests.

Want to know more about Bolivia's history, taking into account the effects of geography, economy, policy and more? Check out the dense but incisive *A Concise History of Bolivia* (2011) by Herbert S Klein.

1975	**1978**	**1982**	**1985**
Operation Condor, a clandestine program to subvert communist movements and support right-wing governments in South America, gets its blackwater beginnings. Some attribute 60,000 deaths to Condor.	After a decade of reported human rights abuses, Hugo Banzer Suárez schedules general elections and loses. He ignores the results, but is eventually forced to step down by a coup.	The Bolivian Congress appoints a woman, Lidia Gueilar, as interim president during a tumultuous period of several presidential elections and coups. The rule of Bolivia's first woman president is brief.	Paz Estenssoro's New Economic Policy promotes spending cuts and privatization, resulting in strikes and protests by the miners' union; massive unemployment follows the crash of the price of tin.

Following a successful campaign advised by a team of US political consultants that he hired, Goni was again appointed president in August 2002. The following year his economic policies were met with widespread demonstrations which resulted in the loss of 67 lives during a police lockdown in La Paz. In October 2003, Goni resigned amid massive popular protests and fled to the US. He currently faces charges related to the deaths during the demonstrations, both in the US and Bolivia, and a formal extradition process is underway.

Protests, rising fuel prices and continued unrest pushed Goni's successor, Carlos Mesa, to resign in 2005.

The Morales Era

In December 2005 Bolivians elected their country's first indigenous president. A former *cocalero* (coca grower) and representative from Cochabamba, Evo Morales of Movimiento al Socialismo (MAS) won nearly 54% of the vote, having promised to alter the traditional political class and to empower the nation's poor (mainly indigenous) majority. After the election, Morales quickly grabbed the lefty spotlight, touring the world and meeting with Venezuela's Hugo Chávez, Cuba's Fidel Castro, Brazil's Luis Inácio Lula da Silva and members of South Africa's African National Congress. Symbolically, on May Day 2006, he nationalized Bolivia's natural gas reserves and raised taxes on energy investors in a move that would consolidate Bolivia's resources in Bolivian hands. Nationalizations continue to this day.

In July 2006, Morales formed a National Constituent Assembly to set about rewriting the country's constitution. In January 2009, the new socially focused constitution was approved by 67% of the voters in a nationwide referendum. The first constitution in Bolivia approved by popular vote, it gave greater power to the country's indigenous majority and allowed Morales to seek a second five-year term, which he won that same year. The constitution also limited the size of landholdings in order to redistribute Bolivia's land from large ranchers and landowners to poor indigenous farmers.

While Evo Morales has near-universal support among the indigenous people of Bolivia, his radical social changes aren't without resistance. In the eastern part of the country – the four departments known as La Media Luna (Half Moon, after their geographic shape) – where much of the natural resources lie, a strong right-wing opposition has been challenging Morales, accusing him of being an ethnocentric despot.

The polarization in Bolivia is very real, with the province of Santa Cruz constantly requesting more autonomy and threatening to secede from the western highlands. However, Morales has been surprisingly

COCA

About 1.2 million kilos of coca leaf are consumed monthly in Bolivia, leading Evo Morales to declare it an intrinsic part of Bolivia's heritage in the new constitution. Millions have been invested in alternative uses for coca.

1987	1989	1993	2002–03
The US begins sending Drug Enforcement Administration anti-coca squadrons into the Beni and Chapare regions, where coca has generated substantial income for the growers and traffickers.	With no candidate winning a majority in the presidential election, the National Congress is left to select Jaime Paz Zamora of the MIR as the 73rd president of Bolivia.	Gonzalo 'Goni' Sánchez is elected president on a center-left free-marketeering ticket and, with his government, proceeds to introduce landmark social, economic and constitutional reforms.	Goni wins the presidency with only 22.5% of the vote. After massive protests against his unpopular economic policies lead to more than 60 deaths, he resigns in October 2003.

successful in pushing his initiatives through, despite the fervent opposition (following the September 2008 protests, he expelled the US ambassador, Philip S Goldberg, reproaching him for fuelling the right-wing separatists). And it's not just opposition from the east: Morales has seriously alienated businesspeople and industrialists throughout the nation, not to mention international investors, causing the country to become even more fractured along economic, cultural and racial lines. It seems the dual society in one of South America's poorest nations will last a while longer.

2005	2008	2009
After a string of more than 70 presidents throughout its tumultuous history, Bolivia elects the country's first indigenous leader, Evo Morales, who wins with nearly 54% of the vote.	Right-wing factions' opposition to Morales' renationalization of Bolivia's gas wealth culminates in pitched street battles in Santa Cruz that leave 11 dead and more than 50 wounded.	The new constitution is approved with more than 60% support, giving greater rights to the majority indigenous population and allowing Morales to run for – and win – his second term.

» Morales election banner

Life in Bolivia

The National Psyche

Bolivia is a remarkably stratified society. While the hierarchies defined over 500 years of rule by Spanish descendants are slowly starting to fade, your place in society and the opportunities you will have throughout life are still largely defined by the color of your skin, the language you speak, the clothes you wear and the money you have.

Attitude depends on climate and altitude. *Cambas* (lowlanders) and *kollas* (highlanders) enjoy expounding on what makes them different (ie better) than the other. Lowlanders are said to be warmer, more casual and more generous to strangers; highlanders are supposedly harder working but less open-minded. While the jesting used to be good-natured, regional tensions have increased over the past few years, with Santa Cruz' threats of secession constantly in the news.

Thanks in part to Evo Morales, many Bolivians have been redefining and even questioning what it means to be Bolivian. From the beginning, Evo Morales vigorously stressed that Bolivian identity was based on an individual's ethnic origins. Despite his claims that all Bolivians are equal, Morales has been quick to espouse the status of indigenous groups. Some accuse him of political maneuvering and of further polarizing the country according to race, class and economic status. He has been seen as favoring indigenous groups over others, including mestizos who, as descendants of the Spanish colonists and indigenous people, are also proud of their Bolivian status.

And while the political power is shifting toward the indigenous majority, the money stays in the hands of the ruling elite (at least in the hands of those who have not left since Evo Morales took power).

Not many Bolivians are especially proud of their nation, and talking with people from all walks of life you can't help but get a sense of poor self-esteem and fatalism. And while many could attribute this to poverty, not many 'poor' Bolivians consider themselves poor. For example, in the Altiplano, many 'poor' llama herders have up to 80 head of llama (worth about US$8000). Wealth is found in lasting assets such as land and family, connection with the earth and health.

Life's not easy – it's actually really tough for most Bolivians – so many try to take joy from the little things: soccer, the rising of the sun, good rains and harvests, birthdays, religious festivals, coca, *cerveza* (beer), births and christenings.

AYMARÁ

The Wiphala flag (square-shaped and consisting of 49 small squares in a grid with graduating colors of the rainbow) has been adopted as a symbol of the Aymará people. Whether the colors used originate from Inca times or more recently, is cause for debate.

Lifestyle

Day-to-day life varies from Bolivian to Bolivian, mostly depending on whether they live in the city or in the country and whether they are rich or poor. Many *campesinos* (subsistence farmers) live without running water, heat or electricity, and some wear clothing that has hardly changed in style since the Spanish arrived. But in the Bolivian cities, especially

ARE YOU LOST, MY FRIEND?

Rather than give no response at all, some Bolivians will provide you with incorrect answers or directions. They're not being malicious; they merely want to appear helpful and knowledgeable. It's also worth remembering that street numbers are hardly used – people give directions by landmarks instead. Sometimes it's best to ask several people the same question – the most common response is likely to be correct.

Santa Cruz (the country's richest city), La Paz, Cochabamba and Sucre, thousands of people enjoy the comforts of contemporary conveniences and live very modern lifestyles.

Life in this fiercely self-reliant nation begins with the family. No matter what tribe or class one comes from, it's likely that they have close ties to their extended family. In the highlands, the concept of *ayllu* (the traditional peasant system of communal land ownership, management and decision making) that dates back to the Inca times is still important today.

For many in Bolivia's lower class, the day is about making enough money to eat, attending church, doing chores, the children studying, and a bit of laughter and forgetting. For the richer city class, there are distractions that come from economic surplus such as theater, cuisine, the arts, and the ever-important country club. In these circles, the last name still defines where a person can get to. Young people are increasingly flaunting these rules, but it is still relatively rare to see intermarriage between people from disparate ethnic groups or economic classes.

Homosexuality is legal in Bolivia but isn't openly displayed in this society of machismo. Despite a growing number of gay bars in some larger cities, gay culture remains fairly subtle.

Religion

Roughly 95% of Bolivia's population professes Roman Catholicism and practices it to varying degrees. The remaining 5% are Protestant, agnostic or belonging to other religions. Strong evangelical movements are rapidly gaining followers with their fire-and-brimstone messages of the world's imminent end. Despite the political and economic strength of Christianity, it's clear that most religious activities have incorporated some Inca and Aymará belief systems. Doctrines, rites and superstitions are commonplace, and some *campesinos* still live by a traditional lunar calendar.

Despite the high prevalence of llama fetuses in the markets (used for sacrificial offerings), llamas are not killed especially for them. About 3000 llamas are slaughtered daily on the Altiplano for wool and meat; the fetuses are removed from those animals subsequently found to be pregnant.

Sports

Like for many of its Latin American neighbors, Bolivia's national sport is *fútbol* (soccer). La Paz' Bolívar and The Strongest usually participate (albeit weakly) in the Copa Libertadores, the annual showdown of Latin America's top clubs. Professional *fútbol* matches are held every weekend in big cities, and impromptu street games are always happening. While small towns lack many basic services, you can be sure to find a well-tended *cancha* (soccer field) almost everywhere you go – and you'll be welcome to join in. Some communities still bar women from the field, but women's teams have started popping up in the Altiplano, where they play clad in *polleras* (skirts) and jerseys.

In rural communities, volleyball is a sunset affair, with mostly adults playing a couple of times a week. Racquetball, billiards, chess and *cacho* (dice) are also popular. The unofficial national sport, however, has to be feasting and feting – the competition between dancers and drinkers knows no bounds.

Indigenous Culture

Bolivia is a multiethnic society with a remarkable diversity of linguistic, cultural and artistic traditions. In fact, the country has the largest population of indigenous peoples in South America, with most sociologists and anthropologists agreeing that more than 60% of the population is of indigenous descent.

Bolivia has 36 identified indigenous groups. The vast majority of those who identify themselves as indigenous are Aymará (about 25%) and Quechua (about 30%), many of whom are located in the highlands. The remaining groups (including Guaraní and Chiquitano) are located almost entirely in the lowlands.

Mestizos (people of mixed indigenous and Spanish blood) make up a substantial portion of the population. Mestizos sometimes fall into mainstream society, while others retain their roots within the indigenous societal makeup.

Political & Social Change

Until recently Bolivia's indigenous groups have lacked a significant political voice, though they make up the majority of the nation's poor. With the election of Evo Morales, and a new constitution that grants expanded rights to indigenous groups and establishes Bolivia as a plurinational and secular state, the role of indigenous peoples in the nation's economy and policy is rapidly evolving. Nowadays there are numerous high-level indigenous ministers and technocrats, many of whom came from humble beginnings. This new awareness is creating a growing sense of pride within indigenous communities, where centuries-old traditions of terrace farming, respect for the land and communal decision making still play a strong role in everyday life, as do satellite TVs, cell phones, trucks, new rural schools, westernized dress and changing artistic, musical and political attitudes.

For centuries, women of indigenous descent who lived in the cities were known as *cholas*. Today, many consider this term to be derogatory, and some now go with the politically correct *mestiza* moniker. The only problem is that *mestizo/a* also describes people of mixed Spanish and indigenous descent. *Indígenas* is a commonly accepted term for indigenous peoples, as are the simpler and more effective *gente* (people), *persona* (person), *ser humano* (human being).

Visitors to indigenous communities, especially in the Altiplano where communities are particularly wary of outsiders, may be turned off by the aloofness and insular nature of these people. But keep in mind that Bolivia has lived under a highly structured, hierarchical societal framework since the rise of Tiwanaku and that your visit is but a distraction from the daily chores of survival. Many indigenous communities are slowly

The Aymará and Quechua spiritual worlds embrace three levels: Alajpacha (the world above or eternal sky, representing light and life); Akapacha (located between the sky and hell, and between life and death); and Mankapacha (located below, symbolizing death and obscurity).

embracing tourism and a stay in places such as Curahuara de Carangas can provide a unique introduction to these communities.

Religious Life

Based on animism, indigenous religions revolve around natural gods and spirits that date back to Inca times and earlier. Pachamama, the ubiquitous Mother Earth, is the most popular recipient of sacrificial offerings, since she shares herself with human beings, helps bring forth crops and distributes riches to those she favors. She has quite an appetite for coca, alcohol and the blood of animals, particularly white llamas. If you're wondering about all the llama fetuses in the markets, they are wrapped up and buried under new constructions, especially homes, as an offering to Pachamama.

Among the Aymará and Quechua mountain gods, the *apus* and *achachilas* are important. The *apus,* mountain spirits who protect travelers, are often associated with a particular *nevado* (snowcapped peak). Illimani, for example, is an *apu* who looks over inhabitants of La Paz. *Achachilas* are spirits of the high mountains; believed to be ancestors of the people, they look after their *ayllu* (loosely translated as 'tribe') and provide bounty from the earth.

Ekeko, which means 'dwarf' in Aymará, is the jolly little household god of abundance. Since he's responsible for matchmaking, finding homes for the homeless and ensuring success for businesspeople, he's well looked after, especially during the Alasitas festival in La Paz.

BOLIVIA'S INDIGENOUS GROUPS

It's impossible to capture the remarkable linguistic, artistic and spiritual traditions of Bolivia's myriad ethnic groups in just a few words, but here's an overview.

Highlands

» **Aymará** The Aymará culture emerged on the southern shores of Lake Titicaca after the fall of Tiwanaku. These strong, warlike people lived in city-states and dominated the areas around the lake. Today, Aymará live in the areas surrounding the lake and in the Yungas, with La Paz' El Alto area being the capital of Aymará culture. They speak – you guessed it – Aymará.

» **Chipaya** Perhaps the direct descendants of the Tiwanaku.

» **Kallawaya** A remote tribe with a dying language.

» **Quechua** Descended from the Inca, some 9 to 14 million Quechua speakers live in Bolivia, Peru, Ecuador, Chile, Colombia and Argentina today. These people lived across the former Inca empire. With the decline of mining in the 1980s, many Quechua speakers moved to the Chapare to harvest coca.

Lowlands

» **Chiquitano** Living primarily in the Chiquitania tropical savanna outside Santa Cruz, but also in Beni and in Brazil, there are about 180,000 Chiquitanos in Bolivia and about a quarter of them speak Chiquitano. Before the arrival of the Jesuits in the region there were numerous disparate ethnic groups. During the evangelization they were forced to live in small townships where a common language and dress were adopted.

» **Guaraní** This tribe shares a common language and lives in Paraguay, Brazil and parts of Uruguay and Bolivia. You can learn about their culture at the Guaraní Museum in Santa Cruz.

» **Mojeño** This significant ethnic group from the Beni department was quite large before the 17th century, with more than 350,000 people. Many were killed off by European diseases, but the language and culture survives today. Many early European explorers believed El Dorado would be found in Mojeño territory.

One of the most bizarre and fascinating Aymará rituals is the Fiesta de las Ñatitas (Festival of Skulls), which is celebrated one week after Day of the Dead. *Ñatitas* (skulls) are presented at the cemetery chapel in La Paz to be blessed by a Catholic priest. Parish priests shy away from associating this rite with Mass, but have begrudgingly recognized the custom. The skulls are adorned with offerings of flowers, candles and coca leaves, and many even sport sunglasses and a lit cigarette between their teeth. While some people own the skulls of deceased loved ones and friends (who they believe are watching over them), many anonymous craniums are believed to have been purchased from morgues and (so it is claimed) medical faculties. After the blessings, the decorated *ñatitas* are carted back to the owners' houses to bring good luck and protection. This ancient Aymará ritual was practiced in secret but, nowadays, the chapel's head count is growing every year.

Shamans oversee religious festivals, read fortunes and provide homemade traditional cures throughout Bolivia. Your closest experiences with shamans will be near Copacabana during religious festivals, or in remote regions in the Amazon jungle where packaged-for-tourists Ayahuasca healers ply their craft – be aware that Ayahuasca is a powerful hallucinogenic and that there have been tourist deaths related to its effects.

Stone talismans are also used in daily life to encourage prosperity or to protect a person from evil. A turtle is thought to bring health, a frog or toad carries good fortune, an owl signifies wisdom and success in school, and a condor will ensure a good journey. You can buy these in La Paz' Mercado de Hechicería (Witches' Market) and throughout the country.

Further Study

» **La Misk'isimi** (Sweet Mouth in Quechua) Story by Adolfo Costa du Rels.

» **www.mamani. com** Contemporary Aymará artist Mamani Mamani.

» **Sayari** Breakthrough film with an all-indigenous cast directed by Mela Márques.

Weaving

Bolivian textiles come in diverse patterns displaying a degree of skill resulting from millennia of artistry and tradition. The most common piece is a *manta* or *aguayo,* a square shawl made of two handwoven strips joined edge to edge. Also common are the *chuspa* (coca pouch), *chullo* (knitted hat), *falda* (skirt), woven belts and touristy items such as camera bags made from remnants.

Regional differences are manifested in weaving style, motif and use. Weavings from Tarabuco often feature intricate zoomorphic patterns, while distinctive red-and-black designs come from Potolo, northwest of Sucre. Zoomorphic patterns are also prominent in the wild Charazani country north of Lake Titicaca and in several Altiplano areas outside La Paz, including Lique and Calamarka.

Some extremely fine weavings originate in Sica Sica, one of the many dusty and nondescript villages between La Paz and Oruro, while in Calcha, southeast of Potosí, expert spinning and an extremely tight weave – more than 150 threads per inch – produce Bolivia's finest textiles.

Vicuña fibers, the finest and most expensive in the world, are produced in Apolobamba and in Parque Nacional Sajama.

Music & Dance

While all Andean musical traditions have evolved from a series of pre-Inca, Inca, Spanish, Amazonian and even African influences, each region of Bolivia has developed distinctive musical traditions, dances and instruments.

The instrument Bolivia is most known for, and understandably proud of, is the *charango,* considered the king of all stringed instruments. Modeled after the Spanish *vihuela* and mandolin, it gained initial popularity in Potosí during the city's mining heyday. Another instrument commonplace in the gringo markets is the *quena,* a small flute made of cane, bone or ceramic. The instrument predates Europeans by many centuries and

INDIGENOUS CULTURE WEAVING

MESTIZA DRESS

The characteristic dress worn by many Bolivian indigenous women was imposed on them in the 18th century by the Spanish king, and the customary central parting of the hair was the result of a decree by the Viceroy of Toledo.

This distinctive ensemble, both colorful and utilitarian, has almost become Bolivia's defining image. The most noticeable characteristic of the traditional Aymará dress is the ubiquitous dark green, black or brown bowler hat. Remarkably, these are not attached with hat pins but merely balanced on the head.

The women normally braid their hair into two long plaits that are joined by a tuft of black wool known as a *pocacha*. The *pollera* skirts they wear are constructed of several horizontal pleats, worn over multiple layers of petticoats. Traditionally, only a married woman's skirt was pleated, while a single female's was not. Today, most of the synthetic materials for these brightly colored *polleras* are imported from South Korea.

The women also wear a factory-made blouse, a woolen *chompa* (sweater/jumper), a short vestlike jacket and a cotton apron, or some combination of these. Usually, they add a shawl, known as a *manta*. Fashion dictates subtleties, such as the length of both the skirt and the tassels on the shawl.

Some sling an *aguayo* (also spelled *ahuayo*), a rectangle of manufactured or hand-woven cloth decorated with colorful horizontal bands, across their backs. It's used as a carryall and is filled with everything from coca or groceries to babies.

The Quechua of the highland valleys wear equally colorful, but not so universally recognized, attire. The hat, called a *montera*, is a flat-topped affair made of straw or finely woven white wool. It's often taller and broader than the bowlers worn by the Aymará. The felt *monteras* (aka *morriones*) of Tarabuco, patterned after Spanish conquistadors' helmets, are the most striking. Women's skirts are usually made of velour and are shorter in length.

the earliest examples, made of stone, were found near Potosí. A curious instrument known as a jaguar-caller comes from the Amazon region. This hollowed-out calabash, with a small hole into which the player inserts his hand, seems to do the trick in calling the big cats to the hunt.

Traditional Altiplano dances celebrate war, fertility, hunting prowess, marriage and work. After the Spanish arrived, European dances and those of the African slaves were introduced, resulting in the hybrid dances that now characterize many Bolivian celebrations.

Oruro's Carnaval draws huge local and international crowds. Potosí is famed for its re-creations of the region's *tinku* (ritual fighting) tradition, while La Paz is renowned for La Morenada, which re-enacts the dance of African slaves brought to the courts of Viceroy Felipe III.

The Natural World

When people think of Bolivia they generally conjure up images of somewhere high (La Paz), dry (Altiplano) and salty (Uyuni salt plains). While this may be true for large areas of the country, there's much more to the Bolivian landscape than just mountains. The range of altitude – from 130m in the jungles of the Amazon Basin to 6542m on the peaks of the rugged Andes – has resulted in a huge variety of ecological and geological niches supporting a bewildering variety of nature. Environmentally it is one of the most diverse countries on the continent.

The country has 1415 bird species and 5000 described plant species, some of the highest numbers in the world. It's also among the neotropical countries with the highest level of endemism (species which exist only in Bolivia), with 21 birds, 28 reptiles, 72 amphibians and 25 mammals found nowhere else on earth.

But while it may seem obvious that Bolivia's natural resources are one of its greatest assets, not everybody values assets that don't have a direct monetary value. From the lush tropical forests of Amboró National Park to the wetlands of the Pantanal, the scrub that obscures the Chaco gas fields and the *Polylepis* woodlands of the Andes, the Bolivian environment is under constant threat from destruction for economic exploitation.

A 2008 World Bank report concluded that climate change would eliminate many glaciers in the Andes within 20 years, threatening the existence of nearly 100 million people.

The Land

Two Andean mountain chains define the west of the country, with many peaks above 6000m. The Cordillera Occidental, in the west, stands between Bolivia and the Pacific coast. The eastern Cordillera Real runs southeast, then turns south across central Bolivia, joining the other chain to form the southern Cordillera Central.

The haunting Altiplano (altitude 3500m to 4000m) is boxed in by these two great cordilleras. It's an immense, nearly treeless plain punctuated by mountains and solitary volcanic peaks. At the Altiplano's northern end, straddling the Peruvian border, Lake Titicaca is one of the world's highest navigable lakes. In the far southwestern corner, the land is drier and less populated. The salty remnants of two vast ancient lakes, the Salar de Uyuni and the Salar de Coipasa, are there as well.

East of the Cordillera Central are the Central Highlands, a region of scrubby hills, valleys and fertile basins with a Mediterranean-like climate. North of the Cordillera Real, the rainy Yungas form a transition zone between arid highlands and humid lowlands.

More than half of Bolivia's total area is in the Amazon Basin, with sweaty tropical rainforest in the western section, and flat *cerrados* (savannas) and extensions of the Pantanal wetland in the east. In the country's southeastern corner is the nearly impenetrable scrubland of the Gran Chaco, an arid, thorny forest that experiences the highest temperatures in the country.

At 1,098,581 sq km, landlocked Bolivia is South America's fifth-largest country, three-and-a-half times the size of the British Isles.

Wildlife

Animals

Bolivia is one of the best places on the continent to observe wildlife, and even seasoned wildlife watchers will be impressed by the diversity on show.

The distribution of wildlife is dictated by the country's geography and varies considerably from region to region. The Altiplano is home to vicuñas, flamingos and condors; the Chaco to secretive jaguars, pumas and peccaries; the Pantanal provides refuge for giant otters, marsh deer and waterbirds; and the Amazon Basin contains the richest density of species on earth, featuring an incredible variety of reptiles, parrots, monkeys, hummingbirds, butterflies, fish and bugs (by the zillion!).

Of course, the animals that steal the show are the regional giants: the majestic jaguar, the continent's top predator; the elephant-nosed tapir *(anta)* and the giant anteater. The ostrich-like rhea or *ñandú*, the continent's biggest bird, is here too and it can be surprisingly common in some areas. You may even be lucky enough to spot the breathtaking Andean condor – revered by the Inca – soaring on mountain thermals.

River travelers are almost certain to see capybaras (like giant aquatic guineapigs) and caimans (alligators). It's not unusual to see anacondas in the rivers of the department of Beni, and a spot of piranha fishing is virtually an obligation for anybody spending time in the Amazon.

Overland travelers frequently see armadillos, foxes, *jochis* (agoutis) and the gray-faced, llama-like guanaco. Similar, but more delicately proportioned, is the fuzzy vicuña, once mercilessly hunted for its woolly coat but now recovering well. You won't have to work quite as hard to spot their domesticated relatives, the llama and the alpaca.

The Andean condor, one of the world's heaviest flying birds, has a 3m wingspan and can effortlessly drag a 20kg carcass.

Plants

Because of its enormous range of altitudes, Bolivia enjoys a wealth and diversity of flora rivaled only by its Andean neighbors. No fewer than 895 plants are considered endemic to the country, including 16 species of passionfruit vines and at least three genera of orchids.

In the overgrazed highlands, the only remaining vegetable species are those with some defense against grazing livestock or those that are not suitable for firewood. Much of what does grow in the highlands grows slowly and is endangered, including the globally threatened

---

ENVIRONMENTAL ISSUES

Bolivia's environmental problems may not yet have reached apocalyptic proportions, but environmentalists are concerned that accelerating economic growth is not being tempered by the necessary measures to maintain a sound ecological balance. Besides extensive land clearing for agricultural monocultures (particularly soybean), ranching and hydrocarbon exploration, there are also concerns about the future of freshwater supplies, with glaciers melting and the rivers increasingly polluted.

Many nonprofit organizations are working on countrywide environmental conservation efforts, including the following local groups:

» **Asociación Armonía** (www.armonia-bo.org) Everything you need to know about bird-watching and bird conservation.

» **Fundación Amigos de la Naturaleza** (p250) One of the most active of the local conservation groups, working at the national level.

» **Protección del Medioambiente del Tarija** (Prometa; www.elgranchaco.com/prometa) Works in the Gran Chaco region on a series of social and conservation initiatives.

genus of *Polylepis* shrubs which form dense, low forests at altitudes of up to 5300m, making them the highest growing arborescent plants in the world.

The lower elevations of the temperate highland hills and valleys support vegetation superficially reminiscent of that of Spain or California. The area around Samaipata is particularly rich in endemic plants, including a cactus *Samaipaticereus* and a bromeliad *Tillandsia samaipatensis*, while the gigantic Bolivian mountain coconut *Parajubaea torallyi* of the inter-Andean valleys is the world's highest growing palm.

The moist upper slopes of the Yungas are characterized by dwarf forest. Further down the slopes stretches the cloud forest, where the trees grow larger and the vegetation thicker. Northern Bolivia's lowlands consist of islands of true rainforest dotted with vast wetlands and endangered *cerrados*, while the Amazon Basin contains the richest botanical diversity on earth.

The national flower of Bolivia is the *kantuta*; not only is it aesthetically beautiful, but it also reflects the color of the national flag.

Threatened Species

Though it's the anteaters and jaguars that get all the headlines, these species are widespread throughout South America, and the most threatened members of the Bolivian fauna are not necessarily the most conspicuous or famous. There are exceptions, of course: the endangered Chaco peccary, an enormous piglike creature known only from fossil remains until 1976; the elusive spectacled bear; or the Golden Palace titi monkey, which hit the world headlines when a Canadian casino paid a fortune for the rights to name it.

Among the most threatened wildlife in the highlands are the little-known deer, the North Andean huemul, the Andean hairy armadillo and the endemic short-tailed chinchilla, sought out for its luxurious fur. The windswept lakes of the southern Altiplano are the exclusive habitat of the rare James flamingo, while the charming Cochabamba mountain finch has a total range of just 3500 sq km perilously close to the outskirts of the city of Cochabamba.

The Amazon Basin may be famous for its pink river dolphins, but rather lesser-known is the blue-throated macaw *(barba azul)*, a species considered critically endangered and thought to number fewer than 300 individuals. The mythical unicorn bird of the Yungas, more properly known as the horned currasow, was long thought to be extinct until its recent rediscovery. In the Pantanal region the golden spear-nosed bat lives only in a handful of caves, while the hyacinth macaw has suffered for its comical appearance through capture for the pet trade.

More than 40% of the Bolivian territory is affected by desertification caused by climate change, population increase and indiscriminate forest felling.

Some of Bolivia's most remarkable threatened species, however, won't win any awards for attractiveness. Consider the bizarre marsupial frogs of the genus *Gastrotheca*, which includes five species in Bolivia that are all threatened with extinction, and the Jabba the Hutt–like Titicaca giant frog, confined to Bolivia's most famous lake. The latter can weigh up to 400g and is under extreme pressure because of a local belief that drinking the juice from the liquidized amphibian has aphrodisiacal properties. You can find more information about them online at http://bolivianamphibianinitiative.org.

National Parks & Reserves

Bolivia has protected 18% of its total land by declaring 22 national protected areas and additional regional reserves under what is known as the Sistema Nacional de Áreas Protegidas (SNAP). The system is one of the most extensive on the continent, but even though it covers much of Bolivia's most amazing landscapes, the reality is that most reserves are only nominally protected.

EL CHAQUEO: THE BIG SMOKE

Each dry season, from July to September, Bolivia's skies fill with a thick pall of smoke, obscuring the air, occasionally canceling flights, aggravating allergies and causing respiratory strife. This is all the result of *el chaqueo*, the slashing and burning of the savannas (and some forest) for agricultural and grazing land. A prevailing notion is that the rising smoke forms rain clouds and ensures good rains for the coming season. In reality the hydrological cycle, which depends on transpiration from the forest canopy, is interrupted by the deforestation resulting in diminished rainfall.

Ranchers in the Beni department have long set fire to the savannas annually to encourage the sprouting of new grass. These days, however, the most dramatic defoliation occurs along the highways in the country's east, the new agricultural frontier. Here the forest is being consumed by expanding cattle ranches and pristine natural habitat is being replaced by seemingly endless monocultures. Although the burned vegetable matter initially provides rich nutrients for crops, those nutrients aren't replenished. After two or three years the land is exhausted and it takes 15 years for it to become productive again. That's too long for most farmers to wait; most just pull up stakes and burn larger areas.

As the rural population increases, so do the effects of *el chaqueo*. Despite the fact that this burning is prohibited by Bolivian forestry statutes, the law has proved impossible to enforce in the vast Bolivian lowlands. The long-term implications aren't yet known but international pressure to reduce the negative effects of the burning has seen the Bolivian government implement a program encouraging lowland farmers to minimize *el chaqueo* in favor of alternatives that don't drain the soil of nutrients, and culminated in the signing of a joint agreement with Brazil and Italy to reduce burning in the Amazon region. Despite this, it seems that *el chaqueo* will be a fact of life in Bolivia for many years to come.

The system of protected areas is managed by the government-run administrative body **Servicio Nacional de Áreas Protegidas** (SERNAP; www.sernap.gob.bo). In order to try to address the chronic financial and staffing issues that this body faces, local and international NGOs have worked with SERNAP to create innovative ways to preserve select habitats, with varying degrees of success.

Such projects have typically aimed to encourage local involvement and co-management of protected areas in an effort to attract tourists to community-based, ecotourism experiences, as well as to produce commercially viable natural products, including medicinal patents. A comprehensive guide to such initiatives in Bolivia was published in 2008: *Desde adentro* (Deep Inside Bolivia).

Survival Guide

Directory A–Z

Accommodations

Bolivian accommodations are among South America's cheapest, though price and value are hardly uniform. Be aware that, with the exception of the international hotel chains, the star ratings for hotels are not based on the recognized international rating system.

The Bolivian hotel-rating system divides accommodations into *posadas* (inns), *alojamientos* (basic accommodations), *residenciales* (simple accommodations), *casas de huéspedes* (family-run guesthouses), *hostales* (hostels) and *hoteles* (hotels). This subjective zero- to five-star rating system reflects the price scale and, to some extent, the quality. (Note that *hostales* are not necessarily hostels as you might normally think; some are in fact up-market hotels.) Rock-bottom places are usually found around bus and train stations, though this area is often the most dangerous in town.

Prices in this book reflect high-season rates (late May to early September). Room availability is only a problem at popular weekend getaways such as Coroico and during fiestas (especially Carnaval in Oruro and festivals in Copacabana), when prices double.

In the Altiplano, heat and hot water make the difference in price, while in lowland areas, air-con and fans are common factors.

The sleeping sections in this book are organized by author preference. Always ask to see a couple of rooms before committing, keep your valuables in a safe when available and check the sheets for bedbugs by searching for their feces beneath pillows. You can sometimes negotiate the room price in cheaper places.

Warning: several readers have alerted us to improper use of propane heaters in Bolivia. These are sometimes offered in cheaper accommodations but are not meant to be used in enclosed spaces, so refrain from using them if supplied.

Camping

Bolivia offers excellent camping, especially along trekking routes and in remote mountain areas. Gear (of varying quality) is easily rented in La Paz and at popular trekking base camps such as Sorata. There are few organized campsites, but you can pitch a tent almost anywhere outside population centers, although it's always a good idea to ask for permission if possible. Remember that highland nights are often freezing.

Theft and assaults have been reported in some areas – always inquire locally about security before heading off to set up camp.

Hostels

Hostelling International (HI; www.hostellingbolivia.org) is affiliated with a network of 15 accommodations in different parts of Bolivia. For affordable accommodations, check out www.boliviahostels.com. Most hostels have common areas, bunk beds in shared rooms, shared bathrooms with or without hot water, book exchanges, wi-fi, and some even come with pubs and Jacuzzis. You can often get cheaper accommodations at low-end hotels, but you'll miss out on the traveler culture.

Hostales & Hotels

Bolivia has pleasant midrange places and five-star luxury resorts, but these are mostly limited to the larger cities and popular vacation and weekend resort destinations. Standard hotel amenities include breakfast, private bathroom with 24/7 hot shower (gas- or electric-heated), phones, wi-fi and color TV, usually with cable. Save big by

---

BOOK YOUR STAY ONLINE

For more accommodations reviews by Lonely Planet authors, check out http://hotels.lonelyplanet.com. You'll find independent reviews, as well as recommendations on the best places to stay. Best of all, you can book online.

PRICE RANGES

The following price ranges refer to a double room with bathroom in high season, including all taxes and fees.

La Paz

$ less than B$180 (US$25)

$$ B$180-560 (US$25-80)

$$$ more than B$560 (US$80)

Rest of Bolivia

$ less than B$160 (US$22)

$$ B$160-400 (US$22-57)

$$$ more than B$400 (US$57)

booking ahead with online aggregators at www.hotels.com and www.expedia.com ilk.

Posadas, Alojamientos, Residenciales & Casas de Huéspedes

The accommodations at the cheapest end can be pretty bad. The worst *posadas* can be smelly, with showers scarce and hot water unheard of. Most *alojamientos* have communal bathrooms with electric showers (to avoid electric shock, don't touch the shower while the water is running and wear rubber sandals). Most travelers end up at *residenciales* with private or shared bathrooms. C*asas de huéspedes* sometimes offer a more midrange, B&B-like atmosphere.

Business Hours

Standard banking hours are 9am to 4pm or 6pm Monday to Friday, and 10am to noon or 5pm Saturday. Most businesses are closed on Sun-

days, save for restaurants. Markets stir as early as 6am and some are open on Sunday mornings. Shops sometimes close from noon to 2pm on weekdays, and are open from 10am to noon or 5pm on Saturdays. Restaurant hours vary, but they are generally open for breakfast (8am to 10am), lunch (noon to 3pm) and dinner (6pm to 10pm or 11pm).

Children

There are a few things to consider before bringing your children to Bolivia, including the following:

Altitude Potentially tough on tots.

Bugs Bites can be problematic because of potential disease. Your best defense is not to get bitten.

Climate Can be extreme.

Comfort Bumpy roads and long distances can make for unhappy campers.

Food Diarrhea is common.

Political instability There are more than 1000 ongoing conflicts in Bolivia today, and roadblocks and tear gas are not uncommon.

Vaccines You'll probably want them for visits to the lowlands, but many can be dangerous for children younger than two and for breastfeeding moms.

On the plus side, Bolivians love children, it's a one-of-a-kind cultural experience for them, and bringing your children in tow will do wonders for breaking down cultural barriers. All things considered, many still choose to leave their children at home.

As a general rule, civilian airlines charge 10% of adult ticket prices and/or airport taxes and fees for children under the age of two, who must sit on your lap. On long-distance buses, those who occupy a seat will normally have to pay the full fare. Some hotels have family rooms with three or

four beds. Restaurants rarely advertise children's portions, but will often offer a child-sized serving at a lower price, or will allow two kids to share an adult meal.

Cribs, diaper-changing facilities and child-care services are only available in the finest hotels in big cities. Breastfeeding in public is widespread. Formula milk is available in modern supermarkets in big cities, as are disposable diapers. If you plan on driving, bring your car seat from home.

There are fantastic children's museums in La Paz and Sucre, plus a water park in Santa Cruz. Most Bolivians spend Sunday afternoons picnicking with the family in parks and zoos or strolling the traffic-free pedestrian walks of La Paz and Cochabamba.

For more information, advice and anecdotes, see Lonely Planet's *Travel with Children*.

Checklist

» First aid kit including diarrhea tablets, rehydration salts, sunscreen, bug spray, Neosporin, Band-Aids, acetaminophen, thermometer

» Required vaccines, passports and visas, as kids need them too

» Snacks and favorite foods from home

» Clothes and sun hat for all weather

» Parental permission note if traveling solo

» Baby carrier, as strollers are basically pointless

» Favorite toys

» Wipes

Customs Regulations

When entering Bolivia, you can bring in most articles duty-free provided you can convince customs that they are for personal use. There's also a loosely enforced duty-free allowance of 200 cigarettes and 1L of alcohol per person.

Discount Cards

The **International Student Travel Confederation** (ISTC; www.aboutistc.org) is an international network of student travel organizations. It's also the body behind the International Student Identity Card (ISIC), which gives carriers discounts on a few services in Bolivia.

Electricity

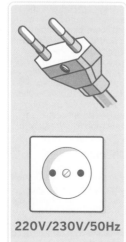

220V/230V/50Hz

220V/230V/50Hz

Embassies & Consulates

For a full list of foreign diplomatic representation in Bolivia, see www.embassies abroad.com/embassies-in/Bolivia.

Argentine Embassy in La Paz (Map p42; ☑2-241-7737; www.mrecic.gov.ar; Aspiazu 475); consulates in Cochabamba (Map p170; ☑4-425-5859; Federico Blanco 929), Santa Cruz (Map p242; ☑3-334-7133; Junín 22), Tarija (Map p224; ☑4-664-4273; Bolívar 696) and Villazón (☑2-596-5253; Saavedra 311)

Australian (Map p42; ☑7061-0626, 2-211-5655; australiaconsbolivia@mac.com; Aspiazu 416, La Paz)

Brazilian Embassy in La Paz (Map p42; ☑2-216-6400; www.brasil.org.bo; Arce 2739, Edificio Multicentro); consulates in Cochabamba (Map p170; ☑4-425-5860; Av Oquendo N-1080), Guayaramerín (☑3-855-3766; 24 de Septiembre 28), Santa Cruz (Map p242; ☑3-334-4400; Germán Busch 330) and Sucre (Map p188; ☑4-645-2661; Arenales 212)

Canadian (☑2-241-5141; international.gc.ca; Victor Sanjinés 2678, 2nd fl, La Paz)

Chilean Consulates in La Paz (☑2-279-7331; www.chile abroad.gov.cl; Calle 14 No 8024, Calacoto) and Santa Cruz (☑3-335-8989; René Moreno 551, 1st fl)

Ecuadorian Embassy in La Paz (Map p42; ☑2-278-4422; Calle 10 No 8054, Calacoto); consulate in Sucre (☑4-646-0622; Los Ceibos 2, Barrio Tucsupaya)

French (☑2-214-9900; www.ambafrance-bo.org; Fernando Siles 5390 at Calle 8, Obrajes, La Paz)

German Embassy in La Paz (Map p42; ☑2-244-0066; www.la-paz.diplo.de; Arce 2395); consulates in Cochabamba (Map p170; ☑4-425-4024; cnr España & Heroínas, Edificio La Promontora, 6th fl) and Sucre (☑4-645-2091; Rosenda Villa 54)

Italian (Map p42; ☑2-278-8506; www.amblapaz.esteri.it; Calle 5 No 458, Obrajes, La Paz)

Paraguayan (Map p42; ☑2-243-3176; Pedro Salazar 351, Edificio Illimani, La Paz)

Peruvian (Map p42; ☑2-244-0631; Av 6 de Agosto 2827, La Paz)

Spanish Embassy in La Paz (☑2-211-7820; www.maec.es; Av 6 de Agosto 2827); consulates in Santa Cruz (☑3-332-8921; Santiesteban 237) and Santa Cruz (☑3-312-1349; cnr Av Cañoto & Peru)

UK Embassy in La Paz (☑2-243-3424; www.ukin bolivia.fco.gov.uk/en; Arce 2732); consulate in Santa Cruz (☑3-353-5035; Santa Cruz International School, Km 7.5)

US Embassy in La Paz (☑2-216-8000; http://lapaz.usembassy.gov; Av Aniceto Arce 2780); consulate in Santa Cruz (☑3-351-3477; Av Roque Aguilera 146)

Food

The eating recommendations provided in this book are ordered by author preference. In larger cities, they are also often broken down by neighborhood where applicable.

Altiplano fare tends to be starchy and full of carbohydrates. In the lowlands, fish, fruit and vegetables feature more prominently. Meat invariably dominates and is usually accompanied by rice, a starchy tuber (usually potato) and shredded lettuce. Often, the whole affair is drowned with *llajua* (a fiery tomato-based salsa). The soups are a specialty.

Desayuno (breakfast) consists of little more than coffee and a bread roll, and is often followed by a mid-morning street snack such as a *salteña* (meat and vegetable pasty), *tucumana* (an empanada-like pastry) or empanada.

Almuerzo (lunch) is the main meal of the day. The best-value meals are found in and around markets (often under B$10) and at no-frills restaurants offering set lunches (usually between B$15 and B$40). *Cena*, the evening meal, is mostly served à la carte. Many highlanders prefer a light *té* (tea) instead of an evening meal.

Vegetarian options are on the rise, but you'll be stuck with lots of overly cooked vegetables, rice, potatoes, pizza and pasta. Quinoa is a super grain, perfect for vegetarians.

Got a nut allergy? *Maní* means 'peanut' and is a popular ingredient, especially in soups.

Basics

Do not drink tap water, or eat unpeeled vegetables and fruits. You will likely get traveler's stomache (a nice euphemism for diarrhea), and if you do, stay hydrated and eat plain food.

Formal tipping is haphazard except in the nicer restaurants. Elsewhere, locals leave coins amounting to a maximum of 10% of the total in recognition of good service.

Snacks & Soups

Scrumptious street snacks include empanadas, *tucumanas*, *salteñas*, *tamales* (cornmeal-dough pockets filled with spiced beef, vegetables, potatoes and/or cheese) and *humintas* (or *humitas*; cornmeal filled with cheese, onion, egg and spices, baked in the oven or boiled). For a hearty snack, try *anticuchos* (grilled cow heart on skewers), served at markets or street stalls.

A large bowl of *sopa* (soup) – whether vegetarian or meat-based – is the start of every great Bolivian meal. The most popular soups are the delicious *maní* (peanut) soup and *chairo*, a hearty soup using many Andean ingredients including *chuños* (freeze-dried potatoes),

meat and vegetables, and often topped with crispy fried pigskin. *Chupe*, *cha'que* and *lawa* (aka *lagua*) are the most common thick, stew-like soups. Quinoa and *maní* are often used to thicken broth.

Meats

Beef is typically *asado* (barbecued) or *parrillada* (grilled) in various cuts, including *lomo* (filet), *brazuelo* (shank) and *churrasco* (skirt steak). Jerked beef, llama or other red meat is called *charque*. A popular dish is *pique a lo macho*, a plate of chopped grilled beef and sausage served with potatoes, onions, lettuce, tomatoes and *locoto* (chili peppers). On the Altiplano, beef is often served with *choclo* (corn), corn on the cob, or *mote* (rehydrated dried corn kernels); in the lowlands it's served with yuca or mashed plantain. In the Beni, beef may be served as *pacumutus*, enormous chunks of grilled meat accompanied by yuca, onions and other trimmings.

Pollo (chicken) is either *frito* (fried), *al spiedo* or *a la broaster* (cooked on a spit), *asado*, or *dorado* (broiled). Cheap chicken restaurants are ubiquitous in Bolivia, where a meal of chicken and potatoes costs around B$7.

On the Altiplano the most deservedly popular *pescado* (fish) are *trucha* (trout) and *pejerrey* (kingfish), introduced species from Lake Titicaca.

Fruits

Many deliciously juicy South American fruits are cultivated in Bolivia. Most notable are the *chirimoya* (custard apple), *tuna* (prickly pear cactus) and *maracuya* and *tumbo* passion fruits.

In the lowlands, the range of exotic tropical fruits defies middle-latitude expectations. Among the more unusual are the human hand–shaped *ambaiba*; the small, round, green-and-purple *guaypurú*;

PRICE RANGES

The following price ranges refer to the cost of a main meal:

$ less than B$30 (US$4.20)

$$ B$30-60 (US$4.20-8.50)

$$$ more than B$60 (US$8.50)

the spiny yellow *ocoro;* the lemon-like *guapomo;* the bean-like *cupesi;* the *marayau*, which resembles a bunch of giant grapes; the currant-like *nui;* the scaly onion-looking *sinini;* and the stomach-shaped *paquio.*

Drinks

Top *cervezas* (beers) include Paceña, Huari, Sureña, Taquiña, Potosina and Tropical Extra. *Vino* (wine) is good, especially around Tarija. *Singani* is a white grape brandy, popular in a *chufflay* (mixed drink with soda or lemonade). *Chicha* is a fermented corn drink popular in the countryside.

On the nonalcoholic drink side, *Api* is made from a ground purple corn, while *mate de coca* is an infusion of water and dried coca leaves. Another wonderful hot drink is *trimate,* a combination of chamomile, coca and anise. A must try is a *mocochinche,* a sugary peach drink made from boiled cane sugar, cinnamon sticks and featuring a floating dried peach (another Andean food-preservation marvel). Also popular are the sweet and nutty *tostada* and the corn-based *horchata* and *licuados* (fruit shakes blended with water or milk).

Gay & Lesbian Travelers

Homosexuality is legal in Bolivia but still not widely accepted.

Gay bars and venues are limited to the larger cities, especially Santa Cruz and La Paz, but these are still somewhat clandestine affairs. As for hotels, sharing a room is no problem – but discretion is still in order.

Gay-rights lobby groups are active in La Paz (MGLP Libertad), Cochabamba (Dignidad) and, most visibly, in progressive Santa Cruz, which held Bolivia's first Gay Pride march in 2001. La Paz is known for La Familia Galán, the capital's most fabulous group of cross-dressing queens who aim to educate Bolivians around issues of sexuality and gender through theater performances. The feminist activist group Mujeres Creando is based in La Paz and promotes the rights of oppressed groups.

Insurance

A good travel insurance policy to cover theft, loss and medical mishaps is important.

There is a wide variety of policies available: shop around and scrutinize the fine print. Some policies specifically exclude 'dangerous activities,' which can include skiing, motorcycling, mountain biking and even trekking. Check that the policy covers ambulances and emergency airlift evacuations.

Worldwide travel insurance is available at www.lonely planet.com/travel_services. You can buy, extend and claim online anytime – even if you're already on the road.

Some other companies include the following:

ETA (www.eta.co.uk)

Insure My Trip (www.insuremytrip.com)

Travel Guard (www.travel guard.com)

World Nomads (www.world nomads.com)

Internet Access

Nearly every corner of Bolivia has a cyber cafe, and wi-fi is now standard in most midrange and top-end hotels (and many cafes). Rates run from B$2 to B$5 per hour. In smaller towns, expect to pay more – check the local Entel offices and be ready for slow satellite connections.

Language Courses

Language courses are offered in Cochabamba, Coroico, La Paz, Oruro and Sucre. Including a homestay will greatly expand your cultural exposure and increase your learning curve.

Legal Matters

The biggest legal problems include trafficking and possession of cocaine and other drugs, minor traffic violations and sex-related crimes.

If you are arrested, foreign embassies should be contacted immediately. Note, however, that they don't have the power to resolve the legalities (or illegalities) if you break the law.

Be aware that more recently incidences of fake police have been on the rise.

See also the La Paz chapter (p58) for more on safety issues for travelers.

Maps

Maps are available in La Paz, Cochabamba and Santa Cruz through Los Amigos del Libro and other book-

---

PRACTICALITIES

Addresses In addresses s/n means sin número (no street number). In smaller cities, landmarks are preferred to street names to get around.

Electricity Most electricity currents are 220V AC, at 50Hz. Most plugs and sockets are the two-pin, round-prong variety, but a few anomalous American-style two-pin, parallel flat-pronged sockets exist.

Newspapers Most locals take their coca tea or cafecito ('little' coffee) with La Razón (www.la-razon.com, in Spanish), the nation's biggest daily newspaper. In Sucre seek out El Correo del Sur (www.correodelsur.com, in Spanish); in Santa Cruz, El Deber (www.eldeber.com.bo, in Spanish). International periodicals are sold in bigger cities.

Radio For a 24/7 stream of Andean artists, browse Bolivia Web Radio (www.boliviaweb.com/radio). Radio Panamericana (www.panamericana-bolivia.com) is popular all around Bolivia.

Television Switch on the TV to watch the government-run Canal 7 (www.boliviatv.bo, in Spanish) or the private ATB TV (www.atb.com.bo, in Spanish) network. Opposition to the government is shown on UNITEL (www.unitel.tv, in Spanish) out of Santa Cruz. Cable TV with international stations is available in most upmarket hotels.

Weights and measures Use the metric system, except when buying produce at street markets, where everything is sold in libras (pounds; 1lb = 0.45kg).

stores. Government 1:50,000 topographical and specialty sheets are available from the Instituto Geográfico Militar (IGM), with offices in La Paz and in most other major cities.

International sources for hard-to-find maps include the US-based **Maplink** (www.maplink.com) and **Omnimap** (www.omnimap.com), and the UK-based **Stanfords** (www.stanfords.co.uk). In Germany, try **Deutscher Alpenverein** (www.alpenverein.de), which publishes its own series of climbing maps.

See the Bolivia Outdoors chapter (p24) for more about maps and guidebooks.

Money

ATMs

Sizeable towns have *cajeros automáticos* (ATMs) – usually Banco Nacional de Bolivia, Banco Bisa, Banco Mercantil Santa Cruz and Banco Unión. They dispense bolivianos in 50 and 100 notes (sometimes US dollars as well) on Visa, MasterCard, Plus and Cirrus cards; note that in the past, many Europeans have reported trouble using their cards. In smaller towns, the local bank Prodem is a good option for cash advances on Visa and MasterCard (3% to 6% commission charged) and many branches are meant to be open on Saturday mornings; the hours and machines are unreliable. Don't rely on ATMs; always carry some cash with you, especially if venturing into rural areas.

Change

Finding change for bills larger than B$10 is a national pastime, as change for larger notes is scarce outside big cities. When exchanging money or making big purchases, request the *cambio* (change) in small denominations. If you can stand the queues, most banks will break large bills. Also, check any larger bills for damage

A NOTE ABOUT PRICES

Prices in this guidebook are generally listed in bolivianos. However, many higher-end hotels will only quote prices in US dollars; likewise for many travel agencies and tour operators. Therefore, prices in this book are listed in bolivianos, except in cases where a business quotes its costs in US dollars. The currency is fairly stable.

as you may not be able to change them if they're torn or taped together.

Counterfeits

Counterfeit bolivianos and US dollars are less common than they used to be, but it still happens more often than you'd like.

Credit Cards

Brand-name plastic – such as Visa, MasterCard and (less often) American Express – may be used in larger cities at the better hotels, restaurants and tour agencies.

Currency

Bolivia uses the boliviano (B$). Most prices are pegged to the US dollar. Only crisp US dollar bills are accepted (they are the currency for savings).

The boliviano is divided into 100 centavos. Bolivianos come in 10, 20, 50, 100 and 200 denomination notes, with coins worth 1, 2 and 5 bolivianos as well as 10, 20 and 50 centavos. Often called 'pesos' (the currency was changed from pesos to bolivianos in 1987), bolivianos are extremely difficult to unload outside the country.

Exchanging Money

Visitors fare best with US dollars (travelers have reported that it's difficult to change euros). Currency may be exchanged at *casas de cambio* (exchange offices) and at some banks in larger cities. You can often change money in travel agencies, hotels and sometimes in stores selling touristy items. *Cambistas*

(street money changers) operate in most cities but only change cash dollars, paying roughly the same as *casas de cambio*. They're convenient after hours, but guard against rip-offs and counterfeit notes. The rate for cash doesn't vary much from place to place, and there is no black-market rate. Currencies of neighboring countries may be exchanged in border areas and at *casas de cambio* in La Paz. Beware, too, mangled notes: unless both halves of a repaired banknote bear identical serial numbers, the note is worthless. Also note that US$100 bills of the CB-B2 series are not accepted anywhere, neither are US$50 bills of the AB-B2 series.

International Transfers

The fastest way to have money transferred from abroad is with **Western Union** (www.westernunion.com). A newer, alternative option is through **Money Gram** (www.moneygram.com), which has offices in all major cities – watch the hefty fees, though. Your bank can also wire money to a cooperating Bolivian bank; it may take a couple of business days.

PayPal is increasingly used to make bank transfers to pay for hotels.

Photography

Keep in mind that the combination of high-altitude ultraviolet rays and light reflected off snow or water will conspire to fool both your eye and your light meter.

A polarizing filter is essential when photographing the Altiplano, and will help to reveal the dramatic effects of the exaggerated UV element at high altitude. In the lowlands, conditions include dim light, humidity, haze and leafy interference.

La Paz is generally the best place to buy equipment and for repairs.

Photographing People

While some Bolivians are willing photo subjects, others may be superstitious about your camera, suspicious of your motives or interested in payment. Many children will ask for payment, often after you've taken their photo. It's best to err on not taking such shots in the first place – be sensitive to the wishes of locals. Ask permission to photograph if a candid shot can't be made; if permission is denied, you should neither insist nor snap a picture.

Post

Even the smallest towns have post offices – some are signposted 'Ecobol' (Empresa Correos de Bolivia). From major towns, the post is generally reliable (although often involving long delays), but when posting anything important, it's better to pay extra to have it registered or send it by courier. **DHL** (www.dhl.com) is the most reliable courier company with international service.

Parcels

To mail an international parcel in La Paz, take it downstairs in the central post office (the stairs are halfway along the ground floor and to the right). You may be charged a small fee to have the belongings wrapped or your box officially labeled. You'll need two copies of your

passport – one will be included in your package. Complete the necessary forms (at the time of research these included a customs declaration form and a list of contents, known as a CN-23: Declaración de Aduana and CP-71 Boletín de Expedición). Take your parcel to the office marked 'Encomiendas.' If your package is less than 2kg, it's easier to send by regular mail. Pay the cost of postage and complete the CN-23. A 1kg parcel to the US will cost about B$150 by air and B$238 by faster courier service.

In some cities, you might have your parcels checked by customs at the post office; in cities without inhouse customs agents, you may have to trek across town to the *aduana* (customs office). A parcel's chances of arriving at its destination are inversely proportional to its declared value, and to the number of 'inspections' to which it is subjected.

Postal Rates

Airmail *postales* (postcards) or letters weighing up to 20g cost about B$7.50 to the US, B$9 to Europe and B$10.50 to the rest of the world. Relatively reliable express-mail service is available for rates similar to those charged by private international couriers.

Receiving Mail

Reliable, free *lista de correos* (poste restante) is available in larger cities. Mail should be addressed to you, c/o Lista de Correos (Poste Restante), Correo Central, La Paz (or whatever city), Bolivia. Using only a first initial and capitalizing your entire last name will help avoid confusion. Mail is often sorted into foreign and Bolivian stacks, so those with Latin surnames should check the local stack as well as checking for your first name. La Paz holds poste restante for two months. You will need your passport to collect the mail.

Public Holidays

Public holidays vary from province to province. The following is a list of the main national and provincial public holidays; for precise dates (which vary from year to year), check locally.

Nuevo Año (New Year's Day) January 1

Carnaval February/March

Semana Santa (Easter Week) March/April

Día del Trabajo (Labor Day) May 1

Corpus Christi May/June

Día de la Independencia (Independence Day) August 6

Día de Colón (Columbus Day) October 12

Día de los Muertos (All Souls' Day) November 2

Navidad (Christmas) December 25

Departmental Holidays

Not about to be outdone by their neighbors, each department has its own holiday.

Beni November 18

Chuquisaca May 25

Cochabamba September 14

La Paz July 16

Oruro February 10

Pando September 24

Potosí November 10

Santa Cruz September 24

Tarija April 15

Safe Travel

Crime against tourists is on the increase in Bolivia, especially in La Paz and, to a lesser extent, Cochabamba, Copacabana and Oruro. Scams are commonplace, and fake police, false tourist police and 'helpful' tourists are on the rise. Be aware, too, of circulating counterfeit banknotes.

There is a strong tradition of social protest in Bolivia: with more than 1000 ongoing conflicts, demonstrations are a regular occurrence and this can affect travelers. While generally peaceful, they can turn threatening in nature at times: agitated protesters throw stones and rocks and police occasionally use force and tear gas to disperse crowds. *Bloqueos* (roadblocks) and strikes by transportation workers often lead to long delays. Be careful if using taxis during transportation strikes – you may end up at the receiving end of a rock, which people pelt at those who are not in sympathy with them.

The rainy season means flooding, landslides and road washouts, which in turn means more delays. Getting stuck overnight behind a landslide can happen; you'll be a happier camper with ample food, drink and warm clothes on hand.

Note that the mine tours in Potosí, bike trips outside La Paz and the 4WD excursions around Salar de Uyuni have become so popular that agencies are willing to forgo safety. Make sure you do your research before signing up for the tour.

Shopping

Each town or region has its own specialty *artesanía* (locally handcrafted items). For traditional musical instruments, head for Tarija or Calle Sagárnaga in La Paz (although the latter will be overpriced). For weavings, the Cordillera Apolobamba or the environs of Sucre are your best bet. Ceramics are a specialty around Cochabamba, and crafts in tropical woods are sold in the lowlands around Santa Cruz, Trinidad and the Amazon Basin.

You'll find a range of reasonably priced artwork from all over the country in La Paz and Copacabana, but prices are generally lower at the point of original production. All sorts of clothing are available in llama and alpaca wool; vicuña wool is the finest and most expensive. Some pieces are hand-dyed and woven or knitted while others are mass-produced by machine.

Many articles are made by cooperatives or profit companies with ecofriendly and culturally responsible practices.

Solo Travelers

As always when traveling, safety is in numbers; solo travelers should remain alert when traveling, especially at night. On the whole, however, the benefits of solo travel can be huge, as being alone often opens up many doors to meeting local people as well as other travelers.

On the well-trodden gringo circuit, solo travelers should have little trouble meeting up with others. Some hostels and hotels have notice boards for those wanting to form groups to do activities. In places like Uyuni it's relatively easy to meet other travelers around town to make up the numbers needed for excursions.

Hostel prices are often based on a per-person rate, although more upmarket hotels have separate prices for single and double, with the latter being more economical.

The recent increase in tourism to Bolivia has meant that locals are becoming more accustomed to seeing Western travelers, including unaccompanied women. This has significantly reduced the incidence of sexual harassment and the concept of the 'loose gringa,' but in some places you may still face unwanted attention.

If you are traveling without a male companion and/or alone, it's wise to avoid testosterone-filled domains such as bars, sports matches, mines and construction sites. It's generally safe to catch a lift on a *camión* (flatbed truck) if you see lots of other people waiting; don't get on board if anything seems fishy. Women should never hitchhike alone. Especially in urban areas and at night, women – even in groups – should be careful, and avoid isolation. Hiking alone is discouraged under any circumstances.

Telephone

Numerous carriers – such as Entel, Viva, Boliviatel, Cotel and Tigo – offer local and long-distance rates on both landlines and cellular phones. Bolivia's first company, Empresa Nacional de Telecomunicaciones (Entel), is still the most prevalent in smaller towns but other companies are making an entrance. Local calls cost just a few bolivianos from these offices. *Puntos,* run by all of the above companies, are small, privately run outposts offering similar services and are open late. Alternatively, street kiosks are often equipped with telephones

GOVERNMENT TRAVEL ADVICE

The following government websites offer travel advisories and information on current hot spots:

Australian Department of Foreign Affairs (www.smartraveller.gov.au)

British Foreign Office (www.fco.gov.uk)

Canadian Department of Foreign Affairs (www.dfait-maeci.gc.ca)

US State Department (www.travel.state.gov)

that charge B$1 for brief local calls.

In some tiny villages you'll find card-phone telephone boxes – phones take both magnetic and computer chip varieties. Both card types (tarjetas) come in denominations of B$10, B$20, B$50 and B$100. Touts in fluorescent jackets with cellular phones chained to themselves offer calls for B$1 per minute.

Cellular SIM cards are cheap (starting at B$40, inclusive of B$20 to B$30 credit) and available from larger carrier outlets as well as small private phone shops. If you buy from a private outlet, activate the number and check that the phone works before purchasing. Make sure your phone has tri-band network capabilities (similar to the US system). To top up your call amount, buy cards (ask for crédito, ie credit) from the numerous puntos in any city or town.

Phone Codes

In this book, when the given phone number is in another city or town (eg some rural hotels have La Paz reservation numbers), the single-digit telephone code is provided along with the number.

International Calls

Bolivia's country code is ☏591. The international direct-dialing access code is ☏00. Calls from telephone offices are getting cheaper all the time, especially now that there's competition between the carriers – they can vary between B$1.50 and B$8 per minute.

In La Paz the cheapest of cheap calls can be made from international calling centers around Calle Sagárnaga for about B$2 per minute.

Some Entel offices accept reverse-charge (collect) calls; others will give you the office's number and let you be called back. For reverse-charge calls from a private line, ring an international operator: for the US (☏800-10-1110, 800-10-2222), Canada (☏800-10-0101) or UK (☏800-10-0044) be aware that these calls can be bank-breakers.

Internet Calls

Most internet places have Skype installed, which you can use at no extra cost – you just have to pay for the time online.

DIALING IN TO THE TELEPHONE NETWORK

Even Bolivians struggle with their own telephone network. Here's a quick kit to get you dialing.

Numbers Líneas fijas (landlines) have seven digits; cellular numbers have eight digits. Numerous telecommunications carriers include, among others, Entel, Cotel, Tigo, Boliviatel and Viva. Each carrier has an individual code between ☏010 and ☏021.

Area codes Each department (region) has its own single-digit area code, which must be used when dialing from another region or to another city, regardless of whether it's the same area code as the one you're in. The department codes are: ☏2 La Paz, Oruro, Potosí; ☏3 Santa Cruz, Beni, Pando; ☏4 Cochabamba, Chuquisaca, Tarija.

Public phones Dialing landlines from public phone booths is easy; ask the cashier for advice.

Placing calls To make a call to another landline within the same city, simply dial the seven-digit number. If you're calling another region, dial ☏0 plus the single-digit area code followed by the seven-digit number, eg ☏02-123-4567. If calling a cell phone, ask the cashier for instructions; most puntos have different phones for calls to cellulars and landlines, so you may have to swap cabins if calling both.

Cellular phones Cellular-to-cellular calls within the same city are simple – just dial the eight-digit number. A recorded message (in Spanish) may prompt you for a carrier number, indicating that the person is either not within the same city or region or has a SIM card from another region, in which case you must then redial using a ☏0 plus the two-digit carrier number plus the eight-digit cellular number. For cellular-to-landline calls within the same city, in most cases, you must dial the single-digit area code, and then the seven-digit number. For cellular-to-landline calls to another region, in most cases, you must dial a ☏0 plus the two-digit carrier code, followed by the single-digit area code, and then the seven-digit number. For example, if dialing Sucre from La Paz, dial ☏0 then ☏10 (or any one of the carrier codes – ☏10 is Entel's network carrier) then ☏4 (Sucre's area code) then the seven-digit number.

International calls For international calls, you must first dial ☏00 followed by a country code, area code (without the first zero) and the telephone number.

Time

Bolivian time is four hours behind Greenwich Mean Time (GMT), and an hour ahead of the US Eastern Standard Time. When it's noon in La Paz, it's 4pm in London, 11am in New York, 8am in San Francisco, 4am the following day in Auckland and 2am the following day in Sydney.

Toilets

Toilet humor becomes the norm in Bolivia. First and foremost, you'll have to learn to live with the fact that facilities are nonexistent on nearly all buses (except for a few of the luxury ones). Smelly, poorly maintained *baños públicos* (public toilets) abound and charge about B$1 in populated areas and B$5 in the wilderness, such as around the Salar de Uyuni. Carry toilet paper with you wherever you go, at all times! Toilet paper isn't flushed down any Bolivian toilet – use the wastebaskets provided. In an emergency, you can always follow the locals' lead and drop your drawers whenever and wherever you feel the need. Some of the most popular spots seem to be below 'No Orinar' (Don't Urinate) signs threatening *multas* (fines) equal to the average Bolivian monthly wage. Use the facilities at your hotel before heading out.

Tourist Information

Despite the fact that tourism has taken off in recent years, the Bolivian tourist industry is still in its formative stages, and government tourist offices still concentrate more on statistics and bureaucratic spending than on promotion of the country's attractions or imposing safety regulations. Most real

development and promotion has been courtesy of the private sector, which is the chief source of brochures and promotional programs.

There are often offices covering the *prefectura* (department) and *alcaldía* (local municipality) of a particular city. The major cities, such as Santa Cruz and La Paz, have offices for both, although the different tourism bodies range from helpful to useless, often flying under the new InfoTur banner. Most municipal offices can provide street plans and answer specific questions about local transportation and attractions. The most worthwhile are those in La Paz, Santa Cruz and Oruro, while those in other major cities seem to be considerably less useful. Note that the posted opening hours are not always followed. There are no tourist offices abroad. Servicio Nacional de Áreas Protegidas (SERNAP) is the best source of information about Bolivia's national parks.

Travelers with Disabilities

The sad fact is that Bolivia's infrastructure is ill-equipped for travelers with disabilities. You will, however, see locals overcoming myriad obstacles and challenges while making their daily rounds. If you encounter difficulties yourself, you'll likely find locals willing to go out of their way to lend a hand. For general information, visit the **Global Access – Disabled Travel Network** (www.globalaccess news.com).

Visas

Passports must be valid for six months beyond the date of entry. Entry or exit stamps are supposed to be free, but in remote border areas you will often be charged anywhere from B$15 to B$30 for an exit stamp. Personal

documents – passports and visas – must be carried at all times, especially in lowland regions. It's safest to carry photocopies rather than originals.

Bolivian visa requirements can be arbitrarily changed and interpreted. Regulations, including entry stays, are likely to change. Each Bolivian consulate and border crossing may have its own entry procedures and idiosyncrasies.

In 2007, as an act of reciprocity, the Morales government introduced visas for US citizens visiting Bolivia (a 90-day visa valid for five years costs US$135). At the time of writing, it was possible to obtain the visa upon arrival in Bolivia; check with the **Bolivian embassy** (202-483-4410; www.bolivia -usa.org) before traveling.

Citizens of most South American and Western European countries can get a tourist card on entry for stays up to 90 days (depending on the nationality). Citizens of Canada, Australia, New Zealand and Japan are granted 30 days, while citizens of Israel are granted 90 days. This is subject to change; always check with your consulate prior to entry. If you want to stay longer, you have to extend your tourist card (this is accomplished at the immigration office in any major city with a letter requesting the extension; it's free for some nationalities – for others, it costs B$198 per 30-day extension). The maximum time travelers are permitted to stay in the country is 180 days in one year. Alternatively, you can apply for a visa. Visas are issued by Bolivian consular representatives, including those in neighboring South American countries. Brazilian visas can be complicated, so check ahead. Costs vary according to the consulate and the nationality of the applicant, but hover around B$2500.

Overstayers can be fined B$14 per day (or more, depending on the nationality) – payable at the immigration office or airport – and may face ribbons of red tape at the border or airport when leaving the country.

In addition to a valid passport and visa, citizens of many Communist, African, Middle Eastern and Asian countries require 'official permission' from the Bolivian Ministry of Foreign Affairs before a visa will be issued.

More up-to-date visa information can be found at www. lonelyplanet.com.

Vaccination Certificates

Border agents may or may not request a yellow-fever vaccination certificate, and there are occasional checkpoints heading into the lowlands, where you will need to produce a certificate. Many neighboring countries, including Brazil, require anyone entering from Bolivia to have proof of a yellow-fever vaccination. If necessary, a jab can often be administered at the border but it is preferable to take care of this at home.

Volunteering

There are hundreds of voluntary and nongovernmental organizations (NGOs) working in Bolivia, making this a popular spot to volunteer. Many of the opportunities included here follow the pay-to-volunteer model, and often include room and board, costing anywhere from US$200 to US$1000 per month.

Be aware that some profit organizations offer 'internship' or 'volunteer' opportunities, when in reality it's unpaid work in exchange for free trips or activities.

There are a few options to do genuine volunteer work. Government-sponsored organizations or NGOs offer longer-term programs (usually two years) for which you receive an allowance, pre-departure briefings and ongoing organizational support; church-affiliated or religious organizations offer short-term opportunities, often on a group basis; and smaller volunteer organizations (often profit-based) offer independent travelers the opportunity to work on community projects. These usually have a two- or four-week minimum for which you pay.

Volunteer Organizations

Animales S.O.S (☑2-230-8080; www.animalessos.org; Av Chacaltaya 1759, La Paz) An animal-welfare group caring for mistreated or abused stray animals.

Parque Machía (☑4-413-6572; www.intiwarayassi. org; Villa Tunari, Chapare) Volunteer-run wild-animal refuge; previous experience of working with animals is needed, and the minimum commitment is 15 days.

Senda Verde (☑7472-2825; www.sendaverde.com; Yolosa) Just outside Coroico, this wildlife refuge has a two-week volunteer program.

Sustainable Bolivia (☑4-423-3786; www.sustainable bolivia.org; Julio Arauco Prado 230, Cochabamba) Cochabamba-based non-profit organization with a variety of volunteering programs, both short- and long-term, through 22 local organizations.

Volunteer Bolivia (Map p170; ☑4-452-6028; www. volunteerbolivia.org; Ecuador 0342, Cochabamba) Arranges short- and long-term volunteer work, study and homestay programs throughout Bolivia.

WWOOOF Latin America (www.wooflatinamerica.com) Sets you up with volunteer opportunities on organic farms.

International Programs

Amizade (www.amizade .org)

Bridge Abroad (www. volunteeradventures.com)

Earthwatch Institute (www.earthwatch.org)

Global Crossroad (www. globalcrossroad.com)

GoAbroad.com (www. volunteerabroad.com)

GVI (www.gvi.co.uk)

i-to-i (www.i-to-i.com)

Projects Abroad (www. projects-abroad.co.uk)

Real Gap (www.realgap. co.uk)

UN Volunteers (www.unv .org)

Wayna Hilaña Yanapaña (W.H.Y) (www.whybolivia .org)

World Volunteer Web (www.worldvolunteerweb .org)

Women Travelers

Women's rights in Bolivia are nearing modern standards, and cities are more liberal than country regions. But despite the importance of women in Bolivian society and the elevation of females in public life (including a female ex-president and women mayors), the machismo mindset still pervades Bolivia. In the home women rule, while external affairs are largely managed by men. As a female traveling alone, the mere fact that you appear to be unmarried and far from your home and family may cause you to appear suspiciously disreputable.

Bear in mind that modesty is expected of women in much of Spanish-speaking Latin America. Local women who wear Western dress in the warmer and lower areas tend to show more flesh than elsewhere in the country. That said, as a foreigner, avoid testing the system alone in a bar wearing a miniskirt. Conservative dress and confidence without arrogance are a must for gringas, more to be respectful than anything else. Men are generally more forward and flirtatious in the lowlands, where the Latino culture is more prevalent, than in the Altiplano where indigenous cultures prevail. The best advice is to watch the standards of well-dressed Bolivian women in any particular area and follow their example.

As a safety measure for a woman traveler, try to avoid arriving at a place at night. If you need to take a taxi at night, it's preferable to call for a radio taxi than to flag one down in the street. Note that during the period leading up to Carnaval and during the festivities, a woman traveling solo can be a popular target for water bombs, which can feel like quite a harassment or at least an annoyance.

Women should avoid hiking alone, and should never walk alone at night.

Work

For paid work, qualified English teachers can try the professionally run **Centro Boliviano-Americano** (CBA; Map p42; ☎2-243-0107; www.cba.edu.bo; Parque Zenón Iturralde 121) in La Paz; there are also offices in other cities. New, unqualified teachers must forfeit two months' salary in return for their training. Better paying are private school positions teaching math, science or social studies. Accredited teachers can expect to earn up to US$500 per month for a full-time position. Other travelers find work in gringo bars, hostels or with tour operators. Keep in mind that you are likely taking the job from a Bolivian by doing this.

Transportation

GETTING THERE & AWAY

A landlocked country, Bolivia has numerous entry/exit points, and you can get here by boat, bus, train, plane, bike and on foot. Some places are easier to travel through and more accessible than others.

Flights, cars and tours can be booked online at www.lonelyplanet.com.

Entering the Country

If you have your documents in order and are willing to answer a few questions about the aim of your visit, entering Bolivia should be a breeze. If crossing at a small border post, you may be asked to pay an 'exit fee.' Unless otherwise noted in the text, such fees are strictly unofficial.

Note that Bolivian border times can be unreliable at best and you should always check with a *migración* (immigration) office in the nearest major town. If you plan to cross the border outside the stated hours, or at a point where there is no border post, you can usually obtain an exit/entry stamp from the nearest *migración* office on departure or arrival.

Air

Only a few US and European airlines offer direct flights to Bolivia, so airfares are high. There are direct services to most major South American cities and the flights to/from Chile and Peru are the cheapest. Santa Cruz is an increasingly popular entry point from Western European hubs. Due to altitude-related costs, it is more expensive to fly into La Paz than Santa Cruz. High season for most fares is from early June to late August, and from mid-December to mid-February.

Airports & Airlines

Bolivia's principal international airports are La Paz' **El Alto International Airport** (LPB), formerly known as John F Kennedy Memorial, and Santa Cruz' **Viru-Viru International** (VVI).

The bigger airlines operate international flights and have offices in La Paz.

Aerolíneas Argentinas (AR; ☎3-333-9776; www.aerolineas.com.ar)

Amaszonas (☎2-222-0848; www.amaszonas.com)

American Airlines (AA; ☎2-334-1314; www.aa.com)

BOA (☎901-105-010; www.boa.bo) This is the new national airline, but at the time of writing its service was still irregular.

Grupo Taca (TA; ☎800-10-8222; www.taca.com)

LAN Airlines (LA; ☎800-100-521; www.lan.com)

TAM (PZ; ☎2-244-3442; www.tam.com.br)

Tickets

Ticket prices in this chapter do not include taxes or fuel levies, which can significantly increase air travel costs. Save money by using online aggregators and deal sites or make a cost-saving flight/land connection via Lima, Cuzco, Santiago or Buenos Aires.

ROUND-THE-WORLD TICKETS

Round-the-world (RTW) tickets can be real bargains if you are traveling to South America from the other side of the world. Generally put together by airline alliances, RTW tickets allow you a limited period (usually a year) in which to circumnavigate the globe.

An alternative to a RTW ticket is one put together by a travel agent. These tickets are more expensive than airline RTW fares, but you get to choose your itinerary.

Travel agents can also combine tickets from two low-cost airlines to offer multidestination fares that are cheaper than a RTW ticket and allow for two stops on the way to and from South America.

Some online sites offer intercontinental tickets.

Oneworld (www.oneworld.com) An airline alliance.

Round the World Flights (www.roundtheworldflights.com) An excellent site that allows you to build your own trip from the UK.

Star Alliance (www.staralliance.com) An airline alliance.

STA Travel (www.statravel.com) Student travel.

Australia & New Zealand

Travel between Australasia and South America isn't cheap, so it makes sense to consider a RTW ticket or travel via Buenos Aires or Santiago. Round-trip fares from Sydney to La Paz via Auckland and Santiago start at about A$2500/3000 return in low/high season. Fares via the US are considerably more expensive, starting at about A$3200 return in low season. RTW tickets including La Paz start at about A$3300. The most direct routes are from Sydney to Santiago on LAN/Qantas, or to Buenos Aires with Qantas/LAN and Aerolíneas Argentinas.

Destination Holidays (☎03-9725-4655; www.south-america.com.au) and **South American Travel Centre** (☎03-9642-5353; www.satc.com.au) specialize in Latin American travel.

Continental Europe

The best places in Europe for cheap airfares are student travel agencies (you don't have to be a student to use them) and online aggregators.

Some fares include a stopover in the US. Note that passengers traveling through New York (JFK) or Miami must pass through American immigration procedures, even if they aren't visiting the US. That means you'll either need to have a US visa or be eligible for the Visa Waiver Program, which is open to Australians, New Zealanders

and most Western Europeans unless they're traveling on a non-accredited airline (which include most Latin American airlines).

By the time you read this, BOA's planned daily service from La Paz to Madrid should be up and running.

South America

BOA connects La Paz to São Paolo and Buenos Aires several times a week. Aerolíneas Argentinas flies daily between Santa Cruz and Buenos Aires, and Varig-Gol Airlines flies between Santa Cruz and Rio de Janeiro (among other destinations). At the time of writing, Amaszonas was planning a daily service between Cuzco and La Paz.

LanChile connects La Paz with Santiago daily and there are connecting flights to Iquique. Brazilian-owned TAM connects Asuncíon with Santa Cruz. LanPeru flies from La Paz to Cuzco (often via Lima) daily.

UK

From London, all flights go via the US or South American countries. Save money by booking online or with a RTW ticket. Expect to pay from about £400 one-way in the low season. RTW tickets from London that take in South America (Santiago and Rio de Janeiro) start from about £1400.

London-based South American specialists include **Journey Latin America** (JLA; ☎020-3468-1460; www.journeylatinamerica.co.uk) and **Western & Oriental** (☎020-7666-1260; www.wandotravel.com).

US & Canada

Tickets from North American gateways usually have restrictions – often a two-week advance-purchase requirement, and you must usually stay at least one week and no longer than three months (prices can double for longer periods). Miami departures are the cheapest options.

Save money online and through deal-watcher or price-alerts sites such as www.travelzoo.com, www.groupon.com or www.kayak.com. Look for agencies that specialize in South America, such as **eXito** (☎800-655-4053; www.exitotravel.com).

Most flights from Canada involve connecting via a US gateway such as Miami or Los Angeles.

Land & River

Border Crossings

ARGENTINA

Two major overland crossings between Argentina and Bolivia are **Villazón/La Quiaca** (open 7am to 11pm) and **Yacuiba/Pocitos** (7am to 4pm). Villazón is connected by train with Oruro or Tupiza. The Yacuiba/Pocitos crossing is 5km from Yacuiba, in the Chaco region. Buses traveling further into Argentina leave every couple of hours.

The minor border crossing at **Bermejo/Agua Blanca** (8am to 5pm) south of Tarija is at an international bridge that leads onto a highway going further into Argentina.

BRAZIL

Note that proof of yellow-fever vaccination is needed when crossing into Brazil. If you don't have one, you can get a shot at the border (in relatively sanitary conditions).

Bolivia can be accessed via the **Quijarro/Corumbá** crossing.

Frequent motorboats (B$10) provide a novel water entry/exit via Río Mamoré at **Guayaramerín/Guajará-Mirim** (8am to 8pm). There

---

DEPARTURE TAX

Departure taxes vary according to the airport and destination. All are payable at the airport (either at the counter or a separate window) and are not included in ticket prices. Domestic departure taxes range from B$11 to B$15. International departure tax is US$25. Some airports also levy a municipal tax of up to B$7.

CLIMATE CHANGE & TRAVEL

Every form of transportation that relies on carbon-based fuel generates CO_2, the main cause of human-induced climate change. Modern travel is dependent on airplanes, which might use less fuel per kilometer per person than most cars but travel much greater distances. The altitude at which aircraft emit gases (including CO_2) and particles also contributes to their climate change impact. Many websites offer 'carbon calculators' that allow people to estimate the carbon emissions generated by their journey and, for those who wish to do so, to offset the impact of the greenhouse gases emitted with contributions to portfolios of climate-friendly initiatives throughout the world. Lonely Planet offsets the carbon footprint of all staff and author travel.

are no restrictions when entering Guajará-Mirim for a quick visit, but if you intend to travel further into Brazil, you must pick up an entry/exit stamp. For departure stamps from Bolivia, head to the Polícia Federal in **Bolivian immigration** (☺8am-8pm) by the dock.

Alternative ferry options are becoming less common, but can provide short hops across borders in the Amazon Basin at far-flung locales such as Parque Nacional Noel Kempff Mercado and Pimienteras in Bolivia, and Cobija and Brasiléia in Brazil.

CHILE

Note that meat, fruit and food produce (including coca leaves) cannot be taken from Bolivia into Chile and will be confiscated at the border.

The most popular route between Chile and Bolivia is by bus from La Paz to Arica through the border at **Chungará/Tambo Quemado** (8am to 8pm). A convenient alternative for those doing the 4WD Southwest Circuit tour is to be dropped off on the last day at **Hito Cajón** (8am to 11pm, although it's wise to be there before 6pm) and head for San Pedro, Chile (many tour operators now offer transfers). From here, you can pick up a bus. Note the one-hour trip between the Bolivian border and San Pedro – it's better to arrange transport for this in advance, in case taxis aren't waiting. Alternatively, there is a less used road between Oruro and Iquique with a border at **Pisiga/Colchane** (8am to 8pm).

A crossing can be made by train or road from Uyuni to Calama, where the border crossing is **Ollagüe/Avaroa** (8am to 8pm).

PARAGUAY

The easiest route between Paraguay and Bolivia is to cross from Pedro Juan Caballero (in Asunción, Paraguay) to Ponta Porã (Brazil), and then travel by bus or train to Corumbá (Brazil) and Quijarro (Bolivia).

The trans-Chaco bus trip between Santa Cruz in Bolivia and Asunción in Paraguay is a daily service. This is a notorious smuggling route, so expect to be lined up with your bags while customs officials and sniffer dogs rifle through your possessions.

For the adventurous, traveling by river between Asunción and Bolivia (via Corumbá, Brazil) is likely to involve a series of short journeys and informal arrangements with individual boat captains. From Asunción, there's an irregular river service to Concepción (Paraguay), and beyond here is where the informal boat arrangements begin. You'll probably wind up doing it in two stages: from Concepción to Bahía Negra (northern Paraguay), and Bahía Negra to Corumbá.

PERU

Bolivia is normally reached overland from Peru via Lake Titicaca. If you have time, the border crossing at **Kasani/Yunguyo** (8am to 6pm) via Copacabana is more appealing than the faster, less secure

and least interesting one at **Desaguadero** (9am to 9pm).

If departing Bolivia directly from La Paz, it's easiest to catch an agency bus to Puno (Peru); the bus stops in Copacabana and for immigration formalities in Yunguyo. A similar service goes direct to Cuzco. A cheaper way from Copacabana is by minibus from Plaza Sucre to the Kasani/Yunguyo border, with onward transportation to the border at Yunguyo (five minutes) and to Puno.

Bus

Depending on which country you enter from, some intercountry buses booked through an agency might cover your entire route; at other times you'll switch to an associated bus company once you cross the border. If traveling by local bus, you'll usually need to catch onward buses once you've made your border crossing. **Bolivia en tus Manos** (www.boliviaentusmanos.com/terminal) provides online bus schedules from major cities, including Cochabamba, La Paz, Potosí and Sucre.

Car & Motorcycle

You can enter Bolivia by road from any of the neighboring countries. The route from Brazil is improving but can still be a little rough, and roads from Paraguay should be considered only if driving a 4WD. The routes from Argentina, Chile and Peru pose no significant problems.

Foreigners entering Bolivia from another country need

the *hoja de ruta* (circulation card), available from the Servicio Nacional de Tránsito/Aduana at the border. This document must be presented and stamped at all police posts – variously known as *trancas, tránsitos* or *controles* – which are sited along highways and just outside major cities. *Peajes* (tolls) are often charged at these checkpoints, and vehicles may be searched for contraband.

GETTING AROUND

Bolivian roads are getting better, with several new paved routes popping up in recent years. Air transit is also easier, and slightly more cost-effective and prevalent, especially in the lowlands. Most of Bolivia is covered by small bus, boat, train and airline companies. It still takes a while to get around, and roads blocked by protesters, construction and landslides are common, as are flooded roads, and rivers with too little water to traverse.

Air

Air travel within Bolivia is inexpensive and the quickest and most reliable way to reach out-of-the-way places. It's also the only means of transportation that isn't washed out during the wet season. When weather-related disruptions occur, planes eventually get through, even during summer flooding in northern Bolivia. Schedules tend to change frequently and cancellations are frequent, so plan ahead.

Airlines in Bolivia

The closure of two large Bolivian carriers, Lloyd Aéro Boliviano and AeroSur, has left a gap in national air services. There is now a new national airline, **BOA** (☑901-105-010; www.boa.bo). **Transporte Aéreos Militares** (TAM; Map p38; ☑2-268-1111; www.tam.bo; Ismael Montes 738, Prado, La Paz) also offers flights around the country.

AeroCon (☑901-105-252; www.aerocon.bo) Connects the country's major cities, as well as some more remote corners.

Amaszonas (☑2-222-0848; www.amaszonas.com) Small planes fly from La Paz to Uyuni, Rurrenabaque, Trinidad, Santa Cruz and other lowland destinations. By now, a planned service to Cuzco should be operating.

Bicycle

For cyclists who can cope with the challenges of cold winds, poor road conditions, high altitudes and steep terrain, Bolivia is a paradise. With the number of dirt roads, mountain bikes are common. While traffic isn't a serious problem (though cliffs are), intimidating buses and *camiones* (flatbed trucks) can leave cyclists in clouds of dust or embedded in mud. Finding supplies may prove difficult, so cyclists in remote areas must carry ample food and water. Given these challenges, many prefer to leave the work to a tour company.

If you're considering any biking in Bolivia, make sure you purchase a comprehensive travel insurance policy.

Bolivia has its fair share of inexpensive bikes, mostly supermarket beaters from China. Quality new wheels are rarer. Your best bet for buying a used, touring-worthy stead is through agencies in La Paz. Try **Gravity Assisted Mountain Biking** (Map p42; ☑2-231-3849; www.gravitybolivia.com; 16 de Julio 1490 No 10, Edificio Avenida, Prado, La Paz) for spare parts and help with repairs. Bringing your own bicycle into the country is generally hassle-free.

Boat
Ferry

The only public ferry service in Bolivia operates between San Pedro and San Pablo, across the narrow Estrecho de Tiquina (Straits of Tiquina) on Lake Titicaca. You can travel by launch or rowboat to any of Lake Titicaca's Bolivian islands. Boats and tours are available from Huatajata to the Huyñaymarka islands in the lake's southernmost extension.

To visit Isla del Sol, you can take a tour, hire a launch or catch a scheduled service from Copacabana, or look for a lift in Yampupata or the villages along the way. A couple of well-established tour companies provide cruises by motorboat or hydrofoil. Book your trips from **Copacabana Beach** (Map p74) or from Huatajata.

River Boat

There's no scheduled passenger service on the Amazon, so travelers almost invariably wind up on some sort of cargo vessel. The most popular routes are from Puerto Villarroel to Trinidad, and Trinidad to Guayaramerín. There are also much less frequented routes from Rurrenabaque or Puerto Heath to Riberalta, but these are increasingly hard to arrange.

Bus

Bus travel is cheap and relatively safe in Bolivia, but can also be quite uncomfortable and nerve-racking at times. Buses are the country's most popular type of transport, and come in various forms. Long-distance bus services are called *flotas*, large buses are known as *buses*, three-quarter (usually older) ones are called *micros*, and minibuses are just that.

If looking for a bus terminal, ask for *la terminal terrestre* or *la terminal de buses*. Each terminal charges a small fee (a couple of bolivianos), which you pay to an agent upon boarding or when purchasing a ticket at the counter.

There have been numerous reports of items disappearing from buses' internal

TOP TIPS FOR GETTING AROUND

Air

Save time Flights will save you days of travel, but can add to your overall budget. In the Amazon, flying is now much preferred to boat travel.

Cancellations are common Call ahead to make sure you are still booked. You may need to wait until the next day, and if not you may be able to get a 70% refund.

Carry heavy stuff Weight limits are often 15kg for checked bags.

Save money Book online or with the airline office.

Boat

Less common Boat services are less common in the lowlands than they used to be. Adventurous spirits will find unique experiences if they are willing to seek services out.

Protect valuables Keep them padlocked.

Keep comfortable Bring a hammock, book and mosquito repellent.

Bus

Go direct Direct *cama* (reclining seat), semi-*cama* (partially reclining seat) and tourist-class services cost more but can save several hours.

Safeguard valuables Keep them with you on the bus (not in the overhead bin). You should padlock your bag if it's going on top.

---

overhead compartments. Hold on tight to your day-packs and bags if they are with you in the bus. Backpacks and bags are generally safe when stored in the baggage compartment, but try to watch as your luggage is loaded – there have been instances of bags becoming 'lost' or 'disappeared.' You will be given a baggage tag, which you must show when reclaiming your bag. A lock is a good idea.

Except on the most popular runs, most companies' buses depart at roughly the same time, regardless of how many companies are competing for the same business. Between any two cities, you should have no trouble finding at least one daily bus. On the most popular routes, you can choose between dozens of daily departures.

It's always a good idea to check the vehicles of several companies before purchasing your ticket. Some buses are ramshackle affairs with broken windows, cracked windshields and worn tires; it's better to stay away from these and look for a better

vehicle, even if it means paying a little more. Don't try to save on safety.

Classes & Costs

The only choices you'll have to make are on major, long-haul routes, where the better companies offer *coche* (or 'bus'), *semi-cama* (half-sleeper, with seats that recline a long way and footrests) and *cama* (sleeper) services. The cost can double for sleeper service, but could be worth it. Tourist buses to major destinations like Copacabana and Uyuni are twice the price of standard buses, but are safer and more comfortable. The VCR on the newest buses will be in better shape than the reclining seats (expect Van Damme all night), heaters *may* function, snacks *may* be served and toilets (yes, toilets) *may* work.

Prices vary according to the different standard of bus (from the more luxurious *bus cama* service to the ancient Bluebird-style buses) and the length of trip (whether overnight or short day-hop).

Reservations

To be certain, reserve bus tickets at least several hours in advance. Many buses depart in the afternoon or evening and arrive at their destination in the small hours of the morning. On most major routes there are also daytime departures. **Bolivia en tus Manos** (www.bolivia entusmanos.com/terminal) has online bus schedules for departures from major cities, including Cochabamba, La Paz, Potosí and Sucre.

Car & Motorcycle

The advantages of a private vehicle are flexibility, access to remote areas and the chance to seize photo opportunities. More Bolivian roads are being paved (most recently, between La Paz and Potosí), but others are in varying stages of decay, making high-speed travel impossible (unless you're a Bolivian bus driver) and inadvisable.

The undaunted should prepare their expeditions carefully. Bear in mind that

Stay warm Bring warm clothes and even a sleeping bag if going anywhere in the Altiplano. Roadside vendors offer snacks along the way, but bring some just in case, as well as some water.

Times may change Expect transit times to vary by up to three hours. Getting stranded overnight is not hugely uncommon.

Stay safe If your driver is drunk, don't get on, or get down. Accidents caused by drunk bus drivers are all too common in Bolivia. Daytime driving is the safest.

Car & Motorcycle

Speak Spanish Only drive or ride if you speak Spanish moderately well.

Expect delays There might be speed traps, potholes and closures on the road.

Supplies Bring a GPS, a good map, extra food and water, sleeping bag, clothes.

Don't drive at night Stick to daytime travel.

Train

Expect delays Timetables are more like guidelines than strict schedules.

Plan for comfort Bring snacks, games and sleeping bags.

Watch out Pickpockets and bag snatchers often operate at stops.

spare parts are a rare commodity outside cities. A high-clearance 4WD vehicle is essential for off-road travel. You'll need tools, spare tires, a puncture repair kit, extra gas and fluids, and as many spare parts as possible. For emergencies, carry camping equipment and plenty of rations. You'll also need to purchase a good travel insurance policy back home (check with your credit card to see if it covers rental insurance in Bolivia).

Low-grade (85-octane) gasoline and diesel fuel is available at *surtidores* (gas stations) in all cities and major towns. Gas costs about B$3.74 per liter, and more in remote areas. Expect some lines.

In lowland areas where temperatures are high and roads are scarce, motorbikes are popular for zipping around the plazas, as well as to explore areas not served by public transport. They can be rented for about B$80 to B$100 per day from moto-taxi stands. Note that many travel insurance policies will not cover you for injuries arising from motorbike accidents.

Driver's License

Most Bolivian car-rental agencies will accept your home driver's license, but if you're doing a lot of driving, it's wise to back it up with an International Driver's License.

Bolivia doesn't require special motorcycle licenses, but neighboring countries do. All that is normally required for motorcycle and moped rentals is a passport.

Private Drivers

Hiring a driver can be a more comfortable and efficient alternative to being squashed in a bus for long periods on bad roads. Alternatively, many people just want transportation to trailheads or base camps, rather than a tour.

Private 4WD service with a driver costs about B$250 to B$300 per hour for the entire car (four to six people). Private taxi service and/or driver service costs B$40 to B$80 per hour.

You can hire drivers through car rental companies and tour operators. Private taxi drivers may also be hired.

Rental

Few travelers in Bolivia rent self-driven vehicles. Only the most reputable agencies service their vehicles regularly, and insurance purchased from rental agencies may cover only accidental damage – breakdowns may be considered the renter's problem. Check ahead, and make sure your credit card covers incidentals, like the US$80 Budget charges to clean cars.

You must be aged over 25, have a driver's license from your home country and provide a major credit card or cash deposit (typically around US$1000). You'll be charged a daily rate and a per-kilometer rate (some agencies allow some free kilometers). They'll also want you to leave a copy of your passport.

To save money, book online or through an aggregator. Weekly rentals will save you money. Daily rates are about US$50 for cars, while 4WDs cost US$55 to US$90 per day.

For listings of better-known agencies, see Getting Around sections for the major cities.

Road Rules

Traffic regulations are similar to those in North America or Europe. Speed limits are infrequently posted, but in most cases the state of the road would prevent you from exceeding them anyway. If stopped, you should show your driver's license rather than your passport. If your passport is requested, only show a copy. Bribes are common here.

Bolivians keep to the right. When two cars approach an uncontrolled intersection from different directions, the driver who honks (or gets there first) tends to have the right of way if passing straight through – but this can be somewhat hit and miss. In La Paz, those going uphill have right of way at an intersection. When two vehicles meet on a narrow mountain road, the downhill one must reverse until there's room for the other to pass.

Hitchhiking

Thanks to relatively easy access to camiones and a profusion of buses, hitchhiking isn't really necessary or popular in Bolivia. Still, it's not unknown and drivers of movilidades – coches (cars), camionetas (pickup trucks), NGO vehicles, gas trucks and other vehicles – are usually happy to pick up passengers when they have room. Always ask the price, if any, before climbing aboard, even for short distances. If they do charge, it should amount to about half the bus fare for the same distance.

Please note that hitchhiking is never entirely safe in any country. If you decide to hitchhike, you should understand that you are taking a small but potentially serious risk. Travel in pairs and let someone know where you're planning to go.

Local Transportation

Camión

Prior to today's expansive bus network, camiones (trucks) were often the only way for travelers to venture off the beaten track. These days, in the more populated areas you might consider a camión trip more for the novelty value than necessity; it is how many campesinos (subsistence farmers) choose to travel.

Camiones generally cost about half of the bus fare. You'll need time and a strong constitution, as travel can be excruciatingly slow and rough, depending on the cargo and number of passengers. A major plus is the raw experience, including the best views of the countryside.

On any camión trip, especially in the highlands by day or night, be sure to take plenty of warm clothing as night temperatures can plunge below freezing and at best they can be chilly.

To get on a camión, wait on the side of the road and flag it down as it passes.

Micros, Minibuses & Trufis

Micros (half-size buses) are used in larger cities and are Bolivia's least expensive form of public transportation. They follow set routes, with the route numbers or letters usually marked on a placard behind the windshield. There is also often a description of the route, including the streets taken to reach the end of the line. They can be hailed anywhere along their route, though bus stops are starting to pop up in some bigger cities. When you want to disembark, move toward the front and tell the driver or assistant where you want them to stop.

Minibuses and trufis (cars, vans or minibuses), also known as colectivos, are prevalent in larger towns and cities, and follow set routes that are numbered and described on placards. They are always cheaper than taxis and nearly as convenient. As with micros, board or alight anywhere along their route.

Taxis

In cities and towns, taxis are relatively cheap. Few are equipped with meters, but in most places there are standard per-person fares for short hauls. In some places, taxis are collective and more like trufis, charging a set rate per person. However, if three or four people are all headed for the same place, you may be able to negotiate a reduced rate for the entire group.

Radio taxis always charge a set rate for up to four people; if you squeeze in five people, the fare increases by a small margin.

When using taxis, try to have enough change to cover the fare, as drivers often like to plead a lack of change in the hope that you'll give them the benefit of the difference. As a general rule, taxi drivers aren't tipped, but if one goes beyond the call of duty, a tip of a couple of bolivianos wouldn't be inappropriate.

In larger cities, especially if traveling alone at night, it's advisable to opt for a radio taxi, which is booked by phone, instead of hailing one in the street; ask your hotel or restaurant to call one for you.

Tours

Many organized tours run out of La Paz or towns closest to the attractions you're likely to wish to visit. Tours are a convenient way to visit a site when you are short of time or motivation, and are frequently the easiest way to visit remote areas. They can also be relatively cheap, depending on the number of people in your group and the mode of transportation.

Scores of companies offer trekking, mountain-climbing and rainforest-adventure packages around Bolivia. For climbing in the Cordilleras, operators offer customized expeditions and can arrange anything from guide and transportation right up to equipment, porters and even a cook. Some also rent trekking equipment.

It's best to check an agency's website before making contact and bookings.

Akapana Tours (☎2-242-0013; www.akapanatours.com; Av Sanchez Lima 2512, Edificio Melissa, Piso 11D, Sopocachi, La Paz) A German-run agency offering personalized tours all over Bolivia with a focus on adventure, culture, trekking and climbing. It specializes in off-the-beaten-path destinations such as Cordillera Apolobamba, Cordillera Quimsa Cruz and Torotoro.

America Tours (Map p42; ☎2-237-4204; www.america-ecotours.com; 16 de Julio 1490 No 9, Prado, La Paz) This warmly recommended English-speaking agency organizes a wide range of community-based ecotourism projects and tours around La Paz and Bolivia.

Bolivia Millenaria (☎2-241-4753; www.millenariantours.com; Av Sanchez Lima 2193, Sopocachi, La Paz) This agency manages the Tomarapi ecolodge in Sajama and offers cultural tours around Bolivia.

Bolivia Specialist (Map p188; ☎4-643-7389; www.boliviaspecialist.com; Ortiz 30, Sucre) Tours organized all over Bolivia as well as in the region around Sucre. If the office in Sucre is closed, ask at the bar/restaurant **Florín** (Map p188; Bolívar 567).

Bolivian Journeys (Map p38; ☎7-201-4900; www.bolivianjourneys.org) A specialist in climbing, mountaineering and trekking, this company does guided climbs to Huayna Potosí. Equipment rental is available, with maps and gas for MSR stoves for sale.

Candelaria Tours (Map p188; ☎4-644-0340; www.candelariatours.com; Plazuela Cochabamba, Sucre) Reliable agency, with staff fluent in English, which runs many types of trips. Particularly recommendable for trips to Tarabuco and Candelaria. It also has participatory programs where visitors can work in indigenous communities, especially with textiles.

Forest Tours (☎3-337-2042; www.forestbolivia.com; Junín & 21 de Mayo, Galería Casco Viejo, Office 115, Santa Cruz) English-speaking and extremely helpful, offering tours in the Santa Cruz region and elsewhere, including Samaipata, the Che Trail and Parque Nacional Amboró.

Fremen Tours (Map p38; ☎2-244-0242; www.andes-amazonia.com; cnr Av 6 de Agosto & Perez, Edificio V Centenario, Oficina 6-C, La Paz) Upmarket agency specializing in soft adventure in the Amazon and Chapare; there are also offices in **Cochabamba** (Map p170; ☎4-425-9392; Tumusla N-245) and **Uyuni** (Map p146; ☎2-693-3543; Sucre 325).

Inca Land Tours (☎2-231-6760; www.incalandtours.com; Sagárnaga 233 No 3, La Paz) An established Peruvian budget operation specializing in tours out of Rurrenabaque and Coroico.

Madidi Travel (Map p38; ☎2-231-8313; www.madidi-travel.com; Linares 968, Rosario, La Paz) Specializing in trips to Madidi, this tour operator's 4000-hectare private reserve within the park adds another layer of protection.

Magri Turismo (Map p42; ☎2-244-2727; www.magriturismo.com; Capitán Ravelo 2101, Prado, La Paz) A range of tours organized around Bolivia.

Topas Bolivia (☎2-211-1082; www.topas.bo; Carlos Bravo 299, La Paz) A joint venture between Topas Denmark and Akhamani Trekking, this English-speaking adventure travel agency is run by experienced people and offers high-quality tours all over Bolivia, with a special focus on trekking and climbing.

Turisbus (Map p38; ☎2-244-1756; www.turisbus.com; Illampu 704, Hotel Rosario, Rosario, La Paz) A large range of day and multiday tours organized for groups and individuals around Bolivia.

Train

Passenger rail services have been cut back since privatization in the mid-1990s. The western network operated by the **Empresa Ferroviaria Andina** (FCA; www.fca.com.bo) runs from Oruro to Villazón on the Argentine border and a branch line runs southwest from Uyuni to Avaroa on the Chilean border.

The east is operated by **Ferroviaria Oriental** (www.ferroviariaoriental.com), which operates a line from Santa Cruz to the Brazilian frontier at Quijarro, where you cross to the Pantanal. An infrequently used service goes south from Santa Cruz to Yacuiba on the Argentine border, and at the time of writing there was a pilot project running tourist trains from La Paz to Tiwanaku.

Train fares range fron B$32 to B$224, depending on the class and distance. In terms of price, they are competitive with bus fares.

Reservations

Even in major towns along the routes, tickets can be reserved only on the day of departure. At smaller stations, they may not be available until the train has arrived. Larger intermediate stations have only a few seat reservations, and tickets go on sale literally whenever employees decide to open up. The best info is usually available from the *jefe de la estación* (station master).

When buying tickets, make sure you have a passport for each person for whom you're buying a ticket. This is a remnant from the days when ticket scalping was profitable.

Health

BEFORE YOU GO

The only required vaccine for Bolivia is yellow fever, and that's only if you're arriving from a yellow fever–infected country in Africa or the Americas. However, a number of other vaccines are recommended, such as hepatitis A, rabies, tetanus/diphtheria and typhoid.

Since most vaccines don't produce immunity until at least two weeks after they're given, visit a physician four to eight weeks before departure. Ask your doctor for an International Certificate of Vaccination, containing a list of your vaccinations.

Bring medications in their original containers, clearly labeled, and a signed, dated letter from your physician describing all medical conditions and medications. If carrying syringes or needles, carry a physician's letter documenting their medical necessity.

Insurance

If your health insurance does not cover you for medical expenses abroad, consider supplemental insurance. Check the Travel Insurance section of Lonely Planet's website (www.lonelyplanet.com/travel-insurance) for more information. Find out in advance if your insurance plan will make payments directly to providers or reimburse you later for overseas health expenditures. Most private-practice providers in Bolivia expect cash payment and should provide receipts for your insurance company claims and reimbursement. Credit cards are usually not accepted for medical services.

IN BOLIVIA

Availability & Cost of Healthcare

Good medical care is available in the larger cities, but may be difficult to find in rural areas. Many doctors and hospitals expect payment in cash, regardless of whether you have travel health insurance. See the Information section of each city or town for recommended emergency and medical services. Note that a taxi may get you to the emergency room faster than an ambulance.

If you develop a life-threatening medical problem, you'll probably want to be evacuated to a country with state-of-the-art medical care. Since this may cost tens of thousands of dollars, be sure the insurance covers this before you depart.

Bolivian pharmacies offer most of the medications available in other countries. In general it's safer to buy pharmaceuticals made by international manufacturers rather than local companies; buy the brand name prescribed by your doctor, not the generic-brand drugs that may be offered at lower prices. These medications may be out of date or have no quality control from the manufacturer.

Infectious Diseases

Cholera

Cholera is an intestinal infection acquired through ingestion of contaminated food or water. The main symptom is profuse, watery diarrhea, which may be so severe that it causes life-threatening dehydration. The key treatment is drinking an oral rehydration solution. Antibiotics are also given, usually tetracycline or doxycycline, though quinolone antibiotics such as ciprofloxacin and levofloxacin are also effective.

Cholera sometimes occurs in Bolivia, but it's rare among travelers. A cholera vaccine is no longer required. There are effective vaccines, but they're not available in many countries and are only recommended for those at particularly high risk.

Dengue Fever

Dengue fever is a viral infection found throughout South America. Dengue is transmitted by Aedes mosquitoes, which bite preferentially during the daytime and are usually found close to human habitations, often indoors.

They breed in artificial water containers, such as jars, barrels, cans, cisterns, metal drums, plastic containers and discarded tires. As a result, dengue is especially common in densely popu-lated, urban environments.

Dengue causes flu-like symptoms, including fever, muscle aches, joint pains, headache, nausea and vomit-ing, often followed by a rash. The body aches may be quite uncomfortable, but most cases resolve uneventfully in a few days. Severe cases usually occur in children under the age of 15 who are experiencing their second dengue infection.

There is no specific anti-virus (antibiotics) treatment for dengue fever except to take analgesics such as acetaminophen/paracetamol (Tylenol) and drink plenty of fluids. Severe cases may re-quire hospitalization for intra-venous fluids and supportive care. There is no vaccine. The cornerstone of prevention is insect protection (see p351).

MEDICAL CHECKLIST

» antibiotics

» antidiarrheal drugs (eg loperamide)

» acetaminophen (Tylenol) or aspirin

» anti-inflammatory drugs (eg ibuprofen)

» antihistamines (for hay fever and allergic reactions)

» antibacterial ointment (eg Bactroban) for cuts and abrasions

» steroid cream or cortisone (for poison ivy and other allergic rashes)

» bandages, gauze, gauze rolls

» adhesive or paper tape

» scissors, safety pins, tweezers

» thermometer

» pocket knife

» DEET-containing insect repellent for the skin

» permethrin-containing insect spray for clothing, tents and bed nets

» sunscreen

» oral rehydration salts

» iodine tablets (for water purification)

» syringes and sterile needles

» acetazolamide (Diamox) for altitude sickness

Hepatitis A

Hepatitis A is the second most common travel-related infection (after travelers' diarrhea). It's a viral infec-tion of the liver that is usu-ally acquired by ingestion of contaminated water, food or ice, or by direct contact with infected persons. The illness occurs throughout the world, but the incidence is higher in developing nations. Symp-toms may include fever, malaise, jaundice, nausea, vomiting and abdominal pain. Most cases resolve without complications, though hepatitis A occasion-ally causes severe liver dam-age. There is no treatment.

Malaria

Malaria occurs in nearly every South American country. It's transmitted by mosquito bites, usually between dusk and dawn. The main symptom is high spik-ing fever, which may be ac-companied by chills, sweats,

headache, body aches, weak-ness, vomiting or diarrhea. Severe cases may affect the central nervous system and lead to seizures, confusion, coma and death.

Taking malaria pills is strongly recommended for areas below 2500m (8202 ft) in the departments of Beni, Santa Cruz and Pando, where the risk is highest. Falciparum malaria, which is the most dangerous kind, occurs in Beni and Pando. No malaria is currently present in the cities of these departments.

There is a choice of three malaria pills, all of which work about equally well. Meflo-quine (Lariam) is taken once weekly in a dosage of 250mg, starting one to two weeks before arrival, and continuing through the trip and for four weeks after return. The prob-lem is that a certain percent-age of people (the number is controversial) develop neuropsychiatric side effects, which may range from mild

to severe. Stomachache and diarrhea are also common. Atovaquone/proguanil (Ma-larone) is taken once daily with food, starting two days before arrival and continuing daily until seven days after departure. Side effects are typically mild. Doxycycline is relatively inexpensive and easy to obtain, but it is taken daily and can cause an exag-gerated sunburn reaction.

For longer trips it's prob-ably worth trying mefloquine; for shorter trips, Malarone will be the drug of choice for most people.

Protecting yourself against mosquito bites is just as important as taking malaria pills, since none of the pills are 100% effective.

If you may not have ac-cess to medical care while traveling, you should bring along additional pills for emergency self-treatment, which you should take if you can't reach a doctor and you develop symptoms that

ONLINE RESOURCES

MD Travel Health (www.mdtravelhealth.com)

World Health Organization (www.who.int/ith)

Your government's travel health website can also be helpful:

Australia (www.smartraveller.gov.au/tips/travelwell.html)

Canada (www.hc-sc.gc.ca/english/index.html)

UK (www.direct.gov.uk/en/TravelAndTransport/index.htm)

US (www.cdc.gov/travel)

suggest malaria, such as high spiking fevers. One option is to take four tablets of Malarone once daily for three days. However, Malarone should not be used for treatment if you're already taking it for prevention. An alternative is to take 650mg quinine three times daily and 100mg doxycycline twice daily for one week. If you start self-medication, see a doctor at the earliest possible opportunity.

If you develop a fever after returning home, see a physician, as malaria symptoms may not occur for months.

Typhoid Fever

Typhoid fever is caused by the ingestion of food or water contaminated by a species of salmonella known as salmonella typhi. Fever occurs in virtually all cases. Other symptoms may include headache, malaise, muscle aches, dizziness, loss of appetite, nausea and abdominal pain. Either diarrhea or constipation may occur. Possible complications include intestinal perforation, intestinal bleeding, confusion, delirium or (rarely) coma.

A typhoid vaccine is a good idea. It's usually given orally, but is also available as an injection. Neither vaccine is approved for use in children under the age of two.

It is not a good idea to self-treat for typhoid fever as the symptoms may be indis-

tinguishable from malaria. If you show symptoms for either, see a doctor immediately – treatment is likely to be a quinolone antibiotic such as ciprofloxacin (Cipro) or levofloxacin (Levaquin).

Yellow Fever

Yellow fever is a life-threatening viral infection transmitted by mosquitoes in forested areas. The illness begins with flu-like symptoms, such as fever, chills, headache, muscle aches, backache, loss of appetite, nausea and vomiting. These symptoms usually subside in a few days, but one person in six enters a second, toxic phase characterized by recurrent fever, vomiting, listlessness, jaundice, kidney failure and hemorrhage, leading to death in up to half of the cases. There is no treatment except for supportive care.

Yellow-fever vaccine is strongly recommended for all those visiting areas where yellow fever occurs, which at time of publication included the departments of Beni, Cochabamba, Santa Cruz and La Paz. For the latest information on which areas in Bolivia are reporting yellow fever, see the website of Centers for Disease Control & Protection (CDC; www.cdc.gov).

Proof of vaccination is required from all travelers arriving from a yellow fever–infected country in Africa or the Americas.

Yellow-fever vaccine is given only in approved yellow-fever vaccination centers, which provide validated International Certificates of Vaccination (yellow booklets). The vaccine should be given at least 10 days before any potential exposure to yellow fever, and remains effective for approximately 10 years. Reactions to the vaccine are generally mild and may include headaches, muscle aches, low-grade fevers, or discomfort at the injection site. Severe, life-threatening reactions have been described but are extremely rare. In general, the risk of becoming ill from the vaccine is far smaller than the risk of becoming ill from yellow fever, and you're strongly encouraged to get the vaccine.

Taking measures to protect yourself from mosquito bites is an essential part of preventing yellow fever.

Other Infections

A number of rare but serious diseases are carried by insects and rodents, such as bartonellosis, Bolivian hemorrhagic fever, Chagas' disease, leishmaniasis, typhus and the plague. Rabies is also a concern, especially in the southeastern part of the country. Do not attempt to pet, handle or feed any animal. Any bite or scratch by a mammal, including bats, should be promptly and thoroughly cleansed with large amounts of soap and water, followed by application of an antiseptic such as iodine or alcohol. The local health authorities should be contacted immediately for possible post-exposure rabies treatment, whether or not you've been immunized against rabies. It may also be advisable to start an antibiotic, since wounds caused by animal bites and scratches frequently become infected. Or use one of the newer quinolones, such as levofloxacin (Levaquin), which many travelers carry in case of diarrhea.

Travelers' Diarrhea

To prevent diarrhea, avoid tap water unless it has been boiled, filtered or chemically disinfected (with iodine tablets); only eat fresh fruits or vegetables if peeled or cooked; be wary of dairy products that might contain unpasteurized milk; and be highly selective when eating food from street vendors.

If you develop diarrhea, be sure to drink plenty of fluids, preferably an oral rehydration solution containing lots of salt and sugar. A few loose stools don't require treatment but if you start having more than four or five stools a day, you should start taking an antibiotic (usually a quinolone drug) and an antidiarrheal agent (such as loperamide). If diarrhea is bloody, or persists for more than 72 hours, or is accompanied by fever, shaking chills or severe abdominal pain, you should seek medical attention.

Environmental Hazards

Altitude Sickness

Altitude sickness may develop in those who ascend rapidly to altitudes greater than 2500m (8100 ft). In Bolivia this includes La Paz (altitude 4000m). Being physically fit offers no protection. Those who have experienced altitude sickness in the past are prone to future episodes. The risk increases with faster ascents, higher altitudes and greater exertion. Symptoms may include headache, nausea, vomiting, dizziness, malaise, insomnia and loss of appetite. Severe cases may be complicated by fluid in the lungs (high-altitude pulmonary edema) or swelling of the brain (high-altitude cerebral edema).

The best treatment for altitude sickness is descent. If you are exhibiting symptoms, do not ascend. If symptoms are severe or persistent, descend immediately.

To protect yourself against altitude sickness, take 125mg or 250mg acetazolamide (Diamox) twice or three times daily, starting 24 hours before ascent and continuing for 48 hours after arrival at altitude. Possible side effects include increased urinary volume, numbness, tingling, nausea, drowsiness, myopia and temporary impotence. Acetazolamide should not be given to pregnant women or anyone with a history of sulfa allergy.

For those who cannot tolerate acetazolamide, the next best option is 4mg dexamethasone taken four times daily, best with medical supervision. Unlike acetazolamide, dexamethasone must be tapered gradually on arrival at altitude if taken for longer than 10 days, since there is a risk that altitude sickness will occur as the dosage is reduced. Dexamethasone is a steroid, so it should not be given to diabetics or anyone for whom steroids are contra-indicated. A natural alternative is gingko, which helps some people.

When traveling to high altitudes, it's also important to avoid overexertion, eat light meals and abstain from alcohol.

If your symptoms are more than mild or don't resolve promptly, see a doctor immediately. Altitude sickness should be taken seriously; it can be life-threatening when severe.

Insect Bites & Stings

To prevent mosquito bites, wear long sleeves, long pants, hats and shoes (rather than sandals). Bring along a good insect repellent, preferably one containing DEET, which should be applied to exposed skin and clothing, but not to eyes, mouth, cuts, wounds or irritated skin. Products containing lower concentrations of DEET are as effective, but for shorter periods of time. In general, adults and children over 12 should use preparations containing 25% to 35% DEET, which usually lasts about six hours. Children between two and 12 years of age should use preparations containing no more than 10% DEET, applied sparingly, which will usually last about three hours. Neurologic toxicity has been reported from DEET, especially in children, but appears to be extremely uncommon and generally related to overuse. DEET-containing compounds should not be used on children under the age of two.

Insect repellents containing certain botanical products, including eucalyptus oil and soybean oil, are effective but last only 1½ to two hours. DEET-containing repellents are preferable for areas where there is a high risk of malaria or yellow fever. Products based on citronella are not effective.

For additional protection you can apply permethrin to clothing, shoes, tents and bed nets. Permethrin treatments are safe and remain effective for at least two weeks, even when items are laundered. Permethrin should not be applied directly to skin.

Don't sleep with the window open unless there is a screen. If sleeping outdoors or in accommodations that allow entry of mosquitoes, use a fine-mesh bed net, preferably treated with permethrin, with edges tucked in under the mattress. If the sleeping area is not protected, use a mosquito coil, which will fill the room with insecticide through the night. Repellent-impregnated wristbands are not effective.

Snake Bites

In Bolivia there are two species of poisonous snakes: pit vipers (rattlesnakes) and coral snakes. These are found chiefly on the sugar and banana plantations, and in the dry, hilly regions. In the event of a venomous snake bite, place the victim at rest, keep the bitten area immobilized and move the victim to the nearest medical facility immediately. Avoid tourniquets, which are no longer recommended.

Sunburn & Heat Exhaustion

To protect yourself from excessive sun exposure, stay out of the midday sun, wear sunglasses and a wide-brimmed sun hat, and apply sunscreen with SPF 15 or higher, with both UVA and UVB protection. Sunscreen should be generously applied to all exposed parts of the body approximately 30 minutes before sun exposure and should be reapplied after swimming or vigorous activity. Travelers should also drink plenty of fluids and avoid strenuous exercise in high temperatures.

Water

Tap water in Bolivia is not safe to drink. Vigorous boiling for one minute is the most effective means of water purification. At altitudes greater than 2000m (6500ft), boil for three minutes.

Another option is to disinfect water with iodine pills such as Globaline, Potable-Aqua and Coghlan's, available at most pharmacies. Instructions are enclosed and should be carefully followed. Or you can add 2% tincture of iodine to one quart or liter of water (five drops to clear water, 10 drops to cloudy water) and let it stand for 30 minutes. If the water is cold, longer times may be required. The taste of iodinated water may be improved by adding vitamin C (ascorbic acid). Iodinated water shouldn't be consumed for more than a few weeks. Pregnant women, those with a history of thyroid disease and those allergic to iodine should not drink iodinated water.

A number of water filters are on the market. Those with smaller pores (reverse osmosis filters) provide the broadest protection, but they are relatively large and are readily plugged by debris. Those with larger pores (microstrainer filters) are ineffective against viruses, although they remove other organisms. Manufacturers' instructions must be carefully followed.

Women's Health

There are English-speaking obstetricians in Bolivia, listed on the US Embassy website (http://bolivia.usembassy.gov/uploads/images/eOd9_kCdEzOZa_poIlKATw/PHYSICIANSLIST1.pdf). However, medical facilities will probably not be comparable to those in your home country. It's safer to avoid travel to Bolivia late in pregnancy, so that you don't have to deliver there.

If pregnant, you should avoid travel to high altitudes. The lower oxygen levels that occur at high altitudes can slow fetal growth, especially after the 32nd week. Also, it's safer not to visit areas where yellow fever occurs, since the vaccine is not safe during pregnancy.

If you need to take malaria pills, mefloquine (Lariam) is the safest during pregnancy.

WANT MORE?

For in-depth language information and handy phrases, check out Lonely Planet's *Latin American Spanish Phrasebook* and *Quechua Phrasebook*. You'll find them at **shop.lonelyplanet.com**, or you can buy Lonely Planet's iPhone phrasebooks at the Apple App Store.

Language

Latin American Spanish pronunciation is easy, as most sounds have equivalents in English. Read our colored pronunciation guides as if they were English, and you'll be understood. Note that kh is a throaty sound (like the 'ch' in the Scottish *loch*), v and b are like a soft English 'v' (between a 'v' and a 'b'), and r is strongly rolled, although you may hear some Bolivians pronounce it as the 's' in 'pleasure' at the beginning of a word or after *l*, *n* or *s*. There are some variations in spoken Spanish across Latin America, the most notable being the pronunciation of the letters *ll* and *y*. In our guides they are represented with y because they are pronounced as the 'y' in 'yes' in Bolivia, as is the case in most parts of Latin America. In some parts of the continent they sound like the 'lli' in 'million'. The stressed syllables are in italics in our pronunciation guides.

The polite form is used in this chapter; where both polite and informal options are given, they are indicated by the abbreviations 'pol' and 'inf'. Where necessary, both masculine and feminine forms of words are included, separated by a slash and with the masculine form first, eg *perdido/a* (m/f).

BASICS

Hello.	*Hola.*	o·la
Goodbye.	*Adiós.*	a·dyos
How are you?	*¿Qué tal?*	ke tal
Fine, thanks.	*Bien, gracias.*	byen gra·syas
Excuse me.	*Perdón.*	per·don
Sorry.	*Lo siento.*	lo syen·to
Please.	*Por favor.*	por fa·vor
Thank you.	*Gracias.*	gra·syas
You are welcome.	*De nada.*	de na·da
Yes.	*Sí.*	see
No.	*No.*	no

My name is ...
Me llamo ... me ya·mo ...

What's your name?
¿Cómo se llama Usted? ko·mo se ya·ma oo·ste (pol)
¿Cómo te llamas? ko·mo te ya·mas (inf)

Do you speak English?
¿Habla inglés? a·bla een·gles (pol)
¿Hablas inglés? a·blas een·gles (inf)

I don't understand.
Yo no entiendo. yo no en·tyen·do

ACCOMMODATIONS

I'd like a single/double room.
Quisiera una kee·sye·ra oo·na
habitación a·bee·ta·syon
individual/doble. een·dee·vee·dwal/do·ble

How much is it per night/person?
¿Cuánto cuesta por kwan·to kwes·ta por
noche/persona? no·che/per·so·na

Does it include breakfast?
¿Incluye el desayuno? een·kloo·ye el de·sa·yoo·no

campsite	*terreno de cámping*	te·re·no de kam·peeng
guesthouse	*pensión*	pen·syon
hotel	*hotel*	o·tel
youth hostel	*albergue juvenil*	al·ber·ge khoo·ve·neel

air-con	aire acondi-cionado	ai·re a·kon·dee·syo·na·do
bathroom	baño	ba·nyo
bed	cama	ka·ma
window	ventana	ven·ta·na

DIRECTIONS

Where's ...?
¿Dónde está ...?   don·de es·ta ...

What's the address?
¿Cuál es la dirección?   kwal es la dee·rek·syon

Could you please write it down?
¿Puede escribirlo,   pwe·de es·kree·beer·lo
por favor?   por fa·vor

Can you show me (on the map)?
¿Me lo puede indicar   me lo pwe·de een·dee·kar
(en el mapa)?   (en el ma·pa)

at the corner	en la esquina	en la es·kee·na
at the traffic lights	en el semáforo	en el se·ma·fo·ro
behind ...	detrás de ...	de·tras de ...
in front of ...	enfrente de ...	en·fren·te de ...
left	izquierda	ees·kyer·da
next to ...	al lado de ...	al la·do de ...
opposite ...	frente a ...	fren·te a ...
right	derecha	de·re·cha
straight ahead	todo recto	to·do rek·to

EATING & DRINKING

Can I see the menu, please?
¿Puedo ver el menú,   pwe·do ver el me·noo
por favor?   por fa·vor

What would you recommend?
¿Qué recomienda?   ke re·ko·myen·da

Do you have vegetarian food?
¿Tienen comida   tye·nen ko·mee·da
vegetariana?   ve·khe·ta·rya·na

I don't eat (red meat).
No como (carne roja).   no ko·mo (kar·ne ro·kha)

That was delicious!
¡Estaba buenísimo!   es·ta·ba bwe·nee·see·mo

Cheers!
¡Salud!   sa·loo

The bill, please.
La cuenta, por favor.   la kwen·ta por fa·vor

I'd like a table for ...	Quisiera una mesa para ...	kee·sye·ra oo·na me·sa pa·ra ...
(eight) o'clock	las (ocho)	las (o·cho)
(two) people	(dos) personas	(dos) per·so·nas

KEY PATTERNS

To get by in Spanish, mix and match these simple patterns with words of your choice:

When's (the next flight)?
¿Cuándo sale   kwan·do sa·le
(el próximo vuelo)?   (el prok·see·mo vwe·lo)

Where's (the station)?
¿Dónde está   don·de es·ta
(la estación)?   (la es·ta·syon)

Where can I (buy a ticket)?
¿Dónde puedo   don·de pwe·do
(comprar un billete)?   (kom·prar oon bee·ye·te)

Do you have (a map)?
¿Tiene (un mapa)?   tye·ne (oon ma·pa)

Is there (a toilet)?
¿Hay (servicios)?   ai (ser·vee·syos)

I'd like (a coffee).
Quisiera (un café).   kee·sye·ra (oon ka·fe)

I'd like (to hire a car).
Quisiera (alquilar   kee·sye·ra (al·kee·lar
un coche).   oon ko·che)

Can I (enter)?
¿Se puede (entrar)?   se pwe·de (en·trar)

Could you please (help me)?
¿Puede (ayudarme),   pwe·de (a·yoo·dar·me)
por favor?   por fa·vor

Do I have to (get a visa)?
¿Necesito   ne·se·see·to
(obtener   (ob·te·ner
un visado)?   oon vee·sa·do)

Key Words

appetisers	aperitivos	a·pe·ree·tee·vos
bottle	botella	bo·te·ya
bowl	bol	bol
breakfast	desayuno	de·sa·yoo·no
children's menu	menú infantil	me·noo een·fan·teel
(too) cold	(muy) frío	(mooy) free·o
dinner	cena	se·na
food	comida	ko·mee·da
fork	tenedor	te·ne·dor
glass	vaso	va·so
hot (warm)	caliente	kal·yen·te
knife	cuchillo	koo·chee·yo
lunch	comida	ko·mee·da
main course	segundo plato	se·goon·do pla·to
plate	plato	pla·to
restaurant	restaurante	res·tow·ran·te

spoon	*cuchara*	koo·*cha*·ra
with	*con*	kon
without	*sin*	seen

Meat & Fish

beef	*carne de vaca*	*kar*·ne de *va*·ka
chicken	*pollo*	*po*·yo
duck	*pato*	*pa*·to
fish	*pescado*	pes·*ka*·do
lamb	*cordero*	kor·*de*·ro
pork	*cerdo*	*ser*·do
turkey	*pavo*	*pa*·vo
veal	*ternera*	ter·*ne*·ra

Fruit & Vegetables

apple	*manzana*	man·*sa*·na
apricot	*albaricoque*	al·ba·ree·*ko*·ke
artichoke	*alcachofa*	al·ka·*cho*·fa
asparagus	*espárragos*	es·*pa*·ra·gos
banana	*plátano*	*pla*·ta·no
beans	*judías*	khoo·*dee*·as
beetroot	*remolacha*	re·mo·*la*·cha
cabbage	*col*	kol
carrot	*zanahoria*	sa·na·o·*rya*
celery	*apio*	*a*·pyo
cherry	*cereza*	se·*re*·sa
corn	*maíz*	ma·*ees*
cucumber	*pepino*	pe·*pee*·no
fruit	*fruta*	*froo*·ta
grape	*uvas*	*oo*·vas
lemon	*limón*	lee·*mon*
lentils	*lentejas*	len·*te*·khas
lettuce	*lechuga*	le·*choo*·ga
mushroom	*champiñón*	cham·pee·*nyon*
nuts	*nueces*	*nwe*·ses
onion	*cebolla*	se·*bo*·ya
orange	*naranja*	na·*ran*·kha
peach	*melocotón*	me·lo·ko·*ton*
peas	*guisantes*	gee·*san*·tes
(red/green) pepper	*pimiento (rojo/verde)*	pee·*myen*·to (*ro*·kho/*ver*·de)
pineapple	*piña*	*pee*·nya
plum	*ciruela*	seer·*we*·la
potato	*patata*	pa·*ta*·ta
pumpkin	*calabaza*	ka·la·*ba*·sa
spinach	*espinacas*	es·pee·*na*·kas
strawberry	*fresa*	*fre*·sa

tomato	*tomate*	to·*ma*·te
vegetable	*verdura*	ver·*doo*·ra
watermelon	*sandía*	san·*dee*·a

Other

bread	*pan*	pan
butter	*mantequilla*	man·te·*kee*·ya
cheese	*queso*	*ke*·so
egg	*huevo*	*we*·vo
honey	*miel*	myel
jam	*mermelada*	mer·me·*la*·da
oil	*aceite*	a·*sey*·te
pasta	*pasta*	*pas*·ta
pepper	*pimienta*	pee·*myen*·ta
rice	*arroz*	a·*ros*
salt	*sal*	sal
sugar	*azúcar*	a·*soo*·kar
vinegar	*vinagre*	vee·*na*·gre

Drinks

beer	*cerveza*	ser·*ve*·sa
coffee	*café*	ka·*fe*
(orange) juice	*zumo (de naranja)*	*soo*·mo (de na·*ran*·kha)
milk	*leche*	*le*·che
red wine	*vino tinto*	*vee*·no *teen*·to
sparkling wine	*vino espumoso*	*vee*·no es·poo·*mo*·so
tea	*té*	te
(mineral) water	*agua (mineral)*	*a*·gwa (mee·ne·*ral*)
white wine	*vino blanco*	*vee*·no *blan*·ko

EMERGENCIES

Help!	*¡Socorro!*	so·*ko*·ro
Go away!	*¡Vete!*	*ve*·te

Signs	
Abierto	Open
Cerrado	Closed
Entrada	Entrance
Hombres/Varones	Men
Mujeres/Damas	Women
Prohibido	Prohibited
Salida	Exit
Servicios/Baños	Toilets

Call ...!	¡Llame a ...!	ya·me a ...
a doctor	un médico	oon me·dee·ko
the police	la policía	la po·lee·see·a

I'm lost.
Estoy perdido/a.   es·toy per·dee·do/a (m/f)

I'm ill.
Estoy enfermo/a.   es·toy en·fer·mo/a (m/f)

I'm allergic to (antibiotics).
Soy alérgico/a a   soy a·ler·khee·ko/a a
(los antibióticos).   (los an·tee·byo·tee·kos) (m/f)

Where are the toilets?
¿Dónde están los   don·de es·tan los
baños?   ba·nyos

SHOPPING & SERVICES

I'd like to buy ...
Quisiera comprar ...   kee·sye·ra kom·prar ...

I'm just looking.
Sólo estoy mirando.   so·lo es·toy mee·ran·do

Can I look at it?
¿Puedo verlo?   pwe·do ver·lo

I don't like it.
No me gusta.   no me goos·ta

How much is it?
¿Cuánto cuesta?   kwan·to kwes·ta

That's too expensive.
Es muy caro.   es mooy ka·ro

Can you lower the price?
¿Podría bajar un   po·dree·a ba·khar oon
poco el precio?   po·ko el pre·syo

There's a mistake in the bill.
Hay un error   ai oon e·ror
en la cuenta.   en la kwen·ta

ATM	cajero automático	ka·khe·ro ow·to·ma·tee·ko
credit card	tarjeta de crédito	tar·khe·ta de kre·dee·to
internet cafe	cibercafé	see·ber·ka·fe
market	mercado	mer·ka·do
post office	correos	ko·re·os
tourist office	oficina de turismo	o·fee·see·na de too·rees·mo

Question Words		
How?	¿Cómo?	ko·mo
What?	¿Qué?	ke
When?	¿Cuándo?	kwan·do
Where?	¿Dónde?	don·de
Who?	¿Quién?	kyen
Why?	¿Por qué?	por ke

TIME & DATES

What time is it?	¿Qué hora es?	ke o·ra es
It's (10) o'clock.	Son (las diez).	son (las dyes)
It's half past (one).	Es (la una) y media.	es (la oo·na) ee me·dya

morning	mañana	ma·nya·na
afternoon	tarde	tar·de
evening	noche	no·che

yesterday	ayer	a·yer
today	hoy	oy
tomorrow	mañana	ma·nya·na

Monday	lunes	loo·nes
Tuesday	martes	mar·tes
Wednesday	miércoles	myer·ko·les
Thursday	jueves	khwe·ves
Friday	viernes	vyer·nes
Saturday	sábado	sa·ba·do
Sunday	domingo	do·meen·go

January	enero	e·ne·ro
February	febrero	fe·bre·ro
March	marzo	mar·so
April	abril	a·breel
May	mayo	ma·yo
June	junio	khoon·yo
July	julio	khool·yo
August	agosto	a·gos·to
September	septiembre	sep·tyem·bre
October	octubre	ok·too·bre
November	noviembre	no·vyem·bre
December	diciembre	dee·syem·bre

TRANSPORTATION

Public Transportation

boat	barco	bar·ko
bus	autobús	ow·to·boos
plane	avión	a·vyon
taxi	taxi	tak·see
train	tren	tren

first	primero	pree·me·ro
last	último	ool·tee·mo
next	próximo	prok·see·mo

Numbers

1	uno	oo·no
2	dos	dos
3	tres	tres
4	cuatro	kwa·tro
5	cinco	seen·ko
6	seis	seys
7	siete	sye·te
8	ocho	o·cho
9	nueve	nwe·ve
10	diez	dyes
20	veinte	veyn·te
30	treinta	treyn·ta
40	cuarenta	kwa·ren·ta
50	cincuenta	seen·kwen·ta
60	sesenta	se·sen·ta
70	setenta	se·ten·ta
80	ochenta	o·chen·ta
90	noventa	no·ven·ta
100	cien	syen
1000	mil	meel

A ... ticket, please.	*Un billete de ..., por favor.*	oon bee·ye·te de ... por fa·vor
1st-class	*primera clase*	pree·me·ra kla·se
2nd-class	*segunda clase*	se·goon·da kla·se
one-way	*ida*	ee·da
return	*ida y vuelta*	ee·da ee vwel·ta

airport	*aeropuerto*	a·e·ro·pwer·to
aisle seat	*asiento de pasillo*	a·syen·to de pa·see·yo
bus stop	*parada de autobuses*	pa·ra·da de ow·to·boo·ses
cancelled	*cancelado*	kan·se·la·do
delayed	*retrasado*	re·tra·sa·do
platform	*plataforma*	pla·ta·for·ma
ticket office	*taquilla*	ta·kee·ya
timetable	*horario*	o·ra·ryo
train station	*estación de trenes*	es·ta·syon de tre·nes
window seat	*asiento junto a la ventana*	a·syen·to khoon·to a la ven·ta·na

I want to go to ...
Quisiera ir a ...   kee·sye·ra eer a ...

Does it stop at ...?
¿Para en ...?   pa·ra en ...

What stop is this?
¿Cuál es esta parada?   kwal es es·ta pa·ra·da

What time does it arrive/leave?
¿A qué hora llega/sale?   a ke o·ra ye·ga/sa·le

Please tell me when we get to ...
¿Puede avisarme cuando lleguemos a ...?   pwe·de a·vee·sar·me kwan·do ye·ge·mos a ...

I want to get off here.
Quiero bajarme aquí.   kye·ro ba·khar·me a·kee

Driving & Cycling

I'd like to hire a ...	*Quisiera alquilar ...*	kee·sye·ra al·kee·lar ...
4WD	*un todo-terreno*	oon to·do·te·re·no
bicycle	*una bicicleta*	oo·na bee·see·kle·ta
car	*un coche*	oon ko·che
motorcycle	*una moto*	oo·na mo·to

child seat	*asiento de seguridad para niños*	a·syen·to de se·goo·ree·da pa·ra nee·nyos
diesel	*petróleo*	pet·ro·le·o
gas	*gasolina*	ga·so·lee·na
helmet	*casco*	kas·ko
hitchhike	*hacer botella*	a·ser bo·te·ya
mechanic	*mecánico*	me·ka·nee·ko
service station	*gasolinera*	ga·so·lee·ne·ra
truck	*camion*	ka·myon

Is this the road to ...?
¿Se va a ... por esta carretera?   se va a ... por es·ta ka·re·te·ra

(How long) Can I park here?
¿(Cuánto tiempo) Puedo aparcar aquí?   (kwan·to tyem·po) pwe·do a·par·kar a·kee

The car has broken down (at ...).
El coche se ha averiado (en ...).   el ko·che se a a·ve·rya·do (en ...)

I had an accident.
He tenido un accidente.   e te·nee·do oon ak·see·den·te

I have a flat tyre.
Tengo un pinchazo.   ten·go oon peen·cha·so

I've run out of gas.
Me he quedado sin gasolina.   me e ke·da·do seen ga·so·lee·na

AYMARÁ & QUECHUA

The few phrases in Aymará and Quechua included here will be useful for those traveling in the Bolivian highlands. Travelers interested in learning more will find language courses in La Paz, Cochabamba and Sucre. Dictionaries and phrasebooks are available through Los Amigos del Libro and larger bookstores in La Paz, but to use them you'll first need a sound knowledge of Spanish.

In the following phrases, Aymará is given first, Quechua second. The principles of pronunciation for both languages are similar to those found in Spanish. An apostrophe (') represents a glottal stop, which is the 'nonsound' that occurs in the middle of 'uh-oh.'

Hi.	Laphi.	Raphi.
Hello.	Kamisaraki.	Napaykullayki.
Please.	Mirá.	Allichu.
Thank you.	Yuspagara.	Yusulipayki.
Yes.	Jisa.	Ari.
No.	Janiwa.	Mana.

It's a pleasure.
Take chuima'hampi. — Tucuy sokoywan.

How do you say ...?
Cun sañasauca'ha ...? — Imainata nincha chaita ...?

It's called ...
Ucan sutipa'h ... — Chaipa'g sutin'ha ...

Please repeat that.
Uastata sita. — Ua'manta niway.

Where is ...?
Kaukasa ...? — Maypi ...?

How much?
K'gauka? — Maik'ata'g?

distant	haya	caru
downhill	aynacha	uray
father	auqui	tayta

food	manka	mikíuy
lodging	korpa	pascana
mother	taica	mama
near	maka	kailla
river	jawira	mayu
snowy peak	kollu	riti-orko
trail	tapu	chakiñan
very near	hakítaqui	kaillitalla
water	uma	yacu

1	maya	u'
2	paya	iskai
3	quimsa	quinsa
4	pusi	tahua
5	pesca	phiska
6	zo'hta	so'gta
7	pakalko	khanchis
8	quimsakalko	pusa'g
9	yatunca	iskon
10	tunca	chunca
100	pataca	pacha'g
1000	waranka	huaranca

GLOSSARY

abra – opening; refers to a mountain pass, usually flanked by steep high walls

achachilas – *Aymará* mountain spirits, believed to be ancestors who look after their people and provide bounty from the earth

aduana – customs office

aguayo – colorful woven square used to carry things on one's back, also called a *manta*

albergue – basic guesthouse

alcaldía – municipal/town hall

Altiplano – High Plain; the largest expanse of level (and, in places, arable) land in the Andes, it extends from Bolivia into southern Peru, northwestern Argentina and northern Chile

Alto Perú – the Spanish colonial name for the area now called Bolivia

anillos – literally 'rings'; the name used for main orbital roads around some Bolivian cities

apacheta – mound of stones on a mountain peak or pass; travelers carry a stone from the valley to place on top of the heap as an offering to the *apus;* the word may also be used locally to refer to the pass itself

api – a local drink made of maize

apu – mountain spirit who provides protection for travelers and water for crops, often associated with a particular *nevado*

arenales – sand dunes

artesanía – locally handcrafted items, or a shop selling them

Aymará – indigenous people of Bolivia; 'Aymará' also refers to the language of these people; also appears as 'Aymara' or *Kolla*

azulejos – decorative tiles, so named because most early Iberian *azulejos* were blue (*azul*) and white

bajones – immense flutes introduced by the Jesuits to the lowland indigenous communities; they are still featured in festivities at San Ignacio de Moxos

balsa – raft; in the Bolivian Amazon, *balsas* are used to ferry cars across rivers that lack bridges

barranquilleros – wildcat gold miners of the Yungas and Alto Beni regions

barrio – district or neighborhood

bloqueo – roadblock

bodega – boxcar, carried on some trains, in which 2nd-class passengers can travel; also wine cellar

boliche – nightclub

bolivianos – Bolivian people; also the Bolivian unit of currency

bus cama – literally 'bed bus'; a bus with fully reclining seats that is used on some international services, as well as a few longer domestic runs; it's often substantially more expensive than normal services

cabaña – cabin

camarín – niche in which a religious image is displayed

camba – a Bolivian from the Eastern Lowlands; some highlanders use this term for anyone from the Beni, Pando or Santa Cruz departments

cambista – street money-changer

camino – road, path, way

camión – flatbed truck; a popular form of local transportation

camioneta – pickup truck, used as local transportation in the Amazon Basin

campesino – subsistence farmer

cancha – open space in an urban area, often used for market activities; also soccer field

cerrado – sparsely forested scrub savanna, an endangered habitat that may be seen in Parque Nacional Noel Kempff Mercado

cerro – hill; this term is often used to refer to mountains, which is a classic case of understatement given their altitudes

cha'lla – offering

chalanas – ferries

chapacos – residents of Tarija; used proudly by *tarijeños* and in misguided jest by other Bolivians

(el) chaqueo – annual burning of Amazonian rainforest to clear agricultural and grazing land; there's a mistaken belief that the smoke from *el chaqueo* forms clouds and ensures good rains

charango – a traditional Bolivian ukulele-type instrument

chicha – fermented corn

chichería – bar specializing in *chicha*

cholo/a (m/f) – Quechua or Aymará person who lives in the city but continues to wear traditional dress

chompa – sweater/jumper

chullo – traditional pointed woolen hat, usually with earflaps

chullpa – funerary tower, normally from the Aymará culture

cocalero – coca grower

cochabambinos – Cochabamba locals

colectivo – minibus or collective taxi

Colla – alternative spelling for *Kolla*

comedor – dining hall

Comibol – Corporación Minera Boliviana (Bolivian Mining Corporation), now defunct

cooperativos – small groups of miners who purchase temporary rights

cordillera – mountain range

corregidor – chief magistrate
cruce – turnoff
cruceños – Santa Cruz locals

DEA – Drug Enforcement Agency, the US drug-offensive body sent to Bolivia to enforce coca-crop substitution programs and to apprehend drug magnates

edificio – building
Ekeko – household god of abundance; the name means 'dwarf' in Aymará
Entel – Empresa Nacional de Telecomunicaciones (Bolivian national communications commission)
entrada – entrance procession
esquina – street corner, often abbreviated *esq*
estancia – extensive ranch, often a grazing establishment

feria – fair, market
ferrobus – passenger rail bus
flota – long-distance bus company
fútbol – soccer

guardaparque – national park ranger

hechicería – traditional Aymará witchcraft
helados – ice creams
hoja de ruta – circulation card
hornecinos – niches commonly found in Andean ruins, presumably used for the placement of idols and/or offerings
huemul – Andean deer

iglesia – church
Inca – dominant indigenous civilization of the Central Andes at the time of the Spanish conquest
ingenio – mill; in Potosí, it refers to silver smelting plants along the Ribera, where metal was extracted from low-grade ore by crushing it with a mill wheel

in a solution of salt and mercury

jardín – garden
jefe de la estación – station-master
jipijapa – the fronds of the cyclanthaceae fan palm (*Carludovica palmata*)
jochi – agouti, an agile, long-legged rodent of the Amazon Basin; it's the only native animal that can eat the Brazil nut

Kallahuayas – itinerant traditional healers and fortune-tellers of the remote Cordillera Apolobamba; also spelled 'Kallaway'
koa – sweet-smelling incense bush (*Senecio mathewsii*), which grows on Isla del Sol and other parts of the Altiplano and is used as an incense in Aymará ritual; also refers to a similar-smelling domestic plant *Mentha pulegium,* which was introduced by the Spanish
Kolla – the name used by the Aymará to refer to themselves; also spelt 'Colla'
Kollasuyo – Inca name for Bolivia, the 'land of the Kolla,' or Aymará people; the Spanish knew the area as Alto Perú, 'upper Peru'

La Diablada – Dance of the Devils, frequently performed at festivals
lago – lake
laguna – lagoon; shallow lake
lancha – motorboat
lavandería – laundry
licuado – fruit shake made with either milk or water
llanos – plains
loma – artificial mounds

Manco Capac – the first Inca emperor
manta – shawl, also called an *aguayo*
mariguí – a small and very irritating biting fly of the Amazon lowlands; the bite

initially creates a small blood blister and then itches for the next two weeks, sometimes leaving scars
mate – herbal infusion of coca, chamomile, or similar
mercado – market
mestizo – person of mixed Spanish and indigenous parentage or descent; also architectural style incorporating natural-theme designs
micro – small bus or minibus
mirador – lookout
moto-taxi – motorbike taxi, a standard means of public transportation in the Eastern Lowlands and Amazon Basin
movilidades – anything that moves (in terms of transportation)
mudéjar – Spanish name for architecture displaying Moorish influences

ñandu – rhea, a large, flightless bird also known as the South American ostrich
nevado – snowcapped mountain peak

orureño/a (m/f) – Oruro local

paceño/a (m/f) – La Paz local
Pachamama – the Aymará and Quechua goddess or 'Mother Earth'
pahuichi – straw-thatched home with reed walls; a common dwelling in the Beni department
paja brava – spiky grass of the high Altiplano
parrilla – barbecue
parrillada – plate of mixed grilled meats
peajes – tolls sometimes charged at a *tranca* or toll station
peña – folk-music program
piso – floor
plata – **silver**
pollera – traditional *chola* skirt
pongueaje – feudal system

of peonage inflicted on the Bolivian peasantry; abolished after the April Revolution of 1952

pullman – 'reclining' 1st-class rail or bus seat; it may or may not actually recline

puna – high open grasslands of the Altiplano

punto – privately run phone office

quebrada – ravine or wash, usually dry

Quechua – highland (Altiplano) indigenous language of Ecuador, Peru and Bolivia; language of the former Inca empire

quena – simple reed flute

queñua – dwarf shaggy-barked tree *(Polylepis tarapana)* that grows at higher altitudes than any other tree in the world; it can survive at elevations of over 5000m

quinoa – highly nutritious grain similar to sorghum, used to make flour and thicken stews; grown at high elevations

quirquincho – armadillo carapace used in the making of *charangos;* nickname for a resident of Oruro

radiales – 'radials', the streets forming the 'spokes' of a city laid out in *anillos,* or rings; the best Bolivian example of this is in Santa Cruz

refugio – mountain hut

río – river

roca – rock

salar – salt pan or salt desert

salteña – pastry shell filled with meat and vegetables

saya – Afro-Bolivian dance that recalls the days of slavery in Potosí; it's featured at festivities

seringueros – rubber tappers in the Amazon region

SERNAP – Servicio Nacional de Áreas Protegidas, government-run environment agency

singani – a distilled grape spirit (local firewater)

soroche – altitude sickness, invariably suffered by newly arrived visitors to highland Bolivia

surazo – cold wind blowing into lowland Bolivia from Patagonia and Argentine pampa

surtidores de gasolina – gas dispensers/stations

tambo – wayside inn, market and meeting place selling staple domestic items

tarijeños – Tarija locals

taxista – taxi driver

termas – hot springs

terminal terrestre – long-distance bus terminal

thola – small desert bush

tienda – small shop, usually family-run

tinku – traditional festival that features ritual fighting,

taking place mainly in the north of the department of Potosí; any bloodshed during these fights is considered an offering to Pachamama

totora – type of reed, used as a building material around Lake Titicaca

tranca – highway police post, usually found at city limits

tranquilo – 'tranquil', the word often used by locals to describe Bolivians' relatively safe and gentle demeanor; it's also used as an encouragement to slow down to the local pace of life

trufi – collective taxi or minibus that follows a set route

vicuña – a small camelid of the high *puna* or Altiplano; a wild relative of the llama and alpaca

viscacha – small, long-tailed rabbit-like rodent *(Lagidium viscaccia)* related to the chinchilla; inhabits rocky outcrops on the high Altiplano

Wara Wara – slow train on the Red Occidental that stops at most stations

yatiri – traditional Aymará healer or witch doctor

zampoña – pan flute made of hollow reeds of varying lengths, lashed together side by side; it's featured in most traditional music performances

FOOD GLOSSARY

ají – chili condiments

anticuchos – beef-heart shish kebabs

api – syrupy form of *chicha* made from sweet purple corn, lemon, cinnamon and white sugar

brazuelo – shoulder

buñuelo – sticky type of doughnut dipped in sugar syrup

cabrito – goat

camote – sweet potato

carne – beef

carne de chancho – pork

cerveza – beer; Taquiña is the best, Huari the fizziest

chairo – mutton or beef soup with *chuños*, potatoes and *mote*

chajchu – beef with *chuño*, hard-boiled egg, cheese and hot red-pepper sauce

chanko – chicken with yellow pepper and a tomato and onion sauce; a Tarija specialty

chaque – like *chupe* but much thicker and contains more grain

charque – meat jerky (often llama meat); the source of the English word 'jerky'

charquekan – meat jerky served with *choclo*, potato and boiled egg

chicha – popular beverage that is often alcoholic and made from fermented corn

chicharrón de cerdo – fried pork

chirimoya – custard apple; a green scaly fruit with creamy white flesh

choclo – large-grain corn (maize)

chuños – freeze-dried potatoes

chupe – thick meat, vegetable and grain soup with a clear broth flavored with garlic, *ají*, tomato, cumin or onion

churrasco – steak

cordero – lamb or mutton

cuñape – cassava and cheese roll

despepitado – (aka *mocachinchi*) a dried and shriveled peach in a boiled cane-sugar and cinnamon liquid

empanada – meat or cheese pasty

escabeche – vinegar-pickled vegetables

fricasé – pork soup; a specialty from La Paz

fritanga – spicy-hot pork with mint and hominy

haba – bean of the palqui plant found on the Altiplano, similar to fava beans

huminta – (aka *humita*) like a *tamale* but filled with cheese only and normally quite dry

kala purkha – soup made from corn that is cooked in a ceramic dish by adding a steaming chunk of heavy pumice; a Potosí and Sucre specialty

lawa – (aka *lagua*) meat-stew broth thickened with corn starch or wheat flour

licuado – fruit shake made with either milk or water

llajhua – spicy-hot tomato sauce

llaucha paceña – a doughy cheese bread

locoto – small, hot pepper pods

lomo – loin (of meat)

maní – peanuts

maracuya – a sweet and delicious fruit (aka passion fruit); also see *tumbo*

masaco – *charque* served with mashed plantain, yuca and/or corn; a Bolivian Amazonian staple sometimes served with cheese

mate – herbal infusion of coca, chamomile, or similar

milanesa – a fairly greasy type of beef or chicken schnitzel (see *silpancho*)

mote – freeze-dried corn

oca – tough edible tuber similar to a potato

papas rellenas – mashed potatoes stuffed with veggies

or meat and fried; especially tasty when piping hot and served with hot sauce

parrillada – meat grill or barbecue

pastel – a deep-fried *empanada;* may be filled with chicken, beef or cheese

pescado – generic term for fish

pollo – chicken

pomelo – large, pulpy-skinned grapefruit

pucacapa – circular *empanada* filled with cheese, olives, onions and hot pepper sauce, and baked in an earth oven

queso – cheese

quinoa – nutritious grain similar to sorghum

saíce – hot meat and rice stew

salteña – delicious, juicy meat and vegetable pasty; a popular mid-morning snack

silpancho – a schnitzel pounded till very thin and able to absorb more grease than a *milanesa* (a properly prepared *silpancho* is said to be perfect to use when viewing a solar eclipse!)

tallarines – long, thin noodles

tamale – cornmeal dough filled with spiced beef, vegetables and potatoes, then wrapped in a corn husk and fried, grilled or baked

tarhui – legume from Sucre

thimpu – spicy lamb and vegetable stew

tomatada de cordero – lamb stew with tomato sauce

tucumana – *empanada*-like pastry stuffed till bursting with meat, olives, eggs, raisins and other goodies; originated in Tucumán, Argentina

tumbo – a variety of passion fruit

tuna – prickly pear cactus

witu – beef stew with pureed tomatoes

yuca – cassava (manioc) tuber

behind the scenes

SEND US YOUR FEEDBACK

We love to hear from travelers – your comments keep us on our toes and help make our books better. Our well-traveled team reads every word on what you loved or loathed about this book. Although we cannot reply individually to postal submissions, we always guarantee that your feedback goes straight to the appropriate authors, in time for the next edition. Each person who sends us information is thanked in the next edition – the most useful submissions are rewarded with a selection of digital PDF chapters.

Visit **lonelyplanet.com/contact** to submit your updates and suggestions or to ask for help. Our award-winning website also features inspirational travel stories, news and discussions.

Note: We may edit, reproduce and incorporate your comments in Lonely Planet products such as guidebooks, websites and digital products, so let us know if you don't want your comments reproduced or your name acknowledged. For a copy of our privacy policy visit lonelyplanet.com/privacy.

OUR READERS

Many thanks to the travelers who used the last edition and wrote to us with helpful hints, useful advice and interesting anecdotes:

Michael Addison, Lisa Arcobelli, Daniel Buck, Errol Burdon, Renee Charpentier, Dick Commandeur, Miriam Cristina, Karen Daley, Peter Dam, Tom De Bock, Hans De Schrijver, Peter Ekblom, Emma Ellis, Malin Enerås, Sabrina Evain, Marty Fokkink, Rink Glazema, Ricia Gordon, Rupert Haag, Jennifer Harwood, Mick Huerta, Therese Jensen, Petra Kaandorp, Annessa Kaufman, Bradley Kendal, Marianne Kerrebrouck, Julia Knopper, Pia Lehtonen-Davies, Samuel Liaigre, Lars Loll, Zara Macalister, Tania Manickchand, Dave Marquart, Veronica McNamee, Anne Meadows, Julia Mehoke, Evan Meyer, Jens Mueller, Christel Mukopadhyay, Neil Murray, Monique Musper, Stuart Nelson, Judith Nijeboer, Andrew Ofstehage, Koos Reitsma, Uwe Richter, Sander Ruitenbeek, Wendy Rushbrooke, William Seager, Aditi Seth, Lezak Shallat, Francois Sonnet, Joao Speck, Shu Tan, Christina Taubert, Florian Ulmer, Michelle Veney

AUTHOR THANKS

Greg Benchwick

Gracias and a huge *abrazo* to my intrepid travel companions Violeta and Alejandra, to Brian for giving me my first job in Bolivia, and to my editor Kathleen and the LP crew for keeping the dream alive. Special thanks go to Eduardo Muñoz and family, previous authors and my coauthor Paul, and to the experts who helped along the way, including Stanford's Herbert Klein (history), Climbing South America's Jeff Sandifort (climbing) and La Paz on Foot's Stephen Taranto (trekking).

Paul Smith

Thanks to Henry Aramayo, Trent and Chari, Luis Aguirre, Bennett and Ruth Hennessey. Elibeth Pereda was a whizz at getting me off the beaten track and David made visiting the missions a pleasure. Greg, Kathleen and Alison made sure everything ran smoothly during the write up, as usual. Carol and Shawn always make sure that coming home is even more fun than traveling. Mum and Dad proofread. Margie, this is another one for you. Miss you loads!

ACKNOWLEDGMENTS

Climate map data adapted from Peel MC, Finlayson BL & McMahon TA (2007) 'Updated World Map of the Köppen-Geiger Climate Classification', Hydrology and Earth System Sciences, 11, 163344.

Cover photograph: Llama and Licancabur volcano, Eduardo Mariano Rivero/Alamy ©

This Book

This 8th edition of Lonely Planet's *Bolivia* guidebook was researched and written by Greg Benchwick and Paul Smith. Professor Herbert S Klein reviewed the History chapter. The previous edition was written by Anja Mutić, Kate Armstrong and Paul Smith. The 6th edition was written by Kate Armstrong, Vesna Maric and Andy Symington. This guidebook was commissioned in Lonely Planet's Oakland office, and produced by the following:

Commissioning Editor Kathleen Munnelly

Coordinating Editors Kate Mathews, Branislava Vladisavljevic

Coordinating Cartographer Brendan Streager

Coordinating Layout Designer Katherine Marsh

Managing Editors Sasha Baskett, Bruce Evans, Annelies Mertens

Managing Cartographer Alison Lyall

Managing Layout Designer Jane Hart

Assisting Editors Andrea Dobbin, Justin Flynn, Lorna Goodyer, Briohny Hooper, Rosemary Neilson, Kristin Odijk, Tracy Whitmey

Assisting Cartographer Enes Basic

Cover Research Naomi Parker

Internal Image Research Aude Vauconsant

Thanks to Imogen Bannister, Laura Crawford, Ryan Evans, Larissa Frost, Jouve India, Catherine Naghten, Trent Paton, Martine Power, Raphael Richards, Dianne Schallmeiner, Amanda Sierp, Gerard Walker

000 Map pages
000 Photo pages

NOTES

how to use this book

These symbols will help you find the listings you want:

👁 Sights   ☞ Tours   🍷 Drinking

🏊 Beaches   🎊 Festivals & Events   ☆ Entertainment

🏃 Activities   🛏 Sleeping   🔒 Shopping

🍴 Courses   🍴 Eating   ℹ Information/Transport

These symbols give you the vital information for each listing:

☑	Telephone Numbers	🛜	Wi-Fi Access	🚌	Bus
☺	Opening Hours	🏊	Swimming Pool	⛴	Ferry
P	Parking	🥗	Vegetarian Selection	M	Metro
⊖	Nonsmoking	📖	English-Language Menu	S	Subway
❄	Air-Conditioning	👪	Family-Friendly	🚋	Tram
@	Internet Access	🐾	Pet-Friendly	🚆	Train

Reviews are organised by author preference.

Look out for these icons:

TOP CHOICE Our author's recommendation

FREE No payment required

🍃 A green or sustainable option

Our authors have nominated these places as demonstrating a strong commitment to sustainability – for example by supporting local communities and producers, operating in an environmentally friendly way, or supporting conservation projects.

Map Legend

Sights
- 🟢 Beach
- 🔵 Buddhist
- 🟠 Castle
- 🟢 Christian
- 🟣 Hindu
- 🔵 Islamic
- 🟢 Jewish
- 🟠 Monument
- 🟤 Museum/Gallery
- 🟢 Ruin
- 🟣 Winery/Vineyard
- 🟢 Zoo
- 🔵 Other Sight

Activities, Courses & Tours
- 🟢 Diving/Snorkelling
- 🟢 Canoeing/Kayaking
- 🔵 Skiing
- 🟡 Surfing
- 🟢 Swimming/Pool
- 🟤 Walking
- 🔵 Windsurfing
- 🟢 Other Activity/Course/Tour

Sleeping
- 🛏 Sleeping
- ⛺ Camping

Eating
- 🍴 Eating

Drinking
- 🟢 Drinking
- ⚪ Cafe

Entertainment
- 🟢 Entertainment

Shopping
- 🔵 Shopping

Information
- 🟢 Bank
- 🔵 Embassy/Consulate
- ➕ Hospital/Medical
- @ Internet
- 🔵 Police
- 🟢 Post Office
- 🟢 Telephone
- 🟢 Toilet
- ℹ Tourist Information
- • Other Information

Transport
- ✈ Airport
- ⊗ Border Crossing
- 🚍 Bus
- ⊷🚡⊶ Cable Car/Funicular
- ⊷🚲⊶ Cycling
- ⊷⛴⊶ Ferry
- ⊷🚝⊶ Monorail
- P Parking
- 🟢 Petrol Station
- 🟢 Taxi
- ⊷🚆⊶ Train/Railway
- ⊷🚋⊶ Tram
- M Underground Train Station
- • Other Transport

Routes
- Tollway
- Freeway
- Primary
- Secondary
- Tertiary
- Lane
- Unsealed Road
- Plaza/Mall
- Steps
- ⊱ Tunnel
- Pedestrian Overpass
- Walking Tour
- Walking Tour Detour
- Path

Geographic
- 🏠 Hut/Shelter
- 🔴 Lighthouse
- 🔵 Lookout
- ▲ Mountain/Volcano
- 🟢 Oasis
- 🟢 Park
-)(Pass
- 🟢 Picnic Area
- 🔵 Waterfall

Population
- ✪ Capital (National)
- ◉ Capital (State/Province)
- 🔴 City/Large Town
- 🔴 Town/Village

Boundaries
- — — — International
- — — State/Province
- — - - Disputed
- — - — Regional/Suburb
- Marine Park
- ⌒⌒⌒ Cliff
- Wall

Hydrography
- River, Creek
- Intermittent River
- Swamp/Mangrove
- Reef
- Canal
- Water
- Dry/Salt/Intermittent Lake
- Glacier

Areas
- Beach/Desert
- + + + Cemetery (Christian)
- × × × Cemetery (Other)
- Park/Forest
- Sportsground
- Sight (Building)
- Top Sight (Building)

OUR STORY

A beat-up old car, a few dollars in the pocket and a sense of adventure. In 1972 that's all Tony and Maureen Wheeler needed for the trip of a lifetime – across Europe and Asia overland to Australia. It took several months, and at the end – broke but inspired – they sat at their kitchen table writing and stapling together their first travel guide, *Across Asia on the Cheap*. Within a week they'd sold 1500 copies. Lonely Planet was born.

Today, Lonely Planet has offices in Melbourne, London, Oakland and Delhi, with more than 600 staff and writers. We share Tony's belief that 'a great guidebook should do three things: inform, educate and amuse.'

OUR WRITERS

Greg Benchwick

Coordinating Author, La Paz, Lake Titicaca, The Cordilleras & Yungas, Southern Altiplano Greg started his career in journalism as the managing editor of the world-famous *Bolivian Times*, covering everything from the war on drugs to human rights abuses and the state of affairs in Bolivia's numerous bars and *discotecas*. Since then he's written dozens of guidebooks to countries throughout Latin America, interviewed Bolivian *campesinos* and *politicos* for the UN's International Fund for Agricultural Development, and continued on a path toward happiness and nonstop adventure. On this research trip, Greg traveled with his beautiful wife Alejandra and 18-month-old daughter Violeta, stopping along the way for parades and protests, diaper breaks and family photos. Violeta got passport stamp number six at La Paz airport.

Paul Smith

Central Highlands, South Central Bolivia & the Chaco, Santa Cruz & Gran Chiquitania, Amazon Basin, The Natural World From an early age, and with a vague and naive ambition to be the next David Attenborough, Paul dreamed of exploring the remotest areas of the globe in search of wildlife. While researching this edition, Paul took 15 flights in six weeks, lost 8kg in 10 days, caught a catfish that weighed more than he did, and reminded himself of why Bolivia is still one of the best countries on earth for adventurous travelers.

Contributing Author

Herbert S Klein is Gouverneur Morris Professor Emeritus, Columbia University and currently Research Fellow, Hoover Institution, Stanford University. He is the author of *Parties and Political Change in Bolivia, 1880–1952* (1969, 2009), *Revolution and the Rebirth of Inequality* (coauthor, 1981); *Haciendas and Ayllus: Rural Society in the Bolivian Andes* (1993) and *A Concise History of Bolivia* (2nd ed, 2011). He reviewed this book's History chapter.

Published by Lonely Planet Publications Pty Ltd
ABN 36 005 607 983
8th edition – June 2013
ISBN 978 1 74179 937 8
© Lonely Planet 2013   Photographs © as indicated 2013
10 9 8 7 6 5 4 3 2 1
Printed in China

Although the authors and Lonely Planet have taken all reasonable care in preparing this book, we make no warranty about the accuracy or completeness of its content and, to the maximum extent permitted, disclaim all liability arising from its use.

All rights reserved. No part of this publication may be copied, stored in a retrieval system, or transmitted in any form by any means, electronic, mechanical, recording or otherwise, except brief extracts for the purpose of review, and no part of this publication may be sold or hired, without the written permission of the publisher. Lonely Planet and the Lonely Planet logo are trademarks of Lonely Planet and are registered in the US Patent and Trademark Office and in other countries. Lonely Planet does not allow its name or logo to be appropriated by commercial establishments, such as retailers, restaurants or hotels. Please let us know of any misuses: lonelyplanet.com/ip.

Bestselling guide to Bolivia – source: Nielsen Bookscan, Australia, UK and USA, December 2011 to November 2012.